2ⁿᵈ EDITION

A HANDBOOK OF CONTEMPORARY

SPANISH
GRAMMAR

D1252177

**A reference and practice book
for students of Spanish**

Ana Beatriz Chiquito
Professor, University of Bergen, Norway
Visiting Researcher, MIT

VISTA®
HIGHER LEARNING

Boston, Massachusetts

Publisher: José A. Blanco
Editorial Development: Judith Bach, Jo Hanna Kurth, Gonzalo Montoya
Project Management: Kayli Brownstein, Sharon Inglis
Rights Management: Jorgensen Fernandez, Caitlin O'Brien
Technology Production: Daniel Ospina, Paola Ríos Schaaf
Design: Gabriel Noreña, Andrés Vanegas
Production: Manuela Arango, Oscar Díez, Erik Restrepo

Student Text ISBN: 978-1-68004-449-2
Library of Congress Control Number: 2015948689

2 3 4 5 6 7 8 9 EBM 22 21 20 19 18 17 16

The Vista Higher Learning Story

Your Specialized Foreign Language Publisher

Independent, specialized, and privately owned, Vista Higher Learning was founded in 2000 with one mission: to raise the teaching and learning of world languages to a higher level. This mission is based on the following beliefs:

- It is essential to prepare students for a world in which learning another language is a necessity, not a luxury.
- Language learning should be fun and rewarding, and all students should have the tools necessary for achieving success.
- Students who experience success learning a language will be more likely to continue their language studies both inside and outside the classroom.

With this in mind, we decided to take a fresh look at all aspects of language instructional materials. Because we are specialized, we dedicate 100 percent of our resources to this goal and base every decision on how well it supports language learning.

That is where you come in. Since our founding, we have relied on the continuous and invaluable feedback from language instructors and students nationwide. This partnership has proved to be the cornerstone of our success by allowing us to constantly improve our programs to meet your instructional needs.

The result? Programs that make language learning exciting, relevant, and effective through:

- an unprecedented access to resources
- a wide variety of contemporary, authentic materials
- the integration of text, technology, and media, and
- a bold and engaging textbook design

By focusing on our singular passion, we let you focus on yours.

The Vista Higher Learning Team

VISTA®
HIGHER LEARNING

500 Boylston Street, Suite 620, Boston, MA 02116-3736 TOLLFREE: 800-618-7375
TELEPHONE: 617-426-4910 FAX: 617-426-5209 **www.vistahigherlearning.com**

To the student

A Handbook of Contemporary Spanish Grammar, Second Edition, is your most reliable Spanish grammar reference and study tool. Through comprehensive and accessible explanations, detailed easy-to-use charts and diagrams, a *Glosario combinatorio* (glossary of collocations, or common word combinations), and substantial auto-graded practical exercises that emphasize grammar points, this useful reference tool will reinforce and expand your knowledge of Spanish grammatical concepts.

Here are some of the features and benefits you will encounter in **A Handbook of Contemporary Spanish Grammar, Second Edition**:

- Updated grammar explanations that incorporate revised rules and recommendations from the *Nueva gramática* most recently published by the **Real Academia Española**

- Coverage of standard usage in Spain and Latin America, including *voseo*

- Regional variations

- An abundance of examples that demonstrate contemporary, real-world usage

- A highly structured, easy-to-navigate design that facilitates the learning of grammar concepts

- A thorough glossary of grammatical and lexical word combinations to expand your vocabulary and improve oral and written communication

- All activities in the book available online, most with auto-grading

- Hundreds of additional online auto-graded activities—at least one per grammar point—with extra support for more complex grammar topics

- Animated grammar tutorials for review of basic concepts

A Handbook of Contemporary Spanish Grammar, Second Edition, serves multiple course configurations:

- Stand-alone text for intermediate and advanced literature and language courses

- Companion grammar and practice tool for any intermediate or advanced Spanish class

- Grammar reference and practice book for heritage speakers as well as intermediate and advanced Spanish students

- Self-study book if you want to go beyond the grammar taught in introductory and intermediate courses

We hope that **A Handbook of Contemporary Spanish Grammar, Second Edition,** will be an invaluable companion as you advance in your study of Spanish.

To the instructor

A Handbook of Contemporary Spanish Grammar, Second Edition, combines thorough, accessible grammar explanations with a unique online component that offers Spanish students an invaluable grammar reference and study tool. The text can serve as a stand-alone textbook for grammar courses, as a companion text for language learning, composition, literature, and culture courses, or as a reference for independent study.

Program features

- A topical structure that is flexible and simple to navigate

- Coverage of all major grammar topics, incorporating key updates and revisions from the *Nueva gramática* published by the **Real Academia Española**

- Concise, comprehensive explanations that include detailed tables and relevant examples

- Lexical and regional variations

- An abundance of examples of contemporary, real-world usage

- A *Glosario combinatorio*

- Activities that allow students to practice the grammar concepts independently

- Additional online practice and assessment (See p. vii.)

The *Nueva gramática* and the *Nueva ortografía*

A Handbook of Contemporary Spanish Grammar, Second Edition, incorporates key updates from the *Nueva gramática*, published by the **Real Academia Española** (RAE) in conjunction with all the regional Spanish language academies (see p. 18). The terminology used by the RAE often differs from that used throughout North America. Though the RAE's terminology is standard in this book, other naming conventions are acknowledged and presented.

The same approach has been applied to the grammar explanations. When appropriate, both the RAE explanation and the traditional explanation are presented. For an example, see the case of demonstratives on p. 63.

The *vos* conjugations covered correspond to those presented in the verb tables in the *Nueva gramática*. Verb tense presentations and verb tables include the *vos* form for the present indicative and affirmative commands (*salís, salí*). The *vos* forms for the present subjunctive and negative commands that do not match the *tú* forms (*salgás, no salgás*) are acknowledged in the verb presentations, but not included in verb tables.

New to this edition

A Handbook of Contemporary Spanish Grammar, Second Edition, offers further support for students, more online resources, and a wealth of new features, including:

- Simplified grammar explanations with more familiar language

- New cross-references to other sections and chapters for easy reference

- New or revised margin notes that provide support and practice on complex grammar and lexical topics, especially for students learning Spanish as a second language

- Open-ended writing activities that facilitate oral and written communication

New to the Supersite

- All textbook activities available online, most with auto-grading

- Additional online-only activities

- Animated grammar tutorials for review of basic concepts

Each section of your text comes with activities on the **A Handbook of Contemporary Spanish Grammar, Second Edition,** Supersite, most of which are auto-graded for immediate feedback. Plus, the Supersite is iPad®-friendly*, so it can be accessed on the go! Visit **vhlcentral.com** to explore this wealth of exciting resources.

- All activities from the student text, with auto-grading for most of them

- Additional, comprehensive practice for each chapter

- Quizzes for self-assessment

- Spanish Mini Dictionary

- Animated grammar tutorials

- vText—online, interactive Student Edition with access to Supersite activities

For instructors

Instructors have access to the entire student site, as well as to these additional resources:

- A robust, time-saving course management system

- Instructor tools to create open-ended and Partner Chat activities

- Live Chat for video chats, audio chats, and instant messaging

- A communications center for announcements, notifications, and help requests

- Voiceboards for oral/audio online discussions

- Answer key for all textbook activities online

*Students must use a computer for audio recording and select presentations and tools that require Flash or Shockwave.

Table of contents

Organization

A Handbook of Contemporary Spanish Grammar, Second Edition, includes the following sections.

Grammar explanations

- 31 chapters divided into clearly marked sections and subsections

Activities

- Around 500 activities
- Additional practice available online (See p. vii.)
- Immediate feedback provided when practice is done on the Supersite

Verb conjugation tables

- Complete verb tables for easy reference

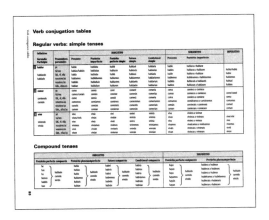

Glosario combinatorio

- See pp. xix and C1 for more details.
- Practical glossary of collocations, or common word combinations

Sidebars and icons

- On the first page of every chapter, a sidebar summarizes the chapter's contents.

Chapter 11

A. Overview

B. Comparisons of inequality

C. Comparisons of equality

D. Superlatives

- Clearly marked and numbered headings help you navigate the grammar explanations and easily locate cross-references.

19.B **Use of the present perfect**

19.B.1 **Life experiences** – *nunca, alguna vez, hasta ahora*

- A sidebar at the end of the chapter includes the specific activity sequence with its corresponding page numbers. The Supersite icon indicates that all of these activities are also available online.

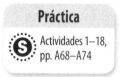

Práctica

Actividades 1–18, pp. A68–A74

- In the *Actividades* section, a mouse icon indicates that all of these activities are also on the Supersite.

Adverbs   **Chapter 10**

- Each activity identifies the chapter (**13**) and section(s) (**A–H**) where the material is presented.

16. Síntesis Escoger Selecciona los pronombres adecuados. **13.A–13.H**

- Additional practice on the Supersite, not available in the text, is indicated at the end of each practice section.

Practice more at **vhlcentral.com.**

Glosario combinatorio

A Handbook of Contemporary Spanish Grammar, Second Edition, features a practical glossary of collocations, or common word combinations. The glossary functions as:

- An invaluable tool for expanding vocabulary and increasing grammatical accuracy
- An excellent reference for improving fluency by learning word combinations commonly used by native speakers

For a detailed description, see p. C1.

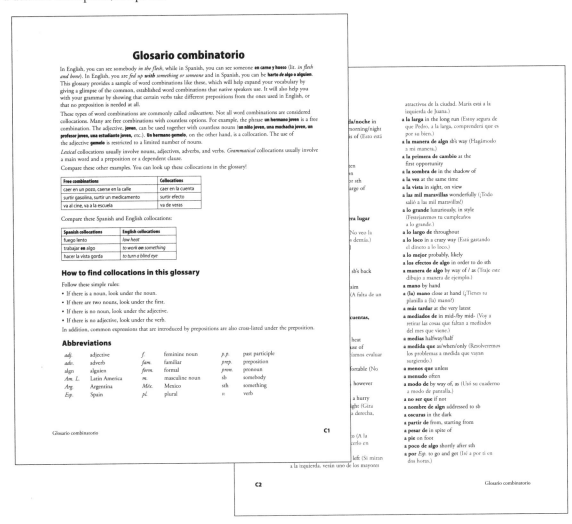

Glosario combinatorio

In English, you can see somebody *in the flesh*, while in Spanish, you can see someone **en carne y hueso** (lit. *in flesh and bone*). In English, you are *fed up **with** something or someone* and in Spanish, you can be **harto de algo o alguien.** This glossary provides a sample of word combinations like these, which will help expand your vocabulary by giving you a glimpse of the common, established word combinations that native speakers use. It will also help you with your grammar by showing that certain verbs take different prepositions from the ones used in English, or that no preposition is needed at all.

These types of word combinations are commonly called *collocations*. Not all word combinations are considered collocations. Many are free combinations with countless options. For example, the phrase **un hermano joven** is a free combination. The adjective, **joven**, can be used together with countless nouns (**un niño joven, una muchacha joven, un profesor joven, una estudiante joven,** etc.). **Un hermano gemelo**, on the other hand, is a collocation. The use of the adjective **gemelo** is restricted to a limited number of nouns.

Lexical collocations usually involve nouns, adjectives, adverbs, and verbs. *Grammatical* collocations usually involve a main word and a preposition or a dependent clause.

Compare these other examples. You can look up these collocations in the glossary!

Free combinations	Collocations
caer en un pozo, caerse en la calle	caer en la cuenta
surtir gasolina, surtir un medicamento	surtir efecto
va al cine, va a la escuela	va de veras

Compare these Spanish and English collocations:

Spanish collocations	English collocations
fuego lento	low heat
trabajar **en** algo	to work **on** something
hacer la vista gorda	to turn a blind eye

How to find collocations in this glossary

Follow these simple rules:
- If there is a noun, look under the noun.
- If there are two nouns, look under the first.
- If there is no noun, look under the adjective.
- If there is no adjective, look under the verb.

In addition, common expressions that are introduced by prepositions are also cross-listed under the preposition.

Abbreviations

adj.	adjective	*f.*	feminine noun	*p.p.*	past participle
adv.	adverb	*fam.*	familiar	*prep.*	preposition
algn	alguien	*form.*	formal	*pron.*	pronoun
Am. L.	Latin America	*m.*	masculine noun	sb	somebody
Arg.	Argentina	*Méx.*	Mexico	sth	something
Esp.	Spain	*pl.*	plural	*v.*	verb

Glosario combinatorio   C1

---

da/noche in morning/night is of (Esto está

ten n or sth arge of

era lugar

No veo la demás.)

sb's back

aim (A falta de un

cuentas,

heat use of íamos evaluar

fortable (No

, however

a hurry ght (Gira a derecha,

o (A la cerlo en

left (Si miran a la izquierda, verán uno de los mayores

atractivos de la ciudad. María está a la izquierda de Juana.)

a la larga in the long run (Estoy segura de que Pedro, a la larga, comprenderá que es por su bien.)
a la manera de algn sb's way (Hagámoslo a mi manera.)
a la primera de cambio at the first opportunity
a la sombra de in the shadow of
a la vez at the same time
a la vista in sight, on view
a las mil maravillas wonderfully (¡Todo salió a las mil maravillas!)
a lo grande luxuriously, in style (Festejaremos tu cumpleaños a lo grande.)
a lo largo de throughout
a lo loco in a crazy way (Está gastando el dinero a lo loco.)
a lo mejor probably, likely
a los efectos de algo in order to do sth
a manera de algo by way of / as (Traje este dibujo a manera de ejemplo.)
a mano by hand
a (la) mano close at hand (¿Tienes tu planilla a (la) mano?)
a más tardar at the very latest
a mediados de in mid-/by mid- (Voy a retirar las cosas que faltan a mediados del mes que viene.)
a medias halfway/half
a medida que as/when/only (Resolveremos los problemas a medida que vayan surgiendo.)
a menos que unless
a menudo often
a modo de by way of, as (Usó su cuaderno a modo de pantalla.)
a no ser que if not
a nombre de algn addressed to sb
a oscuras in the dark
a partir de from, starting from
a pesar de in spite of
a pie on foot
a poco de algo shortly after sth
a por *Esp.* to go and get (Iré a por ti en dos horas.)

C2   Glosario combinatorio

Reviewers

On behalf of the author and its editors, Vista Higher Learning expresses its sincere appreciation to the instructors who participated in the survey that led to the second edition of **A Handbook of Contemporary Spanish Grammar, Second Edition**. Their comments and suggestions were instrumental.

Jeff Barnett
Washington and Lee University, VA

Rosalba Bellen
Archmere Academy, DE

Elizabeth Bruno
University of North Carolina at Chapel Hill, NC

Claudia Costagliola
University of Florida, FL

Mark Cox
Presbyterian College, SC

William O. Deaver, Jr.
Armstrong Atlantic State University, GA

Carmen Marie Diaz
Silver Lake College, WI

Conxita Domenech
University of Wyoming, WY

Debra Faszer-McMahon
Seton Hill University, PA

Chris Foley
Liberty University, VA

Judith Garcia-Quismondo
Seton Hill University, PA

Raquel Gaytan
Rice University, TX

Jill Gibian
Eastern Oregon University, OR

Ryan Hallows
Concord University, WV

Maria H. Hernandez
Georgia Southern University, GA

Jesus David Jerez-Gomez
California State University, San Bernardino, CA

Sharon Knight
Presbyterian College, SC

Izaskun Kortazar
Boise State University, ID

Michael Langer
Wake Technical Community College, NC

Nelson López
Bellarmine University, KY

Kenneth V. Luna
California State University, Northridge, CA

Markus Muller
California State University, Long Beach, CA

Maria del Rosario Ramos
Johns Hopkins University, MD

Jacob Rapp
University of Kansas, KS

Juan Pablo Rodríguez Prieto
Butler University, IN

Clinia Saffi
Presbyterian College, SC

Pedro Sandin
University of North Carolina at Asheville, NC

Gabriel Saxton-Ruiz
University of Wisconsin-Green Bay, WI

David Shook
Georgia Institute of Technology, GA

Paul Siegrist
Fort Hays State University, KS

Bryant Smith
Nicholls State University, LA

Susana Solera Adoboe
Southern Methodist University, TX

Katya Soll
University of Kansas, KS

Dwight TenHuisen
Calvin College, MI

Robert L. Turner III
University of South Dakota, SD

Ines Warnock
Portland State University, OR

Roberto Weiss
University of Florida, FL

Bel Winemiller
Arizona State University, AZ

España y Guinea Ecuatorial

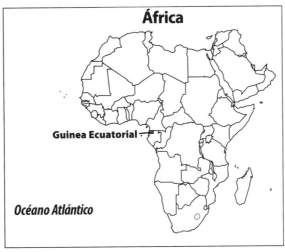

América del Sur

Mar Caribe

Barranquilla

Cúcuta • San Cristóbal

Caracas ✪

VENEZUELA

Océano Atlántico

GUAYANA
SURINAME
GUAYANA FRANCESA (FRANCIA)

• Medellín

✪ Bogotá
• Cali

COLOMBIA

• Mitú

✪ Quito
• Guayaquil

ECUADOR

ISLAS GALÁPAGOS

• Iquitos

• Piura

PERÚ

• Trujillo

BRASIL

✪ Lima
• Ica

• Cusco

BOLIVIA

Océano Pacífico

Arequipa •

Trinidad
✪ La Paz
• Cochabamba
• Santa Cruz
✪ Sucre

• Arica

PARAGUAY

• Antofagasta

✪ Asunción

CHILE

San Miguel de Tucumán
Resistencia •

• Córdoba

Rosario •
• Salto

URUGUAY
✪ Montevideo

Mendoza
• Valparaíso
✪ Santiago

Buenos Aires ✪

ARGENTINA

Océano Atlántico

• Concepción

Mar del Plata

• Valdivia
• San Carlos de Bariloche

ISLAS MALVINAS (R.U.)

500 km
500 mi.

México, América Central y el Caribe

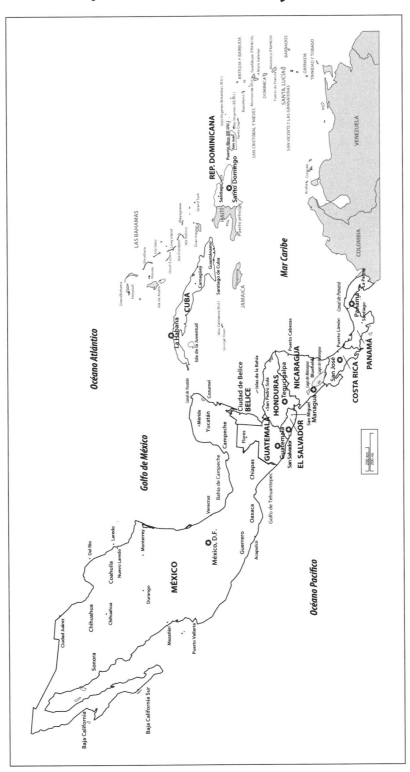

El español en los Estados Unidos

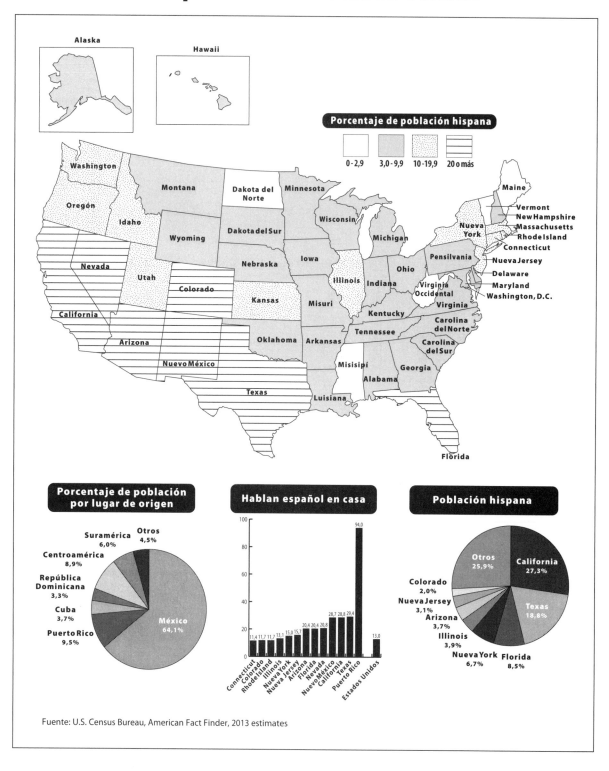

Alaska

Hawaii

Porcentaje de población hispana

0-2,9   3,0-9,9   10-19,9   20 o más

Washington, Oregón, Idaho, Montana, Dakota del Norte, Minnesota, Wisconsin, Nevada, Utah, Wyoming, Dakota del Sur, Nebraska, Iowa, Michigan, California, Colorado, Kansas, Misuri, Illinois, Indiana, Ohio, Arizona, Nuevo México, Oklahoma, Arkansas, Tennessee, Kentucky, Virginia Occidental, Virginia, Pensilvania, Nueva York, Maine, Vermont, New Hampshire, Massachusetts, Rhode Island, Connecticut, Nueva Jersey, Delaware, Maryland, Washington, D.C., Carolina del Norte, Carolina del Sur, Texas, Luisiana, Misisipí, Alabama, Georgia, Florida

Porcentaje de población por lugar de origen

- Suramérica 6,0%
- Otros 4,5%
- Centroamérica 8,9%
- República Dominicana 3,3%
- Cuba 3,7%
- Puerto Rico 9,5%
- México 64,1%

Hablan español en casa

Estado	%
Connecticut	11,4
Colorado	11,7
Rhode Island	11,7
Illinois	13,1
Nueva York	15,0
Nueva Jersey	15,7
Arizona	20,4
Florida	20,4
Nevada	20,8
Nuevo México	28,7
Texas	28,8
California	29,4
Puerto Rico	94,0
Estados Unidos	13,0

Población hispana

- Otros 25,9%
- California 27,3%
- Colorado 2,0%
- Nueva Jersey 3,1%
- Arizona 3,7%
- Illinois 3,9%
- Nueva York 6,7%
- Texas 18,8%
- Florida 8,5%

Fuente: U.S. Census Bureau, American Fact Finder, 2013 estimates

The Spanish language
La lengua española

1.A Letters

Las letras

Letters represent *phonemes*: distinct sounds in a language that are capable of conveying differences in meaning. One letter can represent multiple phonemes, which in turn can change meanings of words. For example, in English the letter *i* in *wind* (as in weather) and *wind* (as in winding a clock) represents two different phonemes that give the words different meanings. This example shows there is no direct correlation between letters and phonemes.

1.B The alphabet

El alfabeto

The Spanish alphabet, or **abecedario**, has twenty-seven letters. It has five vowels and twenty-two consonants. One of the consonants is silent: **h**. **Ch** and **ll** are not letters but **dígrafos** (digraphs). Digraphs are combinations of two letters that represent a single sound, like the English *th* in *those*.

a	a	g	ge	m	eme	s	ese
b	be	h	hache	n	ene	t	te
c	ce	i	i	ñ	eñe	u	u
(ch)	(che)	j	jota	o	o	v	uve/ve
d	de	k	ka	p	pe	w	doble uve / doble ve
e	e	l	ele	q	cu	x	equis
f	efe	(ll)	(elle)	r	ere/erre	y	ye (i griega)
						z	zeta

In the past, **ch** and **ll** had their own entries in dictionaries and reference books, just like the other letters. In 1994, the language academies in Spanish-speaking countries voted to follow the international guidelines for alphabetization. Subsequently, **ch** and **ll** were included under **c** and **l**, respectively. The letter **ñ** retained its own entry. Recent reforms have eliminated **ch** and **ll** from the alphabet.

1.C Pronunciation

Pronunciación

In English and Spanish, spelling, sound, and meaning are interconnected. In English, the vowel often differentiates meaning, as in *pop/pope* or *dove* (a bird)/*dove* (past of *to dive*). In Spanish, the stressed syllable can determine the meaning of a word. Most Spanish words carry the stress on the next-to-last syllable.

Stress and accents: 1.E

hablo	*I speak*	habló	*he spoke*	canto	*I sing*	cantó	*he sang*

Vowels and consonants

The following charts outline how Spanish vowels, consonants, and digraphs are pronounced.

Vocales
a
e
i
o
u

1.C.1 Vowels

The pronunciation of Spanish vowels (**vocales**) is similar to some English vowel sounds. Unlike English, each vowel in Spanish has only one sound.

Spanish vowels	Similar to the following English vowel sounds		Examples	
			Spanish	**English meaning**
a	*ah* sound	*father*	c**a**sa, **a**la	*house, wing*
e	long *a*	*they, day*	m**e**sa, p**e**sa	*table, weight*
i	long *e*	*bee, meat*	s**í**, m**i**	*yes, my*
o	long *o*	*note, snow*	y**o**, c**o**c**o**	*I, coconut*
u	long *u*	*food, rude*	l**u**na, t**u**	*moon, your*

1.C.2 Diphthongs

Diptongos
ai, ay, au
ia, ua
ei, ey, eu
ie, ue
oi, oy, ou
io, uo
iu, ui, uy

In Spanish, there are strong vowels and weak vowels. **A, e,** and **o** are strong vowels, and **i** and **u** are weak. A diphthong (**diptongo**) is a combination of a strong and a weak vowel, or two weak vowels, in a single syllable. A syllable ending in a vowel + **y** is also considered a diphthong.

Diphthongs with *a*			Diphthongs with *e*		
ai	b**ai**le	*dance*	**ei**	s**ei**s	*six*
ay	h**ay**	*there is/are*	**ey**	r**ey**	*king*
ia	famil**ia**	*family*	**ie**	c**ie**n	*one hundred*
au	**au**la	*classroom*	**eu**	**Eu**ropa	*Europe*
ua	c**ua**tro	*four*	**ue**	b**ue**no	*good*

Diphthongs with *o*			Diphthongs with *u, i*		
oi	**oi**go	*I hear*	**iu**	c**iu**dad	*city*
oy	s**oy**	*I am*	**ui**	r**ui**do	*noise*
io	qu**io**sco	*kiosk/newsstand*	**uy**	m**uy**	*very*
ou	t**ou**r	*tour*			
uo	c**uo**ta	*payment/installment*			

Division of words: 1.D.3
Accents on vowel
combinations: 1.E.4
Hiatus and accentuation: 1.E.5

The diphthong **ou** appears in
foreign words.

1.C.3 Triphthongs

When three vowels are pronounced together as one syllable, they create a triphthong (**triptongo**). Triphthongs begin and end with an unstressed **i** or **u** and have a stressed **a, e,** or **o** in the middle: **buey, miau.** Most triphthongs with **i** or **u** carry a written accent over the letter in the middle. Most words with triphthongs are verb forms used with **vosotros** (*you, fam. pl.*): **enviáis** (*you send*), **continuáis** (*you continue*).

Division of words: 1.D.3
Accents on vowel
combinations: 1.E.4
Hiatus and accentuation: 1.E.5

1.C.4 Combinations: *a, e, o*

When any of the vowels **a, e,** or **o** are paired together, they do not form a diphthong or a triphthong. These combinations always form two syllables: hé-**ro-e**, c**a-o**s, le-**er**.

1.C.5 *g, c, d, p,* and *t*

The consonants (**consonantes**) **g** and **c** (before **a, o,** or **u**), and **d** are pronounced with a short audible breath in English. This breath sound does not happen in Spanish. At the beginning of a phrase or after the letter **n**, the Spanish **g** is pronounced like the *g* in *girl*. In any other position, the Spanish **g** has a somewhat softer sound. The consonants **p** and **t** are also pronounced with a short breath sound in English, but not in Spanish.

1.C.6 **Consonants and digraphs**

	Consonants	**Examples**
b, v	represent the same sound. They are pronounced roughly like the English *b* at the beginning of a word and after **m** and **n**. Between vowels, **b** and **v** are pronounced like a soft English *b* sound; the lips do not close.	**b**ueno (*good*) tam**b**ién (*also*) u**v**a (*grape*)
c	is pronounced like the English *k* in *keep* before **a, o,** and **u**, but without breath sound. In Latin America and southern Spain, **c** is pronounced like an **s** before **e** and **i**. In most of Spain, it is pronounced like an English *th*.	**c**asa (*house*) **c**olonia (*colony*) **c**ielo (*sky*) **c**ena (*dinner*)
d	is pronounced roughly like the English *d* at the beginning of a word and after **l** or **n**. Between vowels and in other positions, the **d** has a soft sound (almost like an English *th*).	**d**iez (*ten*) fal**d**a (*skirt*) bo**d**a (*wedding*) Pe**d**ro
f	is pronounced like the English *f*.	**f**in (*end*)
g	is pronounced like the English *g* in *go* before **a, o,** or **u**, and **-ui** or **-ue (gue, gui)**. Before **e** and **i**, the **g** is pronounced like the Spanish **j**. (See below.)	**g**ato (*cat*) **g**uerra (*war*) **g**igante (*giant*) **g**ente (*people*)
h	is silent.	**h**ola (*hello*) a**h**ora (*now*)
j	is pronounced in Spanish like a *guttural sound* with varying strength depending on the region. In Latin America, the pronunciation varies from a strong to a very weak English *h*.	**j**efe (*boss*) a**j**o (*garlic*) **j**oven (*young*)
k	is pronounced like the English *k* without breath sound.	**k**ilo (*kilogram*)
l	is pronounced like the English *l*.	**l**indo (*pretty*)
m	is pronounced like the English *m*.	a**m**or (*love*)
n	is pronounced with the tongue a little higher up (toward the back of the teeth) than the English *n*.	**n**ada (*nothing*) **n**osotros (*we*) A**n**a
ñ	is pronounced like the *ny* sound in the English word *canyon* or the *ni* sound in the English word *onion*.	ni**ñ**a (*girl*) ma**ñ**ana (*morning*) sue**ñ**o (*dream*)
p	is pronounced like the English *p* without breath sound.	**p**a**p**á (*dad*)
q	is pronounced like the English *k* without breath sound; the letter **q** appears in Spanish only in the combinations **que** and **qui**.	**q**ueso (*cheese*) a**q**uí (*here*)
r	is pronounced as a strong trill at the beginning of words and after **n, l,** and **s**. Otherwise the **r** is pronounced with a very short, loose, and simple hit of the tongue. Note that a **rr** combination represents a strong trill between vowels. See the digraphs chart that follows this one.	**r**osa (*rose*) al**r**ededor (*around*) hon**r**ado (*honest*) co**r**o (*choir*)
s	is pronounced like the English *s* in *summer*, but can vary regionally. In parts of Latin America, southern Spain, and the Caribbean, the **s** is pronounced very softly or is omitted at the end of a word and before a consonant. In Madrid, the **s** is pronounced with a whistling sound.	**s**ala (*living room*) ca**s**a (*house*)
t	is pronounced roughly like the English *t*, but without breath sound.	**t**aza (*cup*)
w	is found only in foreign words and can be pronounced like the English *w* or like the Spanish **b/v**.	**W**ashington

Consonantes

b
v
c
d
f
g
h
j
k
l
m
n
ñ
p
q
r
s
t
w

Omission of the letter **p**: 1.G.3

x	varies in pronunciation regionally. It can be pronounced like an English *ks*, *gs*, or *s* between vowels. Before a consonant, it is usually pronounced like an **s**. When **x** appears in the name of a Mexican town, it is pronounced like the Spanish **j** or English *h*.	e**x**amen (*exam*) e**x**acto (*exact*) me**x**icano (*Mexican*) Mé**x**ico, Oa**x**aca
y	acts as a vowel with the Spanish **i** sound when it is part of a diphthong. At the beginning of words and between vowels, **y** sounds like the English *y* in *yes*. (See also **ll** in the digraphs chart for regional variations.)	ho**y** (*today*) **y**uca (*yucca*) pla**y**a (*beach*)
z	is pronounced like an **s** in Latin America, southern Spain, and the Canary Islands. Pronouncing the **z** like an **s** is called **seseo**. The letter **z** is pronounced like the English *th* in most parts of Spain. (See also **c**.)	**z**apato (*shoe*) a**z**ul (*blue*)

Dígrafos

ch
ll
rr

Yeísmo is pronouncing **ll** and ▶ **y** like the English *y* in *yes*. It is a common feature in Latin America and in Spain.

	Digraphs	**Examples**
ch	is pronounced like the English *ch* in *chocolate*.	**ch**ocolate
ll	is pronounced very much like the English *y* in most parts of Latin America and in many areas of Spain. This is called **yeísmo**. (See also the pronunciation of **y**.) In Argentina, Uruguay, and parts of Paraguay, the **ll** is pronounced similarly to the English *sh*. In central parts of Spain and in some Andean regions of Latin America, the **ll** is pronounced like a continuous **lj** sound.	ca**ll**e (*street*) **ll**ave (*key*)
rr	is a strong rolling **r** sound that occurs between vowels, and it is written with a double **rr**.	ba**rr**o (*mud*) a**rr**oz (*rice*)

1.D   Division of words

Separación de las palabras

In writing, it is sometimes necessary to hyphenate words at the end of a line. According to style conventions in Spanish, the words must be divided into syllables; the syllables themselves can't be divided.

1.D.1   Formation of syllables

a. A consonant between two vowels forms a syllable with the second vowel.

ca-**ma**-**ro**-te	*boat cabin*	Ca-**ta**-li-**na**	*Catalina*
gra-**má**-**ti**-**ca**	*grammar*	co-**le**-**gi**o	*school*

b. The consonants **b, c, f, g,** and **p** followed by **l** or **r** form syllables with the next vowel.

a-**crí**-li-co	*acrylic*	en-**crip**-ta-do	*encrypted*	an-**glo**-sa-jo-na	*Anglo-Saxon*
a-**bra**-si-vo	*abrasive*	a-**fri**-ca-no	*African*	em-**ple**-a-do	*employee*

c. The consonants **t** and **d** followed by **r** form syllables with the next vowel.

Pe-**dro**	*Pedro*	ras-**tri**-llo	*rake*	a-**tro**-ci-dad	*atrocity*

d. The combination **tl** stays together in one syllable in Latin America and the Canary Islands; it is split between two syllables in the rest of Spain.

Latin America	**Spain**	
a-**tle**-ta	at-**le**-ta	*athlete*
a-**tlas**	at-**las**	*atlas*

e. Other consonant pairs are split between two syllables when they are in the middle of a word.

pris-**ma**	*prism*	ac-**ci**ón	*action*	con-so-na**n-te**	*consonant*

f. When **l** or **r** comes last in a group of three consonants, the last two consonants begin a new syllable.

co**m**-**pr**o-mi-so	*agreement*	si**m**-**pl**e	*simple*
si**n**-**cr**o-ni-zar	*to synchronize*	a**m**-**pl**iar	*to enlarge/extend*

1.D.2 Diphthongs and triphthongs

Vowel groups that form a diphthong or a triphthong can't be split.

ja-g**ua**r	*jaguar*	qu**ie**-ro	*I want*	v**iei**-ra	*scallop*
s**ue**l-do	*salary*	d**ue**r-mo	*I sleep/am sleeping*	U-ru-g**uay**	*Uruguay*

1.D.3 Other vowels

Vowel groups that do not form a diphthong or triphthong can be split into syllables, but stylistically they should stay together.

◀ However, when hyphenating at the end of a line of text, vowel groups that do not form a diphthong should not be divided: **aho**-ra, **ca**-cao.

a-ho-ra	*now*	c**a**-**o**s	*chaos*	c**a**-**e**r	*to fall*
l**e**-**e**r	*to read*	cr**e**-**o**	*I believe*	ca-c**a**-**o**	*cocoa*

1.D.4 ch, ll, rr

◀ Digraphs: 1.C.6

These letter pairs can't be split.

an-**ch**o	*wide*	a-**ll**í	*there*	ca-**rr**e-ta	*wagon*
te-**ch**o	*ceiling/roof*	ca-**ll**e	*street*	pe-**rr**o	*dog*

1.D.5 The letter x

◀ Variations in the pronunciation of the letter **x**: 1.C.6, 1.G.2a, 3.F.4

X represents two phonemes [ks]. Between vowels, **x** forms a syllable with the second vowel. If **x** is followed by a consonant, it forms a syllable with the previous vowel.

Division of words with *x*			
e-**xa**-men	*exam*	tó-**xi**-co	*toxic*
[e-**ksa**-men]		[tó-ksi-ko]	
ex-cep-ción	*exception*	**ex**-plicar	*to explain*
[e**ks**-cep-ción]		[e**ks**-pli-kar]	

1.E Stress and accents

Acentuación

In Spanish, there are two kinds of accents. The accent that indicates the stressed syllable of a word is the **acento prosódico** (*prosodic accent*). The **acento diacrítico** (*diacritical accent*) distinguishes two words that are otherwise spelled the same: **mi** (*my*), **mí** (*me*).

The following rules explain the regular pronunciation of Spanish words, when to use the **tilde** or **acento gráfico**, and the accentuation of diphthongs and triphthongs.

Acentos
(á)
(é)
(í)
(ó)
(ú)

1.E.1 Stress on the final syllable: *Palabras agudas*

◀ Pronunciation: 1.C

Most words that end in a consonant other than **n** or **s** are stressed on the final syllable. No accent is needed in these cases.

pa-pe**l**	*paper*	ciu-da**d**	*city*	es-cri-bi**r**	*to write*

If a word ends in **n, s,** or a vowel and is stressed on the final syllable, a written accent is needed.

ha-bl**é**	*I spoke*	ca-jó**n**	*drawer*	qui-zá**s**	*maybe*

One exception is when a word ends in *consonant* + **-s**; a written accent is not needed in this case. This rule usually affects technological or foreign words, such as **robots**.

1.E.2 Stress on the next-to-last syllable: *Palabras llanas o graves*

Most words that end in **n, s,** or a vowel are stressed on the next-to-last syllable. No accent is needed in these cases.

me-s**a**   *table*   **can**-ta**n**   *they sing/are singing*   lec-**cio**-ne**s**   *lessons*

If a word ends in any consonant other than **n** or **s**, and is stressed on the next-to-last syllable, a written accent is needed.

fá-ci**l**   *easy*   **ál**-bu**m**   *album*   a-**zú**-ca**r**   *sugar*

Words in this group that end in *consonant* + **-s** carry a written accent (**bíceps**), as do plurals of some foreign words, such as **cómics**.

1.E.3 Other cases: *Palabras esdrújulas y sobreesdrújulas*

If the stress falls before the next-to-last syllable, the stressed syllable must always be marked with a written accent, regardless of the word's ending or length.

cá-ma-ra   *camera*   ce-**rá**-mi-ca   *ceramic*   e-**léc**-tri-co   *electric*
rá-pi-do   *fast*   **más**-ca-ra   *mask*   **sá**-ba-na   *sheet*

When one or more pronouns are added to a command, the number of syllables increases and usually the word will need a written accent on or before the third-to-last syllable.

es**crí**be<u>me</u>   *write to me*   **llá**me<u>los</u>   *call them*
cómpra<u>telos</u>   *buy them for yourself*   ex**plí**ca<u>melo</u>   *explain it to me*
de**mués**tra<u>noslo</u>   *show it to us*   **dí**ga<u>selo</u>   *tell it to him*

1.E.4 Accents on vowel combinations

Diphthongs: 1.C.2 ▶
Triphthongs: 1.C.3

Diphthongs and triphthongs follow the accentuation rules of **palabras agudas, palabras llanas,** and **palabras esdrújulas**. When the stress falls on the syllable with the diphthong or triphthong, there are rules that dictate which vowel will carry the accent mark. In these cases, it is useful to remember that the vowels **a, e,** and **o** are considered **fuertes** (*strong*) and the vowels **u** and **i** are **débiles** (*weak*). Diphthongs and triphthongs are either a combination of strong vowels and unstressed weak vowels (**ai, eu,** etc.) or a combination of weak vowels (**ui, uy, iu**). The combination of two strong vowels never forms a diphthong.

a. When a syllable with a diphthong or triphthong requires an accent for stress, the strong vowel carries the written accent and the pronunciation of the diphthong or triphthong is usually maintained. In the following list, <u>cuen</u>-ta does not carry a written accent because it ends in a vowel and the stress is on the next-to-last syllable (**llana**). **Cuén**-ta-me does have a written accent because the stress is on the third-to-last syllable (**esdrújula**); the accent goes over the strong vowel, **e**.

<u>cue</u>n-ta   <u>cué</u>n-ta-me   can-<u>tas</u>-**teis**   can-**téis**   U-ru-**guay**   en-**viáis**
a-<u>ma</u>-b**ais**   a-**máis**   fun-<u>cio</u>-na   fun-**ción**   **buey**   a-ve-ri-**güéis**

Hiatus and accentuation: 1.E.5 ▶

b. If the stress falls on the weak vowel of a *weak vowel + strong vowel* combination that would normally form a diphthong or triphthong, the vowels split to form part of different syllables. This break in the vowels is called **hiato** (*hiatus*). In this case, the stressed weak vowel always carries a written accent.

Regional differences in ▶
pronunciation can create
a diphthong or hiatus;
for example, **mie-do** is
pronounced with a diphthong,
while the same combination
of vowels can be pronounced
with a hiatus in some regions
of Spain and Latin America:
su-fri-e-ron. 1.C.2,
1.C.3, 1.E.5

One syllable	Hiatus: Different syllables
La serie es continua. (con-<u>ti</u>-n**ua**)	La fiesta continúa. (con-ti-**nú**-a)

When the first weak vowel in a combination of three vowels that would normally form a triphthong is stressed, it stands as a separate syllable while the other two vowels form a diphthong.

oiríais (oi-**rí**-**ais**)   salíais (sa-**lí**-**ais**)   comprendíais (com-pren-**dí**-**ais**)

c. The combination of the weak vowels **i** and **u** forms a diphthong for the purpose of spelling, although it can sometimes be pronounced as either a diphthong or a hiatus.

ciudad (c**iu**-<u>dad</u>)   cuidado (c**ui**-<u>da</u>-do)   ruido (<u>r**ui**</u>-do)
construir (cons-tr**ui**r, also pronounced cons-tr**u**-<u>ir</u>)

d. When two weak vowels are combined and the stress falls on the second vowel in the pair, a diphthong is formed and the word follows the regular rules of accentuation. For example, if the diphthong appears in the third-to-last syllable, the second vowel carries a written accent. Note that the accent is always on the second vowel.

cuídate (<u>c**uí**</u>-da-te)   lingüística (lin-g**üís**-ti-ca)

1.E.5 Hiatus and accentuation

A *hiatus* (**hiato**) is formed when two or more consecutive vowels in a word are not pronounced together as one syllable. In Spanish, a hiatus occurs in the following cases.

a. When the vowels **a, e,** and **o** are combined in pairs, they *always* form a hiatus. This also applies when the letter **h** appears between two of those vowels.

Combinations: *a, e, o*: 1.C.4
Accents on vowel combinations: 1.E.4

ahora	a-<u>ho</u>-ra	*now*	**rea**lidad	re-**a**-li-<u>dad</u>	*reality*
poeta	po-**e**-ta	*poet*	**teo**rema	te-**o**-<u>re</u>-ma	*theorem*

b. Double vowels or double vowels separated by an **h** also form a hiatus.

alb**ah**aca	al-b**a**-<u>ha</u>-ca	*basil*	micr**oo**ndas	mi-cro-**on**-das	*microwave*
chi**i**ta	chi-**i**-ta	*Shiite*	pos**ee**r	po-s**e**-**er**	*to own*
c**oo**rdinar	c**o**-**o**r-di-<u>nar</u>	*to coordinate*			

c. The words that appear in the two previous points do not require a written accent according to the rules of accentuation. For example, **poeta** does not carry a written accent because its pronunciation is regular. The stress falls on the vowel **e** (the next-to-last syllable) and the word ends in a vowel. The following words, however, require a written accent because they are **esdrújulas** (stress on the third-to-last syllable).

Palabras agudas: 1.E.1
Palabras esdrújulas: 1.E.3

aéreo	a-**é**-re-o	*aerial*	cr**ée**me	<u>cr**é**</u>-e-me	*believe me*
ca**ó**tico	ca-**ó**-ti-co	*chaotic*	te**ó**rico	te-**ó**-ri-co	*theoretical*

d. Words that have a strong vowel combined with a weak, stressed vowel always form a hiatus and require a written accent over the stressed vowel. Because the accent is breaking a diphthong, it is required even if other rules for accentuation do not call for it. For example, the word **increíble** is **llana** (stressed on the next-to-last syllable) and ends in a vowel, a case that normally does not call for an accent. However, because the **i** is stressed, an accent is required to reflect the correct pronunciation.

Palabras llanas o graves: 1.E.2

b**aú**l	ba-**úl**	incr**eí**ble	in-cre-**í**-ble	**oí**r	o-**ír**
b**úh**o	b**ú**-ho	m**ío**	m**í**-o	pa**ís**	pa-**ís**
d**ía**	d**í**-a	pr**oh**íbe	pro-h**í**-be	sonr**íe**	son-r**í**-e

1.E.6 Diacritical marks

The written accent, or **tilde**, indicates the stressed syllable of a word and visually marks the stressed vowel. In speech, the stress on a syllable is called the **acento prosódico** (*prosodic accent*). The **acento diacrítico** (*diacritical accent*) is a written accent mark used to distinguish two words that are otherwise spelled the same.

Spanish relative pronouns: 15.A.2, Question words and exclamations: 1.E.7

a. One-syllable words (**palabras monosílabas**) have only one vowel, or, if they have more than one, they do not have a hiatus (**hiato**). One-syllable words usually do not carry a written accent.

bien   mal   no   si   un   cien   muy   pie   sol   vas

b. A diacritical accent is necessary to differentiate these pairs of words.

de	of, from	dé	imperative of **dar** (to give)
el	definite article	él	he
mi	my	mí	me/myself
se	himself, herself, itself, themselves, yourself (formal)	sé	I know; imperative of **ser** (to be)
si	if	sí	yes; yourself/yourselves/ him/himself/her/herself/ themselves (object of a preposition)
tu	your	tú	you
te	you/yourself	té	tea
mas	but	más	more

Somos **de** Nueva York.	*We are from New York.*
Por favor, **dé** usted una donación.	*Please give a donation.*
El chico habla francés y español.	*The boy speaks French and Spanish.*
Hoy viene **él**, ella no.	*He is coming today, but she is not.*
Mi padre es Lorenzo.	*My father is Lorenzo.*
Nora siempre me llama a **mí**.	*Nora always calls me.*
Viviana **se** mira en el espejo.	*Viviana is looking at herself in the mirror.*
Sé mucho español.	*I know a lot of Spanish.*
Sé un buen chico.	*Be a good boy.*
Si vas a viajar, llámame.	*If you're going to travel, call me.*
—¿Quieres viajar a Madrid? —¡**Sí**!	*—Do you want to go to Madrid? —Yes!*
Solamente piensa en **sí** mismo.	*He thinks only of himself.*
Yo soy **tu** amigo.	*I am your friend.*
¿Quién eres **tú**?	*Who are you?*
¿**Te** gusta el **té**?	*Do you like tea?*
Quiero ir, **mas** no puedo.	*I want to go, but I can't.*
No hay nada que me guste **más**.	*There's nothing I like more.*

Aun/aún: 10.B.4, 16.C.6 **c.** *Aun, aún*

The word **aun** can mean *even, until, also,* or *including,* but the written accent on **aún** changes the meaning to *still* or *yet.*

Estoy cansado, **aun** después de pasar una buena noche.	*I am tired, even after a good night´s sleep.*
¡**Aún** estoy esperando a Luisa!	*I am still waiting for Luisa!*

d. *Solo, sólo*

The word **solo** can be an adjective or an adverb. As an adjective, it never carries a written accent. The adverb can carry an accent in case of ambiguity; however, according to the *Nueva ortografía,* it is no longer required. As an adverb, a synonym can also be used: **solamente**, **únicamente**.

¿Estás **solo** en casa?	*Are you home alone?*	**Sólo/Solo** estaré en casa hoy.	*I will only be home today.*

Demonstratives: Ch. 8 **e.** The demonstratives **este, ese,** and **aquel** and their feminine and plural forms used to carry an accent when they functioned as pronouns and there was risk of ambiguity. It is still possible to use the written accent in case of ambiguity, but it is no longer required.

1.E.7 **Question words and exclamations**

a. The following words always carry a written accent when their function is interrogative or exclamatory.

Diacritical marks: 1.E.6
Spanish relative pronouns: 15.A.2
Questions and question words: Ch. 14

cómo	how	dónde	where	quién(es)	who	cuánto/a(s)	how much/many
qué	what	cuándo	when	cuál	which	cuáles	which

¿**Cómo** estás?	*How are you?*
¿**Qué** estudias?	*What are you studying?*
¿**Dónde** estudias?	*Where are you studying?*
¿**Cuándo** vas a la clase?	*When are you going to class?*
¿**Quién** es tu profesor?	*Who is your teacher?*
¿**Cuál** es tu asignatura favorita?	*What is your favorite subject?*
¿**Cuánto** cuesta el libro?	*How much does the book cost?*
¿**Cuáles** son tus libros?	*Which books are yours?*
¡**Qué** hermoso día!	*What a beautiful day!*
¡**Cómo** puedes decir eso!	*How can you say that!*
¡**Cuántos** libros tienes!	*You have so many books!*

b. These words also carry a written accent in sentences with an indirect question.

Indirect questions: 31.B.6d

No sé **cuánto** cuesta el libro.	*I don't know how much this book costs.*
Dime **dónde** vives.	*Tell me where you live.*
En las noticias dicen **qué** sucedió.	*They explain what happened on the news.*
En *Google* encuentras **cómo** llegar aquí.	*You can use Google to find out how to get here.*
No recuerdo **cuándo** es su cumpleaños.	*I don't remember when her birthday is.*

1.E.8 **Adverbs ending in** *-mente*

Adverbs ending in **-mente**: 10.G

Adverbs ending in **-mente** are formed using the feminine adjective as the base. These words are special in Spanish because they have two prosodic accents: that of the adjective and that of the ending **-mente**. In order to determine whether the adverb needs an accent mark, look at the adjective base. If the adjective has an accent, as in **fácil**, the adverb keeps it: **fácilmente**. If the adjective does not have an accent, as in **tranquila**, the adverb does not either: **tranquilamente**.

afortunado	afortunadamente	cortés	cortésmente
claro	claramente	difícil	difícilmente
preferible	preferiblemente	pésimo	pésimamente
terrible	terriblemente	rápido	rápidamente

1.E.9 **Accentuation of plurals and compound words**

Most nouns and adjectives keep the accent on the same stressed syllable in both the singular and plural form: **fácil/fáciles, cámara/cámaras**. However, the use of a written accent can also vary when forming the plural.

Plural formation: 2.B

Palabras esdrújulas: 1.E.3

a. Some words gain a syllable in the plural and become **esdrújulas**. The accented syllable remains the same, but a written accent must be added in the plural to reflect the correct stress.

cri**men**	crí**menes**	jo**ven**	jó**venes**
exa**men**	exá**menes**	orden	órdenes
ima**gen**	imá**genes**	origen	orígenes

Irregular plurals: 2.B.2c

b. The following are examples of words that are irregular because the accented syllable, either written or spoken, is different in the singular and plural.

carácter ⟩ caracteres
régimen regímenes
espécimen especímenes

In the plural, these words are no longer **agudas**. Since they are now **llanas** and end in **-s**, a written accent is not required: 1.E.1, 1.E.2, 2.B.1e

c. When a word ends in a stressed syllable with a written accent, as in **televisión, revés,** and **corazón,** the written accent is not necessary in the plural.

revés	reveses	ecuación	ecuaciones
cortés	corteses	nación	naciones
faisán	faisanes	sillón	sillones
confín	confines	fusión	fusiones
delfín	delfines	misión	misiones
jardín	jardines	pensión	pensiones
pequeñín	pequeñines	televisión	televisiones
sillón	sillones	versión	versiones
belén	belenes	corazón	corazones
sartén	sartenes	razón	razones
edición	ediciones	atún	atunes

Hyphen: 1.F.6a

d. Compound words written as one word follow Spanish rules of accentuation. When the words are separated by a hyphen, they keep their original accentuation.

tragicómico   político-social
lavaplatos   socio-económico
hispanoamericano   técnico-administrativo

1.E.10 Words with varied accentuation

In Spanish, some words allow for different accentuation without changing meaning. Using one form over the other can be regional or personal preference. Here are some common examples.

básquetbol	basquetbol	maníaco/a	maniaco/a
chófer	chofer	olimpíada	olimpiada
cóctel	coctel	paradisíaco/a	paradisiaco/a
fríjol	frijol	período	periodo
fútbol	futbol	policíaco/a	policiaco/a
hipocondríaco/a	hipocondriaco/a	vídeo	video
ícono	icono	zodíaco	zodiaco

1.E.11 Accentuation of capital letters

Use of capital letters: 1.G.1

Capital letters require a written accent according to the rules of accentuation, whether the capital letter is the first letter of the word or the word is written entirely in capitals. Due to past typographical and printing constraints, this rule was not always possible to follow. Therefore, there are still older signs or books that do not follow it.

Él se llama Héctor.   Me llamo Miguel **Á**ngel.   ¡DETÉNGASE!

1.F Punctuation

Puntuación

Punctuation in Spanish is very similar to English. Note these uses.

1.F.1 [.] Period

a. Sentences

As in English, the period (**punto**) marks the end of a sentence. If you are dictating, say **punto [y] seguido** to indicate that the sentence should end and the paragraph should continue. To indicate that the sentence and the paragraph should end, say **punto [y] aparte**.

Sentences ending with an abbreviation do not need an additional period.

Visitaremos los EE. UU.	*We will visit the U.S.*

Sentences ending with an ellipsis, or exclamation or question marks, do not need a period unless the sentence is enclosed in parentheses or quotes.

¡Iremos al Gran Cañón! Es un sitio majestuoso... Llegaremos allí mañana.	*We will go the Grand Canyon! It's a majestic site... We will arrive there tomorrow.*

b. Abbreviations, acronyms, and symbols

Abbreviations are always followed by a period. Symbols never are; acronyms in all capital letters may or may not be.

Abbreviation	Symbol	Acronym
Sr. (señor)	kg (kilo)	ONU (Organización de las Naciones Unidas) *UN*
Ud. (usted)	lb (libra, *pound*)	EE. UU. (Estados Unidos de América) *USA*

Spanish abbreviations of ordinal numbers have a period before the small superscript sign showing the noun's number and/or gender ending.

◀ Abbreviations of ordinal numbers: 6.D.5

1.er piso   *first floor*   3.^a salida   *third exit*

c. Numbers

Hours and minutes are separated by a period or a colon. Number-only dates are separated by slashes, periods, or hyphens (less common).

◀ The standard date format in Spanish is day/month/year: 6.G.1

La fecha y hora de nacimiento de las gemelas fue: 9.10.2010 a las 5:27 p.m.	*The date and time of the twin girls' birth was October 9, 2010, at five twenty-seven in the afternoon.*

Thousands and millions are notated by a period in some countries and by a comma in others. The formal rule requires a space to separate the thousands when the number has five or more digits. The comma is the most common sign used to separate decimals in Spanish, although the decimal point is also used in some countries.

◀ Writing styles for numbers: 6.A.1 Numbers and counting expressions: 6.C.2

Current norm		Period	Comma	Decimals	
1000	10 000	10.000	10,000	10,2	10.2
mil		diez mil		diez coma dos	diez punto dos

A period should not be used in the numerical expression of years, page numbers, street numbers, or zip codes, or in articles, decrees, or laws.

el año 2012   página 2345   calle Príncipe, 1034   28010 Madrid

d. Addresses

Street numbers and postal codes do not have a period, except when there is an abbreviation.

La dirección del Hospital General de México es: Calle Dr. Balmis N.º 148, Col. Doctores, Delegación Cuauhtémoc, C. P. 06726, México, D. F.

Internet URLs and e-mail addresses use periods to separate elements. Note how they are read in Spanish.

http://www.whitehouse.gov	*Hache-te-te-pe-dos puntos-barra doble-uve doble-uve doble-uve doble (o triple uve doble)-punto-white house-punto-gov*
minombre.miapellido@miservidor.com	*Mi nombre-punto-mi apellido-arroba-mi servidor-punto-com*

Spain: **uve doble** (w)
Lat. Am.: **doble ve** (w)

1.F.2 [,] Comma

Non-defining relative clauses: 15.B.1

a. Inserted clauses that are not essential for the meaning of a sentence start and end with a comma (**coma**), as in English.

El doctor, **que es joven**, trabaja mucho.	*The doctor, who is young, works a lot.*

Defining relative clauses: 15.B.2

b. Clauses that are necessary for the meaning of a sentence do not have a comma.

El doctor **que es joven** trabaja mucho; el otro doctor, no.	*The young doctor works a lot; the other doesn't.*

c. Use a comma to separate a person's name from an opening exclamation or question mark.

Hola, **Patricia**, ¿cómo estás?	*Hi, Patricia, how are you?*
Martín, ¡bienvenido a casa!	*Welcome home, Martin!*

d. Use a comma after a **si** clause at the beginning of a sentence.

*Conditional **si** clauses: 23.E.8*

Si vas al mercado, compra manzanas.	*If you go to the market, buy apples.*
Compra manzanas si vas al mercado.	*Buy apples if you go to the market.*

e. A comma may be used to replace an implied verb.

Ana fue al parque; **Paula**, al cine.	*Ana went to the park; Paula, to the movies.*

f. A comma is used before the words **como** and **pero**.

Quiero algo dulce, **como** chocolate.	*I want something sweet, like chocolate.*
Tengo sueño, **pero** quiero jugar.	*I'm tired, but I want to play.*

g. Commas are used to separate items in lists. In Spanish, it is incorrect to use a comma before the last item in the series.

Tengo **libros, papel y lápices**.	*I have books, paper, and pencils.*

1.F.3 [;] Semicolon

a. The semicolon (**punto y coma**) is used to list groups of things that are separated internally by a comma and/or **y**.

Tengo papel, libros y lápices; cuadernos y computadoras.	*I have paper, books, and pencils; notebooks; and computers.*

b. A semicolon is used to link two independent clauses without connecting words.

Voy a la fiesta; no me voy a quedar mucho tiempo.	*I'm going to the party; I'm not going to stay long.*

c. A semicolon is used before a clause that begins with a conjunction or phrase such as **sin embargo, por (lo) tanto, no obstante, por consiguiente, en cambio,** and **en fin**.

Llovió mucho; sin embargo, fuimos al parque.	*It rained heavily; however, we went to the park.*

1.F.4 [:] Colon

a. Colons (**dos puntos**) are used after the person's name in a salutation for a letter or e-mail. The colon is more formal than a comma. In English, a comma is usually used unless the salutation is in a business letter.

Querida Paula: Espero que estés muy bien.   *Dear Paula, I hope all is well with you.*

b. A colon is also used before the listing of several elements.

Tengo muchos amigos: Luis, Marta, Patricia,   *I have many friends: Luis, Marta,*
Frank, Adam y Sarah.   *Patricia, Frank, Adam, and Sarah.*

c. A colon is used to separate a clarification, explanation, cause, consequence, summary, conclusion, or example from a preceding independent clause.

Siempre me dice lo mismo: que busque trabajo.   *He always tells me the same thing: to get a job.*

1.F.5 Questions and exclamations

Questions and question words: Ch. 14

In Spanish, questions can be asked without changing the sentence structure, as is done in English. The opening question mark conveys the intonation that must be used in order to pronounce the statement as a question. The same thing happens with an opening exclamation mark. Opening exclamation marks can be placed anywhere you wish to start an exclamation and where the voice must be raised, even if it is in the middle of the sentence.

a. [¿ ?] Question marks – *Signos de interrogación*
The beginning of a question is marked with an opening (inverted) question mark. As in English, if the question is part of a longer sentence, a comma separates it.

¿Qué día es hoy**?**   *What day is it today?*   Hace frío, **¿**verdad**?**   *It's cold, isn't it?*

b. [¡ !] Exclamation marks – *Signos de admiración o exclamación*
Exclamation marks are always placed at the beginning and end of an exclamation and follow a comma when placed within a sentence.

¡Qué bonito día**!**   *What a lovely day!*   Me gusta la paella, **¡**es deliciosa**!**   *I like paella. It's delicious!*

1.F.6 [-] Hyphen

The hyphen (**guión corto**) is a short dash that is used in writing to join or separate words.

a. The hyphen joins words to form a compound word. When two adjectives are joined, only the last one agrees with the noun in gender and number; the first is always singular and masculine.

Accentuation of plurals and compound words: 1.E.9d

tareas teórico-prácticas   *theoretical and practical homework*
textos histórico-religiosos   *texts about history and religion*

Words that indicate origin (**gentilicios**) can be written with or without a hyphen.

colombo-irlandés/irlandesa   *of Colombian and Irish origin*
franco-alemán/alemana   *of French and German origin*
afroamericano/a   *African American*

It is also possible to use a hyphen to create new concepts.

¡Luis tiene una **casa-mansión** enorme!   *Luis has a huge mansion-like house!*

b. The hyphen separates syllables of a word when the word does not fit on a line of text. In order to divide the word, it is necessary to follow the Spanish rules for dividing words into syllables.

Division of words: 1.D. Abbreviations, acronyms, and symbols: 1.F.1b

pan-ta-lla	co-rres-pon-den-cia	sal-chi-cha	com-pren-sión	cons-ti-tu-ción
(*screen*)	(*correspondence*)	(*sausage*)	(*comprehension*)	(*constitution*)

Stylistically, it is preferable not to leave one or two letters alone on a line. Also, abbreviations (**Srta.**) and acronyms (**ONU, EE. UU.**) should not be divided.

c. The hyphen indicates part of a word in grammar texts, word lists, and dictionaries. The position of the hyphen indicates whether the segment goes at the beginning, middle, or end of a word.

El sufijo **-ito** se usa en los diminutivos: lib**rito**.	*The suffix **-ito** is used in diminutives: lib**rito**.*
La palabra **ante**pasado contiene el prefijo **ante-**.	*The word **ante**pasado (ancestor) has the prefix **ante-**.*
Las consonantes **-zc-** aparecen en varios verbos: cono**zc**o.	*The consonants **-zc-** appear in several verbs: cono**zc**o.*

d. Time periods or ranges are specified with a hyphen.

Tenemos que estudiar los capítulos 1-3.	*We have to study chapters 1–3.*
El Quijote fue escrito por Miguel de Cervantes (1547-1616).	*El Quijote was written by Miguel de Cervantes (1547–1616).*

1.F.7 [—] Dash

The dash (**guión largo** o **raya**) is longer than the hyphen. Its main function is to mark the beginning or end of a segment of text in the following cases.

a. Dashes separate comments that interrupt the text. Commas and parentheses can also serve this function.

Notice that in English there is no space in between the dash and the text. However, in Spanish, the dash is separated by one space from the word that precedes it and attached to the first word of the text that interrupts the sentence.

Celeste —pensativa— contestó mi pregunta.	*Celeste—thoughtful—answered my question.*

b. A dash indicates each new speaker in a dialogue.

—¿Quieres café?	*"Do you want some coffee?"*
—Sí, muchas gracias.	*"Yes, thank you very much."*

c. In narrations with dialogue, the dash separates dialogue from narration.

—Tengo miedo —dijo Pilar cuando escuchó que alguien intentaba abrir la puerta.
—No tengas miedo —le dijo su madre, aunque ella sabía que no podrían escapar.
"I'm scared," said Pilar when she heard someone trying to open the door.
"Don't be afraid," said her mother, though she knew they could not escape.

1.F.8 Quotation marks

Spanish usually uses a different symbol than English to mark quotation marks (**comillas**): « ». However you may also see single or double straight quotes and smart quotes, as in English: ' ' and " ".

a. The main use of quotation marks is to indicate quotes taken from a text, to tell what a person has said, or to cite titles or names of book chapters, articles, reports, or poems. Punctuation of quotes remains inside the quotation marks, but if punctuation is not part of the quoted text, it falls outside the quotes. The period, however, always appears after the quoted text.

Gabriel García Márquez empieza su autobiografía diciendo «Mi madre me pidió que la acompañara a vender la casa».	*Gabriel García Márquez starts his autobiography saying: "My mother asked me to go with her to sell the house."*
Según los estudiantes que han leído el libro, «¡Vale la pena leerlo!».	*According to students who have read the book, "It's worth reading!"*
¿Leíste el artículo «Náufrago en tierra firme»?	*Have you read the article "Shipwrecked on Dry Land"?*

b. Quotation marks can call attention to a word in a text, for example, to explain a word or indicate that it is foreign, improper, wrong, or said with irony.

«**Hablar**» es un verbo regular.	"**Hablar**" (to speak) *is a regular verb.*
Las palabras «**quiosco**» y «**kiosco**» son igualmente aceptables.	*The words "**quiosco**" and "**kiosco**" are equally acceptable.*
¡Pablo dice que «**sabe**» escribir!	*Pablo says he "knows" how to write!*

`1.F.9` [...] Ellipsis

Ellipses (**puntos suspensivos**) may indicate that what is expressed in the sentence is uncertain or unknown, but it also has other uses.

a. Ellipses are used to mean *et cetera* in an incomplete list. A capital letter is used if the following text is a new sentence, and other punctuation marks may be used if necessary.

En el colegio tenemos que estudiar, escribir, leer… ¡No tengo tiempo para nada más!	*At school we have to study, we have to write, we have to read… I have no time for anything else!*
Tengo amigos mexicanos, peruanos, cubanos… de todas partes.	*I have friends from Mexico, Peru, Cuba… from all over the world.*

b. Ellipses can also express suspense or uncertainty in the message, for example, when writing letters, e-mails, and text messages.

Me gané la lotería y… bueno… no sé qué hacer…	*I won the lottery and… well… I don't know what to do…*
Pienso en ti…	*I think of you…*
Estoy esperando tu llamada…	*I'm waiting for your call…*

c. When quoting a text, ellipses in parentheses or brackets indicate that part of the text has been omitted.

Dice García Márquez en su autobiografía: "No nos tuteábamos, por la rara costumbre (…) de tutearse desde el primer saludo y pasar al usted sólo cuando se logra una mayor confianza (…)".

García Márquez says in his autobiography: "We did not use the tú form of address, due to the strange custom (…) of using tú from the first greeting and switching to usted only upon becoming close friends (…)".

`1.F.10` Parentheses and brackets

Parentheses (**paréntesis**) ( ) and brackets (**corchetes**) [ ] have similar functions.

a. Parentheses enclose text that expands on or clarifies what is said in a sentence, for example, data, dates, and names.

Me gusta mucho Nueva York (es una metrópoli impresionante) y quiero volver allí. Es extraño que no sea la capital del estado del mismo nombre (la capital es Albany).

I like New York very much (it is an impressive metropolis) and I want to go there again. It is strange it is not the capital of the state of New York (the capital is Albany).

b. When it is necessary to give alternatives in a text, they can be added in parentheses.

Los (Las) estudiantes tendrán vacaciones pronto.	*The students will be on break soon.*

c. Brackets can replace parentheses. Brackets are also used to add comments or clarifications in text that is already in parentheses. Notes about a text, such as notes from a translator or editor, also go in brackets.

El primer presidente afroamericano, Barack Obama (nacido en Honolulu [Hawai] de madre estadounidense y padre keniano), fue elegido en 2008.	*The first African American president, Barack Obama (born in Honolulu [Hawaii] to an American mother and a Kenyan father), was elected in 2008.*

Ortografía

1.G.1 **Use of capital letters**

Accentuation of capital letters:
1.E.11

a. Days of the week and months are not capitalized in Spanish as they are in English.

lunes	domingo	viernes	mayo	abril	enero
Monday	*Sunday*	*Friday*	*May*	*April*	*January*

b. All proper nouns begin with a capital letter. Articles that are part of the proper noun are also capitalized. Adjectives formed from proper nouns are not written with a capital letter. This rule is also valid for names of religions and their followers (adjectives).

Pedro	Luisita	Júpiter	Google	Facebook
Venezuela	**venezolano/a**	La Habana	**habanero/a**	
Cristianismo	**cristiano/a**	Protestantismo	**protestantes**	

c. Prepositions that are part of a Spanish last name are not capitalized except when the last name appears alone. If only the definite article is present, it is always capitalized.

Alejandro de la Hoz   Sr. De la Hoz   Susana la Salle   Sra. La Salle

d. Only the first word in a title is capitalized in Spanish, unless the title includes a proper noun. However, capital letters at the beginning of all important words of a title are now being used more in official settings.

La isla bajo el mar es una novela de Isabel Allende.   *Island Beneath the Sea* is a novel by Isabel Allende.

Instituto Nacional de Salud (Bogotá)   National Institute of Health *(Bogotá)*

Centro Nacional de Educación Básica a Distancia (Madrid)   National Center for Long-Distance Basic Education *(Madrid)*

e. As in English, the first letter of a sentence is always capitalized. After a colon, capital letters are normally not used in Spanish. However, capital letters are used after a colon in the salutation of a letter or e-mail or if the text that follows a colon is a full quote.

Esta es la primera oración de este párrafo. Continuamos con la segunda oración aquí y terminamos este texto con estas últimas palabras: ¡has leído hasta el final!

This is the first sentence in this paragraph. We continue with the second sentence here and we end this text with these final words: You have read to the end!

f. In Spanish, exclamation marks and question marks can end sentences, in which case the new sentence starts with a capital letter. However, unlike English, a comma can also separate a series of exclamations and/or questions.

¿Sabes cuándo es la fiesta? Creo que será pronto, ¿verdad?   *Do you know when the party is? I think it will be soon, won't it?*

¿Cómo estás?, ¿sigues viviendo en Miami?, ¡cuéntame toda la historia!   *How are you? Still living in Miami? Tell me everything!*

1.G.2 **Place names**

México: 3.F.4

a. The letter **x** in **México** and in other Mexican names and their adjectives is pronounced like the Spanish **j** when it is the first letter of the word or comes between vowels. Its pronunciation is /**ks**/ or /**s**/ in consonant combinations.

Name	Adjective	Name	Adjective
México	mexicano/a	Oaxaca	oaxaqueño/a
Xalapa	xalapeño/a / jalapeño/a	San Jerónimo Xayacatlán	xayacateco/a
Tlaxcala	tlaxcalteca	La Mixteca	mixteco/a

b. Names of cities and regions in Spain where other languages are official may be written in the region's native language.

Catalunya	Euskadi	A Coruña	A Mariña
Cataluña	País Vasco	La Coruña	La Mariña

c. Many cities and geographical places in the world have their own Spanish names or spelling.

Nueva York   Estados Unidos   Venecia   Ginebra   Londres   Holanda   Inglaterra

d. Articles and geographical terms included in the *official* name of a place (city, mountain, river, gulf, etc.) are written in capital letters; otherwise, lowercase is used.

Official name		Description only
la Sierra Nevada	el Río Bravo	la cordillera de los Andes
la Ciudad de México	el Río de la Plata	la ciudad de Miami
la Ciudad del Cabo	El Salvador	el río Amazonas
La Paz	El Cairo	la Argentina

e. The names of planets, stars, and constellations are written with a capital letter unless they are used as common nouns.

Los planetas giran alrededor del **Sol**.	Protégete del **sol**.	Los astronautas ven la **Tierra** desde el espacio.	En California, la **tierra** es fértil.
The planets orbit around the Sun.	*Protect yourself from the sun.*	*Astronauts look at the Earth from space.*	*In California, the land is fertile.*

1.G.3 Omission of the letter *p*

a. The letter **p** is silent in words beginning with **ps-** (**psicólogo, psiquiatra**). These words may also be spelled without the **p** (**sicólogo, siquiatra**). This spelling is accepted, but in formal texts, these words tend to keep the initial **p**. In words containing **-ps-** (**eclipse, cápsula**), the letter **p** is always kept.

b. Among the words that contain the consonant combination **-pt-**, only **septiembre** and **séptimo/a** (*seventh*) can be spelled **setiembre** and **sétimo/a**.

c. The past participles of many verbs ending in **-bir** end in **-to** in most Spanish-speaking countries, except Argentina and Uruguay, where they are spelled with **-pt-**. This is an archaic form that has remained in use in the **Río de la Plata** region.

◀ Irregular past participles: 19.A.2, 25.D.2

Infinitive	English	Past participle	Past participle (Arg./Uru.)
describir	*to describe*	descrito	descripto
inscribir	*to inscribe*	inscrito	inscripto
suscribir	*to subscribe*	suscrito	suscripto

1.H The Spanish language

La lengua española

In the Spanish-speaking world, the terms **español** (*Spanish*) or **castellano** (*Castilian*) are used to refer to the Spanish language, which today is one of the most widely spoken languages in the world. Castilian was the language in **Castilla** (*Castile*), the powerful kingdom that united with the kingdom of **Aragón** to form **España** and reached the coasts of the New World in 1492. Castile's language spread quickly to the new continent and the word *Castilian,* therefore, shows the origin of the Spanish language. The term is still associated in Spain with the language variant spoken in today's Castile, the government's center. Spain's constitution (1978) declares that **castellano** is the national language, but that the autonomous provinces can have their own official language in addition to **castellano**. Today **catalán** (*Catalan*), **euskera** (*Basque*), **gallego** (*Galician*), and **valenciano** (*Valencian*) are official languages, along with Castilian, in their regions. Furthermore, there are other languages that are not official, such as those spoken in Asturias and Mallorca.

In most of Latin America, **español** and **castellano** are synonyms, but the term **español** is more common than **castellano**. The Spanish variant, **español americano** or **español de América,** is the mother tongue of over 90% of the nearly 500 million Spanish-speaking people in the world (including the U.S.). Spanish in Latin America also coexists with other languages, such as **maya** and **náhuatl** (in Mexico and Guatemala), **quechua** (in Ecuador, Peru, and Bolivia), **guaraní** (in Paraguay), and **English** (in the Caribbean). In many new Latin American constitutions from the 1990s, the majority of countries declared themselves multicultural and multilingual nations, naming Spanish as their official language or as one of their official languages.

Ever since the 1700s, when the Royal Academy for the Spanish Language (**La Real Academia Española, RAE**) published its first standard works—a dictionary, *Diccionario de autoridades* (1726–1739); a text on spelling, *Ortografía* (1741); and one on grammar, *Gramática* (1771)—its rules have played an important role in retaining the Castilian variant as the norm in the whole of the Spanish-speaking world. Eventually, with the formation of the Association of Spanish Language Academies (**Asociación de Academias de la Lengua Española, ASALE**) in 1951, the Spanish-speaking world was finally treated as a whole in terms of the development and use of the Spanish language. A goal was set to maintain the Spanish-speaking community, but also to recognize and make known the different variations of the Spanish language. This goal led to the release of a common description of the Spanish language in the form of a spelling text (1999), a common dictionary, and a common grammar text (approved by the ASALE in 2007 and published in 2010). An updated spelling text, the *Nueva ortografía*, was approved in late 2010. **A Handbook of Contemporary Spanish Grammar** is written from this integral perspective of the Spanish language.

Asociación de Academias de la Lengua Española (ASALE), 1951: http://asale.org	
Real Academia Española (RAE), 1713	Academia Hondureña de la Lengua, 1948
Academia Argentina de Letras, 1931	Academia Mexicana de la Lengua, 1875
Academia Boliviana de la Lengua, 1927	Academia Nacional de Letras de Uruguay, 1943
Academia Chilena de la Lengua, 1885	Academia Nicaragüense de la Lengua, 1928
Academia Colombiana de la Lengua, 1871	Academia Norteamericana de la Lengua Española, 1973
Academia Costarricense de la Lengua, 1923	Academia Panameña de la Lengua, 1926
Academia Cubana de la Lengua, 1926	Academia Paraguaya de la Lengua Española, 1927
Academia Dominicana de la Lengua, 1927	Academia Peruana de la Lengua, 1887
Academia Ecuatoriana de la Lengua, 1874	Academia Puertorriqueña de la Lengua Española, 1945
Academia Filipina de la Lengua Española, 1924	Academia Salvadoreña de la Lengua, 1876
Academia Guatemalteca de la Lengua, 1887	Academia Venezolana de la Lengua, 1883

Práctica

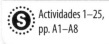 Actividades 1–25, pp. A1–A8

Nouns
Sustantivos

2.A Gender

Género

Nouns are words that refer to people, animals, things, places, events, or ideas. In Spanish, nouns are either feminine or masculine.

2.A.1 People and animals

a. The ending **-a** usually indicates feminine and the ending **-o** usually indicates masculine.

Masculine		Feminine	
el amig**o**	*(male) friend*	**la** amig**a**	*(female) friend*
el chic**o**	*boy*	**la** chic**a**	*girl*
el niñ**o**	*(male) child*	**la** niñ**a**	*(female) child*
el gat**o**	*(male) cat*	**la** gat**a**	*(female) cat*

Determiners and subjects: 4.B.1
Use of definite articles: 5.C

b. An **-a** is added to a noun that ends in **-or** to make it feminine.

Masculine		Feminine	
el profes**or**	*(male) teacher*	**la** profes**ora**	*(female) teacher*
el señ**or**	*man/lord*	**la** señ**ora**	*woman/lady*

c. Nouns that end in **-ista** and **-al** can be either feminine or masculine. This is determined by the article or context.

el/la art**ista**	*artist*	**el/la** intelectu**al**	*intellectual*
el/la correspons**al**	*correspondent*	**el/la** profesion**al**	*professional*
el/la electric**ista**	*electrician*	**el/la** riv**al**	*rival*
el/la fisc**al**	*district attorney*		

Poeta is both masculine and feminine. The feminine **poetisa** is also used.

d. Nouns ending in **-ante, -ente** that refer to people usually can be either masculine or feminine based on the article used.

Masculine	Feminine	
el ag**ente**	**la** ag**ente**	*agent*
el cant**ante**	**la** cant**ante**	*singer*
el estudi**ante**	**la** estudi**ante**	*student*
el paci**ente**	**la** paci**ente**	*patient*
el particip**ante**	**la** particip**ante**	*participant*
el represent**ante**	**la** represent**ante**	*representative*

Some nouns have an **-ente** ending in the masculine form and an **-enta** ending in the feminine form.

Masculine	Feminine	
el asist**ente**	**la** asist**enta**	*assistant*
el dependi**ente**	**la** dependi**enta**	*shop assistant*
el ger**ente**	**la** ger**enta**	*manager*
el pari**ente**	**la** pari**enta**	*relative*
el presid**ente**	**la** presid**enta**	*president*

The forms **la gerente** and **la pariente** are also used.

e. A number of social roles and professions use separate masculine and feminine nouns.

el emperador (*emperor*) → la emperatriz (*empress*)

el padrino (*godfather*) → la madrina (*godmother*)

Masculine		Feminine	
el actor	*actor*	**la** actriz	*actress*
el caballero	*gentleman*	**la** dama	*lady*
el hombre	*man*	**la** mujer	*woman*
el padre, **el** papá	*father*	**la** madre, **la** mamá	*mother*
el príncipe	*prince*	**la** princesa	*princess*
el rey	*king*	**la** reina	*queen*
el yerno	*son-in-law*	**la** nuera	*daughter-in-law*

f. Some nouns can only be masculine or feminine even though they can refer to both men and women.

Mi padre es **una** buena **persona**.   *My father is a good person.*

¡Tu hija es **un encanto**!   *Your daughter is a sweetheart!*

g. For some animals, the *noun* + **macho** is used for males, and the *noun* + **hembra** for females. Some animal names have masculine and feminine forms, while others have different words for males and females. Pets, such as **el** gat**o** or **el** perr**o**, usually follow gender rules and can take an **-a** in the feminine (**la** gat**a**, **la** perr**a**).

Masculine		Feminine	
la jirafa **macho**	*male giraffe*	**la** jirafa **hembra**	*female giraffe*
el oso	*(male) bear*	**la** osa	*(female) bear*
el león	*lion*	**la** leona	*lioness*
el caballo	*horse*	**la yegua**	*mare*
el toro	*bull*	**la vaca**	*cow*
el gallo	*rooster*	**la gallina**	*hen*

2.A.2 Things

a. Nouns that refer to concrete things or abstract ideas are, with a few exceptions, masculine if they end in **-o** and feminine if they end in **-a**.

Singular feminine nouns that begin with a stressed **a** or **ha** take the masculine singular article, but take an adjective with a feminine form. **el agua clara, el alma buena**: 5.A.3

Masculine		Feminine	
el calendari**o**	*calendar*	la ros**a**	*rose*
el florer**o**	*vase*	la calculador**a**	*calculator*
el libr**o**	*book*	la impresor**a**	*printer*
el pensamient**o**	*thought*	la ide**a**	*idea*

20

Nouns • **Chapter 2**

Exceptions:

Masculine		Feminine	
el día	*day*	**la** mano	*hand*
el mapa	*map*	**la** foto	*photo*
el planeta	*planet*	**la** moto	*motorcycle*
el tranvía	*streetcar*	**la** radio	*radio*

La foto and **la moto** are feminine because they are short for **la fotografía** and **la motocicleta**.

La radio is used for radio as a means of communication; **el radio** means the actual radio, as well as *radius* and *radium*.

b. Nouns that end in **-e** can be masculine or feminine.

el cine	*cinema*	**la** gente	*people*
la clase	*class*	**el** puente	*bridge*

c. Most nouns that end in **-i** or **-u** are masculine, but a few are feminine.

el rubí	*ruby*	**el** espíritu	*spirit*
el tabú	*taboo*	**la** tribu	*tribe*

d. Nouns that end in **-aje, -al, -és, -in,** and **-or** are usually masculine.

el pasaje	*fare/ticket*	**el** canal	*canal*	**el** estrés	*stress*
el fin	*end*	**el** sabor	*taste*	**el** valor	*value/worth*

Exceptions:

la catedral	*cathedral*	**la** sal	*salt*
la flor	*flower*	**la** labor	*task*

e. Many nouns that end in **-ma** are masculine. Most are of Greek origin and have cognates in English.

el clima	*climate*	**el** idioma	*language*	**el** programa	*program*
el dilema	*dilemma*	**el** panorama	*panorama*	**el** síntoma	*symptom*
el drama	*drama*	**el** poema	*poem*	**el** sistema	*system*
el enigma	*enigma*	**el** problema	*problem*	**el** tema	*theme/topic*

f. Nouns that end in **-ción, -sión, -dad, -tad, -umbre, -tud, -is,** and **-z** are usually feminine.

la lección	*lesson*	**la** televisión	*television*
la actividad	*activity*	**la** libertad	*freedom*
la costumbre	*custom*	**la** juventud	*youth*
la síntesis	*synthesis*	**la** luz	*light*

Exceptions:

el arroz	*rice*	**el** lápiz	*pencil*

2.A.3 Other nouns

a. Names of colors are masculine.

el azul	*blue*	**el** blanco	*white*	**el** rojo	*red*
el amarillo	*yellow*	**el** negro	*black*	**el** verde	*green*

This is true even for color words that end in **-a** (**el rosa**).

b. Names of days, months, trees, mountains, rivers, numbers, oceans, and lakes are masculine.

Trabajo **los** lunes.	*I work on Mondays.*	**El** Amazonas es largo.	*The Amazon River is long.*
Enero es frío.	*January is cold.*	**El** 13 no es peligroso.	*The number 13 is not dangerous.*
El pino es bonito.	*The pine tree is beautiful.*	**El** Atlántico es inmenso.	*The Atlantic Ocean is enormous.*
El Aconcagua es alto.	*Mount Aconcagua is high.*	**El** Titicaca es hermoso.	*Lake Titicaca is beautiful.*

City names that begin with ▶
San/Santo are masculine:
San Francisco, Santo
Domingo, Santo Tomás.
City names that begin
with **Santa** are feminine:
Santa Marta, Santa
Mónica: 3.D.2

c. The gender of town names varies. Names of towns are often feminine if they end in an unstressed **-a**, and if the town is considered a city (**una ciudad**). If you define a town as a place (**un sitio**), masculine is also possible.

la hermosa Barcelona	*beautiful Barcelona*
la lejana Santiago	*remote Santiago*
el misterioso Machu Picchu	*the mysterious Machu Picchu*

d. Names of letters are feminine: **la letra** (*letter*).

La eñe es española.   *The letter **ñ** is Spanish.*

e. Infinitives used as nouns are masculine.

el deber   *duty*   **el** atardecer   *dusk*

f. Some nouns can be either masculine or feminine, depending on their meaning.

Masculine		Feminine	
el capital	*capital (funds)*	**la** capital	*capital (city)*
el cometa	*comet*	**la** cometa	*kite*
el cura	*priest*	**la** cura	*cure*
el editorial	*editorial*	**la** editorial	*publishing house*
el frente	*front*	**la** frente	*forehead*
el guía	*(male) tour guide*	**la** guía	*(female) tour guide; guidebook*
el mañana	*future*	**la** mañana	*morning*
el modelo	*example; (male) model*	**la** modelo	*(female) model*
el orden	*order*	**la** orden	*command; religious order*
el papa	*pope*	**la** papa	*potato (Lat. Am.)*
el pendiente	*earring*	**la** pendiente	*slope*
el policía	*policeman*	**la** policía	*policewoman/the police*

2.B Number

Número

Accentuation of plurals and ▶
compound words: 1.E.9

2.B.1 Regular plurals

a. Nouns that end in an *unstressed vowel* form the plural with an **-s**.

Singular		Plural	
el amig**o**	*friend*	los amig**os**	*friends*
la cas**a**	*house*	las cas**as**	*houses*
el espírit**u**	*spirit*	los espírit**us**	*spirits*
la noch**e**	*night*	las noch**es**	*nights*

b. Nouns that end in a *stressed* **-a, -o**, or **-e** form the plural with an **-s**.

Singular		Plural	
la mam**á**	*mother*	las mam**ás**	*mothers*
el pap**á**	*father*	los pap**ás**	*fathers*
el sof**á**	*sofa*	los sof**ás**	*sofas*
el caf**é**	*coffee/café*	los caf**és**	*coffees/cafés*

Singular		Plural	
el pie	*foot*	los pies	*feet*
el dominó	*domino*	los dominós	*dominoes*
el buró	*bureau*	los burós	*bureaus*

c. Most nouns that end in a *consonant* form the plural with **-es**. When the noun ends in **-z** in the singular, the **-z** changes to **-c** in the plural.

Singular		Plural	
la actividad	*activity*	las actividades	*activities*
el papel	*paper*	los papeles	*papers*
el monitor	*monitor*	los monitores	*monitors*
el pez	*fish*	los peces	*fish [pl.]*

d. Most nouns that end in a *stressed* **-i** or **-u** can form the plural with **-s** or **-es**, but **-es** is the preferred form. Some words of foreign origin form the plural only by adding **-s**.

Singular		Plural	
el esquí	*ski*	los esquíes, los esquís	*skis*
el rubí	*ruby*	los rubíes, los rubís	*rubies*
el tabú	*taboo*	los tabúes, los tabús	*taboos*
el popurrí	*potpourri*	los popurrís	*potpourris*
el champú	*shampoo*	los champús	*shampoos*
el menú	*menu*	los menús	*menus*

e. Nouns ending in **-n** or **-s** that have an accent on the last syllable form the plural with **-es** and drop the accent in order to keep the original stress.

Singular		Plural	
la transmisión	*broadcast*	**las** transmisiones	*broadcasts*
el autobús	*bus*	**los** autobuses	*buses*

Note that there are also nouns that require an accent in the plural to maintain the correct stress, 1.E.9:

joven ⟶ jóvenes

2.B.2 Irregular plurals

a. Nouns that end in an *unstressed* (**átona**) vowel followed by **-s** do not change form between singular and plural.

el lunes	*Monday*	los lunes	*Mondays*	el análisis	*analysis*	los análisis	*analyses*
el martes	*Tuesday*	los martes	*Tuesdays*	la crisis	*crisis*	las crisis	*crises*
el miércoles	*Wednesday*	los miércoles	*Wednesdays*	el oasis	*oasis*	los oasis	*oases*
el jueves	*Thursday*	los jueves	*Thursdays*	la tesis	*thesis*	las tesis	*theses*
el viernes	*Friday*	los viernes	*Fridays*	el virus	*virus*	los virus	*viruses*

b. Some nouns are used only in the plural.

las afueras	*outskirts*	**las** nupcias	*wedding*	**los** anteojos	*glasses*
las esposas	*handcuffs*	**las** tijeras	*scissors*	**los** alrededores	*surroundings*
las gafas	*glasses*	**las** vacaciones	*vacation*	**los** celos	*jealousy*

los enseres	*belongings*
los prismáticos	*binoculars*
los víveres	*provisions*

c. The following nouns have irregular plural forms.

el carácter	*character*	**los** caracteres	*characters*
el régimen	*regime*	**los** regímenes	*regimes*
el espécimen	*specimen*	**los** especímenes	*specimens*

Accentuation of plural and compound words: 1.E.9b

2.C Expressive suffixes

Sufijos expresivos

2.C.1 Overview

A suffix is an ending that is added to a word. In Spanish, nouns have three types of expressive suffixes: *diminutives* (**diminutivos**), *augmentatives* (**aumentativos**), and *pejoratives* (**despectivos**). They are used to express feelings or judgements about events, people, and things. While diminutives and augmentatives are generally used to express affection or size, pejorative suffixes attach negative meaning to a word. The use and meaning of expressive suffixes varies greatly depending on context, intonation of the speaker, and regional differences. The formation of these suffixes also differs from region to region, but the most common rules are described next.

2.C.2 Structure of diminutives

The most common diminutive suffix is **-ito/a**. Other suffixes are **-illo/a**, **-ico/a**, and **-uelo/a**.

> The spelling changes if the word ends in a syllable with **-c-** or **-g-**: jue**go**/jue**guito**, bar**co**/bar**quito**.

a. Generally, in nouns ending with an *unstressed* **-o** or **-a**, the vowel is dropped to add the diminutive **-ito/a**.

gat**o**/gat**ito**   *cat/kitten*   niñ**a**/niñ**ita**   *girl/little girl*

> In these examples, the ending **-cito/-cita** is more common in Latin America.
> More diminutives of **café**: café**tito**, café**tico**, café**tín**, café**tillo**.

b. If a word ends in a *stressed* vowel, the preferred ending is **-cito/a,** but the diminutive can vary depending on the region.

bebé → bebe**cito**, beb**ito**   papá → papa**cito**, papa**íto**, pap**ito**   café → cafe**cito**, cafe**íto**

c. The most common ending of two-syllable nouns that end in **-e** is **-ecito/a**: madre**cita**. If the word has more than two syllables, the ending is usually **-ito/a**: compadr**ito**, comadr**ita**.

> In general, **-ecito/-ecita** and **-ecillo/-ecilla** are more common in Spain, but they are also used in several parts of Latin America.

d. When a one-syllable word ends in a consonant, both **-cito/-cita** and **-ecito/-ecita** can be used: pan**cito**, pan**cillo**, pan**ecito**, pan**ecillo**, flor**cita**, flor**cilla**, flor**ecita**, flor**ecilla**.

> Words ending in **-z** have a spelling change:
> luz → luce**cita**
> Beatriz → Beatri**cita**

e. Words with two or more syllables that end in **-n** or **-r** usually take the ending **-cito/a**: camion**cito**, amor**cito**, cancion**cita**. If they end in any other consonant, the ending is usually **-ito/-ita**: lapi**cito**, dificil**ito**.

2.C.3 Structure of augmentatives and pejoratives

Augmentatives (**aumentativos**) and pejoratives (**despectivos**) are formed similarly to diminutives, adding **-ote/a** (**-zote/-zota**), **-azo/a**, **-ón/ona** and **-ucho/a**, **-aco/a**, **-ajo/a**, respectively.

casa/cas**ona**   *house/big house*   casa/cas**ucha**   *house/ugly house*

2.C.4 Gender and number

Words with an expressive suffix follow the rules for forming plurals. They also keep their grammatical category and gender, but some feminine nouns can also be converted to a masculine form with the ending **-ón** for greater emphasis.

noticia → notici**ón**/notici**ona**   *really big news/big news*
lámpara → lampar**ón**/lampar**ona**   *great big lamp/big lamp*

2.C.5 Accentuation

> Palabras agudas: 1.E.1
> Palabras llanas: 1.E.2

The expressive suffix always has the stressed syllable of a word. For this reason, most diminutives form **palabras llanas** (words with the stress on the next-to-last syllable): television**cita**, cama**rita**. The endings **-ón, -ín** form **palabras agudas** (words with the stress on the last syllable): camis**ón,** pequeñ**ín**.

2.C.6 Grammatical category

Throughout most of the Spanish-speaking world, expressive suffixes are generally used with just nouns and adjectives. However, in Latin America, diminutives are also used in other grammatical categories. Some examples of the different grammatical categories are listed in the following table.

Base word	Diminutive	Augmentative	Pejorative
camión *n.*	camion**cito**	camion**ón**, camion**zote**, camion**azo**	camion**ucho**, camion**ete**, camion**aco**
casa *n.*	cas**ita**	cas**ota**, cas**ona**	cas**ucha**
libro *n.*	libr**ito**	libr**ote**, libr**ón**, libr**azo**	libr**ucho**, libr**aco**, libr**ajo**
débil *adj.*	debil**ito/a**, debil**cito/a**	debil**ote/a**	debil**ucho/a**
fuerte *adj.*	fuerte**cito/a**	fuert**ote/a**, fuert**ón/ona**	fuert**ucho/a**
ahora *adv.*	ahor**ita**		
aquí *adv.*	aqui**cito**		
nada *pron.*	nad**ita**		
todo *pron.*	tod**ito/a**		
adiós *interj.*	adios**ito**		

Adjectives: 3.A.4
Adverbs: 10.J.1

2.C.7 Combinations

Many nouns and adjectives can combine various suffixes (often repeated), but the final result depends on phonetic factors, number of syllables, specific noun or adjective and, of course, on regional and personal preferences.

chico	chiqu**ito**, chiqu**itico**, chiqu**itito**, chiqu**itiquitico**, chiqu**illo**, chiqu**illito**, chiqu**illico**, chiqu**illote**, chiqu**illazo**, chic**ucho**
joven	joven**citico**, joven**citito**, joven**zotote**
casa	cas**uchita**

2.C.8 Dictionary words

Some words with diminutive and augmentative suffixes have been used for so long that they appear in dictionaries and are no longer considered diminutives and augmentatives: **ventanilla, bocadillo, sillón**.

2.C.9 Uses of diminutives

a. To indicate smaller size or brevity of events. They can also indicate less intensity when describing people and things.

Tengo un **autito**.	*I have a little car.*
Demos un **paseíto**.	*Let's take a short walk.*
¿Te da **miedito** conducir por esta carretera?	*Aren't you a little scared of driving on this road?*
¿Por qué estás **tristecita** hoy?	*Why are you a little sad today?*

b. To show affection when speaking to loved ones or talking about them: **mamita, papito, amorcito, abuelita, noviecita**. Diminutives are also common with proper names: **Susanita, Eduardito**.

c. To soften requests or orders:

| ¿Me sirve un **cafecito**, por favor? | *Can I get a coffee, please?* |
| ¿Me haces un **favorcito**? | *Can you do me a little favor?* |

d. To soften the meaning of strong words or characteristics:

Esos chicos son unos **ladroncitos**.　　　　　*Those boys are just a couple of little thieves.*

e. To diminish the importance of uncomfortable or disagreeable situations:

La **multita** por la infracción es de cien dólares.　*It's only a little one-hundred dollar fine.*
La **operacioncita** no tiene importancia.　　　*The little procedure is nothing.*

2.C.10　Uses of augmentatives and pejoratives

a. To intensify the positive or negative meaning of a noun or adjective:

¡Tu visita me dio un **alegrón** inmenso!　　　*Your visit (absolutely) made my day!*
Tenemos un **problemazo**.　　　　　　　*We have a very/really big problem.*

Talking about age: 6.H.3

b. To express an exaggerated size. The ending **-azo/a** can be positive, but context and intonation are crucial for its meaning. When referring to age, the ending **-ón/ona** can be derogatory.

Tienes unos **ojazos** que me encantan.　　　*I just love your big eyes.*
Él es un **cuarentón** sin futuro.　　　　　*He's a forty-something with no future.*

c. To communicate a "hard hit" with the object described:

machete → **machetazo**　　balón → **balonazo**　　bate → **batazo**　　codo → **codazo**

Adjectives: 3.A.4

d. Both nouns and adjectives can have pejorative suffixes.

¡Has escrito una **novelucha** sin valor!　　　*You've written a completely worthless novel!*
Esa pobre familia vive en una **casucha**.　　　*That poor family lives in (such) a dump.*
Este bombero **debilucho** casi no empata las mangueras.　*This weakling firefighter has trouble connecting the hoses.*

2.D　Regional variations

Variaciones regionales

2.D.1　Gender

The following nouns can be either masculine or feminine depending on the region.

el/la azúcar	*sugar*		**el/la** lente	*lens*
el/la Internet	*Internet*		**el/la** maratón	*marathon*
el/la interrogante	*query, question*		**el/la** sartén	*frying pan*

2.D.2　Job titles

a. In Spanish-speaking countries, the masculine form is traditionally used for all job titles, for women as well as men (**el/la piloto**). The use of feminine forms for many of these job titles is now common.

la abogad**a**　*lawyer*　　　　　**la** médic**a**　*doctor*

For a better understanding of the differences in pronunciation of the **c** and **z** between Spain and Latin America, see Consonants and digraphs: 1.C.6.

b. Words referring to people, especially job titles, that have historically had only a masculine form can now be found in the feminine.

el general	**la** general**a**	*general*	**el** ingeniero	**la** ingenier**a**	*engineer*
el juez	**la** juez**a**	*judge*	**el** ministro	**la** ministr**a**	*minister*

2.D.3　Common word variations

The most common regional variations in Spanish are expressed through vocabulary, especially nouns. For example, *hunting* is called **caza** in Spain, while in Latin America it is called **cacería**. In Latin America, **caza** is pronounced the same as **casa** (*house*), so a different word is used.

Práctica

(S) Actividades 1–18, pp. A8–A14.

Adjectives
Adjetivos

3.A Gender and number

Género y número

An adjective describes a noun and agrees with the noun in gender and number.

3.A.1 Endings *-o / -a*

Adjectives that end in **-o** in the masculine form change to **-a** for the feminine form and add **-s** to form the plural.

	Singular		**Plural**	
Masculine	el libr**o** blanc**o**	*the white book*	los libr**os** blanc**os**	*the white books*
Feminine	la cas**a** blanc**a**	*the white house*	las cas**as** blanc**as**	*the white houses*

3.A.2 Endings *-e / -ista*

Adjectives that end in **-e** or **-ista** do not change in gender, but they do change in number.

	Singular		**Plural**	
Masculine	**el** libr**o** grand**e**	*the big book*	**los** libr**os** grand**es**	*the big books*
	el país social**ista**	*the socialist country*	**los** países social**istas**	*the socialist countries*
Feminine	**la** cas**a** grand**e**	*the big house*	**las** cas**as** grand**es**	*the big houses*
	la nación social**ista**	*the socialist nation*	**las** naciones social**istas**	*the socialist nations*

If the adjective is augmentative and ends in **-ote,** it forms the feminine with an **-a.**

grandot**ote,** grandot**ota**   *very big*

◀ Diminutives, augmentatives, and pejoratives: 3.A.4

3.A.3 Other endings

a. For adjectives that end in **-or, -án, -ón, -ín,** add **-a** to form the feminine and remove the written accent. To form the plural, add **-es** to the masculine form and **-s** to the feminine form. Bear in mind that in the masculine plural form, the written accent is not needed for the endings **-anes, -ones, -ines**.

conservad**or(es)**	conservad**ora(s)**	*conservative*
encantad**or(es)**	encantad**ora(s)**	*charming*
trabajad**or(es)**	trabajad**ora(s)**	*hard-working*
holgaz**án**/holgaz**anes**	holgaz**ana(s)**	*lazy*
glot**ón**/glot**ones**	glot**ona(s)**	*gluttonous*
pequeñ**ín**/pequeñ**ines**	pequeñ**ina(s)**	*tiny*

b. The following comparative adjectives that end in **-or** do not change in gender, but do add **-es** in the plural.

◀ Comparison of adjectives: 3.E
Comparisons: Ch. 11

anteri**or(es)**	*previous/front*	posteri**or(es)**	*subsequent/back*
mej**or(es)**	*better*	pe**or(es)**	*worse*
interi**or(es)**	*interior*	exteri**or(es)**	*exterior*
may**or(es)**	*older*	men**or(es)**	*younger*
superi**or(es)**	*superior*	inferi**or(es)**	*inferior*

c. Most adjectives ending in **-és** become feminine by adding **-a**. This is the case for adjectives of nationality (**gentilicios**). The feminine singular form and both the masculine and feminine plural forms lose the written accent.

Masculine	Feminine	
danés/daneses	danes**a**(s)	*Danish*
francés/franceses	frances**a**(s)	*French*
inglés/ingleses	ingles**a**(s)	*English*
portugués/portugueses	portugues**a**(s)	*Portuguese*

Exception:

The adjective **cortés** (*polite*) keeps the same form in the feminine. It has the same plural form for both masculine and feminine.

el chico cort**és**   *the polite boy*   **la** chica cort**és**   *the polite girl*

los chicos cort**eses**   *the polite boys*   **las** chicas cort**eses**   *the polite girls*

Many adjectives that form nouns ▶ come from art, science, and technology fields.
La **curva** es peligrosa.
La línea es **curva**.

d. Adjectives that end in **-a, í, -ú** do not change in gender, but do have a plural form. Adjectives that end in **-e** or in the consonants **-z, -l, -r, -s** act in the same way.

Singular		Plural	
problema **agrícola**	*agricultural problem*	problemas **agrícolas**	*agricultural problems*
persona **belga**	*Belgian person*	personas **belgas**	*Belgian people*
marinero **bengalí**	*Bengali sailor*	marineros **bengalíes**	*Bengali sailors*
templo **hindú**	*Hindu temple*	templos **hindúes**	*Hindu temples*
estudiante **feliz**	*happy student*	estudiantes **felices**	*happy students*
clase **útil**, libro **útil**	*useful class, useful book*	clases y libros **útiles**	*useful books and classes*
círculo **polar**	*polar circle*	círculos **polares**	*polar circles*

Remember that **z** changes to ▶ **c** when **-es** is added to a word ending in **-z**.

3.A.4 **Diminutives, augmentatives, and pejoratives**

Expressive suffixes: 2.C ▶

a. Like nouns, adjectives are very flexible when it comes to adding expressive suffixes. The most common diminutive endings are **-ito/a(s)** and in some cases **-cito/a(s), -ecito/a(s),** and **-illo/a(s), -ín(ines)/ina(s)**.

amarill**ito(s)**   *yellowish*   pequeñ**ín(es)**   *tiny*

gord**ito(s)**   *chubby*   verde**cilla(s)**   *greenish*

b. Augmentatives are less common in adjectives than in nouns. The endings are **-ote/a(s), -zote/a(s), -ón(ones)/ona(s)**.

dul**zón**   *"somewhat sweet"*   simpatic**ona**   *very friendly (derogatory)/ "somewhat" nice*

joven**zote**   *handsome young man*   grand**ote**   *very big*

c. The suffix **-ón(ones)/ona(s)** can also be added to nouns to turn them into adjectives. These tend to have a negative connotation.

boca   *mouth*   María, ¡no seas boc**ona**!   *María, don't be a bigmouth!*

barriga   *belly*   Juan es muy barrig**ón**.   *Juan has a big belly.*

d. Some pejorative suffixes are **-acho/a, -ucho/a(s), -ajo/a(s)**. The English translations may lack the negative connotation the Spanish provides.

fe**úcho**	*quite ugly*	fri**úcha**	*very cold*	pequeñ**ajo**	*very small*
flac**ucho**	*too thin*	gord**ote**	*too fat*	ric**acho**	*filthy rich*

3.B   Agreement

Concordancia

3.B.1 Nouns with the same gender

When an adjective describes several nouns of the *same* gender, the adjective takes the same gender in the plural.

un libr**o** y un cuadern**o** nuev**os**	*a new book and notebook*
una lámpar**a** y una mes**a** nuev**as**	*a new lamp and table*

3.B.2 Nouns of different gender

a. When an adjective describes several nouns of *different* gender and comes *after* the nouns, it takes the masculine form in the plural.

una herman**a** y un herman**o** simpátic**os**	*a nice sister and brother*
un libr**o** y una mes**a** nuev**os**	*a new book and table*

b. When an adjective describes several nouns of *different* gender and comes *before* the nouns, it agrees with the nearest noun.

un**os** simpátic**os** amig**os** y amig**as**	*some nice friends*
un**as** simpátic**as** amig**as** y amig**os**	*some nice friends*

3.B.3 Nouns used as adjectives

Nouns can be used as adjectives to modify other nouns. In this usage, they do not vary in number.

la palabra **clave**	*the keyword*	las palabras **clave**	*the keywords*
el programa **piloto**	*the pilot program*	los programas **piloto**	*the pilot programs*
el coche **bomba**	*the car bomb*	los coches **bomba**	*the car bombs*

3.B.4 Colors

a. It is common to use names of flowers, plants, minerals, and seeds as color adjectives. In this case, they are normally considered invariable and are commonly used with **(de) color**. Words in this category include **naranja** (*orange*), **lila** (*lilac*), and **rosa** (*pink*).

la(s) corbata(s) **café/(de) color café**	*the brown tie(s)*
el/los mantel(es) **naranja/(de) color naranja**	*the orange tablecloth(s)*

b. They can also be treated as regular adjectives, in which case they agree with the noun in number but the gender does not vary: **calcetines lilas**. In the case of **naranja** and **rosa**, the adjectives **anaranjado/a(s)** and **rosado/a(s)** can also be used.

las camisas **rosas**/las camisas **rosadas**	*the pink shirts*

c. When colors are modified by other adjectives (**claro, oscuro, pálido**), both the color and the adjective are usually considered invariable. This usage assumes the omission of the masculine singular noun **color**.

medias **verdes**	*green socks*	medias **(color) verde claro**	*light-green socks*
piel **pálida**	*pale skin*	piel **(color) rosa pálido**	*pale pink skin*

3.C Placement

Posición

The adjective usually comes after the noun, but it can also come before the noun.

3.C.1 Placement after the noun

a. An adjective placed after a noun distinguishes that particular noun from others within the same group. It is the most common placement in Spanish.

Me gustan las películas **cómicas**.　　　　　　*I like funny movies.*

In this example, the adjective **cómicas** restricts the meaning of the noun by referring only to *funny* movies and excluding all other movies that are not funny.

Adjectives and determiners with ▶ fixed placement: 3.C.3c

b. "Relational" adjectives that either derive from a noun or classify a noun always come after the noun. Context determines whether an adjective is relational. For example, **grave** can come before or after **enfermedad** to describe an illness. However, **mental** can only come after **enfermedad** because it describes the specific nature of the disease: one related specifically to the brain. These adjectives can usually be paraphrased as "related to" or, in Spanish, as **de** + *noun*: **enfermedad mental = enfermedad de la mente**.

una enfermedad **mental**	una enfermedad **de la mente**
economía **nacional**	economía **de la nación**
actuación **cinematográfica**	actuación **de cine**
ecuación **matemática**	ecuación **de matemáticas**
sitio **web**	sitio **de Internet**
cosas **técnicas**	cosas **de la tecnología**

3.C.2 Placement before the noun

a. Adjectives can come before a noun to emphasize or intensify a particular characteristic or suggest that it is inherent to the noun.

una **oscura** noche de invierno	*a dark winter night*
el **horrible** monstruo	*the horrible monster*

When the adjective comes ▶ before a noun, the noun must be defined by a determiner. See Determiner placement in relation to the noun: 4.B.5

b. Adjectives that come before a noun can create a certain stylistic effect or tone. They can indicate how the speaker feels toward the person or thing being described.

el **talentoso** autor	*the talented author*
las **feas** casas	*the ugly houses*
unas **pequeñas** calles	*some small streets*
un **amplio** jardín	*a spacious garden*

c. Adjectives can also come before a noun to indicate that a characteristic is unique to the noun. This mostly happens in poetry and literature for stylistic effect. Such adjectives are called **epítetos** (*epithets*).

La **famosa** Manhattan con sus **altísimos** rascacielos.	*The famous Manhattan with its very tall skyscrapers.*

d. Adjectives describing known persons and things come before the noun to highlight an inherent quality or trait.

la **hermosa** ciudad de Madrid	*the beautiful city of Madrid*
mis **queridos** padres	*my dear parents*
el **asombroso** Hombre Araña	*the amazing Spiderman*

3.C.3 Adjectives and determiners with fixed placement

a. The following determiners always come *before* the noun.

amb**o/a(s)**	*both*	plen**o/a(s)**	*full*
much**o/a(s)**	*a lot (of)/many/much*	poc**o/a(s)**	*little/few*
otr**o/a(s)**	*other*	tant**o/a(s)**	*as/so much, as/so many*

b. Adjectives that describe origin, nationality, and noun type come *after* the noun.

la casa **alemana**	*the German house*	un chico **cubano**	*a Cuban boy*
una caja **fuerte**	*a safe deposit box*	la calle **principal**	*the main street*

c. Technical and professional characteristics are described by an adjective placed *after* the noun.

◀ Placement after the noun: 3.C.1b

el teléfono **celular**	*the cell phone*	la tesis **doctoral**	*the doctoral thesis*
la página **web**	*the web page*	la impresora **láser**	*the laser printer*

d. Certain adjectives that derive from a noun and convey a direct relationship to it *follow* the noun (**economía → económico; nación → nacional**).

La familia tiene problemas **económicos**.	*The family has financial problems.*
Solo vendemos productos **nacionales**.	*We sell only domestic products.*

e. With comparisons, the adjective comes *after* the noun.

Quiero un café **caliente,** no un café **frío**.	*I want a hot coffee, not a cold coffee.*

f. Adjectives with expressive suffixes come *after* the noun.

◀ Diminutives, augmentatives, and pejoratives: 3.A.4

Pedro está conduciendo un coche **nuevecito**.	*Pedro is driving a newish car.*
No conozco ciudades **feúchas** en el país.	*I don't know any ugly cities in this country.*

3.C.4 Placement and meaning

A number of common adjectives change meaning depending on whether they come before or after the noun.

◀ Determiners:
Agreement: 4.B.4
Placement: 4.B.5

Adjectives	Before the noun		After the noun	
alto	un **alto** ejecutivo	*a senior executive*	un ejecutivo **alto**	*a tall executive*
cierto	una **cierta** persona	*a certain person*	una cosa **cierta**	*a sure thing*
diferente	**diferentes** lugares	*several places*	lugares **diferentes**	*different places*
grande	una **gran** casa	*a grand house*	una casa **grande**	*a big house*
medio	**media** hora	*half an hour*	la clase **media**	*the middle class*
nuevo	mis **nuevos** zapatos	*my new shoes*	mis zapatos **nuevos**	*my brand-new shoes*
pobre	un **pobre** pueblo	*unlucky people*	un pueblo **pobre**	*poor/needy people*
puro	**puro** aire	*only air*	aire **puro**	*pure/clean air*
raro	una **rara** cualidad	*a rare quality*	una persona **rara**	*an unusual person*
rico	un **rico** chocolate	*a delicious chocolate*	una familia **rica**	*a rich family*
triste	un **triste** caso	*an unfortunate case*	una historia **triste**	*a sad history*
único	mi **único** amor	*my only love*	un amor **único**	*a unique love*
viejo	un **viejo** amigo	*an old friend*	un amigo **viejo**	*an elderly friend*

◀ **Grande** is shortened to **gran** before both masculine and feminine singular nouns: 3.D

◀ **Mismo, propio**: 7.E.5

3.D | Adjectives before nouns

Adjetivos antepuestos

3.D.1 | Buen, mal, primer, tercer, algún, ningún

Indefinite quantifiers **algún**, **alguno**, **alguna**; **ningún**, **ninguno**, **ninguna**: 7.B.2

The forms **bueno, malo, primero, tercero, alguno, ninguno** drop the final **-o** and become **buen, mal, primer, tercer, algún, ningún** before masculine singular nouns. This does not happen before feminine and plural nouns.

un **buen** libro	*a good book*	un **mal** ejemplo	*a bad example*
el **primer** día	*the first day*	el **tercer** año	*the third year*

3.D.2 | Gran, san

Placement and meaning: 3.C.4

a. The adjective **grande** is shortened before both masculine and feminine singular nouns. Remember that the meaning changes when **gran** comes before a noun.

un **gran** partido	*a great game*
una **gran** fiesta	*a grand party*

b. The adjective **santo** is shortened to **san** when it comes before a proper noun that does not begin with **To-** or **Do-**.

San Diego	**Santo To**más
San José	**Santo Do**mingo

3.E | Comparison

Comparación

3.E.1 | Structure

Most adjectives have a basic form, called the *positive* form. The *comparative* form expresses higher and lower degrees of a characteristic; the *superlative* form expresses the highest or lowest degrees.

Comparison of adverbs: 10.I
Comparisons: Ch. 11

Positive form		Comparative		Superlative	
verde(s)	*green*	**más** verde(s)	*greener*	**el/la/los/las más** verde(s)	*the greenest*
verde(s)	*green*	**menos** verde(s)	*less green*	**el/la/los/las menos** verde(s)	*the least green*

Todo es **más** verde en verano.	*Everything is greener in the summertime.*
La casa blanca es **la más** alta.	*The white house is the tallest.*
Mis jardines son **los más** bonitos.	*My gardens are the most beautiful.*
Esta flor es **menos** roja que esa.	*This flower is less red than that one.*

3.E.2 | Irregular forms

a. Some common adjectives have irregular comparative and superlative forms.

Comparative adjectives ending in **-or**: 3.A.3b

Positive form		Irregular comparative		Irregular superlative	
bueno/a(s)	*good*	**mejor(es)**	*better*	**(el/la) mejor**	*(the) best*
malo/a(s)	*bad*	**peor(es)**	*worse*	**(el/la) peor**	*(the) worst*
joven/jóvenes	*young*	**menor(es)**	*younger*	**(el/la) menor**	*(the) youngest*
viejo/a(s)	*old*	**mayor(es)**	*older*	**(el/la) mayor**	*(the) oldest*

Rosa es **la mayor** de todos.	*Rosa is the oldest of them all.*
Juan es **el menor** de la familia.	*Juan is the youngest in the family.*

b. The regular comparative forms of **bueno/a** and **malo/a** can be used as well. However, in this case, they exclusively emphasize character judgements.

Mario es **más bueno** que el pan.	*Mario is a very good person.*
Mario es **mejor** deportista que su hermano.	*Mario is a better athlete than his brother.*
Este perro es **más malo** que el diablo.	*This dog is more evil than the devil.*
El problema es **peor** de lo que pensaba.	*The problem is worse than I thought.*

c. Mayor and **menor** are used much more than the regular comparative forms.

Juan es **mayor** que su hermano.	*Juan is older than his brother.*
Juan es **más viejo** que su hermano.	*Juan is older than his brother.*

d. When **pequeño/a** and **grande** refer to age, their comparative and superlative forms are the same as those for **joven** and **viejo/a**.

Mario es el **más grande/pequeño** de los tres hermanos.	*Mario is the biggest/smallest of the three brothers.*
Mario es el **mayor/menor** de los tres hermanos.	*Mario is the oldest/youngest of the three brothers.*

e. Grande and **pequeño/a** also use **mayor** and **menor** as comparative and superlative forms when describing the scope or importance of an issue.

California es el estado con el **mayor** número de hispanohablantes en los EE. UU.
California is the state with the greatest number of Spanish speakers in the U.S.

3.E.3 Superlatives with *-ísimo/a(s)*

muchísimo, poquísimo: 7.C.1
Adverbs: Superlative
constructions: 10.I.2

a. Spanish also forms superlatives with the endings **-ísimo/a(s)**. This form is called the **superlativo absoluto**. For adjectives that end in a vowel, drop the vowel before adding the absolute superlative ending.

La casa es **alta**.	La casa es **altísima**.	*The house is (very) tall.*
El problema es **fácil**.	El problema es **facilísimo**.	*The problem is (very) easy.*

Note that there's no accent over the **a** in **facilísimo**.

b. A number of adjectives have spelling changes in the absolute superlative.

ri**c**o/a	ri**qu**ísimo/a	*rich/very rich*
lar**g**o/a	lar**gu**ísimo/a	*long/very long*
feli**z**	feli**c**ísimo/a	*happy/very happy*
joven	joven**c**ísimo/a	*young/very young*
trabajador(a)	trabajador**c**ísimo/a	*hard-working/very hard-working*

c. Some adjectives have irregular absolute superlatives.

antiguo/a	**antiquísimo/a**	*old/very old*
ardiente	**ardentísimo/a**	*passionate/very passionate*
cruel	**crudelísimo/a** (also **cruelísimo/a**)	*cruel/very cruel*
fiel	**fidelísimo/a**	*loyal/very loyal*

d. Adjectives ending in **-ble** form the absolute superlative with the ending **-bilísimo/a**.

Pedro es **amable**.	Pedro es **amabilísimo**.	*Pedro is (very) kind.*

e. Some adjectives have two absolute superlative forms. However, the regular form is more commonly used.

bueno/a	**buenísimo/a, bonísimo/a**	*good/very good*
fuerte	**fuertísimo/a, fortísimo/a**	*strong/very strong*

f. Some adjectives can take the suffix **-érrimo/a** instead. This is found only in formal writing.

célebre	**celebérrimo/a**	*famous/very famous*
libre	**libérrimo/a**	*free/very free*
mísero/a	**misérrimo/a**	*miserable/very miserable*
pobre	**paupérrimo/a** (also, **pobrísimo/a**)	*poor/very poor*

3.F Regional variations

Variaciones regionales

There aren't many grammatical differences in the use of adjectives in the Spanish-speaking world. The differences depend on which adjectives are used in the different regions.

3.F.1 Colors

a. In Spain, it is more common to use **marrón** than **café** for *brown*, and in Latin America **castaño** is used for *dark hair* (**cabello/pelo castaño**).

b. In some regions of the Spanish-speaking world, **morado/a** and **púrpura** are used instead of **violeta, colorado/a** is more common than **rojo/a,** and **bordó** is heard instead of **granate**.

3.F.2 Nationality

a. People from India are called **hindú** in Latin America and **indio/a** in Spain. The latter word is used in Latin America to refer to the indigenous people of the region. The adjective **indio/a,** however, also has some negative connotations in Latin America; therefore, **indígena** is preferred, especially in written language. **Indiano/a** is used in Spain for the Spaniards who returned home after becoming wealthy in the Americas.

b. The adjective **suramericano/a** is more common in most of Latin America than **sudamericano/a,** which is more common in Spain and Argentina.

3.F.3 ¿Hispano, latino o latinoamericano?

a. In the United States, the terms **hispano/a** and **latino/a** are used interchangeably to refer to people from Spanish-speaking countries. Both terms are correct, and the preference for one or the other comes from one's personal perception of subtle differences between the two words. Outside of the United States, **hispano/a** is used more frequently, since one meaning of the term **latino/a** technically refers to all of the peoples, both European and American, that speak any language derived from Latin.

b. Latinoamericano/a refers to anyone from the Americas that speaks Spanish, Portuguese, or French, while **hispanoamericano/a** refers exclusively to Spanish-speaking individuals from the Americas. **Iberoamericano/a** describes anyone from Spanish- and Portuguese-speaking countries in the Americas, or from these countries as well as Spain and Portugal.

3.F.4 México

Variations in the pronunciation of the letter **x**: 1.C.6, 1.D.5, 1.G.2a

Although at some point the adjectives **mejicano** and **mexicano** coexisted, the official name of the country is **México** and the official adjective is **mexicano**. This use of the **x** is common in many Mexican place names and in their corresponding adjectives. Although some cities have lost the **x** spelling (such as **Jalisco**), most have kept it. In most cases, this **x** is pronounced like a **j**.

México	mexicano/a	Oaxaca	oaxaqueño/a

Práctica

Actividades 1–15, pp. A15–A20.

Adjectives • **Chapter 3**

Determiners
Determinantes

4.A Overview

Aspectos generales

Determiners are words that come before a noun to indicate which person, place, thing, or idea the noun represents. They can be used to refer to something or someone nonspecific (**un** chico) or to something or someone very specific (like **el** coche or **esta** casa). Determiners can also refer to the quantitative nature of a noun, stating its exact number, as in **tres amigos**, or an indefinite amount: **varias** cosas, **muchas** chicas, **unos** estudiantes. Determiners state and clarify the nature of the noun.

Determiners		
	Groups	**Examples**
Articles *Artículos*	Specific reference: definite articles	**El** parque es grande.
	Nonspecific reference: indefinite articles	**Unos** niños juegan.
Quantifiers *Cuantificadores*	Specific quantity: numbers	Hay **tres** árboles.
	Nonspecific quantity: affirmative and negative quantifiers	Hay **muchas** personas; **algunos** chicos y **pocas** chicas.
Demonstratives *Demostrativos*	Three-level system for describing relative distance	**Este** árbol y **esas** flores me gustan. **Aquellas** no.
Possessives *Posesivos*	Forms before and after nouns	**Mi** casa es **tuya**.

It is important to note that many determiners can have several functions in a sentence. For example, quantifiers often act as adverbs. The words **mucho, bastante, más, menos** are determiners that function like adjectives when they support the noun, but they are adverbs when they support the verb.

En verano hay **muchos** conciertos.　*There are many concerts in the summer.*

(**Muchos** is a determiner and modifies **conciertos** by stating its quantity.)

Los conciertos me gustan **mucho**.　*I like concerts very much.*

(**Mucho** is an adverb of quantity and modifies the verb **gustar** by stating how much the speaker likes concerts.)

En la Florida hay **bastantes** playas.　*There are a lot of beaches in Florida.*

(**Bastantes** is a determiner and modifies **playas** by stating its quantity.)

¡Cuando voy allí, nado **bastante**!　*When I go there, I swim a lot!*

(**Bastante** is an adverb of quantity and modifies the verb **nadar** by stating how much the speaker swims.)

¡No digas **más** mentiras!　*Don't tell any more lies!*
No voy a mentir **más**.　*I won't lie anymore.*
Debes trabajar **menos**.　*You should work less.*

Articles: Ch. 5
Quantifiers: Numbers, Ch. 6
Indefinite quantifiers and pronouns: Ch. 7
Demonstratives: Ch. 8
Possessives: Ch. 9

Most determiners agree in gender and/or number with the noun they modify. Adverbs never change form. Agreement: 4.B.4 Determiners and adverbs: 4.B.7

Notice that **más** and **menos** do not change form.

Características comunes

4.B.1 Determiners and subjects

a. One of the functions of a determiner is to indicate the subject of a sentence.

Tu casa es bonita. **Las** casas son bonitas.

Such sentences without a determiner are grammatically incorrect in Spanish. This does not apply to proper nouns: **La** ciudad es hermosa. (*The city is beautiful.*), Madrid es hermosa. (*Madrid is beautiful.*)

b. When the subject is a *plural* noun, the determiner can be left out in specific written contexts such as newspapers, magazines, and commercials: **Investigadores** encuentran nuevo virus (*Researchers find new virus*), **Presos** se amotinan contra guardias (*Prisoners riot against guards*).

c. The determiner can be left out when an uncountable noun *follows* a verb that means (*not*) *to exist, to be lacking, to remain*: **Falta** azúcar. (*There's no sugar.*), **No hay** leche. (*There isn't any milk.*)

d. Countable nouns must have determiners when there's a specific quantity: Queda **un** pan. (*There is one loaf left.*), Quedan **dos** panes. (*There are two loaves left.*)

e. Plural countable nouns can follow the verb without determiners when the reference isn't specific: Faltan tenedores y cuchillos. (*There aren't any forks or knives.*)

f. The same rule applies to direct objects. A plural noun that functions as a direct object can also follow the verb without a determiner when the reference isn't specific: Compré libros. (*I bought books.*), Comemos manzanas. (*We are eating apples.*)

g. Indirect objects, however, must always be specified by a determiner: Le compré un libro a **la niña**. (*I bought a book for the girl.*)

h. Personal pronouns and proper nouns can always be the subject without a determiner: **Ella** lee. (*She is reading.*), **Pedro** habla. (*Pedro is talking.*)

4.B.2 Determiners as pronouns

Indefinite pronouns: 7.C.3, 7.D

a. When determiners stand alone, they act as pronouns. This happens only when there's no noun. To understand what the determiner is referring to, you can often use the context.

Algunos vienen, **otros** se van.	*Some are coming, others are going.*
Esta casa es cara, **esa** no.	*This house is expensive, but not that one.*
Tú tienes amigos; yo no tengo **ninguno**.	*You have friends; I have none.*

Demás: 7.C.10
Cada: 7.C.8

b. Some determiners can never stand alone as a pronoun and appear only next to other determiners. This applies to **demás,** which must always come after a definite article and is often also used with **todo**. **Cada** must be followed by a noun.

Dame **las demás** cosas.	*Give me the rest of the things.*
Todo lo demás puede esperar.	*Everything else can wait.*
Cada persona tiene sus ideas.	*Each person has his/her own ideas.*
Os visitaremos **a cada uno** de vosotros.	*We're going to visit every/each one of you.*

c. The following words are always indefinite pronouns: **algo, alguien, nada, nadie**. They can never act as determiners.

¿Vais a hacer **algo** hoy?	*Are you [pl.] going to do anything today?*
¿Hay **alguien** en casa?	*Is anyone home?*

d. Negative indefinite pronouns and negative determiners require double negation when they come after the verb.

No tenemos **ningún** plan.   *We have no plans./We don't have (any) plans.*

No hay **nadie** en casa.   *There is nobody home.*

4.B.3   Determiners and adjectives

a. An adjective describes a noun and agrees with it in gender and number. Determiners are therefore related to adjectives, but illustrate other aspects of a noun. The main difference between them is that determiners belong to *closed word groups*. This means that there is a limited number of determiners of the same type in each group. It can take hundreds of years for new determiners to develop in a language. New adjectives, on the other hand, are forming continuously in order to describe new things. For example, by following the rules for adjective formation in Spanish, one can create new ones such as in this sentence: ¡Mi hijo es **hispano-inglés, cibernavegante** y **chateadorcísimo**!

Adjectives: Ch. 3

b. Suffixes and prefixes can't be added to determiners, with the exception of **mucho** and **poco** (**muchísimo, poquísimo**).

4.B.4   Agreement

Most determiners agree in gender and number with the noun they support (**esta** casa, **algunos** libros, **pocas** chicas), but **cada, más,** and **menos** never change form (**menos** tiempo, **más** libros).

Comparison of adjectives: 3.E

4.B.5   Placement in relation to the noun

a. It is common for a determiner to come before a noun: **este** chico, **el** estudiante. If there's a descriptive adjective before the noun, the determiner must come before the adjective: **este** simpático chico, **el** buen estudiante.

Adjective placement before the noun: 3.C.2

b. Some determiners can come before or after the noun. Determiners placed after the noun highlight a feature of the noun or create a different emphasis.

Demonstratives after a noun: 8.A.2b

El chico **ese** no es simpático.   *That boy isn't nice.*

No soy una persona **cualquiera**.   *I'm not just anyone.*

*The word **ese/a** after a noun has a pejorative effect and may even convey contempt.*

4.B.6   Combination of two determiners

a. Determiners can be used together in pairs: **estos dos** libros (*these two books*), **mis otras** cosas (*my other things*). Three determiners together are rare, and in such cases the third one is usually a number word: **los otros cinco** chicos.

b. Of all determiners, only **todo/a(s)** can *come before* a definite article: **todos los** días. The following determiners (in all their forms) can *follow* the article: **el mucho** amor, **el poco** dinero, **la otra** vez, **los varios** países, **los tres** amigos.

Use of definite articles: 5.C

c. The indefinite article **un(a)** must come after **todo/a** and can only be used in its singular form in this combination. **Un(a)** must come before **cierto/a(s)**, and can be used in its singular or plural form. **Un(a)** can never be combined with **otro** like *another* in English.

Eres **todo un** caballero.   *You're a real gentleman.*

Ellos pagaron **una cierta** suma.   *They paid a certain amount.*

Ahora vivo en **otra** ciudad.   *Now, I live in another city.*

d. Demás always comes before the noun with a plural definite article: **los/las demás**. The article agrees with the noun's gender and number. It is common to add **todo/a(s)** to a definite or neuter article: **todas las demás** casas (*all those other houses*), **todo lo demás** (*all the rest*).

Demás: 7.C.10

Indefinite quantifiers and
pronouns: Ch. 7
Adverbs of quantity: 10.D.2

4.B.7 Determiners and adverbs

a. The following indefinite determiners that refer to a noun's quantity can also act as adverbs: **bastante, demasiado, más, menos, mucho, poco, tanto, todo**. Like all other adverbs, they can modify verbs, adjectives, or other adverbs.

¡Tú siempre te quejas **tanto**!	*You always complain so much!*
Trabajamos **demasiado**.	*We work too much.*
¡Chateas **bastante** en la red!	*You chat quite a bit online!*
Mi computadora es **un poco** lenta.	*My computer is a bit slow.*

b. Mucho can never be used with adjectives and adverbs; only **muy** can come before them.

El barco navega **muy** rápidamente.	*The boat is sailing very fast.*
El viento está **muy** fuerte hoy.	*The wind is very strong today.*

c. Only **tanto** and **todo** agree in gender and number when they come before an adjective.

Ella está **toda** entusiasmada.	*She is all excited.*
Mis zapatos están **todos** mojados.	*My shoes are completely soaked.*

d. The word **tan** can only be used before adjectives and adverbs.

¡El tiempo para almorzar es **tan** corto y pasa **tan** rápidamente!	*Lunchtime is so short and goes so fast!*

Comparisons: Ch. 11

4.B.8 Comparisons with *más, menos, mucho, tanto (tan)*

Comparative structures in Spanish use **que** or **como** and determiners.

El avión es **más** rápido **que** el tren.	*The plane is faster than the train.*
El rock británico es **tan** bueno **como** el estadounidense.	*British rock is just as good as American.*

Práctica

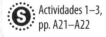 Actividades 1–3,
pp. A21–A22

Articles
Artículos

Chapter 5

Determiners (2)
A. Definite and
indefinite articles
B. Use of indefinite articles
C. Use of definite articles
D. Regional variations

5.A Definite and indefinite articles

Artículos definidos e indefinidos

5.A.1 Forms of definite and indefinite articles

Both definite and indefinite articles can be masculine or feminine, singular or plural.
They come before a noun and take the same gender and number as that noun.

	Definite articles		Indefinite articles	
	Masculine	**Feminine**	**Masculine**	**Feminine**
Singular	el	la	un	una
Plural	los	las	unos	unas

el amigo	*the friend*	**un** amigo	*a friend*
los amigos	*the friends*	**unos** amigos	*some friends*
la escuela	*the school*	**una** escuela	*a school*
las escuelas	*the schools*	**unas** escuelas	*some schools*

Note that **uno** is an *indefinite pronoun* and can never be used with a noun: 7.C.4 and 7.D.3

5.A.2 *Lo*

The neuter article **lo** is used before adjectives, possessive pronouns, and adverbs like **mejor** and **peor** in order to express abstract ideas. It can't come before nouns.

lo bueno	*the good (thing)*	**lo** mío	*my thing*

Lo mejor, lo peor: 11.D.3

5.A.3 Use of *el* and *un* with feminine nouns

El and **un** are used before feminine nouns that begin with a stressed **a-** or **ha-**. The gender of the noun does not change. It is still feminine in the plural: **el** agua, **las** aguas.

el águila bonit**a**	*the beautiful eagle*	**el ha**cha negr**a**	*the black axe*
un águila bonit**a**	*a beautiful eagle*	**un ha**cha negr**a**	*a black axe*

5.A.4 Contractions with the article *el*

When the prepositions **a** or **de** come before the definite article **el**, they combine to form a contraction: **a** + **el** = **al** and **de** + **el** = **del**.

Viajo **al** Perú.	*I'm going to Peru.*	el libro **del** chico	*the boy's book*

The article **el** does not form a contraction with the preposition when it is part of a proper name: **Viajo a El Salvador**: 5.C.6

5.B Use of indefinite articles

Uso de los artículos indefinidos

Indefinite determiners: 7.C.4

5.B.1 Placement and agreement of indefinite articles

a. Indefinite articles always come before the noun and agree with it in gender and number.

Tengo **un** libro.	*I have a book.*
Escribo **una** carta.	*I'm writing a letter.*

b. Indefinite articles often come before nouns used as subjects.

Unos turistas visitaron la Casa Blanca.	*Some/A few tourists visited the White House.*
Un chico ya la había visitado.	*A boy had already visited it.*

c. Two other determiners that can appear together with indefinite articles are **poco/a(s)** and **cada**.

Tengo **un poco** de café.	*I have some coffee.*
Tengo **unas pocas** amigas mexicanas.	*I have a few Mexican friends.*
Cada uno debe cuidar sus cosas.	*Everyone should look after his/her possessions.*

5.B.2 Reference to quantity

Indefinite determiners: 7.C.4 ▶

a. The singular indefinite articles **un** and **una** may refer to exactly one person or thing, especially in contrasts and to stress the lack of something countable (*not even one, not a single one*).

No tengo **un** hermano, sino **tres**.	*I don't have **one** brother, but **three**.*
Voy a comprar **una** torta, no **dos**.	*I'm going to buy **one** cake, not **two**.*
No hay ni **una** (sola) silla libre.	*There isn't a single vacant seat.*

b. The plural indefinite articles **unos** and **unas** refer to an undefined quantity and, with numbers, to an approximate one.

Hay **unas** estudiantes polacas.	*There are **some** Polish students.*
Me quedan **unos cuatro** dólares.	*I have **around** four dollars left.*

5.B.3 Exclamations

In exclamations, it is common to use an indefinite article in cases where it may not be required in order to add emphasis.

Hace frío.	*It's cold.*
¡Hace **un** frío!	*It's so cold!*

5.B.4 *Otro/a(s)*

Un and **una** are not used before **otro/a(s)** (*one more, another*).

¡Por favor, **otro** café!	*Another coffee, please!*	¡**Otra** vez!	*One more time!*

5.C Use of definite articles

Uso de los artículos definidos

5.C.1 General uses

Unlike English, Spanish uses the definite article when talking about people, things, or events in general.

Los estudiantes son trabajadores.	*Students are hard-working.*
Me gusta **la** leche.	*I like milk.*

5.C.2 Days and dates

a. The definite article is *not* used with months or to tell which day it is.

Hoy es lunes.	*Today is Monday.*
Ayer fue jueves.	*Yesterday was Thursday.*
Voy a Medellín en noviembre.	*I'm going to Medellín in November.*

b. The definite article is used to refer to something on a specific day or date.

Estudio **los** martes.	*I study on Tuesdays.*
La Nochebuena es **el** 24 de diciembre.	*Christmas Eve is December 24.*

5.C.3 Time

Time is indicated by **ser** + **(a) las** + *number* for plurals, and **ser** + **(a) la una** for *one o'clock*.

La clase de español **es a las** tres.	*Spanish class is at three o'clock.*
Son las cuatro de la tarde.	*It is four o'clock in the afternoon.*
La cita **es a la una**.	*The appointment is at one o'clock.*

◀ **Ser** in calendar and time expressions: 29.C.2a

5.C.4 Direct address and titles

Definite articles are not used with titles or proper names when addressing someone directly. However, when talking about someone, the article is used with most titles and matches the person in gender and number. The polite forms **don** and **doña** (which have no exact English equivalent) are used in the singular without an article and are usually followed by a first name.

Addressing someone	
Señora Gómez, ¿es usted peruana?	*Are you Peruvian, Mrs. Gómez?*
Doctor Medina, ¿cómo está usted?	*How are you, Dr. Medina?*
Don Pedro, ¿habla usted inglés?	*Do you speak English, Don Pedro?*

Talking about someone	
La señora Gómez es peruana.	*Mrs. Gómez is Peruvian.*
El doctor Medina está bien.	*Dr. Medina is well.*
Don Pedro no habla inglés.	*Don Pedro doesn't speak English.*

5.C.5 Names of languages

The names of languages take a definite article except after the preposition **en** or with the verbs **hablar** (*to talk, to speak*), **aprender** (*to learn*), **comprender** (*to understand*), **enseñar** (*to teach*), **escribir** (*to write*), **leer** (*to read*), and **saber** (*to know*).

El español es fácil.	*Spanish is easy.*
¿Cómo se dice eso **en** español?	*How do you say that in Spanish?*
John, ¿**hablas** español?	*Do you speak Spanish, John?*

5.C.6 Country names

a. Definite articles are frequently used with the names of some countries and regions. The article can be left out if it's not part of the official name.

la Argentina	**los** Estados Unidos	**el** Paraguay
el Brasil	**la** Florida	**el** Perú
el Canadá	**la** India	**la** República Dominicana
el Ecuador	**el** Japón	**el** Uruguay

b. If the article is a part of the official name, it is capitalized. In this case, the masculine article does not form a contraction with the prepositions **a** or **de**.

◀ Contractions with the article **el**: 5.A.4

Vivo en **El** Salvador.	*I live in El Salvador.*
Llegué a **El** Dorado, en Bogotá.	*I arrived at El Dorado in Bogotá.*

Possessives before nouns: 9.B

5.C.7 Expressing ownership with an article

The definite article replaces possessives before a noun when ownership is obvious, for example, when you talk about parts of the body or personal belongings.

Article instead of possessives: 9.D.4

Me duelen **los** pies.	*My feet hurt.*
¡Ponte **los** zapatos!	*Put your shoes on!*

5.C.8 Position of the definite article

a. The definite article must always come before the noun. Adjectives and adjective phrases (e.g., *adverb + adjective*) can come between the article and noun.

Combination of two determiners: 4.B.6

la hermosa Barcelona	*beautiful Barcelona*
los cada vez más altos precios	*ever-increasing prices*

b. No determiners other than **todo/a(s)** can come before the definite article.

todos los profesores	*all of the professors*

5.C.9 Articles without nouns

When the noun can be identified from context, the definite article can be used alone with an adjective, adverb, or pronoun.

No quiero tu bolsa azul; dame **la** roja.	*I don't want your blue bag; give me the red one.*
Nos gusta su auto, pero es mejor **el** nuestro.	*We like his car, but ours is better.*

5.C.10 Articles in exclamations

Lo: 5.A.2

The definite article and the neuter **lo** can be used with an adjective in exclamations. In English, you would normally use *how many/much* or *how + adjective*.

¡Es increíble **la** gente que hay!	*It's amazing how many people there are!*
¡**Lo** bien que estamos aquí!	*How great life is here!*

5.C.11 Family names

A plural definite article is used before last names (in the singular) to refer to the whole family.

Los Johnson están en Madrid.	*The Johnsons are in Madrid.*
Pronto vendrán **los** Romero.	*The Romero family will come soon.*

5.D Regional variations

Variaciones regionales

5.D.1 Proper names

In some regions of Latin America and Spain, the definite article is used before proper names in spoken language. Normally, it is used only when referring to close friends or family. In regions where this use of the definite article is less common, some native speakers may consider it incorrect.

Quiero mucho a **la** Juana.	*I'm very fond of Juana.*
¡Debemos visitar **al** Miguel!	*We must visit Miguel!*

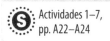

Práctica

Actividades 1–7, pp. A22–A24

Quantifiers: Numbers
Cuantificadores: Los números

6.A Cardinal numbers

Números cardinales

0–199 Números del cero al ciento noventa y nueve

0	cero	10	diez	20	veinte	30	treinta
1	uno	11	once	21	veintiuno	40	cuarenta
2	dos	12	doce	22	veintidós	50	cincuenta
3	tres	13	trece	23	veintitrés	60	sesenta
4	cuatro	14	catorce	24	veinticuatro	70	setenta
5	cinco	15	quince	25	veinticinco	80	ochenta
6	seis	16	dieciséis	26	veintiséis	90	noventa
7	siete	17	diecisiete	27	veintisiete	100	cien
8	ocho	18	dieciocho	28	veintiocho	101	ciento uno
9	nueve	19	diecinueve	29	veintinueve	199	ciento noventa y nueve

200–1000 Números del doscientos al mil

200	doscientos/as	700	setecientos/as
300	trescientos/as	800	ochocientos/as
400	cuatrocientos/as	900	novecientos/as
500	quinientos/as	1000	mil
600	seiscientos/as		

1001–1 000 000 Números del mil uno a un millón

1001	mil uno	100 000	cien mil
1002	mil dos	200 000	doscientos/as mil
2000	dos mil	1 000 000	un millón

2 000 000 Números mayores de dos millones

2 000 000	dos millones
1 000 000 000	mil millones (*a billion*)
1 000 000 000 000	un billón (*a trillion*)

Spanish	U.S. English	U.K. English								
mil	*thousand*	*thousand*	1000							
un millón	*million*	*million*	1000	000						
mil millones/millardo	*billion*	*thousand million/milliard*	1000	000	000					
un billón	*trillion*	*billion*	1000	000	000	000				
mil billones	*quadrillion*	*billiard*	1000	000	000	000	000			
trillón	*quintillion*	*trillion*	1000	000	000	000	000	000		
mil trillones	*sextillion*	*trilliard*	1000	000	000	000	000	000	000	
cuatrillón	*septillion*	*quadrillion*	1000	000	000	000	000	000	000	000

España tiene alrededor de **cuarenta y siete millones** de habitantes.	*Spain has approximately forty-seven million inhabitants.*
México tiene más de **cien millones** de habitantes.	*Mexico has more than a hundred million inhabitants.*
Ecuador tiene **doscientos ochenta y tres mil quinientos sesenta y un** kilómetros cuadrados.	*Ecuador is 283,561 km².*

6.A.1 Writing styles for numbers

Punctuation of numbers: 1.F.1c

a. Numbers (not decimals) of four digits or fewer are written without a space, period, or comma: **1000; 230**. This also applies to years, pages, postal codes, law paragraphs, and line numbers.

b. Numbers (not decimals) of more than four digits are divided into groups of three, as in English. If the number of digits is not evenly divisible by three, the one or two digits left over form a separate group. Each group is separated by a space: **10 000 000; 23 005; 100 500**. The traditional way of writing these numbers with a comma or a period as separator every three digits is no longer required. When the number is very large, it can be shortened by writing digits and words: **3 trillones de euros**. Numbers with **mil**, however, can't be written with both digits and words.

Numbers and counting expressions: 6.C.2
Ordinal numbers: 6.D.2

c. Decimals are usually marked with a comma, but a period can also be used: 0.23 (**cero punto veintitrés**); 0,23 (**cero coma veintitrés**). This figure can also be read as (**cero con**) **veintitrés centésimos** (*zero and twenty-three hundredths*).

6.B Use of cardinal numbers

Uso de los números cardinales

6.B.1 Number combinations

hay (*there is/are*): 29.B.1

Uno/un	**Un** is used before masculine nouns. *51 books:* cincuenta y **un** libros *541 books:* quinientos cuarenta y **un** libros The term **uno** is used only when it is not followed by a noun. —¿Cuántos estudiantes hay? *How many students are there?* —Hay **uno**. / Hay treinta y **uno**. *There is one. / There are thirty-one.*
Una	**Una** is used before feminine nouns. *31 pounds:* treinta y **una** libras *1001 pounds:* mil (y) **una** libras Note that **uno** and **una** do not have a plural form even if they are part of a number greater than 1.
Y	**Y** is used between the tens and ones. 1492: mil cuatrocientos noventa **y** dos 2 010 095: dos millones diez mil noventa **y** cinco But: 409 001: cuatrocientos nueve mil uno
21–29	Combinations of the number 20 are written as one word. It's less common to use three words. 21: **veintiuno/a** (**veintiún** before masculine nouns) / veinte y uno/a 26: **veintiséis** / veinte y seis 225: doscientos **veinticinco** / doscientos veinte y cinco
31–99	Combinations of numbers from 31 to 99 are written as three words. 32: **treinta y dos**; 92: **noventa y dos** 2255: dos mil doscientos **cincuenta y cinco**

100 **Cien**	**Cien** by itself expresses *a hundred/one hundred*. **Cien** does not agree in gender or number with the noun. *100 books*: **cien** libros *100 boxes*: **cien** cajas El cien es mi número favorito. *One hundred is my favorite number.* ¿Cuántos estudiantes hay? *How many students are there?* Hay **cien** estudiantes. *There are one hundred students.*
101–199 **Ciento**	**Ciento** is used from **101** to **199** before nouns and does not change in gender or number. *103 books*: **ciento** tres libros *169 boxes*: **ciento** sesenta y nueve cajas
200–999 **Cientos/as**	**Cientos/as** is used from **200** to **999** and agrees with the noun's gender. Unlike English, multiple hundreds are expressed in one word (though the following numbers are separate). *200 schools*: **doscientas** escuelas *301 houses*: **trescientas** una casas *999 teachers*: **novecientos noventa y nueve** profesores
1000 **Mil**	**Mil** does not change in gender. In some Latin American countries, the indefinite article **un** can be used before **mil** in financial and legal documents when the number is exactly a thousand. *1000 dollars / girls:* **(un) mil** dólares / **(un) mil** niñas *2000 dollars / girls:* **dos mil** dólares / **dos mil** niñas
1 000 000 **Millón /** **Millones** **Millón de** **Millones de**	**Millón** is used when referring to a single million (**un millón, este millón**). When referring to two million or more, always use **millones** (**dos millones** de personas; *two million people*). *1 021 101 pesos:* **un millón veintiún mil ciento un** pesos *2 100 341 rupees:* **dos millones cien mil trescientas cuarenta y una** rupias Round numbers in *whole millions* are followed by **de**. *1 000 000 pesos:* **un millón de** pesos *131 000 000 dollars:* **ciento treinta y un millones de** dólares But: *131 001 000 dollars:* **ciento treinta y un millones mil** dólares
Cientos de **Miles de** **Millones de**	**Cientos de** and **miles de** are not used for counting. The expressions are used the same way in English and Spanish. **Millones de** can also indicate an unspecified high number of countable nouns. Hay **cientos de / miles de /** *There are hundreds/thousands/* **millones de** personas en las calles. *millions of people in the streets.*

6.B.2 The word *número*

The word **número** is masculine and its article agrees in gender, whether the word **número** is stated or not.

El (**número**) trece me gusta.   *I like the number thirteen.*

El **primer** trece de la lista tiene que ir en color rojo.   *The first (number) thirteen on the list must be in red.*

The word **número** is implied for page numbers, so you'd say **la página veintiuno**.

6.B.3 Plurals

a. Numbers' plural forms follow the same rules as other nouns.

Plural of nouns: 2.B

¿Tienes billetes de **cinco** pesos?   *Do you have five-peso bills?*

No, solamente tengo **dieces** y **veintes**.   *No, I only have tens and twenties.*

b. As in English, the number **cero** is used with plural nouns, even with fractions.

Hace cero grados Celsius de temperatura.   *The temperature is zero degrees Celsius.*

El bebé creció solo 0,5 centímetros el último mes.   *Last month the baby grew only 0.5 centimeters.*

6.C   Collective numbers and counting expressions

Expresiones numéricas colectivas y expresiones para contar

6.C.1   *Decena, veintena*

Collective numbers are followed by **de** before the noun.

Década and other words for ▶ periods of time: 6.J.2

decena(s)	*ten(s)*	cincuentena	*about fifty*
docena(s)	*dozen(s)*	sesentena	*about sixty*
veintena	*about twenty*	setentena	*about seventy*
treintena	*about thirty*	centenar(es)	*a hundred/hundreds*
cuarentena	*about forty*	millar(es)	*a thousand/thousands*

En la biblioteca hay **millares** de libros.   *There are thousands of books in the library.*
La **docena** de huevos cuesta dos dólares.   *A dozen eggs cost two dollars.*

6.C.2   Numbers and counting expressions

a. Percentages can come after the definite article **el** or the indefinite article **un**.

Los precios suben (el/un) **2%** mañana.   *The prices go up 2% tomorrow.*
Mi casa vale hoy un **diez por ciento** más   *My house is worth about ten percent more today*
   que cuando la compré.   *than when I bought it.*

Writing styles for ▶ numbers: 6.A.1

b. In most Spanish-speaking countries, the period is still used after thousands (although it can be left out, as recommended by new **Real Academia** grammar rules) and the comma with decimals.

1.000   mil   **0,5   cero coma cinco**

c. The use of the comma for thousands is still common in some countries, like Mexico and Peru. The period is used for decimals.

1,000   mil   **0.5   cero punto cinco**

d. The preposition **con** is used to indicate decimals in prices.

$ 45,60   cuarenta y cinco pesos **con** sesenta centavos   *forty-five pesos and sixty cents*

e. Numbers over a thousand can't be read in hundreds in Spanish as they are in English.

€ 1250   mil doscientos cincuenta euros   *twelve hundred and fifty euros*

The verb **dar** is also used ▶ with calculations. Veinte más ocho **da** veintiocho.

f. The verb **ser** (**es/son**) and the following expressions are used to describe calculations in Spanish. The singular form (**es**) is used if the calculation is equal to the numbers 0 or 1 only. The symbols **:** and **/** are also used for division. The symbols **·** or **∗** are also used for multiplication.

	Mathematical operations		Examples
+	**La suma**	$1 + 2 = 3$	Uno **más/y** dos **es igual a / son** tres.
−	**La resta**	$2 - 2 = 0$	Dos **menos** dos **es igual a / es** cero.
×	**La multiplicación**	$3 \times 4 = 12$	Tres **por** cuatro **es igual a / son** doce.
÷	**La división**	$4 \div 2 = 2$	Cuatro **dividido (por/entre)** dos **es igual a / son** dos.
=	**El resultado:** *igual a*	$10 - 7 = 3$	Diez menos siete **es igual a / son** tres.

6.D | Ordinal numbers

Números ordinales

6.D.1 Ordinal numbers for 1–99

a. The ordinal numbers for **1** through **10** are the most used in Spanish. In everyday speech it is also common to use **décimo primero/a** and **décimo segundo/a** instead of **undécimo/a** and **duodécimo/a**, which are not used in many countries. In most Spanish-speaking countries, the **planta baja** (*ground floor*) is not considered the first floor, as it is in the U.S. Therefore, in Spanish the **primer piso** (*first floor*) is usually equivalent to the *second floor* in U.S. English, and so on.

Ordinal numbers			
primer(o/a)	*first*	**séptimo/a**	*seventh*
segundo/a	*second*	**octavo/a**	*eighth*
tercer(o/a)	*third*	**noveno/a**	*ninth*
cuarto/a	*fourth*	**décimo/a**	*tenth*
quinto/a	*fifth*	**undécimo/a**	*eleventh*
sexto/a	*sixth*	**duodécimo/a**	*twelfth*

b. In formal situations, the following ordinal numbers are also used. However, in everyday language there is a growing tendency to avoid complex ordinal numbers by replacing them with the corresponding cardinal number. Note that the ordinal number usually comes before the noun but that the cardinal number comes after.

vigésimo/a	*twentieth*	**sexagésimo/a**	*sixtieth*
trigésimo/a	*thirtieth*	**septuagésimo/a**	*seventieth*
cuadragésimo/a	*fortieth*	**octogésimo/a**	*eightieth*
quincuagésimo/a	*fiftieth*	**nonagésimo/a**	*ninetieth*

Perdí la carrera en la **vigésima** vuelta.
Perdí la carrera en la vuelta veinte. *I lost the race in the twentieth lap.*

Hoy celebramos el **septuagésimo**
  aniversario de la escuela. *Today, we're celebrating the school's*
Hoy celebramos el aniversario setenta *seventieth anniversary.*
  de la escuela.

6.D.2 Centésimo, milésimo, millonésimo

The numbers **centésimo/a(s)** (*hundredth[s]*), **milésimo/a(s)** (*thousandth[s]*), **millonésimo/a(s)** (*millionth[s]*) are used mostly for fractions or figuratively to mean a large number.

◀ Writing styles for numbers: 6.A.1

Esta es la **centésima** llamada. *This is the hundredth call.*
1/1000 es un(a) **milésimo/a**. *1/1000 is a thousandth.*

6.D.3 Milenario, centenario, millonario

Milenario/a and **centenario/a** are terms for age, while **millonario/a** describes wealth, just like in English.

Madrid es una ciudad **milenaria**. *Madrid is a thousand-year-old city.*
Roberta Martínez es **millonaria**. *Roberta Martínez is a millionaire.*
Para el **bicentenario** de la Independencia *There were many official ceremonies for the*
  hubo muchos actos oficiales. *bicentennial of our independence.*

6.D.4 Agreement

Ordinal numbers are adjectives and agree in gender and number with the noun they modify. **Primero** and **tercero** are shortened to **primer** and **tercer** before a masculine singular noun.

el décimo **tercer** aniversario | *the thirteenth anniversary*
el **primer** puesto | *the first position*

6.D.5 Abbreviations

In abbreviations of ordinal numbers, a superscript **a** or **o** is written to the right of the number to indicate gender and number. The superscript letter is separated from the number with a period. The superscript **-er** is used to abbreviate **primer** and **tercer**.

Viajo en **1.ª** clase. | *I travel in 1st class.*
Marta vive en el **10.º** piso. | *Marta lives on the 10th floor.*
Está en **3.er** grado. | *She is in 3rd grade.*

6.D.6 Proper names

The names of kings, queens, and popes with numbers from **1** to **10** are written with Roman numerals and are read as ordinal numbers. Starting from the Roman numeral **XI**, the numerals are read as cardinal numbers.

Isabel II	Isabel **segunda**	*Elizabeth II*
Papa Juan Pablo II	Papa Juan Pablo **segundo**	*Pope John Paul II*
Luis XV	Luis **quince**	*Louis XV*
Papa Juan XXIII	Papa Juan **veintitrés**	*Pope John XXIII*

6.D.7 Ordinals used as nouns

With the definite article, ordinals may function as nouns.

Soy **la primera** de la fila y tú, **el tercero**. | *I am the first one in this line; you are the third.*

6.E Fractions and multiples

Números fraccionarios y múltiplos

6.E.1 Numerators and denominators

a. The *numerator* (**numerador**) in Spanish is read as a cardinal number. *Denominators* (**denominadores**) are usually read as ordinal numbers. The exceptions are 1/2, which is read as **un medio** or **la mitad**, and the masculine form for 1/3 or 2/3, which uses the word **tercio(s)**. The ordinal number agrees in gender and number with the noun.

1/2	un medio, la mitad	**1/10**	un(a) décimo/a, una décima parte
2/3	dos tercios, dos terceras partes	**1/7**	un sé(p)timo, una sé(p)tima parte
1/4	un cuarto, una cuarta parte	**5/8**	cinco octavos, cinco octavas partes
3/5	tres quintos, tres quintas partes	**2/9**	dos novenos, dos novenas partes

b. Starting from 11, **-avo/a** is added to the cardinal numbers in denominators, with the exception of **centésimo/a(s)**, **milésimo/a(s)**, **millonésimo/a(s)**.

Tenemos una **doceava** parte de la compañía. | *We own a twelfth of the company.*
Erré la estimación por cinco **centésimas**. | *I misestimated by five hundredths.*

c. Fractions are followed by **de** before a noun.

El corredor ganó por una **milésima de** segundo.	*The runner won by a thousandth of a second.*
Mil dólares es la **mitad del** precio.	*A thousand dollars is half the price.*

Medio is used without **de** before **kilo**, **litro**, etc. **De** can sometimes be omitted before **cuarto**. **Medio litro** de leche. Un **cuarto (de) kilo** de harina.

6.E.2 Multiples

a. The following are the most common words in Spanish to express multiple amounts. They can function as nouns or adjectives.

Most used	
doble	*double*
triple	*triple*

Less used	
cuádruple	*quadruple*
quíntuple	*quintuple*
séxtuple	*sextuple*

En el dormitorio hay una cama **doble**.	*There is a double bed in the bedroom.*
Dame un café expreso **triple**.	*Give me a triple espresso.*
Veinticinco es el **quíntuple** de cinco.	*Twenty-five is five times five.*

b. To express exponential quantities, use *number* + **veces más/menos** (*times more/less*).

Mi auto costó **cinco veces más** que el tuyo.	*My car cost five times more than yours.*

Comparisons with **más/menos**: 11.B

6.F Time

La hora

6.F.1 *Es/son*

a. Use the verb **ser** in the plural (**son**) to give most times. The singular (**es**) is used for one o'clock.

Use of **ser** with the time: 29.C.2

Es la una en punto.	*It's one o'clock on the dot.*
Son las ocho de la noche.	*It's eight at night.*
Son las cuatro de la mañana.	*It's four in the morning.*

b. It is the norm to use **es** to ask about the time, but in some parts of Latin America the plural form is also used.

¿Qué hora es? / ¿Qué horas son?	*What time is it?*

6.F.2 Time after the hour

Time after the hour is expressed with the *hour* plus **y** and the *number of minutes*. **Cuarto** or **quince** can be used for *quarter past* and **media** or **treinta** for *half past*.

Son las ocho **y** diez.	*It's ten past eight.*
Es la una **y cuarto/quince**.	*It's quarter past one.*
Son las seis **y media/treinta**.	*It's half past six.*

6.F.3 Time before the hour

Time before the hour is expressed with **menos**, primarily in Spain. In Latin America, the expression **falta(n)** is also used with the number of minutes remaining until the next hour.

Son las dos **menos** diez.	*It's ten to two.*
Faltan diez **para** las dos.	
Es la una **menos** cuarto.	*It's quarter to one.*
Falta un cuarto **para** la una.	

6.F.4 Time (appointments and events)

The verb **ser** followed by **a** + **la(s)** + *clock time* expresses the time of an appointment or event.

—¿**Es a las** dos de la tarde la cita?   *Is the appointment at two p.m.?*

—No, **es a la** una de la tarde.   *No, it's at one p.m.*

ser and estar with the calendar and time: 29.C.2

6.F.5 The 24-hour clock

In Latin America, the 12-hour clock is more commonly used in everyday speech. In Spain, the 24-hour clock, sometimes called military time, is also used.

La conferencia es a las **19:30** (diecinueve [y] treinta) **horas**.   *The conference is at seven-thirty p.m.*

La boda es a las **15** (quince) **horas**.   *The wedding is at three p.m.*

6.F.6 Time expressions: *de la mañana / tarde / noche*

You can use **de la madrugada** to indicate that it's early morning.

With the 12-hour clock, add whether it is the morning, afternoon, or evening.

Es la una **de la mañana**.   *It's one in the morning.*

Son las cinco **de la tarde**.   *It's five in the afternoon.*

Son las nueve **de la noche**.   *It's nine at night.*

6.G Dates

La fecha

6.G.1 Structure

a. The date is expressed with the verb **ser**. For day, month, and year, cardinal numbers are used with the following structures.

15 de mayo de 2015   Hoy **es** (el) quince de mayo de dos mil quince.   15/05/2015

b. The first of the month is expressed with **primero** in Latin America and with **uno** in Spain.

Hoy es (el) **primero** de enero.
Hoy es (el) **uno** de enero.   *Today is January first.*

6.G.2 Letters

In letters and other documents, place and date are separated by a comma, like in English. Months can also come before the day's date.

Nueva York, 2 de mayo de 2020   Nueva York, dos de mayo de dos mil veinte

Nueva York, abril 19 de 2010   Nueva York, abril diecinueve de dos mil diez

Writing styles for numbers: 6.A.1a
Década and other words for periods of time: 6.J.2

6.G.3 Years

In Spanish, years are not read as hundreds as they are in English. The year is always read as a cardinal number.

4 de julio de 1776:
Cuatro de julio de mil setecientos setenta y seis   *July fourth, seventeen seventy-six*

6.G.4 The calendar

In many Latin American countries, the calendar starts with Sunday like in the U.S. In Spain, the calendar goes from Monday to Sunday.

6.G.5 Expressions of time for dates

Todo/a(s), **próximo/a(s)**, **dentro de**, and **en** are often used in expressions of time.

◀ **todo**: 7.C.9

todos los días / meses, **todas las** semanas	*every day/month/week*
todos los años	*every year*
dentro de / en **ocho** días dentro de / en **una** semana	*in a week*
dentro de / en **unos** días	*in a few days*
dentro de / en **quince** días dentro de / en **dos** semanas	*in two weeks*
la semana **próxima**; el mes/año **próximo** la **próxima** semana, el **próximo** mes/año	*next week/month/year*
Mi cumpleaños es dentro de **ocho** días.	*My birthday's in a week.*
La escuela empieza dentro de / en **quince** días.	*School begins in two weeks.*

6.H Age

La edad

6.H.1 Structure

In Spanish, age is expressed with the verb **tener**.

◀ **tener** with age: 29.D

Juliana **tiene** tres años.	*Juliana is three years old.*

6.H.2 Birthdays

The verb **cumplir** describes how many years a person is turning or how old a person is.

Juliana **cumple** tres años hoy.	*Juliana is turning three today.* *Juliana is three today.*

6.H.3 Talking about age

In English, it is common to include age when talking about people, for example, in the news (*A sixty-year-old won the lottery.*). In Spanish, it's less common to use age when talking about people, except when it is of significance to the context. Note the following age expressions.

Expressions of age	Use
quinceañero/a	Term used to refer to fifteen-year-olds. **La fiesta de quince años** is a celebration for girls turning fifteen to mark their passage into adulthood.
veinteañero/a	A less common term for people in their twenties, primarily used to emphasize that they are still young.
cuarentón/cuarentona **cincuentón/cincuentona** **sesentón/sesentona**	Derogatory terms used to refer to men or women over forty, fifty, sixty years of age: *forty-year-old, fifty-year-old, sixty-year-old.*
octogenario/a, **nonagenario/a,** **centenario/a**	Neutral terms referring to elderly men and women: *eighty-year-old, ninety-year-old, hundred-year-old.*

◀ Augmentative suffixes: 2.C.10b

6.I | Temperature

Temperatura

6.I.1 | Structure

a. Temperature can be expressed using the following structures.

Hacer and **estar** with weather expressions 29.C.1

¿Qué temperatura **hace**?	*What's the temperature?*
Hace tres grados **bajo cero**.	*It's three degrees below zero.*
¿Cuántos grados **hace**?	*How many degrees is it?*
Hace veinte **grados**.	*It's twenty degrees.*
¿A qué temperatura **estamos**?	*What's the temperature (now)?*
Estamos a cero **grados**.	*It's freezing (It's zero degrees).*

b. Temperature is measured in degrees Celsius (**grados Celsius/centígrados**) in Latin America and Spain. The exception is Puerto Rico, which uses both the system used in the U.S., Fahrenheit (**grados Fahrenheit**), and Celsius.

In Spanish, there should be a space between the number and the degree symbol, and no space between the degree symbol and *C* or *F*.

15 °C es aproximadamente 60 °F.	*15°C is about 60°F.*

6.I.2 | Words and expressions

temperatura **máxima/mínima**	*highest/lowest temperature*
temperatura **media/promedio**	*average temperature*
temperatura **normal**	*normal temperature*

6.J | Idiomatic expressions

6.J.1 | The expressions *y pico, y tantos*

To express *a bit* in relation to quantities (prices, amounts), the expression *number* + **y pico / y tantos** can be used: **treinta y pico** (*thirty and a bit*). In Chile, **y tantos** is preferred because **y pico** is considered taboo.

6.J.2 | *Década* and other words for periods of time

The periods of time **quinquenio** (*5 years*), **decenio** (*10 years*), and **centenio** (*100 years*) refer only to the numbers of years. **Década** (*decade*), **siglo** (*century*), and **milenio** (*millennium*), on the other hand, are specific periods of years. **Edad** and **era/época** are used to refer to long or remote periods of time: **Edad de Hierro** (*Iron Age*), **era moderna**. Most of these terms are formal and are used primarily in written language.

Collective numbers and counting expressions: 6.C

Alejandro y Sara vivieron en la **década de los treinta**, en el **siglo XX**.	*Alejandro and Sara lived in the thirties, in the 20th century.*
El **nuevo milenio** trae muchas incógnitas.	*The new millennium brings many unknowns.*
El presupuesto es solamente para un **quinquenio**. Es **quinquenal**.	*The budget is only for a five-year period. It's every five years.*

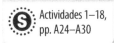

Práctica

Actividades 1–18, pp. A24–A30

Indefinite quantifiers and pronouns

Cuantificadores y pronombres indefinidos

7.A   Determiners and pronouns

Determinantes y pronombres

Among determiners, words like **alguno/a(s)** (*some*) and **muchos/as** (*many*) are considered *indefinite quantifiers*. The indefinite articles **un** and **una** can also be considered indefinite quantifiers. Just like all other determiners, indefinite quantifiers support the noun. They make the noun indefinite when they refer to identity, quantity, or size. In addition to indefinite quantifiers, this chapter also introduces *indefinite pronouns*. Some indefinite quantifiers can function as *determiners, pronouns,* and *adverbs*.

Había **mucha** gente. *(determiner)*	*There were a lot of people.*
Necesitaba uno, pero compré **muchos**. *(pronoun)*	*I needed one, but I bought a lot.*
Mi hermano trabaja **mucho**. *(adverb)*	*My brother works a lot.*

Indefinite quantifiers as adverbs: 7.E.4

7.B   Affirmative and negative indefinite quantifiers

Cuantificadores indefinidos con formas afirmativas y negativas

There are two groups of indefinite quantifiers. One group has both affirmative and negative forms, as shown in the chart, and the other group has only affirmative forms (see **7.C**). Most quantifiers in these groups can agree in gender and number, but none of them have comparative or superlative forms.

Affirmative		Negative	
algún, alguno/a	*some/any*	**ningún, ninguno/a**	*no/not any/none*
algunos/as	*some [pl.]*	**ningunos/as**	*no/not any [pl.]*

7.B.1   Double negation of *ninguno/a*

The negative forms **ningún** and **ninguno/a** require a double negation when they come after the verb; the same applies to the pronouns **nadie** and **nada**.

¡No tienes **ningún** perfil personal actualizado en tu sitio web!	*You don't have an updated personal profile on your website!*
No hay **nadie** en el restaurante.	*There is no one in the restaurant.*

Double negation is considered incorrect in English.

Double negation with **ningún** and **tampoco**: 7.E.1

7.B.2   *Algún, alguno/a(s); ningún, ninguno/a*

a. Algún and **ningún** function only as determiners and are used only before masculine singular nouns. Before feminine singular nouns that begin with a stressed **a** or **ha**, **algún** is commonly used (**algún arma**), but **alguna** is also possible (**alguna arma**). **Alguno(s)** can be both a pronoun and a determiner. As a determiner, the singular form appears only after the noun. **Alguna(s)** can also function as both a pronoun and a determiner. As a determiner, the singular form can be used before or after a noun. The plural forms **algunos/as** can only be used before a noun.

—¿Hay **algún** cine cerca?	*Are there any movie theaters nearby?*
—No, no hay **ningún** cine cerca.	*No, there are no movie theaters nearby.*
¿Tienes **alguna** propuesta?	*Do you have a suggestion?*
Si hay **algún** problema, avísame.	*If there is any problem, let me know.*
No hay problema **alguno**.	*There is no problem.*
Tengo **algunas** dudas.	*I have some doubts.*

Other shortened adjective forms: **buen, mal, primer, tercer**: 3.D

ninguno/a with relative ⊙
clauses: 23.D.2e

b. Alguno/a(s) and **ninguno/a** (but *not* **ningunos/as**) can be used with the preposition **de** or a relative clause.

Leímos **algunas de las** nuevas novelas. *We read some of the new novels.*

No hay **ninguna que** nos guste mucho, *There aren't any that we like in particular,*
pero **algunas de ellas** son muy populares. *but some of them are very popular.*

c. Alguno/a(s) always comes after the noun in negative sentences. The following pairs of sentences have the same meaning.

No hay alternativa **alguna**.
No hay **ninguna** alternativa. *There isn't an/any alternative.*

No habrá viaje **alguno** este año.
No habrá **ningún** viaje este año. *There won't be any trip this year.*

The plural forms **ningunos/as** ⊙
are rarely used.

d. The plural forms **ningunos/as** can be used before or after the noun in negative sentences, but the form **ninguno/a de** + *plural article* or *pronoun* is more common.

No he visitado **ninguna de las** *I haven't visited any of the oil rigs.*
plataformas de petróleo.

e. Ninguno/a de + *pronoun* is also used in Spanish to express *none of.* In such cases, **nadie** can't be used. However, the same idea can be expressed with **nadie** without the **de** + *pronoun.*

Ninguna de nosotras tiene vacaciones. *None of us have vacation.*
Ninguno de ellos sabe español. *None of them know any Spanish.*
Nadie sabe español. *No one knows Spanish.*

7.C Indefinite quantifiers with only affirmative forms

Cuantificadores indefinidos solo con formas afirmativas

Adverbs of quantity: 10.D ⊙

There are many indefinite quantifiers with only affirmative forms. Some refer to the noun's indefinite identity (**cualquiera**), indefinite quantity (**muchos**), or degree (**más, menos**), while others refer to a whole (**todo**) or to a part of something (**cada**).

cualquiera que + subjunctive:
23.D.2d
Le venderé mi casa a **cualquiera
que** pague un buen precio.
*I will sell my house to whoever
pays the best price.*

ambos/as	both	muchos/as	many/lots/a lot of
bastante	quite/quite a lot/enough	otro/a	another/another one
bastantes	quite/quite a lot/enough [pl.]	otros/as	other [pl.]
cada	each/every	poco/a	little/bit
cualquier, cualquiera (de)	whichever/whoever/any (of)	pocos/as	few
cualesquiera (de)	which/whoever/any (of) [pl.]	tanto/a	so much
demás	rest/remainder	tantos/as	so many
demasiado/a	too much	todo/a	all/every/whole/everything
demasiados/as	too many	todos/as	all [pl.]
más	more	un, una	a
menos	fewer, less	unos/as	some
mucho/a	a lot of/much	varios/as	various/several

7.C.1 **Form and agreement**

Indefinite quantifiers that agree in gender and/or number with the noun can't be compared the way adjectives can. However, the determiners **mucho, poco,** and **tanto** can take the absolute superlative ending **-ísimo/a: muchísimo/a, poquísimo/a, tantísimo/a**.

◀ mucho - muchísimo:
4.B.3b
Comparison of adjectives: 3.E
Comparison of adverbs: 10.I
Comparisons: Ch. 11

Ambos novios se han casado **varias** veces.	*Both partners have been married several times.*
Ella tiene **muchísimos** hijos y él tiene solo **una** hija.	*She has a lot of children and he has only one daughter.*
Todos son muy felices con **tantísima** gente en casa.	*Everyone is very happy with so many people at home.*
Cada familia es diferente.	*Every family is different.*

7.C.2 **Affirmative quantifiers with double placement**

Quantifiers with only affirmative forms generally come before the noun, but the following quantifiers can also come after the noun. Note that when **cualquiera, más,** and **menos** come after the noun, they must be used with an indefinite article or **otro/a(s)** (or a cardinal number).

◀ Combination of two
determiners: 4.B.6

◀ Bastante(s): 7.C.7

◀ Varios/as: 7.C.6

bastante(s)	**bastante** dinero	*quite a lot of money*
	dinero **bastante**	*enough money*
varios/as	**varias** galletas	*several cookies*
	galletas **varias**	*an assortment of cookies*
cualquier(a)/ cualesquiera	**cualquier** día	*whichever/any day*
	cualesquiera días	
	un día **cualquiera**	
	unos días **cualesquiera**	
más, menos	**más/menos** pan	*more/less bread*
	un pan **más/menos**	*one more loaf/one loaf less*
	otro pan **más/menos**	*another loaf/another loaf less*
	otros panes **más/menos**	*some more loaves/a few loaves less*

7.C.3 **Indefinite quantifiers as pronouns**

a. With a few exceptions, quantifiers can function as pronouns when the noun they refer to is not stated.

◀ Determiners as pronouns:
4.B.2

En Argentina **todo** me gusta. Hay **bastante** que ver y **mucho** que hacer.	*I like everything in Argentina. There's quite a lot to see and do.*

b. The shortened forms **un, algún, ningún,** and **cualquier** can't function as pronouns, while the corresponding longer forms in both singular and plural can: **uno/a(s), alguno/a(s), ninguno/a(s), cualquiera, cualesquiera**.

—¿Hay estudiantes franceses aquí?	*Are there French students here?*
—No, este año no hay **ninguno,** pero a veces vienen **algunos**.	*No, there aren't any this year, but sometimes there are some.*

c. In order to function as pronouns, **demás** must be accompanied by an article (**los, las, lo**) and **cada** must always be used with **uno/a** or a noun.

Dos estudiantes de la clase tienen A en todo. **Los demás,** tienen B.	*Two students in the class have an A in everything. The rest have a B.*
Cada uno hizo un gran esfuerzo.	*Every one of them tried very hard.*

d. The following example shows **varios/as, otro/a(s),** and **poco/a(s)** used as pronouns.

Varios recibieron un premio, **otros** recibieron dos premios y muy **pocos,** muchos premios.	*Some received one prize, others received two prizes, and very few, a lot of prizes.*

7.C.4 *Un, uno/a, unos, unas*

Use of indefinite articles: 5.B
Indefinite pronouns: 7.D

a. Only the forms **un, una,** and **unos/as** can come before the noun, while **uno** can only be used as an indefinite determiner in the form **uno de los** (*one of the*) before the noun. In any other context, **uno** is used as a pronoun.

b. Un and **una** can usually be omitted in negative sentences (*not any*).

No hay policía en la calle.	*There are no policemen on the street.*
Ella no tiene familia.	*She doesn't have any family.*
No tenemos pan en casa.	*We don't have any bread in the house.*

c. Un poco de (*a little*) is used before the noun.

Hace **un poco de** calor aquí.	*It's a little warm here.*

d. Unos/as means *about, approximately* when used before numbers.

El boleto de autobús cuesta **unos** cincuenta dólares.	*The bus ticket costs about fifty dollars.*

7.C.5 *Cualquier, cualquiera, cualesquiera*

a. Before all singular (masculine and feminine) nouns, the shortened form **cualquier** is always used. After both masculine and feminine nouns, only **cualquiera** can be used. When used after the noun, **cualquiera** can also mean *ordinary.*

Cualquier persona puede ser admitida en la universidad.	*Any person can be admitted to the university.*
Él no es una persona **cualquiera**.	*He is not an ordinary person.*
Le pediré un favor a **cualquiera de** mis amigos.	*I will ask any of my friends a favor.*
Cualquiera que llegue tarde no podrá entrar.	*Whoever arrives late will not be allowed in.*

Cualquiera in relative clauses: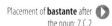
15.B.7, 23.D.2d

b. The plural form, **cualesquiera,** is rarely used.

Cualesquiera (que) sean tus motivos, no estoy de acuerdo con tu decisión.	*Whatever your reasons may be, I don't agree with your decision.*
Tráeme dos libros **cualesquiera**.	*Bring me any two books.*

7.C.6 *Ambos/as, varios/as*

Different meanings of
varios/as: 7.C.2

Ambos/as (*both*) is always plural and can never be followed by **dos**. However, it can be replaced by **los/las dos**. **Ambos/as** can function alone as a pronoun when the noun is not stated. **Varios/as** expresses a quantity greater than two.

Ambas chicas hablan español.	*Both girls speak Spanish.*
Las dos chicas estudian mucho.	*The two girls study a lot.*
Varias personas son suecas.	*Several people are Swedish.*
Llegaron dos invitados y **ambos** son alemanes.	*Two guests arrived, and both are German.*

7.C.7 *Bastante(s)*

This quantifier must agree in number with the noun, and usually comes before it.

Placement of **bastante** after
the noun: 7.C.2

Hay **bastante** gente en el concierto.	*There are quite a lot of people at the concert.*
En este libro hay **bastantes** ejemplos de gramática.	*In this book there are quite a lot of grammar examples.*

7.C.8 *Cada, cada uno/a*

a. Cada does not change form and indicates only a part of a whole. It can't stand alone without a noun. It's used in the phrase **cada uno/a (de)**. **Todo** + *singular noun* means *every (single) one* and is a synonym for **cada uno de los/las** + *noun*.

Determiners as pronouns: 4.B.2b
Todo: 7.C.9

Cada estudiante debe hacer el trabajo individualmente.	*Every student should do the work individually.*
Revisaremos el contenido de **cada uno de** los contratos.	*We will go through the contents of every one of the contracts.*
Todo contrato/**Cada uno de** los contratos debe estar firmado.	*Every single contract should be signed.*

b. Cada and **cada uno de los/las** + *noun* bring attention to each member of a group.

Cada animal es único.	*Each animal is unique.*
Cada uno de los animales es único.	*Each of the animals is unique.*

c. In Spanish, periods of time are expressed with **todo**: **todos los días, todas las semanas. Cada** is used to convey periodic repetition rather than a whole period of time.

Pienso en ti **cada** segundo del día, **todos** los días.	*I think about you every second of the day, every day.*
Hay que tomar la medicina **cada** dos horas.	*The medicine must be taken every two hours.*

7.C.9 *Todo*

a. When **todo** indicates something abstract (*everything*), it's an indefinite pronoun.

Todo es muy sencillo.	*It's all very simple.*
¿Lo terminaste **todo**?	*Did you finish everything?*

b. When it refers to an implied noun and appears alone, **todo** is a pronoun and agrees in gender and number with the noun.

—¿Enviaste los paquetes?	*Did you send all the packages?*
—Sí, los envié **todos**.	*Yes, I sent them all.*
Dice que no le gusta la polenta, pero siempre se la come **toda**.	*He says he doesn't like polenta, but he always eats it all.*

c. Todo/a + *singular noun* is a synonym for **todos/as los/las** + *plural noun*.

Todo ser vivo tiene células.	*Every living being has cells.*
Todos los seres vivos tienen células.	*All living beings have cells.*

d. Todo lo, todo el, and **toda la** refer to something as a whole.

Eso es **todo lo** que sé.	*That's all/everything I know.*
¡**Todo el** año pasó volando!	*The whole year flew by!*
Te querré **toda la** vida.	*I will love you my whole life.*

e. Todo/a un(a) intensifies the noun.

todo/a un(a): 4.B.6c

Es buenísimo tener **todo un** día libre.	*It's awesome to have a whole day free.*
¡Los glaciares de Alaska son **toda una** maravilla!	*The glaciers in Alaska are all so amazing!*

Determiners as pronouns: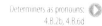
4.8.2b, 4.8.6d

Don't confuse demás with
de más or además
(besides).

7.C.10 *Demás*

Demás does not change form and usually needs a plural definite article when it comes before a noun. It's often used with the neuter article **lo** to mean *the rest, the remainder* and with **todo** as an intensifier: **todo lo demás** (*everything else*). On rare occasions, **demás** can be used without an article.

Usted debe firmar **los demás** documentos.	You must sign the rest of the documents.
Dime **todo lo demás**.	Tell me the rest/everything else.
Saludos para tu familia y **todos los demás** parientes.	Greetings to your family and all your other relatives.
Los jefes y **demás** colegas vendrán a la fiesta de Navidad.	The bosses and other colleagues will come to the Christmas party.

7.C.11 *Demasiado/a(s)*

With uncountable nouns (*water, pollution*), **demasiado/a** means *too much*. With countable nouns, it means *too many*. It can be combined with **poco** but not with **mucho/a(s)**.

Hay **demasiada** contaminación.	There is too much pollution.
Tenéis **demasiadas** cosas que hacer.	You [pl.] have too many things to do.
Se come mucha carne y **demasiado poco** pescado.	They eat a lot of meat and not enough fish.

7.C.12 *Más, menos, mucho/a(s), poco/a(s)*

These quantifiers are very flexible. Their most important function is in comparisons, but they also form many common expressions. Note the use of **un poco más/menos de, varios/as**.

Expressions with *más, menos, mucho, poco*	
muchas más horas	*many more hours*
muchos menos amigos	*far fewer friends*
un poco más de café	*a little more coffee*
algunos pocos ejemplos **más**	*a few more examples*
bastante más dinero	*quite a lot more money*
bastantes menos cosas	*far fewer/very few things*
otras cosas **más**	*several other things*
varias cosas **menos**	*fewer things*

Invitaron a **mucha más** gente de lo que habían dicho.	They invited a lot more people than they'd said they would.
Tendrías que poner **un poco menos de** chocolate y **un poco más de** azucar.	You should use a little less chocolate and a little more sugar.
No pienso esperar **muchas** horas **más**.	I won't wait many more hours.
Te presto **un** libro **más** y basta.	I'll lend you one more book, and that's it.

7.C.13 *Otro/a(s)*

a. Otro/a can never be combined with **un(a)**, but it can come after the definite article: **el/la otro/a, los/ las otros/as** (*the other, the others*). **Otro/a** is used in many Spanish expressions.

¡Otra pizza, por favor!	Another pizza, please!
Te vi **el otro** día.	I saw you the other day.
Este café no es bueno; compra **otra** marca.	This coffee isn't good; buy another brand.
Viajaré el lunes y regresaré **al otro** día.	I will travel on Monday and return the following day.

b. Otro/a(s) can be combined with many quantifiers.

Otro/a(s) **with other quantifiers**	
ningún otro estudiante	*no other student*
alguna otra casa	*another house/some other house*
muchos otros países	*many other countries*
cualquier otro día	*any other day*
otro poco de leche	*a little more milk*
otros pocos casos	*a few other cases*
pocas otras personas	*few other people*
varios otros sitios	*several other places*
bastantes otras cosas	*many other things*
todos los otros muebles	*all the other furniture*
todo lo otro	*all the rest*
otra vez **más/menos**	*once more/less*
otras cosas **más/menos**	*some more/fewer things*
otros tres ejemplos	*three other examples*

7.D Indefinite pronouns

Pronombres indefinidos

7.D.1 Form and placement

Indefinite pronouns can function just like common personal pronouns in a sentence. With the exception of **una** for females, they do not agree in gender. They can *never* directly support nouns like the determiners do (**algún auto**). **Cada uno/a** (*each one*) is included as a compound indefinite pronoun.

◀ **un, uno, una** as indefinite determiners: 7.C.4

Indefinite pronouns			
Affirmative		**Negative**	
uno/a	*one/someone*	**nadie**	*no one/nobody*
alguien	*someone*		
algo	*something*	**nada**	*nothing*

7.D.2 Features of indefinite pronouns

a. Indefinite pronouns are used with singular verbs. They do not have a plural form. If it's necessary to refer to an indefinite group of people, an indefinite quantifier must be used.

◀ Indefinite quantifiers with only affirmative forms: 7.C

¿Hay **alguien** en casa?	*Is anyone home?*
Tengo que decirte **algo**.	*I have to tell you something.*
Uno no puede saberlo todo.	*One can't know everything.*
Como abogada, **una** trabaja muchas horas diarias.	*As a lawyer, one works many hours a day.*

b. The negative forms need double negation when they come after the verb.

◀ Double negation of **ninguno/a**: 7.B.1

No hay **nada**.	*There is nothing. / There isn't anything.*
No vemos a **nadie** allí.	*We don't see anyone there.*

c. The preposition **a** must be used before indefinite pronouns that refer to a person when they function as objects: **a uno/a, a alguien, a nadie**.

◀ Use of the preposition **a** with direct objects: 12.B.2c, 13.E.2

Ellos no conocen **a nadie**.	*They know no one./They don't know anyone.*
Si **a uno** le gusta el sol, debe ir a Miami.	*Someone who likes the sun ought to go to Miami.*

uno in impersonal **se** sentences:
28.E.2b

7.D.3 Uno/a

a. Uno/a is used in impersonal expressions that also imply personal experience. **Uno** is used for males, and **una** is used for females. However, it is also common to use **uno** for females.

En la playa puede **uno** acostarse y descansar.	*On the beach one can lie down and rest.*
Uno se siente satisfecho con un trabajo bien hecho.	*One feels satisfied after a job well done.*
Aquí se siente **uno** muy bien.	*One feels very good here.*
Como le dije a mi mamá, **una** a veces tiene que quejarse.	*As I told my mom, you have to complain sometimes.*

b. When the noun is not stated, the determiners **unos** and **unas** also function as pronouns.

¿Tienes **unas** tijeras? Sí, tengo **unas** aquí.	*Do you have a pair of scissors? Yes, I've got a pair here.*

7.D.4 Nadie más

The expression **nadie más** means *nobody else.*

Nadie más tiene buenas notas.	*Nobody else has good grades.*
No conocemos a **nadie más** que a ti en la ciudad.	*We don't know anyone else but you in the city.*

7.D.5 Nada

As a pronoun and an adverb, **nada** forms many idiomatic expressions.

Este aparato **no** sirve para **nada**.	*This gadget isn't useful for anything.*
Tú **no** sirves para **nada**.	*You're completely useless.*
Tus notas **no** son **nada** buenas.	*Your grades aren't good at all.*
Luisa **no** es **nada** simpática.	*Luisa isn't nice at all.*
El príncipe se casó **nada menos que** con una plebeya.	*The prince married a commoner, no less.*
No queremos **nada más**.	*We don't want anything else.*
¡Por favor, **nada de** tonterías!	*Please, none of that silliness!*

7.E Common features of indefinite quantifiers and pronouns

Características comunes de cuantificadores y pronombres indefinidos

Affirmative and negative
indefinite quantifiers: 7.B
Indefinite quantifiers with
only affirmative forms: 7.C

7.E.1 Double negation

A special characteristic in the Spanish language is that the negative indefinite determiners **ningún, ninguno/a(s)** and the indefinite pronouns **nadie** and **nada** require *double negation* when they come after the verb. In this case, **no** or another negative expression must come before the verb.

No tengo **nada**.	*I don't have anything.*
Hoy **no** viene **nadie**.	*Nobody is coming today.*
Tampoco hay **ninguna** explicación.	*There isn't any explanation either.*

7.E.2 Reference: person or thing?

The indefinite pronouns **alguien** and **nadie** are used *only* for people, while **algo** and **nada** can *only* be used for things. The indefinite determiners **algún, alguno/a, ningún, ninguno/a, cualquier(a), todo/a(s), un, uno/a** and all the other indefinite quantifiers in tables **7.B** and **7.C** can be used for both people and things.

Hoy **no** trabaja **nadie** porque **no** hay **nada** que hacer.		Nobody is working today because there is nothing to do.	
Algunos trabajadores creen que **algo** raro sucede en la fábrica.		Some workers believe that something strange is happening in the factory.	
Todos los empleados están seguros de que **alguien** sabe la verdad.		All the employees are sure that someone knows the truth.	

7.E.3 The preposition *a* before an indefinite pronoun

The preposition **a** must be added before all indefinite pronouns and indefinite quantifiers that function as direct or indirect objects and refer to people.

Use of the preposition **a** with direct objects: 12.B.2c, 13.E.2

No conozco **a nadie** en la universidad todavía.

I don't know anyone at the university yet.

Le preguntaré **a algún** estudiante qué actividades hay hoy.

I will ask one of the students what activities there are today.

7.E.4 Indefinite quantifiers and *algo, nada* as adverbs

Algo and **nada** can function as adverbs of quantity. **Tan, tanto, más**, and **menos** are also used as adverbs in comparisons. The adverb **muy** can only be used before adjectives and adverbs, while **mucho** can only be used after the verb.

Comparisons: Ch. 11

Adverbs of quantity: 10.D

Quantifiers and adverbs			
algo	*somewhat / a little*	**nada**	*(not) at all / not very*
mucho, muy	*a lot/very*	**poco**	*little*
demasiado	*too much*	**bastante**	*quite*
tan	*as/very/so*	**tanto**	*so much*
más	*more*	**menos**	*less*

Trabajo **mucho** y **muy** bien.

I work a lot and very well.

¡Los canadienses esquían **tanto** y son **tan** buenos!

Canadians ski so much and are very good!

A veces esquío **mucho,** otras veces **poco**.

Sometimes I ski a lot, other times not so much.

Me siento **bastante** bien esquiando, pero **algo** insegura porque mis esquíes no son **nada** modernos.

I feel quite good when I ski, but somewhat insecure because my skis aren't very new.

Últimamente en Colorado nieva **menos**. Antes nevaba **mucho más**.

Lately it's been snowing less in Colorado. It used to snow a lot more.

7.E.5 *Mismo, propio*

a. The words **mismo/a, mismos/as** (*self/selves*) and **propio/a, propios/as** (*own*) are considered *semi-determiners* (**cuasideterminantes**). They come after a personal pronoun or proper noun. Both agree in gender and number but do not have comparative or superlative forms. **Propio/a** intensifies possessive determiners and proper nouns (with the definite article): **mi propio auto** (*my own car*); **el propio Juan,** which means the same as **Juan mismo** (*Juan himself*). **Propio /a** can't be used with personal pronouns the same way as **mismo/a**.

Adjectives: **mismo** (*same*), comparisons with **el mismo** (*the same*): 11.C.5
Mismo with reflexives: 27.A.2
Expressions with **propio**: 9.D.3e

¿Quieres tener casa **propia**?

Do you want your own house?

Tú mismo debes decidir sobre tu **propia** vida.

You, yourself, should make decisions about your own life.

Indefinite quantifiers and pronouns • **Chapter 7**

61

b. In both English and Spanish, *self* must follow the pronoun. Note that *self* can't always be translated as **mismo/a(s),** which can also be an adjective.

él mismo, ella misma, etcétera	*himself, herself, etc.*
el mismo, la misma, los mismos, las mismas	*the same*

Use of pronoun in contrasts: 13.A.1b

Por mi parte/Personalmente, me siento rico, pero no tengo ni un centavo.	*I **myself** feel rich, but I don't have a cent to my name.*
Mi blog lo escribo **yo misma/yo sola**.	*I write my blog **myself**.*
Hoy nos visitará el presidente **en persona**.	*Today the president **himself** will visit us.*
Dijo que todo había salido mal, pero **él mismo** se veía contento.	*He said that everything had gone wrong, but he **himself** seemed happy.*
¿Tienes todavía **la misma** dirección?	*Do you still have the same address?*

c. Mismo/a can also intensify a direct or indirect object. **Mismo** can also be used to intensify adverbs such as **ya, ahora,** and **allí.**

Mismo/a with reflexive pronouns: 27.A.2

¿Os veis a vosotros **mismos** como buenos estudiantes?	*Do you see yourselves as good students?*
¿Te darás a ti **misma** un buen regalo?	*Will you give yourself a good present?*
Ven aquí ya **mismo**.	*Come here right now.*

7.E.6 *Sendos*

The determiner **sendos/as** (*each*) can only come before a plural noun and is used in written, formal language.

Los ganadores recibieron **sendos** premios.	*The winners each received a prize.*
Ellos escribieron **sendas** entradas en sus blogs.	*They each wrote their own blog post.*

7.F Regional variations

Variaciones regionales

7.F.1 *Más*

As an intensifier, **más** comes after the indefinite pronouns **nada** and **nadie: No hay nada/nadie más.** (*There isn't anything/anyone else.*) In southern Spain, the Caribbean, and some parts of South America, **más** can come before **nada** and **nadie** with the same meaning: **No queremos más nada.**

7.F.2 *Poca de, (de) a poco, por poco*

a. In central Spain, **un poco de** can agree in gender: **una poca de sal.**

b. In everyday language, the Mexican expression **a poco** is used to express surprise: **¿A poco crees que soy tonta?** (*You surely don't think I'm stupid, do you?*) It can also be used to seek confirmation or agreement (*isn't it? right? don't you think so?*).

c. De a poco / de a poquito(s) (*little by little*) is a common expression in Latin America: **Dame la medicina de a poquitos.** (*Give me the medicine little by little.*)

d. Por poco is often used colloquially to mean *almost*.

Por poco me caigo.	*I almost fell.*

7.F.3 *Con todo y* + **clause or noun**

Práctica

 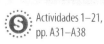
Actividades 1–21, pp. A31–A38

This expression, which means *despite*, is common in some Latin American countries and in northeast Spain.

Con todo y tus disculpas, no te perdono.	*Despite your excuses, I don't forgive you.*

Demonstratives
Demostrativos

8.A **Demonstrative determiners and pronouns**

Determinantes y pronombres demostrativos

8.A.1 Structure

Demonstrative determiners and pronouns show where people and things are in relation to the speaker. English has a two-level system: (*this/that*, *these/those*), which can sometimes be strengthened with *here* and (*over*) *there*. Spanish has a three-level system that specifies whether the item is close to the person speaking, close to the person being spoken to or a short distance from both people, or far away from both.

	Determiners				Pronouns
	Masculine		**Feminine**		**Neuter**
Relative placement	**Singular**	**Plural**	**Singular**	**Plural**	**Singular**
close to the person speaking	est**e**	est**os**	est**a**	est**as**	**esto**
close to the person being spoken to	es**e**	es**os**	es**a**	es**as**	**eso**
far away from both people	aquel	aquel**los**	aquel**la**	aquel**las**	**aquello**

8.A.2 *Este, ese, aquel*

a. Demonstrative determiners in the singular and plural usually come before the noun and agree with it in gender and number. These forms can come before numbers.

Aquella cas**a** es grande.	*That house (over there) is big.*
Estos tres libr**os** son míos.	*These three books are mine.*

b. Demonstratives placed after a noun can convey a condescending or ironic attitude. **Aquel /aquella** has a more neutral attitude than the other forms.

¡No sé qué dice **el** profesor **ese**!	*I don't know what that professor is saying!*
El niño **este** no para de hablar.	*This child won't stop talking.*
¡Qué tiempos **aquellos**!	*Those were good times!*

c. Demonstrative determiners with masculine and feminine forms can stand alone (without a noun). In this case, they act as pronouns and have traditionally carried a written accent to differentiate them from the forms that come before nouns. For years, the written accent was considered a requirement only in cases of ambiguity. The **Real Academia** no longer requires the accent, even in cases of ambiguity, since such cases are rare and easily avoided.

8.A.3 Reference to time and items in a text

a. Demonstrative determiners can also refer to events in the past or near future, or to specific items or ideas in a text. **Este/a** and **estos/as** appear in many expressions to refer to the nearest moment in time within the present time period. **Esta mañana, esta tarde,** and **esta noche** are equivalent to **hoy por la mañana, hoy por la tarde,** and **hoy por la noche**.

esta mañana	*this morning*	**esta semana**	*this week*
esta tarde	*this afternoon*	**este mes**	*this month*
esta noche	*tonight*	**este año**	*this year*

En **estos** días voy a trabajar mucho.   *I'm going to work a lot these (next few) days.*
Nos veremos **esta** noche.   *We're meeting up tonight.*
Este año será difícil.   *This year will be difficult.*

b. Ese/a and **aquel/aquella** refer primarily to the past, but can also refer to the future.

En **esa/aquella** época, todo era mejor.   *At that time, everything was better.*
Las ventas empiezan a las ocho y, en **ese**   *The sales start at eight o'clock and, at*
   momento, abrirán las puertas.   *that moment, the doors will open.*

8.A.4   *Esto, eso, aquello*

a. The neuter demonstratives **esto, eso,** and **aquello** can function only as pronouns.

Esto que me dijiste me dejó preocupada.   *What you told me made me worried.*
Tengo mucho trabajo y **eso** no me gusta nada.   *I have so much work, and I don't like that at all.*
¿Aquello te parece bien?   *Does that sound good to you?*

b. The neuter demonstratives are used mostly to refer to things or ideas. When used to refer to people, they can be derogatory, unless the meaning of the demonstrative is actually explained. They are rarely used to refer to animals.

¡Esto es mi equipo de trabajo! (*derog.*)   *This (thing over here) is my work team!*
Mi equipo de trabajo era **eso**, un excelente   *My work team was just that, a wonderful group*
   grupo humano.   *of people.*

Lo que: 15.B.7b   **c. Aquello** can replace **lo** in relative clauses. In that case, it does not indicate proximity/distance.

¡Haz **aquello/lo** que te dije!   *Do what I told you!*

Todo: 7.C.9   **d.** Neuter demonstratives can be used with **todo**.

Todo esto es mentira.   *This is all a lie.*

8.A.5   *Aquí, allí*

Adverbs of place: 10.E.1   A few adverbs naturally go with demonstratives: **acá/aquí, allí/ahí, allá**.

A estas personas que están **aquí** no las conozco.   *These people here, I don't know them.*
Ese señor que está **allí** es Luis.   *That man there is Luis.*

8.B   Regional variations

Variaciones regionales

Esto and **este** are often used to fill pauses in speech, as are words like **pues, ah,** and **eh**.

Este... no sé qué decir...   *Well... I don't know what to say...*
Luisa, ... **esto**... ¿me prestas dinero?   *Luisa, ... um... can I borrow some money?*

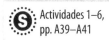

Práctica

Actividades 1–6,
pp. A39–A41

Possessives
Posesivos

Chapter 9

Determiners (6)
A. Possessive determiners
B. Possessives before nouns
C. Possessives after nouns
D. Features
E. Regional variations

9.A Possessive determiners

Determinantes posesivos

Possessives are determiners that express ownership or belonging. The short, unstressed forms (**átonos**) come before the noun. The long, stressed forms (**tónicos**) must always come after the noun, but they can also stand alone as pronouns. Possessives always agree with what is owned, regardless of placement. The short forms are used more than the long forms.

mi libro	*my book*	el libro **mío**	*my book*
tus amigos	*your friends*	los amigos **tuyos**	*your friends*
nuestra casa	*our house*	la casa **nuestra**	*our house*
vuestro país	*your [pl.] country*	el país **vuestro**	*your [pl.] country*

9.B Possessives before nouns

Determinantes posesivos prenominales

Short possessives come before the noun (the thing owned) and agree with that noun in number. Two forms, **nuestro/a(s)** and **vuestro/a(s)**, agree in both gender and number. **Tú** and **vos** use **tu(s)**, and all third persons, including **usted(es)**, use **su(s)**.

Cuyo/a: 15.A.2, 15.B.1-2, 15.B.6

Possessives before nouns			
	Singular	**Plural**	
yo	mi	mis	*my*
tú	tu	tus	*your*
vos	tu	tus	*your*
usted	su	sus	*your*
él	su	sus	*his*
ella	su	sus	*her*
nosotros/as	nuestr**o/a**	nuestr**os/as**	*our*
vosotros/as	vuestr**o/a**	vuestr**os/as**	*your*
ustedes	su	sus	*your*
ellos/as	su	sus	*their*

mi libro	*my book*	**su** escuela	*your/his/her/their school*
mis hermanos	*my siblings*	**sus** escuelas	*your/his/her/their schools*
tu casa	*your house*	**nuestra** casa	*our house*
tus libros	*your books*	**nuestras** familias	*our families*
nuestro amigo	*our friend*	**nuestros** amigos	*our friends*
vuestros amigos	*your friends*	**vuestras** casas	*your houses*

9.C Possessives after nouns

Determinantes posesivos posnominales

9.C.1 Structure

Like adjectives, possessives after nouns agree in gender and number with those nouns.

Possessives after nouns			
	Singular	**Plural**	
yo	mí**o/a**	mí**os/as**	*mine*
tú	tuy**o/a**	tuy**os/as**	*yours*
vos	tuy**o/a**	tuy**os/as**	*yours*
usted	suy**o/a**	suy**os/as**	*yours*
él	suy**o/a**	suy**os/as**	*his*
ella	suy**o/a**	suy**os/as**	*hers*
nosotros/as	nuestr**o/a**	nuestr**os/as**	*ours*
vosotros/as	vuestr**o/a**	vuestr**os/as**	*yours*
ustedes	suy**o/a**	suy**os/as**	*yours*
ellos/as	suy**o/a**	suy**os/as**	*theirs*

Definite article: 5.A.1 ▶
Indefinite quantifiers
(determiners): 7.B–7.C

9.C.2 Use

a. The long possessive forms must be used when a definite article, an indefinite article, or one or more determiners come before the noun.

el libro **mío**	*my book (the book of mine)*	**la** casa **mía**	*my house*
los libros **míos**	*my books*	**las** casas **mías**	*my houses*
un amigo **mío**	*a friend of mine*	**varios** libros **vuestros**	*various books of yours*
todas estas cosas **tuyas**	*all these things of yours*	**bastantes** ideas **nuestras**	*quite a lot of our ideas*
el teléfono **tuyo** es mejor que el mío	*your phone is better than mine*	**un** compañero **nuestro**	*a classmate of ours*

Comparisons with possessives ▶
after nouns: 11.B.1f

b. The long forms can stand alone like pronouns when the noun is not mentioned. They agree in gender and number with the noun they replace and are used with a definite article.

Este es mi número de teléfono, ¿cuál es **el tuyo**?	*This is my phone number; what's yours?*
Estos papeles son **los míos** y esos son **los tuyos**.	*These papers are mine, and those are yours.*
Haz el pastel con tu receta, no con **la mía**.	*Make the cake with your recipe, not with mine.*
Esta cámara es **la nuestra**, no **la tuya**.	*This camera is ours, not yours.*
Lo tuyo es mío y **lo mío** es tuyo.	*What is yours is mine, and what is mine is yours.*
Vuestra casa es muy grande. **La nuestra** es más pequeña.	*Your [pl.] house is very big. Ours is smaller.*

c. With **ser** and **parecer,** the long forms can emphasize ownership without an article or other determiner.

Ese lápiz es **mío**.	*That pencil is mine.*
¿Es **tuyo** todo esto?	*Is all this yours?*
Las demás cosas parecen **mías**.	*The remaining things seem to be mine.*

Using possessives before and ▶
after nouns: 9.D.7

d. In Spanish, when several possessives are put together, a combination of short and long possessive forms or a combination of **de** + *noun/pronoun* and long forms is used.

Mañana vienen **tus** amigos y **los míos**.	*Tomorrow, your friends and mine are coming.*
Las preferencias **de ellos** y **las mías** son iguales.	*Their preferences and mine are the same.*
El carro **de Juan** y **el nuestro** son del mismo modelo.	*Juan's car and ours are the same model.*

66   Possessives • **Chapter 9**

e. Long possessive forms are often used instead of compound prepositions made up of *noun + preposition*.

Compound prepositions 12 A, b

alrededor de ellos / alrededor **suyo**	*around them*
al lado de ella / al lado **suyo**	*next to her*
en torno a mí / en torno **mío**	*around me*

9.D Features

Características generales

9.D.1 Use of *de + pronoun* to clarify possessor

The possessives **su(s)** and **suyo/a(s)** have multiple meanings: *your(s), his, her(s), its, their(s)*. If the context is ambiguous or to establish contrast, use **de** + *pronoun* or *noun* to identify the owner clearly.

Benito no lavará su auto sino el **de ella**.	*Benito will not wash his car, but hers.*
La familia **de ellos** es muy grande.	*Their family is very large.*
Ellos son los padres **de Leonor**.	*They are Leonor's parents.*
Estos documentos son **de ustedes**.	*These documents are yours.*
¿Este libro es **de usted**?	*Is this book yours?*

9.D.2 Use of *de nosotros/as* in Latin America

In Latin America, **de** + **nosotros/as** frequently replaces **nuestro/a(s)** in oral and written Spanish.

Una prima **de nosotras** vive en Miami.	*A cousin of ours lives in Miami.*
El auto **de nosotros** es un modelo viejo.	*Our car is an old model.*

9.D.3 Uses of *propio*

In Spanish, **propio/a(s)** (*own, of one's own*) can be used before or after a noun, with or without a possessive, and can have several meanings.

a. To stress ownership, place **propio/a(s)** *before* a noun and after a possessive, as in English.

Compared with mismo 7.E.3

Mary vio el robo con **sus propios** ojos.	*Mary saw the robbery with her own eyes.*
Prefiero tener **mi propia** habitación.	*I prefer to have my own room.*
Crea **tu propio** blog.	*Create your own blog.*
Juan construyó **su propia** casa.	*Juan built his own house.*

b. **Propio/a(s)** is used to express characteristics of people and things. Note the use of **de** + *pronoun* or *noun*.

Ser with nouns 10.B.1

Jugar bien es **propio** de campeones.	*Playing well is the way of champions.*
¡Esa risa es **propia** de Luisa!	*That laugh is typical of Luisa!*
El tango es **propio** de Argentina.	*Tango is typical of Argentina.*
La salsa tiene un ritmo muy **propio**.	*Salsa music has a unique rhythm.*
Las travesuras son **propias** de los niños.	*Mischief is typical of children.*

c. **Propio/a** can be a synonym of **mismo/a** + *place*. This use is equivalent to the English *proper*.

Vivo en la misma...

Vivo en la **propia** capital.	*I live in the capital proper.*

d. **Propio/a(s)** can also mean *appropriate*, *proper*, or *suitable*, as in the following examples.

Este diccionario es **propio** para estudiantes.	*This dictionary is suitable for students.*
Te daré botas **propias** para el invierno.	*I'll give you proper winter boots.*

Other meanings of **propio**: 7.E.5 ▶

e. Propio/a appears in many common useful expressions.

Rita vive en su **propio mundo**.	*Rita lives in her own world.*
Es cuestión de **amor propio**.	*It's a matter of pride.*
El acusado actuó en **defensa propia**.	*The defendant acted in self-defense.*
Eso lo sé por **experiencia propia**.	*I know that from my own experience.*
Esto lo decides por **cuenta propia**.	*You should decide this on your own.*
Aprendo español a mi **propio ritmo**.	*I learn Spanish at my own pace.*

9.D.4 **Article instead of possessives**

Expressing ownership ▶
with an article: 5.C.7

a. The definite article is used instead of a possessive with parts of the body or personal belongings. However, with verbs like **ser** and **parecer,** the possessive is used to make ownership clear.

¡Niños, tenéis **las** manos sucias!	*Children, your hands are dirty!*
¿Dónde he dejado **las** gafas?	*Where did I leave my glasses?*
Tengo puestos **los** zapatos nuevos.	*I have my new shoes on.*
Mis zapatos son de cuero.	*My shoes are made of leather.*
Tu piel parece muy seca.	*Your skin looks very dry.*

b. The definite article is used instead of the possessive when the verb is reflexive because the reflexive pronoun already indicates the owner.

Tienes que poner**te los** lentes.	*You have to put in your contact lenses.*
Voy a lavar**me la** cara.	*I'm going to wash my face.*
El perro **se** rasca **el** lomo.	*The dog is scratching his back.*

Verbs like **gustar**: 13.F.3, 17.B.4 ▶

c. Verbs that express physical reactions and ailments, such as **arder, doler,** and **picar,** are used with indirect object pronouns. The affected part of the body, which is the subject of the sentence, uses a definite article, not a possessive.

¿**Te** arden **los** ojos?	*Do your eyes burn?*
A ellos **les** duelen **los** pies.	*Their feet hurt.*

d. When ownership is not obvious, using possessives helps clarify who the owner is.

La madre paseaba con **los/sus** hijos.	*The mother was walking with the/her children.*
Hoy visité a **la/mi** vecina.	*I visited the/my neighbor today.*
La/Mi familia me visitará el Día de Acción de Gracias.	*The/My family will visit me on Thanksgiving.*

9.D.5 *Lo* **+ possessives**

With the neuter article **lo**, the long possessive forms express general ownership or areas of interest.

Lo tuyo es el arte.	*Art is your thing.*
Lo nuestro no es un secreto.	*Our relationship is not a secret.*
Lo mío es tuyo.	*What's mine is yours.*
Y ahora, cada uno va a **lo suyo**.	*And now, it's every man for himself.*
Lo vuestro es la literatura.	*Literature is your [pl.] thing.*

9.D.6   Definite and indefinite meaning of possessives

a. The short possessive forms always refer to something definite: **mis amigos = los amigos míos** (*my friends*). The long possessive forms are much more flexible and may also convey ownership of unspecified things or unspecified quantity: **unos/muchos/varios/los otros amigos míos** (*some/many/ several/other friends of mine*).

b. Definite articles can never accompany a short possessive form because it is already definite, as explained in part **a**. In this case, the long forms must be used.

Tu trabajo es muy interesante.	
El trabajo **tuyo** es muy interesante.	*Your work is very interesting.*

c. Unlike the short possessive forms, the long forms can be used with demonstratives and many indefinite determiners.

Possessive determiners: 9.A

Ese viaje **vuestro** tendrá que esperar.	*That trip of yours will have to wait.*
¡No te diré **ningún** secreto **mío**!	*I won't tell you any of my secrets!*
Olvidamos **varias** cosas **nuestras** en el hotel.	*We forgot several of our things at the hotel.*
¡**Esa** idea **tuya** es fantástica!	*That idea of yours is fantastic!*

d. Short possessive forms (which are definite) are generally used with **estar** and long forms (which are indefinite) with **haber**. When using the long possessive forms with **estar,** you usually need a definite article or another determiner. Compare the following examples.

Uses of **estar** and **haber**: 29.B.1, 30.C.7

Aquí **están los** cinco dólares **tuyos** y **los** cuatro **míos**.	*Here are your five dollars and my four.*
Aquí **están tus** cinco dólares y **mis** cuatro dólares.	*Here are your five dollars and my four dollars.*
Somos tres hermanos: primero **está mi** hermana mayor que tiene veinte años y luego **está mi** hermano menor que tiene quince.	*There are three of us (siblings): first there's my older sister, who is twenty years old, and then there is my younger brother, who is fifteen.*
En el garaje **están mis** libros viejos y hay, además, **varias** cosas **tuyas**.	*In the garage, there are my old books and there are also several things of yours.*
Aquí **hay** cinco dólares **tuyos** y cuatro **míos**.	*Here are five dollars that are yours and four that are mine.*

9.D.7   Using possessives before and after nouns

Short possessive forms can be combined with long forms. Several long forms can also be combined, but two short forms can't be combined unless the noun is repeated.

Use of possessives after nouns: 9.C.2d

Los planes **tuyos y míos** son incompatibles.	*Your plans and mine are incompatible.*
Hoy vendrán **vuestras** amigas y las **mías**.	*Your friends and mine will come today.*
Mi cumpleaños y **el tuyo** son el mismo día.	*My birthday and yours are on the same day.*
Mi cumpleaños y **tu** cumpleaños son el mismo día.	

9.D.8 Use of possessives in direct address

a. The long possessive forms are more common than the short forms when addressing someone by name, title, or nickname.

¡Querida Alicia mía, escúchame bien!	*My dear Alicia, listen to me very carefully!*
Amigos míos, ¡la cena está servida!	*Dear friends, dinner is served!*
Cariño mío, te extraño.	*I miss you, my dear.*

b. Particularly in Latin America, the short possessive forms are frequently used to address someone.

amor **mío**	**mi** amor	*my love*
cielito **mío**	**mi** cielito	*my darling*
corazón **mío**	**mi** corazón	*my darling*
hijo/a **mío/a**	**mi**jito/**mi**jita, **m'**hijito/**m'**hijita	*my son/daughter*

c. In military circles, the norm is to use short possessive forms with titles. Kings, nobles, cardinals, and the pope are addressed in similar ways.

mi capitán	*my captain*	**Su** Alteza Real	*Your Royal Highness*
mi general	*my general*	**Su** Excelencia	*Your Excellence*
mi sargento	*my sergeant*	**Su** Santidad	*Your Holiness*
mi soldado	*my soldier*	**Su** Señoría	*Your Honor*

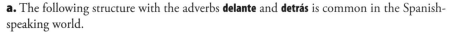

9.E Regional variations

Variaciones regionales

9.E.1 Adverbs of place used with possessives

Compound prepositions: 12.A.2b ▶

a. The following structure with the adverbs **delante** and **detrás** is common in the Spanish-speaking world.

El perro camina **delante de ella**.	*The dog walks in front of her.*

b. Although not as common, the long possessive forms are also used with adverbs of place. Many Spanish speakers consider this usage incorrect.

El perro camina **delante suyo**.	*The dog walks in front of her.*

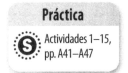

Práctica

Ⓢ Actividades 1–15, pp. A41–A47

Adverbs
Adverbios

10.A Overview

Aspectos generales

Adverbs describe *when*, *how*, *where*, and *why* something happens or is done. Adverbs can modify a verb, another adverb, an adjective, or a whole sentence. Although they modify other words, adverbs do not change form to agree with any other word in a sentence.

Adverbs can be used together with:		
1. Verbs	Camino **rápidamente**.	*I walk **quickly**.*
2. Other adverbs	Camino **muy** rápidamente.	*I walk **very** quickly.*
3. Adjectives	Estoy **bastante** cansado.	*I'm **quite** tired.*
4. Sentences	**Generalmente**, estudio los lunes.	***Usually**, I study on Mondays.*

10.B Adverbs of time

Adverbios de tiempo

10.B.1 Cuándo, cuando

Question		Answer	
¿cuándo?	*when?*	**cuando**	*when*

Cuándo with a written accent is used in direct and indirect questions. Without a written accent, **cuando** is used in subordinate clauses.

—¿**Cuándo** hacéis las tareas? — *When do you [pl.] do your homework?*

—Las hacemos **cuando** podemos. — *We do it when we can.*

◀ **Cuándo** 14.B.8
Cuando in subordinate clauses: 23.E.2a
Conjunctions of time: 16.C.3
Relative adverbs: 15.C.1
Indirect questions: 14.B.9, 31.B.6d

10.B.2 Common adverbs of time

ahora	*now*	**entonces**	*then*
antes	*before*	**después**	*after(ward), later, then*
		luego	*later*
hoy	*today*	**mañana**	*tomorrow*
		pasado mañana	*day after tomorrow*
		ayer	*yesterday*
		anteayer	*day before yesterday*
		anoche	*last night*
		anteanoche	*night before last*
siempre	*always*	**nunca**	*never, ever*
		jamás	*never, ever (emphatic)*
tarde	*late*	**temprano**	*early*
todavía, aún	*still*	**todavía no, aún no**	*not yet*
ya	*already, now*	**ya no**	*no longer*
mientras	*meanwhile, in the meantime*		

Podemos descansar **después**.	*We can rest **later**.*
Ana viene **mañana**.	*Ana is coming **tomorrow**.*
Siempre estudio mucho.	*I **always** study a lot.*
No estudiaste **ayer**.	*You didn't study **yesterday**.*
Hoy es martes.	***Today** is Tuesday.*
Pronto termino.	*I'll finish **soon**.*
Los estudiantes se reunían en parejas. El profesor, **mientras**, explicaba la actividad.	*The students got together in pairs. The professor, **meanwhile**, explained the activity.*
Primero trabajamos y **luego/después** descansamos.	***First** we'll work and **later/then** we'll rest.*
Siempre llegas **antes** y yo **después**.	*You always arrive **before** and I arrive **after**.*

Mientras is set off by commas when it used as an adverb, but not when it is used as a conjunction: 16.C.3

10.B.3 *Nunca, jamás*

Nunca and **jamás** mean *never* or, sometimes, *ever*, but **jamás** is more emphatic. They can be used together to make an even stronger negation, **nunca jamás** (*never ever*). These adverbs can come before or after a verb, but both require a double negative when they follow a verb.

Nunca te olvidaré./**No** te olvidaré **nunca**.	*I will **never** forget you.*
Jamás nos diremos adiós./**No** nos diremos adiós **jamás**.	*We will **never** say goodbye.*
Nunca jamás te olvidaré./**No** te olvidaré **nunca jamás**.	*I will **never ever** forget you.*

10.B.4 *Ya, ya no; todavía, todavía no; aún, aún no*

a. Note how these adverbs are used in the following sentences.

Ya lo he pagado todo.	*I've **already** paid for everything.*
Ya no estudio literatura.	*I'm **not** studying literature **anymore**.*
Todavía vivo en Nueva York.	*I **still** live in New York.*
Todavía no hablo bien español.	*I **don't** speak Spanish well **yet**.*

b. Here are some common expressions with **ya**.

Note that **ir**, not **venir**, is used to say *I'm coming*.

¡**Ya** voy!	*I'm coming!*	**Ya** (lo) sé.	*I already know that.*
¡**Ya** vengo/regreso/vuelvo!	*I'll be right back!*	**Ya** verás/veremos.	*You'll see. / We'll see.*

Diacritical marks: 1.E.6c

c. Aún is a synonym of **todavía**. **Aun** (without an accent) can mean *even*, *also*, or *including*.

Aún vivo en Nueva York.	*I **still** live in New York.*
Aún no hablo bien español.	*I don't speak Spanish well **yet**.*
Sigo cansado **aun** después de dormir la siesta.	*I am tired **even** after taking a nap.*
Todos, **aun** los que al principio se opusieron, apoyaron la decisión.	*Everyone supported the decision, **including** those who had initially opposed it.*

10.B.5 *Después, luego*

The adverbs **luego** and **después** are synonyms.

Después/Luego vuelvo.	*I'll come back **later**.*

10.B.6 Adverbs of frequency

Adverbial phrases: 10.H

a. These adverbs express how often something happens. They can be arranged on a scale where **siempre** and **nunca** are opposites, with adverbs of various frequencies in between.

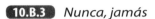

Más frecuencia ←---→ Menos frecuencia							
siempre	*always*	**casi siempre**	*almost always*	**casi nunca**	*almost never*	**nunca, jamás**	*never*
todo/a(s) + def. article + time	*every + time*	**muchas veces**	*many times*	**pocas veces**	*a few times*	**nunca jamás**	*never ever*
		a veces, de vez en cuando	*sometimes, once in a while*	**rara vez**	*seldom, rarely*		
		frecuentemente, con (mucha) frecuencia, a menudo	*frequently, often*	**con poca frecuencia**	*infrequently*		

Trabajo **todos los días**.

Siempre estudio por la mañana.

A veces practico el vocabulario.

Casi siempre escribo en mi blog.

Nunca me canso de chatear.

Rara vez vamos a la playa.

I work every day.

I always study in the morning.

Sometimes I practice the vocabulary.

I almost always write in my blog.

I never get tired of chatting.

We rarely go to the beach.

b. In addition to these adverbs of frequency, Spanish uses **cada** + *time expression* to emphasize incremental actions or events.

Cada día aprendo más español.

I learn more Spanish each day.

10.C Adverbs of manner

Adverbios de modo

10.C.1 Cómo, como

Question		Answer	
¿Cómo?	*How?*	**como**	*as, like*

Cómo with a written accent is used in direct and indirect questions. **Como** is used without a written accent in comparisons and subordinate clauses that express the way something is done.

El clima está tan bueno hoy **como** ayer.

Viaja **como** quieras, en avión o en tren.

—¿**Cómo** quieres el café?

—¡Exactamente **como** tú lo preparas!

*The weather is just as good today **as** yesterday.*

*Travel **as** you wish, by plane or train.*

***How** do you want your coffee?*

*Exactly **how** you prepare it!*

Como in subordinate clauses: 23.E.1
Relative adverbs: 15.C.1
Cómo: 14.B.6

Conjunctions of comparison: 16.C.8
Expressing manner - **como**: 16.C.9

10.C.2 Common adverbs of manner

bien	*well*	**mal**	*badly*
mejor	*better*	**peor**	*worse*
así	*this way, like this/that*	**regular**	*so-so*

Quiero el café **así**: ¡caliente!

*I want my coffee **like this**: hot!*

The adverb **bien** can be used as an adjective: **Ellos son gente bien.** (*They are good people.*) Also in exclamations: **¡Qué bien!** (*That's great!*)

a. The adverbs **bien** and **mal** have their own comparative forms.

¡Este nuevo chef cocina **peor** las pastas!

Un pediatra examina **mejor** a los niños.

*This new chef cooks the pasta **worse**!*

*A pediatrician examines children **better**.*

10.C.3 *Bien*

The adverb **bien** before an adjective adds force or emphasis.

La película es **bien** divertida.	*The film is **quite** funny.*
¡Tienes un auto **bien** bonito!	*You have a **really** nice car!*

10.D Adverbs of quantity

Adverbios de cantidad

10.D.1 *Cuánto, cuanto*

Cuán is a short form of **cuánto** used mainly in exclamations and can be replaced by **qué**:
¡**Cuán/Qué** listo es este chico!
(*What a bright kid he is!*)

Question		Answer	
¿Cuánto?	*How much?*	**cuanto**	*as much (as)*

a. Cuánto with a written accent is used in direct and indirect questions. **Cuanto** is used without a written accent in subordinate clauses to express *quantity* or *degree*.

Cuánto: 14.B.5
Indirect questions:
14.B.9, 31.B.6d

—¿**Cuánto** trabajas?	***How much** do you work?*
—Trabajo **cuanto** puedo.	*I work **as much as** I can.*

b. In speech and in less formal texts, **todo lo que** (*as much as*) is more common than **cuanto**.

Todo: 7.C.9d

Trabajo **todo lo que** puedo.	*I work **as much as** I can.*

10.D.2 Other common modifiers and adverbs of quantity

Suficiente = bastante

más (*more*)	←---------------------------→		**menos** (*less*)
demasiado *too much*	**mucho, muy** *a lot, very*	**bastante, suficiente** *enough/quite a lot/quite*	**poco** *little*
tanto, tan *so much*	**casi** *almost*	**apenas** *barely, hardly*	**solo, solamente** *only*

Me comí **casi** todo el paquete.	*I ate **almost** the whole package.*
Apenas tengo tiempo libre.	*I **barely** have free time.*
Duermes **mucho** y trabajas **poco**.	*You sleep **a lot** and work **little**.*
Solo estudio español.	*I **only** study Spanish.*
Tú trabajas **más** que yo.	*You work **more** than I do.*
¡Nieva **tanto** hoy!	*It's snowing **so much** today!*

a. Más, menos, and **tanto** are the most common adverbs used in all types of comparisons.

Comparisons: Ch. 11

Estudiamos **más que** vosotros.	*We study **more than** you [pl.].*
Viajo **menos que** antes.	*I travel **less than** before.*
Sabes **tanto como** yo.	*You know **as much as** I do.*

b. Casi is used mostly with the present tense in Spanish, while *almost*, in English, can also be used in the past tense.

Casi compro un auto nuevo.	*I **almost** bought a new car.*

c. The adverb **bastante** can stand alone or be combined with adjectives or other adverbs.

Trabajo **bastante**.	*I work **quite a lot**.*
Mary está **bastante** cansada.	*Mary is **quite** tired.*
Tu trabajo está **bastante** bien.	*Your work is **quite** good.*
No comes **bastante**.	*You don't eat **enough**.*

◀ Bastante before and after a noun: 7.C.2

d. The adverbs **muy, mucho,** and **demasiado** can't appear together. Note how their equivalents are used in English.

Hablas **mucho**.	*You talk **a lot**.*
Trabajas **demasiado**.	*You work **too much**.*
Estamos **demasiado** cansados.	*We are **too** tired.*
El problema es **muy** difícil.	*The problem is **very** difficult.*

◀ Demasiado/a: 7.C.11

10.E Adverbs of place

Adverbios de lugar

There are two groups of adverbs that express where an action takes place. One group expresses relative distance from the perspective of the speaker. The other group expresses the specific location of people and things.

10.E.1 Relative distance

Close to the person speaking		Far from the person speaking	
aquí	*here*	allí, ahí	*there*
acá	*here*	allá	*(over) there*

a. Aquí and **allí** work the same way as *here* and *there*, and are used primarily to indicate location.

Aquí siempre hace buen tiempo.	*It's always good weather here.*
Allí están tus libros.	*There are your books.*

b. Ahí is more general than **allí** and expresses an indefinite location when used with **por**.

Tus zapatos están **por ahí**.	*Your shoes are around somewhere.*
—¿Dónde entrenas los domingos?	*Where do you train on Sundays?*
—**Por ahí**, en la ciudad o en el parque.	*Around, in the city or the park.*

c. Acá and **allá** are often used with verbs of motion. In contrast to **allí,** the adverb **allá** can be used with **más** and **muy**.

Ven **acá**.	*Come here.*
Isabel va para **allá**.	*Isabel is on her way there.*
El correo está **más allá**.	*The post office is farther away.*

10.E.2 Adverbs of place and direction: *adónde/adonde; dónde/donde*

Adverbs of place can refer to specific locations of people and things, and some of them also indicate direction.

◀ Dónde: 14.B.8
Donde/adonde: 16.C.10

a. These adverbs are used to ask and answer a question about a location or direction.

Question		Answer	
¿adónde?	*where?*	**adonde**	*where (in, on, at)*
¿a dónde?	*to where?*	**a donde**	*to where*
¿dónde?	*where?*	**donde**	*where*

b. Dónde is a question adverb that refers to location. **Donde** can be used to answer a question with **dónde** and refers to a location already mentioned.

Donde in subordinate ▶
clauses: 23.E.1
Relative adverb **donde**:
15.C.1

—¿**Dónde** vive tu familia?　　　　　　　　*Where does your family live?*
—Vive en la ciudad **donde** nací.　　　　　　*They live in the city **where** I was born.*

c. It is common to use *preposition* + **el/la/los/las que** in relative clauses as a synonym for **donde**.

—¿**Dónde** estudias?　　　　　　　　　　　　*Where are you studying?*
—En una escuela **en la que** hay buenos maestros.　*At a school **where** there are good teachers.*

d. Adónde is a question adverb used to refer to location with verbs of motion. **Adonde** can be used to answer questions with **adonde**. In this case, **adonde** is a relative adverb referring to a definite location. Both can be written as two words: **a dónde, a donde**.

Donde, adonde are used ▶
informally for the meaning *at
(somebody's house)*:
Estoy donde Juan. *I'm at Juan's.*

—¿**Adónde** viajas en verano?　　　　　　　*Where do you travel in the summer?*
—Este año iré a Londres, **adonde** viajé　　　*This year I'll go to London, **where** I traveled*
el año pasado.　　　　　　　　　　　　　*last year.*
—Viajo **a donde** vive mi familia.　　　　　*I'm going **to where** my family lives.*

Ser, estar with adverbs: ▶
30.C.1, 30.E

`10.E.3`　**Other common adverbs of place and direction**

The following adverb pairs look similar, but their meanings and uses are different. The adverbs in the *Place* column describe location only. The adverbs in the other column express location relative to a specific *direction*.

Place		Direction	
delante	*in front*	**adelante**	*forward, ahead, in front, at the front*
detrás	*behind, in the back*	**atrás**	*behind, back, at the back*
encima	*on top*	**arriba**	*above, up*
debajo	*underneath*	**abajo**	*below, down*
dentro	*within, inside*	**adentro**	*inside*
fuera	*out, outside*	**afuera**	*outside*
cerca	*close (by)*		
lejos	*far (away)*		
alrededor	*around*		
enfrente	*opposite, in front*		

Compound prepositions: 12.A.2b ▶

a. Adverbs of place that describe location usually form compound prepositions with **de**: **delante de** (*in front of*), **encima de** (*on top of*), **alrededor de** (*around*), etc. The adverbs that convey direction are not used with **de**.

One common exception is ▶
de arriba abajo (*from top to
bottom, from head to toe*).

Delante de la iglesia hay una plaza.　　　*In front of the church there is a square.*
Hay mucha gente **dentro de** la iglesia.　　*There are lots of people inside the church.*

b. Only adverbs of place that convey direction can be used with prepositions indicating movement: **hacia adelante** (*in a forward direction*), **hasta atrás/arriba** (*all the way back/up*), **hacia/para abajo** (*downward*), and similar expressions.

La chica miraba **para arriba y para abajo**.　　*The girl looked up and down.*

Cerca, lejos: 10.E.3h ▶

c. Adverbs of quantity can be used with adverbs of place that convey direction to indicate how much distance in a specific direction. Adverbs of place that do not convey direction do not take adverbs of quantity (except **cerca** and **lejos**).

más adelante	farther on, later	muy abajo	very far down
bastante arriba	very high up	un poco atrás	a little bit behind
muy cerca	very close	mucho más lejos	much farther away
demasiado atrás	too far back	nada lejos	not very far away

d. Delante and **detrás** express location exclusively, while **adelante** and **atrás** convey a sense of movement or placement (*forward* and *backward*) in addition to location.

El parque está allí **delante**.	*The park is there, right in front.*
El parque está allí **adelante**.	*The park is there, farther on.*
La fuente está **detrás**.	*The fountain is in back.*
La fuente está más **atrás**.	*The fountain is farther back.*
Los niños viajan **atrás** y los adultos **adelante**.	*The children ride in the back and the adults in the front.*

Adverbs of place used with possessives: 9.E.1

e. Arriba and **abajo** express location, but always with a sense of direction, *up* or *down*. Therefore, these two adverbs can be used to mean *upstairs, downstairs* or figuratively as in the expressions **los de arriba** (*upper class*) and **los de abajo** (*lower class*). **Encima** and **debajo** express only location.

En el texto, los títulos van **arriba** y las notas van **abajo**.	*In the text, the titles go above and the notes go below.*
En la caja, encuentras los libros **debajo** y los papeles **encima**.	*In the box, you'll find the books underneath and the papers on top.*

f. Dentro and **fuera** generally don't appear alone. They are usually combined with prepositions to refer to physical or figurative places.

Los rayos X muestran el cuerpo **por dentro**.	*X-rays show the inside of the body.*
Por fuera, la casa se ve chica.	*The house looks small from the outside.*
Hay mucha gente **fuera del** cine.	*There are a lot of people outside the movie theater.*

g. Adentro and **afuera** must be used with a stated or implied verb of motion.

No te muevas, quédate **afuera**.	*Don't move; stay outside.*
Hace frío, vamos **adentro**.	*It's cold; let's go inside.*

h. Cerca and **lejos** express location only. They are often used with adverbs of quantity (**muy, bastante,** etc.) and **de**. They can *never* be used with prepositions indicating movement.

Adverbs + **hacia, hasta**: 10.E.3b

El centro de la ciudad queda **lejos**.	*The city center is far away.*
Alaska queda **muy lejos de** Nueva York.	*Alaska is very far from New York.*

10.E.4 **Adverbs of place and prepositions**

There is an important difference between adverbs of place and prepositions. Prepositions are followed by a noun, while adverbs of place can stand alone.

Compound prepositions: 12.A.2b

Prepositions	
El perro está **debajo de** la cama.	*The dog is **under** the bed.*
Las cartas están **encima de** la mesa.	*The letters are **on** the table.*

Adverbs of place	
En la caja encuentras los libros **debajo** y los papeles **encima**.	*In the box, you'll find the books **underneath** and the papers **on top**.*

10.F Affirmative, negative, and doubting adverbs

Adverbios de afirmación, de negación y de duda

10.F.1 Common affirmative and negative adverbs

¿no?	right (true)?	¿sí?	yes? is it true?
sí	yes	no	no, not
bueno	OK, well	también	also
tal vez, quizá(s)	maybe	tampoco	neither

a. In negative sentences, **no** comes before the verb. Note how you answer negatively in Spanish: **No, no...** *No... not.* Both **¿sí?** and **¿no?** are added at the end of the sentence in order to ask a question, which is equivalent to a *tag question* in English.

Tag questions: 14.A.3 ▶

—Vives en Chicago, **¿no?**   *You live in Chicago, **don't you**?*
—**No, no** vivo en Chicago.   *No, I **don't** live in Chicago.*
—**Sí,** vivo en Chicago.   *Yes, I live in Chicago.*

b. In spoken language, it is common to add **sí** in order to add emphasis to an affirmative statement, especially when contrasting affirmative and negative.

¿Tú **no** quieres ir? ¡Yo **sí** quiero!   *You don't want to go? I sure do!*

c. También is used like the English *also*. **Tampoco** is used in negative sentences to mean *neither*.

Gabriel viene y Carolina **también**.   *Gabriel is coming, and Carolina too.*
Tú **no** quieres ir y yo **tampoco**.   *You don't want to go, and neither do I.*

Use of the subjunctive in ▶ independent clauses: 23.B.1

d. Tal vez and **quizá(s)** are synonyms. Both can be used with the indicative and the subjunctive.

Quizás es/sea Luisa.   *It might be Luisa.*
Tal vez viajamos/viajemos pronto.   *We might go soon.*

10.G Adverbs ending in *-mente*

Adverbios terminados en *-mente*

10.G.1 Structure

Adverbs ending in *-mente*: 1.E.8 ▶

Many common adverbs in Spanish end in **-mente** and are formed using the feminine form of an adjective. When the adjective does not have a feminine form, **-mente** is added to the basic form. Adjectives keep written accents when they form adverbs.

Adjectives: 3.A ▶

Adjectives		Adverbs	
Masculine	**Feminine**	**Adjective + *-mente***	
correcto	correct**a**	correcta**mente**	*correctly*
fácil	fácil	fácil**mente**	*easily*
feliz	feliz	feliz**mente**	*happily*

Felizmente, aprobé el examen.   *Happily, I passed my exam.*
Hablas **correctamente**.   *You speak correctly.*

10.G.2 Adjectives as adverbs

In modern Spanish, some common adjectives are also used as adverbs without the
-mente ending. Note that these short forms are always masculine and singular.

Respiro **hondo**.	*I'm breathing deeply.*	Juegan **duro**.	*They play hard.*
Escribes **claro**.	*You write clearly.*	Camino **rápido**.	*I walk quickly.*
Juegas **limpio**.	*You're playing fairly.*	Hablan **raro**.	*They speak in a strange way/strangely.*

10.G.3 Placement of adverbs

a. Adverbs that end in **-mente** almost always come after the verb. Adverbs that support an
adjective or other adverbs usually come before the verb, close to the word they modify.

Laura canta **maravillosamente**.	*Laura sings marvelously.*
Mike **casi siempre** está ocupado.	*Mike is almost always busy.*
La explicación es **poco clara**.	*The explanation is not very clear.*

b. When there are several **-mente** adverbs in a row, only the final adverb keeps the **-mente** ending.

La profesora explica la lección clara, pausada y excelente**mente**.	*The professor explains the lesson clearly, slowly, and very well.*

10.H Adverbial phrases

Locuciones adverbiales

Adverbial phrases combine adverbs, prepositions, or nouns, and express time, manner, quantity,
place, assertion, doubt, and negation.

10.H.1 Adverbial phrases vs. adverbs ending in *-mente*

Some common adverbs ending in **-mente** may be replaced by a prepositional phrase with the
same meaning, formed with the corresponding noun.

Adverb ending in *-mente*	Adverbial phrase	
cariñosamente	con cariño	*affectionately*
claramente	con claridad	*clearly*
cortésmente	con cortesía	*courteously*
cuidadosamente	con cuidado	*carefully*
difícilmente	con dificultad	*with difficulty*
firmemente	con firmeza	*firmly*
frecuentemente	con frecuencia	*frequently*
locamente	con locura	*madly*
rápidamente	con rapidez	*quickly*
repentinamente	de repente	*suddenly*
sinceramente	con sinceridad	*sincerely*
telefónicamente	por teléfono	*by phone*

Adverbs • **Chapter 10**

79

10.H.2 **Useful adverbial phrases**

a la larga	in the long run	**A la larga**, conseguirás trabajo. *You will get a job in the long run.*
a las mil maravillas	wonderfully	¡Se preparó **a las mil maravillas**! *It was prepared wonderfully!*
a lo grande	luxuriously, in style	Celebrarán la boda **a lo grande**. *They will celebrate their wedding in style.*
a (la) mano	close at hand	Lleva tu pasaporte **a (la) mano**. *Have your passport close at hand.*
a menudo	frequently, often	Viajamos en avión **a menudo**. *We travel frequently by plane.*
a veces	sometimes	**A veces** duermo la siesta. *I take naps sometimes.*
al final	at/in the end	**Al final** decidimos irnos en tren. *In the end, we decided to travel by train.*
alguna vez	sometime (ever)	¿Has ido a México **alguna vez**? *Have you ever been to Mexico?*
con frecuencia	frequently, often	Escribo en Twitter **con frecuencia**. *I write on Twitter frequently.*
de primera mano	firsthand	Sé la noticia **de primera mano**. *I know the news firsthand.*
en algún momento	at some point, sometime	**En algún momento** debes decidirte. *You will have to decide sometime.*
en alguna parte	somewhere	He dejado mis gafas **en alguna parte**. *I left my glasses somewhere.*
en buenas manos	in good hands	Este trabajo está **en buenas manos**. *This job is in good hands.*
en fin	finally, well then	**En fin**, tenemos que irnos ya. *Well then, we have to go now.*
por fin	at last, finally	**Por fin** has terminado el trabajo. *You have finished your work at last.*
por las buenas o por las malas	one way or the other	Tendrás que estudiar **por las buenas o por las malas**. *You will have to study one way or the other.*
por necesidad	out of necessity	Trabajamos **por necesidad**. *We work out of necessity.*
por poco	almost	**Por poco** pierdo el autobús. *I almost missed the bus.*

por poco: 7.F.2

10.I Comparison of adverbs

Comparación del adverbio

10.I.1 Comparative constructions

Comparisons: Ch. 11
Comparison of adjectives: 3.E

a. Adverbs have a basic form, as well as a comparative form. Most adverbs form the comparative using **más** or **menos**. Some have irregular forms.

Adverbs	Basic	Comparative
Regular	**eficazmente** *efficiently*	**más/menos eficazmente** *more/less efficiently*
Irregular	**bien** *well*	**mejor** *better*
	mal *badly*	**peor** *worse*
	mucho *much/a lot*	**más** *more*
	poco *little/a bit*	**menos** *less*

Actualmente, la gente vive **mejor**.

Nowadays, people live better.

El médico cree que como **mal**, pero mi hermano come **peor** que yo.

The doctor thinks I eat badly, but my brother eats worse than I do.

b. Comparisons using adverbs can be formed with the following structures: **más/menos** + *adverb* + **que** or **tan** + *adverb* + **como**.

Viajamos **más frecuentemente que** antes.

We travel a lot more than before.

Leemos **tan bien como** vosotros.

We read as well as you [pl.] do.

10.I.2 Superlative constructions

a. Absolute superlatives of adverbs can be formed by adding -**mente** to the absolute superlative feminine form of an adjective with an -**ísima** ending. In English, the superlative is produced with other intensifying adverbs: *very, unbelievably*, etc.

Superlatives of adverbs: 11.D.2

Adjectives		Adverbs	
Basic	Superlative	Superlative of adjective + -*mente*	
lento	**lentísima**	**lentísimamente**	*very slowly*
claro	**clarísima**	**clarísimamente**	*very clearly*
fuerte	**fuertísima**	**fuertísimamente**	*very strongly/hard*

¡Explicas todo **clarísimamente**!

You explain everything very clearly!

Te comportas **tontísimamente**.

You're behaving really stupidly.

b. Short adverbs that are identical to masculine singular adjectives take the ending -**ísimo**.

Adjectives as adverbs: 10.G.2

Corre **rápido**.   *He runs fast.*

Corre **rapidísimo**.   *He runs very fast.*

c. Some adverbs that are not derived from adjectives also have absolute superlatives. The absolute superlative keeps the ending of the adverb.

lejos → lejísimos   *very far*

poco → poquísimo   *very little*

cerca → cerquísima   *very close*

mucho → muchísimo   *a lot*

Los fines de semana duermo **poquísimo**.

I sleep very little on weekends.

Mis primos viven **lejísimos**.

My cousins live very far away.

d. Relative superlatives can be formed using a comparative form (sometimes coming after a definite article).

Fue **la pintura más cuidadosamente** realizada.

*It was **the most carefully** done painting.*

De todas las pinturas, esta es **la más cuidadosamente realizada**.

*Of all the paintings, this is **the most carefully done**.*

Juan es quien **más dedicadamente** trabaja.

*Juan is the one who works **the most diligently**.*

e. Lo más/menos + *adverb* + *adjective/clause* is usually equivalent to the English *as much as* + *adjective/clause* or *as little as* + *adjective/clause*. The adjective most commonly used in this construction is **posible**.

Entreno **lo más frecuentemente posible**.	*I train as much as possible.*
Trabaja **lo más rápidamente que puede**.	*She works as fast as she can.*

Lo más/menos + *adverb* + *adjective/clause* is also commonly used in time expressions.

Lo más tarde que llegué al trabajo es las diez.	*The latest I arrived at work is ten.*
Hazlo **lo más pronto que puedas**.	*Do it as soon as you can.*

f. When English uses a superlative adverb, Spanish can use either a sentence containing a relative clause or a comparative sentence. Note in the examples that when using a comparative sentence, a person is compared with everyone else in the group.

Él es el que más rápido corre.	
Él corre más rápido que todos.	*He runs **the fastest**.*
Todos nos sentimos mal, pero ella es la que peor se sintió.	
Todos nos sentimos mal, pero ella se sintió peor que todos.	*We all felt bad, but she felt **the worst**.*
Ella es la que resolvió el problema más inteligentemente.	
Ella resolvió el problema más inteligentemente que el resto.	*She resolved the problem **the most intelligently**.*

10.J Regional variations

Variaciones regionales

10.J.1 Diminutives

In Latin America, diminutives of adverbs are common in daily language.

Diminutives, augmentatives, and pejoratives: 2.C.6, 3.A.4

ahora	*now*	**ahorita**	*right now/in a moment*
allá	*there*	**allacito**	*over there*
aquí	*here*	**aquicito**	*exactly here*
después	*later/after*	**despuesito**	*right away/in just a moment*
enseguida	*soon*	**enseguidita**	*in a tiny little bit*

10.J.2 *Vale, bien, de acuerdo, claro que sí*

a. In daily language, **vale** is used in Spain for questions with the meaning *OK?* The answer may include the same word.

—Nos vemos más tarde, **¿vale?**	*We'll meet up later, OK?*
—**¡Vale!**	*OK!*

b. In Latin America, there are many local variations of *OK.* Some of the most common expressions are **está bien, de acuerdo, dale, sí, ok.**

—Regreso pronto, **¿de acuerdo?**	*I'll be back soon, OK?*
—**¡De acuerdo!**	*OK!*
—Nos juntamos más tarde.	*We'll get together later.*
—**Dale.**	*OK.*

c. In the Spanish-speaking world, some of the most common expressions of agreement, disagreement, and consent are **claro, claro que sí, claro que no, por supuesto que sí, cómo no, por supuesto que no.**

—¿Puedo abrir la ventana?	*Can I open the window?*
—**¡Claro que sí!** ¡Ábrela!	*Of course! Open it!*
—¿Estás irritada?	*Are you annoyed?*
—**¡Claro que no!**	*Of course not!*

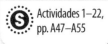

Práctica

Actividades 1–22,
pp. A47–A55

Adverbs • **Chapter 10**

Comparisons
Comparaciones

11.A Overview

Aspectos generales

Some English adjectives have a comparative form that takes the suffix *-er* (*longer*), while others use *more* and *less* (*more/less popular*). English adverbs use *more* and *less* for comparative forms (*more slowly*). Nouns are compared using *as many as*, *more/fewer than*. Spanish uses a much more regular structure to compare things or people (*nouns, pronouns*), characteristics (*adjectives*), actions (*verbs*), and how the actions happen (*adverbs*).

11.B Comparisons of inequality

Desigualdad

11.B.1 Adjectives, adverbs, nouns, and verbs

a. Inequality is expressed in the following ways in Spanish.

Comparisons of adjectives, adverbs, and nouns		
más (*more*) / **menos** (*less*) +	*adjectives/adverbs/nouns*	+ **que** (*than*)

For comparisons of inequality with verbs, **más/menos que** comes after the verb.

Adjectives	Las películas son **más** *largas* **que** las telenovelas.	*Films are longer than soap operas.*
	Antonio es **menos** *famoso* **que** yo.	*Antonio is less famous than I am.*
Adverbs	La impresora grande imprime **más** *rápidamente* **que** la pequeña.	*The big printer prints more quickly than the little one.*
	Escribo **mejor** en español **que** en francés.	*I write better in Spanish than in French.*
Nouns	Tengo **más** *libros* **que** Betty.	*I have more books than Betty.*
	Hoy tengo **menos** *dinero* **que** ayer.	*Today I have less money than yesterday.*
Verbs	*Viajas* **más que** yo.	*You travel more than I do.*
	Entreno **menos que** tú.	*I train less than you do.*

Note that the subject pronoun is used in comparisons (**yo, tú, él,** etc.).

b. Some adjectives and adverbs have irregular comparative forms.

Adjectives		Irregular comparatives	
bueno/a(s)	*good*	**mejor(es)**	*better*
malo/a(s)	*bad*	**peor(es)**	*worse*
joven/jóvenes	*young*	**menor(es)**	*younger*
viejo/a(s)	*old*	**mayor(es)**	*older*

Adverbs		Irregular comparatives	
bien	*well*	**mejor**	*better*
mal	*badly*	**peor**	*worse*
mucho	*a lot/very*	**más**	*more*
poco	*little*	**menos**	*less*

◄ Comparison of adjectives: 3.E

◄ **Inferior** and **superior** are irregular comparatives of **bajo** and **alto**. See table in 11.D.1b.

◄ Comparison of adverbs: 10.I

c. The regular comparative forms of **bueno/a** and **malo/a** can also be used. However, in this case, they exclusively emphasize character judgements.

María es **más buena** que el pan.	*María is a very good person./María is kindness itself.*
María es **mejor** cocinera que su madre.	*María is a better cook than her mother.*

d. Mayor and **menor** are used much more than the regular comparative forms. They are also used as comparative forms of **grande** and **pequeño** when these refer to age.

Carlos es **menor / más joven** que yo.	*Carlos is younger than I am.*

e. Grande and **pequeño** also use **mayor** and **menor** as superlative forms when describing the scope or importance of an issue.

Mi ciudad tiene el **mayor** número de desocupados.	*My city has the largest number of unemployed people.*

f. After **que,** a long possessive form always follows a definite article: **el mío, la suya,** etc.

Possessives after nouns: 9.C ▶

Mi auto gasta menos gasolina **que el tuyo**.	*My car consumes less gasoline than yours.*
Nuestras vacaciones son (mucho) más largas **que las vuestras**.	*Our vacations are (much) longer than yours [pl.].*

g. When numbers are compared, **que** is replaced by **de**.

Asisto a **más de** tres clases todos los días.	*I attend more than three classes every day.*
El libro costó **menos de** veinte euros.	*The book cost less than twenty euros.*

Adverbs: **mucho, muy**: 7.E.4 ▶

h. Comparative forms can be strengthened with the help of other adverbs. The most common are **mucho, bastante,** and **(un) poco**. The adverb **muy** can't appear before **más** or **menos,** and can come only before adjectives or adverbs.

El tiempo está hoy **mucho peor** que ayer.	*The weather today is much worse than yesterday.*
Los billetes de avión son **bastante más** caros que los pasajes de tren.	*Plane tickets are quite a lot more expensive than train tickets.*

i. The following comparative expressions indicate that something is different: **diferente a/de, distinto/a(s) + a/de** (*different from*).

Su último libro es **diferente a** los otros.	*His latest book is different from the others.*
Tú eres **distinta a** todas las otras chicas.	*You're different from all the other girls.*

j. In English, comparative forms of an adjective can be used without stating a comparison: *We live in a bigger city in Ecuador.* In Spanish, this is not possible, and such expressions must be said in a different way.

Vivimos en una ciudad **muy/relativamente** grande en Ecuador.	*We live in a very/relatively big city in Ecuador.*

k. In affirmative comparisons, **nadie/ninguno/nunca/nada** express *more/less than anyone, ever, anything,* etc.

Ellos son **más** hábiles **que nadie**.	*They are more skilled than anyone.*
Puedes bailar **mejor que ninguno**.	*You can dance better than anybody.*
Hoy habéis actuado **mejor que nunca**.	*Today you [pl.] have performed better than ever.*
Me encanta el helado **más que nada**.	*I love ice cream more than anything.*

Sino: 16.B.1, 16.B.5b ▶

l. The expression **no... más que** in *negative* sentences is not comparative and is equivalent to **no... sino** or **solamente** as in the following examples.

No hablo **más que** español.	*I speak nothing but Spanish.*
No hablo **sino** español.	*I speak nothing but Spanish.*
Solamente hablo español.	*I only speak Spanish.*

84   Comparisons • **Chapter 11**

11.B.2 **Comparisons with** *de* + ***definite article*** + *que*

a. The second element of a comparison can be a relative clause that refers to the noun in the first part of the comparison. In this case, the second element is introduced by **de** + *definite article* + **que**. The definite article agrees in gender and number with the noun in the first part of the comparison.

más/menos +	*masc. sing. noun* + **del que**	+ *clause*
	fem. sing. noun + **de la que**	
	masc. pl. noun + **de los que**	
	fem. pl. noun + **de las que**	

Gastamos **más** *dinero del* **que** teníamos. — We spent more money than we had.
(gastamos dinero; teníamos dinero)

Había **más** *gente* **de** *la* **que** esperábamos. — There were more people than we expected.
(había gente; esperábamos gente)

Fuimos a **menos** *museos* **de** *los* **que** planeábamos — We went to fewer museums than we were
visitar. (fuimos a museos; planeábamos visitar museos) — planning to visit.

Había **menos** *plazas* **de** *las* **que** hay en mi ciudad. — There were fewer squares than there are in
(había plazas; hay plazas) — my city.

b. **De lo que** is used when the second part of a comparison is a clause and the first is a verb, an adjective, or an adverb.

◀ **Lo**: 5.A.2

Verb	*Trabajó* **más de lo que** esperábamos.	He worked more than we expected.
Adjective	Los precios allí son bastante **más** *altos* **de lo que** dice la gente.	The prices there are quite a lot higher than people say.
Adverb	El tiempo pasó **más** *rápidamente* **de lo que** pensábamos.	The time passed more quickly than we thought.

c. **De lo que** can also be used when the first part of the comparison is a noun. In this case, the verb in the second part of the comparison does not refer specifically to the noun in the first part. This happens particularly with the noun **vez** or when the first part of the comparison expresses a measurement.

Gasté *cinco dólares* **más de lo que** habíamos acordado. — I spent five dollars more than we had agreed.
Vine de visita *tres veces* **más de lo que** viniste tú. — I came to visit three times more than you did.

◀ Multiples: 6.E.2b

d. **De lo que** can also be used when the clause in the second part of the comparison refers to a general idea rather than to the specific noun in the first part of the comparison. In this case, agreement with the noun is also possible.

Gastamos **más** *dinero* **de lo que/del que** pensábamos. — We spent more money than we thought.
(gastamos dinero; pensábamos gastar menos dinero)

Compare with this sentence, in which **de lo que** can't be used.

Gastamos **más** *dinero* **del que** teníamos en el banco. — We spent more money than we had in the bank.
(gastamos dinero; teníamos dinero)

e. **De lo** is also used with adjectives like **aconsejable, autorizado, esperado, habitual, justo, necesario, normal, permitido, previsto,** and **requerido**. It is also possible to use **que** in this case.

Trabajé más **de/que lo** esperado. — I worked more than expected.
Me parece más complicado **de/que lo** previsto. — It seems more complicated than anticipated.

11.C Comparisons of equality

Igualdad

The structures for comparing similar characteristics, people, and things depend on what is being compared.

11.C.1 Tan

Adjectives and adverbs are compared in the same way when emphasizing similarities.

tan *(as)* + adjective/adverb + **como** *(as)*

Adjectives	Las películas no son **tan *cortas* como** las telenovelas.	*Films are not as short as soap operas.*
	Antonio es **tan *famoso* como** yo.	*Antonio is as famous as I am.*
Adverbs	La impresora grande imprime **tan *rápidamente* como** la pequeña.	*The big printer prints just as quickly as the little one.*
	Escribo **tan bien** en español **como** en francés.	*I write as well in Spanish as in French.*

Indefinite quantifiers (determiners): 7.E.4

11.C.2 Tanto/a(s)

Nouns (people and things) are compared using the word **tanto/a(s),** which agrees with the noun that follows it.

tanto/a(s) *(as much/many)* + noun + **como** *(as)*

Nouns	Tengo **tantos libros como** Betty.	*I have as many books as Betty.*
	Hoy, tengo **tanto dinero como** ayer.	*Today, I have just as much money as yesterday.*

11.C.3 Tanto

Verbs are compared using **tanto,** which does not change form and comes after the verb. The verb after **como** is implied and is normally not repeated.

Tanto... como:
16.B.2d

verb + **tanto** *(just as much/as much)* + **como** *(as)*

Verbs	**Viajas tanto como** yo.	*You travel as much as I do.*
	Entreno tanto como tú.	*I train just as much as you do.*

11.C.4 Igual, tal como

The expression **igual de... que** is used for both adjectives and adverbs. With nouns, **igual a** and **(tal) como** are used, and with verbs, **igual que**.

Adjectives	Rita es **igual de** joven **que** yo.	*Rita is just as young as I am.*
Adverbs	Yo no escribo **igual de** bien **que** tú.	*I don't write as well as you do.*
Nouns	Mi camisa es **igual a** / **tal como** la tuya.	*My shirt is just like yours.*
Verbs	Nosotros trabajamos **igual que** / **como** ellos.	*We work just like they do.*

11.C.5 *Mismo/a(s)*

Similarity can be expressed using a definite article and **mismo/a(s)** (*same*).

Tengo **la misma** camisa que tú.   *I have the same shirt as you.*

Tenemos **la misma** camisa.   *We have the same shirt.*

Hago **lo mismo** de siempre.   *I'm doing the same as always.*

Siempre ponen **las mismas** películas año tras año.   *They always show the same films year after year.*

◄ **Mismo**: Other meanings: 7.E.5 and 27.D.1

◄ **Similar a** and **parecido/a a** can also be used to express similarity.

11.D Superlatives

El superlativo

Superlatives refer to the highest or lowest degree of a characteristic (adjectives), how something is done (adverbs), or to the greatest or smallest number of people or things (nouns). In English, the superlative is formed with the ending *-est* (*biggest, smallest, youngest*) or with *most, least*.

11.D.1 Adjectives

a. The superlative of adjectives is formed using **el/la/los/las más/menos** + *adjective*.

Me gustan varios deportes, pero el fútbol es   *I like many sports, but soccer is the*
el más interesante.   *most interesting.*

b. The following adjectives have irregular superlatives.

Adjectives		Comparatives		Superlatives	
alto	high	más alto superior	higher	el más alto el superior supremo	the highest
bajo	low	más bajo inferior	lower	el más bajo el inferior ínfimo	the lowest
bueno	good	más bueno mejor	better	el más bueno el mejor óptimo	the best, optimal
grande	big	más grande mayor	bigger	el más grande el mayor máximo	the biggest, the maximum
joven	young	menor	younger	el menor	the youngest
malo	bad	más malo peor	worse	el más malo el peor pésimo	the worst
pequeño	small	más pequeño menor	smaller	el más pequeño el menor mínimo	the smallest, the minimum
viejo	old	mayor	older	el mayor	the oldest

◄ Comparison of adjectives: 3.E, 11.B.1

◄ **Más bueno** and **más malo** are used exclusively to refer to character traits: 3.E.2b, 11.B.1c

◄ **Mayor** and **menor** as comparative forms of **grande** and **pequeño**: 11.B.1d-e

Esta es **la peor** noticia **que** he recibido.   *This is the worst news I've (ever) received.*

Esta película es **la peor que** he visto.   *This film is the worst I've (ever) seen.*

Mario y Carlos son malos diseñadores,   *Mario and Carlos are bad designers, but*
   pero Pedro es **el peor**.   *Pedro is the worst.*

Mis dos gatitos son muy buenos.	*My two kittens are very good.*
No muerden ni rasguñan a nadie.	*They don't bite or scratch anyone.*
Pero el gatito de mi vecino es **el más bueno** de todos.	*But my neighbor's kitten is the nicest of all.*
Los resultados no son **óptimos**,	*The results are not optimal, but they*
pero son aceptables.	*are acceptable.*

Todo: 7.C.9 ▶ **c.** It is common to add **todos/as** (*all*) in superlative sentences. **Todos/as** is always plural and agrees in gender with the noun that follows it or with the context of the sentence.

Rita es **la** estudiante **más** lista **de todos/as**.	*Rita is the smartest student of all.*

(**todos**: there are male students in the group; **todas**: all students in the group are female)

Rita es **la más** lista **de todos** los estudiantes.	*Rita is the smartest of all the students.*

d. De, not **en**, is used if a group is indicated.

Nueva York es **la** ciudad **más** grande **del** país.	*New York is the biggest city in the country.*
Este libro es **el menos** caro **de** estos.	*This book is the least expensive of these.*

Superlatives with ▶ -**ísimo/a(s)**: 3.E.3 **e.** The endings -**ísimo/a(s)** can be added to adjectives to form the *absolute superlative*.

grandísimo	*unbelievably big*	**facilísimo**	*very, very easy*

f. The following superlative adjectives are used in daily language.

Esa ropa es de **ínfima** calidad.	*Those clothes are of the lowest quality.*
Tu solución no es **óptima**.	*Your solution isn't the best.*
La diferencia es **mínima**.	*The difference is minimal.*
La temperatura **máxima** fue de 3 grados.	*The maximum temperature was 3 degrees.*

g. People's ages are compared with **mayor/menor,** while their height and size are compared using **alto/bajo** and **grande/pequeño**.

Marcos es **el mayor** de los tres, pero es	*Marcos is the oldest of the three, but he is*
el más pequeño.	*the smallest.*
Olivia es **la menor** de la clase, pero	*Olivia is the youngest in the class, but she is*
es la más alta.	*the tallest.*

h. Adjectives can also be strengthened using many adverbs, such as **bien, enormemente, extraordinariamente, impresionantemente, increíblemente, terriblemente, totalmente,** and **verdaderamente**.

Bien as an adverb: 10.C.3 ▶
Adverbs ending in ▶ -**mente**: 10.G

El problema es **bien** grave.	*The problem is really serious.*
Lucía es **enormemente** rica.	*Lucía is extremely wealthy.*
Eso es **extraordinariamente** extraño.	*That is extraordinarily strange.*
Ella es **impresionantemente** bella.	*She is strikingly beautiful.*
El tráfico está **increíblemente** malo.	*The traffic is incredibly bad.*
La comida es **terriblemente** mala.	*The food is terribly bad.*
La caja está **totalmente** vacía.	*The box is totally empty.*
Eres **verdaderamente** listo.	*You are truly clever.*

11.D.2 **Adverbs**

Comparison of adverbs: 10.I ▶ **a.** Absolute superlatives of adverbs ending in -**mente** can be formed by adding -**mente** to the absolute superlative feminine form of an adjective with an -**ísima** ending. Short adverbs that are identical to masculine singular adjectives take the ending -**ísimo**.

Ríe **locamente**.	*He laughs wildly.*	Ríe **loquísimamente**.	*He laughs extremely wildly.*
Corre **rápido**.	*He runs fast.*	Corre **rapidísimo**.	*He runs very fast.*

Adjectives as adverbs: 10.G.2 ▶

b. Some adverbs that are not derived from adjectives also have absolute superlatives. The absolute superlative keeps the ending of the adverb.

Superlative constructions with adverbs: 10.I.2

In some Latin American countries, the superlative form of **lejos** is **lejísimo**.

lejos → **lejísimos**	*very far*	**cerca** → **cerquísima**	*very close*
poco → **poquísimo**	*very little*	**mucho** → **muchísimo**	*a lot*
Vivo **lejísimos**.	*I live very far away.*	Comes **poquísimo**.	*You eat very little.*

c. Superlative constructions can be formed using the comparative form (sometimes following a definite article).

Es el caso **más cuidadosamente** investigado.	*It is the most carefully investigated case.*
De todos los casos, este es **el más cuidadosamente** investigado.	*Of all the cases, this one is the most carefully investigated.*
Es el detective que **más cuidadosamente** investiga.	*He is the detective that most carefully investigates.*

d. Lo más/menos + *adverb* + *adjective/clause* is usually equivalent to the English *as much/little as* + *adjective/clause*. The most common adjective in this construction is **posible**. This is also used in time expressions.

Entreno **lo más frecuentemente** posible.	*I train as much as possible.*
Trabaja **lo más rápidamente** que puede.	*She works as fast as she can.*
Lo más temprano que llego a la oficina es a las ocho.	*The earliest I get to the office is eight o'clock.*

e. The Spanish equivalent of an English sentence that contains a superlative adverb can be a sentence containing a relative clause or a comparative sentence (in which the first part is compared with everything/everyone else in the group).

Él es el que mejor canta.	
Él canta mejor que todos.	*He sings **the best**.*
Él es el que trabajó más incansablemente.	
Él trabajó más incansablemente que el resto.	*He worked **the most tirelessly**.*

11.D.3 *Lo*

The neuter article **lo** forms abstract noun phrases that can also have a superlative meaning.

Lo: 5.A.2

lo mejor	**Lo mejor** del verano es el calor.	*The best thing about summer is the heat.*
lo más increíble	¡Eso es **lo más increíble** de todo!	*That is the most incredible thing of all!*
lo menos posible	Debes decir **lo menos posible**.	*You should say as little as possible.*
lo más romántico	La ceremonia fue **lo más romántico** de la boda.	*The ceremony was the most romantic part of the wedding.*
lo peor	Ese libro es **lo peor** que he leído.	*That book is the worst thing I have (ever) read.*
lo más sensato	Eso es **lo más sensato** que puedes hacer.	*It's the most sensible thing to do.*

11.D.4 Superlatives with *que*

Que in defining clauses: 15.B.3 ▶

a. Besides **de** + *group*, it is possible to form superlative constructions using **más/menos** and the relative pronoun **que**.

Este libro es **el más interesante de** todos los que he leído.	*This is the most interesting book of all the books I have read.*
Este libro es **el más interesante que** jamás haya leído.	*This is the most interesting book (that) I have ever read.*
Es **el libro que más** me gusta.	*It's the book (that) I like best.*

Lo que: 15.B.7b ▶

b. The neutral **lo** is used instead of **el/la/los/las** when there's no reference to a specific noun. The constructions with **lo que más/menos** are usually translated as *the thing that* or *what*.

El que más me gusta es este libro. (**el** = el libro)	*The one I like best is this book.*
Lo que más me gusta es jugar al tenis. (**lo** = jugar al tenis)	*What I like best is to play tennis.*

c. When the comparison focuses on an adjective or adverb, the adjective or adverb comes between **más/menos** and **que**.

Lo más valioso que tiene mi país es su gente.	*The most valuable thing my country has is its people.*
Lo más rápidamente que puedes viajar allí es en avión.	*The fastest you can travel there is by plane.*

Práctica

 Actividades 1–14, pp. A55–A60

Prepositions
Las preposiciones

Chapter 12
A. Overview
B. Use of prepositions
C. Regional variations

12.A Overview

Aspectos generales

Prepositions are words or word phrases that can come before a noun to indicate the relationship between that noun and another word in the sentence. They never change form. Most prepositions indicate a relationship between two words in terms of time, location, direction, or origin.

Since Spanish and English use prepositions in different ways, a preposition used in Spanish may not have a direct English translation.

Use of prepositions: 12.B

Examples		
Location	Roberto está **en** Sevilla.	*Roberto is in Seville.*
Time	Mi vuelo es **a** la una.	*My flight is at one.*
Ownership	la casa **de** José María	*José María's house*

12.A.1 Simple prepositions

a. There are a limited number of single-word prepositions in Spanish.

Simple prepositions			
a	*at, to*	**excepto, salvo**	*except, apart from*
ante	*before, facing*	**hacia**	*toward*
bajo	*under*	**hasta**	*until*
con	*with*	**mediante**	*through, by means of*
contra	*against*	**para**	*for, to, in order to, by*
de	*of, from*	**por**	*for, because of, by*
desde	*from, since*	**según**	*according to*
durante	*during*	**sin**	*without*
en	*on, in, at*	**sobre**	*over, about*
entre	*between*	**tras**	*after, behind*

Verbs with prepositions: 17.B.2

Other simple prepositions are found mainly in poetry: **allende** (*beyond*), **cabe** (*near*), **so** (*under*), etc.

Por favor, siéntate con la espalda **contra** la pared.   *Please sit with your back against the wall.*
Ángel ha estado viajando **desde** ayer.   *Ángel has been traveling since yesterday.*
Según Elisa, va a llover.   *According to Elisa, it's going to rain.*
El perrito corre **tras** su dueño.   *The little dog runs after his owner.*

b. Spanish prepositions always come between two words and can never end a sentence as they do informally in English.

Relative pronouns: 15.A.3b

Rita es la chica **con** la que salgo.   *Rita is the girl I go out **with**.*

c. In English, two prepositions can be joined using *and* or *or*, while in Spanish, they appear separately in the sentence. The noun or phrase that the preposition refers to is repeated, but in the second instance can be replaced by a pronoun.

Tomo el autobús para ir **a** la escuela **y** regresar **de** la escuela.   *I take the bus **to and from** school.*
Plantaremos árboles **delante de** la casa **o detrás de** ella.   *We will plant trees **in front of or behind** the house.*

d. The words **pro**, **versus**, and **vía** are sometimes counted as prepositions. **Pro** comes before nouns: **grupos *pro* derechos humanos** (*pro-human rights groups*). In Spanish, the meaning of **versus (vs.)** is **contra**, **frente a**; it's used only in formal texts: **las grandes economías *versus* las economías de menor escala** (*large economies vs. small-scale economies*). The preposition **vía** indicates how something is done: the medium, the route, etc.: **El viaje es de San Francisco a Nueva York *vía* Chicago.** (*The trip is from San Francisco to New York, via Chicago*).

12.A.2 **Compound prepositions and prepositional phrases**

Compound prepositions (**locuciones preposicionales**) are formed by two simple prepositions: **por entre** (*through*); a combination of preposition(s) and an adverb: **(por) delante de** (*in front of*), **cerca de** (*near*); or combining preposition(s) and a noun: **en contraste con** (*in contrast with*).

a. Here are examples of compound prepositions formed by two or more simple prepositions.

a por: 12.C.1 ▶

Compound prepositions: *preposition + preposition*		
a por (*Spain*)	Iremos **a por** café.	*We will go **to get** coffee.*
de a	Nos tocan **de a** tres chocolates a cada uno.	*We get three chocolates **each**.*
de entre	Un día **de entre** semana podré trabajar contigo.	*On any **working** day, I will be able to work with you.*
en contra (de)	No actúes **en contra de** tus propios principios.	*Don't act **against** your own principles.*
	¿Estáis **en contra** mía?	*Are you [pl.] **against** me?*
en pro, en contra de	¿Estás **en pro** o **en contra de** la propuesta?	*Are you **for** or **against** the proposal?*
para con	Ella es generosa **para con** todos.	*She is generous **with** everyone.*
por entre	El perro se metió **por entre** los arbustos y se escondió.	*The dog squeezed **in between** the bushes and hid.*

b. The prepositions **de** and **por** form many compound prepositions with adverbs. Some adverbs take **por** when movement is involved (*around the back of, passing by the front of,* etc.).

Adverbs of place and ▶ direction: 10.E.3

Compound prepositions: *adverb + preposition*			
(por) delante de	in front of, opposite, across from	**(por) detrás de**	behind, in back of
enfrente de			
frente a			
al lado de	beside, next to	**lejos de**	far from
cerca de	near, close to		
junto a	close to, next to		
encima de	on top of, on	**debajo de**	under, underneath
por encima de	over	**por debajo de**	
dentro de	in, inside of	**fuera de**	out, outside of
por dentro de		**por fuera de**	
alrededor de	around		
antes de	before	**después de**	after
		luego de	

El autobús pasa **por delante de** la catedral.

*The bus passes **in front of** the cathedral.*

La catedral está **enfrente del / frente al** parque.

*The cathedral is **opposite** the park.*

En el parque, los niños juegan **al lado de** sus madres.

*In the park, the children play **next to** their mothers.*

Vivimos **cerca del** centro de la ciudad.

*We live **close to** downtown.*

Mis abuelos viven **junto a** nosotros.

*My grandparents live **next to** us.*

Dentro de la casa hay un pequeño patio y **alrededor de** él hay plantas.

***Inside** the house there is a small courtyard and there are plants **around** it.*

La casa se veía vieja **antes de** pintarla. **Después de** pintarla, parece nueva.

*The house looked old **before** it was painted. It looks new **after** being painted.*

◀ al lado suyo/mío, etc.: 9.C.2e

◀ antes de que, después de que: 23.E.2

c. There are many prepositional phrases formed with a *noun* and *one or more prepositions*, usually **a**, **de**, **en**, **por**, and **con**. Most of these phrases function in a sentence as adverbs or adverbial transitions.

◀ In some of these examples, other words (like **lo mejor**) function like nouns.

Prepositional phrases: *preposition + noun (+ preposition)*		
a base de	Las tortillas se preparan **a base de** maíz.	*Tortillas are made **with** corn.*
a bordo de	Los pasajeros pasaron **a bordo del** avión.	*Passengers got **on board** the plane.*
a cargo de	La profesora está **a cargo de** la clase.	*The teacher is **in charge of** the class.*
a causa de	Nos retrasamos **a causa del** mal tiempo.	*We were delayed **because of** bad weather.*
a costa de	No hagas nada **a costa de** los demás.	*Don't do anything **at the expense of** others.*
a eso de	Llegaremos **a eso de** las tres de la tarde.	*We will arrive **around** three in the afternoon.*
a falta de	**A falta de** computadora, escribiré a mano.	***Lacking** a computer, I will write by hand.*
a fondo	Estudiaremos los documentos **a fondo**.	*We will study the documents **in depth**.*
a fuerza de	**A fuerza de** voluntad, has logrado tener éxito.	***Through** willpower, you have managed to succeed.*
a la hora de	**A la hora de** pagar, ¿no tienes dinero?	***When it's time to** pay the bill, you don't have money?*
a la sombra de	Ese chico creció **a la sombra de** su famoso padre.	*That kid grew up **in the shadow of** his famous father.*
a la vez	¿Haces todo **a la vez**?	*Do you do everything **at the same time**?*
a lo largo de	Fue un hombre ejemplar **a lo largo de** toda su vida.	*He was an exemplary man **throughout** his whole life.*
a lo mejor	**A lo mejor** va a llover hoy.	***Maybe** it will rain today.*
a mediados de	Su pedido llegará **a mediados de** mayo.	*Your order will arrive **in mid**-May.*
a menudo	Estudiamos en la biblioteca **a menudo**.	*We study at the library **often**.*
a modo de	Leeré un corto texto **a modo de** introducción.	*I will read a short text **by way of** introduction.*
a partir de	**A partir del** lunes habrá conciertos mensuales.	***Starting** Monday, there will be monthly concerts.*
a pesar de	Compraremos la casa **a pesar del** precio.	*We will buy the house **in spite of** the price.*
a pie	Los estudiantes van a la universidad **a pie**.	*Students go to the university **on foot**.*
a principios de	El pago se enviará **a principios de** mes.	*The payment will be sent **at the beginning of** the month.*
a prueba de	Nuestros productos son **a prueba de** agua.	*Our products are water**proof**.*
a raíz de	**A raíz de** la crisis, los precios han subido.	***As a result of** the crisis, prices have risen.*

◀ en pie = *standing*

a razón de	Los precios han subido **a razón del** dos por ciento anual.	*Prices have risen **at a rate of** two percent annually.*
a tiempo	Finalmente, todo se hizo **a tiempo**.	*Finally, everything was done **on time**.*
a veces	**A veces** salimos temprano del trabajo.	***Sometimes** we leave work early.*
al menos	¿Me prestas dinero? ¿**Al menos** cinco dólares?	*Can you lend me some money? **At least** five dollars?*
con base en	El informe se realizó **con base en** datos confiables.	*The report was carried out **based on** reliable data.*
con miras a	Los presidentes se reunirán hoy **con miras a** firmar un acuerdo.	*The presidents will meet today **with the intention of** signing an agreement.*
con motivo de	La cena es **con motivo de** tu visita.	***The reason for** this dinner is your visit.*
con respecto a	No sé nada **con respecto a** este problema.	*I don't know anything **regarding** this problem.*
de acuerdo con	Estoy **de acuerdo con** tu opinión. **De acuerdo con** el profesor, el examen será pronto.	*I **agree with** your opinion.* ***According to** the professor, the exam will be soon.*
de lo contrario	Tengo que anotar tu teléfono, **de lo contrario**, lo olvidaré.	*I have to write down your phone number; **if not**, I will forget it.*
de nuevo	¡Qué gusto verte **de nuevo**!	*So good to see you **again**!*
de pie	Debes ponerte/estar **de pie** cuando tocan el himno nacional.	*You should **stand up / be standing** when they play the national anthem.*
de regreso a	¿Cuándo estará usted **de regreso a** su trabajo?	*When will you **be back at** work?*
de repente	Hacía sol y **de repente**, empezó a llover.	*It was sunny and **suddenly**, it started to rain.*
de veras	¡**De veras** sabes mucho sobre cine!	*You **really** know a lot about movies!*
de vez en cuando	Vamos al cine **de vez en cuando**.	*We go to the movies **once in a while**.*
en cuanto a	**En cuanto a** películas, me gustan las comedias.	***Regarding** movies, I like comedies.*
en vez de, en lugar de, en cambio de	¿Prefiere usted café **en lugar/cambio/ vez de** té?	*Do you prefer coffee **instead of** tea?*
en cambio	La lechuga me gusta, **en cambio** las espinacas no.	*I like lettuce; **on the other hand**, I don't like spinach.*
enseguida	¡Ven **enseguida**!	*Come here **immediately**!*
en torno a	La clase será **en torno a** la literatura moderna.	*The class will be **about** modern literature.*
frente a frente, cara a cara	Los equipos se encontrarán pronto **frente a frente / cara a cara**.	*The teams will soon meet **face to face**.*
para siempre	El petróleo no durará **para siempre**.	*Oil won't last **forever**.*
por eso	Quiero cuidar el ambiente, **por eso** ¡reciclo!	*I want to take care of the environment; **that's why** I recycle!*
por fin	¡**Por fin** acaba de llegar el autobús!	*The bus has **finally** arrived!*
por lo general	**Por lo general**, en España la cena es tarde.	***In general**, dinner in Spain is late.*
por lo menos	Hace mucho frío, pero **por lo menos** hace sol.	*It's cold, but **at least** it's sunny.*
por otra parte, por otro lado	Mi auto es bueno y, **por otra parte / por otro lado**, no es caro.	*My car is nice and **besides**, it's not expensive.*
por poco	¡**Por poco** olvido tu cumpleaños!	*I **almost** forgot your birthday!*
por supuesto	Este es nuestro mejor precio, **por supuesto**.	*This is our best price, **of course**.*
sin embargo	Esta novela no es popular y, **sin embargo**, es excelente.	*This novel is not very popular. **However**, it's excellent.*

Al menos = por lo menos ▶

De repente = de pronto ▶

Por poco is generally used with the present indicative. ▶

Sin embargo: 16.B.5c ▶

12.B Use of prepositions

Uso de las preposiciones

12.B.1 Overview

After a preposition, the pronouns for the first- and second-person singular (**yo**, **tú**) change to **mí**, **ti**, except after the prepositions **entre**, **según**, **excepto**, and **salvo**. After these prepositions, subject pronoun forms are always used: **yo**, **tú**. The pronoun **vos** does not change form after a preposition: **para vos** (*for you*), **con vos** (*with you*).

◀ **Vos**: 13.B.2, 13.B.5
Pronouns after prepositions: 13.C

Ven, siéntate cerca de **mí**.	*Come and sit down close to me.*
Los libros son para **ti**.	*The books are for you.*
Esto queda entre **tú** y **yo**.	*This stays between you and me.*

12.B.2 The preposition *a*

a. The preposition **a** is used in the following cases.

Clues for use	Examples	
Time	La cita es **a las tres**.	*The appointment is at three.*
Time that has passed before something happens/happened	Me **gradúo a** los dos años.	*I'll graduate after two years.*
	Me **gradué a** los dos años.	*I graduated after two years.*
Destination with verbs of motion	**Llegamos a** casa.	*We arrived home.*
	Bajamos al primer piso.	*We went down to the first floor.*
	Vamos a la reunión.	*We're going to the meeting.*
Distance from a location	El correo está **a dos calles** de la iglesia.	*The post office is (located) two streets/blocks from the church.*
al + *infinitive*	**Al contar** el dinero, faltaba un dólar.	*When I counted the money, one dollar was missing.*
	Pagué **al recibir** el paquete.	*I paid upon receiving the package.*

◀ Other verb phrases with the infinitive: 26.C

b. When the preposition **a** is followed by the article **el**, the two words combine to form the contraction **al**.

Voy **al** mercado.	*I'm going to the market.*
Le di la información **al** profesor.	*I gave the information to the professor.*

c. One of the most important uses of the preposition **a** is to indicate that the direct object in a sentence is a person. This use is called *the personal* **a**.

Clues for use	Examples	
Comes before the direct object when it's a person (or it's personified).	Conozco **a** mis vecinos.	*I know my neighbors.*
	Quiero mucho **a** mi mascota.	*I love my pet very much.*
Must be used before indefinite pronouns when they refer to people: **nadie**, **alguno**, **todos**, etc.	Admiro **a todos** mis profesores.	*I admire all my professors.*
	Conozco **a algunos** de mis profesores personalmente.	*I know some of my professors personally.*
It's omitted when the direct object does not have a determiner.	Necesitamos ingenieros especializados.	*We need specialized engineers.*
It's omitted after **tener** as long as no indefinite pronoun follows.	Tenemos muchos amigos. No tenemos **a nadie** para ese trabajo.	*We have many friends. We don't have anyone for that job.*

◀ The preposition **a** with a direct object: 13.E.2

◀ The preposition **a** with indefinite pronouns and quantifiers: 7.D.2c, 7.E.3

◀ Determiners: 4.A

◀ You do use **a** after **tener** when the verb means *keeping* or *holding* someone.

The indirect object: 13.F.1

d. The preposition **a** is used to signal the indirect object in a sentence.

Le doy un regalo **a Luis**.	*I'm giving Luis a gift.*
Les escribo **a mis amigos**.	*I write to my friends.*
¡Agrégale más memoria **a tu PC**!	*Add more memory to your PC!*

12.B.3 The preposition *con*

a. Con is used in the following ways.

Estar con: 30.C.4

Clues for use	Examples	
To mean *with/together with*	Pablo está **con** sus amigos.	*Pablo is with his friends.*
Use of tools	Escribo **con** el lápiz.	*I write with a pencil.*
With nouns in adverbial phrases of frequency or manner	Viajo **con** frecuencia.	*I travel often.*
	Te ayudo **con** gusto.	*I'm happy to help you.*
Condition	**Con** precios tan altos, no puedo comprar nada.	*With such high prices, I can't buy anything.*

b. After the preposition **con**, **mí** changes to **–migo** and **ti** changes to **–tigo**. These pronouns do not vary.

—¿Quieres ir al cine **conmigo**?	*Do you want to go to the movies with me?*
—Sí, quiero ir al cine **contigo**.	*Yes, I want to go to the movies with you.*

Sí: 13.C.2, 27.A.2
Mismo: emphasis: 7.E.5, reflexive: 27.A.2, 27.D.1d

c. The reflexive pronoun **sí** takes the invariable form **consigo** after **con**. **Mismo/a** can be added for emphasis if the action refers back to the subject.

¿Lleva usted su licencia de conducir **consigo**?	*Do you carry your driving license with you?*
Pensé que Lisa hablaba **consigo misma**, pero ¡estaba conversando por su celular!	*I thought that Lisa was talking to herself, but she was talking on her cell phone!*

12.B.4 The preposition *de*

a. De has many uses in Spanish.

Use of **ser**: 30.B.3

Clues for use	Examples	
Ownership	los zapatos **de** Rita	*Rita's shoes*
	el club **de** los estudiantes	*the students' club*
Nationality	Soy **de** México.	*I'm from Mexico.*
Point of departure or origin	El avión llega **de** Vancouver.	*The plane arrives from Vancouver.*
	Salí **de** casa temprano.	*I left home early.*
Placed before an infinitive to express purpose	la escoba **de** barrer	*the broom for sweeping*
	la mesa **de** planchar	*the ironing board*
To indicate what something is made of	la caja **de** plástico	*the plastic box*
	la cuchara **de** plata	*the silver spoon*

Clues for use	Examples	
Subject	los estudiantes **de** español	*the students of Spanish*
	el libro **de** química	*the chemistry book*
Physical appearance	la persona **de** gafas	*the person wearing glasses*
	el niño **de** pantalón corto	*the child wearing shorts*
	la casa **de** ventanas verdes	*the house with green windows*
estar de + *new or temporary occupation*	**estar de** profesora/enfermero/ayudante	*to be a teacher/a nurse/an assistant (for now, currently)*
estar de + *noun*: describes conditions	estar **de** mal humor	*to be in a bad mood*
	estar **de** viaje/vacaciones	*to be traveling/on vacation*
	estar **de** regreso	*to be back*
	estar **de** buenas/malas	*to be lucky/unlucky*
	estar **de** visita	*to be visiting*
	estar **de** amigos	*to be friends*

◀ Use of **estar de** to express a temporary profession, work: 30.C.3

b. When the preposition **de** is followed by the article **el**, the two words form the contraction **del**.

El libro **del** que te hablé cuesta 20 dólares.   *The book I talked to you about costs 20 dollars.*

12.B.5 The preposition *en*

En is used to express the following relationships.

Clues for use	Example	
Specifies where someone/something is located	Estamos **en** Portugal. Elisa vive **en** la ciudad. El papel está **en** el cajón. Marta está **en** el dormitorio. El país está **en** Europa.	*We're in Portugal.* *Elisa lives in the city.* *The paper is in the drawer.* *Marta is in the bedroom.* *The country is in Europe.*
To mean *on, on top of*	La cena está **en** la mesa.	*Dinner is on the table.*
With ordinals and the infinitive in expressions like *the first who...*	Rosa siempre es la primera **en** llegar. Ernesto es el último **en** pagar.	*Rosa is always the first to arrive.* *Ernesto is the last one to pay.*
With months, years, and other time expressions (*not used with days*)	**En** junio hay vacaciones. Lisa llamó **en** ese instante. Estaba feliz **en** esa época.	*There is vacation in June.* *Lisa called just then.* *I was happy during that time.*
Expressions with **estar** + **en**	estar **en** silencio	*to be silent*
	estar **en** la pobreza	*to be poor*
	estar **en** la ignorancia	*to be ignorant*
	estar **en** la cúspide	*to be at the height/peak (of fame, wealth, etc.)*
	estar **en** la oscuridad	*to be in the dark*

◀ **Estar en** + place: 30.D.1

◀ Llegué **el lunes**.

12.B.6 **The prepositions** *para* **and** *por*

Both **para** and **por** mean *to* or *for*, but they are not interchangeable.

Para		
Clues for use	**Examples**	
With a person: refers to the recipient of something	Llegó una carta **para** ti.	*A letter arrived for you.*
	Hay comida **para** todos.	*There's food for everyone.*
With verbs of motion: provides destination	Hoy salimos **para** Chile.	*We're leaving for Chile today.*
	¿Vas **para** la clase?	*Are you going to the class?*
	Ven **para** acá.	*Come here.*
With action verbs: provides purpose	Trabajo **para** vivir.	*I work to live.*
	Estudiamos **para** aprender.	*We study to learn.*
	Las discotecas son **para** divertirse.	*Nightclubs are for having fun.*
With expressions of time: provides a deadline or a closing date	El documento es **para** el lunes.	*The document is due on Monday.*
	Termino el trabajo **para** las tres.	*I'll finish the job by three o'clock.*
With verbs connected to work/tasks: refers to the employer or a client	Trabajo **para** el gobierno. Escribo **para** la televisión.	*I work for the government.* *I write for TV.*
To express *for being so,* using the formula **para ser tan** + *adjective/ adverb*	**Para** ser tan joven, es muy maduro.	*For a young guy, he's very mature.*
With *tool* + **ser** + **para**: provides area of use	El lápiz es **para** escribir, no **para** jugar.	*Pencils are for writing, not for playing.*
With **estar para** + *infinitive* to say that something is about to happen	Ya estoy **para** salir.	*I'm ready to leave. / I'm about to leave.*

Use of **ser** + **para**: 30.B.4 ▶

See **estar por** in the next chart. ▶

Por		
Clues for use	**Examples**	
Refers to cause or justification	Cancelaron el carnaval **por** la lluvia.	*They canceled the carnival because of the rain.*
Describes movements through or around an area	Salimos **por** la puerta principal. Paseáis **por** el parque. Mañana paso **por** tu casa.	*We left through the main door.* *You stroll through the park.* *I'll stop by your house tomorrow.*
Provides a time frame	Estaré en Madrid **por** unos días.	*I'll be in Madrid for a few days.*
With communication and transmission: television, telephone, mail, Internet, fax, radio	Envíame el paquete **por** correo. Transmiten los partidos de fútbol **por** radio y televisión. Mi profesor enseña **por** la red. Hablas mucho **por** teléfono.	*Send me the package by mail.* *They broadcast the soccer games on the radio and TV.* *My professor teaches online.* *You talk a lot on the telephone.*
Describes an exchange	Cambié mi auto viejo **por** uno nuevo. Compramos la bicicleta **por** muy poco dinero.	*I traded in my old car for a new one.* *We bought the bicycle for very little money.*
With **estar** + **por** to express the possibility of doing something in the very near future	**Estoy por** ponerme a estudiar un rato. Ella dice que **está por salir** en cualquier momento.	*I think I'm going to study for a bit.* *She says she's going to leave at any moment.*

See **estar para** in the ▶ previous chart.

Shows that someone is acting on behalf of someone else	¿Puedes asistir a la reunión **por** mí?	Can you attend the meeting instead of/for me?
With percentages	3%: tres **por** ciento	three percent
With verbs of motion in the sense of *collecting, getting*	Vamos **por** los niños a las tres. ¿Vas **por** el periódico?	We'll pick up the children at three o'clock. Are you going to go get the newspaper?
Refers to tasks that still need to be done (with **quedar, hay, tener**)	Quedan/Hay/Tengo varias cuentas **por** pagar.	There are/I have several bills left to pay.

12.B.7 Expressing location, direction, and time with prepositions

The following prepositions convey physical or figurative movement from one point to another, as well as periods of time.

◀ Prepositions used with adverbs of place and direction: 10.E.3

a. The preposition pair **desde-hasta** indicates a precise origin and arrival point, while **de-a** conveys a less concrete *from–to* direction. The preposition **por** conveys a *through* movement, while **hacia** and **para** refer to a *forward* destination without any reference to origin.

¿**Para** dónde vas?	**Where** are you going?
Voy **de** la biblioteca **al** gimnasio y **desde** allí tomo el autobús **hasta** el teatro.	I'm going **from** the library **to** the gym and **from** there, I take the bus **to** the theater.
El autobús pasa **por** el centro de la ciudad y sigue **hacia** las afueras.	The bus passes **through** downtown and continues **toward** the suburbs.

b. The prepositions in the diagram can also refer to *time*. **Desde-hasta** conveys a limit, while **de-a** describes a direction in time. **Hacia** is used for approximate time, and **por** forms specific time expressions: **por la mañana, por la noche, por la tarde**. The preposition **durante** refers to a progressive period of time, while **a** tells the exact time. **En** is used with months and years (not days of the week) and to express how much time is left for something to be completed: **en un mes** (*within/in a month*), **en tres días** (*within/in three days*).

—¿**Para** cuándo terminarás el proyecto?	**(For) when** will you finish the project?
—Lo tendré listo **en** tres días. Hoy martes trabajaré **de** tres **a** cuatro de la tarde y después **desde** mañana **hasta** el viernes. Es decir, trabajaré **durante** tres días.	I will have it ready **in** three days. Today, Tuesday, I will work **from** three **to** four in the afternoon, and then **from** tomorrow **until** Friday. In other words, I will work **during** three days.
Terminaré el trabajo **hacia** fines de esta semana.	I will finish the work **toward** the end of this week.
¡El viernes **por** la tarde, **a** las tres en punto!	Friday **in** the afternoon **at** three o'clock sharp!

c. The preposition pair **ante-tras** describes opposite horizontal locations (*in front of–back of*), while **sobre-bajo** expresses vertical opposites (*above–under*). **Entre** describes a neutral location *in between* any of these points.

Ante el juez está la acusada y **tras** ella, su familia.	**Facing** the judge sits the defendant, and **behind** her, her family.
Sobre la mesa están las pruebas y **bajo** estas, los documentos del juez.	**On** the table are the exhibits and **under** them, the judge's documents.
Los guardias están de pie **entre** el juez y la acusada.	The guards are standing **between** the judge and the defendant.

Compound prepositions: 12.A.2
Adverbs of place and direction:
10.E.3

d. In modern Spanish, the prepositions **ante**, **tras**, and **bajo** are used mostly in idioms, and in formal and figurative language. **Delante de**, **detrás de**, and **debajo de** may replace them if they refer to a *physical* place.

La chica no se rinde **ante** los desafíos.	*The girl doesn't give up when **facing** a challenge.*
Tras la crisis, han aumentado los problemas.	***After** the crisis, the problems have grown.*
Bajo ningún concepto llegues tarde.	*Don't be late **for** any reason at all.*

encima: adverbs of place:
10.E.3

e. Sobre is a synonym of **encima de** only when it refers to a physical place. It can be replaced by **en** only if there is *physical contact* with a horizontal surface. **Contra** implies physical contact *against* a surface (usually vertical). It can also be used figuratively for an effort *against* someone or something (a direction, a location, a person, etc.).

La taza de café está **sobre / encima de / en** la mesa.	*The cup of coffee is **on** the table.*
La mesa está **contra** la pared.	*The table is **against** the wall.*
Protégete **contra** el sol.	*Protect yourself **against** the sun.*

f. The preposition **sobre** is also used figuratively to express *about* and *above* or *beyond* a limit (distance, time, quantity, importance, etc.).

El folleto es **sobre** los precios de Internet.	*The brochure is **about** Internet prices.*
Me importas tú **sobre** todas las cosas.	*You matter to me **above** everything else.*

g. The preposition pair **con-sin** (*with–without*) is situational and does not refer to location. **Excepto** and **salvo** (*except*) are synonyms. **Salvo** is formal and used in writing and fixed phrases.

Con mi nuevo teléfono, siempre estoy en la red.	***With** my new phone, I am always online.*
El teléfono es bueno, **excepto** su cámara.	*The phone is good, **except** its camera.*

h. Mediante (*by means of, through*) is formal. Its more common synonyms in Spanish are **con la ayuda de**, **por medio de**, and **a través de**. The preposition **con** may replace it in specific contexts.

Los desacuerdos se resuelven **mediante/con** el diálogo.	*Disagreements are resolved **by means of/ through** dialogue.*
Mediante/Con su colaboración, ayudaremos a muchos niños.	***With** your help, we will help many children.*

12.C Regional variations

Variaciones regionales

12.C.1 A por

In Spain, **a por** is used with verbs of motion and nouns (*verb* + **a por** + *noun*) to mean *in search of*. It is sometimes used to clarify meaning. For example, **Voy por agua** could mean *I'm going by water*. But **Voy a por agua** means *I'm going to get some water*.

Voy **a por** la escalera.	*I'm going to get the ladder.*
Pronto iremos **a por** Juan.	*We will pick up Juan soon.*

12.C.2 Entrar en, entrar a

The verb **entrar** is usually followed by **en** in Spain and **a** in Latin America.

Entro **en** la sala. (*Spain*) Entro **a la** sala. (*Latin America*)	*I'm going into the living room.*

Práctica

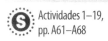
Actividades 1–19,
pp. A61–A68

Personal pronouns
Pronombres personales

13.A Subject pronouns

Pronombres personales sujeto

Pronouns are words that replace nouns. Some English examples are *I, you, me, it, him/her, them.* A pronoun has different forms depending on how it is used in a sentence. The subject form is used when a pronoun is the subject of a sentence.

There are two important regional differences for the subject forms of personal pronouns. In Spain, there are two pronouns for *you* plural: a formal pronoun, **ustedes**, and an informal one, **vosotros/as**. In Latin America, **ustedes** is used both formally and informally. The other difference is the use of **vos** instead of **tú** as the informal singular word for *you* in many areas of Latin America.

Spain			
Singular		**Plural**	
yo	*I*	**nosotros, nosotras**	*we*
tú	*you*	**vosotros, vosotras**	*you*
usted	*you (formal)*	**ustedes**	*you (formal)*
él, ella	*he, she*	**ellos, ellas**	*they*

Latin America			
Singular		**Plural**	
yo	*I*	**nosotros, nosotras**	*we*
tú, vos	*you*	**ustedes**	*you*
usted	*you (formal)*		
él, ella	*he, she*	**ellos, ellas**	*they*

Map of Spain and Equatorial Guinea: p. xxi
Map of South America: p. xxii
Map of Mexico, Central America, and the Caribbean: p. xxiii
Map of **voseo** regions in Latin America: p. B21

13.A.1 Use of pronouns

a. When Spanish verbs are conjugated, their endings provide information about the subject. For that reason, the subject pronoun is often omitted in both written and spoken language.

Habl**o**.   *I am talking.*   Habl**amos**.   *We are talking.*

Verb forms: 17.A.2b

b. Subject pronouns are used when the subject of a sentence is unclear. Although conjugated verbs provide information about the subject, in some cases verbs take the same forms for different pronouns, like **él/ella/usted** and **ellos/ellas/ustedes**, so the pronoun is often needed for clarification. Subject pronouns are also used for emphasis when comparing and contrasting.

Yo soy profesora y **tú** eres dentista.	*I'm a teacher and you're a dentist.*
Ella es simpática; **él** no lo es.	*She's friendly; he's not.*
Nosotros somos profesores y **vosotros** sois médicos.	*We're teachers and you're [pl.] doctors.*
¿Pagan **ustedes** la cuenta o la pagan **ellos**?	*Are you [pl.] paying the bill or are they paying it?*

c. Usted and **ustedes** are often abbreviated as **Ud.** and **Uds.**, respectively.

¿Cómo está **Ud.**?	*How are you?*
Les damos a **Uds.** una cordial bienvenida.	*We give you [pl.] a warm welcome.*

13.A.2 It, this/that

a. There is no exact equivalent of the English subject pronoun *it*.

Es un problema.	*It's a problem.*
Es una novela.	*It's a novel.*

esto, eso, aquello: 8.A.4 ▶
b. The demonstratives **esto** and **eso** are often used to express an idea or talk about something in general.

Eso está bien.	*That is good.*
No comprendemos **esto**.	*We don't understand this.*

c. Ello is a rarely used synonym of **eso**.

No pienses en **ello**.	*Don't think about it/that.*
No pienses en **eso**.	

Ello is also used in expressions like these.

a pesar de **ello**	*despite that*
cuenta con **ello**	*count on it*

este/a, ese/a: 8.A.2 ▶
d. Este/a and **ese/a** can replace the subject noun.

—¿Es importante el Premio Nobel?	*Is the Nobel Prize important?*
—Sí, **ese** es importante.	*Yes, that one is important.*

e. Lo can replace a whole sentence or idea.

—¿Es importante el Premio Nobel?	*Is the Nobel Prize important?*
—Sí, **lo** es.	*Yes, it is.*

13.B Formal and informal address

Formas de tratamiento

Spanish speakers can choose between *formal* and *informal* address, but the alternatives differ regionally. The differences can be explained through a historical context. When the Spanish language arrived in the Americas at the end of the 15th century, the informal forms of address for one person were **tú** and **vos**, while **Vuestra Merced** (*Your Grace*) was formal. To address several people, **vos** and **Vuestras Mercedes** (*Your Graces*) were used. By the 17th century, **Vuestra(s) Merced(es)** had evolved into the pronouns **usted** and **ustedes**. At the same time, **vosotros/as** had become the informal plural pronoun to avoid confusion with the singular **vos**, which was used less and less frequently in Spain. By 1800, **vos** was no longer used in Spain or its political centers across the Atlantic—Mexico, Peru, and the Caribbean—, where **tú** became the preferred form. The use of **vos** continued in the rest of the Spanish-speaking world, either as the only informal pronoun (as in Argentina) or together with **tú** (as in Colombia). During the same time period, the use of **vosotros/as** became common in parts of Spain, but it never took root in Latin America, the Canary Islands, or parts of Andalusia. Today's forms of address in the Spanish-speaking world reflect this history.

Vuestra merced became ▶ vuesarced, then vusted, and finally, usted.

Subject pronoun chart: 13.A ▶

13.B.1 Tú - usted

The use of **tú** as the informal singular word for *you* is called **tuteo**. In **tuteo** regions, **usted** is the formal word for *you* singular. In these regions, **tú** is used with peers, friends, and family, while **usted** is used with strangers or those to whom one wishes to show respect. This applies to Spain, Mexico (except Chiapas), the Caribbean (Puerto Rico, the Dominican Republic, most of Cuba, Panama, and the Caribbean coast of Colombia and Venezuela), and many Spanish speakers in the United States.

Map of Spanish speakers in the ▶ U.S.: p. xxiv

13.B.2   *Vos*

The use of **vos** as the informal singular word for *you*, called **voseo**, is common in many Latin American countries.

a. There are pure **voseo** regions as well as regions where both **tú** and **vos** are used. Argentina, Uruguay, Paraguay, and parts of Central America, Colombia, and Venezuela are pure **voseo** regions.

b. Regions with both **voseo** and **tuteo** are Bolivia, Chile, Peru, Ecuador, parts of Colombia and Venezuela, and Chiapas (Mexico). In these regions, **usted** is the formal singular word for *you*. However, the roles of **tú**, **vos**, and **usted** vary. **Usted** might be used to address children or acquaintances (Central America and parts of Colombia), or **vos** might be used with close friends and family, while **tú** is used with others. In Argentina and Uruguay, where only **voseo** is used in informal address, **usted** is used in formal address.

c. The publication of the *Nueva gramática* by the Real Academia Española in 2010 treats **voseo** as an integral part of the Spanish language. The increasing use of informal written language on the Internet, in chat rooms, and in social media has helped make **voseo** more visible as a way to communicate informally in many regions of Latin America. In Argentina, Uruguay, Paraguay, Central America, and the **voseo** regions of Colombia, Venezuela, and Ecuador, **vos** is used with its own verb forms, some of which are presented in the verb tables in this book. In Chile, the pronoun **vos** itself is not common and its verb forms are slightly different from those mentioned in the verb tables: **¿Cómo *estái*?**

Map of **voseo** regions in Latin America: p. B21

Voseo. Present indicative: 17.D

d. In all **voseo** regions, **vos** adopted the direct and indirect object pronouns of **tú** (***Te digo a vos.*** *I tell you.*) as well as its possessive forms and reflexive pronouns (**Vos *te* sentás en *tu* silla.** *You sit in your chair.*).

13.B.3   *Vosotros/as - ustedes*

a. In Spain, there are two plural address forms: the informal **vosotros/as** (for family, friends, and peers) and the formal **ustedes** (for strangers and those to whom you wish to show respect).

b. In Latin America, **ustedes** is the only plural form of address. It is used in both formal and informal contexts. **Vosotros/as** is not used in Latin America except to a very limited degree in specific contexts, such as political speeches and religious sermons.

13.B.4   *Nosotros/as, vosotros/as, ellos/as*

For groups made up exclusively of females, the feminine forms **nosotras**, **vosotras**, and **ellas** are used. For groups of males or groups of males *and* females, the masculine forms **nosotros**, **vosotros**, and **ellos** are used.

13.B.5   *Tú, vos, usted*

Age, gender, and social status play an important role in the choice of address, and it is important to be aware of regional differences, especially in formal contexts. Throughout the Spanish-speaking world, **usted(es)** can be used with strangers, even in **voseo** areas. Those who do not use **vos** in their own region can use **tú** with friends and acquaintances in **voseo** areas, but it is helpful to master the **vos** forms.

13.C Pronouns after prepositions

Pronombres preposicionales

13.C.1 Mí, ti, conmigo, contigo

a. The pronouns **yo** and **tú** take a new form after a preposition: **mí** and **ti**, respectively. The other pronouns (including **vos**) do not change form after a preposition. After the preposition **con**, **mí** and **ti** change to **–migo** and **–tigo**.

conmigo/contigo:
12.B.3b, 27.A.2

Mí has an accent mark to distinguish it from **mi** (*my*): 1.E.6b

Pronouns after prepositions: 12.B.1

Subject pronoun	Pronouns after prepositions			
	After preposition		**After preposition** *con*	
yo	**mí**	*me*	**conmigo**	*with me*
tú	**ti**	*you*	**contigo**	*with you*

—¿**Para** quién es el libro?　　　　*Who is the book for?*
—Es **para mí**.　　　　　　　　　　*It's for me.*

—¿Queréis trabajar **para** nosotros?　*Do you [pl.] want to work for us?*
—Sí, queremos trabajar **para** vosotros.　*Yes, we want to work for you [pl.].*

—¿Vas al cine **con** tus amigos?　　*Are you going to the movies with your friends?*
—No, hoy voy **sin** ellos.　　　　　*No, today I'm going without them.*

—¿Está Isabel **contigo**?　　　　　*Is Isabel with you?*
—Sí, Isabel está **conmigo**.　　　　*Yes, Isabel is with me.*

13.C.2 Sí, consigo

consigo: 12.B.3b–c, 27.A.2

The *reflexive pronoun* **se** changes to **sí** after a preposition, except after the preposition **con**.

Sí has an accent mark to distinguish it from **si** (*if*): 1.E.6b

Subject pronoun	Reflexive pronoun		Pronoun after prepositions		
			After preposition	**After preposition** *con*	
él, ella, usted	**se**	*self*	**sí**	**consigo**	*with himself, herself, yourself*
ellos, ellas, ustedes		*selves*			*with themselves*

Ella se compró unos zapatos y también　*She bought a pair of shoes and also*
compró **para sí** una cartera.　　　　　*bought a purse for herself.*

¿Tiene usted su pasaporte **consigo**?　*Do you have your passport with you?*

13.C.3 With the prepositions *entre, según*

The subject pronouns **yo** and **tú** are used after the prepositions **entre, según, excepto,** and **salvo.**

Entre **tú** y **yo** hay amor.　　　　*There is love between you and me.*
Según **tú**, tengo un problema.　　*According to you, I have a problem.*

13.D Direct and indirect objects

Complementos de objeto directo e indirecto

Sentences consist of a subject and a predicate. The verb is the central part of the predicate, which says something about the subject. In the sentence *I am sleeping,* the verb gives enough information to make the sentence meaningful. In *I'm giving,* however, more information is needed about the action. An *object* complements the information provided by the verb. In *I'm giving,* a direct object provides information about *what* is given (for example, *a book*) and an indirect object provides information about *to whom* it is given (for example, *my sister*): *I'm giving **a book** to **my sister.***

Transitive and intransitive verbs: 17.B.1

Direct and indirect object nouns can be replaced by object pronouns: *I'm giving **it** to **her.***

13.E Direct object pronouns

Pronombres de objeto directo

13.E.1 The direct object

The direct object tells *what* or *who* receives the action of the verb directly in the sentence.

Leo **el libro**.	*I'm reading the book.*
¿Compraste nuevos **zapatos**?	*Did you buy new shoes?*

Note that direct object nouns generally follow the verb in both Spanish in English.

13.E.2 The preposition *a* before a person

When the direct object is a person, it comes after the preposition **a**. This also applies to interrogative, possessive, and indefinite pronouns.

Conozco **a Griselda**.	*I know Griselda.*
Esperamos **al Sr. Luis Romero**.	*We're waiting for Mr. Luis Romero.*
Visito **a mis papás**.	*I'm visiting my parents.*
¿**A quién** vas a visitar en Nueva York?	*Who are you going to visit in New York?*
Veo a mi novia, pero no veo **a la tuya**.	*I see my girlfriend, but I don't see yours.*
No espero **a nadie**.	*I'm not waiting for anyone.*

The personal **a**: 12.B.2c
Use of the preposition **a** when indefinite pronouns and other determiners are direct objects: 7.D.2c and 7.E.3

13.E.3 Direct object pronouns

a. A direct object noun can be replaced by a direct object pronoun to avoid repetition. The pronoun agrees in gender and number with the noun it replaces.

Spanish verbs like **buscar** (*to look for*), **escuchar** (*to listen to*), **esperar** (*to wait for*), and **mirar** (*to look at*) are transitive, which means that they take a direct object, while their English equivalents are not.

Direct object pronouns		
yo	**me**	*me*
tú, vos	**te**	*you*
usted	**la, lo**	*you*
él	**lo**	*him*
ella	**la**	*her*
nosotros/as	**nos**	*us*
vosotros/as	**os**	*you*
ustedes	**las, los**	*you*
ellos	**los**	*them*
ellas	**las**	*them (female)*

In Spain, **le** and **les** may be used as direct object pronouns instead of **lo** and **los**: 13.E.4

The pronoun **os** is used only in Spain.

Lo, **la**, **los**, and **las** can also refer to things (*it*, *them*).

Me visitan mis amigos.	*My friends are visiting me.*
Te llaman.	*They're calling you.*
Lo espero.	*I'm waiting for him/you.*
Las espero.	*I'm waiting for you/them.*
Nos invitan.	*They're inviting us.*
Os invito.	*I'm inviting you [pl.].*

b. When a preposition comes before an object pronoun in a sentence, the pronouns **yo** and **tú** take new forms: **mí** and **ti**.

Pronouns after prepositions: 13.C

Nos llaman **a ti** y **a mí**.	*They're calling **you** and **me**.*

13.E.4 *Le/les* **instead of** *lo/los* **as direct object pronouns** - *leísmo*

In Spain, **le/les** is often used as the direct object pronoun for males instead of **lo/los**. In Latin America, **le/les** can be used as the direct object pronoun in some regions, especially with **usted** in sentences that are gender neutral. The use of **le/les** in this case is called **leísmo**.

Loísmo is the use of **lo/los** as indirect object pronouns.
Laísmo is the use of **la/las** as indirect object pronouns.
Both can be used in Spain.

Conozco **a Juan**.	*I know **Juan**.*
Le conozco. (Spain)	*I know **him**.*
Lo conozco. (Latin America)	

13.F Indirect object pronouns

Pronombres de objeto indirecto

13.F.1 The indirect object

The *indirect object* indicates who or what receives the action of the verb indirectly.

An indirect object is a noun or pronoun that answers the question *to whom* or *for whom* an action is done. In Spanish, it is common to find sentences with both indirect object nouns and pronouns.

Le hicimos un favor **a Eric**.	*We did a favor **for Eric**.*
Le hicimos un favor **a él**.	*We did a favor **for him**.*
Le envié una foto **a Eva**.	*I sent a photo **to Eva**.*
Le envié una foto **a ella**.	*I sent a photo **to her**.*

13.F.2 Indirect object pronouns

Except for **le** and **les**, the indirect object pronouns have the same forms as the direct object pronouns. The indirect object pronoun agrees in number but not in gender with the noun it replaces.

Le and **les** become **se** when followed by the direct object pronouns **lo(s)** and **la(s)**: 13.G.5c

Indirect object pronouns		
yo	**me**	*me*
tú, vos	**te**	*you*
usted, él, ella	**le (se)**	*you, him, her*
nosotros/as	**nos**	*us*
vosotros/as	**os**	*you*
ustedes, ellos, ellas	**les (se)**	*you, them*

¿**Te** dio Pedro la noticia?	*Did Pedro give you the news?*
La universidad **os** dio las notas.	*The university gave you [pl.] the grades.*
¿**Le** pago la cuenta?	*Shall I pay the bill for him/her/you?*
¿**Me** dices la verdad?	*Are you telling me the truth?*

In Spanish, a sentence with an indirect object should have an indirect object pronoun, but it does not need an indirect object noun.

13.F.3 Verbs like *gustar*

Verbs like **gustar**: 17.B.4

a. Many Spanish verbs are conjugated using the indirect object pronouns in a way similar to the English expression *It is pleasing to me*. In this sentence, the *grammatical* subject is *it* and the *logical* subject, *I*, is expressed with its object pronoun: *me*. The corresponding Spanish sentence is **Eso me gusta**. In this sentence, **eso** is the grammatical subject, while the logical subject, **yo**, is expressed with the indirect object pronoun: **me**. In the sentence *I like it.*, the grammatical subject is *I* and the direct object is *it*.

The subject of each sentence is in *italics* in the following examples. Note that **gustar** takes the singular form **gusta** when the subject is a verb or a singular noun and takes the plural form **gustan** when the subject is a plural noun.

Verbs agree with the sentence's grammatical subject.

Nos gusta mucho *caminar*.	*We really like to walk.*
¿**Os molesta** *el tráfico*?	*Does traffic bother you [pl.]?*
¡**Le encantan** *los paseos*!	*He/She loves outings!*

b. The indirect object can be spelled out with **a** + *pronoun/noun* for emphasis or clarity, especially with **le** and **les** since they have multiple meanings.

A Ramiro le aburre *el teatro*.	*Ramiro finds theater boring.*
A todos nos gustan *las buenas noticias*.	*We all like good news.*
¿Les interesa *la música* **a ustedes**?	*Are you [pl.] interested in music?*

13.G Placement of direct and indirect object pronouns

Posición de los pronombres de objeto directo e indirecto

13.G.1 Before conjugated verbs

Direct and indirect object pronouns come before a conjugated verb, one that can stand alone as the main verb in a sentence.

Placement of pronouns with nonpersonal verbal forms: 25.B.4, 25.C.8
Personal and nonpersonal verb forms: 17.A.2, 25.A

Direct object pronouns	
Nos visitas.	*You're visiting **us**.*

Indirect object pronouns	
Os damos un regalo.	*We're giving **you** [pl.] a present.*

13.G.2 Conjugated verbs plus an infinitive or a present participle

a. In verbal expressions with a conjugated verb plus an infinitive or a present participle, direct and indirect object pronouns can either come before the conjugated verb or be attached to the infinitive or present participle.

Verb phrases with infinitives: 26.B-C
Verb phrases with the present participle: 26.D

Direct object pronouns	
Te voy a invitar.	*I'm going to invite you.*
Voy a invitar**te**.	
Nos estáis esperando.	*You're waiting for us.*
Estáis esperándo**nos**.	

Indirect object pronouns	
Os voy a dar una gran noticia.	*I'm going to give you [pl.] some big news.*
Voy a dar**os** una gran noticia.	
Luisa **nos** está preparando la cena.	*Luisa is preparing dinner for us.*
Luisa está preparándo**nos** la cena.	

b. When a direct or indirect object pronoun is attached to the end of a present participle, a written accent is added to indicate the stressed syllable.

Accents: 1.E.3

es-pe-**ran**-do	*The word ends in a vowel and the stress falls on the next-to-last syllable (**llana**). The word is regular and does not need an accent.*
es-pe-**rán**-do-nos	*The stressed syllable is now the third-to-last one (**esdrújula**) and needs a written accent.*

Impersonal expressions with **ser**: 23.C.8

13.G.3 **Impersonal expressions with** *ser*

In impersonal expressions with **ser** that are followed by an adjective and the infinitive, the direct and indirect object pronouns are always attached to the infinitive.

Direct object pronouns	
—¿Es bueno estudiar **la lección**?	*Is it good to study **the lesson**?*
—Claro, es bueno estudiar**la**.	*Of course it's good to study **it**.*

Indirect object pronouns	
—¿Es necesario dar**te** instrucciones?	*Is it necessary to give **you** instructions?*
—No, no es necesario dar**me** instrucciones.	*No, it's not necessary to give **me** instructions.*

13.G.4 **Compound verb forms with** *haber*

In all compound forms with **haber**, object pronouns and reflexive pronouns come before **haber**. They can never be added to the participle or come after the participle form.

Direct and indirect object pronouns must always come before the forms of **haber** in compound tenses with a past participle.

Direct object pronouns	
—¿Dónde está Lisa?	*Where is Lisa?*
—No **la** he visto.	*I haven't seen **her**.*

Indirect object pronouns	
—¿**Te** han dado el dinero?	*Have they given **you** the money?*
—No, no **me** han dado el dinero.	*No, they haven't given **me** the money.*

13.G.5 **Indirect and direct object pronouns in the same sentence**

Placement of pronouns in verb phrases with:
Infinitives: 25.B.4,
Present participles: 25.C.8a
Past participles: 19.A.1

a. When both indirect and direct object pronouns appear together in the same sentence, the indirect object pronoun is always first.

—¿Quién **te** regaló **las flores**? *Who gave you the flowers?*
—Mis amigos **me las** regalaron. *My friends gave them to me.*

b. Note that the order of the pronouns also applies when both are attached to the infinitive or the present participle.

—¿Quién **te** va a dar **las flores**? *Who is going to give you flowers?*
—Mis amigos **me las** van a dar.
—Mis amigos van a dár**melas**. *My friends are going to give them to me.*

Accents: 1.E.3

When both pronouns are attached, an accent mark is always needed to keep the original stress.

c. The indirect object pronouns **le** and **les** change to **se** when followed by the direct object pronouns **lo**, **la**, **los**, and **las**.

—¿**Le** enviaste la foto a Pilar? *Did you send the photo to Pilar?*
—Sí, **se la** envié. *Yes, I sent it to her.*

—**Les** diste las galletas a los niños? *Did you give the cookies to the children?*
—No, no **se las** di. *No, I didn't give them to them.*

13.G.6 **With commands**

Object pronouns are attached to the verb in affirmative commands and come before the verb in negative commands. The indirect object pronoun always comes before the direct object. See the following examples with formal (**usted**) commands.

Placement of pronouns in commands: 24.F

Affirmative	
¡De**me el libro**, por favor!	*Please give **me the book**!*
¡Dé**melo**, por favor!	*Please give **it to me**!*

Note that affirmative commands usually need a written accent to keep the original stress.

Accents: 1.E.3

Negative	
¡No **nos** mande **los paquetes** todavía, por favor!	*Don't send **the packages to us** yet, please!*
¡No **nos los** mande todavía, por favor!	*Don't send **them to us** yet, please!*

13.H Repetition of direct and indirect objects

There is no repetition of direct and indirect objects in English.

Repetición del objeto directo e indirecto

13.H.1 **Optional repetition of an object**

a. Object pronouns with prepositions (**a mí, a ti, a él**, etc.) can be added after the verb to clarify or emphasize the direct or indirect object. This applies particularly to **usted/él/ella** and **ustedes/ellos/ellas**, which have the same indirect object pronouns (**le** and **les**).

Direct object pronouns	
La respeto.	*I respect **her/you**.*
La respeto **a usted**, Sra. Acosta.	*I respect **you**, Mrs. Acosta.*

Indirect object pronouns	
Les diré la verdad.	*I'll tell **them/you** [pl.] the truth.*
Les diré la verdad **a ustedes**.	*I'll tell **you** [pl.] the truth.*

b. An object pronoun with a preposition can also be used for all other persons for emphasis.

Direct object pronouns	
Me ven **a mí**.	*They see **me**.*
Te llaman **a ti**.	*They're calling **you**.*
Lo espero **a usted**, Sr. Pérez.	*I'm waiting for **you**, Mr. Pérez.*
Las espero **a ellas**.	*I'm waiting for **them**.*
Nos invitan **a nosotros**.	*They're inviting **us**.*
Os invito **a vosotros**.	*I'm inviting **you** [pl.].*

Indirect object pronouns	
¿**Te** dio Miguel la noticia **a ti**?	*Did Miguel tell **you** the news?*
Os envié las notas **a vosotros**.	*I sent the notes to **you** [pl.].*
Le hablo del viaje **a él / a ella / a usted**.	*I'm talking to **him/her/you** about the trip.*
¿**Me** dices la verdad **a mí**?	*Are you telling **me** the truth?*
Les pido un favor **a ellos**.	*I'm asking **them** for a favor.*

13.H.2 **Necessary repetition of objects**

a. When direct or indirect objects in the form of proper nouns or pronouns come before a verb, a corresponding object pronoun is needed *after* the object and *before* the verb.

Direct objects	
A la abuela *la* quiero.	*I love Grandma.*
A Juan *lo* visito.	*I'm visiting Juan.*
A ti *te* respeto.	*I respect you.*

Indirect objects	
A los chicos *les* doy un regalo.	*I'm giving the boys a present.*
A María *le* di mi teléfono.	*I gave María my phone number.*
A vosotros *os* envío postales.	*I'm sending you [pl.] postcards.*

In the examples, the objects come before the verb: **a la abuela**, **a Juan**, **a ti** (direct objects) and **a los chicos**, **a María**, **a vosotros** (indirect objects). This requires a direct or indirect object pronoun between the object and the verb.

b. This placement of objects and object pronouns before the verb also applies to things and abstract ideas.

Direct objects	
Esto no *lo* entiendo.	*I don't understand this.*
Tus cartas *las* recibí ayer.	*I got your letters yesterday.*

Indirect objects	
A la pared *le* di una capa de pintura.	*I gave the wall a coat of paint.*
A mi cámara *le* compré más memoria.	*I bought more memory for my camera.*

13.H.3 *Todo/a(s)*

Direct and indirect object pronouns usually appear when **todo/a(s)** is the direct or indirect object in the sentence.

Todo: 7.C.9 ▶

La policía **lo** sabe **todo**.	*The police know everything.*
Las invitaron **a todas**.	*They invited all the girls.*
Les enviamos invitaciones **a todos**.	*We sent invitations to everyone.*

13.H.4 **Questions and answers**

Personal **a**: 12.B.2c, 13.E.2 ▶

Note that the preposition **a** must be included when answering a question with a direct or indirect object pronoun that refers to a person.

—¿A quién llamó Viviana?	*Who did Viviana call?*
—¡**A mí**!	*Me!*
—¿A quiénes les das el regalo?	*Who are you giving the present to?*
—Claro, ¡**a vosotros**!	*To you [pl.], of course!*

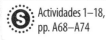

Práctica

Actividades 1–18, pp. A68–A74

Questions and question words
Preguntas y palabras interrogativas

14.A Direct questions

Preguntas directas

In Spanish, there are three ways to ask a question that requires a *yes*-or-*no* answer.

14.A.1 Change of usual word order

Just as in English, the usual word order of a statement in Spanish is *subject + verb*.

Roberto es estudiante.	*Roberto is a student. (statement)*
Roberto está enfermo.	*Roberto is sick. (statement)*

In questions, the verb usually comes before the subject. Although the intonation may vary, this word order implies a question. Note that the subject can come immediately after the verb or at the end of the sentence.

¿**Es** estudiante **Roberto**?	*Is Roberto a student? (question)*
¿**Está Julia** en casa?	*Is Julia home? (question)*

◀ Remember that the beginning of a question in Spanish is indicated by an opening (inverted) question mark: 1.F.5a

14.A.2 Intonation

A question can also keep the usual word order of a statement, *subject + verb*. In this case, the rising intonation indicates that it is a question.

¿**Pedro está** enfermo?	*Pedro is sick?*
¿**Julia está** en casa?	*Julia is home?*

14.A.3 Tag questions

When the usual statement word order is used, a tag question can be added to the end of the sentence: ¿**no**?, ¿**verdad**?, ¿**no es cierto**?, ¿**no es verdad**?, ¿**no es así**?, ¿**ah**?, ¿**eh**?, etc.

◀ Adverbs in tag questions: 10.F.1a

—Hace buen tiempo hoy, ¿**no**?	*It's nice weather today, isn't it?*
—Sí, hace muy buen tiempo.	*Yes, it's very nice weather.*
—Te llamas Alberto, ¿**no es cierto**?	*Your name is Alberto, isn't it?*
—No, me llamo Arturo.	*No, my name is Arturo.*
—Vienes mañana, ¿**verdad**?	*You're coming tomorrow, right?*
—Sí, vengo mañana.	*Yes, I'm coming tomorrow.*

14.B Interrogatives

Interrogativos

14.B.1 Structure

a. Questions that require more than a simple *yes*-or-*no* answer start with an interrogative word. All interrogatives carry an accent.

◀ Accents with question words: 1.E.7

Interrogatives		
Qué	*what, which*	¿**Qué** vas a preparar hoy? *What are you going to prepare today?*
Cuál(es)	*which, what*	¿**Cuál** es tu mejor plato? *Which one is your best dish?*
		¿**Cuáles** son los ingredientes? *What are the ingredients?*
Quién(es)	*who*	¿**Quiénes** vienen a cenar? *Who is coming to dinner?*
	whom	¿Con **quién** fuiste a la fiesta? *With whom did you go to the party?*
	whose	¿**De quién** es la receta? *Whose recipe is it?*
Cuánto	*how much + verb*	¿**Cuánto** vale la cena? *How much does dinner cost?*
Cuánto/a	*how much + noun*	¿**Cuánto** azúcar quieres? *How much sugar do you want?*
Cuántos/as	*how many + noun*	¿**Cuántos** invitados hay? *How many guests are there?*
Cómo	*how + verb*	¿**Cómo** está la comida? *How is the food?*
Dónde	*where*	¿**Dónde** está el postre? *Where is the dessert?*
Cuándo	*when*	¿**Cuándo** se sirve la cena? *When is dinner served?*
Por qué	*why*	¿**Por qué** está fría la sopa? *Why is the soup cold?*

Indirect questions:
14.B.9, 31.B.6

b. Interrogatives can also be used with indirect questions.

Van a averiguar **quién** es el chef.   *They're going to find out who the chef is.*
Quisiera saber **cuándo** estará lista la cena.   *I'd like to know when dinner will be ready.*

14.B.2 *Qué*

a. Qué does not change form and can come before nouns or verbs.

¿**Qué** plato prefieres?   *Which dish do you prefer?*
¿**Qué** quieres beber?   *What do you want to drink?*
¿**Qué** le pasa a Ramiro?   *What's happening/wrong with Ramiro?*
¿**Qué** significa eso?   *What does that mean?*
¿**Qué** opinas?   *What do you think?*

b. Qué is used with the verb **ser** to ask for definitions and explanations.

¿**Qué** es esto?   *What is this?*
¿**Qué** son estas cosas?   *What are these things?*
¿**Qué** es *house* en español?   *What is* house *in Spanish?*

14.B.3   Cuál, cuáles

a. Cuál(es) is used in questions that require choosing something or someone from several alternatives. The choices usually come after a definite article.

¿**Cuáles** son **tus** amigos?	*Which (ones) are your friends?*
¿**Cuál** era **la** contraseña?	*What was the password?*
¿**Cuál** quieres, **la** sopa o **la** ensalada?	*Which one do you want, the soup or the salad?*

Cuál(es) may be followed by a noun, especially in parts of Latin America: 14.D.a

b. If the alternatives in a question do not come after a definite article or other determiner (possessive, demonstrative, etc.), the meaning changes and **qué** is more common.

¿**Qué** quieres, sopa o ensalada?	*What would you like, soup or salad?*

Determiners: Ch. 4

c. Cuál(es) de followed by *definite article* or *demonstrative* + *noun* clearly restricts the choices.

¿**Cuál de las** ensaladas prefieres?	*Which one of the salads do you prefer?*
¿**Cuáles de estos** postres son buenos?	*Which of these desserts are good?*

Demonstratives: Ch. 8

14.B.4   Quién, quiénes

a. Quién(es) refers only to people. The plural **quiénes** is used if a plural answer is expected.

—¿**Quién** es Luisa?	*Who is Luisa?*
—Luisa es mi hermana.	*Luisa is my sister.*
—¿**Quiénes** vienen a cenar?	*Who is coming to dinner?*
—Vienen Gabi y Rodrigo.	*Gabi and Rodrigo are coming.*

b. De quién means *whose*. Note that the preposition comes before the question word.

—¿**De quién** son las botas?	*Whose boots are these?*
—Son mías.	*They are mine.*

14.B.5   Cuánto/a(s), cuánto, cuán

a. Cuánto/a (*how much*) and **cuántos/as** (*how many*) agree in gender and number with the noun they modify.

¿Cuánt**o** diner**o** necesitamos?	*How much money do we need?*
¿Cuánt**a** agu**a** mineral quieres?	*How much mineral water do you want?*
¿Cuánt**as** person**as** vienen hoy?	*How many people are coming today?*
¿Cuánt**os** plat**os** vamos a servir?	*How many dishes are we going to serve?*

b. Use **cuántos/as de** to ask specifically how many of something there are.

¿**Cuántos de los** estudiantes están aquí hoy?	*How many of the students are here today?*
¿**Cuántas de estas** palabras comprendes?	*How many of these words do you understand?*

c. Cuánto does not change form when it stands alone before a verb.

¿**Cuánto** cuesta la cena?	*How much does dinner cost?*
¿**Cuánto** pagaste por el postre?	*How much did you pay for the dessert?*

d. Cuánto is shortened to **cuán** before *adjectives* and sometimes before *adverbs*. The shortened version is formal and appears more in exclamations than in questions.

¿**Cómo son de caros** los pasajes?	*How expensive are the tickets?*
¿**Cuán caros** son los pasajes?	

Cuánto, cuanto: 10.D.1

Cómo: 14.B.6

qué tanto/a(s): 14.D.c ▶

e. In Latin America, **qué tan**, a common interrogative structure, has the same meaning as **cuán**.

Qué tan + *adjective* or *adverb*	
¿Qué tan *caros* son los boletos?	*How expensive are the tickets?*
¿Qué tan *rápidamente* llegas en tren?	*How fast do you get there by train?*

Cómo, como: 10.C.1 ▶

14.B.6 *Cómo*

a. Cómo is invariable and can *only* be followed by verbs.

¿Cómo estás?	*How are you?*
¿Cómo os parece Barcelona?	*How do you [pl.] like Barcelona?*
¿Cómo se enciende la tele?	*How do you turn on the TV?*

b. Unlike the Spanish **cómo**, the English *how* may appear before adjectives and adverbs (usually of manner). English sentences with *how + adjective/adverb* must be expressed in Spanish with other structures, like this common one.

cuán + *adjective*: 14.B.5d ▶
qué tan + *adjective*:
14.B.5e, 14.D.b

Cómo + ser + de + *adjective*	
¿Cómo es de *difícil* el problema?	*How difficult is the problem?*
¿Cómo son de *caros* los libros?	*How expensive are the books?*
¿Cómo es de *grande* la ciudad?	*How large is the city?*

c. Cuál es + *noun* or **qué** + *noun* + **tener** are other alternatives. The Spanish noun in these constructions corresponds to the English adjective/adverb in the parallel English structure, *how + adjective/adverb*.

¿Cómo es de alto el edificio?	
¿Cuál es la altura del edificio?	*How **tall** is the building?*
¿Qué altura tiene el edificio?	
¿Cómo es de importante la carta?	
¿Cuál es la importancia de la carta?	*How **important** is the letter?*
¿Qué importancia tiene la carta?	

d. *How* questions concerning weight, height, length, and age are asked with specific verbs.

¿Cuánto **pesa** el bebé?	*How much does the baby weigh?*
¿Cuánto **pesa** tu portátil?	*How heavy is your laptop?*
¿Cuánto **miden** las ventanas?	*How big are the windows?*
¿Cuánto **mide** usted?	*How tall are you?*
¿Cuántos años **tiene** usted?	*How old are you? (What is your age?)*
¿Qué edad **tiene** usted?	

e. The purpose of the *how* question determines which options are used: degree of distance (*how far*), frequency of time (*how often*), degree of a quality (*how well, how tired*), etc. Combinations of adverbs and prepositions with interrogatives, **que** + *noun*, and other structures can convey the same meaning in Spanish as a *how* question in English.

qué tan: 14.B.5e, 14.D.b ▶
cuán: 14.B.5d

¿Hasta dónde vas?	***How far*** *are you going?*
¿Cada cuánto visitas a tu familia?	***How often*** *do you visit your family?*
¿Con qué frecuencia para el autobús?	***How often*** *does the bus stop?*
¿A qué distancia queda?	***How far*** *is it?*
¿A qué altura saltas?	***How high*** *can you jump?*
¿A qué velocidad escribes?	***How fast*** *can you write?*
¿Cómo escribes **de** rápido?	

14.B.7 *Qué tal*

a. Qué tal is a very informal expression equivalent to **cómo**. It is used as a greeting, to ask about people and daily events, or to make informal invitations.

¡Hola! ¿**Qué tal**?	*Hi! How are you?*
¿**Qué tal** la película?	*How is/was the movie?*
¿**Qué tal** tu familia?	*How is your family?*
¿**Qué tal** por casa?	*How is everyone at home?*
¿**Qué tal** es Juan como médico?	*How good a doctor is Juan?*
¿**Qué tal** un cafecito?	*How about a coffee?*
¿**Qué tal** si vamos al cine hoy?	*How about going to the movies today?*

b. A question with **qué tal** can be rephrased with **cómo** only if it's followed by a verb.

¿**Qué tal** (está) la comida?	*How is the food?*
¿**Cómo está** la comida?	

14.B.8 *Dónde, cuándo, por qué*

a. Dónde (*where*), **cuándo** (*when*), and **por qué** (*why*) are invariable, and their use is similar to English.

¿**Dónde** vives?	***Where** do you live?*
¿**Cuándo** sales para el trabajo?	***When** do you leave for work?*
¿**Por qué** regresaste tarde?	***Why** did you return so late?*

b. Dónde is replaced by **adónde** or **a dónde** with verbs of motion.

¿**Adónde** te mudaste?	*Where did you move to?*

14.B.9 **Indirect questions**

Indirect questions are also asked with interrogative words.

No sé **qué** quieres.	*I don't know what you want.*
Dime **cómo** estás.	*Tell me how you are.*
Avísame **cuándo** llegas.	*Let me know when you arrive.*
Quiero saber **quién** es tu profesor.	*I want to know who your teacher is.*
Queremos saber **cuánto** dinero hay.	*We want to know how much money there is.*

14.B.10 *El qué, el cómo, el cuánto, el cuándo, el dónde, el porqué*

Some common interrogatives can be used as nouns. These nouns are masculine and singular, and carry an accent mark: **el qué, el cómo, el cuánto, el cuándo, el dónde, el porqué**.

No conocemos **el porqué** de la crisis.	*We don't know the reason for the crisis.*
Sabrás **el cuándo** y **el cómo** de la situación después.	*You will find out the when and the how of the situation later.*

14.C Exclamations with question words

Exclamaciones con expresiones interrogativas

Question words with a written accent are also used in exclamations in the following way.

Do not confuse the interrogative **por qué** with **porque** (*because*).

Cuándo, cuando: 10.B.1

Adverbs of place and direction: 10.E.2

Indirect questions: 31.B.6

Remember that the beginning of an exclamation in Spanish is indicated by an opening (inverted) exclamation mark: 1.F.5b

Qué + *noun/ adjective/adverb*	¡**Qué** maravilla!	*How wonderful!*
	¡**Qué** bonito!	*How beautiful!*
	¡**Qué** bien!	*Great! (That's wonderful!)*
Cómo + *verb*	¡**Cómo** te quiero!	*I love you so much!*
Cómo + *verb* + **de** + *adj.*	¡**Cómo** es **de** alto!	*It's so tall!*
Cuánto + *verb*	¡**Cuánto** estudias!	*You study a lot!*
Cuánto/a(s) + *noun*	¡**Cuánta** gente!	*So many people! (There were many…)*
	¡**Cuántos** libros!	*So many books! (There were many…)*
Quién + *verb*	¡**Quién** fuera rico!	*Oh, to be rich!*

Exclamations with the subjunctive: 23.B.2

14.D Regional variations

Variaciones regionales

a. In many Latin American countries, **cuál** comes before the noun when a choice is implied. In the rest of the Spanish-speaking world, it is considered incorrect to use **cuál** before a noun.

¿De **cuál** país hispano eres?　　　*Which Hispanic country are you from?*

¿**Cuál** restaurante te gusta más?　　*Which restaurant do you like the most?*

¿**Cuáles** recetas vas a preparar?　　*Which recipes are you going to prepare?*

cuán: 14.B.5 d–e

b. In Latin America, the following expressions can be used for direct and indirect questions, as well as exclamations. The intonation of the speaker indicates whether the sentence is a question or an exclamation.

Qué tan + *adjective*	¿**Qué tan** bueno es ese café?	*How good is that coffee?*
	¡**Qué tan** fantástico!	*How fantastic!*
	Me pregunto **qué tan** caro es.	*I wonder how expensive it is.*
Qué tan + *adverb*	¿**Qué tan** bien hablas español?	*How well do you speak Spanish?*
	¡**Qué tan** bien escribes!	*You write so well!*
Qué tanto + *verb*	¿**Qué tanto** tienes que esperar el autobús?	*How long do you have to wait for the bus?*
	¡**Qué tanto** trabajas!	*You work so much!*
	Le pregunté **qué tanto** le interesa la política.	*I asked him how interested he is in politics.*

Indirect questions: 14.B.9, 31.B.6

c. In questions, **cuánto/a(s)** is preferred to **qué tanto/a(s)**, but both can be used in questions and exclamations.

Qué tanto/a(s) + *noun*	¿**Cuánta** gente hay? ¿**Qué tanta** gente hay?	*How many people are there?*
	¡**Cuánta** gente hay! ¡**Qué tanta** gente hay!	*There are so many people!*
	¿**Cuántos** amigos tienes? ¿**Qué tantos** amigos tienes?	*How many friends do you have?*
	¡**Cuántos** amigos tienes! ¡**Qué tantos** amigos tienes!	*You have so many friends!*

d. In the Caribbean, primarily the Dominican Republic, Puerto Rico, and Cuba, it is common to put a subject pronoun before the verb in short **qué** questions.

¿**Qué tú** vas a hacer hoy?　　*What are you going to do today?*

¿**Qué tú** quieres?　　　　　*What do you want?*

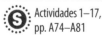

Práctica

Actividades 1–17, pp. A74–A81

116

Relative pronouns and adverbs
Pronombres y adverbios relativos

Chapter 15

A. Relative pronouns
B. Choosing relative pronouns
C. Relative adverbs
D. Nonspecific relative constructions

15.A Relative pronouns

Pronombres relativos

15.A.1 Structure

A relative pronoun refers to a noun (person, thing, or idea) and can link two descriptions of the noun into a single, complex sentence, made up of a main clause and a *relative clause* or *adjective clause*.

El profesor enseña español.	*The professor teaches Spanish.*
El profesor es inglés.	*The professor is English.*
El profesor **que** enseña español es inglés.	*The professor who teaches Spanish is English.*

The noun described, **el profesor**, is called the *antecedent* (**antecedente**). The relative pronoun, **que**, introduces a relative clause (**que enseña español**) that refers to the noun.

15.A.2 Spanish relative pronouns

Que is the most common relative pronoun in spoken Spanish. In written language, many other pronouns are used.

Relative pronouns		Antecedents
que does not change form	*which/who/that*	people, things, ideas
el/la que **el/la cual** article agrees with gender and number of antecedent	*the one/thing which/who/that*	people, things, ideas, whole sentences, actions, events
los/las que **los/las cuales** article agrees with gender and number of antecedent	*those which/ who/that*	people, things, ideas, whole sentences, actions, events
lo que, lo cual not used with people, does not change form	*the one/thing which/that*	whole sentences, actions, or events
quien, quienes agrees in number with antecedent	*who*	only people
cuyo/a, cuyos/as expresses ownership or connection, agrees in gender and number with item owned	*whose*	people, things

lo que/cual: Se ofendió mucho, **lo que/cual** me pareció extraño. (*He was very offended, which I thought was strange.*)

cuyo/a: El hombre **cuya** voz es melodiosa. (*The man whose voice is melodious.*)

15.A.3 Important differences between Spanish and English

There are three important differences between English and Spanish relative pronouns.

a. In Spanish, relative pronouns are required, while in English they are sometimes optional.

El auto **que** tienes es fabuloso.	*The car (**that**) you have is fabulous.*
¿Es bueno el libro **que** estás leyendo?	*Is the book (**that**) you're reading good?*
No tengo ningún teléfono **que** funcione bien.	*I don't have a phone **that** works well.*

Use of the subjunctive in relative clauses: 23.D

Prepositions: 12.A.1.b ▶

b. In English, a preposition can come after the relative pronoun, but in Spanish, the preposition must *always* come before the relative pronoun.

Spain: **el ordenador** = ▶
the computer

Esta es la computadora **con la que** siempre escribo.	*This is the computer (**that**) I always write **with**.*
La casa **en la que** vivimos es pequeña.	*The house (**that**) we live **in** is little.*
La chica **con quien / con la que** salgo se llama Anita.	*The girl (**that**) I go out **with** is named Anita.*

Personal **a**: 12.B.2c, 13.E.2 ▶

c. In Spanish, when the relative pronoun refers to a person that is a direct or indirect object in the sentence, the preposition **a** must come before the relative pronoun.

Pedro fue **a quien** vi ayer.	*It was Pedro I saw yesterday.*
Camila es la estudiante **a quien** le envié la información.	*Camila is the student I sent the information to.*
Janet, **a quien/a la que/a la cual** conozco bien, está de visita.	*Janet, whom I know well, is visiting.*

15.B Choosing relative pronouns

Elección del pronombre relativo

In order to select an appropriate relative pronoun, the antecedent must first be identified by asking: *Who is the person or what is the thing or idea being described?* In Spanish, the use of the relative pronoun depends on whether the clause is *defining* or *non-defining*. If it's non-defining, it is important to note whether the relative pronoun follows a preposition.

These clauses are also known as ▶
restrictive and *nonrestrictive*.

15.B.1 Non-defining clauses

Comma: 1.F.2 ▶

a. *Non-defining clauses* provide additional information about the antecedent and are always set off by commas in Spanish. These clauses can be omitted from a sentence without affecting the meaning. They are introduced by a relative pronoun (or a relative adverb), sometimes with a preposition.

Relative adverbs: 15.C ▶

Que means *who* or *which* in a ▶
non-defining clause.

Mario, **que/quien** siempre llega tarde, no tiene auto.	*Mario, who always arrives late, doesn't have a car.*
Nuestra escuela, **cuya** reputación es excelente, es muy cara.	*Our school, whose reputation is excellent, is very expensive.*

b. When **que** is ambiguous, a *definite article* + **que/cual** can be used to make the antecedent clear.

La esposa del señor Juárez, **la que/cual** siempre es elegante, llega hoy.	*Mr. Juárez's wife, who is always elegant, arrives today.*

15.B.2 Defining clauses

Defining clauses provide information that is necessary for the meaning of a sentence. These are never separated from the antecedent with a comma. Which relative pronoun is used in a defining clause is determined by whether a preposition is used.

Choosing relative pronouns in defining clauses		
Relative pronoun	**With a preposition**	**Without a preposition**
que	Yes: after **a, de, en, con**	Yes
el/la/los/las que	Yes	No
el/la/los/las cuales	Yes	No
quien(es)	Yes	No
cuyo/a(s)	Yes	Yes

¿Sabías que cerró el restaurante **en (el) que / en el cual** nos conocimos?	*Did you know that the restaurant where we met has closed?*
El libro **que** me prestaste es muy interesante.	*The book you lent me is very interesting.*
La película **de la cual** hablamos se estrena mañana.	*The movie we talked about opens tomorrow.*

a. In defining clauses that do not require a preposition, **que** can be used alone (without an article).

Que means *who* or *that* in a defining clause.

Los amigos **que** tengo son estudiantes.	*The friends (that) I have are students.*
La paz **que** hemos logrado es inestable.	*The peace (that) we've attained is unstable.*
Eso **que** me contaste es muy interesante.	*What you told me is very interesting.*
El rock es la música **que** más me gusta.	*Rock is the music (that) I like best.*

b. Que is generally used with an article after all prepositions, but can be used without the article in defining clauses with the prepositions **a**, **de**, **en**, and **con** when the clause does not refer to a person. This usually happens only in informal speech.

La ciudad **en (la) que** vivo es grande.	*The city (that) I live in is big.*
El aceite **con (el) que** se preparan las tapas es español.	*The oil (that) you make tapas with is Spanish.*
Los problemas **a (los) que** me refiero son graves.	*The problems I'm referring to are serious.*
La causa **por la que** lucho es justa.	*The cause (that) I'm fighting for is just.*
El banco **para el que** trabajo es internacional.	*The bank (that) I work for is international.*

15.B.4 *El/la que/cual, los/las que/cuales* **in defining clauses**

In defining clauses, these pronouns must always be used *after a preposition* for both people and things. The article must agree in gender and number with the antecedent.

El señor **al que** llamé no contestó.	*The man I called didn't answer.*
Los estudiantes **a los que** enseño español son estudiosos.	*The students I teach Spanish to are studious.*
Las carreteras **por las que** conduzco son peligrosas.	*The roads I drive on are dangerous.*
La universidad **en la que** estudio queda en Madrid.	*The university I study at is in Madrid.*
Hoy enviamos las facturas **en las cuales** está toda la información.	*Today we sent the invoices that have all the information.*

Personal **a**: 12.B.2c, 13.E.2

15.B.5 *Quien(es)* **in defining clauses**

Quien(es) can't be used without a preposition in defining clauses. The preposition **a** comes before **quien** if the antecedent is a direct or indirect object.

Hablé **con quien** contestó el teléfono.	*I talked to the one/person who answered the phone.*
Le escribí **a quien** tú recomendaste.	*I wrote to the one/person you recommended.*
En Navidad solo les daré regalos **a quienes** más quiero.	*For Christmas, I will only give presents to those I love most.*
Puedes pedirle ayuda **a quien** quieras.	*You can ask whomever you like for help.*
Hay que hablar **con quien** pueda resolver el problema.	*You must talk to someone who is able to solve the problem.*

Use of the subjunctive with unknown antecedent: 23.D.1

15.B.6 *Cuyo/a(s)*

Cuyo/a(s) is a formal relative pronoun used only in written Spanish. It agrees in gender and number with what is owned and can be used in defining and non-defining clauses. In speech and in less formal texts, **cuyo** is replaced by **que/cual** and the verb **tener**.

> **Cuyo/a(s)** is sometimes referred to as a *relative adjective*.

> Remember to use **¿de quién?** to ask *whose*?

Las personas **cuya** nacionalidad es inglesa…	*People whose nationality is English…*
Las personas **que tienen** nacionalidad inglesa…	*People who have English nationality…*

15.B.7 Indefinite antecedents

> **Cualquiera**: 7.C.5

a. **El que** (*the one who*) refers to a male or an indefinite person and **la que** refers to an indefinite female (in an all-female group). **Cualquiera que/quien** (*whoever*) refers to anyone, without specifying gender.

> Use of the subjunctive with indefinite antecedents: 23.D.2

El que / Cualquiera que / Quien fume aquí, recibirá una multa.	*Anyone who smokes here will get a fine.*

> **lo que**: 8.A.4c, 11.D.4b

b. **Lo que** (*what, that which*) is a neuter relative pronoun that refers to an indefinite idea (not a person).

Lo que me interesa es la salud.	*What interests me is health.*
Lo que dices es muy importante.	*What you say is very important.*

15.B.8 Emphatic constructions

In English, the description of an event often uses the following structures, especially in a news context: *It was yesterday when…, There was a four-year-old who…, It was here in the city where…* In Spanish, similar structures are rare, used only to emphasize special aspects of an event (time, person, location, manner, etc.).

> Common word order in a sentence: 14.A.1
> Other structures using **ser**: 30.B.8
> **Cuando, donde**, and **como** are relative adverbs. See 15.C.

Fue ayer **cuando** Laura Valle resolvió el problema de los robos en la universidad.	*It was yesterday when Laura Valle solved the problem of the robberies at the university.*
Fue en Londres **donde** sucedieron los hechos.	*It was in London where the events took place.*
Fue Laura Valle **quien** / **la que** lo descubrió todo; no fue Felipe, su jefe.	*It was Laura Valle who discovered it all; it wasn't Felipe, her boss.*
Fue así **como** se supo quién era el culpable.	*That was how it was revealed who the culprit was.*
La manera **como/en la que** lo supe es un secreto.	*The way I found it out is a secret.*

15.B.9 Special cases of agreement

a. In emphatic relative clauses similar to **Yo soy el que/quien**, the verb usually agrees with the relative pronoun (**el que/quien**) and not with the subject of **ser** (**yo**). This also happens with **tú** and **vos**.

Tú eres *quien* más **trabaja**.	*You're the one who works the most.*
Yo soy *el que* **enseña** español.	*I'm the one who teaches Spanish.*
Vos sos *la que* **llamó**.	*You're the one who called.*

This is also the case when the relative clause comes first.

La que **sabe** eres tú.	*The one who knows is you.*

b. The verb may agree with the subject of **ser** (**yo**, **tú**, or **vos**) only in informal speech.

Tú eres la que **llegas** tarde.	*You're the one who arrives late.*
Yo soy quien **pagaré** la cuenta.	*I'm the one who will pay the bill.*
Vos sos la que no **tenés** tiempo.	*You're the one who doesn't have time.*

c. If the expression **uno/a de los que** (*one of those who...*) is the relative clause, the verb normally follows its subject, the relative pronoun **los/las que**. Sometimes the pronoun **uno/a** is omitted, but the verb in the relative clause still agrees with the plural relative pronoun.

Tú eres **uno** de *los que* **escriben** blogs.

Tú eres de *los que* **escriben** blogs.

You're one of those who write blogs.

d. When the subject of **ser** is a plural pronoun (**nosotros**, **vosotros**), the verb always agrees with it.

Vosotros sois los que **habláis** mejor español.

Nosotros somos los que **vendremos**.

You're [pl.] the ones who speak the best Spanish.

We're the ones who will come.

15.C Relative adverbs

Adverbios relativos

15.C.1 *Donde, cuando, como*

a. The adverbs **adonde**, **donde**, **cuando**, and **como** can also introduce a relative clause. They are equivalent to **en el/la que** or **en el/la cual** when referring to the *location*, *time*, or *manner* in which an event takes place. They do not change form and do not have a written accent.

Dónde, **cuándo**, and **cómo** as question words: 14.B

La casa **donde** vivo es grande.

Me gusta la manera **como** trata a los niños.

Extraño la época **cuando** íbamos a la escuela primaria.

The house I live in is big.

I like the way she treats the kids.

I miss the times when we were in elementary school.

b. In speech and informal texts, **donde** is often replaced by a preposition of place + **el/la/los/las que** when a definite location is given.

La universidad (**en**) **donde / en la que** estudio está en Connecticut.

Paseamos en un parque **donde / en el que** hay un lago.

The university where I study is in Connecticut.

We take walks in a park where there is a lake.

c. Cuando refers to time in an indicative or subjunctive clause. The subjunctive indicates time in the future.

Use of the subjunctive with conjunctions of time: 23.E.2

Me alegro **cuando** mi abuela viene de visita.

Volví a casa **cuando** empezó a llover.

Llámame **cuando** tengas tiempo.

Te llamaré **cuando** pueda.

I'm glad when my grandmother visits us.

I went back home when it started to rain.

Call me when you have time.

I'll call you when I can.

d. When there is no stated antecedent, **donde**, **cuando**, and **como** have traditionally been regarded as conjunctions that introduce an adverbial clause. The current interpretation adopted by the RAE also classifies **donde**, **cuando**, and **como** as relative adverbs when there is no antecedent and refers to these clauses as *free relative adverbial clauses*.

Fui **donde** me dijiste.

Llegué **cuando** la película había comenzado.

Lo pinté **como** tú me pediste.

I went where you told me.

I arrived when the film had begun.

I painted it the way you asked me.

e. Como refers to how something is done and can be replaced by **de la manera que / del modo que**.
Como is a neutral or less specific word in these clauses, but can be emphasized with the word **tal**.

Use of the subjunctive with ▶
relative adverbs: 23.D.1c

Vístete **como / de la manera que** quieras.

Las cosas **como / del modo que** tú las
ves no son ciertas.

Debéis escribir los textos **tal como / de la manera
que** ha dicho el profesor.

Dress as you want.

*Things the way you see them
are not true.*

*You [pl.] ought to write the texts just as the
professor has said.*

15.D Nonspecific relative constructions

Relativos inespecíficos

15.D.1 (A)dondequiera, cuandoquiera, comoquiera

a. Nonspecific relative constructions are formed combining the indefinite quantifiers
(a)dondequiera, cuandoquiera, and **comoquiera** with a defining relative clause. These indefinite
quantifiers are compound words formed by a relative adverb (**donde, cuando, como**) + **-quiera**.
They refer to people and things that are not identified.

Doquier, usually following ▶
por, is a short version
of dondequiera used
primarily in literary
contexts.

Te acompañaré **adondequiera** que vayas.

Cuandoquiera que mi jefe tome una decisión, te aviso.

Comoquiera que te llames, yo te voy a decir Pepe.

I'll go with you wherever you go.

When my boss makes a decision, I'll let you know.

Whatever your name is, I'm going to call you Pepe.

Cualquiera: 7.C.5, 15.B.7 ▶
Use of the subjunctive with
cualquiera: 23.D.2d

b. Cualquiera also belongs to this group when it comes before a defining relative clause. It has a
plural form, **cualesquiera**.

Cualquiera que sea tu propuesta, la quiero escuchar.

Whatever your proposal is, I want to hear it.

c. Quienquiera is another compound word used with a defining relative clause. It is formed by
the pronoun **quien** + **-quiera** and refers to an unidentified person. Its plural form is **quienesquiera**.

Quienquiera que venga, será recompensado.

Whoever comes will be rewarded.

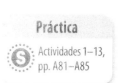

Práctica

Actividades 1–13,
pp. A81–A85

Relative pronouns and adverbs • **Chapter 15**

Conjunctions
Conjunciones

16.A Overview

Aspectos generales

Conjunctions are words that join words, phrases, or clauses together in a sentence. *Coordinating conjunctions* join similar or equal parts of a sentence. *Subordinating conjunctions* make the subordinate clause dependent on the main clause. Conjunctions do not vary.

16.B Coordinating conjunctions

Conjunciones coordinantes

16.B.1 Structure

a. Coordinating conjunctions join together two (or more) similar words, phrases, or sentences. Two sentences joined by a coordinating conjunction can each stand alone.

Words	En la escuela hay estudiantes **y** profesores.	*At the school there are students **and** teachers.*
Sentences	Podemos ver televisión **o** podemos jugar al ajedrez.	*We can watch TV, **or** we can play chess.*

b. The following are the most common coordinating conjunctions in Spanish.

Coordinating conjunctions			
y (e)	*and*	Isabel **y** Ana estudian **y** trabajan.	*Isabel **and** Ana study **and** work.*
o (u)	*or*	¿Quieres café **o** té?	*Do you want coffee **or** tea?*
no... ni **ni... ni**	*neither... nor*	Hoy **no** llueve **ni** nieva.	*It's **neither** raining **nor** snowing today.*
pero	*but (rather)*	Llueve, **pero** no hace frío.	*It's raining, **but** it's not cold.*
sino		**No** quiero café **sino** té.	*I don't want coffee **but** rather tea.*

16.B.2 The conjunction *y*

a. The conjunction **y** expresses sum or addition, and can join words or sentences together.

Tenemos tiempo **y** oportunidad.	*We have time and opportunity.*
Estoy feliz **y** satisfecho.	*I am happy and satisfied.*
La profesora enseña **y** corrige las tareas.	*The professor teaches and corrects the homework.*

b. When there are more than two elements, a comma is used to separate them, except before **y**. In English, there is usually a comma before *and*.

◀ Comma: 1.F.2g

Compré peras, manzanas **y** naranjas.	*I bought pears, apples, and oranges.*

c. The conjunction **y** changes to **e** before words that start with **i-** or **hi-**, except when **hi-** is part of a diphthong. This change in pronunciation and spelling helps keep the conjunction from blending into the following word.

Ana **e I**sabel conversan por teléfono.	*Ana and Isabel are chatting on the phone.*
Mamá siempre lleva aguja **e hi**lo en su bolso.	*Mom always carries a needle and thread in her bag.*
En la acera hay nieve **y hie**lo.	*On the sidewalk there is snow and ice.*

Do not confuse this structure ▶ with **tanto/a(s)... como** in comparisons of equality: 11.C

d. *And* can be expressed with the invariable **tanto... como** and **y** in Spanish. This structure appears primarily in written Spanish.

Tanto Lisa **como** Pedro vienen hoy.	*Both Lisa and Pedro are coming today.*
El profesor lo explica todo **tanto** rápido, **como** simple **y** claramente.	*The teacher explains everything quickly, simply, and clearly.*
La casa es **tanto** grande **como** bonita **y** moderna.	*The house is big, nice, and modern.*

16.B.3   The conjunction *o*

a. The conjunction **o** expresses two or more alternatives. In Spanish, unlike English, there is no comma before the last element.

Podéis pedir carne, pollo **o** pescado.	*You [pl.] can order beef, chicken, or fish.*

In English, the verb is always ▶ singular when singular words are joined together with *or*.

b. The verb is often plural when singular words are joined together with **o**.

Olga **o** Roberto **van** a hablar.	*(Either) Olga or Roberto is going to talk.*

c. Before words that begin with **o-** or **ho-**, **u** is used instead. This change in pronunciation and spelling helps keep the conjunction from blending into the following word.

Tengo siete **u o**cho pesos.	*I have seven or eight pesos.*
¿Regresaste ayer **u ho**y?	*Did you get back yesterday or today?*

d. Traditionally, when **o** appeared between numbers, it was written with an accent mark in order to avoid confusing it with the number zero. According to the RAE's *Nueva ortografía*, modern typography has eliminated the risk of confusing the **o** and the zero. Therefore, the accent mark is no longer required.

Necesitamos 350 **o** 400 pesos.	*We need 350 or 400 pesos.*

e. Bien... bien is used instead of **o... o** to indicate that the options are mutually exclusive. This is used mostly in written language.

Podéis viajar, **bien** en auto, **bien** en tren.	*You [pl.] can travel either by car or train.*
Bien me escribes o **bien** me llamas.	*You can either write or call me.*

f. When **bien** is added to **o... o**, the options are mutually exclusive.

Recibió **o bien** un premio, **o bien** una mención especial.	*He received either an award or a special mention.*

16.B.4 **The conjunction** *ni*

a. The conjunction **ni** joins negative elements together. It always follows another negative word.

Pedro **no** llama **ni** escribe.	*Pedro neither calls nor writes.*
Nunca tenemos pan **ni** leche.	*We never have bread or milk.*

b. Ni can come before each element or just before the last one.

No tenemos leche **ni** azúcar.	*We don't have milk or sugar.*
¡**No** tenemos **ni** leche **ni** azúcar!	*We don't have milk or sugar!*

c. When the compound conjunction **ni... ni** is used with nouns in the subject, the verb should be plural.

Ni Juan **ni** Marcos **fueron** a la fiesta.	*Neither Juan nor Marcos went to the party.*

◀ In English, singular nouns joined together with *neither... nor* take a singular verb; if one noun is singular and the other is plural, the verb agrees with the noun that is closer.

16.B.5 *Pero, sino, mas, sin embargo*

a. Pero is used the same way as *but* in English. **Mas** is a synonym of **pero** used primarily in formal texts.

Voy al supermercado, **pero** regreso pronto.	*I'm going to the supermarket, but I'll be back soon.*

◀ Remember to use a comma before **pero**: 1.F.2f

b. After a negative word, **sino** is used instead of **pero** to indicate an alternative. **Sino que** is used before a conjugated verb.

La clase **no** es hoy **sino** mañana.	*The class isn't today, but tomorrow.*
No me llamó **sino que** me escribió.	*He didn't call me, but rather he wrote to me.*

c. The expression **sin embargo** has the same meaning as **pero**, but is more formal and used mostly in written language. In formal texts, **sin embargo** is preferred for starting a sentence.

Los precios subieron mucho. **Sin embargo,** los consumidores siguen comprando.	*The prices went up a lot. **However,** consumers continue to buy.*
Los precios subieron mucho, **pero/sin embargo** los consumidores siguen comprando.	*Prices went up a lot, **but/however** consumers continue to buy.*

d. Pero (que) muy acts as an intensifier.

El libro es muy **pero (que) muy** difícil.	*The book is very very difficult.*

16.B.6 **Conjunctions that express consequence or introduce an explanation**

Conjunctions that introduce an explanation (**esto es, es decir, o sea**) and that express consequence (**por consiguiente, pues, así pues, de manera que,** etc.) are usually grouped with coordinating conjunctions. **Pues** can also be a subordinating conjunction when it expresses cause.

Mi jefe me llamó porque hubo una emergencia. **Por lo tanto/Así pues**, tuve que ir a trabajar el domingo.	*My boss called me because there was an emergency. Therefore, I had to go to work on Sunday.*

16.C Subordinating conjunctions

Conjunciones subordinantes

Subordinate clauses begin with subordinating conjunctions. A subordinate clause (*...if she should come*) is dependent on a main clause (*Nora asked...*) in order to make sense. Subordinating conjunctions form two types of subordinate clauses: **que** clauses (*that* clauses) and adverbial subordinate clauses introduced by simple conjunctions like **porque** (*because*), **aunque** (*although*), or compound expressions like **tan pronto como** (*as soon as*), **a fin de que** (*in order that*).

Use of the subjunctive in
noun clauses: 23.C

Indirect discourse: Ch. 31

Interrogatives: 14.B

Indirect questions: 31.B.6

Use of the subjunctive in
adverbial subordinate
clauses: 23.E

Adverbs of time: 10.B

Use of the subjunctive with
conjunctions of time: 23.E.2

16.C.1 *Que* **clauses (noun clauses)**

a. Que is the most common subordinating conjunction in Spanish and is equivalent to *that*. **Que** can't be left out in Spanish.

Main clause	Subordinate clause	Main clause	Subordinate clause
Creo	**que** va a llover.	I think	(**that**) it's going to rain.
Rosita dijo	**que** está cansada.	Rosita said	(**that**) she's tired.

b. Que is often added before an interrogative word in everyday speech. This construction is rare in written Spanish.

Main clause	Subordinate clause	Main clause	Subordinate clause
Te preguntan	**que cuál** es tu dirección.	They're asking you	**what** your address is.
Me preguntaron	**que dónde** había ido.	They asked me	**where** I had gone.

c. In indirect questions without interrogative words, **si** is used. **Que** can come before **si** in everyday speech.

Nos preguntaron (**que**) **si** podíamos ayudar.   *They asked us if we could help.*

16.C.2 **Adverbial subordinate clauses**

Adverbial subordinate clauses begin with conjunctions that express time, manner, purpose, etc., that expand on the action in the main clause.

Main clause	Subordinate clause	Main clause	Subordinate clause
Luis se enferma	**cuando** come helado.	Luis gets sick	**when** he eats ice cream.
Luis estaba bien	**hasta que** comió helado.	Luis was fine	**until** he ate ice cream.
Luis se enfermó	**porque** comió helado.	Luis got sick	**because** he ate ice cream.
Luis come helado	**aunque** se enferme.	Luis eats ice cream	**even though** he gets sick.

16.C.3 **Conjunctions of time**

These conjunctions describe when the action happens and introduce subordinate clauses of time.

Conjunctions of time – *Conjunciones temporales*			
al mismo tiempo que	at the same time as	**en cuanto**	as soon as
antes de que	before	**hasta que**	until
apenas	as soon as	**mientras (que)**	while/so long as
cada vez que	each time/every time (that)	**siempre que**	whenever
cuando	when	**tan pronto como**	as soon as
después de que, luego de que	after/as soon as	**una vez que**	as soon as/once

Siempre visito el Museo del Prado **cuando** estoy en Madrid.

I always visit the Prado Museum when I'm in Madrid.

Te llamaré **apenas** termine de estudiar.

I'll call you as soon as I finish studying.

Leemos el periódico **mientras** desayunamos.

We read the newspaper while we eat breakfast.

Cada vez que me olvido el paraguas, ¡llueve!

Every time I forget my umbrella, it rains!

Levántate **antes de que** sea tarde.

Get up before it's late.

16.C.4 Conjunctions of cause

a. Cause is primarily expressed with **porque** in Spanish. The indicative is normally used after conjunctions of cause. If the sentence is negative, the subjunctive can be used.

◀ Use of the subjunctive with conjunctions of cause: 23.E.5

Conjunctions of cause – *Conjunciones causales*		
a causa de que / dado que	puesto que	because (of) / given that / since
porque (como)	ya que	

Rita habla bien español **porque** estudió en Madrid.

*Rita speaks Spanish well **because** she studied in Madrid.*

No estudio español **porque** esté de moda, sino **porque** es el idioma de mis abuelos.

*I don't study Spanish **because** it's popular, but **because** it's the language my grandparents spoke.*

La casa es cara, **dado que** está en el centro.

*The house is expensive **because** it's downtown.*

b. Subordinate clauses of cause usually come after the main clause. When the cause comes first, **como** is used as the conjunction.

Como Rita estudió en Madrid, habla bien español.

***Because/Since** Rita studied in Madrid, she speaks Spanish well.*

16.C.5 Conjunctions of consequence

a. These conjunctions always follow the main clause and express consequence when used with the indicative. The most common conjunction of consequence is **así que**.

◀ Use of the subjunctive with conjunctions of consequence: 23.E.4

Conjunctions of consequence – *Conjunciones consecutivas*	
así que	
de (tal) forma/manera/modo que	so
de (tal) suerte que	

Mi casa está lejos, **así que** tengo que tomar dos autobuses.

My house is far away, so I have to take two buses.

El profesor no llegó, **de (tal) modo que** ayer no tuvimos clase.

The professor didn't come, so we didn't have class yesterday.

Ana no tiene trabajo, **de (tal) manera que** tampoco tiene dinero.

Ana doesn't have a job, so she doesn't have any money either.

b. **Tal** can also be used after **forma/modo/manera**.

No encuentro el libro, **de manera tal que** no puedo estudiar.

I can't find the book, so I can't study.

c. **De (tal) manera** and **de (tal) modo que** followed by the subjunctive express purpose.

◀ Conjunctions of purpose: 16.C.7

Deben ustedes cumplir la ley, **de tal manera que** no tengan problemas.

You must comply with the law so that you won't have any problems.

Colgó el cuadro **de tal modo que** le dé la luz.

He hung the painting in such a way that the light would hit it.

Use of the subjunctive with conjunctions of concession: 23.E.6

16.C.6 Conjunctions of concession

Clauses introduced by conjunctions of concession indicate an objection, obstacle, or difficulty in carrying out the action in the main clause. This objection or obstacle doesn't impede the action in the main clause.

Aun, aún: 1.E.6c

Conjunctions of concession – *Conjunciones concesivas*		
aunque	**a pesar de que**	*although, even though, despite, in spite of*
aun cuando	**pese a que**	

Elena obtiene buenas notas **pese a que** nunca estudia.

Elena gets good grades even though she never studies.

Aunque es joven, Roberto es muy responsable.

Even though he is young, Roberto is very responsible.

A pesar de que la película no parece interesante, creo que voy a ir a verla.

Despite the fact that the film doesn't sound interesting, I think I'll go see it.

Aun cuando me lo pidiera de rodillas, no iría a la fiesta con él.

Even if he (got down on his knees and) begged me, I wouldn't go to the party with him.

16.C.7 Conjunctions of purpose

Use of the subjunctive with conjunctions of purpose: 16.C.5c, 23.E.3

a. A fin de que and **para que** always require the subjunctive. **De manera que** and **de modo que** take the subjunctive when they express purpose. The indicative can be used, but the subordinate clause becomes a clause of consequence. Only subordinate clauses of purpose that begin with **para que** can come before the main clause.

Conjunctions of purpose – *Conjunciones de finalidad*	
para que	*in order to, so that*
a fin de que, de modo que / de manera que	

Para que tengas buena salud, debes comer bien.

In order to have good health, you must eat well.

Debéis planear bien **a fin de que** no tengáis problemas más tarde.

You [pl.] should plan well so that you [pl.] don't have problems later on.

Te compré entradas para el cine **de modo que** tuvieras algo que hacer el viernes.

I got you movie tickets so that you'd have something to do on Friday.

Conjunctions of consequence: 16.C.5

b. When the indicative is used with **de manera/modo que**, the subordinate clause becomes a clause of consequence. Compare these examples.

Está nevando, **de manera que tienes** que usar botas.

It's snowing, so you have to wear boots.

Te compré un par de botas **de manera que puedas** salir cuando nieva.

I bought you a pair of boots so that you can go out when it snows.

16.C.8 Conjunctions of comparison

Comparisons: Ch. 11

Comparisons can be made using these structures.

Conjunctions of comparison – *Conjunciones comparativas*			
más... que	*more... than*	**tanto... como**	*as much... as*
menos... que	*less... than*	**igual... que**	*just as much... as*
tan... como	*as... as*		

Me preocupo **tanto como** te preocupas tú.

I worry as much as you do.

16.C.9 **Expressing manner** – *como*

a. The relative adverb **como** describes *how* something is done or happens. Followed by the indicative, it refers to past and present actions. The subjunctive is used to express uncertainty about the way the action will be performed, or when the action refers to the future.

Escribí el ensayo **como** quería el profesor.　　*I wrote the essay the way the teacher wanted.*
Escribiré el ensayo **como** quiera el profesor.　　*I will write the essay however the teacher wants.*

b. The expression **como si** is used to talk about assumptions and always comes before a form of the past subjunctive.

Beatriz habla español **como si** fuera española.　　*Beatriz speaks Spanish as if she were Spanish.*
Te quejas **como si** el examen hubiera sido difícil.　　*You're complaining as if the exam had been difficult.*

◀ **Como** as a relative adverb: 15.C.1
Subjunctive in adverbial subordinate clauses: 23.E.1

◀ The past subjunctive: 22.C

16.C.10 **Expressing location** – *donde/adonde*

The relative adverb **donde** can also act as a conjunction.

Iremos **adonde** querráis.　　*We'll go where you [pl.] want.*
Vivo **por donde** está la escuela.　　*I live around where the school is.*

◀ **Donde** as a relative adverb: 15.C.1
Adonde is used with verbs of motion: 10.E.2d

16.D Conditional conjunctions

Conjunciones condicionales

16.D.1 Conditional clauses

Conditional conjunctions are used to make an assumption about something that will or won't happen. The most important conditional conjunction in Spanish is **si**. The subjunctive is always used with all conditional conjunctions except **si**, which has special rules and sometimes takes the indicative, and **siempre que**, which expresses habit (*whenever*) with the indicative and condition with the subjunctive (*as long as*).

◀ Conditional subordinate clauses: 23.E.7

Conditional conjunctions – *Conjunciones condicionales*			
si	*if/whether*	**con tal de que**	*provided that / as long as*
en caso de que	*in case*	**siempre y cuando**	
a menos (de) que	*unless*	**siempre que**	*provided that / as long as (whenever)*

Lleva el paraguas **en caso de que** llueva.　　*Carry the umbrella **in case** it rains.*

Os escribiré **siempre y cuando** me escribáis.　　*I'll write to you [pl.] **as long as** you [pl.] write to me.*

No podremos ir de paseo **a menos que** tengamos tiempo.　　*We will not be able to go for a walk **unless** we have time.*

Siempre que vamos al mercado, compramos demasiado.　　***Whenever** we go to the market, we buy too much.*

Iremos al parque, **siempre que** terminemos temprano.　　*We will go to the park **as long as** we finish early.*

Conditional **si** clauses:
17.E.9, 23.E.8

16.D.2 Conditional clauses with *si*

a. Spanish distinguishes between real and possible conditional clauses, and *imaginary* (hypothetical) and *contrary-to-fact* (impossible) conditional clauses. Real and possible conditional clauses take the indicative. The subjunctive expresses what is imagined (*If I were rich...*) or impossible (*If the sky were green...; If I had done it...*).

Conditional clauses with *si*		Result
Real/true	**Si** Luis come helado, *If Luis eats ice cream,*	se enferma. *he gets sick.*
	Si Luis come helado, *If Luis eats ice cream,*	se enfermará. *he will get sick.*
Imagined/hypothetical	**Si** Luis comiera helado, *If Luis ate ice cream,*	se enfermaría. *he would get sick.*
Not fullfilled in the past / impossible	**Si** Luis hubiera comido helado, *If Luis had eaten ice cream,*	se habría enfermado. *he would have gotten sick.*

The past perfect subjunctive with -**era** (but not -**ese**) can also be used to express the unfulfilled/ impossible situation: **Si** Luis hubiera comido helado, se **hubiera** enfermado. Past perfect subjunctive: 22.E

b. When the **si** clause comes before the main clause, a comma is needed.

Si me invitas, allí estaré.   *If you invite me, I'll be there.*
Allí estaré **si me invitas**.   *I'll be there if you invite me.*

c. Donde, como, and **mientras** can express a condition when they are followed by the subjunctive.

Donde no **encuentre** trabajo, no tendré dinero.   *If I don't find work, I won't have money.*
Como no me **digas** la verdad, les voy a   *If you don't tell me the truth, I'm going to ask*
preguntar a tus padres.   *your parents.*
Mientras yo **tenga** salud, trabajaré diariamente.   *As long as I have my health, I'll work every day.*

Práctica

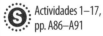
Actividades 1–17,
pp. A86–A91

The present indicative
Presente de indicativo

17.A Verbs

Verbos

17.A.1 The sentence

a. A sentence is a self-contained unit that relates a subject to a predicate. The verb is the main element in the predicate. The other elements of the predicate can be nouns or pronouns that function as *objects*, as in Juan tiene **un libro**; adverbs or adverbial expressions that explain the circumstances around the subject's actions, as in Juan comió **rápidamente** or Juan comió **en la cocina**; prepositions that are required by the verb, as in Juan piensa **en** María; and conjunctions, which link sentences, as in Juan comió **porque** su mamá había preparado su plato favorito.

b. The subject can be represented by a pronoun, a name, a noun, or any expression that can replace it.

Determiners and subjects: 4.B.1

Subject	Predicate	
Ellos **Luis y Ana**	estudian	las lecciones todos los días.
Todos los estudiantes de español **Las personas de las que te hablé**	son	excelentes estudiantes.

17.A.2 Verb forms

a. Verbs describe actions: what you do or what happens. Verb forms are divided into two main groups: personal forms that are conjugated and nonpersonal forms that can't be conjugated: infinitives, present participles, and past participles.

b. Verbs consist of two parts: a stem and an ending. Spanish verbs are divided into three conjugation groups based on their infinitive endings: **-ar**, **-er**, and **-ir**. What remains after dropping the **-ar**, **-er**, or **-ir** ending is the verb stem. Verbs are conjugated in Spanish by changing the infinitive ending to other endings that indicate person, number, time, and mood. For that reason, in Spanish it is not always necessary to include the subject.

cantar *to sing*			
Stem	**Ending**		***Ending indicates:***
cant-	**-o**	*I sing*	*present indicative, 1st-person singular*
cant-	**-arás**	*you will sing*	*simple future, 2nd-person singular*
cant-	**-ó**	*he/she sang*	*preterite, 3rd-person singular*
cant-	**-aríamos**	*we would sing*	*conditional, 1st-person plural*
cant-	**-aban**	*they used to sing*	*imperfect, 3rd-person plural*

17.B Verb objects and complements

Objetos y complementos verbales

17.B.1 Linking, transitive, and intransitive verbs

a. Verbs are classified into three main categories.

Types	Characteristics	Examples	English
Linking	connects the subject and its complements	María **es** traductora. El agua **está** caliente.	*María is a translator.* *The water is hot.*
Transitive	takes one or more direct objects	María **habla** español e inglés con su novio. María **hierve** agua.	*María speaks Spanish and English with her boyfriend.* *María is boiling water.*
Intransitive	does not take a direct object	María **habla** demasiado sobre sus amigas. El agua **hierve** desde hace diez minutos.	*María talks too much about her friends.* *The water has been boiling for ten minutes.*

Look in a dictionary to determine whether a verb can be transitive, intransitive, or both. A verb might be transitive in Spanish but intransitive in English and vice versa.

b. Some verbs can be both transitive and intransitive.

Carlos **habla** portugués.   *Carlos speaks Portuguese.*

Carlos **habla** mucho.   *Carlos speaks a lot.*

17.B.2 Verbs with prepositions

Glosario combinatorio: pp. C1–C44

a. While some verbs can be followed by a direct object (transitive verbs), others require a prepositional phrase called **complemento de régimen**. Sometimes the same verb can be used with a direct object or with a preposition.

No **creo en** los fantasmas.   *I don't believe in ghosts.*

Disfruté (de) las vacaciones.   *I enjoyed my vacation.*

b. The choice of preposition is not predictable. Verbs with similar meanings might take different prepositions or a direct object. A verb in Spanish might take a different preposition than the one required by its English counterpart, or a verb in one language might use a preposition while its equivalent in the other language does not.

No **confío en** él.   *I don't trust him.*

No **me fío de** él.   *I don't trust him.*

Consiguió diez dólares.   *He got hold of ten dollars.*

Se hizo con diez dólares.   *He got hold of ten dollars.*

Asistí a la conferencia.   *I attended the conference.*

c. The most common prepositions used in **complementos de régimen** are **a, con, de,** and **en**. Verbs that require **por** or **para** are rare.

Preposition	Verb with prepositions			
a	asistir a	*to attend*	jugar a	*to play (a sport or game)*
con	encontrarse con	*to meet up with*	soñar con	*to dream about/of*
de	disfrutar de	*to enjoy*	sufrir de	*to suffer from*
en	confiar en	*to trust*	influir en	*to influence / to have influence on*
por	preocuparse por	*to worry about*	interesarse por	*to be interested in*

¿**Asistió** usted **a** la conferencia?	Did you attend the conference?
¡**Disfruta (de)** tu tiempo libre!	Enjoy your free time!
Jugaremos al ajedrez profesionalmente.	We will play chess professionally.
Ellos **sueñan con** un mundo mejor.	They dream of a better world.

d. In most cases, the preposition is followed by a noun or pronoun. However, many verbs with prepositions can be followed by infinitives.

◀ Prepositions: Ch. 12

Me encontré con **Marcos**.	I met up with Marcos.
Soñé con **ella**.	I dreamt of her.
Sueño con **ir** a Europa.	I dream of going to Europe.

e. Some verbs with prepositions can only be followed by an infinitive. These expressions usually take **a** or **de**.

◀ Verb phrases with the infinitive: 26.C

verb + preposition + infinitive			
empezar a	to start	acabar de	to have just
volver a	to repeat	tratar de	to try to

La película **acaba de empezar**.	The movie has just begun.
Traté de alcanzar el autobús.	I tried to catch the bus.
Ana **vuelve a leer** la novela.	Ana is reading the novel again.

17.B.3 **Reflexive verbs**

◀ Reflexive pronouns and verbs: 27.A

a. In reflexive verbs the subject performing the action is also the recipient, directly or indirectly.

Subject	Predicate		
	Reflexive pronoun	Verb	Adverbial expression
(Yo)	Me	lavo	frecuentemente.

Subject	Predicate			
	Reflexive pronoun	Verb	Direct object	Adverbial expression
(Yo)	Me	lavo	las manos	frecuentemente.

b. Many daily routines are expressed with reflexive verbs.

◀ Reflexive verbs for daily routines: 27.D.1e

| Ella **se cepilla** los dientes. | She brushes her teeth (herself). |
| **Te pones** los zapatos. | You put on your shoes (yourself). |

c. Verbs that take reflexive pronouns are not always reflexive in meaning.

◀ Reflexive verbs with reciprocal meaning: 27.D.3
◀ Verbs that change meaning: 27.E
◀ Verbs that express change: 27.G

Reciprocal meaning	**Nos** ayuda**mos** siempre.	We always help each other.
Change in meaning	Hoy cayeron diez centímetros de nieve. **Se me cayó** el libro.	Ten centimeters of snow fell today. I dropped the book.
Physical, social, or mental change	Ana **se casó** con Luis y sus familias **se alegraron**.	Ana married Luis, and their families were happy.
Verbs of change	Luis **se hizo** ingeniero.	Luis became an engineer.

Verbs with prepositions: 17.B.2

d. Many reflexive verbs require specific prepositions.

Reflexive verbs with prepositions			
atreverse a	*to dare to*	encontrarse con	*to meet up with*
decidirse a	*to decide to*	enojarse con	*to get angry with*
despedirse de	*to say goodbye to*	convertirse en	*to become / turn into*
reírse de	*to laugh at*	interesarse por	*to be interested in*

El público **se ríe de** los payasos.	*The audience is laughing at the clowns.*
La chica **se convirtió en** una atleta.	*The girl became an athlete.*
Nos despediremos de ella para siempre.	*We will say goodbye to her forever.*
No **me atrevo a** preguntar qué pasó.	*I don't dare ask what happened.*
¿Dónde **os encontráis con** vuestros amigos?	*Where do you [pl.] meet up with your friends?*

17.B.4 Verbs like *gustar*

Indirect object pronouns: 13.F
Verbs like **gustar**: 9.D.4, 13.F.3
Reflexive verbs that can also be conjugated with an indirect object pronoun: 27.G.2b
Use of the subjunctive in subordinate clauses with verbs like **gustar**: 23.C.3

Pronouns after prepositions: 13.C

a. The Spanish verb **gustar** functions differently from its English counterpart, *to like*. In Spanish, the person or object liked is the subject of the sentence and usually appears after the verb. The person that likes something usually appears before the verb and is expressed with an indirect object pronoun. The indirect object is emphasized by adding **a** + *noun/prepositional pronoun*.

Me gusta el helado de chocolate.	*I like chocolate ice cream.*
A mí me gusta el helado de fresa.	*I like strawberry ice cream.*
A mi hermana le gustan los dos.	*My sister likes both.*

b. The verb agrees with the person or thing that is liked. If the subject is an infinitive, the singular form **gusta** is used.

A María **le gustan los hombres altos**.   *María likes tall men.*
(**los hombres altos**: *third-person plural subject* ⟶ **gustan**: *third-person plural verb*)

A María **le gusta su vecino, Luis**.   *María likes her neighbor, Luis.*
(**su vecino, Luis**: *third-person singular subject* ⟶ **gusta**: *third-person singular verb*)

A Marcos y a mí **nos gusta nadar**.   *Marcos and I like swimming / to swim.*
(**nadar** *is an infinitive: third-person singular subject* ⟶ **gusta**: *third-person singular verb*)

The singular form is used even when more than one infinitive is the subject.

c. Gustar is most often used with third-person singular or plural subjects. However, it is possible to use other subjects.

Me **gustaste** desde el momento en que te vi.   *I liked you from the moment I saw you.*
(*implied subject*: **tú**, *second-person singular* ⟶ **gustaste**: *second-person singular*)

¿Te **gusto**?   *Do you like me?*
(*implied subject*: **yo**, *first-person singular* ⟶ **gusto**: *first-person singular*)

Nos **gustáis** mucho.   *We like you [pl.] a lot.*
(*implied subject*: **vosotros**, *second-person plural* ⟶ **gustáis**: *second-person plural*)

When **gustar** is used with a person as the subject, it usually implies a romantic attraction.

d. Many other Spanish verbs function like **gustar**.

Verbs like *gustar*			
aburrir	*to bore/tire*	entristecer	*to sadden*
agradar	*to please/gratify*	entusiasmar	*to delight / carry away*
alarmar	*to alarm/startle*	extrañar	*to miss*
alegrar	*to be/make happy*	faltar	*to lack/need*
apenar	*to distress*	fascinar	*to fascinate/ like very much*
asustar	*to scare*	fastidiar	*to annoy/bother/upset*
complacer	*to please*	frustrar	*to frustrate*
convenir	*to suit*	importar	*to be important / care about*
desesperar	*to despair/exasperate*	indignar	*to outrage*
disgustar	*to dislike*	interesar	*to interest / be interested in*
divertir	*to amuse/entertain*	irritar	*to irritate*
doler	*to hurt/ache*	molestar	*to bother/annoy*
emocionar	*to thrill/excite*	preocupar	*to worry*
encantar	*to delight/love*	quedar	*to be left over / fit*
enfadar	*to anger*	sorprender	*to surprise*

Los fumadores **me irritan**.	*Smokers irritate me.*
La oscuridad **me asusta**.	*Darkness scares me.*
Nos conviene reunirnos mañana.	*It suits us to meet tomorrow.*
¿**Te divierten** las comedias?	*Do comedies amuse you?*
Me alegra que tengas éxito.	*I'm happy that you are successful.*
Nos interesa el español.	*We're interested in Spanish. / Spanish interests us.*
Nuestros clientes **nos importan**.	*Our clients are important to us.*

◀ Article instead of possessives with verbs of physical reactions and ailments: 9.D.4

e. Some of these verbs can also be used reflexively.

Me alegro por tu éxito.	*I'm happy for your success.*
Nos interesamos por el español.	*We're interested in Spanish.*

17.C Tense and mood

Tiempo y modo

17.C.1 Verb tense

Verb tense tells when an action takes place: past, present, or future. There is not always a direct correlation between the grammatical verb tense and the time expressed in the sentence. For example, the present indicative can convey future actions in Spanish: **Vengo mañana.** (*I'm coming tomorrow.*)

17.C.2 Verb mood

Verb mood tells how the speaker feels about an action. Spanish has three moods, like English. Each mood has its own conjugations and follows specific rules of use.

a. Indicative: Usually expresses facts.

b. Subjunctive: Expresses doubt or uncertainty, feelings or emotions, wishes, preferences, assumptions, the unknown, and imaginary situations or events.

◀ Subjunctive: Ch. 22–23

c. Imperative: Expresses orders and requests.

◀ Imperative: Ch. 24

17.D The present indicative

Presente de indicativo

17.D.1 Regular verbs

a. All three conjugation groups (**-ar, -er, -ir**) have both regular and irregular verbs. Regular verbs do not have any changes in the stem, and each group has its own conjugation patterns.

Subject pronoun		cantar *to sing*	correr *to run*	vivir *to live*
I	yo	cant**o**	corr**o**	viv**o**
you	tú	cant**as**	corr**es**	viv**es**
you	vos	cant**ás**	corr**és**	viv**ís**
you (formal), he, she	usted, él, ella	cant**a**	corr**e**	viv**e**
we	nosotros/as	cant**amos**	corr**emos**	viv**imos**
you [pl.]	vosotros/as	cant**áis**	corr**éis**	viv**ís**
you [pl.], they	ustedes, ellos/as	cant**an**	corr**en**	viv**en**

Map of the spread of **vos** in ▶ Latin America: p. B21
Voseo: 13.B.2 , 13.B.5, 17.D.1c–d

b. Verbs ending in **-ar** are the largest group. New verbs usually have the **-ar** ending. The following are some of the most common regular verbs of the three groups.

Regular verbs, present tense: ▶ Verb conjugation tables, p. B5

-*ar* verbs					
acabar	*to finish*	ganar	*to win*	pasar	*to pass/spend (time)*
amar	*to love*	investigar	*to investigate*	practicar	*to practice*
bailar	*to dance*	lavar	*to wash*	saltar	*to jump*
buscar	*to look for*	llamar	*to call*	terminar	*to end*
caminar	*to walk*	llegar	*to arrive*	tomar	*to take/drink/eat*
comprar	*to buy*	llevar	*to take/carry*	trabajar	*to work*
desear	*to desire*	mandar	*to order/send*	usar	*to use*
empacar	*to pack*	mirar	*to look at*	viajar	*to travel*
escuchar	*to listen to*	necesitar	*to need*	visitar	*to visit*

-*er* verbs	
aprender	*to learn*
beber	*to drink*
comer	*to eat*
comprender	*to understand*
creer	*to believe*
leer	*to read*
responder	*to answer*
temer	*to fear*
vender	*to sell*

-*ir* verbs	
abrir	*to open*
asistir	*to attend (something)*
describir	*to describe*
decidir	*to decide*
escribir	*to write*
insistir	*to insist*
permitir	*to permit/allow*
recibir	*to receive*
subir	*to climb/go up*

—¿Qué deportes **practicas**?   *Which sports do you play/practice?*
—No **practico** deportes.   *I don't play/practice any sports.*
Bailo y **camino** mucho.   *I dance and walk a lot.*

   The present indicative • **Chapter 17**

c. The verb forms of **vos** and **vosotros/as** are similar because these two pronouns share a common origin. Most of their forms are regular, even when the verb is stem-changing or has other irregularities. This regularity is especially striking when **vos** forms are compared to the forms of **tú**, which have many irregularities.

◀ **vos**: 13.B, 13.B.2, 13.B.5

d. In the present indicative, **vos** is conjugated by adding **-ás** to **-ar** verbs, **-és** to **-er** verbs, and **-ís** to **-ir** verbs. There are very few irregular forms: **vos sos** (*you are*).

Vos **and** *vosotros/as*: **regular present indicative**			
Personal pronoun	*-ar* **pensar** *to think*	*-er* **tener** *to have*	*-ir* **decir** *to say*
vos	pens**ás**	ten**és**	dec**ís**
vosotros/as	pens**áis**	ten**éis**	dec**ís**

Note that **-ir** verbs have the same endings for **vos** and **vosotros/as**, except for the verb **ir** (*to go*): **vos vas, vosotros/as vais**.

17.D.2 Verbs with spelling changes in the *yo* form

In Spanish, there are a number of verbs that have spelling changes in order to keep the same sound when conjugating the verb. The spelling changes always happen in the last letters of the verb stem, before adding the endings. The endings usually are regular, but can be irregular in some cases.

◀ Pronunciación of consonants: 1.C.6

a. Verbs that end in **-cer**, **-cir** and **-ger**, **-gir**, **-guir** have spelling changes in the verb stem, but take regular endings.

◀ Verbs with spelling changes: Verb conjugation tables, pp. B1–B20. For **c:z**, see verb patterns 32, 72, 75; for **c-zc**, see verb patterns 14, 15, 43.

-cer, -cir **verbs with spelling changes**			
When the letter before the final **c** is a **vowel**, a **z** is added before the **c** in the **yo** form.		When the letter before the final **c** is **n** or **r**, the **c** becomes a **z** in the **yo** form.	
cono**cer** *to know*	yo cono**zco**	conven**cer** *to convince*	yo conven**zo**
condu**cir** *to drive*	yo condu**zco**	espar**cir** *to spread/sprinkle*	yo espar**zo**

Other *-cer, -cir* **verbs**					
Verbs with **-zco** ending in the **yo** form		Verbs with **-zo** ending in the **yo** form		Verbs with **-zo** ending in the **yo** form with **o → ue** stem change	
agrade**cer**	*to appreciate/thank*	ejer**cer**	*to exercise*	co**cer** → cuezo	*to cook*
apete**cer**	*to feel like*	ven**cer**	*to beat/defeat*	tor**cer** → tuerzo	*to twist*
dedu**cir**	*to deduce*				
desapare**cer**	*to disappear*				
introdu**cir**	*to introduce*				
obede**cer**	*to obey*				
ofre**cer**	*to offer*				
pare**cer**	*to seem*				
recono**cer**	*to recognize*				
tradu**cir**	*to translate*				

◀ Stem-changing verbs: 17.D.4c–d

—Yo condu**zco** limusinas. ¿En qué trabajas tú?   *I drive limousines. What do you do?*
—Tradu**zco** del español al inglés para un canal de televisión.   *I translate from Spanish into English for a TV station.*

b. In the **yo** form of verbs ending in **-ger** and **-gir**, **g** is changed to **j**, but the pronunciation remains the same.

-*ger*, -*gir* **verbs with spelling changes**		
Subject pronoun	diri**gir** *to lead/direct/manage/run*	exi**gir** *to require/demand*
yo	diri**jo**	exi**jo**

Other -*ger*, -*gir* **verbs**			
aco**ger**	*to welcome*	infrin**gir**	*to infringe*
afli**gir**	*to afflict*	prote**ger**	*to protect*
corre**gir**	*to correct*	reco**ger**	*to collect / pick up*
ele**gir**	*to choose/elect*	restrin**gir**	*to restrict*
esco**ger**	*to choose*	sumer**gir**	*to submerge*
fin**gir**	*to pretend*	sur**gir**	*to emerge*

Corregir and **elegir** also ▶ have a stem change: **corrijo, elijo**: 17.D.4g–h Verb conjugation tables, pp. B1–B20. See verb patterns 26, 35, 54.

Diri**jo** una organización ecológica.	*I run an ecological organization.*
Reco**jo** y reciclo la basura.	*I collect and recycle the trash.*
Prote**jo** la naturaleza.	*I protect nature.*
Exi**jo** una ciudad más limpia.	*I demand a cleaner city.*

c. In **-guir** verbs, **gu** changes to **g** in the **yo** form, but the pronunciation remains the same.

-*guir* **verbs with spelling changes**	
Subject pronoun	extin**guir** *to extinguish / put out (fires)*
yo	extin**go**

Other -*guir* **verbs**			
conse**guir**	*to get/obtain/achieve*	prose**guir**	*to continue*
perse**guir**	*to pursue/persecute*	se**guir**	*to follow*

These verbs also have ▶ a stem change: **sigo, persigo**: 17.D.4g–h Verb conjugation tables, pp. B1–B20. See verb patterns 36, 64.

Soy policía y persi**go** a los criminales.	*I'm a police officer and I chase criminals.*
No extin**go** incendios porque no soy bombero.	*I don't put out fires because I'm not a firefighter.*

17.D.3 **Verbs without spelling changes in** *nosotros/as, vosotros/as, vos*

Some verbs have spelling changes in the present indicative in all forms except **nosotros/as**, **vosotros/as**, and **vos**. The endings are regular.

a. In **-uir** verbs, **i** changes to **y** before **e** or **o** in all forms except **nosotros/as**, **vosotros/as**, and **vos**.

Conjugation of -*uir* **verbs**	
Subject pronoun	constr**uir** *to build*
yo	constru**yo**
tú	constru**yes**
vos	constru**ís**
usted, él, ella	constru**ye**
nosotros/as	constru**imos**
vosotros/as	constru**ís**
ustedes, ellos/as	constru**yen**

Verbs with spelling changes: ▶ Verb conjugation tables, pp. B1–B20. See verb pattern 23.

Other *-uir* **verbs**			
conclu**ir**	*to conclude*	hu**ir**	*to escape/flee*
constitu**ir**	*to constitute*	inclu**ir**	*to include*
contribu**ir**	*to contribute*	influ**ir**	*to influence*
destitu**ir**	*to dismiss*	intu**ir**	*to sense*
destru**ir**	*to destroy*	reclu**ir**	*to imprison/confine*
disminu**ir**	*to diminish*	reconstru**ir**	*to reconstruct*
distribu**ir**	*to distribute*	sustitu**ir**	*to substitute/replace*

La gente hu**y**e cuando hay un huracán. People flee when there is a hurricane.
Los huracanes destru**y**en las ciudades. Hurricanes destroy cities.

b. Several verbs that end in **-iar** and **-uar** take a written accent on the **-í** and **-ú** except in the **nosotros/as**, **vosotros/as**, and **vos** forms.

-iar, -uar **verbs with spelling changes**		
Subject pronoun	env**iar** *to send*	contin**uar** *to continue*
yo	env**ío**	contin**úo**
tú	env**ías**	contin**úas**
vos	env**iás**	contin**uás**
usted, él, ella	env**ía**	contin**úa**
nosotros/as	env**iamos**	contin**uamos**
vosotros/as	env**iáis**	contin**uáis**
ustedes, ellos/as	env**ían**	contin**úan**

Verbs that need an accent: Verb conjugation tables, pp. B1–B20. For **i:í**, see verb patterns 29, 34, 53; for **u:ú**, see verb patterns 37, 57, 59.

Other *-iar, -uar* **verbs**			
acent**uar**	*to emphasize*	enfr**iar**	*to cool down / chill*
act**uar**	*to act*	evac**uar**	*to evacuate*
ampl**iar**	*to enlarge/extend*	eval**uar**	*to evaluate*
ans**iar**	*to long for*	grad**uar**se	*to graduate*
conf**iar**	*to confide/trust*	gu**iar**	*to guide*
cr**iar**	*to grow*	insin**uar**	*to insinuate*
deval**uar**	*to devalue*	perpet**uar**	*to perpetuate*
efect**uar**	*to carry out / execute*	sit**uar**	*to locate*

Lucía gu**í**a a los turistas. Ellos conf**í**an en ella. *Lucía guides the tourists. They trust her.*
Pronto me grad**ú**o como maestra. *I will graduate as a teacher soon.*

17.D.4 Stem-changing verbs

Many verbs in all three conjugation groups have a stem change. This happens in all forms except for **nosotros/as**, **vosotros/as**, and **vos**. Most stem-changing verbs have regular endings, but some are irregular. A few verbs also have an irregular **yo** form.

Spanish verbs have several types of stem changes in the present indicative: **e → ie**, **o → ue**, **i → ie**, **u → ue**, and **e → i**.

a. Conjugation of stem-changing verbs: $e \rightarrow ie$

	empezar to begin/start	**perder** to lose	**preferir** to prefer
yo	emp**ie**zo	p**ie**rdo	pref**ie**ro
tú	emp**ie**zas	p**ie**rdes	pref**ie**res
vos	empezás	perdés	preferís
usted, él, ella	emp**ie**za	p**ie**rde	pref**ie**re
nosotros/as	empezamos	perdemos	preferimos
vosotros/as	empezáis	perdéis	preferís
ustedes, ellos/as	emp**ie**zan	p**ie**rden	pref**ie**ren

Stem-changing verbs: Verb conjugation tables, pp. B1–B20. See verb patterns 24, 27, 28, 45, 49, 56, 65.

b. Other stem-changing verbs: $e \rightarrow ie$

-ar **verbs**	
atrav**e**sar	to cross
cal**e**ntar	to warm up
c**e**rrar	to close
com**e**nzar	to start/begin
desp**e**rtar	to wake up
gob**e**rnar	to govern
n**e**gar	to deny/refuse
p**e**nsar	to think
recom**e**ndar	to recommend
s**e**ntarse	to sit down

-er **verbs**	
def**e**nder	to defend
desc**e**nder	to descend
enc**e**nder	to light / switch on
ent**e**nder	to understand
qu**e**rer	to want

-ir **verbs**	
cons**e**ntir	to consent
div**e**rtirse	to have fun
m**e**ntir	to lie
s**e**ntir	to be sorry

¿Qu**ie**res ir al cine hoy?   *Do you want to go to the movies today?*
Lo s**ie**nto, hoy pref**ie**ro estudiar.   *Sorry, I prefer to study today.*

c. Conjugation of stem-changing verbs: $o \rightarrow ue$

	contar to count	**volver** to return	**dormir** to sleep
yo	c**ue**nto	v**ue**lvo	d**ue**rmo
tú	c**ue**ntas	v**ue**lves	d**ue**rmes
vos	contás	volvés	dormís
usted, él, ella	c**ue**nta	v**ue**lve	d**ue**rme
nosotros/as	contamos	volvemos	dormimos
vosotros/as	contáis	volvéis	dormís
ustedes, ellos/as	c**ue**ntan	v**ue**lven	d**ue**rmen

Stem-changing verbs: Verb conjugation tables, pp. B1–B20. See verb patterns 6, 9, 16, 25, 44, 50, 61, 67, 72.

d. Other stem-changing verbs: $o \rightarrow ue$

-ar **verbs**	
alm**o**rzar	to have lunch
c**o**star	to cost
enc**o**ntrar	to find
m**o**strar	to show
pr**o**bar	to try/taste
rec**o**rdar	to remember
s**o**nar	to ring
s**o**ñar	to dream

-er **verbs**	
dev**o**lver	to give back
ll**o**ver	to rain
m**o**ver	to move
p**o**der	to be able
prom**o**ver	to promote
rem**o**ver	to remove
res**o**lver	to resolve

-ir **verbs**	
m**o**rir	to die

Oler (*to smell*) is a unique **o:ue** verb: **hue**lo, **hue**les/olés, **hue**le, olemos, oléis, **hue**len.

The present indicative • **Chapter 17**

—¿Cuánto c**ue**sta el libro?　　　　　　　　*How much does the book cost?*
—No rec**ue**rdo. Unos veinte dólares.　　　*I don't remember. About twenty dollars.*

e. Conjugation of stem-changing verbs: *i → ie*

	adquirir *to acquire*	**inquirir** *to inquire*
yo	adqu**ie**ro	inqu**ie**ro
tú	adqu**ie**res	inqu**ie**res
vos	adquirís	inquirís
usted, él, ella	adqu**ie**re	inqu**ie**re
nosotros/as	adquirimos	inquirimos
vosotros/as	adquirís	inquirís
ustedes, ellos/as	adqu**ie**ren	inqu**ie**ren

Stem-changing verbs: Verb conjugation tables, pp. B1–B20. See verb pattern 4.

En mis cursos adqu**ie**ro conocimientos especializados.　　*In my courses I gain specialized knowledge.*

f. Conjugation of stem-changing verbs: *u → ue*

	jugar *to play*
yo	j**ue**go
tú	j**ue**gas
vos	jugás
usted, él, ella	j**ue**ga
nosotros/as	jugamos
vosotros/as	jugáis
ustedes, ellos/as	j**ue**gan

Stem-changing verbs: Verb conjugation tables, pp. B1–B20. See verb pattern 41.

Jugar is the only verb with the **u → ue** stem change.

—¿**Jue**gas algún deporte?　　　　　*Do you play any sports?*
—Sí, j**ue**go al fútbol.　　　　　　　*Yes, I play soccer.*

g. Conjugation of stem-changing verbs: *e → i*

Only **-ir** verbs have an **e → i** stem change in the present indicative.

	pedir *to ask for*
yo	p**i**do
tú	p**i**des
vos	pedís
usted, él, ella	p**i**de
nosotros/as	pedimos
vosotros/as	pedís
ustedes, ellos/as	p**i**den

Stem-changing verbs: Verb conjugation tables, pp. B1–B20. See verb patterns 20, 26, 48, 58, 64.

h. Other stem-changing verbs: $e \rightarrow i$

Other -*ir* verbs with stem change $e \rightarrow i$					
competir	*to compete*	elegir	*to choose*	repetir	*to repeat*
conseguir	*to obtain*	impedir	*to impede*	seguir	*to follow*
corregir	*to correct*	medir	*to measure*	servir	*to serve*
despedir	*to fire*	perseguir	*to pursue*	vestirse	*to get dressed*

Siempre pido tapas en el restaurante español. *I always order tapas at the Spanish restaurant.*
Allí nunca repiten los mismos platos. *They never repeat the same dishes there.*

17.D.5 Irregular verbs in the present indicative
a. Verbs with the ending –*go* in the *yo* form

	caer *to fall*	hacer *to do/ make*	salir *to leave / go out*	poner *to put*	traer *to bring*	valer *to cost / be worth*
yo	caigo	hago	salgo	pongo	traigo	valgo
tú	caes	haces	sales	pones	traes	vales
vos	caés	hacés	salís	ponés	traés	valés
usted, él, ella	cae	hace	sale	pone	trae	vale
nosotros/as	caemos	hacemos	salimos	ponemos	traemos	valemos
vosotros/as	caéis	hacéis	salís	ponéis	traéis	valéis
ustedes, ellos/as	caen	hacen	salen	ponen	traen	valen

Irregular verbs are found alphabetically in the Verb conjugation tables, pp. B1–B20. See verb patterns 8, 13, 39, 51, 63, 73, 74, 79.

Other verbs like *hacer*					
deshacer	*to undo*	rehacer	*to redo*	satisfacer	*to satisfy*

Other verbs like *poner*			
componer	*to make up / compose*	oponerse	*to oppose*
disponer	*to arrange/stipulate*	proponer	*to propose*
imponer	*to impose*	suponer	*to suppose*

Other verbs like *traer*			
atraer	*to attract*	extraer	*to extract*
contraer	*to contract*	retraer	*to retract*
distraer	*to distract*	sustraer	*to subtract*

Soy un gran esquiador. ¡No **me caigo** nunca! *I'm a great skier. I never fall!*
Me pongo las botas y los esquíes. *I'm putting on my boots and skis.*
Salgo de casa muy optimista. *I leave home in an optimistic mood.*
Traigo muchas fotos del paseo. *I'm bringing many photos from the outing.*

b. Verbs with the ending -go in the yo form and other changes

	decir	**oír**	**tener**	**venir**
	$e \rightarrow i$	$i \rightarrow y$	$e \rightarrow ie$	$e \rightarrow ie$
	to say/tell	to hear	to have	to come
yo	di**go**	oi**go**	ten**go**	ven**go**
tú	di**ce**s	o**ye**s	**tie**nes	**vie**nes
vos	decís	oís	tenés	venís
usted, él, ella	di**ce**	o**ye**	**tie**ne	**vie**ne
nosotros/as	decimos	oímos	tenemos	venimos
vosotros/as	decís	oís	tenéis	venís
ustedes, ellos/as	di**cen**	o**yen**	**tie**nen	**vie**nen

Other verbs like decir					
desdecir	to deny	maldecir	to curse/swear	predecir	to predict

Other verbs like tener					
abstenerse	to abstain	detener	to detain/stop	obtener	to obtain
atenerse	to abide	entretener	to entertain	retener	to retain
contener	to contain	mantener	to maintain	sostener	to sustain

Other verbs like venir			
convenir	to agree/suit	prevenir	to prevent
intervenir	to intervene	sobrevenir	to happen suddenly

Verb conjugation tables, pp. B1–B20. See verb patterns 11, 20, 46, 52, 69, 76.

—¿Qué **dices**? No te **oigo**.   *What are you saying? I can't hear you.*

—**Digo** que no **vengo** mañana.   *I'm saying that I'm not coming tomorrow.*

—No **tengo** tiempo.   *I don't have time.*

c. Verbs with irregular yo forms

	caber to fit	**dar** to give	**saber** to know	**ver** to see
yo	**quepo**	**doy**	**sé**	**veo**
tú	cabes	das	sabes	ves
vos	cabés	das	sabés	ves
usted, él, ella	cabe	da	sabe	ve
nosotros/as	cabemos	damos	sabemos	vemos
vosotros/as	cabéis	dais	sabéis	veis
ustedes, ellos/as	caben	dan	saben	ven

Verb conjugation tables, pp. B1–B20. See verb patterns 12, 19, 62, 77.

Sé has an accent to distinguish it from the reflexive pronoun **se**: 1.E.6b

—¡No **quepo** aquí!   *I don't fit here!*

—¿Te **doy** más espacio?   *Shall I give you more room?*

—No **sé**. **Veo** que este escritorio es muy estrecho.   *I don't know. I can see that this desk is very narrow.*

d. Completely irregular verbs

The verb **haber** has two conjugation forms: a personal form like the auxiliary verb *to have*, and an impersonal form with the meaning *there is/are*.

	estar	ser	haber *to have*	ir *to go*
	to be			
yo	est**oy**	**soy**	**he**	**voy**
tú	est**ás**	**eres**	**has**	**vas**
vos	est**ás**	**sos**	**has**	**vas**
él, ella, usted	est**á**	**es**	**ha**	**va**
nosotros/as	estamos	**somos**	**hemos**	**vamos**
vosotros/as	estáis	**sois**	habéis	**vais**
ustedes, ellos/as	est**án**	**son**	**han**	**van**

Verb conjugation tables, pp. B1–B20. See verb patterns 33, 38, 40, 66. Impersonal form of **haber**: 29.B.1

—Hola, ¿dónde **estás**?	*Hello, where are you?*
—Hola, **estoy** en la cafetería.	*Hi, I'm in the cafeteria.*
—Ya **voy**. ¡Espérame!	*I'm coming. Wait for me!*
No **he** cenado todavía.	*I haven't eaten dinner yet.*
En la escuela **hay** muchos estudiantes.	*There are many students in the school.*

17.E Use of the present indicative

Uso del presente de indicativo

17.E.1 Present actions

The present indicative is used for actions that take place currently: *now, today, this month, this year.*

Estoy aquí.	*I'm here.*
Ahora mismo **salgo**.	*I'm leaving right now.*
Este año **estudio** español.	*I'm studying Spanish this year.*

17.E.2 Habits

Just like in English, the present indicative can be used to express habits. Adverbs or other time expressions emphasize the time period.

Entreno todos los días.	*I train every day.*
Abrimos de 6 de la mañana a 5 de la tarde.	*We open from six in the morning until five in the afternoon.*
Los domingos no **trabajamos**.	*We don't work on Sundays.*

17.E.3 Timeless facts

As in English, the present indicative in Spanish is used in definitions, descriptions, and other timeless statements.

El Sol **es** una estrella.	*The Sun is a star.*
En Chile **se habla** español.	*They speak Spanish in Chile.*
Diez más diez **son** veinte.	*Ten plus ten is twenty.*

The future: Ch. 20

17.E.4 The present with future meaning

The present indicative can express the future with the help of context or time adverbs.

Mañana te **llamo**.	*I'll call you tomorrow.*
Y ahora, ¿qué **hago**?	*And what do I do now?*
Me caso el viernes.	*I'm getting married on Friday.*

17.E.5 Historical present

Stories in the past with verbs in the present indicative convey involvement. This approach is common in historical texts and in lively oral stories.

Cristóbal Colón **llega** al Nuevo Mundo en 1492.	*Christopher Columbus arrives in the New World in 1492.*
México **se independiza** en 1821.	*Mexico becomes independent in 1821.*
España **pierde** Puerto Rico en 1898.	*Spain loses Puerto Rico in 1898.*

17.E.6 The present with imperative meaning

The use of the present indicative with imperative meaning happens primarily in spoken language.

¡**Os calláis** de inmediato!	*Be quiet at once!*
¡Ahora mismo **vienes** aquí!	*Come here at once!*
¡**Escribes** esa carta hoy mismo!	*Write that letter today!*

17.E.7 Confirming present

In spoken questions, the present indicative is used to convey or confirm wishes or requests. Note the corresponding expressions in English.

¿Te **doy** más espacio?	*Shall I give you / Would you like more room?*
¿**Compramos** un helado?	*Shall we / Would you like to buy an ice cream?*
¿Os **recojo** mañana?	*Shall I / Would you like me to pick you [pl.] up tomorrow?*

17.E.8 Time expressions: *desde, desde hace, hace... que*

Verbs in the present indicative can refer to actions from the past that continue into the present. The expressions **desde, desde hace,** and **hace** + *time expression* + **que** indicate this continuity in the present.

hace + *time* + que, llevar + gerundio: 18.E.11

¿**Desde** cuándo trabajas en el banco?	*How long have you worked at the bank?*
Trabajo en el banco **desde hace** dos años.	*I have worked at the bank for two years.*
Hace dos años **que** trabajo en el banco.	

17.E.9 Conditional clauses

Real and possible conditions in **si** clauses are expressed with the present indicative.

Indicative or subjunctive in conditional sentences: 16.D.2, 23.E.8

Si no **desayuno** bien, siempre me da hambre muy rápido.	*If I don't eat well at breakfast, I always get hungry very quickly.*

17.F The present progressive

El presente progresivo

17.F.1 Progressive tenses

Spanish can express progressive actions in various ways, but **estar**, in any tense, followed by the present participle, forms the closest equivalent to the English progressive tenses. The Spanish *present progressive* is formed with the present indicative of **estar: Estoy escribiendo**. (*I am writing.*); the *past progressive* is formed with the preterite or the imperfect of **estar: Estuve/Estaba escribiendo**. (*I was writing.*); the *future progressive* is formed with the simple future of **estar: Estaré escribiendo**. (*I will be writing.*) All the other tenses (simple and compound) are formed following the same pattern. Although the structure of the progressive tenses in both languages is similar, they aren't always used in the same way.

Formation of the present participle: 25.C

Progressive tenses: 25.C.3 Verb phrases with the present participle: 26.D

17.F.2 Simple present vs. present progressive

The simple present describes habitual actions. To refer to actions that are not habitual, the present progressive can be used. It is used mostly to emphasize actions that are in progress or are happening *now* or *at this moment*.

Simple present	Present progressive
Elisa **trabaja** desde casa.	Elisa **está trabajando** desde casa.
Elisa works from home.	*Elisa is working from home (lately, now).*
Me duele la rodilla.	**Me está doliendo** la rodilla.
My knee hurts.	*My knee is hurting (right now).*
¿Me **oyes** bien?	¿Me **estás oyendo** bien?
Can you hear me well?	*Can you hear me well (now)?*

17.F.3 Modal verbs

Modal verbs: 26.B

Modal verbs (such as **poder** and **deber**) and **estar** can't be used as present participles in the progressive tenses, but **ser** can, as long as it refers to a temporary situation, usually with passive meaning. This use is limited to formal written language and to current ongoing events.

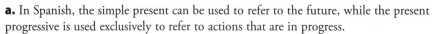

Passive voice with *ser*	Present progressive
El país **es afectado** por el huracán.	El país **está siendo afectado** por el huracán.
The country is affected by the hurricane.	*The country is being affected by the hurricane.*

17.F.4 Using the present to refer to the future

Progressive tenses: 25.C.3d-f

a. In Spanish, the simple present can be used to refer to the future, while the present progressive is used exclusively to refer to actions that are in progress.

Estoy llegando.	*I'm arriving (now).*
Llego mañana.	*I'm arriving tomorrow.*
¿Qué estás haciendo?	*What are you doing (now)?*
¿Qué haces mañana?	*What are you doing tomorrow?*

ir a + *infinitive*: 26.C.1

b. The simple present forms of **ir a** + *infinitive* can be used to refer to the future.

Voy a comprarme un carro.	*I'm going to buy myself a car.*
¿**Vas a salir** esta noche?	*Are you going out tonight?*

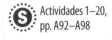

Práctica

Actividades 1–20, pp. A92–A98

The preterite and the imperfect
Pretérito perfecto simple e imperfecto

18.A Past-tense forms and verbal aspect

Formas del pasado y aspecto verbal

18.A.1 Past-tense forms

Spanish has two simple tenses to express the past: the *preterite* and the *imperfect*. Both can be similar to the English preterite, but are used differently, depending on the context.

Spanish preterite	Spanish imperfect	English preterite
Hablaste.	Hablabas.	*You spoke.*
Subiste.	Subías.	*You went up.*

18.A.2 Aspect

a. The Spanish preterite and imperfect tenses convey different *aspects* of actions, events, and states of being, and indicate how they are perceived in relation to time. The preterite action has a starting and/or finishing point and clearly shows that an action took place at a definite time or has been completed. On the other hand, the imperfect action does not have a concrete beginning or end; rather, it expresses an ongoing, habitual, repeated, or frequent action in the past or an action with an indefinite time frame.

Preterite	Imperfect
Al chico le dio frío cuando caminó a la escuela hoy.	Al chico le daba frío cuando caminaba a la escuela.
The boy got cold when he walked to school today.	*The boy used to get cold when he walked to school.*

b. The Spanish preterite and imperfect tenses can sometimes be translated the same way into English, even though the meanings of preterite and imperfect actions are different.

El perro **saltó** por encima de la cerca.	*The dog jumped over the fence.*
El perro **saltaba** por encima de la cerca.	*The dog jumped over the fence. (over and over again)*

18.B The preterite

Pretérito perfecto simple

18.B.1 Regular verbs

Regular **-er** and **-ir** verbs have the same endings in the preterite. Note that the **yo** and **usted/él/ella** forms carry a written accent. The **tú** and **vos** endings are the same.

	-ar **viajar** to travel	-er **comer** to eat	-ir **salir** to go out
yo	viaj**é**	com**í**	sal**í**
tú/vos	viaj**aste**	com**iste**	sal**iste**
usted, él, ella	viaj**ó**	com**ió**	sal**ió**
nosotros/as	viaj**amos**	com**imos**	sal**imos**
vosotros/as	viaj**asteis**	com**isteis**	sal**isteis**
ustedes, ellos/as	viaj**aron**	com**ieron**	sal**ieron**

Preterite of regular verbs: p. B5

Ver is regular but does not have any written accents: **vi, viste, vio, vimos, visteis, vieron**.

Note that regular **-ar** and **-ir** verbs have the same **nosotros/as** form in both the present indicative and the preterite. Context will usually indicate the tense.

18.B.2 Verbs with spelling changes

Pronunciation of consonants: 1.C.6

Some verbs have minor spelling changes in the preterite in order to keep the same consonant sound. The endings are regular.

a. Spelling changes in the **yo** form only:

Verb conjugation tables, pp. B1–B20. For **c:qu**, see verb patterns 71, 78; for **g:gu**, see 41, 42, 45, 61; for **g:gü**, see 10; for **z:c**, see 6, 9, 18, 27, 34.

	c → qu **buscar** to look for	g → gu **jugar** to play	g → gü **averiguar** to find out / check	z → c **empezar** to start/begin
yo	bus**qu**é	ju**gu**é	averi**gü**é	empe**c**é
tú/vos	buscaste	jugaste	averiguaste	empezaste
usted, él, ella	buscó	jugó	averiguó	empezó
nosotros/as	buscamos	jugamos	averiguamos	empezamos
vosotros/as	buscasteis	jugasteis	averiguasteis	empezasteis
ustedes, ellos/as	buscaron	jugaron	averiguaron	empezaron

Ayer bus**qu**é a Carlos todo el día.   *I looked for Carlos all day long yesterday.*
Por la noche averi**gü**é su dirección.   *At night I found out his address.*
Visité a Carlos y ju**gu**é al ajedrez con él un rato.   *I visited Carlos and played chess with him for a while.*

Other verbs like **buscar**: **empacar, volcar**
Other verbs like **jugar**: **investigar, rogar**
Other verbs like **empezar**: **avergonzar, cruzar, tropezar**

c → qu **Verbs like** *buscar*		g → gu **Verbs like** *jugar*	
explicar, expli**qu**é	*to explain*	llegar, lle**gu**é	*to arrive*
practicar, practi**qu**é	*to practice*	pagar, pa**gu**é	*to pay (for)*
tocar, to**qu**é	*to play (an instrument) / to touch*	entregar, entre**gu**é	*to deliver*
sacar, sa**qu**é	*to take (out) / withdraw*	negar, ne**gu**é	*to deny/refuse*
gu → gü **Verbs like** *averiguar*		z → c **Verbs like** *empezar*	
apaciguar, apaci**gü**é	*to appease/pacify*	abrazar, abra**c**é	*to hug*
atestiguar, atesti**gü**é	*to attest/testify*	alcanzar, alcan**c**é	*to reach*
desaguar, desa**gü**é	*to drain*	almorzar, almor**c**é	*to have lunch*
santiguarse, me santi**gü**é	*to make the sign of the cross*	comenzar, comen**c**é	*to start/begin*

Ayer comen**c**é mis estudios universitarios.   *I began my college studies yesterday.*
Practi**qu**é la pronunciación con Ana.   *I practiced my pronunciation with Ana.*
Almor**c**é en la cafetería.   *I ate lunch in the cafeteria.*
Por la tarde sa**qu**é dinero del banco y pa**gu**é los libros nuevos.   *In the afternoon, I withdrew money from the bank and paid for the new books.*

b. Other spelling changes:

	caer *to fall*	leer *to read*	concluir *to conclude*	oír *to hear*
yo	caí	leí	concluí	oí
tú/vos	caíste	leíste	concluiste	oíste
usted, él, ella	ca**y**ó	le**y**ó	conclu**y**ó	o**y**ó
nosotros/as	caímos	leímos	concluimos	oímos
vosotros/as	caísteis	leísteis	concluisteis	oísteis
ustedes, ellos/as	ca**y**eron	le**y**eron	conclu**y**eron	o**y**eron

Verb conjugation tables, pp. B1–B20. See verb patterns 13, 17, 23, 46, 60.

Note that **i** changes to **y** in the **usted/él/ella** and **ustedes/ellos/ellas** forms of all these verbs and that the **tú**, **nosotros/as**, and **vosotros/as** forms of **caer**, **leer**, and **oír** (but not **concluir**) have written accents to reflect the correct pronunciation.

Stress and accents: 1.E

Verbs like *caer*		Verbs like *leer*	
decaer	*to decay/deteriorate*	creer	*to believe*
recaer	*to have a relapse*	poseer	*to have/own*
		proveer	*to provide/supply*
Verbs like *concluir*			
constituir	*to constitute*	huir	*to escape/flee*
construir	*to build/construct*	incluir	*to include*
contribuir	*to contribute*	influir	*to influence*
destituir	*to dismiss*	intuir	*to sense*
destruir	*to destroy*	recluir	*to imprison*
disminuir	*to diminish*	reconstruir	*to reconstruct*
distribuir	*to distribute*	sustituir	*to substitute/replace*

El gobierno constru**y**ó calles nuevas.   *The government built new roads.*
El ministerio distribu**y**ó los fondos.   *The ministry distributed the funds.*
Los grupos de presión influ**y**eron en la decisión.   *The pressure groups influenced the decision.*

18.B.3 Stem-changing verbs

All **-ir** verbs with **e → ie**, **o → ue**, or **e → i** stem changes in the present indicative also have a stem change in the **usted/él/ella** and **ustedes/ellos/ellas** forms in the preterite.

Verb conjugation tables, pp. B1–B20. See verb patterns 25, 26, 48, 58, 64, 65.

Note that there are no stem changes in the preterite for **-ar** and **-er** verbs.

Verbs like **pedir**: 17.D.4h
Verbs like **sentir**: **consentir**, **divertirse**, **mentir**, **preferir**: 17.D.4a-b
Verbs like **dormir**: **morir**: 17.D.4d

According to the RAE, **rio** (not **rió**) is now the correct form.

	e → i			o → u
	pedir *to ask for*	reír *to laugh*	sentir *to feel*	dormir *to sleep*
yo	pedí	reí	sentí	dormí
tú/vos	pediste	reíste	sentiste	dormiste
usted, él, ella	p**i**dió	rio	s**i**ntió	d**u**rmió
nosotros/as	pedimos	reímos	sentimos	dormimos
vosotros/as	pedisteis	reísteis	sentisteis	dormisteis
ustedes, ellos/as	p**i**dieron	r**i**eron	s**i**ntieron	d**u**rmieron

Ayer, en la fiesta, Lisa p**i**dió tapas de jamón.   *At the party yesterday, Lisa ordered ham tapas.*
Sus amigos p**i**dieron la tortilla española.   *Her friends ordered the Spanish omelet.*
Todos se r**i**eron mucho y se s**i**ntieron muy bien.   *Everyone laughed a lot and felt great.*
Nadie d**u**rmió nada.   *Nobody slept at all.*

18.B.4 Verbs with irregular stems

There are three groups of verbs with irregular stems. The endings of these verbs are the same as regular **-er** and **-ir** verbs except for the **yo** and **usted/él/ella** forms. Note that these two forms do not have written accents.

a. Irregular stems: **u** group

Verb conjugation tables, pp. B1–B20. See verb patterns 7, 12, 33, 38, 50, 51, 62, 69.

Personal form of **haber**: Verb conjugation tables, p. B13 Impersonal form of **haber**: 29.B.1

Verbs like **poner**: 17.D.5a Verbs like **tener**: 17.D.5b

Infinitive	Stem
andar	and**uv**-
caber	c**up**-
estar	est**uv**-
haber	h**ub**-
poder	p**ud**-
poner	p**us**-
saber	s**up**-
tener	t**uv**-

Endings	
Subject	**andar**
yo	anduv**e**
tú/vos	anduv**iste**
usted, él, ella	anduv**o**
nosotros/as	anduv**imos**
vosotros/as	anduv**isteis**
ustedes, ellos/as	anduv**ieron**

Rita **estuvo** muy poco tiempo en Madrid.   *Rita was in Madrid for a very short time.*
Ella no **pudo** visitar el Museo del Prado.   *She couldn't visit the Prado Museum.*
No **tuve** oportunidad de verla.   *I didn't get the chance to see her.*

b. Irregular stems: **i** group

Verb conjugation tables, pp. B1–B20. See verb patterns 39, 56, 76.

Verbs like **hacer**: 17.D.5a Verbs like **venir**: 17.D.5b

Infinitive	Stem
hacer	h**ic**-
querer	qu**is**-
venir	v**in**-

Endings	
Subject	**hacer**
yo	hic**e**
tú/vos	hic**iste**
usted, él, ella	hiz**o**
nosotros/as	hic**imos**
vosotros/as	hic**isteis**
ustedes, ellos/as	hic**ieron**

Hacer also has a spelling change in the **usted/él/ella** form: **hizo**.

Patricia no **hizo** nada hoy.   *Patricia didn't do anything today.*
Los invitados no **vinieron** a tiempo.   *The guests didn't arrive on time.*

c. Irregular stems: **j** group

*Decir also has vowel changes in the stem.

Verb conjugation tables, pp. B1–B20. See verb patterns 11, 14, 20, 52, 73.

Note that the **ustedes/ellos/ ellas** preterite form drops the **i** in the ending.

Verbs like **decir**: 17.D.5b Verbs like **traer**: 17.D.5a Verbs like **conducir**: **deducir, reducir**

Infinitive	Stem
conducir	conduj-
decir*	dij-
introducir	introduj-
producir	produj-
traducir	traduj-
traer	traj-

Endings	
Subject	**decir**
yo	dij**e**
tú/vos	dij**iste**
usted, él, ella	dij**o**
nosotros/as	dij**imos**
vosotros/as	dij**isteis**
ustedes, ellos/as	dij**eron**

—¿**Trajiste** suficiente dinero?   *Did you bring enough money?*
—No, no **traje** dinero.   *No, I didn't bring any money.*

—¿**Dijisteis** la verdad?   *Did you [pl.] tell the truth?*
—Sí, **dijimos** toda la verdad.   *Yes, we told the whole truth.*

18.B.5 Irregular verbs

Ir, **ser**, and **dar** are irregular in the preterite. Note that **ser** and **ir** have identical preterite forms. Context clarifies which of the two verbs is being used.

The preterite of *ir, ser,* **and** *dar*		
	ir / ser *to go / to be*	**dar** *to give*
yo	**fui**	**di**
tú/vos	**fuiste**	**diste**
usted, él, ella	**fue**	**dio**
nosotros/as	**fuimos**	**dimos**
vosotros/as	**fuisteis**	**disteis**
ustedes, ellos/as	**fueron**	**dieron**

◄ Verb conjugation tables, pp. B1–B20. See verb patterns 19, 40, 66.

◄ Note that **dar** is irregular because it ends in **-ar** but has the preterite endings of **-er** and **-ir** verbs with no accents.

—¿**Fuiste** a pasear con Alicia?   *Did you go for a walk with Alicia?*
—Sí, **di** un paseo con ella.   *Yes, I went for a walk with her.*
—Y dime, ¿**fuiste** amable con ella?   *And tell me, were you nice to her?*
—Claro que sí. Le **di** unos aretes y tomamos un helado.   *Of course. I gave her a pair of earrings, and we had some ice cream.*

18.C Use of the preterite

Uso del pretérito perfecto simple

In Spanish, the preterite is used in the following ways.

18.C.1 To mark the beginning and end of an action

The Spanish preterite indicates the start, the end, or the completion of events and actions in the past. Specific verbs or expressions like *in the end* or *finally* can be used in English to convey this information about the action.

Escribí las cartas.   *I wrote the letters.*
¿Cuándo **empezasteis** el semestre?   *When did you [pl.] start the semester?*
Finalmente **encontré** mis llaves.   *I finally found my keys.*
El perro **se bebió** el agua.   *The dog drank up the water.*

18.C.2 To indicate that an action took place in the past

a. The preterite indicates that an action or situation actually happened and ended or did not happen in the past. Some time expressions that signal the preterite are **anoche**, **anteayer**, **ayer**, **la semana pasada**, and **el mes/año/siglo pasado**.

Fui a Madrid el año pasado.   *I went to Madrid last year.*
Las clases **me gustaron** mucho.   *I liked the classes a lot.*
Lina no **estuvo** enferma ayer.   *Lina wasn't sick yesterday.*
Mi abuelo **fue** un gran hombre.   *My grandfather was a great man.*
Ayer no **llovió** en Nueva York.   *Yesterday, it didn't rain in New York.*
Hubo un incendio en un hotel.   *There was a fire in a hotel.*

b. The preterite is used to state historical facts.

Hernán Cortés **llegó** a México en 1519.   *Hernán Cortés arrived in Mexico in 1519.*
Costó mucho ganar la Segunda Guerra Mundial.   *It cost a lot to win World War II.*
La Constitución de Estados Unidos **fue escrita** en 1787.   *The U.S. Constitution was written in 1787.*

◄ In Bolivia, the north of Argentina, and central Spain, events that have recently happened can be stated using the *present perfect*: **Hoy ha llovido.** *It has rained today.* See Regional variations: 19.C

◄ Passive voice with **ser**: 28.B

18.C.3 To indicate a sequence of events

a. The preterite can be used to describe actions that were part of a list or chain of events. In this context, the preterite marks the end of one action and the beginning of the next.

Rosa **se levantó** temprano. **Se vistió** rápidamente, no **comió** nada y **salió** corriendo a tomar el autobús.	*Rosa got up early. She got dressed quickly, didn't eat anything, and rushed out to catch the bus.*

b. Using the imperfect in the same context would indicate habitual or repeated actions in the past.

Rosa **se levantaba** temprano, **se vestía** rápidamente, no **comía** nada y **salía** corriendo a tomar el autobús.	*Rosa used to get up early, get dressed quickly, eat nothing, and rush out to catch the bus.*

18.D The imperfect

Pretérito imperfecto

18.D.1 Regular verbs

Most Spanish verbs are regular in the imperfect. There are no stem changes. The same endings are used for **-er** and **-ir** verbs.

Imperfect of regular
verbs: p. B5

	-ar **cantar** to sing	-er **comer** to eat	-ir **vivir** to live
yo	cant**aba**	com**ía**	viv**ía**
tú/vos	cant**abas**	com**ías**	viv**ías**
usted, él, ella	cant**aba**	com**ía**	viv**ía**
nosotros/as	cant**ábamos**	com**íamos**	viv**íamos**
vosotros/as	cant**abais**	com**íais**	viv**íais**
ustedes, ellos/as	cant**aban**	com**ían**	viv**ían**

Note that the **nosotros/as** form of **-ar** verbs is the only one with a written accent and that all imperfect forms of **-er** and **-ir** verbs have accent marks.

Flora **vivía** en Bogotá.	*Flora used to live / lived in Bogotá.*
Tenía muchos amigos allí.	*She had many friends there.*
Se sentía muy contenta.	*She felt very happy.*

18.D.2 Irregular verbs

Only three verbs are irregular in the imperfect.

Verb conjugation tables,
pp. B1–B20. See verb
patterns 40, 66, 77.

Ver is considered irregular
because an **e** is added to its
stem in the imperfect.

	ser	ir	ver
yo	**era**	**iba**	**veía**
tú/vos	**eras**	**ibas**	**veías**
usted, él, ella	**era**	**iba**	**veía**
nosotros/as	**éramos**	**íbamos**	**veíamos**
vosotros/as	**erais**	**ibais**	**veíais**
ustedes, ellos/as	**eran**	**iban**	**veían**

Todo **era** mejor antes.	*Everything was better before.*
Íbamos al parque todos los días.	*We would / used to go to the park every day.*
La gente siempre **se veía** feliz.	*People always looked happy.*

18.E Use of the imperfect

Uso del pretérito imperfecto
In Spanish, the imperfect is used in the following ways.

18.E.1 Background information and setting

a. The imperfect can be used to *set the scene* for past actions. For example, it can be used to describe the time of day, how someone felt, or what was happening when another action took place.

Eran las seis.	*It was six o'clock.*
El sol **brillaba**.	*The sun was shining.*
Me sentía optimista.	*I felt optimistic.*
Había paz en el mundo.	*There was peace in the world.*

b. The descriptions in **a** give background information about specific actions that can be expressed in the preterite.

Eran las seis cuando sonó el despertador.	*It was six o'clock when the alarm went off.*
El sol **brillaba** cuando **viajé** ayer.	*The sun was shining when I traveled yesterday.*
Me sentía optimista y todo **salió** bien.	*I felt optimistic, and everything went well.*
Había paz en el mundo, pero todo **cambió** en un instante.	*There was peace in the world, but everything changed in an instant.*

c. In stories, the imperfect is used for a description in the past or to tell about what was happening when a specific action took place. Time expressions like **de pronto** (*suddenly*) and **en ese momento** (*at that moment*) indicate the beginning of a specific past action that interrupts ongoing actions. This interrupting action is expressed with the preterite.

Había paz en el mundo. El sol **brillaba** y **me sentía** optimista, pero ese mismo día **cambió** mi vida para siempre.	*There was peace in the world. The sun was shining and I felt optimistic, but on that same day my life changed forever.*
Anoche **iba** para mi casa. Todo **parecía** muy tranquilo. **Era** tarde y no **se veía** ni un alma, cuando de pronto **escuché** un grito desgarrador.	*I was on my way home last night. Everything seemed very peaceful. It was late and there wasn't a soul to be seen, when suddenly I heard a bloodcurdling scream.*

18.E.2 Weather

a. The imperfect is used to describe the weather with actions that are expressed in the preterite.

Ayer **nevaba** mucho cuando **salí**.	*It was snowing a lot yesterday when I went out.*

b. When describing the weather during a specific period in the past, the preterite can be used.

Ayer **nevó** mucho.	*It snowed a lot yesterday.*

18.E.3 Age

Age is often expressed with the imperfect. The verb **tener** is used in the imperfect to indicate that someone *was a certain age* when something happened. The verb **cumplir** is used in the preterite to indicate that someone turned a certain age.

Cuando **tenía** dieciocho años, conocí al amor de mi vida.	*When I was eighteen, I met the love of my life.*
Cuando **cumplí** diecinueve años, todo había terminado ya.	*When I turned nineteen, it (our relationship) was over.*

◀ Expressing age with **tener**: 29.D

18.E.4 Characteristics

The imperfect is used to describe the characteristics of people, things, or conditions in the past.

Luis y yo **nos queríamos** mucho.	*Luis and I loved each other a lot.*
Mis abuelos **eran** personas extraordinarias.	*My grandparents were extraordinary people.*

18.E.5 Habits and preferences

The English equivalent ▶ is *used to* or *would.*

a. With action verbs, the imperfect often describes habits, routines, or events that used to happen repeatedly or at regular intervals in the past. Time expressions like **todos los días**, **cada año**, and **siempre** are often used to emphasize the repetition of an action.

¿**Ibais** a la escuela todos los días?	*Did you [pl.] go to school every day?*
Estudiaba mucho cada año.	*I would study hard every year.*

b. The imperfect can also be used to express two or more past actions that used to happen at the same time.

Siempre **me caía** cuando **montaba** en bicicleta.	*I always used to fall when riding my bike.*

18.E.6 Incomplete actions

After **ya**, the imperfect expresses an action in the past that was about to happen, but was interrupted. **Ir a** + *infinitive* can also be used in the imperfect to express the same thing.

ir a + *infinitive*: 26.C.1 ▶

Ya **salía** cuando sonó el teléfono.	*I was on my way out when the phone rang.*
Iban a salir cuando llegaste.	*They were just about to leave when you arrived.*

18.E.7 Courtesy

Use of the conditional for ▶ polite requests: 21.B.4

The imperfect can be used to make polite requests.

Quería pedirte una cosa.	*I wanted to ask you for something.*
Venía a solicitar información.	*I came to ask for some information.*

18.E.8 Dreams and children's games

When children invent games based on fantasy or imagination, the context is created using the imperfect. When dreams are talked about, the start of the story is often **Soñé que...** and the rest is told in the imperfect and other past structures. The preterite is rarely used.

Juguemos a que **estábamos** en una nave espacial, que tú **eras** un monstruo y que yo te **perseguía**.	*Let's pretend that we're in a spaceship, you're a monster, and I'm chasing you.*
Soñé que era el día del examen y que no **había estudiado** nada.	*I dreamt that it was exam day and that I hadn't studied anything.*

18.E.9 Completed actions with the imperfect

In news reports and historical texts, the imperfect is sometimes used in place of the preterite to describe a completed action. This stylistic choice lends greater immediacy and a descriptive tone to the narration.

La boda real se realizó ayer en La Almudena. Unas horas después, Madrid **celebraba** la boda del siglo con fiestas en toda la ciudad.	*The royal wedding was held yesterday in La Almudena. Some hours later, Madrid celebrated the wedding of the century with parties all over the city.*

18.E.10 **Indirect discourse**

a. Indirect discourse is a way to report what someone said without using a direct quote. Indirect discourse is expressed using a subordinate clause with **que**. Quotation marks are not used.

Indirect discourse: Ch. 31
Que clauses: 16.C.1

Direct discourse	Indirect discourse
Él **dice**: "No tengo dinero". *He says: "I don't have any money."*	Él **dice que** no **tiene** dinero. *He says that he doesn't have any money.*
Tú **dijiste**: "Ella **quiere** viajar". *You said: "She wants to travel."*	Tú **dijiste que** ella **quería** viajar. *You said that she wanted to travel.*
Él **decía**: "Ellas no **saben** nada". *He said: "They don't know anything."*	Él **decía que** ellas no **sabían** nada. *He said that they didn't know anything.*
Ellos **dijeron**: "**Esperamos** que no **suban** los precios". *They said: "We hope the prices won't go up."*	Ellos **dijeron que esperaban** que no **subieran** los precios. *They said that they hoped the prices wouldn't go up.*

b. The imperfect replaces the present tense in indirect discourse with the preterite of **decir**, **preguntar**, **comentar**, or other reporting verbs.

When the verbs express will or emotion, the subjunctive is used in the subordinate clause, but the structure to express indirect discourse is the same.

Rita dijo que no **tenía** dinero.
Rita said she didn't have any money.

Te pregunté que si **querías** cenar.
I asked you if you wanted to have dinner.

c. Ir a + *infinitive* expresses the future in Spanish. The imperfect of **ir** is often used in indirect discourse to describe what someone *was going to do*.

ir a + *infinitive*: 26.C.1

Jaime me contó que **iba** a viajar.
Jaime told me that he was going to travel.

Te pregunté que si **ibas** a cenar.
I asked you if you were going to have dinner.

18.E.11 **Expressions with** *hace/hacía* + **period of time** + *que (no)*

a. Hace/Hacía + *period of time* + **que (no)** is used to express *how long since something has/had (not) been done*. In affirmative sentences, it is equivalent to the verb phrase **llevar** + *time expression* + **gerundio**. In negative sentences, it is equivalent to **llevar** + *time expression* + **sin** + *infinitive*.

llevar + *time expression* + **gerundio**: 26.D

Hace tres años **que vivo** en Madrid.
Llevo tres años **viviendo** en Madrid.
I have lived in Madrid for three years.

Hace un año **que no voy** a Londres.
Llevo un año **sin ir** a Londres.
It's been a year since I was last in London. / I haven't been in London for a year.

¡**Hacía** mucho tiempo **que no** te **veía**!
¡**Llevaba** mucho tiempo **sin verte**!
I hadn't seen you for ages.

b. The imperfect is often used to indicate that a certain amount of time is over.

Llevo mucho tiempo **sin verte**.
I haven't seen you in a long time. (I still haven't seen you.)

Llevaba mucho tiempo **sin verte**.
It's been so long since I've seen you. (But now I've seen you.)

18.E.12 **Impersonal constructions** *había, hubo*

The preterite of **haber**, **hubo**, expresses an action or state that has ended, while the imperfect, **había**, describes the existence of something in the past without stating that it ended.

Impersonal form of **haber**: 29.B.1

En el siglo XX **hubo** muchas guerras.
In the 20th century, there were many wars.

Casi en ningún país **había** paz en esa época.
Almost no country had peace during that period.

18.F Verbs that change meaning

Verbos cuyo significado cambia

Some common verbs have different meanings in the preterite and the imperfect. Note that the meaning may also change depending on whether the statement is affirmative or negative.

The examples in this chart ▶ describe scenes and narrate events in the story *La siesta del martes* by Gabriel García Márquez.

Saber: 26.B.7 ▶

Querer: 26.B.6 ▶

Poder: 26.B.5 ▶

Verb	Preterite	Imperfect
tener	*to get; to receive* El sacerdote **tuvo** una visita inesperada: la madre y la hermana del difunto. *The priest got an unexpected visit: the mother and the sister of the deceased.*	*to have* La hija **tenía** dificultades para mover la persiana. *The daughter was having a hard time moving the blinds.*
saber	*to find out; to discover* **Supieron** que Carlos se murió el lunes anterior. *They found out that Carlos died the previous Monday.*	*to know* El padre no **sabía** quiénes eran. *The father didn't know who they were.*
querer	*to try (without necessarily succeeding)* La mujer **quiso** visitar el cementerio donde estaba enterrado su hijo. *The woman tried to visit the graveyard where her son was buried.*	*to want* La gente del pueblo se asomaba a la ventana porque **quería** ver qué sucedía. *The townspeople looked out their windows because they wanted to see what was happening.*
no querer	*to refuse* La mujer **no quiso** irse de la casa del cura sin verlo. *The woman refused to leave the priest's house without seeing him.*	*not to want* La mujer **no quería** despertar al cura. *The woman didn't want to wake up the priest.*
conocer	*to meet (for the first time)* Cuando el cura **conoció** a la mujer, se quedó muy sorprendido. *When the priest met the woman, he was very surprised.*	*to know, to be familiar with* Nadie **conocía** a Carlos en ese pueblo. *Nobody in that town knew Carlos.*
poder	*to manage to; to succeed in* La mujer **pudo** convencer a la hermana del cura de que fuera a buscarlo. *The woman managed to convince the priest's sister to go fetch him.*	*to be able to; can* En la distancia, **se podía** escuchar la música que tocaba la banda. *The music the band was playing could be heard in the distance.*
no poder	*to be unable to; to fail to* La chica **no pudo** subir la ventana del tren. *The girl was unable to close the window in the train.*	*to be unable to (in a general sense)* **No se podía** respirar en el tren a causa del calor. *It was so hot inside the train that one couldn't breathe.*

Práctica

 Actividades 1–14, pp. A99–A104

The present perfect and the past perfect

Pretérito perfecto compuesto y pluscuamperfecto

19.A The present perfect

Pretérito perfecto compuesto

The present perfect is used to talk about what someone has done or what has happened. In Spanish, it is formed with the present indicative of the auxiliary verb **haber** (see table below) and the past participle of the main verb.

¿**Has leído** este libro?   *Have you read this book?*

19.A.1 Regular past participles

a. Most Spanish verbs have a regular past participle. To form regular past participles, the ending **-ado** is added to the stem of **-ar** verbs and the ending **-ido** is added to the stem of **-er** and **-ir** verbs. The present perfect forms of **tú** and **vos** are the same.

				Regular past participles	
Subject pronoun	**Present indicative of** *haber*	**+**	**-ar verbs: -ado**	**-er and -ir verbs: -ido**	
			hablar	**querer**	**venir**
yo	**he**				
tú/vos	**has**				
usted, él, ella	**ha**	**+**	habl**ado**	quer**ido**	ven**ido**
nosotros/as	**hemos**				
vosotros/as	**habéis**				
ustedes, ellos/as	**han**				

b. In the present perfect, the past participle always ends in **-o**. Unlike in English, in Spanish, no word can come between **haber** and the past participle. Object and reflexive pronouns must come before **haber**.

Siempre **he trabajado** mucho.   *I have always worked a lot.*
Lo **he buscado** por todos lados.   *I have looked for it all over the place.*
Lucas **se ha quedado** dormido.   *Lucas has overslept.*

c. When the stem of an **-er** or **-ir** verb ends in **a**, **e**, or **o**, a written accent must be added to the participle, forming the ending **-ído**. The combination of **u** + **i** usually forms a diphthong and does not have a written accent (constr**uido**, h**uido**).

Infinitive	Verb stem	Past participle	
creer	**cre-**	creído	*thought, believed*
leer	**le-**	leído	*read*
oír	**o-**	oído	*heard*
sonreír	**sonre-**	sonreído	*smiled*
traer	**tra-**	traído	*brought*

¿Has **leído** novelas españolas?   *Have you read Spanish novels?*

The past participle: 25.D

The present tense of **haber**: 17.D.5d
Compound tenses: Verb conjugation tables, p. B5

The present perfect used to be called the **pretérito perfecto**. Nowadays, it is referred to as **pretérito perfecto compuesto**.

Do not confuse the auxiliary verb **haber** with the main verb **tener**.

Pronoun placement with **haber**: 13.G.4, 27.A.1b
The past participle in passive **ser** clauses: 28.B.3
Compound tenses using **haber**: Verb conjugation tables, p. B5

Diphthongs: 1.C.2, 1.E.4
-uir verbs: 17.D.3a

Verbs like **traer** also have the written accent (**atraer, atraído**): 17.D.5a

19.A.2 Irregular past participles

a. A number of verbs have an irregular past participle. Most irregular past participles end in **-to**.

The past participle of **ir** is **ido**. ▶

Infinitive	Irregular past participle	
abrir	**abierto**	opened
cubrir	**cubierto**	covered
decir	**dicho**	said, told
describir	**descrito**	described
escribir	**escrito**	written
hacer	**hecho**	done, made
morir	**muerto**	died
poner	**puesto**	placed
resolver	**resuelto**	resolved
romper	**roto**	broken
satisfacer	**satisfecho**	satisfied
ver	**visto**	seen
volver	**vuelto**	returned

Las tiendas no **han abierto** todavía.   *The shops **haven't opened** yet.*

Other verbs like **decir**, **hacer**, and **poner**: 17.D.5a–b ▶

Verbs derived from these infinitives have the same irregularity in the past participle: **contradecir, contradicho; descubrir, descubierto; deshacer, deshecho; suponer, supuesto; devolver, devuelto.**

b. The verbs **freír, imprimir,** and **proveer** (as well as their derivatives: **refreír, sofreír, reimprimir, sobreimprimir, desproveer**) have two equally accepted participles, a regular and an irregular form. Both can be used to form compound tenses and passive sentences. The irregular participles **frito, impreso,** and **provisto** are becoming more common than the regular participles in Spanish-speaking countries.

Passive voice with **ser**: 28.B ▶
Past participles with two forms: 25.D.3 ▶

Infinitive	Past participle	
	Regular	Irregular
freír (*to fry*)	fre**ído**	**frito**
imprimir (*to print*)	imprim**ido**	**impreso**
proveer (*to provide*)	prove**ído**	**provisto**

El chef **ha frito (freído)** las cebollas.
Las cebollas **han sido fritas (freídas)** por el chef.
El secretario **ha impreso (imprimido)** la agenda.
La agenda **ha sido impresa (imprimida)** por el secretario.
La agencia de viajes **ha provisto (proveído)** los itinerarios.
Los itinerarios **han sido provistos (proveídos)** por la agencia de viajes.

The chef has fried the onions.
The onions have been fried by the chef.
The secretary has printed the agenda.
The agenda has been printed by the secretary.
The travel agency has provided the itineraries.
The itineraries have been provided by the travel agency.

Adjectives: Ch. 3 ▶

c. Only the irregular forms can function as adjectives.

las papas *fritas* (*Latin America*)
las patatas *fritas* (*Spain*)   *fried potatoes (potato chips / French fries)*
los documentos *impresos*   *printed documents*
los uniformes *provistos*   *provided uniforms*

19.B Use of the present perfect

Uso del pretérito perfecto compuesto

The use of the present perfect has regional differences. The following examples show common uses of this tense in most Spanish-speaking regions.

19.B.1 Life experiences – *nunca, alguna vez, hasta ahora, en mi vida*

a. The present perfect can be used to describe life experiences up to the present moment. Adverbs like **alguna vez, nunca, hasta ahora/hoy,** and **en mi vida** (*never before*) are often used.

◀ Adverbs: Ch. 10

¿Has viajado en barco **alguna vez**?	*Have you ever traveled by boat?*
Nunca he probado el alcohol.	*I have never tried alcohol.*
Hasta ahora, todo ha salido bien.	*Everything has gone well until now.*
¡En mi vida he estudiado tanto!	*I have never studied so much in my life!*

b. Context usually implies the point in time when the adverb is not stated.

Amy hace un café delicioso,	*Amy makes a delicious coffee.*
¿lo has probado (**alguna vez**)?	*Have you (ever) tried it?*

19.B.2 Incomplete actions – *todavía no*

The present perfect is used with **todavía no** (*not yet*) to express actions that are not yet complete.

◀ To talk about something you have just done or that just happened, use **acabar de** + *infinitive*, not the present perfect.

¿**No** has salido **todavía**?	*Haven't you gone out / left yet?*
No, **todavía no** he salido.	*No, I haven't gone out / left yet.*

19.B.3 Continuous actions – *siempre*

Siempre and other time expressions like **muchas veces** and **todos los días** are used with the present perfect to extend the action into the present.

Siempre te he querido.	*I have always loved you.*
Hemos ido al cine **todos los días**.	*We have been to the movies every day.*

19.C Regional variations

Variaciones regionales

The following examples show the major differences when using the present perfect in Spain and Latin America. There are also variations within regions.

19.C.1 Recently completed actions – *ya, por fin, finalmente*

a. Ya (*already*), **por fin** (*in the end*), and **finalmente** (*finally*) indicate completed actions. In Spain, these expressions are generally used with the present perfect, while the preterite is preferred in most of Latin America.

Spain	¡Por fin **has llegado**!	*You have finally arrived!*
Latin America	¡Por fin **llegaste**!	

b. Questions and answers with **ya** and **todavía no** are generally used with different verb tenses in Spain and Latin America.

Spain	—¿Ya **has cenado**?	Have you had dinner yet?
	—No, todavía no **he cenado**.	No, I haven't had dinner yet.
	—Sí, ya **he cenado**.	Yes, I have already had dinner.

Latin America	—¿Ya **cenaste**?	Did you eat dinner yet?
	—No, todavía no **he cenado**.	No, I haven't had dinner yet.
	—Sí, ya **cené**.	Yes, I already ate dinner.

c. In central Spain, the present perfect is used to convey actions completed in the recent past. The length of this time period in the past can be subjective and is indicated by time expressions such as **hace un momento, este año,** and **hoy**. This use is also common in northwest Argentina and in Bolivia.

Spain (central)	Hace un momento **he visto** a Ernesto.	*I saw Ernesto a short time ago.*
Latin America	Hace un momento **vi** a Ernesto.	

19.C.2 Interpreting time using the present perfect

When the period of time is specified, the present perfect is interpreted differently in central Spain than it is in most of Latin America.

Spain (central)	Este verano **hemos ido** mucho al cine.	This summer, we've been to the movies a lot. (The summer is over.)
Latin America		This summer, we've been to the movies a lot. (The summer is not over yet.)

19.C.3 Cause and effect

Cause-and-effect relationships in the recent past are expressed with the present perfect in Spain and the preterite in Latin America.

Spain	—¿Por qué **has llegado** tan tarde hoy? —¡**He perdido** el autobús!	Why did you arrive so late today? I missed the bus!
Latin America	—¿Por qué **llegaste** tan tarde hoy? —¡**Perdí** el autobús!	

19.D The past perfect

Pretérito pluscuamperfecto

The past perfect is formed using the imperfect of **haber** and the past participle of the main verb: **había hablado** (*I had talked*).

Pretérito pluscuamperfecto					
Subject pronoun	**Imperfect of** *haber*	+	**Regular past participles**		
			-ar **verbs:** *-ado*	*-er* **and** *-ir* **verbs:** *-ido*	
			hablar	**querer**	**venir**
yo	**había**				
tú/vos	**habías**				
usted, él, ella	**había**	+	habl**ado**	quer**ido**	ven**ido**
nosotros/as	**habíamos**				
vosotros/as	**habíais**				
ustedes, ellos/as	**habían**				

> ◀ Compound tenses: Verb conjugation tables, p. B5
> Past participles: 19.A, 25.D

19.E Use of the past perfect

Uso del pretérito pluscuamperfecto

19.E.1 Previous past action

In Spanish, the past perfect expresses what someone *had done*, or what *had happened* before another action or condition in the past.

Cuando Lina llamó, Pedro ya **había salido**.　　　*When Lina called, Pedro had already left.*

19.E.2 Questions and answers with *ya, todavía no* in the past

Antes, aún, nunca, todavía, and **ya** are often used with the past perfect to indicate the order of past actions. These adverbs, as well as pronouns and the word **no**, can't come between **haber** and the past participle. Pronouns and **no** must come before **haber**, but the adverbs can come before **haber** or after the participle.

> ◀ Pronoun placement with **haber**: 13.G.4, 27.A.1b
> Adverbs: Ch. 10

—¿Ya **habías estudiado** español cuando viajaste a Santiago?　　　*Had you already studied Spanish when you traveled to Santiago?*

—Claro, ya **había estudiado** español y sabía bastante.　　　*Of course, I had already studied Spanish and I knew quite a lot.*

—Cuando llegué a Santiago, no **había estudiado** español todavía.　　　*When I arrived in Santiago, I had not studied Spanish yet.*

19.E.3 Indirect discourse

In indirect discourse, the preterite becomes the past perfect.

> ◀ Indirect discourse: Ch. 31

Camilo dijo: "Vi los fiordos chilenos".　　　*Camilo said, "I saw the Chilean fjords."*
Camilo me contó que **había visto** los fiordos chilenos.　　　*Camilo told me that he had seen the Chilean fjords.*

19.F The *pretérito anterior*

The **pretérito anterior** is formed using the preterite of **haber** and the past participle of the main verb. This form of the past perfect is rare in today's spoken Spanish and is generally used only in written language.

The preterite of **haber**: 18.B.4a
Past participles: 19.A, 25.D

Pretérito anterior				
Subject pronoun	**Preterite of** *haber*	+	**Regular past participles**		
			-ar **verbs:** *-ado*	*-er* **and** *-ir* **verbs:** *-ido*	
			hablar	**querer**	**venir**
yo	**hube**				
tú/vos	**hubiste**				
usted, él, ella	**hubo**	+	habl**ado**	quer**ido**	ven**ido**
nosotros/as	**hubimos**				
vosotros/as	**hubisteis**				
ustedes, ellos/as	**hubieron**				

19.G Use of the *pretérito anterior*

Uso del pretérito anterior

a. The **pretérito anterior** marks the end of an action that happened before another action in the past.

Cuando **se hubo tomado** la
  decisión, concluyeron la reunión.

When the decision had been made,
  they ended the meeting.

The preterite: 18.B

b. The **pretérito anterior** can be replaced with the preterite (**pretérito perfecto simple**).

Cuando **se tomó** la decisión,
  concluyeron la reunión.

When the decision was made,
  they ended the meeting.

Práctica

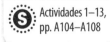
Actividades 1–13,
pp. A104–A108

The present perfect and the past perfect • **Chapter 19**

The future
Futuro

Chapter 20

A. Future expressions
B. The simple future
C. Use of the simple future
D. Other future expressions
E. The future perfect
F. Use of the future perfect
G. Regional variations

20.A Future expressions

Estructuras para expresar el futuro
In Spanish, the future can be expressed using the following structures.

Spanish future expressions		
1. Simple future	Te **devolveré** tus libros muy pronto.	*I will give* you *back* your books very soon.
2. *ir a + infinitive*	**Vamos a construir** una nueva casa.	*We are going to build* a new house.
3. Present indicative	**Regreso** el lunes.	*I am coming back* on Monday. (lit. *I come back* on Monday.)

As you can see, future actions and events can be expressed in Spanish and English using the simple future and *going to + infinitive* expressions. In English, the present progressive may also refer to a future event or action. Note that the Spanish present progressive *can't* be used to refer to the future, but the simple present can.

Present progressive: 17.F
The present with future meaning: 17.E.4

Other future expressions: 20.D

20.B The simple future

Futuro simple
The future tense of regular verbs is formed by adding future endings to the infinitive. The future endings for all **-ar**, **-er**, and **-ir** verbs are identical. Irregular verbs use the same endings, but have changes in the stems. The **tú** and **vos** endings are the same.

20.B.1 Regular verbs

All regular verbs have a written accent in the future tense except the **nosotros/as** form.

Regular verbs: verb conjugation tables, p. B5

	-ar	*-er*	*-ir*
yo	trabajar**é**	comer**é**	ir**é**
tú/vos	trabajar**ás**	comer**ás**	ir**ás**
usted, él, ella	trabajar**á**	comer**á**	ir**á**
nosotros/as	trabajar**emos**	comer**emos**	ir**emos**
vosotros/as	trabajar**éis**	comer**éis**	ir**éis**
ustedes, ellos/as	trabajar**án**	comer**án**	ir**án**

20.B.2 Irregular verbs

Some verbs are irregular in the simple future. The verbs that are irregular have a stem change, but take the same endings as regular verbs in the future.

Infinitive	Stem	Infinitive	Stem	Infinitive	Stem
caber	**cabr-**	poder	**podr-**	salir	**saldr-**
decir	**dir-**	poner	**pondr-**	tener	**tendr-**
haber	**habr-**	querer	**querr-**	valer	**valdr-**
hacer	**har-**	saber	**sabr-**	venir	**vendr-**

Verb conjugation tables, pp. B1–B20.
See verb patterns 12, 20, 38, 39, 50, 51, 52, 56, 62, 63, 69, 74, 76.

Note that the **e** is dropped from the infinitive ending in **caber**, **haber**, **poder**, **querer**, and **saber** and that a **d** replaces the vowel of the infinitive ending in **poner**, **salir**, **tener**, **valer**, and **venir**. **Decir** and **hacer** have completely irregular stems.

—¿**Vendrás** pronto?　　　*Will you come soon?*

—Sí, lo **haré**.　　　*Yes, I will (come).*

Verbs like **decir**, **hacer**, **poner**,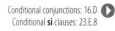
tener, and **venir**: 17.D.5a–b
Verbs derived from **decir**, **hacer**, **poner**, **tener**, and **venir** have the same irregularity in the future tense. Two exceptions are **bendecir** and **maldecir**, and **predecir** has both regular and irregular forms.

20.C　Use of the simple future

Uso del futuro simple

20.C.1　Future actions

The simple future is generally used to express future actions and events.

¿**Viajaréis** de vacaciones en julio?　　　*Will you [pl.] travel / go away on vacation in July?*

20.C.2　Suppositions

The simple future tense can be used to express suppositions or guesses about present or future actions or states. Whether the present or future is referred to depends on the context.

Assumptions about events
in the past: 20.F.2, 21.B.2
a. Suppositions about the present:

—¿Quién **será** ese hombre?　　　*I wonder who that man is. / Who can that man be?*

—No lo sé. **Será** alguna persona importante.　　　*I don't know. He must be an important person.*

b. Suppositions about the future:

—¿Quién **hará** el trabajo? ¿Tú?　　　*Who will do the job? You?*

—¿Yo? No, lo **hará** Rubén. (Supongo que lo **hará** Rubén.)　　　*Me? No, Rubén will do it. (I suppose Rubén will do it.)*

20.C.3　Predictions

The simple future is used in forecasts, horoscopes, and predictions.

Mañana **nevará** en las montañas.　　　*Tomorrow, it will snow in the mountains.*

Las personas de Aries **tendrán** una
agradable sorpresa esta semana.　　　*People born under Aries will have a pleasant
surprise this week.*

Predicen que los precios **subirán**.　　　*They predict that prices will go up.*

Todo **saldrá** bien, ya **verás**.　　　*Everything will be all right, you'll see.*

Conditional conjunctions: 16.D
Conditional **si** clauses: 23.E.8
20.C.4　Conditional constructions

The simple future can be used to describe something that will happen under certain imagined conditions. When the condition is seen as possible, it is expressed with the present indicative in a **si** clause.

Si nos ganamos la lotería, **compraremos** la casa.　　　*If we win the lottery, we'll buy the house.*

20.C.5　Decrees

In written language, the simple future is used for laws, regulations, and decrees.

No **matarás**.　　　*Thou shall not kill.*

20.C.6　Impersonal constructions – *habrá*

Impersonal form of **haber**:
18.E.12, 20.F.3, 21.B.8,
21.D.4, 29.B.1
When **haber** is used as an impersonal verb in the third-person singular of the future tense, it indicates future existence (*there will [not] be*).

No **habrá** reunión mañana.　　　*There won't be a meeting tomorrow.*

Habrá vacaciones en julio.　　　*There will be vacation in July.*

No **habrá** lluvia mañana.   *There won't be rain tomorrow.*
Creo que **habrá** tiempo suficiente.   *I think there will be enough time.*

20.C.7 **Contrast** *– shall, will*

a. In U.S. English, the simple future is formed by adding the auxiliary *will*, but pay attention to the following uses of *shall* and its Spanish equivalents.

Communicative function	Spanish	English
Express formal obligation	**Habrá** sanciones.	*There **shall** (will) be sanctions.*
Express suggestions and requests	¿**Empezamos** (ya)?	***Shall** we start?*

b. These Spanish equivalents of *will* are used for making announcements, asking polite questions, offering or refusing to help, ordering in a restaurant, and selecting items in a store.

◀ Use of the conditional for polite requests: 21.B.4

Se abrirá un nuevo centro comercial.   *A new shopping mall will be opened.*
¿**Asistirá** usted a la reunión?   *Will you attend the meeting?*
¡Yo **abro**!   *I'll get it! (I will open the door.)*
¡Yo no **abro**! (Yo no **abriré**.)   *I won't get it! (I won't open the door.)*
Tráigame una ensalada, por favor.   *I'll have a salad, please.*
Me llevo la blusa roja.   *I'll take the red blouse.*

20.D Other future expressions

Otras expresiones del futuro

20.D.1 *Ir a* + **infinitive**

a. This form is used to express plans or intentions to be carried out immediately or in the very near future.

◀ **Ir a** + infinitive: 26.C.1

—¿Qué **vas a hacer** esta tarde?   *What are you going to do this afternoon?*
—Estoy rendido y **voy a descansar**.   *I'm exhausted and I'm going to rest.*

b. The form **ir a** + *infinitive* describes events that are likely to happen in the near future.

Es muy tarde. ¡**Vas a perder** el tren!   *It's very late. You're going to miss the train!*

c. Ir a + *infinitive* is used with **ya** to describe an impending event.

Ya **va a empezar** el noticiero.   *The newscast is going to start now.*

20.D.2 **The present indicative to express future**

The present indicative can only be used to describe future actions if the context refers to the future. Adverbs of time are often part of the sentence.

◀ The present with future meaning: 17.E.4
Adverbs of time: 10.B.2

Las clases **empiezan** mañana.   *School starts tomorrow.*

20.E The future perfect

Futuro compuesto

The future perfect is formed with the simple future of the auxiliary verb **haber** and the past participle of the main verb. **Tú** and **vos** have the same future perfect forms.

The future tense ▶
of **haber**: 20.B.2
Past participles:
19.A.1–2, 25.D

Simple future of *haber*		+	Regular past participles		
			-*ar* **verbs:** -*ado*	-*er* **and** -*ir* **verbs:** -*ido*	
			hablar	**querer**	**venir**
yo	**habré**				
tú/vos	**habrás**				
usted, él, ella	**habrá**	+	habl**ado**	quer**ido**	ven**ido**
nosotros/as	**habremos**				
vosotros/as	**habréis**				
ustedes, ellos/as	**habrán**				

As with other compound ▶
tenses, the past participle
never varies in the future
perfect. It always
ends in **-o**.

20.F Use of the future perfect

Uso del futuro compuesto

20.F.1 A complete action in the future

Prepositions: Ch. 12 ▶

The future perfect describes an action that will already be complete (*will have happened*) by some point in time in the future. Words like **en**, **para**, and **dentro de** are used in time expressions with the future perfect.

Mañana a esta hora, **habremos regresado** a casa.	*By this time tomorrow, we'll have returned home.*
En junio, ya **habrás terminado** tus estudios.	*By June, you'll have already finished your studies.*

20.F.2 Assumptions about the past

The conditional for assumptions ▶
about the past: 21.B.2
Suppositions about the
present or future: 20.C.2

The future perfect can express an assumption or guess about the probability of an action or state in the past.

¿Cómo me **habrá ido** en el examen ayer?	*I wonder how I did on the exam yesterday.*
Jaime no vino a trabajar el lunes.	*Jaime didn't come to work on Monday.*
¿Dónde **habrá estado**?	*Where could he have been?*

20.F.3 Impersonal constructions – *habrá habido*

Impersonal form of **haber**: ▶
18.E.12, 20.C.6, 21.B.8,
21.D.4, 29.B.1

The impersonal form of **haber** can be used to express assumptions about what could have been.

¿**Habrá habido** algún problema?	*Could there have been a problem?*
¿**Habrá habido** buenos resultados en el examen?	*Could there have been good exam results?*

20.F.4 Conditional constructions

Conditional conjunctions: 16.D ▶
Conditional **si** clauses: 23.E.8

The future perfect expresses what the speaker believes will have happened if a present condition is fulfilled. The **si** clause describing the condition uses the present indicative.

Si no estudias, **habrás perdido** el tiempo en la escuela.	*If you don't study, you will have wasted your time at school.*

20.G Regional variations

Variaciones regionales

There are few regional differences in future verb forms in Spanish. It is a bit more common to use **ir a** + *infinitive* in Latin America to refer to both the near and distant future.

Spain	Este año me **graduaré**.	*I'm going to / I will graduate this year.*
Latin America	Este año me **voy a graduar**.	

Práctica

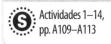 Actividades 1–14,
pp. A109–A113

The conditional
Condicional

Chapter 21

A. The conditional
B. Use of the conditional
C. The conditional perfect
D. Use of the conditional perfect

21.A The conditional

Condicional simple

In English, the conditional is expressed with the word *would*. In Spanish, the conditional tense is expressed with its own verb forms.

Me alegraría verte de nuevo.	*It would make me happy to see you again.*
Roberto dijo que te **llamaría**.	*Roberto said that he would call you.*

Remember that the imperfect can also mean *would*, but in the sense of a habitual past action: 18.E.5

The conditional of Spanish verbs is formed by adding the conditional endings to the infinitive. The conditional endings for **-ar**, **-er**, and **-ir** verbs are identical. The **tú** and **vos** endings are the same.

21.A.1 Regular verbs

All forms have a written accent.

	-ar	-er	-ir
yo	trabajar**ía**	comer**ía**	subir**ía**
tú/vos	trabajar**ías**	comer**ías**	subir**ías**
usted, él, ella	trabajar**ía**	comer**ía**	subir**ía**
nosotros/as	trabajar**íamos**	comer**íamos**	subir**íamos**
vosotros/as	trabajar**íais**	comer**íais**	subir**íais**
ustedes, ellos/as	trabajar**ían**	comer**ían**	subir**ían**

Regular verbs: Verb conjugation tables, p. B5

21.A.2 Irregular verbs

Irregular verbs have the same stem changes in the conditional as in the simple future tense.

Infinitive	Stem	Infinitive	Stem
caber	**cabr-**	querer	**querr-**
decir	**dir-**	saber	**sabr-**
haber	**habr-**	salir	**saldr-**
hacer	**har-**	tener	**tendr-**
poder	**podr-**	valer	**valdr-**
poner	**pondr-**	venir	**vendr-**

Irregular verbs in the simple future: 20.B.2

Verb conjugation tables, pp. B1–B20.
See verb patterns 12, 20, 38, 39, 50, 51, 52, 56, 62, 63, 69, 74, 76.

—¿**Podrías** hacerme un favor?	*Could you do me a favor?*
—Lo **haría** si pudiera.	*I would (do it) if I could.*

Most verbs derived from **decir**, **hacer**, **poner**, **tener**, and **venir** have the same irregularity in the conditional.

Verbs like **decir**, **hacer**, **poner**, **tener**, and **venir**: 17.D.5a–b

21.B Use of the conditional

Uso del condicional simple

21.B.1 Imagined possibility or characterisitic

The conditional expresses a possibility in the near future.

Llegaríamos más rápido en avión.	*We would arrive faster by plane.*
Estarías mejor en otro trabajo.	*You would be better off at another job.*

21.B.2 Assumptions about the past

The future perfect for
assumptions about
the past: 20.F.2

The conditional can be used to express assumptions about the past.

Jaime no vino a trabajar el lunes. ¿Dónde **estaría**?	*Jaime didn't come to work on Monday. Where could/would he have been?*
Supongo que hace mil años la gente **hablaría** de forma muy distinta.	*I suppose that a thousand years ago people would/could have spoken very differently.*
¿Cómo me **iría** en el examen ayer?	*I wonder how it went (for me) / I did on my exam yesterday.*

21.B.3 Wishes

Verbs like **gustar**: 17.B.4 ▶

The conditional is used with verbs like **gustar, preferir, desear, encantar,** and **alegrar** to express wishes or preferences.

Me encantaría ir al teatro.	*I would love to go to the theater.*
¿**Te gustaría** estudiar español?	*Would you like to study Spanish?*

21.B.4 Courtesy

Use of the imperfect for ▶
polite requests: 18.E.7
The imperative and
politeness: 24.G.3b

The conditional is used to communicate polite inquiries and requests.

¿**Podrías** ayudarme con esto?	*Could/Would you help me with this?*
¿**Sería** posible realizar la reunión el lunes?	*Could/Would it be possible to hold the meeting on Monday?*

21.B.5 Advice

The conditional is used to give advice with verbs like **deber** and impersonal expressions like **ser bueno, ser mejor,** and **ser conveniente.**

Subjunctive with impersonal ▶
expressions: 23.C.8

Deberíais dejar de fumar.	*You [pl.] should stop smoking.*
Sería conveniente que fueras al médico.	*It would be good if you went to the doctor.*
En tu lugar, yo no **haría** eso.	*If I were you, I wouldn't do that.*

21.B.6 Indirect discourse

Indirect discourse: Ch. 31 ▶

The conditional is used to express what *would happen* in the future, from a point in the past.

Has prometido varias veces que **iríamos** de compras hoy.	*You've promised several times that we would go shopping today.*
Supe que **habría** una conferencia y he venido para escucharla.	*I found out that there would be a lecture and I've come to listen to it.*

21.B.7 Conditional constructions

Conditional conjunctions: 16.D ▶
Conditional **si** clauses: 23.E.8

The conditional is used to express what would happen in hypothetical circumstances. The past subjunctive is used in the **si** clause.

The past subjunctive: 22.C ▶

Si no estudiaras, **perderías** el tiempo en la escuela.	*If you didn't study, you would waste your time at school.*
No me **quedaría** en casa el fin de semana si no tuviera que estudiar.	*I wouldn't stay home this weekend if I didn't have to study.*
Si pudierais viajar a cualquier parte, ¿adónde **iríais**?	*If you [pl.] could travel anywhere, where would you go?*

The conditional • **Chapter 21**

21.B.8 **Impersonal constructions** – *habría*

The conditional form of **haber, habría** (*there would be*), is used to express the possibility that something could happen or could exist.

Impersonal form of **haber**: 18.E.12, 20.C.6, 20.F.3, 21.D.4, 29.B.1

Con menor velocidad en las carreteras, **habría** menos accidentes.	*With slower speeds on the roads, there would be fewer accidents.*

21.C The conditional perfect

Condicional compuesto

The conditional perfect is formed with the conditional of the auxiliary verb **haber** + *past participle*.

Past participles: 19.A.1–2, 25.D

Conditional of *haber*		+	Regular past participles		
			-ar **verbs:** *-ado*	*-er* **and** *-ir* **verbs:** *-ido*	
			hablar	**querer**	**venir**
yo	**habría**				
tú/vos	**habrías**				
usted, él, ella	**habría**	+	habl**ado**	quer**ido**	ven**ido**
nosotros/as	**habríamos**				
vosotros/as	**habríais**				
ustedes, ellos/as	**habrían**				

As with other compound tenses, the past participle never varies in the conditional perfect. It always ends in **-o**.

21.D Use of the conditional perfect

Uso del condicional compuesto

21.D.1 **Imagined possibility or characterisitic**

The conditional perfect can be used to describe an imagined state in contrast to a present situation (what *would [not] have* happened).

Habríamos llegado más rápido en avión.	*We would have arrived faster by plane.*
Habrías estado mejor en otro trabajo.	*You would have been better off at another job.*
Me aseguraste que hoy, a esta hora, ya **habríamos salido** de compras.	*You assured me that today, by this time, we would already have gone out shopping.*
En tu lugar, yo no **habría gastado** tanto dinero en un auto.	*If I were you, I wouldn't have spent so much money on a car.*
La semana pasada **habrías podido** comprar mejores boletos.	*Last week you would have been able to buy better tickets.*

21.D.2 **Conditional constructions**

The conditional perfect can also be used to express what would have happened in a hypothetical past circumstance. The past perfect subjunctive is used in the **si** clause.

Conditional conjunctions: 16.D
Conditional **si** clauses: 23.E.8

Si hubieras estudiado, no **habrías perdido** el tiempo en la escuela.	*If you had studied, you wouldn't have wasted time in school.*
Te **habría invitado** si me hubieras dicho que querías ir.	*I would have invited you if you had told me you wanted to go.*

The past perfect subjunctive: 22.E

Modal verb phrases with ▶
the infinitive: 26.B.2

21.D.3 English *should have*

The conditional of **deber / tener que** + **haber** + *past participle* is used to express that something *should have been done.*

Deberías haber estudiado más si
  querías aprobar el examen.

*You should have studied more if you
  wanted to pass the exam.*

Tendrías que haber estudiado
  más si querías aprobar el examen.

*You should have studied / would have had to
  study more if you wanted to pass the exam.*

21.D.4 Impersonal constructions – *habría habido*

Impersonal form of **haber:** ▶
18.E.12, 20.C.6, 20.F.3,
21.B.8, 29.B.1

The impersonal conditional perfect form of **haber**, **habría** (*there would have been*), is used to express the possibility that something *could have existed* or *could have been.*

Con menor velocidad en las carreteras,
  habría habido menos accidentes.

*With slower speeds on the roads, there
  would have been fewer accidents.*

Práctica

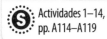

Actividades 1–14,
pp. A114–A119

The subjunctive
Subjuntivo

22.A Overview

Aspectos generales

Like English, Spanish has three verb moods: *imperative, indicative,* and *subjunctive.* The imperative is used to give commands, the indicative is used to express certainty and objectivity, and the subjunctive is used to express uncertainty and subjectivity, such as doubts, wishes, emotions, or imagined realities. The subjunctive mood is rarely used in English, but is essential in Spanish.

The Spanish name for the subjunctive, **subjuntivo**, refers to the dependency of the verb on another element, usually a *governing verb.* The governing verb in the sentence generally indicates whether the subjunctive will be used in the dependent clause. When the governing verb communicates a wish (**desear, necesitar, querer,** etc.), emotion (**desilusionar, gustar, enojar, temer,** etc.), doubt (**dudar, negar,** etc.), or request (**insistir, pedir, prohibir,** etc.), the subjunctive is used.

22.B The present subjunctive

Presente de subjuntivo

a. Most of the examples of *subjunctive* used in this chapter appear in groups of three sentences. The first sentence shows the subjunctive in a *noun* (**que**) clause. The second sentence shows the subjunctive in a relative, *adjective* clause, and the third sentence shows the subjunctive in an *adverbial* clause.

b. In **voseo** regions, the **vos** endings for the present subjunctive can vary. In some areas, the **vos** endings and the **tú** endings are the same: **Quiero que tú/vos salgas de aquí ya mismo**. This is the conjugation presented in this book. The most common **vos** endings for the present subjunctive are **-és** and **-ás: Quiero que caminés/comás/escribás**. Other regional variations exist as well.

22.B.1 Regular verbs

The following endings are added to the verb stem to form the present subjunctive. Note that **-er** and **-ir** verbs have the same endings and that for each type of verb, the **yo** and **usted/él/ella** forms are identical.

Present subjunctive · regular verbs			
Subject pronoun	**hablar** *to speak/talk*	**comer** *to eat*	**subir** *to go up, to climb*
yo	habl**e**	com**a**	sub**a**
tú/vos	habl**es**	com**as**	sub**as**
usted, él, ella	habl**e**	com**a**	sub**a**
nosotros/as	habl**emos**	com**amos**	sub**amos**
vosotros/as	habl**éis**	com**áis**	sub**áis**
ustedes, ellos/as	habl**en**	com**an**	sub**an**

No es bueno que **hables** cuando comes.   *It's not nice to talk with your mouth full (when you're eating).*

Quiero un perrito que no **coma** mucho.   *I want a little dog that doesn't eat much.*

¡Compre ya, antes de que **suban** los precios!   *Buy now, before the prices go up!*

The governing verb: When there is a main clause and a subordinate clause, there are two verbs. The verb in the main clause is the governing verb: 23.C

Noun (**que**) clause: 23.C
Adjective clause (relative clause): 23.D
Adverbial clause: 23.E

Regional variations: 22.H

Map of **voseo** regions in Latin America: p. B21

Verbs that are regular in the present indicative: 17.D.1

Notice that **-ar** verbs have endings that begin with **e-**, while **-er** and **-ir** verbs have endings that begin with **a-**.

Present indicative verbs
with spelling changes:
17.D.2 and 17.D.3
Pronunciación of
consonants: 1.C.6

Verb conjugation tables,
pp. B1–B20.
See verb patterns 23, 26,
35, 36, 54, 64.

Verbs like **corregir, elegir,
conseguir, proseguir,**
and **seguir** have a stem
change as well as a spelling
change: 17.D.4g–h

Stem-changing verbs: 17.D.4a–f

Verbs with a spelling change:
Verb conjugation tables,
pp. B1–B20. See verb
patterns 6, 10, 18, 27, 34,
41, 42, 45, 61, 71, 78.

Verbs with spelling changes in
the preterite: 18.B.2a

22.B.2 Verbs with a spelling change

Verbs with a spelling change in the **yo** form in the present indicative also have spelling changes in the present subjunctive in order to keep the same sound. The verb endings are regular.

a. **-ger, -gir, -guir, -uir** verbs with spelling changes in the present subjunctive:

Ending	Spelling change	Example	yo form Present indicative	yo form Present subjunctive
-ger	g → j	escoger	escojo	escoja
-gir	g → j	elegir	elijo	elija
-guir	gu → g	extinguir seguir	extingo sigo	extinga siga
-uir	i → y	construir	construyo	construya

Queremos que **se elija** a un nuevo alcalde. — *We want a new mayor to be elected.*

Los bomberos necesitan equipos que **extingan** mejor los incendios. — *The firemen need equipment that can extinguish fires better.*

Necesitamos fondos para que **se construyan** parques. — *We need funds to build parks.*

b. **-car, -gar, -guar, -zar** verbs with spelling changes in the present subjunctive:

The following verbs do not have spelling changes in the present indicative, but do have spelling changes in the present subjunctive, in order to maintain the verb's pronunciation when it is conjugated. The verb endings are regular. Note that several of these verbs also have a stem change.

Ending	Spelling change	Example	yo form Present indicative	yo form Present subjunctive
-car	c → qu	tocar	toco	toque
-gar	g → gu	llegar	llego	llegue
-guar	gu → gü	averiguar	averiguo	averigüe
-zar	z → c	alcanzar	alcanzo	alcance

More examples of **-car, -gar, -guar, -zar** verbs with spelling changes:

-car		-gar	
buscar	to look for	agregar	to add
machacar	to crush	entregar	to deliver/turn in
picar	to bite/sting	jugar (u → ue)	to play
roncar	to snore	negar (e → ie)	to deny/refuse
sacar	to take out	pagar	to pay (for)
salpicar	to splash	rogar (o → ue)	to beg
-guar		-zar	
apaciguar	to appease	abrazar	to hug
atestiguar	to attest	almorzar (o → ue)	to have lunch
desaguar	to drain	cruzar	to cross
menguar	to fade/wane	empezar (e → ie)	to start/begin
		enderezar	to straighten
		rezar	to pray

Pídele al pianista que **toque** nuestra canción.	Ask the pianist to play our song.
Quiero viajar en un tren que **llegue** al centro de París.	I want to take a train that arrives in downtown Paris.
Te ayudaré para que **alcances** tus metas.	I will help you so that you reach your goals.

c. **-cer** and **-cir** verbs with spelling changes in the present subjunctive:

Ending	Spelling change	Example	yo form	
			Present indicative	**Present subjunctive**
-cer	c → zc	cono**c**er	cono**zc**o	cono**zc**a
	c → z	conven**c**er	conven**z**o	conven**z**a
-cir	c → zc	condu**c**ir	condu**zc**o	condu**zc**a
	c → z	espar**c**ir	espar**z**o	espar**z**a

◀ Verb conjugation tables, pp. B1–B20. For **c:z**, see verb patterns 32, 72, 75; for **c-zc**, see verb patterns 14, 15, 43.

Necesito que **se traduzca** la carta.	I need the letter translated.
No hay nadie que **cueza** bien.	There isn't anyone who cooks well.
Ven a la fiesta para que **conozcas** a mis amigos.	Come to the party so you can meet my friends.

◀ Other **-cer**, **-cir** verbs: 17.D.2a

◀ Verbs like **cocer** and **torcer** have a spelling change and a stem change.

22.B.3 **Verbs with accents**

Verbs that end in **-iar** and **-uar** take an accent in the present subjunctive just as in the present indicative.

◀ Present indicative: Verb conjugation tables, pp. B1–B20. For **i:í**, see verb patterns 29, 34, 53; for **u:ú**, see verb patterns 37, 57, 59.

Ending	Spelling change	Example	yo form	
			Present indicative	**Present subjunctive**
-iar	i → í	env**i**ar	env**í**o	env**í**e
-uar	u → ú	contin**u**ar	contin**ú**e	contin**ú**e

◀ Present indicative of **-iar**, **-uar** verbs: 17.D.3b

Other -iar, -uar **verbs**			
acent**uar**	to emphasize	enfr**iar**	to cool down / chill
act**uar**	to act	evac**uar**	to evacuate
ampl**iar**	to enlarge/extend	eval**uar**	to evaluate
ans**iar**	to long for	grad**uar**se	to graduate
conf**iar**	to confide/trust	gu**iar**	to guide
cr**iar**	to grow	insin**uar**	to insinuate
deval**uar**	to devalue	perpet**uar**	to perpetuate
efect**uar**	to carry out / execute	sit**uar**	to locate

◀ **Prohibir** and **europeizar** also have an **i:í** change; **rehusar** and **reunir** also have an **u:ú** change.

Es necesario que **envíes** tu solicitud a tiempo.	It's necessary that you send in your application on time.
Queremos invertir en monedas que no **se devalúen**.	We want to invest in currencies that won't be devalued.
Cuando **te gradúes**, tendrás mejor sueldo.	When you graduate, you'll get a better salary.

22.B.4 **Verbs with irregular** yo **forms in the present indicative**

When the **yo** form is irregular in the present indicative, the present subjunctive is also irregular. The endings are regular.

Irregular verbs are found alphabetically in the verb conjugation tables, pp. B1–B20. Irregular verbs in the present indicative: 17.D.5

Infinitive		yo form	
		Present indicative	**Present subjunctive**
caber	*to fit*	**quep**o	**quep**a
caer	*to fall*	**caig**o	**caig**a
decir	*to say/tell*	**dig**o	**dig**a
hacer	*to do/make*	**hag**o	**hag**a
oír	*to hear*	**oig**o	**oig**a
poner	*to put/place*	**pong**o	**pong**a
salir	*to go out*	**salg**o	**salg**a
tener	*to have*	**teng**o	**teng**a
traer	*to bring*	**traig**o	**traig**a
valer	*to be worth*	**valg**o	**valg**a
venir	*to come*	**veng**o	**veng**a
ver	*to see*	**ve**o	**ve**a

Other verbs like **decir**, **tener**, **venir**: 17.D.5b
Other verbs like **hacer**, **poner**, **traer**: 17.D.5a

¡Espero que **haga** un poco de sol hoy!   *I hope there's some sunshine today!*

Compraremos un auto que no **valga** mucho.   *We will buy a car that doesn't cost much.*

Venid a visitarme cuando **tengáis** tiempo.   *Come and visit me when you [pl.] have time.*

22.B.5   Stem-changing *-ar* and *-er* verbs

Stem-changing verbs in the present indicative: 17.D.4

All **-ar** and **-er** verbs that have stem changes in the present indicative also have them in the present subjunctive. As with the present indicative, the change takes place in all forms except **nosotros/as** and **vosotros/as**. The endings stay the same.

a. Conjugation of **-ar** and **-er** verbs with stem change **e → ie**:

	pensar *to think*	**querer** *to want/love*
yo	p**ie**nse	qu**ie**ra
tú/vos	p**ie**nses	qu**ie**ras
usted, él, ella	p**ie**nse	qu**ie**ra
nosotros/as	pensemos	queramos
vosotros/as	penséis	queráis
ustedes, ellos/as	p**ie**nsen	qu**ie**ran

Verb conjugation tables, pp. B1–B20. See verb patterns 27, 28, 45, 49, 56.

Other verbs with stem change *e → ie*			
-ar **verbs**		*-er* **verbs**	
atrav**e**sar	*to cross/go through*	asc**e**nder	*to ascend/rise*
cal**e**ntar	*to warm up / heat*	at**e**nder	*to pay attention*
c**e**rrar	*to close*	def**e**nder	*to defend*
com**e**nzar (**z → c**)	*to start*	desc**e**nder	*to descend/drop*
conf**e**sar	*to confess*	enc**e**nder	*to light / switch on*
desp**e**rtar	*to wake up*	ent**e**nder	*to understand*
emp**e**zar (**z → c**)	*to start*	ext**e**nder	*to extend/spread*
gob**e**rnar	*to govern*	p**e**rder	*to lose/miss*
n**e**gar	*to deny/refuse*	trasc**e**nder	*to become known*
recom**e**ndar	*to recommend*	v**e**rter	*to pour/spill*

¡Esperamos que nos **entendáis**!

Voy a conseguir un reloj que **me despierte** con música.

Enciende la chimenea para que **nos calentemos** un poco.

We hope you [pl.] understand us!

I'm going to get a clock that will wake me up with music.

Light the fire so we can warm up a bit.

b. Conjugation of **-ar** and **-er** verbs with stem change **o → ue**:

	contar *to relate/count*	**volver** *to return*
yo	cuente	vuelva
tú/vos	cuentes	vuelvas
usted, él, ella	cuente	vuelva
nosotros/as	contemos	volvamos
vosotros/as	contéis	volváis
ustedes, ellos/as	cuenten	vuelvan

Other verbs with stem change *o → ue*			
-ar **verbs**		*-er* **verbs**	
almorzar (**z → c**)	*to have lunch*	devolver	*to give back*
costar	*to cost / be difficult*	llover	*to rain*
encontrar	*to find*	mover	*to move*
mostrar	*to indicate/show*	poder	*to be able to*
probar	*to try/taste*	promover	*to promote*
recordar	*to remember*	remover	*to remove/stir*
soñar	*to dream*	resolver	*to resolve*
volar	*to fly*	soler	*to usually do*

Verb conjugation tables, pp. B1–B20. See verb patterns 6, 9, 16, 44, 50, 61, 67, 72.

More **o:ue** stem-changing verbs: **rogar, sonar, morder, torcer**

Es necesario que **recuerdes** tu contraseña.

Haré lo que **pueda** para ayudarte.

Debes tener una buena educación aunque te **cueste** mucho.

You need to remember your password.

I'll do what I can to help you.

You should have a good education even if it's hard work / difficult for you.

c. The verb **oler** (*to smell*) is a unique **o → ue** verb.

h**ue**la, h**ue**las, h**ue**la, **o**lamos, **o**láis, h**ue**lan

Me gusta que la casa **huela** a flores.

I like the house to smell of flowers.

Verb conjugation tables, pp. B1–B20. See verb pattern 47.

22.B.6 Stem-changing *-ir* verbs

All **-ir** verbs with a stem change in the present indicative have the same one in the present subjunctive. These verbs also have a stem change in the **nosotros/as** and **vosotros/as** forms.

Stem-changing verbs in the present indicative: 17.D.4

	e → ie **and** *e → i* **preferir** *to prefer*	*o → ue* **and** *o → u* **dormir** *to sleep*	*e → i* **pedir** *to ask for*
yo	prefiera	duerma	pida
tú/vos	prefieras	duermas	pidas
usted, él, ella	prefiera	duerma	pida
nosotros/as	prefiramos	durmamos	pidamos
vosotros/as	prefiráis	durmáis	pidáis
ustedes, ellos/as	prefieran	duerman	pidan

Verb conjugation tables,
pp. B1–B20. See verb patterns
25, 26, 48, 58, 64, 65.

More e:i verbs: **conseguir,
corregir, despedir,
elegir, medir,
sonreír, vestirse**

Other -*ir* verbs with stem changes					
e → ie and *e → i*		*o → ue* and *o → u*		*e → i*	
di**v**ertirse	to have fun	**m**orir	to die	re**í**r	to laugh
herir	to hurt			repe**t**ir	to repeat
mentir	to lie			se**g**uir	to follow
sentirse	to feel			ser**v**ir	to serve

Me alegra que **te sientas** mejor.
Prepara el plato que **prefieras**.
Acuesta al niño para que **duerma**.

I'm glad you feel better.
Prepare whichever dish you prefer.
Put the boy to bed so that he'll sleep.

22.B.7 The verbs *adquirir* and *jugar*

The verb **adquirir** has the stem change **i → ie**, but does not have a stem change in the **nosotros/as** and **vosotros/as** forms like other stem-changing **-ir** verbs. The verb **jugar** is an **-ar** verb with a **u → ue** stem change and the spelling change **g → gu** in the stem.

Verb conjugation tables,
pp. B1–B20. See verb
patterns 4, 41.

Adquirir and **jugar** in
the present indicative:
17.D.4e–f

The verb **inquirir** is
conjugated like **adquirir** in
the present subjunctive.

	i → ie **adquirir** *to acquire*	*u → ue* **jugar** *to play*
yo	adqu**ie**ra	j**ue**g**u**e
tú/vos	adqu**ie**ras	j**ue**g**u**es
usted, él, ella	adqu**ie**ra	j**ue**g**u**e
nosotros/as	adquiramos	ju**gu**emos
vosotros/as	adquiráis	ju**gu**éis
ustedes, ellos/as	adqu**ie**ran	j**ue**g**u**en

Es fantástico que mi equipo **juegue** hoy.
Apoyaremos al equipo que mejor **juegue**.
Necesitamos capital para que el equipo **adquiera** más jugadores.

It's fantastic that my team is playing today.
We're going to support the team that plays the best.
We need capital so that the team acquires/gets more players.

22.B.8 Completely irregular verbs in the present subjunctive

Diacritical marks: 1.E.6b

The following verbs are irregular in the present subjunctive. Note that **dé** has an accent in order to distinguish the subjunctive form of the verb **dar** from the preposition **de**.

Verb conjugation tables,
pp. B1–B20. See verb
patterns 19, 33, 38.

Verbs that are irregular
in the present
indicative: 17.D.5c–d

	dar *to give*	**estar** *to be*	**haber** *(auxiliary verb)*
yo	**dé**	**esté**	**haya**
tú/vos	**des**	**estés**	**hayas**
usted, él, ella	**dé**	**esté**	**haya**
nosotros/as	**demos**	**estemos**	**hayamos**
vosotros/as	**deis**	**estéis**	**hayáis**
ustedes, ellos/as	**den**	**estén**	**hayan**

	ir *to go*	**saber** *to know*	**ser** *to be*
yo	**vaya**	**sepa**	**sea**
tú/vos	**vayas**	**sepas**	**seas**
usted, él, ella	**vaya**	**sepa**	**sea**
nosotros/as	**vayamos**	**sepamos**	**seamos**
vosotros/as	**vayáis**	**sepáis**	**seáis**
ustedes, ellos/as	**vayan**	**sepan**	**sean**

Verb conjugation tables, pp. B1–B20. See verb patterns 40, 62, 66.

These six irregular verbs have **yo** forms in the present indicative that do not end in **-o**.

Es estupendo que **seas** profesor.　　　*It's great that you're a teacher.*

Buscamos un profesor que **sepa**　　　*We're looking for a teacher who knows how*
　hablar español.　　　　　　　　　　　*to speak Spanish.*

Puedes empezar en cuanto **estés** listo.　*You can begin as soon as you're ready.*

22.C The past subjunctive

Pretérito imperfecto de subjuntivo

The past subjunctive is also called the imperfect subjunctive.

22.C.1 Regular verbs

The following endings are added to the verb stem to form the past subjunctive. The **-ra** and **-se** endings are equal in meaning, but the **-ra** ending is more common, especially in Latin America. Note that **nosotros/as** is the only conjugated form with a written accent and that **-er** and **-ir** verbs have the same endings.

Regular verbs: Verb conjugation tables, p. B5

	hablar *to talk*	**comer** *to eat*	**subir** *to go up*
yo	habl**ara** habl**ase**	com**iera** com**iese**	sub**iera** sub**iese**
tú/vos	habl**aras** habl**ases**	com**ieras** com**ieses**	sub**ieras** sub**ieses**
usted, él, ella	habl**ara** habl**ase**	com**iera** com**iese**	sub**iera** sub**iese**
nosotros/as	habl**áramos** habl**ásemos**	com**iéramos** com**iésemos**	sub**iéramos** sub**iésemos**
vosotros/as	habl**arais** habl**aseis**	com**ierais** com**ieseis**	sub**ierais** sub**ieseis**
ustedes, ellos/as	habl**aran** habl**asen**	com**ieran** com**iesen**	sub**ieran** sub**iesen**

Note that the **yo** and **usted/él/ella** forms are the same in the past subjunctive as well as in the present subjunctive.

Me extrañó que nadie **hablara/hablase**　*I thought it was strange that nobody spoke*
　español en la clase.　　　　　　　　　　*Spanish in the class.*

Quería viajar en un teleférico que me　　*I wanted to ride in a cable car that could take me*
　llevara/llevase hasta la cima de la montaña.　*up to the top of the mountain.*

Vimos el menú y salimos de la cafetería sin　*We looked at the menu and then left the cafeteria*
　que nadie **comiera/comiese** nada.　　　*without eating anything.*

22.C.2 Irregular verbs

Many verbs are irregular in the past subjunctive. Irregularities are primarily stem changes and consonant changes in the stem. The endings, however, follow a regular pattern. Note that all irregular verbs in the **ustedes/ellos/ellas** form of the preterite will also be irregular in the past subjunctive. The most important irregularities are listed in this section.

Stem-changing verbs in the preterite: 18.B.3
Stem-changing -ir verbs in the present subjunctive: 22.B.6

a. Verbs with stem changes **e → i** and **o → u**:

	e → i **pedir** to ask for	**o → u** **dormir** to sleep
yo	pidiera/pidiese	durmiera/durmiese
tú/vos	pidieras/pidieses	durmieras/durmieses
usted, él, ella	pidiera/pidiese	durmiera/durmiese
nosotros/as	pidiéramos/pidiésemos	durmiéramos/durmiésemos
vosotros/as	pidierais/pidieseis	durmierais/durmieseis
ustedes, ellos/as	pidieran/pidiesen	durmieran/durmiesen

Verb conjugation tables, pp. B1–B20. See verb patterns 25, 26, 48, 58, 64, 65.

Other -*ir* verbs with stem changes		
o → u	morir	*to die*
e → i	divertirse	*to have fun*
	herir	*to hurt*
	mentir	*to lie*
	reír	*to laugh*
	sentirse	*to feel*

¡Fue un éxito que la gente **se riera/riese** tanto!	*It was great that people laughed so much!*
¡Necesitábamos un espectáculo que **nos divirtiera/divirtiese** de verdad!	*We needed a show that truly entertained us!*
Todo estaba planeado para que **nos sintiéramos/sintiésemos** bien.	*Everything was planned in such a way as to make us feel good.*

b. Verbs with irregular **u**-stem:

Verb conjugation tables, pp. B1–B20. See verb patterns 7, 12, 33, 38, 50, 51, 62, 69.

Verbs with irregular u-stem in the preterite: 18.B.4a

Other verbs like **poner**, **tener**: 17.D.5a–b

Infinitive	Stem
andar	**anduv-**
caber	**cup-**
estar	**estuv-**
haber	**hub-**
poder	**pud-**
poner	**pus-**
saber	**sup-**
tener	**tuv-**

andar *to walk*	
yo	**anduv**iera/**anduv**iese
tú/vos	**anduv**ieras/**anduv**ieses
usted, él, ella	**anduv**iera/**anduv**iese
nosotros/as	**anduv**iéramos/**anduv**iésemos
vosotros/as	**anduv**ierais/**anduv**ieseis
ustedes, ellos/as	**anduv**ieran/**anduv**iesen

¡Me gustaría que **tuviéramos/tuviésemos** más dinero!	*I wish we had more money!*
Necesitábamos un auto que **estuviera/estuviese** en perfecto estado.	*We needed a car in perfect condition.*
Compré un auto grande para que **cupiera/cupiese** toda la familia.	*I bought a big car so that the whole family would fit.*

c. Verbs with irregular **i**-stem:

Infinitive	Stem
dar	**di-**
hacer	**hic-**
querer	**quis-**
venir	**vin-**

hacer *to do/make*	
yo	**hic**iera/**hic**iese
tú/vos	**hic**ieras/**hic**ieses
usted, él, ella	**hic**iera/**hic**iese
nosotros/as	**hic**iéramos/**hic**iésemos
vosotros/as	**hic**ierais/**hic**ieseis
ustedes, ellos/as	**hic**ieran/**hic**iesen

Verb conjugation tables, pp. B1–B20. See verb patterns 19, 39, 56, 76.

Verbs with irregular **i**-stem in the preterite: 18.B.4b

Other verbs like **hacer**, **venir**: 17.D.5a–b

Fue muy molesto que no **vinieras/vinieses** a la reunión.

It was very annoying that you didn't come to the meeting.

No había nada que yo **quisiera/quisiese**.

There was nothing that I wanted.

Te llamé para que me **dieras/dieses** una explicación.

I called you to get an explanation.

d. Verbs with irregular **y**-stem: **-caer, -eer, -uir, oír**

Infinitive	Stem
caer	ca**y-**
leer	le**y-**
concluir	conclu**y-**
oír	o**y-**

caer *to fall*	
yo	**ca**yera/**cay**ese
tú/vos	**ca**yeras/**cay**eses
usted, él, ella	**ca**yera/**cay**ese
nosotros/as	**ca**yéramos/**cay**ésemos
vosotros/as	**ca**yerais/**cay**eseis
ustedes, ellos/as	**ca**yeran/**cay**esen

Verb conjugation tables, pp. B1–B20. See verb patterns 13, 17, 23, 46.

Verbs with **i:y** spelling change in the preterite: 18.B.2b

Other verbs with the same changes			
Other verbs like *caer*			
decaer	*to decay*	recaer	*to have a relapse*
Other verbs like *leer*			
creer	*to believe/think*	proveer	*to supply/provide*
poseer	*to have/own*	releer	*to read again*
Other verbs like *concluir*			
constituir	*to constitute*	huir	*to escape/flee*
construir	*to build/construct*	incluir	*to include*
contribuir	*to contribute*	influir	*to influence*
destituir	*to dismiss*	intuir	*to sense*
destruir	*to destroy*	recluir	*to imprison*
disminuir	*to diminish*	reconstruir	*to reconstruct*
distribuir	*to distribute*	sustituir	*to substitute/replace*

Fue importante que **reconstruyeran/reconstruyesen** la ciudad antigua.

It was important to rebuild the ancient city.

No había nada que **disminuyera/disminuyese** la importancia del proyecto.

There was nothing that would/could diminish the project's significance.

Trabajamos mucho para que el proyecto **concluyera/concluyese** con éxito.

We worked a lot so that the project would be successful.

e. Verbs with irregular **j**-stem:

Verb conjugation tables,
pp. B1–B20. See verb
patterns 14, 20, 73.

Verbs with irregular **j**-stem
in the preterite: 18.B.4c

Other verbs like **decir**,
traer: 17.D.5a–b

Infinitive	Stem
decir	dij-
traer	traj-
conducir	conduj-
introducir	introduj-
producir	produj-
reducir	reduj-
traducir	traduj-

decir *to say/tell*	
yo	dijera/dijese
tú/vos	dijeras/dijeses
usted, él, ella	dijera/dijese
nosotros/as	dijéramos/dijésemos
vosotros/as	dijerais/dijeseis
ustedes, ellos/as	dijeran/dijesen

Fue un milagro que no **se produjera/produjese** un accidente.

Fue un milagro que no **se produjera/produjese** un accidente.   *It was amazing that there wasn't an accident.*

No había nadie que **condujera/condujese** bien.   *There wasn't anybody who could drive well.*

No te creería aunque **dijeras/dijeses** la verdad.   *I wouldn't believe you even if you were telling the truth.*

f. The past subjunctive of **ir** and **ser**:

Verb conjugation tables,
pp. B1–B20. See verb
patterns 40, 66.

Verbs that are irregular
in the preterite: 18.B.5

You can use context to figure
out which verb is meant.

yo	**fuera/fuese**
tú/vos	**fueras/fueses**
usted, él, ella	**fuera/fuese**
nosotros/as	**fuéramos/fuésemos**
vosotros/as	**fuerais/fueseis**
ustedes, ellos/as	**fueran/fuesen**

El director nos pidió que **fuéramos/fuésemos** a la reunión de padres de familia.   *The principal asked us to go to the parents' meeting.*

Yo quería comprar un auto que **fuera/fuese** seguro y confiable.   *I wanted to buy a car that was safe and reliable.*

Quería llamarte antes de que **fuera/fuese** demasiado tarde.   *I wanted to call you before it was too late.*

22.D The present perfect subjunctive

Pretérito perfecto de subjuntivo

The present perfect subjunctive is formed with the present subjunctive of the auxiliary verb **haber** and the past participle of the main verb.

Present subjunctive
of **haber**: 22.B.8
Regular and irregular past
participles: 19.A.1 and 19.A.2

Present subjunctive of *haber*		+	Past participle		
			-ar **verbs:** *-ado*	*-er* **and** *-ir* **verbs:** *-ido*	
			hablar	querer	venir
yo	**haya**				
tú/vos	**hayas**				
usted, él, ella	**haya**	+	**hablado**	**querido**	**venido**
nosotros/as	**hayamos**				
vosotros/as	**hayáis**				
ustedes, ellos/as	**hayan**				

Espero que **hayas tenido** un buen viaje.

En mi escuela no hay nadie que **haya reprobado** el examen.

Trabajarás mejor cuando **hayas instalado** una buena conexión a Internet.

I hope you have had a good trip.

In my school, there isn't anybody who has failed the exam.

You will be able to work better when you have installed a good Internet connection.

22.E The past perfect subjunctive

Pretérito pluscuamperfecto de subjuntivo

The past perfect subjunctive is formed with the past subjunctive of the auxiliary verb **haber** (**hubiera/hubiese**) and the past participle of the main verb.

Past subjunctive of **haber**: 22.C.2b
Regular and irregular past participles: 19.A.1 and 19.A.2

Past perfect subjunctive *haber*		+	Past participle		
			-ar **verbs:** *-ado*	*-er* **and** *-ir* **verbs:** *-ido*	
			hablar	**querer**	**venir**
yo	**hub**iera/**hub**iese				
tú/vos	**hub**ieras/**hub**ieses				
usted, él, ella	**hub**iera/**hub**iese	+	**hablado**	**querido**	**venido**
nosotros/as	**hub**iéramos/**hub**iésemos				
vosotros/as	**hub**ierais/**hub**ieseis				
ustedes, ellos/as	**hub**ieran/**hub**iesen				

No pensé que **hubieras/hubieses tenido** un buen viaje.

No hubo nadie que **hubiera/hubiese reprobado** el examen.

Trabajarías mejor si **hubieras/hubieses instalado** una buena conexión a Internet.

I didn't think you had had a good trip.

There wasn't anybody who had failed the exam.

You would work better if you had installed a good Internet connection.

22.F The future subjunctive

Futuro de subjuntivo

The future subjunctive is used in modern Spanish only in legal texts, laws, and regulations.

a. The future subjunctive is formed with the same verb stem as the past subjunctive and the following endings.

Past subjunctive: 22.C

	hablar *to talk*	**comer** *to eat*	**subir** *to go up, to climb*
yo	hablar**e**	comier**e**	subier**e**
tú/vos	hablar**es**	comier**es**	subier**es**
usted, él, ella	hablar**e**	comier**e**	subier**e**
nosotros/as	hablár**emos**	comiér**emos**	subiér**emos**
vosotros/as	hablar**eis**	comier**eis**	subier**eis**
ustedes, ellos/as	hablar**en**	comier**en**	subier**en**

b. Irregular verbs have the same irregularities in the verb stems as the past subjunctive. The endings are the same as they are for regular verbs: **fuere, tuviere, hubiere, hiciere**, etc.

c. In everyday speech, the future subjunctive appears only in proverbs or idiomatic expressions. It also appears in formal speeches of a legal nature.

Habrá multa cualquiera que **fuere** el exceso de velocidad.	*There will be a fine whatever the speed limit violation may be.*
Adonde **fueres,** haz lo que **vieres**.	*When in Rome, do as the Romans do.*
Sea quien **fuere** el embajador, la situación no cambiará.	*Whoever the ambassador is, the situation will not change.*

22.G The future perfect subjunctive

The future subjunctive: 22.F
Regular and irregular
past participles: 19.A.1
and 19.A.2

Futuro perfecto de subjuntivo

The future perfect subjunctive is formed with the future subjunctive of **haber** and the past participle of the verb: **hubiere hablado**, **hubieres hablado**, etc. This verb tense is used in legal texts, but is not common.

Se aceptarán las solicitudes siempre y cuando **hubieren llegado** antes de expirar el plazo.	*Applications will be accepted as long as they have arrived before the deadline.*

22.H Regional variations

Variaciones regionales

Voseo: 22.B.b

The use of **vos** forms in the present subjunctive varies regionally. Here are the three main forms.

	1. Voseo (using **tú** form)	2. Voseo (most **voseo** countries)	3. Voseo (Chile)
amar	**ames**	**amés**	**amí(s)**
comer	**comas**	**comás**	**comái(s)**
recibir	**recibas**	**recibás**	**recibái(s)**

Option 2 is common in most **voseo** countries, especially in Central America and the Andes of South America. In Argentina, it coexists with option 1, while option 2 is the most common for informal negative commands (which use the present subjunctive form): **no vayás; no digás**. Option 3 is used primarily in Chile.

Negative **vos** commands: 24.D.1b

Práctica

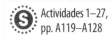
Actividades 1–27, pp. A119–A128

Use of the subjunctive

Uso del subjuntivo

23.A Overview

Aspectos generales

The use of the subjunctive in Spanish follows a fairly regular pattern, depending on the type of clause in which it appears.

23.A.1 Independent clauses

The use of the subjunctive in independent clauses is very limited and happens mainly in clauses with adverbs of doubt and possibility (where the indicative is also possible) or in exclamations.

23.A.2 Subordinate clauses

The subjunctive is used primarily in subordinate clauses governed by a main clause. An understanding of the basic structure of subordinate clauses in Spanish is important for using the subjunctive correctly.

There are three main types of subordinate clauses in which the subjunctive is used:

a. *noun* clauses

b. relative, or *adjective*, clauses

c. *adverbial* clauses

Since the subjunctive is rarely used in English, the translations of examples in this chapter are written to show the nuances of the subjunctive meaning in Spanish.

◀ Here's an example of the subjunctive in English: *If I were a rich man…*

23.B The subjunctive in independent clauses

El subjuntivo en oraciones independientes

23.B.1 Probability, doubt

In independent clauses with adverbs or other expressions of doubt or possibility such as **quizá(s), tal vez, posiblemente**, and **probablemente**, both the indicative and the subjunctive can be used. The verb mood used expresses the degree of probability of the outcome. The indicative expresses a higher probability than the subjunctive.

◀ Expressions of doubt with the subjunctive in **que** clauses: 23.C.6
Tal vez/quizás: 10.F.1d

Subjunctive	Indicative
Posiblemente llegue tarde a casa hoy. *I might get home late today.*	**Posiblemente** llego tarde a casa hoy. *I'll probably be home late today.*
Quizás fuera gripe lo que tenías. *Maybe you had the flu.*	**Quizás era** gripe lo que tenías. *You probably had the flu.*

◀ **A lo mejor** (*maybe, perhaps*) is a very common expression for possibility in everyday language.

23.B.2 Exclamations

a. The subjunctive is *always* used in simple wish clauses in the form of exclamations, usually with **vivir**. In English, this is mostly expressed with *hurrah/hooray, go,* or *long live!*

¡**Viva** el Barcelona!	*Go, Barcelona!*
¡**Vivan** los nuevos estudiantes!	*Hooray for the new students!*
¡**Viva** España!	*Long live Spain! / Hooray for Spain!*

Such simple exclamations are accompanied by **que** when expressing wishes or requests. These exclamations can be interpreted as containing an implied verb of will (**querer, desear, esperar**) that governs what is said.

¡Que se besen los novios!	*The bride and groom may now kiss!*
¡Que llegue pronto mi amigo!	*I hope my friend arrives soon!*

These simple wish clauses are common in social contexts where expressions of good (or bad) wishes are given.

¡Que tengas un feliz viaje!	*Have a good trip!*
¡Que te vaya bien en el examen!	*I hope the exam goes well!*
¡Que os divirtáis mucho!	*Have a lot of fun!*
¡Que cumplas muchos años más!	*Many happy returns!*
¡Que te parta un rayo!	*Damn you!*

b. The word **ojalá** comes from the Arabic *in sha'a Allah* meaning *if Allah/God wills*. It is used in the same way as *God willing* in English and expresses a strong desire that something happen. **Ojalá** is used in noun clauses and is *always* followed by a verb in the *subjunctive*.

Note that the use of **que** is optional.

Future	**¡Ojalá** (que) tengas un buen viaje!	*I hope you have a good trip!*
Past	**¡Ojalá** (que) hayas tenido un buen viaje!	*I hope you've had a good trip!*
Contrary to fact	**¡Ojalá** (que) hubieras tenido un buen viaje!	*I wish you'd had a good trip!*

23.C The subjunctive in noun clauses

El subjuntivo en subordinadas sustantivas

That clauses are also called *noun clauses* because they act like nouns and can be the *subject, direct object,* or *indirect object* of the sentence. Noun clauses in Spanish start with the conjunction **que**, which can never be omitted the way *that* can in English.

Que clauses: 16.C.1

The verb in the main clause is the governing verb: **espero**.

Main clause	Subordinate clause
Espero	**que** estés bien.
I hope	*(that)* you are well.

The use of the subjunctive in Spanish noun clauses is always dependent on the meaning of the governing verb. This verb can fall into one of various verb groups, each with its own rules for the use of subjunctive. The following are the most important verb groups.

23.C.1 Verbs that express will, influence, or necessity

If there's no change in subject, use the infinitive: **Quiero ir al cine**.

a. The *subjunctive* is always used in noun clauses when the main verb either directly or indirectly expresses *will, influence,* or *necessity*. Examples of this type of verb follow.

aconsejar	*to advise*	permitir	*to permit/allow*
desear	*to desire*	preferir	*to prefer*
exigir	*to require/demand*	prohibir	*to prohibit*
gustar	*to like*	proponer	*to propose*
impedir	*to prevent*	querer	*to want*
insistir	*to insist*	recomendar	*to recommend*
mandar	*to order*	requerir	*to require / call for*

necesitar	to need	rogar	to beg
oponerse	to oppose	solicitar	to request
ordenar	to order/arrange	sugerir	to suggest
pedir	to ask (for)	suplicar	to plead

Te aconsejo que no **fumes**.	I advise you not to smoke.
Le pido a usted que me **ayude**.	I'm asking you to help me.
Te sugiero que no **compres** algo caro.	I suggest you don't buy anything expensive.
Recomendamos que **revise** su correo.	We recommend that you check your mail.
Le solicito que me **envíe** el cheque.	I request that you send me the check.
Os ruego que me **prestéis** dinero.	I beg you [pl.] to lend me money.

◀ Note that indirect object pronouns are used with many of these verbs of will and influence.

b. The expression **hacer que** expresses influence and should be followed by the subjunctive.

La nieve **hará que** el tráfico **se vuelva** imposible.	The snow will make traffic impossible.

c. The expression **el hecho de que** (*the fact that*) is used mostly with the *subjunctive*. This also applies to the shortened form **(el) que** (*that*). Note that **el que** in this context is not the same as the relative pronoun **el que** (*the one who/that*).

◀ Relative pronouns: 15.A.2

El (hecho de) que suban los precios es bastante común.	(The fact) That prices go up is quite common.
Que todo **sea** tan caro es producto de la globalización.	That everything is so expensive is a result of globalization.
El que te gusten los medios sociales es muy positivo.	(The fact) That you like social media is very positive.

d. The expression **es que** (*it's that*) describes a causal relationship. The *indicative* is used in affirmative clauses and the *subjunctive* in negative subordinate clauses. This expression is a shortened form of **lo que ocurre/pasa/sucede es que** (*the thing is that*).

No **es que estemos** aburridos, **es que tenemos** que irnos ya.	It's not that we are bored; it's just that we have to go now.
No **es que** yo no **quiera** ayudarte, **es que** no **puedo**.	It's not that I don't want to help you; I just can't.

23.C.2 *Decir* **and other reporting verbs**

◀ Indirect discourse: Ch. 31

The verb **decir** and a few others can convey information or express a wish or a request. With these verbs, the *subjunctive* is used when giving an order or when asking for something, and the *indicative* is used when conveying information. The following are examples of reporting verbs.

◀ Reporting information and commands: 31.B.2

advertir	to warn	indicar	to indicate
decir	to say/tell	insistir	to insist

Subjunctive	Indicative
Isabel dice que **vengas** pronto. *Isabel says that you must come soon.*	Isabel dice que **vienes** pronto. *Isabel says that you are coming soon.*
La luz roja indica que **te detengas**. *The red light tells you to stop.*	La luz roja indica que **debes** detenerte. *The red light indicates that you should stop.*
Mis amigos insisten en que **compre** un auto. *My friends insist that I buy a car.*	Mis amigos insisten en que **necesito** un auto. *My friends insist that I need a car.*

Verbs like **gustar**: 17.B.4

23.C.3 Verbs that express emotions

a. The subjunctive is always used in subordinate clauses when the verb in the main clause expresses an emotion or an emotional reaction to something. This happens primarily with a verb like **gustar**. The subordinate clause describes what a person likes, or finds amazing, frustrating, etc.

Main clause	Subordinate clause
Me alegra	que **tengamos** tantos días libres.
I'm pleased/happy/delighted	*that we have so many free days.*

Verbs in this group:

aburrir	*to bore*	enfadar	*to anger*
agradar	*to please*	entristecer	*to sadden*
alarmar	*to alarm*	entusiasmar	*to excite/delight*
alegrar	*to please*	extrañar	*to surprise*
apenar	*to sadden*	fascinar	*to fascinate/like very much*
asustar	*to frighten/scare*	fastidiar	*to irritate*
complacer	*to satisfy/please*	frustrar	*to frustrate*
convenir	*to suit*	gustar	*to like*
desesperar	*to exasperate*	importar	*to matter / care about*
disgustar	*to disgust*	indignar	*to infuriate / to make indignant/angry*
divertir	*to amuse*	interesar	*to interest*
doler	*to hurt*	irritar	*to irritate*
emocionar	*to excite*	molestar	*to annoy/bother*
encantar	*to enjoy/love*	sorprender	*to surprise*

¿Os molesta que **abra** la ventana?   *Do you [pl.] mind if I open the window?*
Nos conviene que la reunión **sea** el martes.   *It's fine with / better for us that the meeting be on Tuesday.*
Me gusta que me **enseñes** a hablar español.   *I like that you teach me to speak Spanish.*

b. Several of these verbs (but not all) can also be used without a subjunctive clause.

Note that the verbs in the first two examples are reflexive.

Me alegro de/por tu éxito.   *I'm pleased about your success.*
Nos interesamos por el español.   *We're interested in Spanish.*
Nuestros clientes **nos importan**.   *Our clients are important to us.*

c. The verbs **temer** (*to fear, to be afraid of*) and **esperar** (*to hope, to expect*) are used with the *subjunctive* in negative and affirmative clauses.

La gente **teme** que **suban** los precios.   *People fear that prices will go up.*
No espero que siempre **tengas** tiempo para todo.   *I don't expect you to always have time for everything.*

d. The verb **temer** can also mean *to believe*. With this meaning, the *indicative* can be used with **temer** in affirmative clauses. The verb **esperar** can also express a thought rather than an intention or expectation. In this case, the *indicative* is used (except the present indicative, which can't be used in this case).

Subjunctive	Indicative
La gente **teme** que **suban** los precios. *People are worried that prices will go up.*	La gente **teme** que **subirán** los precios. *People believe (fearfully) that prices will go up.*
Esperaba que **tuvierais** tiempo en diciembre. *I hoped you [pl.] would have time in December.*	**Esperaba** que **tendríais** tiempo en diciembre. *I imagined you [pl.] would have time in December.*

e. The expression **esperar a que** (*to wait for something to happen*) always requires the subjunctive.

Espero con alegría **a que llegue** el día de la boda.   *I'm very much looking forward to the wedding day.*
No esperaré a que te calmes para darte la noticia.   *I won't wait for you to calm down to give you the news.*

23.C.4 **The verb** *sentir* **and other sense verbs**

a. When **sentir** is used with the meaning *to be/feel sorry* in affirmative and negative main clauses, the subjunctive must be used in the subordinate clause. Used with the indicative, **sentir** means *to have a feeling, to feel, to sense.*

Subjunctive	Indicative
Sentimos que no **puedas** asistir al seminario. *We're sorry that you can't attend the seminar.*	**Siento** que **vamos a tener** problemas. *I sense that we're going to have problems.*

b. When sense verbs like **oír, escuchar, ver, percibir, notar,** and **observar** are used in a negative main clause, the subjunctive is generally used in the subordinate clause. The indicative is rarely used in spoken language to state a real and undeniable physical state in negative clauses.

Subjunctive	Indicative
No oímos que **se acerque** el autobús. *We can't hear that the bus is approaching/coming.*	**Oímos** que **se acerca** el autobús. *We can hear the bus approaching/coming.*
No veo que **haya** desorden en mi habitación. *I don't see that my room is a mess.*	**Veo** que **hay** desorden en mi habitación. *I see that my room is a mess.*

23.C.5 **Personal opinions, thoughts, and reviews**

a. With verbs that express personal opinions, thoughts, and appraisals in negative main clauses, the *subjunctive* is used in the subordinate clause.

no admitir	*not to admit*	no opinar	*not to think/believe*
no conceder	*not to concede*	no pensar	*not to think*
no creer	*not to believe*	no recordar	*not to remember*

No creo que la lección **sea** fácil.   *I don't think that the lesson is easy.*
No sospecho que aquí **haya** algo raro.   *I don't suspect that there is anything strange here.*

b. When the main verb is affirmative, the *indicative* is used in the subordinate clause.

admitir	*to admit*	opinar	*to think/believe*
conceder	*to concede*	pensar	*to think*
creer	*to believe*	recordar	*to remember*

Creo que la lección **es** fácil. *I think that the lesson is easy.*

Sospecho que aquí **hay** algo raro. *I suspect that there is something strange here.*

c. In affirmative questions, these verbs can be used in spoken language in the *indicative* to signal a desire to confirm or disprove an opinion.

¿Crees que **es** bueno vivir en una ciudad grande? *Do you think it's good to live in a big city?*

The adverb **no** makes the use of the subjunctive more probable.

¿Tú **no crees** que **sea** bueno vivir en una ciudad tan grande? *Don't you believe that it can be good to live in such a big city?*

You can also use **parece** with the indicative and the present subjunctive.
Parece que **va** a nevar.
No parece que **vaya** a nevar.

d. *Parece*

When **parecer** is used to mean *it seems as if*, the *subjunctive* is used. However, with this expression, the present subjunctive can't be used. The most common verb tenses used are the past and past perfect subjunctive.

Parece que **estuviéramos** en Navidad. *It looks as if / seems like we were in the middle of Christmas.*

No parece que **estuviéramos** en Navidad. *It doesn't look as if / seem like we were in the middle of Christmas.*

como si: 23.E.1e **Parece** como si **hubiera sido** ayer. *It seems as though it were yesterday.*

e. *Comprender, entender*

These two verbs convey a meaning of concession or agreement with something previously said when the subjunctive is used. However, with the indicative, they keep the meaning *to understand*.

Entiendo que **te sientas** mal, ¡tienes fiebre! *I understand that you feel bad; you have a fever!*

Comprendo que la primera respuesta **es** incorrecta. *I understand that the first answer is incorrect.*

23.C.6 Verbs of denial or doubt

a. Verbs that express denial and doubt take the *subjunctive* in subordinate clauses.

desconfiar de	to distrust	ignorar	to ignore
dudar	to doubt	negar	to deny

Dudo que **digas** la verdad. *I doubt that you're telling the truth.*

Niego que **hayamos cometido** un error. *I deny that we have made a mistake.*

La policía **desconfía de** que el testigo **diga** la verdad. *The police doubt that the witness is telling the truth.*

b. With statements of certainty, however, use the indicative.

No dudo que les **dirás** la verdad. *I don't doubt that you will tell them the truth.*

No niego que siempre **pagas** tus cuentas. *I don't deny that you always pay your bills.*

23.C.7 Expressions of certainty

Impersonal expressions with **ser**: 30.B.6

Expressions with **ser/estar** + *adjective/noun* and **haber** + *noun* that convey certainty require the *indicative* in affirmative clauses and generally take the *subjunctive* in negative clauses.

a. Ser (*third-person singular*) + *masculine singular adjective* + **que**

cierto	*certain*	evidente	*evident/obvious*	seguro	*certain*
claro	*clear/obvious*	obvio	*obvious*	verdad	*true*

Es seguro que **habrá** fiesta.　　　　　　　　*It's certain that there will be a party.*

No era evidente que **fuera** a ganar el mejor candidato.　　*It was not obvious that the best candidate would win.*

b. Estar + *adjective* + **que**

convencido/a de	*convinced (of)*
seguro/a de	*sure (of)*

Estamos seguros de que **lloverá**.　　　　　*We're sure it's going to rain.*

¿**No estás convencida** de que tu decisión **es/sea** correcta?　　*Aren't you convinced that your decision is the right one?*

c. Haber (*impersonal form*) + *noun* + **de** + **que**

hay certeza de	*it's certain*	hay evidencia de	*there is evidence*
no hay duda de	*there's no doubt*	hay seguridad de	*it's guaranteed/certain*

◀ **No cabe duda de** is another expression of certainty.

Hay certeza de que el tratamiento **es** bueno.　　*It's certain that the treatment is good.*

No hay evidencia de que la medicina **es/sea** efectiva.　　*There is no evidence that the medicine is effective.*

23.C.8 **Expressions of wishes, preferences, advice, necessity, decisions, and emotions**

After expressions with **ser, estar**, and other verbs that convey wishes, preferences, advice, necessity, decisions, and emotions, the *subjunctive* is used. This applies both to affirmative and negative clauses. The following list shows some of the most common expressions that trigger the use of the *subjunctive* in the subordinate clause.

◀ **Estar** with a past participle: 30.C.2

Impersonal expressions with **ser**: 30.B.6

a. Ser + *masculine singular adjective* + **que**: subjunctive

◀ Use the subjunctive unless the impersonal expression is one of certainty: 23.C.7

aconsejable	*advisable*	magnífico	*great/magnificent*
bueno	*good*	malo	*bad*
comprensible	*understandable*	necesario	*necessary*
conveniente	*convenient*	normal	*normal*
dudoso	*doubtful*	(im)posible	*(im)possible*
esencial	*essential*	probable	*probable /likely*
estupendo	*superb/great /marvelous*	recomendable	*advisable*
extraño	*strange*	ridículo	*ridiculous*
horroroso	*horrifying*	sospechoso	*suspicious/suspect*
importante	*important*	suficiente	*sufficient*
(in)admisible	*(in)admissible*	terrible	*terrible*
increíble	*incredible*	triste	*sad*
(in)justo	*(un)fair*	urgente	*urgent*
(i)lógico	*(il)logical*	(in)útil	*useful (useless)*

Fue magnífico que nos **dieran** una habitación con vista al mar.　　*It was great that they gave us a room with a view of the sea.*

Es probable que **haga** buen tiempo mañana.　　*It's likely that it'll be nice out tomorrow.*

No es justo que **tengáis** que trabajar doce horas diarias.　　*It's not fair that you [pl.] have to work twelve hours a day.*

b. Ser + **mejor/peor /mucho menos/más,** etc. + **que:** subjunctive

mejor	better	peor	worse

Es mejor que **regreses** en avión.
It's better/best that you take a flight back.

Fue peor que **mintieras**.
It was worse that you lied.

Sería más cómodo que **viajáramos** en tren.
It would be more comfortable if we traveled by train.

c. Ser + **un(a)** + *noun* + **que:** subjunctive

error	error/mistake	injusticia	injustice
fastidio	nuisance	lástima	pity/shame
horror	horror	locura	madness
peligro	danger	milagro	miracle
robo	robbery	suerte	luck
costumbre	custom	tontería	silliness/nonsense
delicia	delight/joy	vergüenza	shame/embarrassment

Es una delicia que **nos atiendan** como a reyes.
It's a delight to be treated as kings.

¡Fue un milagro que **llamaras**!
It was a miracle that you called!

Antes **no era una costumbre** que los hombres **cuidaran** a los niños.
In the past, it wasn't customary for men to take care of the children.

Impersonal expressions with **estar**: 30.C.5

d. Estar + *adverb/participle* + **que:** subjunctive

bien	good/fine	permitido	permitted/allowed
decidido	decided	prohibido	prohibited
mal	bad	resuelto	resolved

Está bien que **pagues** con tarjeta.
It's fine to pay with a credit card.

Está prohibido que **bebamos** aquí.
It's prohibited to drink here.

e. Estar + *adjective* + *preposition* + **que:** subjunctive

acostumbrado/a a	accustomed/used to	encantado/a de	glad/delighted to
asustado/a de	afraid of	harto/a de	fed up with / sick of
cansado/a de	tired of	ilusionado/a con	hopeful for
contento/a de	happy/satisfied/content with	orgulloso/a de	proud of
deseoso/a de	longing for/eager to	preocupado/a por	worried about
dispuesto/a a	willing to	satisfecho/a de	satisfied by/with

Estamos hartos de que los vecinos **pongan** la música a todo volumen.
We are fed up with the neighbors playing music so loudly.

Estoy satisfecha de que todo **haya salido** bien.
I'm satisfied that everything has gone well.

f. Other verbs and expressions that take the subjunctive:

basta con que	it's enough / sufficient that/just	más vale que	it's better that
da igual que	it doesn't matter / it's the same as	puede (ser) que	it might/could be
da lo mismo que	it makes no difference	vale la pena que	it's worth

Basta con que envíes la solicitud.
Just send the request.

Más vale que compréis los boletos de avión con tiempo.
It's better that you [pl.] buy your plane tickets in advance.

23.C.9 Verbs of will and emotion: same/different subject

a. Use the infinitive, not the subjunctive, when there's no change of subject.

The infinitive after a conjugated verb: 25.B.5

Queremos que **prepares** la cena.	*We want you to prepare dinner.*
Queremos preparar la cena.	*We want to prepare dinner.*
Siento mucho que no **hayas aprobado** el examen.	*I'm so sorry you didn't pass the exam.*
Siento mucho no **haber aprobado** el examen.	*I'm so sorry not to have passed the exam.*

b. In some cases, the subordinate clause can be replaced by the infinitive even when the subjects are different. This happens when an object pronoun in the main clause refers to the same person in the subordinate clause.

La huelga **les impidió** que **viajaran**.	
La huelga **les impidió viajar**.	*The strike prevented them from traveling.*
Te aconsejo que **hagas** más ejercicio.	
Te aconsejo **hacer** más ejercicio.	*I advise you to exercise more.*
Juan **me pidió** que **fuera** con él.	
Juan **me pidió ir** con él.	*Juan asked me to go with him.*
La invité a que **participara** en el concurso.	
La invité a **participar** en el concurso.	*I invited her to participate in the contest.*

23.C.10 Impersonal expressions with *lo* + adjective/adverb and *lo que*

Lo is a neuter article used to form general expressions: **lo bueno** (*the good thing*), **lo mejor** (*the best thing*), **lo que quiero** (*what I want*).

Abstract ideas with **lo**: 5.A.2
Relative pronouns: 15.A.2

a. The *indicative* is used with **lo** expressions that refer to real situations or past events.

Lo + **adjective**	Indicative
Lo cierto es	que **estudias** muchísimo.
The fact is	*that you study a lot.*
Lo mejor fue	que **aprobaste** el examen.
The best thing was	*that you passed the exam.*
Lo importante es	que **eres** inteligente.
The important thing is	*that you are intelligent.*

b. The *subjunctive* is used after a number of **lo** expressions that refer to norms, rules, personal reactions, and preferences about what is best, worst, normal, logical, etc.: **lo lógico es que** (*the logical thing [to do] is*), **lo normal es que** (*the normal thing [to do] is*), **lo corriente/común es que** (*the usual thing [to do] is*). The tense of the subjunctive varies, based on the tense of **ser**.

Lo + **adjective**	Subjunctive
Lo lógico es	que te **llame** yo.
The logical thing (to do) is	*for me to call you.*
Lo más común era	que **fuéramos** a Torrevieja en verano.
The usual thing we did was	*to go to Torrevieja in the summer.*
Lo mejor fue	que te **conociera**.
The best thing was	*meeting you.*

c. After clauses with **lo que** + *verb in the indicative* + **ser**, the subjunctive is used when the verb expresses *a wish, a preference, an order,* or *a necessity.* The indicative is used when referring to something that happens habitually or is a known fact. In these cases, the statement is purely descriptive and there is no wish or necessity on the part of the speaker.

Lo que más me gusta es que **sirvan** tapas.	*What I like best is that they sirve tapas.*
Lo que más me gusta de Medellín es que nunca **hace** frío.	*What I like best about Medellín is that it's never cold.*

d. Other common expressions with **lo que**:

Lo que menos espero es que…	*What I least expect is that…*
Lo único que te pido es que…	*The only thing I ask is that…*
Lo que más necesito es que…	*What I need most is that…*
Lo que no me conviene es que…	*What doesn't suit me is that…*

23.C.11 Tense sequencing

The choice of tense used in a subordinate clause depends on whether the action happened before, at the same time as, or after the action in the main clause.

The present subjunctive: 22.B ▶
The present perfect
subjunctive: 22.D

a. When the *present* or *present perfect subjunctive* appears in the subordinate clause, the main verb is in the present indicative, future, or present perfect. The tense depends on the context.

Main clause		Subordinate clause	
Indicative		**Subjunctive**	
Present	Te **pido** *I ask you*	**Present**	que no **fumes**. *not to smoke.*
Future	Siempre te **pediré** *I will always ask you*		
Present perfect	Te **he pedido** *I have asked you*		
	Me **ha molestado** *It has annoyed me*	**Present perfect**	que **hayas fumado** tanto. *that you have smoked so much.*

The past subjunctive: 22.C ▶

b. When the main verb is not in the present, present perfect, or future, the verb in the subordinate clause can be in the *past subjunctive.* Choice of tense depends on the context.

Main clause		Subordinate clause
Indicative		**Past subjunctive**
Preterite	Ayer te **pedí** *Yesterday, I asked you*	que no **fumaras**. *not to smoke.*
Imperfect	Antes te **pedía** *I used to ask you*	
Conditional	Te **pediría** *I would like to ask you*	
Conditional perfect	Te **habría pedido** *I would have asked you*	

Use of the subjunctive • **Chapter 23**

23.D The subjunctive in relative clauses

El subjuntivo en subordinadas relativas

Relative clauses (*adjective clauses*) start with a relative pronoun: **(el, la, los, las) que, quien(es),** **(el, la) cual, (los, las) cuales, cuya(s), (todo) lo que** or with a relative adverb **(cuando, donde, como).** Relative clauses describe their antecedent.

Main clause (antecedent)	Relative clause (characteristic)
Compra **los libros**	**que necesites**.
Buy the books	*you need.*

In the example, **los libros** is the antecedent for the relative clause **que necesites**.

The use of the *subjunctive* in the relative clause is always determined by the speaker's perspective of the antecedent.

23.D.1 Unknown/Known antecedent

a. The *indicative* is used in relative clauses to refer to *specific* people, things, ideas, or events that the speaker already knows about. The *subjunctive* is used to refer to something or someone *unknown* that has *imagined* or *desired* characteristics.

Subjunctive: unknown	Indicative: known
Queremos comprar **una casa** que **tenga** tres dormitorios. *We want to buy a house that has three bedrooms.*	Vamos a comprar **una casa** que **tiene** tres dormitorios. *We're going to buy a house that has three bedrooms.*
El hotel contratará **un chef** que **tenga** experiencia. *The hotel wants to hire a chef who has experience.*	El hotel contratará a **un chef** que **tiene** experiencia. *The hotel will hire a chef who has experience.*
Queremos ir a **un restaurante** que **tenga** buena comida. *We want to go to a restaurant that has good food.*	Iremos a **un restaurante** que **tiene** buena comida. *We're going to a restaurant that has good food.*

Note that you do not use the personal **a** with hypothetical people.

b. Verbs like **querer, necesitar, buscar**, and **desear** usually appear in relative clauses that describe *imagined* people, things, events, or situations. The indicative is used to describe *specific* or *concrete* people, things, events, or situations.

Subjunctive: imagined	Indicative: specific
Buscamos **un libro** que **explique** bien el subjuntivo. *We're looking for a book that can explain the subjunctive well.*	Buscamos **el libro** que **explica** bien el subjuntivo. *We're looking for the book that explains the subjunctive well.*
Queríamos **una bebida** que no **tuviera** azúcar. *We'd like a drink that doesn't have sugar.*	Queríamos **la bebida** que no **tiene** azúcar. *We wanted the drink that doesn't have sugar.*

Specific things are usually indicated by a definite article. Imagined things are usually indicated by an indefinite article.

c. The subjunctive is also used in relative clauses with a relative adverb that refers to *unknown* and *nonspecific* locations, times, or ways. The adverb, or **que** and a suitable preposition, starts the relative clause.

Relative adverbs: 15.C

Subjunctive: unknown	Indicative: known
Iremos a un restaurante **donde/en el que haya** sitio para todos. *We'll go to a restaurant where there is room for everyone. (The speaker does not know of a specific restaurant.)*	Iremos al restaurante **donde/en el que hay** sitio para todos. *We're going to the restaurant where there is room for everyone. (The speaker knows of a specific restaurant.)*
Puedes preparar la cena **como/del modo que quieras**. *You can prepare dinner however you want. (The speaker does not know how you want to prepare it.)*	Puedes preparar la cena **como/del modo que quieres**. *You can prepare dinner the way you want. (The speaker knows how you want to prepare it.)*

23.D.2 Denied / Undenied and indefinite antecedent

Affirmative and negative indefinite quantifers: 7.B

a. When the main clause indicates or implies that a person or thing does not exist, the subjunctive is used in the subordinate clause.

Negation using *haber*	
Subjunctive: denied/nonexistent	**Indicative: concrete/existing**
En España **no había platos** que **me gustaran** más que el bacalao. *In Spain, there were no dishes I liked more than cod.*	En España **había platos** que **me gustaban** más que el bacalao. *In Spain, there were other dishes I liked more than cod.*
No hay otra persona que me **importe** más que tú. *There is no one more important to me than you.*	**Hay otras personas** que me **importan** más que tú. *There are others who are more important to me than you.*

b. The existence of the person or thing can be denied by negating the whole clause using **nunca, jamás,** or other negative expressions such as **en modo alguno** (*in no way / not in any way*) or **en ninguna parte** (*nowhere*).

Negation using *nunca, jamás*	
Subjunctive	**Indicative**
Nunca/Jamás he sido **una persona** que **lea** mucho. *I have never been a person who reads a lot.*	**Siempre** he sido **una persona** que **lee** mucho. *I have always been a person who reads a lot.*
En ninguna parte hay **plataformas petroleras** que **sean** totalmente seguras. *Nowhere are there oil rigs that are completely safe.*	**En muchas partes** hay **plataformas petroleras** que **son** totalmente seguras. *In many places, there are oil rigs that are completely safe.*

c. Affirmative indefinite pronouns and quantifiers used as antecedents describe something or someone that can't be identified, so they trigger the use of the subjunctive. However, the indicative can be used with affirmative indefinite pronouns and quantifiers to indicate that the speaker knows the person or thing but does not want to identify it.

Affirmative indefinite pronouns	
Subjunctive	**Indicative**
¿Hay **algo** que **quieras** decirme? *Is there something you want to say to me?*	¿Hay **algo** que **quieres** decirme? *Is there something specific you want to say to me?*
Quiero **a alguien** que me **quiera**. *I want someone who loves me.*	Quiero **a alguien** que me **quiere**. *I love someone who loves me.*

Note that you use the personal **a** with **alguien**: 12.B.2c

Indefinite quantifiers with only affirmative forms: **cualquiera,** *anyone*: 7.C.5

d. Cualquier(a) is used with the subjunctive whether it appears before the noun or independently as the pronoun.

*Cualquier(a) – **anybody/who(m)ever/whichever***	
Subjunctive	
Cualquiera que **tenga** visa puede viajar a España. *Whoever has a visa can travel to Spain.*	Puedes preguntarle la dirección a **cualquier** persona que **encuentres** por la calle. *You can ask whomever/anybody you find along the street about the address.*

e. The *subjunctive* must be used when an indefinite pronoun or quantifier is negative: **nadie, nada, ninguno/a(s)**, or **ningún/ninguna** + *noun*.

◀ Algún, alguno/a(s); ningún, ninguno/a: 7.B.2
Indefinite pronouns: 7.D

Negative indefinite pronouns/determiners	Affirmative indefinite pronouns/determiners
Subjunctive	**Indicative**
No hay **ningún** equipo que **sea** mejor que el nuestro. *There is no other team that is better than ours.*	Hay **otro** equipo que **es** mejor que el nuestro. *There is another team that is better than ours.*
No existe **nadie** que **juegue** mejor que nosotros. *There is no one who plays better than we do.*	Hay **alguien** que **juega** mejor que nosotros. *There is someone who plays better than we do.*
La revista **no** publicó **nada** que me **interesara** mucho. *The magazine didn't publish anything that interested me.*	La revista publicó **algo** que me **interesó** mucho. *The magazine published something that interested me a lot.*

◀ Double negation with negative indefinite pronouns and quantifiers: 7.E.1

f. The phrase **el/la/los/las que** or **quien(es)** (*the one[s] that/who*) is used with the *subjunctive* when it refers to someone or something unknown. Note that this applies to defining relative clauses where **lo/el/la cual** can't be used.

◀ Relative pronouns: 15.A

el/la/los/las que, quien(es) – *the one who / those which*	
Subjunctive	**Indicative**
Elena irá con **los que deseen** ir al museo. *Elena will go with anyone who wants to go to the museum.*	Elena irá con **los que desean** ir al museo. *Elena will go with those who want to go to the museum.*
Quienes hayan comprado boletos pueden entrar. *Anyone who has bought tickets can get in.*	**Quienes han comprado** boletos pueden entrar. *Those who (already) have bought tickets can get in.*

g. Clauses with **lo que** take the indicative when they refer to something specific.

lo que – *what/whatever*	
Subjunctive	**Indicative**
Lo que digas será muy importante. *Whatever you say will be very important.*	Lo que **dices** es muy importante. *What you say is very important.*

23.D.3 Tense sequencing

The tense of the verbs in the main and relative clauses depends on the context of the sentence. The examples that follow show some of the most common combinations.

a. When the main verb is in the *present indicative* or *future*, the verb in the relative clause is in the *present subjunctive*. When the main verb is in the *present perfect*, the verb in the relative clause is in the *present perfect subjunctive*.

◀ The present subjunctive: 22.B
The present perfect subjunctive: 22.D

Main clause			Relative clause	
Indicative			Subjunctive	
Present	**Necesito** una impresora *I need a printer*		**Present**	que **funcione** bien. *that works well.*
Future	**Necesitaré** una impresora *I will need a printer*			
Present perfect	Jamás **he tenido** una impresora *I've never had a printer*		**Present perfect**	que **haya funcionado** bien. *that has worked well.*

b. When the main verb is in the indicative and refers to the past, the verb in the subordinate clause is in the *past subjunctive*.

The past subjunctive: 22.C

Main clause		Relative clause	
Indicative		**Subjunctive**	
Preterite	**Necesité** una impresora *I needed a printer*	**Past**	que **funcionara** bien. *that worked well.*
Imperfect	**Necesitaba** una impresora *I needed a printer*		
Conditional	**Querría** una impresora *I would like a printer*		
Conditional perfect	**Habría querido** una impresora *I would have liked a printer*		

23.E The subjunctive in adverbial clauses

El subjuntivo en subordinadas adverbiales

Subordinating conjunctions: 16.C

Adverbial clauses start with conjunctions that express time, manner, purpose, concession, cause, condition, and other relationships.

23.E.1 Place, manner, quantity

Relative adverbs: 15.C

a. In a relative clause, the relative adverbs (**como, donde, cuando**) refer back to the antecedent, which is mentioned and can be identified.

Main clause	Relative clause with antecedent
Estaremos en **un parque** *We'll be in a park*	**donde / en el que podamos** jugar. *where we can play.*

b. When the antecedent is omitted, the adverb does not refer to a specific place, manner, or quantity. These clauses have traditionally been considered adverbial clauses introduced by conjunctions that describe the action (the verb) directly. The *Nueva gramática* regards them as *free relative adverbial clauses* that refer to an implied antecedent.

Main clause	Adverbial clause
Estaremos *We'll be*	**donde podamos** jugar. *where we can play.*
Vino *He came*	**cuando lo llamamos**. *when we called him.*

c. The *subjunctive* is used in clauses that describe unknown places, ways, and quantities/amounts.

como, donde, cuanto, todo lo que	
Subjunctive: unknown	**Indicative: known**
Busca las llaves **donde** las **hayas dejado**. *Look for your keys wherever you left them.*	Busca las llaves **donde** las **dejaste**. *Look for your keys where you left them.*
Resuelvo los problemas **como pueda**. *I resolve problems however I can.*	Resuelvo los problemas **como puedo**. *I resolve problems the way I am able to.*
Ellos harán **cuanto/todo lo que quieran**. *They will do whatever they want.*	Ellos harán **cuanto/todo lo que quieren**. *They will do everything they want.*

d. When **como** starts the subordinate clause, the *subjunctive* expresses a condition in a specific context, while the *indicative* expresses a cause.

como	
Subjunctive: condition	**Indicative: cause**
Como no **encuentres** tu pasaporte, no podrás viajar. *If you don't find your passport, you won't be able to travel.*	**Como** no **encuentras** tu pasaporte, no podrás viajar. *Since you can't find your passport, you won't be able to travel.*

Conjunctions of cause: 16.C.4, 23.E.5

e. The conjunctions of manner **como si** and **sin que** always require the *subjunctive* in the subordinate clause. The conjunction **como si** conveys an imagined situation and is used with the past or past perfect subjunctive.

Como si: 16.C.9b

como si, sin que	
Subjunctive	
Manuel habla catalán **como si fuera** de Barcelona.	*Manuel speaks Catalan as if he were from Barcelona.*
Manuel aprendió catalán **sin que** nadie le **enseñara**.	*Manuel learned Catalan without anyone teaching him.*

Parece: 23.C.5d

Use **sin** with an infinitive when there's no change of subject.

Infinitive and **que** clauses: 23.C.9

f. In exclamations, **ni que** is used with the past subjunctive as an expression of irritation.

Ese collar es muy caro. ¡**Ni que fuera** de oro!   *That necklace is very expensive, as if it were made of gold!*

23.E.2 Time

Conjunctions of time: 16.C.3

Conjunctions of time			
a medida que	*as*	en cuanto	*as soon as*
al mismo tiempo que	*at the same time as*	luego (de) que	*after*
antes (de) que	*before*	hasta que	*until*
apenas	*as soon as*	mientras (que)	*while (so long as)*
cada vez que	*each time / every time (that)*	según	*according to*
cuando	*when*	siempre que	*whenever (as long as)*
desde que	*since*	tan pronto como	*as soon as / once*
después (de) que	*after*	una vez que	*once*

mientras as conditional conjunction: 16.D.2c

cuando as relative adverb: 15.C.1

a. In general, the *subjunctive* is used in a time clause when the main clause refers to the future. When the main clause refers to a habitual action in the present or a past action, the *indicative* is used. These examples with **cuando** illustrate the sequence of time for most time conjunctions. Usually, the subordinate clause comes first.

cuando	
Subjunctive	**Indicative**
Cuando llegue a la oficina, **leeré** mi correo. (Future) *When I get to the office, I'll read my e-mail.*	**Cuando llego** a la oficina, **leo** mi correo. (Present habit) *When I get to the office, I read my e-mail.*
Cuando haya llegado a la oficina, **leeré** mi correo. (Future) *When I have arrived at the office, I'll read my e-mail.*	**Cuando llegué** a la oficina, **leí** mi correo. (Past) *When I got to the office, I read my e-mail.*
Cuando salga de la oficina, ya **habré leído** mi correo. (Future) *When I leave the office, I will have already read my e-mail.*	**Cuando salí** de la oficina, ya **había leído** mi correo. (Past) *When I left the office, I had already read my e-mail.*

You also use the subjunctive when the main clause expresses a command. **Cuando llegues** a la oficina, **lee** tu correo.

Conditional conjunctions: 16.D

b. Mientras (que) and **siempre que** convey a condition with the *subjunctive* (*if, so/as long as*) and are conjunctions of time with the *indicative*.

mientras, siempre que	
Subjunctive: condition	**Indicative: time**
Mientras estés enfermo, debes quedarte en casa. *As long as you're sick, you should stay at home.*	**Mientras estás** enfermo, debes quedarte en casa. *While you're sick, you should stay at home.*
Siempre que pidas los boletos con tiempo, pagarás poco. *As long as you book the tickets in advance, you won't pay much.*	**Siempre que pides** tus boletos con tiempo, pagas poco. *When you book the tickets in advance, you don't pay much.*

c. The conjunction **antes de que** always requires the *subjunctive* in the subordinate clause, but the infinitive is used with **antes de** when there's no change in subject. The following can also come before the infinitive: **después de**, **luego de**, and **hasta**.

Infinitive when subject is the same: 23.C.9
Infinitive after a conjugated verb: 25.B.5

antes de, después/luego de, hasta	
Subjunctive	**Infinitive**
Ven a visitarme **antes de que** yo viaje. *Come and visit me before I travel.*	Ven a visitarme **antes de viajar**. *Come and visit me before you travel.*
¿Podéis quedaros **hasta que terminemos** el trabajo? *Can you [pl.] stay until we've finished the job?*	¿Podéis quedaros **hasta terminar** el trabajo? *Can you [pl.] stay until you've finished the job?*
Os llamaré **después de que regreséis**. *I'll call you [pl.] after you come back.*	Os llamaré **después de regresar**. *I'll call you [pl.] after I come back.*

23.E.3 Purpose, goal

Conjunctions of purpose: 16.C.7

Conjunctions of purpose			
para que	so that	con el fin/objeto/propósito de que	with the aim of
a fin de que	so that	con vistas a que	with a view to

a. Conjunctions of purpose express purpose, intent, goals, and correspond to the English conjunctions *so that, in order that*. The *subjunctive* is always used with conjunctions of purpose.

Subjunctive	
La constitución fue modificada **a fin de que** el presidente **pudiera** ser reelecto.	*The constitution was changed so that the president could be re-elected.*

b. The infinitive is used when there's no change in subject.

The preposition **para**: 12.B.6

Subjunctive	Infinitive
Te daré dinero **para que compres** los libros. *I will give you money so that you buy the books.*	Tengo dinero **para comprar** los libros. *I have money to buy the books.*

c. With the exception of **para que**, conjunctions of purpose are mostly used in formal situations and written Spanish.

El gobierno aplicará medidas **con el objeto de que** no **suban** los precios.   *The government will introduce measures with the objective of keeping prices from rising.*

d. The conjunctions **de (tal) modo que, de (tal) manera que,** and **de (tal) forma que** (*so that, in such a way that*) are used with the *subjunctive* to convey purpose. With the *indicative* they convey consequence.

23.E.4 Consequence

Conjunctions of consequence			
de (tal) forma que		tan... que	
de (tal) manera que	so	tal... que	so... that
de (tal) modo que		tanto... que	

Conjunctions of consequence: 16.C.5

a. Conjunctions of consequence express the consequence of a condition using the *indicative*. With the *subjunctive*, they convey purpose.

Mándame un mensaje de texto, **de tal modo que estemos** en contacto.
Text me so that we can keep in touch.

Nos escribimos, **de tal modo que estamos** en contacto.
We write to each other, so we keep in touch.

Subjunctive: purpose	Indicative: consequence
Viaja mucho, **de (tal) modo que conozcas** otras culturas. *Travel a lot so that you can get to know other cultures.*	Viaja mucho, **de (tal) modo conoces** otras culturas. *Travel a lot, so you get to know other cultures.*
El profesor enseña **de forma que** todos lo **entiendan**. *The professor teaches in a way that allows everyone to understand him.*	El profesor enseña **de forma que** todos lo **entienden**. *The professor teaches in such a way that everyone understands him.*

b. After affirmative main clauses with **tan** and **tanto/a(s)** in an implied comparison, the *indicative* is used. After negative main clauses, the *subjunctive* is used.

Comparisons of equality: 11.C

Subjunctive: negative	Indicative: affirmative
La nieve no es **tan poca que** no **podamos** esquiar. *There isn't so little snow that we can't ski.*	La nieve es **tan poca que** no **podemos** esquiar. *There's so little snow that we can't ski.*
Los problemas no son **tantos que** yo no **pueda** resolverlos. *The problems are not so many that I can't deal with them.*	Los problemas son **tantos que** no puedo resolverlos. *The problems are so many that I can't deal with them.*

23.E.5 Cause

Conjunctions of cause			
porque	*because*	debido a que	*due to, because*
a causa de que	*because (of)*	puesto que	*since, because*
dado que	*given that*	ya que	*since*

a. Conjunctions of cause in Spanish correspond to the English *because* or *since*. The most common conjunctions of cause are **porque, como,** and **ya que**. In written language, there are more.

Conjunctions of cause: 16.C.4

Indicative: affirmative causes	
Cancelaron los vuelos **debido a que / porque nevaba** mucho.	*The flights were canceled because it was snowing a lot.*
No había buenas habitaciones **dado que / porque era** temporada alta.	*There weren't any good rooms because it was peak season.*

b. Porque, a causa de que, and **debido a que** are followed by the *subjunctive* when the cause is negated.

Subjunctive: negative causes	Indicative: affirmative causes
Estudio español **no porque sea** obligatorio **sino porque** me gusta. *I study Spanish not because it's mandatory, but because I like it.*	Estudio español **porque es** obligatorio. *I study Spanish because it's mandatory.*

23.E.6 Concession

Conjunctions of concession		
aunque	pese a que	*even if, despite, in spite of, although, whether*
aun cuando	si bien	
a pesar de (que)	y eso que	

Conjunctions of concession:
16.C.6

a. The most common conjunction of concession is **aunque**. The *subjunctive* is used when the subordinate clause conveys something *imagined, not real,* or *in the future*. The *indicative* expresses a fact. The subordinate clause can come before the main clause or after it, and the context determines the tense of the subjunctive (*present, past,* or *past perfect*).

Subjunctive: not real	Indicative: real
Siempre hablo español **aunque** me **cueste** mucho. *I always speak Spanish even if it is difficult.*	Siempre hablo español **aunque** me **cuesta** mucho. *I always speak Spanish even though it is difficult.*
Aunque me **hubieras hablado** muy rápido en español, te lo habría entendido todo. *Even if you had spoken very quickly to me in Spanish, I would have understood everything.*	**Aunque** me **has hablado** muy rápido en español, te lo he entendido todo. *Although you have spoken very quickly to me in Spanish, I have understood everything.*

b. The expression **por** + *adjective/adverb/noun* + **que** has a meaning of concession and is used with the *subjunctive*.

Por difícil que parezca, el subjuntivo es realmente fácil.	*As hard as it may seem, the subjunctive is really easy.*
Por poco que tengas, siempre puedes ser generoso.	*As little as you may have, you can always be generous.*
Por mucha gente **que venga**, habrá comida para todos.	*Even if a lot of people come, there will be plenty of food for everyone.*

23.E.7 Use of the subjunctive in conditional clauses

Conditional conjunctions: 16.D

Conditional conjunctions			
si	*if*	en caso de que	*in case*
a no ser que	*unless*	excepto que	*if not*
a menos que	*unless*	siempre y cuando	*if*
con tal (de) que	*provided that / as long as*	siempre que	*provided that / as long as*

a. Conditional conjunctions in the previous table take the *subjunctive* in the subordinate clause, except **si**, which has special rules.

Te llamaré **en caso de que quieras** ir conmigo en el coche.	*I'll call you in case you want to go with me in the car.*
Iremos al cine **con tal de que** los chicos **se calmen**.	*We'll go to the movies provided that the kids calm down.*

b. The expression **por si acaso** (*in case*) is very common in everyday speech. It is mainly used with the *indicative*.

Lleva ropa de abrigo **por si acaso nieva**.	*Take warm clothes in case it snows.*
Llevaré la tarjeta de crédito **por si acaso necesito** más dinero.	*I will bring my credit card in case I need more money.*

23.E.8 Conditional *si* clauses

Conditional clauses with **si**: 16.D.2

A subordinate **si** (*if*) clause conveys a condition, while the main clause expresses the consequence or the result if the condition is fulfilled. The main clause can express a fact, a probability, a hypothetical situation, or a command. Each type of clause carries its own rules.

a. *Facts:* When the condition is real and the consequence is certain, both clauses are in the indicative.

Using the *present indicative* in both clauses indicates that the same result happens every time a condition is fulfilled.

The present indicative: Ch. 17

Condition: *present indicative*	Result: *present indicative*
Si **trabajas**,	**ganas** dinero.
If you work,	*you earn money.*

Expressing the condition in the *present indicative* and the result in the *future* (*future tense* or **ir a** + *infinitive*) indicates a clear cause-and-effect relationship.

The future tense: Ch. 20

Condition: *present indicative*	Result: *future indicative*
Si **trabajas** allí,	**ganarás / vas a ganar** mucho dinero.
If you work there,	*you will earn a lot of money.*

Using the *imperfect indicative* in both clauses indicates that something happened each time a condition was fulfilled.

The imperfect tense: 18.D

Condition: *imperfect indicative*	Result: *imperfect indicative*
Si **trabajabas** horario completo,	**ganabas** mucho dinero.
If you worked full-time,	*you earned a lot of money.*

With the *preterite* or *present perfect,* conditional clauses with **si** usually communicate an assumption about something that happened, has happened, or will have happened because a condition was fulfilled. These assumptions are often expressed as questions.

The preterite tense: 18.B
The present perfect: 19.A

Condition: *preterite/present perfect*	Result: *several possible verb tenses*
Si **trabajaste / has trabajado** allí,	**ganaste / has ganado / habrás ganado** mucho dinero, ¿no?
If you worked/have worked there,	*you earned/have earned/must have earned a lot of money, right?*

b. *Probability:* The condition is an assumption and the result is possible.

When the *conditional tense* is used in the main clause to express a probable result (*what would happen*) if a condition were fulfilled, the *past subjunctive* is used in the subordinate **si** clause.

The conditional tense: Ch. 21
The past subjunctive: 22.C

Condition: *past subjunctive*	Result: *conditional*
Si **trabajaras** allí,	**ganarías** mucho dinero.
If you worked there,	*you would earn a lot of money.*

c. Hypothetical: Both the condition and the result are only assumptions.

To express what could have happened if an imagined condition had been fulfilled, the *past perfect subjunctive* is used in the subordinate **si** clause and the *conditional perfect* in the main clause.

The past perfect ▶
subjunctive: 22.E
The conditional perfect: 21.C

Condition: *past perfect subjunctive*	Result: *conditional perfect*
Si **hubieras trabajado** allí,	**habrías ganado** mucho dinero.
If you had worked there,	*you would have earned a lot of money.*

Using the past perfect subjunctive in the main clause (**hubieras ganado**) intensifies the assumption that the outcome would have been highly unlikely, but in daily speech the conditional perfect (**habrías ganado**) is preferred. The **-ese** form of the past perfect subjunctive (**hubieses ganado**) is not used in the main clause of a conditional sentence.

Condition: *past perfect subjunctive*	Result: *past perfect subjunctive*
Si **hubieras trabajado** allí,	**hubieras/habrías ganado** mucho dinero.
If you had worked there,	*you could have earned a lot of money.*

The imperative: Ch. 24 ▶

d. The imperative in the main clause: If a condition *is*, *was*, or *will be* fulfilled, the result can be a command.

Condition: *several possible verb tenses*	Result: *imperative*
Si **trabajas/trabajaste/has trabajado** mucho hoy,	¡**acuéstate** temprano!
If you work/worked/have worked a lot today,	*go to bed early!*

23.F Regional variations

Variaciones regionales

a. The use of the subjunctive is fairly uniform throughout the Spanish-speaking world. The exception is the use of the *present* subjunctive instead of the *past* subjunctive in noun clauses in the past. This happens mainly in southern parts of Latin America and only when the action in the subordinate clause still pertains to the future.

Past subjunctive	Present subjunctive
Susana me pidió ayer que **fuera** con ella al centro comercial.	Susana me pidió ayer que **vaya** con ella al centro comercial.
Susana asked me yesterday to go with her to the mall.	

b. The **-ra** and **-se** endings in the past and past perfect subjunctive are equivalent (**hablara, hablase, hubiera/hubiese hablado**), and are used in both Spain and Latin America.

Queríamos una novela que **fuera/fuese** más interesante.	*We wanted a novel that was more interesting.*
No creía que **hubiera/hubiese** problemas.	*I didn't believe that there were problems.*
Habría sido bueno que **hubieras/hubieses dejado** de fumar.	*It would have been good if you had stopped smoking.*

Práctica

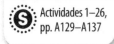
Actividades 1–26,
pp. A129–A137

The imperative
Imperativo

24.A Formal and informal commands

Imperativo formal e informal

The imperative expresses direct requests or commands with personal verb forms. Spanish has formal command forms for **usted** and **ustedes**; informal commands for **tú, vos**, and **vosotros**; and **nosotros** commands (*let's*). All negative informal commands are the same as the corresponding present subjunctive forms. The affirmative and negative formal and **nosotros** commands are also formed using the corresponding present subjunctive forms. Verbs with stem changes in the present indicative and the present subjunctive have the same changes in the imperative.

24.B Affirmative *tú* commands

Imperativo afirmativo de tú

24.B.1 Regular affirmative *tú* commands

Regular affirmative **tú** commands are the same as the **usted/él/ella** forms in the present indicative. This means that verbs with stem changes in the present indicative have the same changes in the affirmative **tú** command.

Regular verbs		Verbs with stem changes	
cantar	canta	d**o**rmir	d**ue**rme
comer	come	p**e**nsar	p**ie**nsa
escribir	escribe	p**e**dir	p**i**de

¡**Habla** más lento, por favor!	*Speak more slowly, please!*
¡**Escribe** un blog!	*Write a blog!*
¡**Piensa** bien las cosas!	*Think carefully about things!*

24.B.2 Irregular affirmative *tú* commands

There are only a few irregular affirmative **tú** commands.

Completely irregular affirmative *tú* commands			
decir (*to say*)	**di**	salir (*to leave, to go out*)	**sal**
hacer (*to do*)	**haz**	ser (*to be*)	**sé**
ir (*to go*)	**ve**	tener (*to have*)	**ten**
poner (*to put*)	**pon**	venir (*to come*)	**ven**

¡**Sal** a jugar, pero **ten** cuidado con los autos!	*Go out and play, but watch out for cars!*
¡**Ve** y **pon** las cartas en el buzón!	*Go and put the letters in the mailbox!*
Sé valiente y **di** la verdad.	*Be brave and tell the truth.*
Haz lo que te parezca mejor.	*Do what you think is best.*

◀ Formal and informal address: 13.B

◀ The present indicative: 17.D

◀ Stem-changing verbs: verb conjugation tables, pp. B1–B20. See verb patterns 25, 48, 49.

◀ Verb conjugation tables, pp. B1–B20

◀ Since **ir** and **ver** have the same affirmative **tú** command (**ve**), you can use context to figure out which verb is being used.

Formal and informal ◗ address: 13.B

24.C Affirmative *vos* and *vosotros* commands

Imperativo afirmativo de *vos* y *vosotros*

24.C.1 Formation of affirmative *vos* and *vosotros* commands

The regular affirmative commands for **vos** and **vosotros** are formed by dropping the **-r** ending from the infinitive and adding an accent to the final vowel for **vos** (**cantá**), or adding a **-d** for **vosotros** (**cantad**). Affirmative **vos** and **vosotros** commands are regular, with the exception of the **vos** command for the verb **ir**, which uses the imperative form of **andar** (**¡Andá!**).

Affirmative *vos*, *vosotros* commands			
Verbs		**vos**	**vosotros**
cant**ar**	canta-	cant**á**	canta**d**
corr**er**	corre-	corr**é**	corre**d**
escrib**ir**	escribi-	escrib**í**	escribi**d**

¡Recordad la contraseña!	*Remember the password!*
Llamá a tu padre.	*Call your father.*
Encendé la luz.	*Turn on the light.*
Andá a buscar a tu hermano.	*Go find your brother.*
Buscad las herramientas.	*Look for the tools.*

24.C.2 Use of *vos* and *vosotros* commands

a. In Spain, **vosotros** is used with its corresponding command forms.

¡Venid a visitarme pronto!	*Come and visit me soon!*
Recordad lo que os dije.	*Remember what I told you.*
Proteged la naturaleza.	*Protect nature.*

b. When **vosotros** is used in Latin America as a formal address (to church congregations and less frequently to voters in political speeches), its command forms are also used. The structure is identical to that used in Spain for **vosotros**.

¡Ayudad a vuestra parroquia!	*Help your parish!*

c. In the **voseo** regions of Argentina, Uruguay, Paraguay, Costa Rica, Guatemala, Honduras, Nicaragua, El Salvador, Colombia, Venezuela, and Panama, the **vos** command is used.

¡Estudiá bien la propuesta!	*Study the proposal well!*
Recordá lo que te dije.	*Remember what I told you.*
Llamá a tu hermano.	*Call your brother.*
Decí la verdad.	*Tell the truth.*

Voseo with the ◗ subjunctive: 22.B, 22.H Map of **voseo** regions in Latin America: p. B21

d. In **voseo** regions in Bolivia, Ecuador, and Chile, the pronoun **vos** is used with the **tú** verb form (**¡Habla, vos!**) in addition to the common form (**¡Hablá, vos!**), or a variant using an **-i** ending (**¡No salgái!**).

24.D Negative *tú, vos,* and *vosotros* commands

Imperativo negativo de *tú, vos* y *vosotros*

24.D.1 Regular negative *tú, vos,* and *vosotros* commands

a. All negative **tú**, **vos**, and **vosotros** commands use the corresponding present subjunctive forms.

◀ The present subjunctive: 22.B

Negative *tú, vos, vosotros* commands			
	cantar	**correr**	**subir**
tú/vos	no cantes	no corras	no subas
vosotros	no cantéis	no corráis	no subáis

b. In **voseo** regions, the **vos** endings for the present subjunctive can vary. Since the negative command matches the present subjunctive form, several negative imperative forms exist for **vos**. In addition to the forms presented in the table (which match the **tú** forms), another common **vos** ending for the present subjunctive and negative command is **-és/-ás**.

◀ **Voseo** with the subjunctive: 22.B, 22.H

No **cantes/cantés**.   No **corras/corrás**.   No **subas/subás**.

◀ **No** always comes before the verb in a negative command.

24.D.2 Irregular negative *tú, vos,* and *vosotros* commands

All verbs with stem changes in the present subjunctive have the same changes in the informal affirmative and negative command forms.

◀ Formal and informal address: 13.B

No me **pidas** que mienta.	*Don't ask me to lie.*
No **seas** así conmigo.	*Don't be like that with me.*
Nunca **hagáis** caso de tonterías.	*Never pay attention to such silliness.*

24.E *Usted, ustedes,* and *nosotros* commands

Imperativo de *usted, ustedes* y *nosotros*

a. Affirmative commands for **usted**, **ustedes**, and **nosotros**, as well as all their negative imperative forms, use the corresponding present subjunctive forms. All verbs with stem changes in the present subjunctive have the same changes in the affirmative and negative command forms for **usted**, **ustedes**, and **nosotros**.

◀ The present subjunctive: 22.B

	cantar	**correr**	**subir**
usted	(no) cante	(no) corra	(no) suba
ustedes	(no) canten	(no) corran	(no) suban
nosotros	(no) cantemos	(no) corramos	(no) subamos

No **venga** muy tarde.	*Don't come too late.*
Digan la verdad.	*Tell the truth.*
Seamos optimistas.	*Let's be optimistic.*

b. Vamos is generally used instead of **vayamos** as the affirmative **nosotros** command form of **ir**.

Vamos al cine.	*Let's go to the movies.*
No **vayamos** al circo.	*Let's not go to the circus.*

◀ You can also use **vamos a** + *infinitive* to say *Let's*.

24.F Placement of pronouns

Posición de los pronombres

Placement of direct
and indirect object
pronouns: 13.G.6
Placement of reflexive
pronouns: 27.A.1c

All pronouns (reflexive pronouns, direct and indirect object pronouns) come *before* negative commands and are *attached* to affirmative commands. The other rules of pronoun placement also apply here: a) The indirect object pronoun always comes before the direct object pronoun. b) The indirect object pronoun **le** becomes **se** when it appears with a direct object pronoun.

Necesito tu dirección. ¡Mánda**mela**!	*I need your address. Send it to me!*
Dá**sela** también al profesor y ¡no	*Give it to the professor too, and don't*
se la des a nadie más!	*give it to anyone else!*

Stress and accents: 1.E.3

Note that an accent mark is usually needed to keep the original stress. In the case of **dé**, the accent is dropped when only one pronoun is added.

De**me** más tiempo.	*Give me more time.*
Dé**melo**.	*Give it to me.*

a. The **-d** ending is dropped from the affirmative **vosotros** command when the pronoun **os** is added (the exception is **irse: idos**). This does not happen with other pronouns. With **-ir** verbs, you will need to add an accent to the **i**.

Quita**os** los zapatos antes de entrar.	*Take off your [pl.] shoes before entering.*
Deci**dme** cómo llego allí.	*Tell me how to get there.*
Vest**íos** de fiesta.	*Get dressed up.*

Hiatus and accentuation: 1.E.5d

b. In **nosotros** commands, the **-s** ending is dropped before the pronouns **nos** and **se**.

Sentémo**nos** a descansar.	*Let's sit down and rest.*
Pongámo**nos** a trabajar ya.	*Let's get to work now.*
¡Vámo**nos**!	*Let's go!*
Démo**selo**.	*Let's give it to him.*

Subject pronouns: 13.A

c. The subject pronoun is used with requests when it is necessary to show a contrast between the people being referred to.

Note that the subject pronoun
follows the command
form of the verb.

Pon la mesa **tú**, Roberto; ayer la puse **yo**.	*You set the table, Roberto; I did it yesterday.*

The subject pronoun is also used for emphasis or politeness.

Asistan a esta clase **ustedes**. Yo iré a	*You go to this class. I'm going to the library.*
la biblioteca.	
Por favor, permita **usted** la entrada	*Please let the musicians enter.*
de los músicos.	

24.G Other imperative constructions

Otras expresiones exhortativas

24.G.1 Infinitives

The infinitive as an
imperative: 25.B.8

a. In everyday language in Spain, the infinitive can be used with **vosotros** instead of the command form.

¡**Dejaros** de tonterías!	*Stop that nonsense!*

b. In both Spain and Latin America, an informal request can be strengthened by adding the preposition **a** before the infinitive.

¡**A trabajar**, todo el mundo!	*Everybody, get to work!*
¡**A acostarse**, niños!	*Go to bed, children!*

24.G.2 Impersonal imperative

a. In contexts where instructions, bans, or commands are expressed to the general public, the *infinitive* is the most common form.

No **fumar**.	*No smoking.*
No **entrar**.	*No entry.*
Leer las instrucciones con cuidado.	*Read the instructions carefully.*
Apagar la luz al salir.	*Turn off the light when you leave.*
¡**Mantener** la calma!	*Stay calm!*

b. Other structures can also be used to express impersonal negative commands. For example, to ban: **Prohibido** + *infinitive* (**Prohibido fumar**) or the **usted** command: **No fume**. Affirmative impersonal commands can also use the **usted** command: **Empuje** (*Push*), **Hale** (*Pull*).

24.G.3 The imperative and politeness

The imperative is softened in everyday language by the use of other verb tenses or expressions.

a. Verb phrases with infinitives can be used as requests.

¡**Ve a traerme** un cafecito!	*Go and get me a coffee!*
¡**Pongámonos a trabajar**!	*Let's get to work!*
¿**Puedes venir** acá, por favor?	*Can you come here, please?*

◀ Modal verb phrases with the infinitive: 26.B

b. Questions with the conditional of **poder** and **querer** can also be used as requests. Adverbs like **ya, ahora**, and **inmediatamente** can be added to strengthen the command.

¿**Podrías** contestarme ahora?	*Could you answer me now?*
¿**Querría** usted hacerlo ya?	*Could you do that immediately?*

◀ The conditional as a polite form: 21.B.4

c. Questions with verbs in the present indicative and statements starting with **A ver** or ending in interrogatives such as ¿**quiere(s)?, ¿puede(s)?, ¿sí?, ¿vale?,** and ¿**eh?** can soften the request as well.

¿**Me dices** tu nombre?	*Can you tell me your name?*
¡**A ver** si terminas pronto!	*Let's see if you can get it done soon!*
Llamas ahora, ¿**vale**?	*Call now, OK?*
¿**Puede decirme** qué hora es?	*Could you tell me what time it is?*
Ayúdame, ¿**eh**?	*Help me, will you?*

◀ Tag questions: 14.A.3

d. The expression ¿**Por qué no...?** is common in everyday speech as a polite, informal request, but good intonation is important, as it can easily be interpreted as a reproachful exclamation.

¿**Por qué no** me ayudas?	*Would (Why don't) you help me?*
¿**Por qué no** te acuestas y descansas un poco?	*Would (Why don't) you lie down and get some rest?*

24.G.4 *Que* + subjunctive

Sentences using the structure **que** + *subjunctive* can be classified as requests (¡**Que siga la fiesta**!), but the verb's meaning can also convey an indirect order or request from someone else (*indirect speech*) using an insistent tone.

◀ The subjunctive in independent clauses: 23.B.2b

Que des una explicación.	*You must give an explanation.*
Que vuelvas a llamar.	*You should / have to call again.*
Que me lo **digas** de nuevo.	*Say it to me again.*
¡**Que** te lo **compres**!	*Go ahead and buy it for yourself!*

◀ Note that in this structure, pronouns come before the verb.

24.H The imperative in colloquial expressions

El imperativo en expresiones coloquiales

The imperative is also used in common colloquial expressions such as **oye, no me digas, mira**, and **anda ya**. In this case, its meaning is not that of a command or request. Instead, it is an idiomatic expression.

—**Oye**, tengo que ir al mercado ahora.   *Listen, I have to go to the market now.*

—**¡No me digas** que te olvidaste del postre!   *Don't tell me that you forgot the dessert!*

—**Oye**, ¿sabes que Eva se va a casar?   *Hey, did you know that Eva is getting married?*

—**¡No me digas!**   *You're kidding! / No way!*

Mira que tu opinión me importa.   *Believe me, your opinion is important to me.*

¡Anda! No esperaba verte aquí.   *Goodness! I didn't expect to see you here!*

—Soy la mejor amiga del mundo.   *I am the best friend in the world.*

—**¡Anda ya!**   *Give me a break! / Come on!*

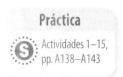

Práctica

Actividades 1–15,
pp. A138–A143

Nonpersonal verb forms
Formas no personales del verbo

25.A Overview

Aspectos generales

In contrast to conjugated personal verb forms, the nonpersonal verb forms do not change according to the person, number, tense, or mood.

Spanish has three nonpersonal forms: the *infinitive*, the **gerundio**, and the *past participle*. Although these are verb forms in Spanish, they can have other non-verb functions in a sentence. The infinitive can act as a *noun*, the past participle can act as an *adjective*, and the **gerundio** is used primarily as an *adverb*.

25.A.1 Simple forms

Both the infinitive and the past participle have corresponding forms in English and Spanish, but the **gerundio** does not. The Spanish **gerundio** and the English present participle (the *-ing* form in *I am talking*) are often equated because they form the progressive tense in both languages: **estar leyendo** (*to be reading*). In spite of this similarity, their areas of use are very different. The present participle can be an adjective or an adverb in English (*a **walking** stick; He died **thinking** about his children.*), while the **gerundio** functions principally as an adverb in Spanish. In addition, the words **gerundio** and *gerund* are false cognates. *Gerund* refers to a verb acting as a noun (***Walking** is good for you.*). In Spanish, the infinitive is used in this case (**Caminar es bueno para la salud**). Therefore, the term **gerundio** is used in this text to refer to this verb form. *Present participle* is used only in reference to the progressive tenses in Spanish.

Progressive tenses: 17.F.1, 25.C.3, 26.D

Simple forms		
Infinitive	**Past participle**	***Gerundio***
habl**ar** (*to talk / to speak*)	habl**ado** (*spoken*)	habl**ando** (*talking/speaking*)
com**er** (*to eat*)	com**ido** (*eaten*)	com**iendo** (*eating*)
sal**ir** (*to go out / to leave*)	sal**ido** (*gone out / left*)	sal**iendo** (*going out / leaving*)

25.A.2 Compound forms

The compound forms of the infinitive and the **gerundio** are composed of **haber** + *past participle*.

Perfect infinitive		*Gerundio compuesto*	
haber (*to have*)	habl**ado** (*spoken*)	**habiendo** (*having*)	habl**ado** (*spoken*)
	com**ido** (*eaten*)		com**ido** (*eaten*)
	sal**ido** (*gone out / left*)		sal**ido** (*gone out / left*)

Deberías **haber comido** antes de salir de casa.   *You should have eaten before you left the house.*
Habiendo salido, pudo hacer la llamada.   *Having stepped out, she was able to make the call.*

Adverbial uses of the **gerundio**: 25.C.5

25.B The infinitive

El infinitivo

The *infinitive* is the base form of the verb. This form can also act as a noun (where English uses the *-ing* gerund form). The infinitive can be the subject or the object of a sentence; it can be modified with articles and other determiners.

The Spanish infinitive can have three endings: **-ar, -er,** or **-ir**. Only a few other Spanish (non-verb) words have these endings: **bazar, bar, néctar, carácter, revólver, mártir, elixir**, etc.

Verbs: 17.A

25.B.1 The infinitive as a noun

a. The infinitive functions as a noun in nonpersonal clauses with **ser** or with other verbs where an infinitive is the grammatical subject. The real (logical) subject of the infinitive is not mentioned.

Es necesario **trabajar**.	*It is necessary to work.*
Tener salud importa mucho.	*It is very important to have good health.*

Determiners: 4.A ▶ **b.** The use of the article and other determiners with an infinitive is possible, but is most often seen in written language, idiomatic expressions, and formal contexts. An article or other determiner is mandatory when the infinitive is the subject and is modified with an adjective or a prepositional phrase.

El hablar de otras personas no me gusta nada.	*I don't like talking about other people at all.*
Este eterno llover me tiene harta.	*I'm tired of this never-ending rain.*

c. Since the infinitive keeps its verbal characteristics, it can be modified by an adverb when it is the subject or object of a sentence. Likewise, it can have a direct object.

Esquiar *bien* es fácil.	*Skiing well is easy.*
Preocuparse *tanto* es totalmente inútil.	*Worrying so much is a complete waste of time.*
Pienso **escribirte** *mucho*.	*I intend to write to you a lot.*
Decirlo es más fácil que **hacerlo**.	*It is easier said than done.*
Estudiar *español* es muy interesante y divertido.	*Studying Spanish is very interesting and fun.*
Quiero recorrer *Latinoamérica* estas vacaciones.	*I want to travel around Latin America over vacation.*

25.B.2 The infinitive with an adverbial function

Prepositions: Ch. 12 ▶ **a. Para** + *infinitive* / **sin** + *infinitive* can start adverbial phrases.

Lo hizo **sin pensar**.	*He did it without thinking.*
Para explicármelo, hizo un dibujo.	*To explain it to me, he made a drawing.*

The article **el** *after the preposition* **a** ▶ **b. Al** + *infinitive* indicates that an action is happening at the same time as something else.
forms the contraction **al**. The time of the action is expressed by the conjugated verb.

Al verte, me enamoré.	*Upon seeing you, I fell in love.*

c. The subject of the infinitive must be stated if it's different from the subject in the main clause.

Cierra la puerta al salir **Marta**.	*Close the door when Marta leaves.*
Cierra la puerta al salir.	*Close the door when you leave.*

d. De + *infinitive* is often used with **ser, seguir**, and **continuar**. It expresses condition or consequence (often negative), assumes a known context, and can have a subject.

De ser tan difíciles las cosas, lo mejor es olvidar el asunto.	*When everything is so difficult, it is best to forget about it.*
De haber continuado así, te habría ido mal.	*If it had continued like that, it would have gone badly for you.*

25.B.3 The infinitive after a noun or adjective

Nouns and adjectives can be modified by a *preposition* + *infinitive*: **problemas por resolver** (*problems to solve*); **trabajo por hacer** (*work to do*).

Vosotros sois **buenos para jugar** al fútbol.	*You [pl.] are good at playing soccer.*
Hay varios **temas a tratar** en la reunión.	*There are several topics to discuss at the meeting.*
Todavía nos queda **mucho por hacer**.	*We still have a lot to do.*

25.B.4 Placement of pronouns

a. When the infinitive follows an *adjective + preposition,* object pronouns are attached to the infinitive.

Las cartas están **listas para enviár*telas***.	*The letters are ready to be sent to you.*
Estoy **contenta de ver*te***.	*I'm glad to see you.*

b. When the infinitive is clearly governed by a conjugated verb or forms a verb phrase (like **ir a** + *infinitive*), the object or reflexive pronoun is added to the end of the infinitive or before the conjugated verb.

Verb phrases with the infinitive: 26.B, 26.C
Placement of direct and indirect object pronouns: 13.G.2

La ley tenéis que cumplir**la**.	*You [pl.] have to follow the law.*
La ley **la** tenéis que cumplir.	

c. When a reflexive verb is followed by an infinitive, object pronouns are attached to the infinitive.

Reflexive pronoun placement: 27.A.1

Me arrepiento de haber**te** mentido.	*I regret lying to you.*
Lina siempre se acuerda de comprar**nos** el diario.	*Lina always remembers to buy us the newspaper.*
¿Te ofreces a ayudar**me**?	*Are you offering to help me?*

25.B.5 The infinitive after a conjugated verb

a. After a verb that expresses a wish, an infinitive is used if the subject is referring to him/herself. When the person in the main clause is expressing a wish about someone else, a noun **que** clause is necessary.

The subjunctive in noun clauses: 23.C.1

Infinitive	Noun clause
Quiero **ser** feliz.	Quiero **que seas** feliz.
I want to be happy.	*I want you to be happy.*

b. After verbs like **creer** and **estimar**, a noun **que** clause can replace the infinitive in formal spoken language and in written language (news headlines, speeches, laws), even if the same subject performs the action.

Infinitive	Noun clause
Creemos saber la razón del problema.	**Creemos que sabemos** la razón del problema.
We think we know the cause of the problem.	*We think that we know the cause of the problem.*
Estimo ganar más dinero en este puesto.	**Estimo que voy a ganar** más dinero en este puesto.
I estimate I'll make more money in this position.	*I estimate that I'll make more money in this position.*

c. Reporting verbs (**decir, asegurar, informar**) in the **usted/él/ella** form are often followed by **que** clauses even if there is no change of subject. The use of the infinitive happens with other persons too, but is less common and more formal than a **que** clause.

Reporting verbs: 23.C.2
Indirect discourse: Ch. 31

Infinitive	Noun clause
El ministro **afirma decir** la verdad.	El ministro **afirma que dice** la verdad.
The minister claims to tell the truth.	*The minister claims that he's telling the truth.*
Informamos haber terminado el proyecto.	**Informamos que terminamos** el proyecto.
We inform you that we have finished the project.	*We inform you that we finished the project.*

d. Most verbs of will and influence (**dejar, permitir, prohibir, recomendar**) can be followed by the infinitive, but a **que** clause followed by the subjunctive is also possible.

Infinitive	Noun clause
No **dejaré salir** a nadie.	No **dejaré que nadie salga**.
I will not have anyone leaving.	*I will not let anyone leave.*
No se te **permitirá viajar** sin visa.	No se te **permitirá que viajes** sin visa.
You won't be allowed to travel without a visa.	*Traveling without a visa won't be allowed.*

25.B.6 The infinitive with verbs of motion

Verbs of motion such as **venir, bajar, entrar, llegar** are usually followed by the prepositions **a** or **de** + *infinitive*. In these sentences, the verb keeps its original meaning of motion and direction in contrast to verb phrases where the meaning of the conjugated verb may be lost (**Voy a estudiar**, *I am going to study*).

Ven **a visitarme**.	*Come and visit me.*
Baja **a abrir** la puerta.	*Go downstairs and open the door.*
Vengo **de trabajar**.	*I'm coming from work.*

25.B.7 The infinitive with sense verbs

Gerundio with sense verbs:  25.C.7

Sense verbs (**ver, oír, sentir**) express a completed action when followed by the *infinitive* and an ongoing action when used with the **gerundio**. Both the infinitive and the **gerundio** describe an action performed by the direct object. In such cases, the infinitive always follows the verb without a preposition.

Infinitive	Gerundio
Os **oí discutir**.	Os **oí discutiendo**.
I heard you [pl.] argue.	*I heard you [pl.] arguing.*
¿Me **viste llegar** a casa?	¿Me **viste llegando** a casa?
Did you see me arrive home?	*Did you see me arriving home?*

25.B.8 The infinitive as an imperative

Infinitive as an imperative: 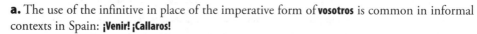 24.G.1

a. The use of the infinitive in place of the imperative form of **vosotros** is common in informal contexts in Spain: **¡Venir! ¡Callaros!**

Other imperative constructions: 24.G.1, 24.G.2

b. Thoughout the Spanish-speaking world, the infinitive is used in commands, instructions, and signs. In spoken language, it is often used with the preposition **a**: **¡A venir todos ya!**

Primero, **conectar** el aparato.	*First, connect the device.*	¡A **trabajar**!	*Let's get to work!*
No **cruzar** la calle.	*Don't cross the street.*	¡A **dormir** ya mismo!	*Go to sleep now!*

25.B.9 Verb phrases with infinitives

Verb phrases: 26.B, 26.C

Many verb phrases in Spanish are formed with the infinitive and often with the preposition **a** or **de**.

Vamos a viajar.	*Let's travel.*
Hay que **dejar de fumar**.	*You must stop smoking.*

25.C The *gerundio*

The Spanish **gerundio** acts as an adverb of manner with an ongoing meaning and, despite a few exceptions, is rarely used as an adjective. It is also used in many verb phrases. The **gerundio** has both regular and irregular forms.

25.C.1 **Regular forms**

The ending **-ando** is added to the stem of **-ar** verbs, and **-iendo** is added to the stem of **-er** and **-ir** verbs.

-ar **verbs**	*-er* **verbs**	*-ir* **verbs**
habl**ar**	com**er**	sub**ir**
habl**ando**	com**iendo**	sub**iendo**

25.C.2 **Irregular forms**

Irregular verbs are often **-er** and **-ir** verbs that form the **gerundio** with **-iendo**, but have spelling or stem changes. This list shows some of the most common examples.

◀ Verb conjugation tables, pp. B1–B20. See verb patterns 11, 13, 17, 20, 23, 25, 26, 46, 48, 50, 52, 58, 60, 64, 65, 73, 76.

-uir, -eer, -aer **and other verbs**		$e \rightarrow i, o \rightarrow u$ **stem change**	
Infinitive	*Gerundio*	**Infinitive**	*Gerundio*
constru**ir**	constru**yendo**	d**e**cir	d**i**ciendo
l**ee**r	l**e**yendo	p**e**dir	p**i**diendo
ca**er**	ca**yendo**	v**e**nir	v**i**niendo
o**í**r	o**y**endo	d**o**rmir	d**u**rmiendo
ro**er**	ro**yendo**	p**o**der	p**u**diendo

◀ Note that **-er** and **-ir** verbs whose stems end in a vowel have a **-yendo** ending.

Verbs derived from these have the same changes in the **gerundio**: **predecir**, **prediciendo**; **convenir**, **conviniendo**, etc.

25.C.3 *Estar +* **present participle** (progressive tenses)

a. The present participle is combined with the verb **estar** to refer to actions that are ongoing. This is sometimes referred to as *progressive* or *continuous* tenses.

◀ Progressive tenses: 17.F.1 Verb phrases with the **gerundio**: 26.D

Estaba trabajando cuando oí la alarma.   *I was working when I heard the alarm.*

b. In Spanish, **estar** + *present participle* can't be used to refer to conditions or states. The past participle is used instead.

◀ The past participle: 25.D

Está parado ahí.   *He is standing over there.*

c. This verb phrase can be used in all indicative and subjunctive mood tenses.

Estar + **present participle: Indicative mood**		
Present	**Estoy trabajando** en este momento.	*I am working right now.*
Simple future	A las ocho **estaré trabajando**.	*I will be working at eight.*
Preterite	**Estuve cocinando** tres horas.	*I was cooking for three hours.*
Imperfect	**Estaba cocinando** cuando sonó el timbre.	*I was cooking when the doorbell rang.*
Conditional	Si fuera rica, **estaría viajando** por el mundo.	*If I were rich, I would be traveling around the world.*
Present perfect	**He estado pensando** mucho en ti.	*I have been thinking a lot about you.*
Future perfect	Para cuando llegue la pizza, **habré estado esperando** más de una hora.	*By the time the pizza arrives, I will have been waiting for over an hour.*
Past perfect	Cuando me di cuenta de que era el libro equivocado, ya **había estado leyendo** tres horas.	*When I realized it was the wrong book, I had already been reading for three hours.*
Conditional perfect	**Habría estado estudiando** si hubiera sabido que tenía examen.	*I would have been studying if I had known that I had an exam.*

Estar + **present participle: Subjunctive mood**		
Present	No creo que **esté durmiendo**.	*I don't think he is sleeping.*
Past	No podía creer que **estuviera dándole** la mano al presidente.	*I couldn't believe I was shaking the president's hand.*
Present perfect	Me extraña que **haya estado trabajando** tantas horas.	*I think it's strange that he's been working so many hours.*
Past perfect	Dudo que **hubiese estado mintiendo**.	*I doubt he had been lying.*

d. In Spanish, the present form of **estar** + *present participle* is never used to refer to the future. The simple present is used instead.

Llegan mañana.   *They are arriving tomorrow.*

e. The future form of **estar** + *present participle* can be used to express probability about the present, while the conditional form can be used to express probability about the past.

—¿Dónde está Carlos?   *Where is Carlos?*
—**Estará trabajando.**   *He must be working.*

—¿Por qué no vino Carlos?   *Why didn't Carlos come?*
—**Estaría trabajando.**   *He must have been working.*

f. The future perfect of **estar** + *present participle* can also be used to express probability in the past.

—¿Por qué no atendió el teléfono?   *Why didn't he answer the phone?*
—**Habrá estado durmiendo.**   *He must have been sleeping.*

25.C.4   **Other verb phrases with the** *gerundio*

In addition to **estar**, other verbs can be combined with the **gerundio**. In some cases, the meaning is similar to that of the phrases with **estar**. In other cases, there are subtle differences.

andar + **gerundio**	*to be + -ing verb*	**Andaba pensando** en ir a Punta Cana.	*I was thinking of going to Punta Cana.*
ir + **gerundio**	*to start + -ing verb*	**Voy poniendo** la mesa mientras te preparas.	*I'll start setting the table while you get ready.*
llevar/pasarse + *time expression* + **gerundio**	*to be doing something for + time expression*	**Llevo** tres años **estudiando** teatro. **Se pasó** todo el verano **estudiando**.	*I've been studying drama for three years. She has been studying all summer.*
seguir/continuar + **gerundio**	*to keep/continue + -ing verb*	**Siguieron planeando** el viaje.	*They kept on planning for the trip.*
venir + **gerundio**	*to be + -ing verb*	**Viene pensando** en cambiar de trabajo.	*He has been thinking about changing jobs.*
vivir + **gerundio**	*to keep + -ing verb (habitual or repeated action)*	**Vive quejándose.**	*She keeps complaining all the time.*

The present with future meaning: 17.E.4
Using the present to refer to the future: 17.F.4

Simple future for assumptions about the present: 20.C.2
Conditional for assumptions about the past: 21.B.2

The future perfect for assumptions about the past: 20.F.2

Verb phrases with the **gerundio**: 26.D

25.C.5 **Adverbial uses of the** *gerundio*

a. The **gerundio** can function like an adverb. The chart that follows describes the main meanings expressed by the **gerundio**.

cause	No **queriendo** escuchar esa conversación, me fui de la reunión.	*Not wanting to listen to that conversation, I left the meeting.*
concession	**Siendo** liberal, sus ideas son un poco conservadoras.	*Being a liberal, his ideas are somewhat conservative.*
condition	**Estando** invitado, sí va.	*If he is invited, he will go.*
manner	Entró **derribando** la puerta.	*He got in by knocking down the door.*
method	Hizo su fortuna **vendiendo** madera.	*He made his fortune selling wood.*
purpose	Me llamó **diciendo** que no iba a venir.	*He called me saying he wasn't going to come.*
simultaneity	Me desperté **queriendo** café.	*I woke up wanting coffee.*

b. To express purpose, the **gerundio** can be used with verbs of communication. It can be replaced by **para** + *infinitive*.

◀ **Para** + *infinitive*: 25.B.2a

Le escribió **diciéndole** que la amaba.　　　*He wrote to her telling her he loved her.*
Le escribió **para decirle** que la amaba.　　*He wrote her to tell her that he loved her.*

c. The action expressed by the **gerundio** should happen before, at the same time, or right after the action expressed with the conjugated verb. Although many Spanish speakers use the **gerundio** to refer to an action that happened after (but not *right* after) the action in the main verb, a relative clause is the preferred form in these cases.

Both actions happened at the same time:
Escuchando los anuncios del gobierno, me deprimí.　　*Listening to the government announcements, I got depressed.*

The action expressed by the **gerundio** happened before:
Alzando el arco, disparó la flecha.　　*Raising the bow, he fired the arrow.*

The action expressed by the **gerundio** happened after:
Aumentaron las tasas de interés **causando** pánico en el mercado.　　*Interest rates rose, causing panic in the market.*

Aumentaron las tasas de interés, **lo que causó** pánico en el mercado.　　*Interest rates rose, which caused panic in the market.*

d. The **gerundio compuesto** can only refer to actions that happened before the action expressed by the conjugated verb.

Habiendo aprobado el examen, salió a festejar.　　*Having passed the exam, he went out to celebrate.*

25.C.6 **The** *gerundio* **vs. the English present participle: use as adjective**

a. Since the **gerundio** normally modifies a verb, the general rule is that it can't be used as an adjective. Therefore, the English present participle used as an adjective is best represented in Spanish by a relative clause, a prepositional phrase, an adjective, or a past participle.

there are growing concerns	cada vez preocupa más
suffering people	personas que sufren
growing problems	problemas crecientes / en aumento
swimming pool	pileta de natación / piscina

b. The **gerundio** can be used in picture captions or titles of paintings.

Pablo Picasso, «Mujer **llorando**», 1937.

Pablo Picasso, "Weeping Woman," 1937.

Foto del príncipe heredero **sonriéndoles**
a los fotógrafos.

*Photo of the crown prince smiling
at the photographers.*

Mi hermana **enseñándome** a nadar
en el verano de 2009.

*My sister teaching me to swim,
summer 2009.*

c. Ardiendo and **hirviendo** can be used as adjectives.

fuego **ardiendo**   *burning fire*   agua **hirviendo**   *boiling water*

25.C.7 Use of the *gerundio* to refer to a direct object

a. With sense verbs like **oír, ver, encontrar, recordar,** and **sentir,** the **gerundio** describes an ongoing action performed by the direct object.

Anoche oímos al perro **ladrando**.

Last night we heard the dog barking.

Hemos encontrado al niño solo y **llorando**.

We found the boy alone and crying.

Placement of the object
pronoun: 13.G

Siempre recordaré a mi profesora **explicándome**
el subjuntivo.

*I will always remember my professor explaining
the subjunctive to me.*

b. The **gerundio** can also be used to refer to the object of a verb that expresses a mental or physical representation (**imaginar, recordar**). The **gerundio** should always express an action, never a state.

Me **lo** imaginé **viajando** por el mundo.

I imagined him traveling around the world.

Los recuerdo **hablando** de sus abuelos.

I remember them talking about their grandparents.

Te hacía **viajando** por Europa.

I thought you were traveling around Europe.

No me puedo imaginar **a Carlos bailando** tango.

I can't imagine Carlos dancing tango.

Recuerdo que Mario tenía problemas.

I remember Mario having problems.

25.C.8 Placement of pronouns

a. When the **gerundio** follows a conjugated verb, the pronoun comes before the conjugated verb or is added to the end of the **gerundio**.

(Te estoy escribiendo la carta.)

(I'm writing the letter to you.)

Te la estoy escribiendo. / Estoy escribiéndo**tela**.

I'm writing it to you.

Gerundio with
sense verbs: 25.C.7

b. Reflexive and object pronouns must be added to the **gerundio** in clauses with sense verbs and objects.

Te vi bajándo**te** del autobús.

I saw you getting off the bus.

Nos oyeron hablándo**les** en francés a los turistas.

They heard us speaking in French to the tourists.

25.D The past participle

El participio

Present and past perfect:
19.A, 19.D
Use of the participle
in passive **ser** clauses: 28.B

The past participle forms all the compound tenses with the auxiliary verb **haber** (*to have*): **Has hablado.** (*You have spoken.*). With **ser**, the past participle forms passive sentences: **La carta fue escrita.** (*The letter was written.*). Apart from these verb functions, the past participle is generally used as an *adjective*.

25.D.1 Regular forms

Regular past participles: 19.A.1
When used as adjectives,
past participles agree in
gender and number: 3.A.1

a. The ending **-ado** is added to the stem of **-ar** verbs to form the past participle. The ending **-ido** is added to the stem of **-er** and **-ir** verbs. Object and reflexive pronouns must *always* come before **haber**.

habl**ar** → hablado   com**er** → comido   sub**ir** → subido

b. When the verb stem ends in **a**, **e**, or **o**, a written accent is needed on the past participle ending **-ido** (**-er** and **-ir** verbs). The combination of **u** + **i** usually forms a diphthong and does not have an accent (**construido, huido**).

Accents on vowel combinations: 1.E.4
Hiatus and accentuation: 1.E.5

Infinitive	Verb stem	Past participle	
creer	**cre-**	creído	*thought*
leer	**le-**	leído	*read*
oír	**o-**	oído	*heard*
sonreír	**sonre-**	sonreído	*smiled*
traer	**tra-**	traído	*brought*

25.D.2 Irregular forms

A number of verbs have an irregular past participle.

Irregular past participles: 19.A.2

Infinitives	Irregular past participles	
abrir	**abierto**	*opened*
cubrir	**cubierto**	*covered*
decir	**dicho**	*said, told*
describir	**descrito**	*described*
escribir	**escrito**	*written*
hacer	**hecho**	*done, made*
morir	**muerto**	*died*
poner	**puesto**	*placed*
resolver	**resuelto**	*resolved*
romper	**roto**	*broken*
satisfacer	**satisfecho**	*satisfied*
ver	**visto**	*seen*
volver	**vuelto**	*returned*

Remember that most verbs derived from these infinitives have the same irregularity in the past participle: **descubrir, descubierto**, etc.

25.D.3 Past participles with two forms

a. The verbs **freír**, **imprimir**, and **proveer** (as well as their derivatives) have two completely equal past participle forms: a regular form and an irregular form that can be used in all the compound verb tenses with **haber** and passive voice with **ser**.

Passive voice with **ser**: 28.B

Infinitive	Past participle	
	Regular	Irregular
imprimir (*to print*)	imprimido	**impreso**
freír (*to fry*)	freído	**frito**
proveer (*to provide*)	proveído	**provisto**

He **impreso/imprimido** la carta.
No hemos **frito/freído** la carne.
A los viajeros se les ha **provisto/proveído** de todo.

I have printed the letter.
We haven't fried the meat.
The travelers have been provided with everything.

b. In the Spanish-speaking world, **freído** and **provisto** are often used as both a participle and an adjective. The irregular form **impreso** is often used in Latin America as both a participle and an adjective.

El formulario está **impreso**.	*The form is printed.*
Las albóndigas ya están **fritas**.	*The meatballs are already fried.*
La bodega está bien **provista**.	*The wine cellar is well supplied.*

Passive voice with **ser**: 28.B ▶

c. All other Spanish verbs that have two past participle forms use only the regular form in compound tenses with **haber** (**He corregido las cartas.**) and the passive voice with **ser** (**Las cartas han sido corregidas.**). The irregular past participle form is only used as an adjective (**Eso es correcto.**). Here is a list of some of these two-participle verbs with their most common meanings.

Gender and number of ▶
adjectives: 3.A

Infinitives	Past participles		Adjectives	
absorber	**absorbido**	*absorbed*	**absorto/a**	*absorbed/engrossed*
atender	**atendido**	*attended/assisted*	**atento/a**	*attentive/alert/courteous*
bendecir	**bendecido**	*blessed*	**bendito/a**	*blessed/holy*
confesar	**confesado**	*confessed*	**confeso/a**	*self-confessed*
confundir	**confundido**	*confused*	**confuso/a**	*confused/confusing*
despertar	**despertado**	*awakened*	**despierto/a**	*awake/bright/alert*
elegir	**elegido**	*chosen/elected*	**electo/a**	*chosen/elected*
maldecir	**maldecido**	*cursed/damned*	**maldito/a**	*cursed/damned*
prender	**prendido**	*caught*	**preso/a**	*imprisoned*
presumir	**presumido**	*presumed*	**presunto/a**	*presumed/alleged*
soltar	**soltado**	*released / let go*	**suelto/a**	*loose/fluid/fluent*

Electo is used mostly in Latin ▶
America as an adjective:
el presidente electo
el preso: the prisoner ▶
estar preso/a: to be
imprisoned

25.D.4 Use of the past participle

a. The past participle forms all the compound verb tenses with **haber** both in the indicative and the subjunctive moods (**ha salido / haya salido**). The participle form always keeps the **-o** ending in all compound tenses.

Passive voice with **ser**: 28.B ▶
Estar and passive voice
with **ser**: 28.C.3

b. The past participle is used in the passive voice with **ser**, where it agrees in gender and number with the subject in the sentence.

La novel**a fue escrita** por Isabel Allende.	*The novel was written by Isabel Allende.*
Las novel**as fueron escritas** por Isabel Allende.	*The novels were written by Isabel Allende.*

Agreement of the past participle ▶
in verb phrases: 26.E

c. With **estar**, the past participle conveys the result of an action. Such sentences often correspond to the passive structure with **ser**.

La carta **fue escrita**. *(passive voice)*	*The letter was written.*
La carta **está escrita**. *(**estar** + past participle)*	*The letter is written.*

Práctica

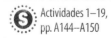
Actividades 1–19,
pp. A144–A150

Verb phrases and modal verbs
Perífrasis verbales y verbos modales

26.A Overview

Aspectos generales

26.A.1 Verb phrases

a. Perífrasis verbales are made up of an auxiliary verb and a main verb. The main verb always uses a nonpersonal form: *infinitive,* **gerundio**, or *past participle*.

Volvió a hablar con su hermano.	*He spoke with his brother again.*
Siguió hablando durante toda la reunión.	*He continued talking during the entire meeting.*
Llevo ganados diez premios.	*I have won ten awards (so far).*

b. Auxiliary verbs are usually conjugated, but can also appear in nonpersonal forms.

Volver a hablar con él fue una alegría.	*Talking to him again was a joy.*
No **pudiendo responder** a la pregunta, se echó a llorar.	*Being unable to answer the question, she began to cry.*

c. Most auxiliary verbs can be used as main verbs.

Volvió a su pueblo.	*He returned to his hometown.*
Sigo su blog todas las semanas.	*I follow your blog every week.*
Llevé a los niños a la fiesta.	*I took the children to the party.*

d. There can be another element, such as a preposition or conjunction, joining the two verbs that form the verb phrase.

◀ Verbs with prepositions: 17.B.2e

Tengo *que* **trabajar** el fin de semana.	*I have to work this weekend.*
Debe *de* **haber llovido** mucho.	*It must have rained a lot.*

e. Not all verb combinations are **perífrasis verbales**. In a **perífrasis verbal**, the meaning of the auxiliary verb is partially or totally different from the meaning of the verb phrase as a whole.

Tengo que trabajar.
(**tener** does not express *possession*)

I have to work.

26.B Modal verb phrases with the infinitive

Perífrasis modales de infinitivo

◀ The infinitive: 25.B

26.B.1 Modal auxiliaries

a. Modal auxiliaries express possibility, obligation, necessity, and other aspects of the speaker's attitude toward the action expressed by the main verb.

◀ Modal verbs: 17.F.3

Bailo.	*I dance.*
Puedo bailar.	*I can dance.*
Quiero bailar.	*I want to dance.*

26.B.2 Aspect expressed by modal verb phrases

Modal verb phrases can express obligation or necessity, possibility, and doubt.

Passive constructions with se and modal verbs: 28.D.3

Modal verb phrases	Aspect expressed	Examples
deber + *infinitive*	obligation	**Debes venir** inmediatamente. *You must come immediately.*
deber de + *infinitive*	doubt or possibility	**Deben de ser** las ocho. *It must be eight o'clock.*
tener que + *infinitive*	obligation	No fui porque **tenía que estudiar**. *I didn't go because I had to study.*
haber de + *infinitive*	obligation	Estos son los documentos que **hemos de darle** al abogado. *These are the documents that we have to give to the lawyer.*
	probability (with perfect infinitive)	Alguien le **ha de haber contado**. *Someone must have told her.*
haber que + *infinitive*	obligation (that can't be avoided; impersonal: used only in the third-person singular)	**Habrá que sobrellevar** la crisis. *The crisis must be endured.*
poder + *infinitive*	capacity, ability	La cerámica **puede resistir** los cambios de temperatura. *Ceramics can withstand changes in temperature.*
	permission	**Puedes venir** mañana si quieres. *You can come tomorrow if you'd like.*
	assumption	**Podría ser** interesante. *It could be interesting.*
venir a + *infinitive*	approximation	El libro **vino a costarme** unos cien pesos. *The book cost me about 100 pesos.*

26.B.3 Other modal verb phrases

The following verb phrases are commonly grouped together with modal verb phrases.

Modal verb phrases	Aspect expressed	Examples
parecer + *infinitive*	conjecture	**Parece haber** mucha gente en la fiesta. *There seem to be a lot of people at the party.*
querer + *infinitive*	wish, desire	**Quiero escuchar** música. *I want to listen to music.*
saber + *infinitive*	skill	**Sé hablar** español muy bien. *I know how to speak Spanish very well.*

26.B.4 *Deber / deber de*

a. Deber expresses obligation, but is weaker than **tener que**. **Deber de** expresses assumption or possibility. In everyday speech, the preposition **de** is often dropped and the meaning becomes ambiguous.

Debes cuidar la naturaleza.	*You should take care of nature.*
Deberías gastar menos.	*You should spend less.*
No **debiste** llegar tarde.	*You shouldn't have arrived late.*
Deberás hacerlo aunque no quieras.	*You should/will do it even though you don't want to.*
Este plato **debe de** ser delicioso.	*This dish must be delicious.*
El huracán **debió de** ser muy fuerte porque hizo mucho daño.	*The hurricane must have been very strong because it caused a lot of damage.*

220   Verb phrases and modal verbs • **Chapter 26**

b. The English *should* is usually translated using the present tense or the conditional of **deber**. It can also be translated using the future tense or passive constructions with **se** without a modal auxiliary, particularly in handbooks and other instructions.

◀ Passive constructions with **se**: 28.D

Deberías/Debes ir al médico.

You **should** go to the doctor.

Al presionar el botón, **escuchará** un sonido.
Al presionar el botón, **se escucha** un sonido.

When you press the button, you **should hear** a beep.

26.B.5 *Poder*

a. In the preterite, **poder** conveys that someone succeeded in doing something, while the imperfect describes whether a person was able to do something or not.

◀ Verbs that change meaning in the preterite: 18.F

La puerta estaba cerrada y no **podíamos** entrar.
Finalmente **pudimos** hacerlo.

The door was locked and we couldn't get in.
Finally, we managed to do it.

b. These examples show the use of **poder** in different verb tenses.

Permission or ban	
Todos **podéis** entrar gratis.	All of you [pl.] may go in for free.
¿**Podrías/Puedes** prestarme tu libro?	Could you / Can you lend me your book? / Could I / Can I / May I borrow your book?
No puedes hacer lo que se te ocurra.	You can't / are not allowed to do whatever you feel like doing.

Possibility/Ability	
¡**No puedo** ponerme las botas!	I can't put my boots on!
Aquí **no se puede** cruzar la calle. ¡Es muy peligroso!	You can't cross the street here. It's very dangerous!
¿**Pudiste** ver la exhibición?	Did you get to see the exhibition?

Assumptions	
Podría ser bueno que vinieras.	It could/might be good if you came.
Eso **pudo/podía** haber sucedido.	It could have happened.
Podrías haber hecho algo.	You could/might have done something.

26.B.6 *Querer*

Querer is translated differently in the imperfect and the preterite. Notice also the difference in the preterite between **querer** and **no querer**.

◀ Verbs that change meaning in the preterite: 18.F

Quería decirle la verdad, pero no pude.
Quise decirle la verdad, pero no pude.
Me invitaron a salir ayer, pero **no quise**.

I wanted to tell him the truth, but I couldn't.
I tried to tell him the truth, but I couldn't.
I was invited to go out yesterday, but I refused.

26.B.7 *Saber*

a. In a verb phrase, **saber** indicates that a person has the skills or the knowledge to perform an action. This is independent of being physically, emotionally, or mentally in a state to do it (**poder**).

—¿**Sabes** esquiar?
—Sí, **sé** esquiar, pero **no puedo** hacerlo.
  Tengo el pie quebrado.

Can you ski?
Yes, I know how to ski, but I can't do it.
  My foot is broken.

Antes **sabía** hablar bien el español,
  pero ya **no puedo** hacerlo.

Before, I knew how to speak Spanish well,
  but I can't do it anymore.

Verbs that change meaning ▶ in the preterite: 18.F

b. As a main verb, **saber** is commonly translated as *to know* or *to discover / find out*.

Marcela **sabía** la verdad.	*Marcela knew the truth.*
Marcela **supo** la verdad.	*Marcela discovered / found out the truth.*

Infinitive: 25.B ▶

26.C | Other verb phrases with the infinitive

Otras perífrasis de infinitivo

26.C.1 | Verb phrases that express time

Use of the present to refer ▶
to the future: 17.F.4b
Use of the imperfect to
refer to incomplete actions:
18.E.6, 18.E.10c

Verb phrases	Aspect expressed	Examples
ir a + *infinitive*	future	**Voy a visitar** a mis primos. *I'm going to visit my cousins.*
	unexpected action or situation	¡Justo **me fui a enamorar** de ti! *Of all people, I fell in love with you!* ¿Puedes creer que mi auto se quedó sin frenos y **fue a dar** precisamente contra la Ferrari de mi jefe? *Can you believe that the brakes failed in my car and it went and hit my boss's Ferrari?*
soler + *infinitive*	repetition, habit	**Suelo levantarme** a las seis. *I usually get up at six.*
acostumbrar (a) + *infinitive* (*Lat. Am.*)	repetition, habit	**Acostumbra (a) tomar** el tren de las cinco. *He usually takes the five o'clock train.*
acabar de + *infinitive*	recent action	**Acabo de preparar** la cena. *I just prepared dinner.*
volver a + *infinitive*	repetition	Prometió que no **volverá a decir** mentiras. *He promised that he wouldn't tell lies again.*

26.C.2 | Verb phrases that express a phase

Some verb phrases refer to the preparation, the beginning, the end, or the interruption of an action.

Verb phrases	Aspect expressed	Examples
estar por + *infinitive*	preparation	**Estaba por preparar** la cena. *I was about to make dinner.*
comenzar/empezar a + *infinitive*	beginning	**Comenzó/Empezó a llover** en cuanto llegamos. *It began to rain as soon as we arrived.*
ponerse a + *infinitive*	beginning	Cuando terminó el espectáculo, todos **se pusieron a aplaudir**. *When the show was over, everyone began to applaud.*
entrar a + *infinitive*	beginning	Todos **entramos a sospechar** de él. *We all started to suspect him.*
dejar/parar de + *infinitive*	interruption	**Dejó de llover** y salió el sol. *It stopped raining and the sun came out.* **¡Para de llorar**, por favor! *Stop crying, please!*
acabar/terminar de + *infinitive*	end	**Terminé de cocinar** a las ocho. *I finished cooking at eight o'clock.*
pasar a + *infinitive*	transition	Después de estudiar italiano, **pasé a estudiar** ruso. *After studying Italian, I went on to study Russian.*

26.C.3 Verb phrases that express order

a. Some verb phrases with infinitives indicate the order of an action in a series.

Modal verb phrases	Aspect expressed	Examples
empezar por + *infinitive*	first action in a series	**Empecé por explicarle** que no me gustaba mi trabajo. *I began by explaining to him that I didn't like my job.*
acabar/terminar por + *infinitive*	last action in a series	**Terminé por comprar** el vestido violeta. *I ended up buying the purple dress.*
venir a + *infinitive*	result, outcome	En ese caso, ambas opciones **venían a ser** lo mismo. *In that case, both options turned out to be the same.*

b. **Empezar/acabar/terminar por** + *infinitive* can be replaced by **empezar/acabar/terminar** + **gerundio**.

Acabó por irse.
Acabó yéndose.   *He ended up leaving.*

26.D Verb phrases with the *gerundio*

Perífrasis de gerundio

All verb phrases with the **gerundio** express an ongoing action. Most verbs used as auxiliaries in these phrases are common verbs of movement (**ir, venir, andar, llevar, pasar, seguir,** etc.).

Verb phrases	Aspect expressed	Examples
estar + **gerundio**	ongoing action	**Estaba trabajando** cuando me llamaste. *I was working when you called me.*
ir + **gerundio**	incremental process with an end limit/result	Sus problemas de salud **fueron aumentando** hasta que finalmente tuvo que dejar de trabajar. *His health problems kept increasing (getting worse) until he finally had to stop working.*
	beginning of an incremental process	¿Podrías **ir pensando** en temas para el último capítulo? *Could you start thinking about topics for the last chapter?*
venir + **gerundio**	process that began in the past and continues up to the current moment	Nos **venía mintiendo**, pero lo descubrimos. *He had been lying to us, but we found out.* ¡Te **vengo diciendo** que comas mejor! *I've been telling you to eat better!*
andar + **gerundio**	current process that usually happens intermittently	El perro **anda olfateando** todos los árboles. *The dog is going around smelling all the trees.*
llevar + *time expression* + **gerundio**	period of time	**Llevo dos años estudiando** español. *I've been studying Spanish for two years.*
pasar(se) + *time expression* + **gerundio**	current process (more emphatic than **estar** + **gerundio**)	**Se pasó la noche llorando** porque extrañaba a su gatito. *He spent the night crying because he missed his kitten.*
vivir + **gerundio** (*Lat. Am.*)	repeated, constant, or habitual action	Mis vecinos **viven gritando**. No me dejan dormir. *My neighbors are always yelling. They don't let me sleep.*
seguir/continuar + **gerundio**	continued process	Ella **sigue estudiando**. *She is still / keeps on studying.*

The **gerundio**: 25.C

Estar + *present participle* (progressive tenses): 25.C.3

Past participle: 19.A.1,
19.A.2, 25.D

26.E Verb phrases with the past participle

Perífrasis de participio

a. All verb phrases with the past participle focus on the result of an action or process.
The participle agrees in gender and number with the subject, or with the object if there is one.

Estar + *past participle*: 28.C.3 ▶

Do not confuse **tener** + *past* ▶
participle with the perfect
tenses: Ch. 19

Verb phrases	Aspect expressed	Examples
estar + *past participle*	resulting state	La carta **está escrita** a mi nombre. *The letter is addressed to me.*
tener + *past participle*	process that has been completed	Eso ya lo **tengo visto**. *I have already looked at that.* Le **tengo prohibido** salir después de las once de la noche. *I have forbidden him to go out after eleven o'clock at night.*
llevar + *past participle*	accumulation up to a certain point in time	**Llevo ganados** cinco premios. *(So far,) I have won five awards.*

The *Nueva gramática* lists ▶
only **estar/tener/llevar** +
past participle.

b. Here are more verb phrases with the past participle.

dejar + *past participle*	Juan **dejó dicho** que lo llames. *Juan left a message for you to call him.*
encontrarse/hallarse + *past participle*	**Se encuentra muy cansado.** *He is feeling very tired.*
ir + *past participle*	Para marzo ya **iban escritos** cuatro capítulos del libro. *By March, four chapters of the book were already written.*
quedar(se) + *past participle*	**Quedé agotada** después de la fiesta. *I was exhausted after the party.*
resultar + *past participle*	La clase media **resultó beneficiada** por la caída de los precios. *The middle class benefited from the drop in prices.*
seguir + *past participle*	Las calles **siguen vigiladas** por la policía. *The streets continue to be patrolled by the police.*
venir + *past participle*	Las instrucciones **vinieron escritas** en la caja. *The instructions came written on the box.*
verse + *past participle*	Juan **se vio obligado** a partir. *Juan felt obligated to leave.*

Práctica

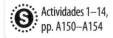

Actividades 1–14,
pp. A150–A154

Reflexive pronouns and verbs
Pronombres y verbos reflexivos

27.A Structure

Estructura

Reflexive pronouns indicate that the subject both does and receives the action in a sentence, directly or indirectly: *You* see *yourself* in the mirror. In Spanish, some verbs can only be used reflexively. These verbs are recorded in dictionaries and word lists with the reflexive pronoun **se** after the infinitive ending, like in **lavarse** (*to wash*), **preocuparse** (*to worry*), and **sentirse** (*to feel*). Reflexive pronouns take the same form as object pronouns except for **usted/él/ella** and **ustedes/ellos/ellas: se**. A different set of pronouns is used after prepositions and is usually followed by the adjective **mismo/a(s)**.

Subject	Reflexive pronouns	lavarse	Translation	After a preposition
yo	**me**	me lavo	*I wash (myself).*	**mí (conmigo)**
tú	**te**	te lavas	*You wash (yourself).*	**ti (contigo)**
vos	**te**	te lavás	*You wash (yourself).*	**vos**
usted, él, ella	**se**	se lava	*You wash (yourself).* *He/She washes (him/herself).*	**sí, usted/él/ella (consigo)**
nosotros/as	**nos**	nos lavamos	*We wash (ourselves).*	**nosotros/as**
vosotros/as	**os**	os laváis	*You wash (yourselves).*	**vosotros/as**
ustedes, ellos/as	**se**	se lavan	*You/They wash (yourselves/themselves).*	**sí, ustedes/ellos/ellas (consigo)**

Reflexive verbs: 17.B.3
Pronouns after prepositions: 13.C

Juan **se despierta** temprano.	*Juan wakes up early.*
Mis padres **se preocupan** mucho.	*My parents worry a lot.*
Hazte la pregunta **a ti mismo**.	*Ask yourself the question.*
Parecía que hablaba **consigo mismo**.	*It seemed he was talking to himself.*

Note that **se** is used for singular and plural subjects.

27.A.1 Placement

a. Reflexive pronouns come before the conjugated verb. With verb expressions using the infinitive or present participle, reflexive pronouns either come before the conjugated verb or are attached to the infinitive/present participle.

Note that reflexive pronouns have the same placement in a sentence as direct and indirect object pronouns, but a reflexive pronoun comes first: 13.G

Ellos **se** lavan.	*They wash (themselves).*
Ellos **se** van a lavar. Ellos van a lavar**se**.	*They are going to wash (themselves).*
Ellos **se** están lavando. Ellos están lavándo**se**.	*They are washing (themselves).*

Note that when a reflexive pronoun is attached to a present participle, an accent mark is added to maintain the original stress.

b. With compound verb forms using **haber** + *past participle*, the pronoun always comes before the conjugated verb.

—¿**Os** habéis lavado?	*Have you [pl.] washed (yourselves)?*
—No, no **nos** hemos lavado.	*No, we have not washed (ourselves).*

c. Reflexive pronouns are attached to affirmative commands and come before negative commands.

Lávate las manos antes de la cena. → *Wash your hands before dinner.*

No **te** preocupes por nada. → *Don't worry (yourself) about anything.*

Stress and accents: 1.E.3 ▶

Note that when a reflexive pronoun is attached to an affirmative command, a written accent mark is usually needed to maintain the original stress.

27.A.2 Reflexive pronouns after a preposition

Pronouns after ▶
prepositions: 13.C

mismo/a(s): 7.E.5 ▶

a. The forms of pronouns used after prepositions (**mí, ti, usted/él/ella, nosotros/as, vosotros/as, ustedes/ellos/as**) can convey a reflexive meaning. After prepositions, the form **sí** can be used instead of **usted, él/ella, ustedes, ellos/as. Sí** is inherently reflexive. When **mí, ti,** and **sí** follow the preposition **con**, they form **conmigo, contigo,** and **consigo.** The adjective **mismo/a(s)** (*self*) usually follows the pronoun to emphasize the reflexive meaning. It agrees in gender and number with the subject.

Pedro solo piensa en **sí** mism**o**. → *Pedro only thinks about himself.*

Marina habla **consigo** mism**a**. → *Marina is talking / talks to herself.*

b. Compare these reflexive and nonreflexive uses of pronouns after prepositions.

Reflexive use	Nonreflexive use
Habla **consigo misma**. *She talks to herself.*	Habla **con ella**. *She talks to her.*
Llevaba **consigo** un bastón. *He carried a cane with him.*	Fui al parque **con él**. *I went to the park with him.*
Me lo guardé **para mí misma**. *I kept it for myself.*	Lo guardé **para ella**. *I kept it for her.*
Se lo repitió **a sí/ella misma**. *She repeated it to herself.*	Se lo repitió **a ella**. *He repeated it to her.*

27.B Reciprocal pronouns

Pronombres recíprocos

27.B.1 Each other

Different meanings of ▶
reflexive verbs: 27.D.3

A plural reflexive pronoun may indicate a *reciprocal* meaning corresponding to the English *each other* or *one another*.

Mis padres y yo **nos queremos** mucho. → *My parents and I love each other very much.*

Vosotros **os llamáis** todos los días. → *You [pl.] call each other every day.*

Las primas **se abrazan**. → *The cousins are hugging each other.*

¿**Os habláis** vosotros? → *Are you [pl.] talking to each other?*

¿**Se escriben** tus amigos y tú? → *Do you and your friends write to each other?*

27.B.2 *El uno al otro*

To emphasize a mutual relationship, **el uno al otro / los unos a los otros** can be added after the verb. The preposition used depends on the verb. The phrase **entre sí** is also common. The adverbs **mutuamente** (*mutually*) and **recíprocamente** (*reciprocally*) are rarely used. They are more common as adjectives in expressions such as the following: **El respeto entre nosotros es mutuo/recíproco.** (*The respect between us is mutual/reciprocal*).

Las primas se abrazan **la una a la otra**.	*The cousins are hugging each other.*
Se pelean todo el tiempo **el uno con el otro**.	*They fight with each other all the time.*
En Navidad nos damos regalos **los unos a los otros**.	*At Christmas, we give each other gifts.*
Para no resbalar, se apoyaron **entre sí**.	*To avoid slipping, they supported each other.*
Los vecinos se ayudan **mutuamente**.	*Neighbors help each other.*

27.C Reflexive verbs

Verbos reflexivos

Reflexive verbs are conjugated with reflexive pronouns. Many verbs have reflexive and nonreflexive forms. These two conjugation forms for the same verb can result in related or completely different meanings.

Reflexive	Nonreflexive
Me **visto** después de bañarme.	**Visto** a la bebé después de **bañarla**.
I get dressed after taking a bath.	*I get the baby dressed after bathing her.*
Te **despiertas** temprano.	**Te despierto** temprano.
You wake up early.	*I wake you up early.*
Las chicas *se* **levantan** tarde.	Las chicas **levantan** pesas.
The girls get up late.	*The girls lift weights.*
No quiero **despedirme** de ti.	Mi jefe **me** va a **despedir**.
I don't want to say goodbye to you.	*My boss is going to fire me.*
Se **lava** el cabello al salir de la piscina.	También **lava** sus gafas de natación.
She washes her hair once she's out of the pool.	*She also washes her swimming goggles.*

◀ Reflexive verbs with prepositions: 17.B.3d

27.D Different meanings of reflexive verbs

Varios significados de los verbos reflexivos

27.D.1 Reflexive meaning

a. This is the meaning implied when reflexive verbs are discussed. The subject (which must refer to something living) performs the action and is also subject to it. In this case, the singular reflexive intensifier **a sí mismo/a** (*self*) can be added.

Ella **se lava** (a sí misma).	*She is washing (herself).*
El perro **se muerde** la cola (a sí mismo).	*The dog is biting its tail.*

◀ Reflexive pronouns: 27.A

b. Reflexive verbs and pronouns are used more often in Spanish than in English, although reflexive pronouns are sometimes used in English in a nonreflexive way.

Yo mismo hice la tarea.	*I did the homework **myself**.*
Me voy a **divorciar**.	*I'm going to get divorced.*
¿No **te avergüenzas** de eso?	*Aren't you ashamed of that?*

c. In genuine reflexive verbs, the subject and object refer to the same person. But if an additional object is added to the sentence (for example, **las manos**), the subject is indirectly affected by the action but the verb is still reflexive.

Los niños **se lavan** las manos.	*The children are washing their hands.*
¿**Te pintaste** las uñas?	*Did you paint your nails?*
Ponte el abrigo.	*Put on your coat.*

◀ Use of article instead of a possessive: 9.D.4b

d. In the previous reflexive sentences, it is not common to use the reflexive intensifier (**a mí mismo, a sí mismo**, etc.), but the reflexive action can be emphasized by adding the phrase **por sí mismo/a** or **por sí solo/a** (*himself/herself*).

El abuelo ya no es capaz de levantarse   *Grandpa can't get up by himself anymore.*
  por sí mismo/solo.

e. A number of verbs that describe daily personal care are reflexive. The intensifier **a sí mismo/a** is not needed with these verbs.

Reflexive verbs for daily routines			
acostarse	*to go to bed*	levantarse	*to get up*
afeitarse/rasurarse	*to shave*	maquillarse	*to put on makeup*
bañarse, ducharse	*to take a bath, to take a shower*	peinarse	*to comb one's hair*
cepillarse	*to brush (hair or teeth)*	ponerse	*to put on (e.g., clothes)*
despertarse	*to wake up*	quitarse	*to take off (e.g., clothes)*
desvestirse	*to get undressed*	secarse	*to dry (off)*
dormirse	*to fall asleep*	vestirse	*to get dressed*

> With an adjective, **ponerse** means *to become*: 27.G.5

Nos acostamos tarde.   *We go to bed late.*
Te levantas temprano.   *You get up early.*
Os despertáis a las siete.   *You [pl.] wake up at seven o'clock.*
No puedo **dormirme**.   *I can't fall asleep.*
Me ducho y **me visto**.   *I take a shower and get dressed.*
Ella **se peina** y **se maquilla**.   *She combs her hair and puts on makeup.*

27.D.2   Verbs with only reflexive forms
A few Spanish verbs have only the reflexive form.

> Verbs that do not have a reflexive meaning but do have a reflexive form are called **verbos pronominales**.

Verbs with only reflexive forms			
abstenerse	*to abstain*	jactarse	*to boast*
arrepentirse	*to regret*	quejarse	*to complain*
atreverse	*to dare*	suicidarse	*to commit suicide*

El abogado **se jacta** de que nunca   *The lawyer boasts that he has never*
  ha perdido ni un solo caso. Nadie **se**   *lost even a single case. Nobody dares*
  atreve a **quejarse** de sus servicios.   *to complain about his services.*

27.D.3   Reciprocal meaning

> el uno al otro: 27.B.2

a. When two or more people are doing an action and are also the recipients of that action, the meaning is reciprocal (**recíproco**). The reciprocal meaning is emphasized by adding **el uno al otro**, **la una a la otra**, **entre sí**, or **mutuamente**. The following verbs are often used with a reciprocal meaning.

Common verbs with reciprocal meaning	
abrazarse	Los novios **se abrazan**. *The couple hugs (each other).*
amarse/quererse	**Nos queremos** desde siempre. *We have always loved each other.*
ayudarse	Mis amigos y yo **nos ayudamos** (**mutuamente**). *My friends and I help each other.*
besarse	En España **nos besamos** al saludar. *In Spain, we kiss when greeting each other.*
comprometerse	¿Vosotros **os** vais a **comprometer**? *Are you [pl.] going to get engaged?*
encontrarse	Julia y Ana **se encontraron** en el cine. *Julia and Ana met up at the movie theater.*
escribirse	Deberíamos **escribirnos** más. *We should write to each other more.*
hablarse	Mi madre y yo **nos hablamos** a diario. *My mother and I talk to each other every day.*
llevarse bien/mal	**Nos llevamos** bien. *We get along well (with each other).*
mirarse	La madre y el bebé **se miran** a los ojos. *Mother and child are looking into each other's eyes.*
odiarse	Los perros y los gatos **se odian**. *Dogs and cats hate each other.*
pelearse	Algunas personas **se pelean** por todo. *Some people fight about anything.*
saludarse	Los presidentes **se saludaron** antes de la cumbre. *The presidents greeted one another before the summit.*
tutearse	Nosotros nunca **nos tuteamos**. *We never address each other informally.*
verse	Mis amigos y yo **nos vemos** los sábados. *My friends and I see each other on Saturdays.*

b. English verbs emphasize reciprocal meaning by adding *each other* or *one another*. Spanish has similar structures with reflexive verbs.

¿**Nos veremos** mañana?	*Will we see each other tomorrow?*
Los jugadores **se reúnen** hoy para entrenar.	*The players are meeting today for training.*
Algunas personas no **se tratan** bien y **se pelean** mucho.	*Some people don't treat each other well and fight a lot.*

27.D.4 To get (something) done: *mandarse a hacer*

When it is obvious that someone other than the subject is doing the action, **hacerse** (*to get [something] done*), **mandarse a** (*to have [something] done*), or similar expressions can be used.

Ella **se hizo construir** una gran casa.	*She had a great house built.*

27.D.5 Verbs that express a complete action

A number of Spanish verbs use the reflexive form and direct object to express that an action is completely fulfilled in relation to the object.

This meaning is conveyed in all verb tenses and used with verbs that express mental and physical activities, such as *to be able to do something perfectly, to learn something by heart, to know somebody inside out, to eat up, to drink up, to climb to the top, to sink to the bottom,* and similar English expressions.

Reflexive verbs that express a complete action	
andarse	**Nos anduvimos** la ciudad entera. *We walked through the whole city.*
aprenderse	¡La profesora **se aprendió** los nombres de pe a pa! *The teacher learned the names from A to Z!*
beberse	¡Ustedes **se bebieron** la limonada hasta la última gota! *You [pl.] drank all the lemonade to the last drop!*
comerse	Y también **se comieron** todas las tapas y los tacos. *And you also finished off (ate up) all the tapas and tacos.*
conocerse	**Me conozco** las calles de Madrid al derecho y al revés. *I know the streets of Madrid like the palm of my hand.*
creerse	Ellos **se creyeron** todo lo que les dijeron. *They believed everything they were told.*
fumarse	¿Usted **se fuma** toda una cajetilla en un día? *Do you smoke a whole pack in one day?*
leerse	**Nos leemos** el libro de principio a fin. *We read the book from cover to cover.*
recorrerse	**Nos recorreremos** el país de un extremo a otro. *We'll travel the country from one end to the other.*
saberse	**Os sabéis** la lección al pie de la letra. *You [pl.] know the lesson by heart.*
tomarse	**Tómate** unas vacaciones, te ves cansado. *Take a vacation; you look exhausted.*
tragarse	¿**Te** puedes **tragar** esas píldoras tan grandes? *Can you swallow such big pills?*
verse	**Nos vemos** todas las películas de Almodóvar. *We see every single Almodóvar movie.*

27.E Verbs that change meaning in the reflexive form

Verbos que cambian de significado en forma reflexiva

Many Spanish verbs have a different but related meaning when conjugated with a reflexive pronoun.

Reflexive verbs with ▶
prepositions: 17.B.3d

Nonreflexive	Meaning	Reflexive	Meaning
acordar	*to agree on*	acordarse de	*to remember*
animar a	*to encourage (to)*	animarse a	*to motivate oneself (to), to dare*
comer	*to eat*	comerse	*to eat up*
decidir	*to decide*	decidirse a/por	*to make up one's mind to*
deshacer algo	*to undo something*	deshacerse de	*to get rid of*
jugar	*to play*	jugarse algo	*to gamble, to risk*
parecer	*to seem*	parecerse a	*to resemble*
saltar	*to jump*	saltarse algo	*to skip, to ignore*
unir	*to unite*	unirse a	*to join*

¡**Cómete** todas las verduras!	*Eat up all your vegetables!*
Debes **comer** alimentos sanos.	*You must eat healthy food.*
Deberías **deshacerte** de tu ropa vieja antes de comprarte nueva.	*You should get rid of your old clothes before you buy new ones.*
Lo hice mal, así que tengo que **deshacerlo**.	*I did it wrong, so I need to undo it.*
No **me animo a** contarle la verdad.	*I don't dare tell her the truth.*
¡Hay que **animar a** nuestro equipo!	*We have to encourage our team!*
Se jugó a todo o nada y perdió.	*He risked it all and lost.*
Jugó al fútbol toda su vida.	*He played soccer all his life.*

27.F Reflexive verbs that express involuntary actions

Verbos reflexivos que expresan acciones involuntarias

27.F.1 Involuntary actions

a. The reflexive form can be used, particularly with inanimate objects, to express an action without indicating the person responsible for the action.

Se cayó el vaso.	*The glass fell.*
Se cerraron las puertas.	*The doors (were) closed.*
El televisor **se rompió**.	*The TV broke.*
La ventana **se hizo trizas**.	*The window broke into pieces.*

b. When an action is perceived as accidental or involuntary, an indirect object pronoun is used to identify the person performing the action or affected by the action. To clarify or emphasize who the person is, **a** + *noun/pronoun* can be added.

◀ Indirect object pronouns: 13.F
Pronouns after prepositions: 13.C

Estaba hablando con mi hermano y **se me cayó** el teléfono.	*I was talking to my brother and I dropped the phone.*
Se le rompió su jarrón favorito.	*Her favorite vase broke.*
Se me cerró la puerta en la cara.	*The door (was) closed in my face.*
Cuando escuché lo que dijo, **se me fue** el alma a los pies.	*When I heard what he said, my heart sank.*
A ti **se te salió** la situación de las manos.	*The situation went out of your control.*

c. Constructions like **caérsele**, **cerrársele**, and **rompérsele** take both the reflexive pronoun **se** and an indirect object pronoun. Other verbs used in this manner include **acabársele**, **antojársele**, **dañársele**, **morírsele**, **ocurrírsele**, **perdérsele**, **quedársele**, and **reírsele**.

Se te acabaron las ideas.	*You're out of ideas.*
¿Qué **se te antoja** comer hoy?	*What do you feel like eating today?*
Se le dañó la computadora.	*He damaged his computer.*
Se me murió el pececito.	*My little fish died.*
Se me han ocurrido dos ideas.	*I've thought of two ideas.*
Se nos perdió el gato.	*We lost our cat.*
Se nos quedaron las llaves adentro.	*We left the keys inside.*
Cuando le conté la verdad, **se me rio** en la cara.	*When I told her the truth, she laughed in my face.*

d. Some of these verbs also have regular reflexive uses without the indirect object pronoun. **Antojársele** and **ocurrírsele** can only be used with a reflexive pronoun and an indirect object pronoun.

Juan **se rio** mucho.	*Juan laughed a lot.*
Se murió el pececito.	*The little fish died.*
Se perdieron dos niños.	*Two children got lost.*
Las llaves **se quedaron** adentro.	*The keys were left inside.*
Se rompió la llave.	*The key broke.*
Mi hermanita **se cayó**.	*My little sister fell.*

Linking, transitive, and intransitive verbs: 17.B.1

e. Quedar(se) can also be used as an intransitive verb.

Las llaves **quedaron** adentro. *The keys were left inside.*

27.F.2 *Olvidarse(le)*

The transitive verb **olvidar** can also be used with a reflexive pronoun in two different constructions.

olvidar	*olvidarse de*	*olvidársele algo a alguien*
Olvidé su nombre.	Me olvidé de su nombre.	Se me olvidó su nombre.
I forgot his name.		

27.G Verbs expressing change: *to become*

Verbos de cambio

27.G.1 Change of state

Some verbs that express a shift from one state to another or suggest that a change exists, such as **emocionarse** (*to get excited, to be moved*), **envanecerse** (*to become conceited*), and **entristecerse** (*to become sad*), are reflexive, and others, like **envejecer** (*to get old, to age*) and **enrojecer** (*to turn red, to blush*), are not.

Me emocioné cuando oí las noticias.	*I got excited when I heard the news.*
La actriz **se entristeció** cuando supo que no había recibido el premio.	*The actress became sad when she found out she had not won the award.*
Juan **envejeció** mucho desde la muerte de su esposa.	*Juan looks a lot older since his wife died.*
Mucha gente **enrojece** cuando la ofenden.	*Many people turn red when they are insulted.*

Expressing change and state: 29.E

27.G.2 Other changes

a. Many reflexive verbs express physical, social, or emotional changes. The table provides some examples. The most important verbs are explained individually.

Other verbs that express emotional changes: **aburrirse, asustarse, calmarse, enojarse, sorprenderse**

Reflexive verbs that express change		
Physical	**Social**	**Emotional**
arrodillarse *to kneel*	**casarse (con)** *to get married (to)*	**alegrarse (de)** *to be happy/glad (about)*
levantarse *to get/ stand up*	**divorciarse (de)** *to get divorced (from)*	**avergonzarse (de)** *to be ashamed (of)*
morirse *to die*	**enriquecerse** *to get rich*	**enamorarse (de)** *to fall in love (with)*
moverse *to move*	**graduarse** *to graduate*	**irritarse** *to get annoyed*
sentarse *to sit down*	**separarse (de)** *to separate (from)*	**preocuparse (por)** *to worry (about)*

Reflexive pronouns and verbs • **Chapter 27**

b. Many Spanish verbs that express emotional reactions have two common conjugation forms. One is reflexive, and the other is conjugated like **gustar**, with an indirect object pronoun.

Indirect object pronouns: 13.F
Verbs like **gustar**: 17.B.4

Reflexive form	Conjugation like *gustar*
Me alegro mucho de que vengas.	**Me alegra** mucho que vengas.
I'm so happy that you're coming.	*It makes me happy that you're coming.*
¿Os preocupáis por la economía mundial?	**¿Os preocupa** la economía mundial?
Are you [pl.] worried about the world economy?	*Does the world economy worry you [pl.]?*

27.G.3 *Convertirse en + noun*

Convertirse en indicates a change that can happen suddenly or after a process, depending on the context. It expresses a significant change, such as a change from boy to man, from a little city to a big city, and so forth.

Nos convertimos en robots con la tecnología.	*Technology turns us into robots.*
La casa **se convierte en** un manicomio cuando Luis hace fiestas.	*The house turns into a madhouse when Luis has parties.*

27.G.4 *Hacerse + noun or adjective*

Hacerse expresses changes that happen as a result of a plan or goal.

Mi hermano **se hizo** cura.	*My brother became a priest.*
Los vikingos **se hicieron** poderosos con su superioridad marítima.	*The Vikings became powerful with their maritime superiority.*
Quiero **hacerme** millonario algún día.	*I want to become a millionaire someday.*

27.G.5 *Ponerse + adjective*

Ponerse expresses relatively rapid changes that are often emotional or physically visible.

Mis amigos **se pusieron** verdes de la envidia cuando vieron mi nuevo auto.	*My friends became green with envy when they saw my new car.*
¡No **te pongas** triste!	*Don't be sad!*
Nos pusimos furiosos cuando vimos el desorden.	*We became furious when we saw the mess.*
Me pongo tan contento cuando me visita mi hermana.	*I get so happy when my sister visits me.*

27.G.6 *Quedarse + adjective or adverb*

Quedarse expresses a long-term result of a change. The reflexive form is more common in Spain, but has the same meaning as the nonreflexive form used in Latin America.

¿**(Te) has quedado** triste con la noticia?	*Has the news made you sad? (Are you sad because of the news?)*
Con la crisis, **(nos) quedamos** sin nada.	*Because of the crisis, we were left with nothing.*
Te estás quedando calvo.	*You're becoming/going bald.*
Me quedé muy solo cuando mi novia se fue.	*I became very lonely when my girlfriend left.*

27.G.7 | Volverse + *adjective* or *noun*

Volverse expresses primarily a mental or physical change of a certain duration and is more permanent than **ponerse**.

Venezuela **se ha vuelto** un país petrolero.	*Venezuela has become an oil country.*
Uno no **se vuelve** rico de la noche a la mañana.	*One doesn't become rich overnight.*
Se volvió loca.	*She went mad/crazy.*
La leche **se volvió** agria.	*The milk became sour / went bad.*

27.G.8 | Llegar a + *infinitive* + *noun* or *adjective*

This verb phrase is a nonreflexive verb of change. It is used when changes are understood as a longer process and assumes some effort to get to the result.

Nunca **llegaré a ser** famoso.	*I will never become famous.*
Roma **llegó a ser** una gran civilización.	*Rome became a great civilization.*
Es posible que **llegues a tener** éxito.	*It's possible you'll be successful.*

27.G.9 | Wishes

It is very common to express wishes or plans of change with these verbs.

Ojalá no **se queden** sin casa.	*I hope they are not left without a home.*
Querría que el mundo **llegara a ser** un lugar pacífico.	*I wish the world would become a peaceful place.*
Espero que **nos convirtamos en** grandes amigos.	*I hope that we will become great friends.*

27.G.10 | Verb aspect and verbs that express change

a. Verbs that express change are often used with the *preterite* and the perfect tenses, which, like the English *to become*, focus on the end result.

Rosa **se ha vuelto** muy antipática.	*Rosa has become very unfriendly.*
Mi ciudad natal **se ha convertido** en una gran metrópoli.	*My hometown has become a big metropolis.*
Se puso furioso cuando le conté la noticia.	*He became furious when I told him the news.*
En la década de 1950, ya **se había convertido** en el hombre más rico de la ciudad.	*By the 1950s, he had already become the richest man in the city.*
Si hubiera estudiado abogacía, **habría llegado a ser** juez.	*If he had studied law, he would have become a judge.*

b. When verbs that express change are used in the *imperfect* or *present* tense, they usually indicate repetition or a description of something that used to happen. Adverbs such as **cada vez más**, **paulatinamente**, and **progresivamente** intensify the verb's meaning.

Me ponía furioso cuando me calificaban una C en el examen.	*I used to become so angry when they would give me a C on an exam.*
Me parece que la gramática **se vuelve** cada vez más fácil.	*It seems to me that grammar is becoming easier and easier.*
En los cuentos de hadas, las ranas **se convierten en** príncipes.	*In fairy tales, frogs turn into princes.*

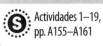

Práctica

Actividades 1–19, pp. A155–A161

Passive and impersonal constructions
Estructuras pasivas e impersonales

28.A Active, passive, or impersonal

Activa, pasiva o impersonal

28.A.1 Passive constructions

Active constructions emphasize the person or thing that carries out an action. In contrast, passive constructions emphasize the action itself, rather than the agent. The direct object of the active sentence becomes the grammatical subject of the passive sentence. The passive voice is used much less in Spanish than in English. Spanish has two ways to express passive actions: the passive voice with **ser** (**voz pasiva con *ser***) and passive constructions with **se** (**pasiva refleja** or **voz pasiva con *se***).

Los aztecas **fundaron** Tenochtitlán. (*active*)	*The Aztecs founded Tenochtitlán.*
Tenochtitlán **fue fundada** por los aztecas. (*passive*)	*Tenochtitlán was founded by the Aztecs.*
¿Sabes en qué año **se fundó** Tenochtitlán? (*passive*)	*Do you know what year Tenochtitlán was founded?*

28.A.2 Impersonal constructions

In Spanish, the impersonal **se** (***se* impersonal**) expresses the idea of an unspecified subject performing an action. In English, this idea is often expressed using *they, you, people, one*, etc.

En esta oficina **se trabaja** muchísimo.	*In this office, people work a lot.*
Se habla de su renuncia.	*People are talking about his resignation.*
Si **se está** tranquilo con uno mismo, **se es** feliz.	*If you are at peace with yourself, you are happy.*
Se invitó a mucha gente.	*Many people were invited.*

Unlike the passive constructions with **se**, impersonal constructions with **se** do not have a grammatical subject and the verb is always singular.

28.B Passive voice with *ser*

Voz pasiva con *ser*

Uses of **ser**: 30.B

28.B.1 The direct object becomes the subject

The passive voice with **ser** can only be formed in Spanish when there is a corresponding active sentence with a *stated direct object*. The direct object of the active sentence becomes the subject, while the real subject is toned down to *agent* or is removed from the sentence. In the active sentence, the preposition **a** indicates that a person is the direct object. In a passive sentence, this preposition is not necessary since the direct object has become the subject.

Use of **a** with a person as a direct object: 12.B.2c, 13.E.2

Active voice	Passive voice with *ser*
El rector recibió a los alumnos.	Los alumnos **fueron recibidos** (por el rector).
The principal welcomed the students.	*The students were welcomed (by the principal).*

28.B.2 Verb tenses of *ser* in the passive voice

The verb in the active sentence becomes a *past participle* in the passive sentence and follows **ser**, which can generally appear in all verb tenses and moods. However, the passive voice with **ser** is most common in the preterite and the perfect tenses. In the present and imperfect, the passive voice with **ser** expresses repetition or habit.

Regular and irregular past participle: 19.A.1, 19.A.2, 25.D

Use of the present indicative: 17.E.2
Use of the imperfect: 18.E.5

Indicative		Subjunctive
El chico es visto	... ha sido visto	Es bueno que el chico sea visto.
... fue visto	... hubo sido visto	Fue bueno que el chico fuera visto.
... era visto	... había sido visto	... fuese visto.
... será visto	... habrá sido visto	... haya sido visto.
... sería visto	... habría sido visto	... hubiera/hubiese sido visto.

Pretérito anterior (hubo sido visto): 19.F

Infinitive	*Gerundio*
ser visto	siendo visto
haber sido visto	habiendo sido visto

Una tragedia nuclear como la de Chernóbil no **ha sido vista** nunca. — *A nuclear tragedy like Chernobyl has never been seen.*
Muchos creen que podría **haber sido prevenida**. — *Many believe that it could have been prevented.*
Las señales de peligro nunca **fueron tomadas** en serio. — *The warning signs were never taken seriously.*
Deberían **haberlo sido**. — *They should have been.*

Use of the past participle: 25.D.4b
The past participle in compound tenses: 19.A.1-2

28.B.3 Agreement of past participle

The past participle in the passive voice with **ser** acts like an adjective and agrees in gender and number with the grammatical subject.

La película fue bien **recibida**. — *The film was well received.*
Las noticias fueron **publicadas** en la red. — *The news was published on the web.*
El problema debe ser **estudiado**. — *The problem should be studied.*
Es necesario que **los gastos** sean **controlados**. — *It is necessary that the expenses be monitored.*

28.B.4 The agent in the passive voice with *ser*

a. In the passive voice with **ser**, the agent is introduced using **por** + *noun*, *pronoun*, or *clause*.

La contaminación es causada **por nosotros**. — *Pollution is caused by us.*
Las reuniones van a ser organizadas **por la ONU**. — *The meetings are going to be organized by the UN.*
Algunas cosas no han sido explicadas **por los responsables**. — *A number of things haven't been explained by those responsible.*
El virus ha sido identificado **por los que conocen su ADN**. — *The virus has been identified by those who recognize its DNA.*

Use of the preposition **por**: 12.B.6

b. It is important to distinguish the agent in passive sentences from causal relationships or other contexts that can also be expressed with **por**. Only the first example indicates the agent.

La velocidad de los autos es controlada **por la policía** (*agent*). — *The speed limit is monitored by the police.*
La velocidad de los autos es controlada **por seguridad**. — *The speed limit is monitored for safety.*
La velocidad de los autos es controlada **por todo el país**. — *The speed limit is monitored across the country.*

28.C | Limitations of the passive voice with *ser*

Limitaciones de la voz pasiva con *ser*

28.C.1 | Use of passive voice with *ser*

The passive voice appears primarily in written formal language, such as in professional articles, contracts, and legal documents. It is used less often in the news. In cases where the agent is still unknown or not mentioned, passive constructions with **se** are preferred.

◀ Passive constructions with **se**: 28.D

28.C.2 | The indirect object in the passive voice with *ser*

Only the direct object of an active sentence can become the subject in the passive voice with **ser**. The indirect object can never become the subject. In English, both the direct and indirect object in the active sentence can become the subject in the passive voice.

El Premio Nobel de Literatura le ha sido otorgado al escritor peruano Mario Vargas Llosa.

The Nobel Prize in Literature was awarded to the Peruvian writer Mario Vargas Llosa. / Mario Vargas Llosa was awarded the Nobel Prize in Literature.

Los honorarios me fueron pagados a mí (por el banco).

The fees were paid to me (by the bank). / I was paid the fees (by the bank).

El contrato os será enviado a vosotros (por Marta).

The contract will be sent to you [pl.] (by Marta). / You will be sent the contract (by Marta).

28.C.3 | Estar + *past participle*

The passive voice with **ser** can only be formed with the past participle and not with participle-like adjectives such as **electo/a** or **bendito/a**. However, these adjectives and past participle forms can convey the result of the action of some verbs by using **estar**.

◀ Past participle: 19.A.1, 19.A.2, 25.D
Verb phrases with the past participle: 26.E
Estar with past participle: 30.C.2

Passive sentence with *ser*	Resulting state with *estar*
La novela **ha sido escrita** por un gran narrador. *The novel has been/was written by a great storyteller.*	La novela **está escrita**. *The novel is written.*
Las tapas **fueron hechas** por el cocinero. *The tapas were made by the cook.*	Las tapas **están hechas**. *The tapas are made.*
Los parques **fueron diseñados** por un arquitecto. *The parks were designed by an architect.*	Los parques **están diseñados**. *The parks are designed.*

28.D | Passive constructions with *se*

Oraciones pasivas reflejas

28.D.1 | The subject in passive constructions with *se*

a. Passive constructions with **se** have a *stated subject* and a *passive meaning.* The subject can be a noun or a clause. The verb agrees with the subject (third-person singular or plural). The verb is always in the third-person singular if the subject is a clause. Passive constructions with **se** do not have a stated agent. They are used mostly when the subject (singular or plural) is not a living being. The subjects in the following Spanish sentences are in italics.

El petróleo venezolano **se exporta** a muchos países.   *Venezuelan oil is exported to many countries.*

Los productos **se venden** en todo el mundo.   *The products are sold all over the world.*

Se espera *que la situación mejore.*   *The situation is expected to improve.*

b. Indefinite nouns that refer to people can also be the subject of a sentence. The preposition **a** is not necessary here because the noun is *not* the object, but the subject.

Se prefieren personas con experiencia.	*People with experience are preferred.*
Se necesitaban ayudantes.	*They needed assistants. / Assistants were needed.*
Se busca un buen economista.	*They are looking for a good economist. / A good economist is sought.*
Se admitirán muchos estudiantes.	*They will admit many students. / Many students will be admitted.*

c. Passive sentences with **se** can also have a clause as the subject. The verb is normally a reporting verb such as **decir, comunicar, informar,** or a verb that provides opinions, beliefs, or knowledge, such as **opinar, creer,** and **saber.** The verb in a passive construction with **se** is *always* singular when a clause is the subject.

Anteriormente **se creía *que*** los gnomos realmente existían.	*Previously it was thought that gnomes really existed.*
No **se sabía *dónde*** vivían.	*It wasn't known where they lived.*
En las leyendas **se narra *cómo*** los gnomos se convertían en montañas.	*In legends, it is told how the gnomes turned into mountains.*
Nunca **se sabrá *si*** eso era cierto.	*It will never be known if that was true.*

28.D.2 No agent

Passive constructions with **se** have no agent. The real performer of the action is not mentioned and remains unknown.

Las tradiciones **se conservan** de generación en generación.	*Traditions are preserved (passed on) from generation to generation.*
Los documentos **se imprimen** automáticamente.	*The documents are printed automatically.*

28.D.3 Passive constructions with *se* and modal verbs

Modal verb phrases with the infinitive: 26.B

In English, modal verbs (*can, could, may, might, must, shall, should, will, would*) are often used to express the passive voice using the construction *modal verb + be + past participle*. In Spanish, the same idea can be conveyed using **se** + *modal verb + infinitive.*

Se podía escuchar todo lo que decían.	*Everything they said could be heard.*
Se debe hacer algo acerca del problema de la contaminación.	*Something should be done about the pollution problem.*

28.D.4 Placement of *se* with verb phrases

Placement of reflexive pronouns: 27.A.1

With verb phrases, **se** usually comes before the conjugated verb, but can also be attached to the the infinitive or present participle.

Las cartas **se** iban a enviar / iban a enviar**se** por correo.	*The letters were going to be sent in the mail.*
El trabajo **se** tiene que hacer / tiene que hacer**se** bien.	*The work must be done well.*
Se está preparando / Está preparándo**se** una gran cena.	*A great dinner is being prepared.*

Remember that you add an accent mark when you attach **se** to the present participle in order to keep the original stress.

28.E Impersonal *se* sentences

Oraciones impersonales con *se*

28.E.1 Impersonal *se* sentences have no subject

Impersonal **se** sentences have a *passive meaning* and *no grammatical subject*, and the verb *always* appears in the third-person singular. The real performer of the action is assumed to be a living being, but is unknown and indefinite. Like passive constructions with **se**, the impersonal **se** is not the subject, but only a structure used to convey that the meaning is impersonal.

28.E.2 General statements

a. Impersonal **se** sentences form general statements with verbs that do not take a direct object (intransitive verbs), such as **vivir, trabajar,** and **llegar,** and with transitive verbs, such as **vender, decir,** and **escribir,** when the object is not mentioned. The verb always appears in the third-person singular. The statement's features are described using an adverb or an adverbial expression.

◀ Transitive and intransitive verbs: 17.B.1

¡Aquí **se trabaja** con gusto!	*Here, people work with pleasure!*
Sin buena salud, no **se vive** bien.	*Without good health, one can't live well.*
En los blogs **se escribe** muy francamente.	*In blogs, people write very honestly.*

b. In general statements with reflexive verbs, the indefinite pronoun **uno** is used. Both male and female speakers can use **uno**. Female speakers, however, can also use **una**.

◀ Indefinite pronoun **uno/a**: 7.D.3

Con esta música, **uno se duerme** de inmediato.	*One falls asleep immediately to this music.*
Este mapa impide que **uno se pierda** en la ciudad.	*With this map, you can't get lost in the city.*
No es posible **sentarse uno** a leer sin interrupciones.	*It's impossible to sit down and read without interruptions.*
¿Puede **uno marcharse** de aquí a cualquier hora?	*Can one leave at any time?*

c. Ser and **estar** form general statements with impersonal **se** sentences, but this use is limited. General statements with modal verbs (**poder, deber**) are more common.

◀ Modal verb phrases: 26.B

Se está muy bien en lugares tranquilos.	*It's very pleasant in peaceful places.*
No siempre **se es** feliz.	*People are not always happy.*
Se puede salir por esta puerta.	*You can go out this door.*
Puede salirse por esta puerta.	

d. If the implied performer of the action is a woman, it is possible to use a feminine adjective.

Cuando se es **honrada**, se llega más lejos.	*If you are honorable, you will go far.*

28.E.3 Direct objects

a. When the direct object is mentioned and it is a person (proper noun, pronoun), it follows the preposition **a** and the verb is always singular.

Se identificará **a los autores** de los robos.	*The perpetrators of the thefts will be identified.*

◀ Use of **a** with a person as a direct object: 12.B.2c, 13.E.2

Direct object pronouns: 13.E.3
Leísmo: 13.E.4

b. When the direct object is mentioned and follows the preposition **a**, it can also be replaced by an object pronoun. In that case, the direct object pronoun will convey information about the agent's gender: **los/las**. It is common to remove the last remnant of the agent's identity by using **le/les** in impersonal **se** constructions.

Se identificará **a los autores /**   *The perpetrators (male/female) of the*
  a las autoras de los robos.   *thefts will be identified.*
Se **los/las** identificará.   *They (male/female) will be identified.*
Se **les** identificará.   *They will be identified.*

c. Impersonal **se** sentences can be used with transitive verbs when the direct object is expressed. This use is common in the present tense and appears in signs and ads. **(Se vende casas. Se repara refrigeradores.)** In these cases, the noun is the direct object of the verb and the performer of the action is not stated.

Impersonal *se* sentence (*los proyectos:* **direct object**)	
Se aprobó los proyectos.	*The projects were approved.*
Se los aprobó.	*They were approved.*

Passive construction with *se* (*los proyectos:* **subject**)	
Se aprobaron los proyectos.	*The projects were approved.*

28.F The indirect object in passive and impersonal sentences

El objeto indirecto en oraciones pasivas e impersonales

The direct object becomes the grammatical subject in the passive voice with **ser** and in passive constructions with **se**. When the indirect object is mentioned, it appears in the different sentence types in the following ways.

28.F.1 Active sentence

Placement of direct and indirect object pronouns: 13.G

In a typical active sentence, you can find a subject (**profesor**), a verb (**entregó**), and a direct object (**textos**) as well as an indirect object (**estudiantes**). The objects can be expressed with the corresponding object pronouns.

El profesor les entregó **los textos**   *The teacher gave the students the texts.*
  a **los estudiantes**.
El profesor **se los** entregó.   *The teacher gave them (to) them.*

28.F.2 Passive voice with *ser*

The real direct object from the previous example sentence (**textos**) becomes the subject in the passive voice with **ser**. The agent and the references to the indirect object (**les, a los estudiantes**) can be omitted. The indirect object in the active sentence can't become the subject in the passive voice.

Los textos les fueron entregados   *The texts were given to the students (by the teacher).*
  a **los estudiantes** (por el profesor).
Los textos les fueron entregados.   *The texts were given to them. (Someone gave them the texts.)*
Los textos fueron entregados.   *The texts were given out. (Someone gave out the texts.)*

28.F.3 Passive constructions with *se*

Passive constructions with **se** have no agent. Information about the indirect object (**les, los estudiantes**) can also be omitted. It is important to note that **se** indicates only that the sentence is impersonal and is not a replacement for the indirect object (**les**), which can be mentioned.

Los textos **se les entregaron** a los estudiantes.	*The texts were given to the students.* *(Someone gave the texts to the students.)*
Los textos **se les entregaron**.	*The texts were given to them.* *(Someone gave them the texts.)*
Los textos **se entregaron**.	*The texts were given out.* *(Someone gave out the texts.)*

28.F.4 Impersonal *se* sentences

In impersonal **se** sentences, the verb is singular and does not have a subject. In general, impersonal **se** sentences use intransitive verbs (without direct objects). When there are both direct and indirect objects, an impersonal **se** sentence would look like this: **Se entregó los textos a los estudiantes**. Such sentences are not common in Spanish, and other solutions are preferred.

◀ Impersonal **se** sentences with direct objects: 28.E.3c
Intransitive verbs: 17.B.1

Passive construction with *se*	Third-person plural
Se entregaron los textos a los estudiantes. / Los textos **se les entregaron** a los estudiantes.	**Les entregaron** los textos a los estudiantes. / **Se los** entregaron.
The texts were given to the students.	*Someone gave the texts to the students. / The texts were given to the students. / They were given to them.*

28.G Comparison of passive constructions with *se* and impersonal *se* constructions

Passive constructions with *se*		Impersonal *se* constructions	
Can only be formed with transitive verbs.	Se enseña inglés.	*Can be formed with intransitive or transitive verbs.*	Se enseña a hablar mejor. Se vive bien aquí.
The object of the active sentence is the grammatical subject.	Se vendió un cuadro de Picasso. ("un cuadro de Picasso" is the subject of the sentence)	*There is no grammatical subject.*	Nunca se está seguro en el puesto de trabajo.
The verb can be singular or plural (it must agree with the subject).	Se firmará el tratado. / Se firmarán los acuerdos.	*The verb is always singular.*	Se firmará los acuerdos. ("los acuerdos" is a direct object; the sentence has no expressed subject)
The indirect object can be expressed.	Se presentaron los textos al jurado. Se le presentaron los textos.	*The indirect object can be expressed.*	Se presentó los textos al jurado.
Plural direct objects that refer to people and do not have an article can become the subject.	Se buscan nuevos maestros. ("nuevos maestros" is the subject)	*When the direct object is a specific person or group of people, the personal **a** is used. The direct object can be replaced by both direct and indirect object pronouns.*	Se invitó a los/las nuevos/as maestros/as. ("a los/las nuevos/as maestros/as" is the direct object) Se los/las invitó. Se les invitó.

◀ Impersonal **se** sentences with direct objects: 28.E.3c

Passive constructions with *se*		Impersonal *se* constructions	
There is no personal **a**, *since the direct object of the active sentence is now the subject.*	Se eligieron los nuevos diputados. Se nombró el nuevo embajador.	*If the direct object is a person, it always requires* **a**. *The verb is always singular.*	Se eligió a los nuevos diputados. Se nombró al nuevo embajador.
The subject can be a noun clause or a reported question. It can also be an infinitive.	Se dice que habrá despidos. Se ha confirmado cómo sucedió el accidente. Se prohíbe fumar.	*(**Note:** Due to their impersonal meaning, the examples on the left are sometimes interpreted as impersonal* **se** *constructions. However, this text follows the interpretation of the RAE's* Nueva gramática *regarding these structures.)*	

Indirect questions: 14.B.9, 31.B.6 ▶

28.H | Other expressions with impersonal meaning

Otras expresiones de impersonalidad

a. The following can be used in an impersonal sense. The most common is the third-person plural, which refers to an impersonal **ellos**.

Impersonal use of the pronoun	
third-person plural	¿Os **atendieron** bien en el restaurante? *Did you [pl.] get good service / Did they serve you well in the restaurant?*
tú	**Tú** nunca **sabes** a qué hora llega el autobús. *You never know when the bus will come.*
la/mucha gente	Que **la gente** crea lo que quiera. *People can think what they want.*
uno/a	**Uno** nunca sabe con seguridad. *One/You can never know with certainty.*

Impersonal form of ▶ **haber**: 29.B.1

b. Every expression with the impersonal forms of **haber** is impersonal. The verb is always singular.

Hay problemas.	*There are problems.*	**Hay** paz/guerra.	*There is peace/war.*
Hay mucho.	*There is a lot.*	**Habrá** algo.	*There will be something.*
Hay poco.	*There isn't much.*	No **habrá** nada.	*There won't be anything.*

Expressing weather ▶ and time: 29.C

c. Hacer, ser, and other verbs in expressions of time and weather are impersonal. The verb is always singular.

Hace frío/calor.	*It's cold/hot.*	Ya **era** hora.	*It's about time.*
Es de día/noche.	*It's day/night.*	**Llueve**.	*It's raining.*
Es Navidad.	*It's Christmas.*	**Nieva**.	*It's snowing.*

d. There are many other verbs that function the same way.

Importa/Conviene hacerlo.	*It's important/useful to do it.*	**Se trata** de estudiar o no estudiar.	*It's about studying or not studying.*

Práctica

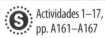

Actividades 1–17, pp. A161–A167

Passive and impersonal constructions • **Chapter 28**

To be and *to become*
Ser, estar, haber, hacer, tener

29.A Structure: *ser* and *estar*

Estructura de *ser* y *estar*

29.A.1 To be: *ser*

a. *To be* is expressed in Spanish using **ser** and **estar**, but **haber, hacer**, and **tener** are also used to convey *to be*. **Ser** describes the *essential qualities* of the subject, while **estar** describes its *condition* or *state*.

b. The verb **ser** can't be used on its own with the meaning *to exist*. An appropriate modern Spanish translation of Hamlet's famous question "To be or not to be?" would be **"¿Existir o no existir?"**. In very short yes/no questions and answers, however, **ser** can be used to answer, in the sense *it is* or *it's not*, to confirm or deny the identity of an item.

◀ Use of **ser** and **estar**: Ch. 30

—Este libro **es** tuyo, ¿verdad?	*This book is yours, isn't it?*
—Sí, sí (lo) **es**. /—No, no (lo) **es**.	*Yes, it is. / No, it isn't.*
—¿**Es** Juan el que va allí?	*Is that Juan over there?*
—Sí, sí (lo) **es**. /—No, no (lo) **es**.	*Yes, it is (him). / No, it isn't (him).*

29.A.2 To be: *estar*

The verb **estar** can also appear alone in short yes/no questions and be used as an answer in the sense *to be present* in a specific or implied location, for example, when a person asks if someone is home.

—¿**Está** Juan?	*Is Juan there?*
—No, no **está**. / —Sí, sí **está**.	*No, he isn't. / Yes, he is.*

29.B To be: there is, there are

Haber para expresar existencia

◀ Ser, estar, and **haber**: 30.C.7

29.B.1 Impersonal form of *haber*

a. The *impersonal* form of **haber** (*there is / there are*; *is/are present*) is used instead of **estar** to refer to the existence of nonspecific people, things, or ideas.

◀ estar and **haber** with possessives: 9.D.6d

—¿**Hay** conexión a Internet?	*Is there an Internet connection?*
—Sí, (la) **hay**. / —No, no (la) **hay**.	*Yes, there is. / No, there isn't.*
—¿**Hay** estudiantes alemanes?	*Are there (any) German students?*
—No, no (los) **hay**. /—Sí, (los) **hay**.	*No, there aren't./Yes, there are.*

b. **Haber** can't be used with subject pronouns or a noun following a determiner. It can be used with indefinite pronouns, numbers, and determiners, except **ambos, cada, los/las demás**, and **cualquiera**.

◀ Indefinite quantifiers and pronouns: Ch. 7

—¿**Hay** alguien (en casa)?	*Is anyone home?*
—No, no **hay** nadie.	*No, there's nobody home.*
—¿Cuántos estudiantes **hay**?	*How many students are there?*
—**Hay** uno.	*There's one.*

◀ Use of cardinal numbers: 6.B.1

c. Subject pronouns and nouns with determiners can be used with **estar** in the same situations.

—¿**Están** Laura y Fernando en casa? *Are Laura and Fernando home?*
—Ella sí **está**, pero él no. *She's home, but he isn't.*

—Hola, ¿dónde **estás** tú? *Hello, where are you?*
—**Estoy** en el parque. *I'm at the park.*

—¿Cuántos de los estudiantes **están** allí? *How many of the students are there?*
—Tres de ellos **están** aquí. *Three of them are here.*

29.B.2 Personal form of *haber*

Haber is conjugated in the compound verb forms of the indicative and subjunctive.

The present perfect and the ▶ past perfect: Ch. 19

¿**Habéis ido** alguna vez a Costa Rica? *Have you [pl.] ever been to Costa Rica?*
En Ecuador se **ha hablado** quechua por mucho tiempo. *In Ecuador, Quechua has been spoken for a long time.*

29.C Expressing weather and time: *hacer, estar, ser*

Hacer, estar, ser para expresar clima y tiempo

Expressing temperature: 6.I.1 ▶

29.C.1 Weather expressions

Hacer and **estar** are used in many weather expressions for which English uses *to be*.

Hace frío.	*It's cold.*	**Hace** sol.	*It's sunny.*
Hace calor.	*It's warm.*	**Hace** mal tiempo.	*It's bad weather.*
Está nublado.	*It's cloudy.*	**Está** lloviendo.	*It's raining.*
Está oscuro.	*It's dark.*	**Está** nevando.	*It's snowing.*

29.C.2 Calendar and time

Time: 5.C.3, 6.F ▶

a. Ser is used with the time, days, months, years, and other periods of time.

Son las tres.	*It's three o'clock.*	**Es** verano.	*It's summer.*
Es lunes.	*It's Monday.*	**Es** 2030.	*It's 2030.*

b. Estar can also be used with days, months, years, and times of the year (but not clock time) as long as there is a preposition (**a, en**) before the noun. The verb is in the **nosotros** form.

Estamos a lunes.	*It's Monday (finally/now).*
Estamos en marzo.	*We're in March now. / It's March (finally/now).*
Estamos en verano.	*It's summer (finally/now).*
Estamos en 2030.	*It's 2030 (finally/now).*

29.D Expressing age and states: *tener*

Tener para expresar edad y cambios físicos

Expressing age: 6.H, 18.E.3 ▶

Tener is used to describe most temporary physical states, or to tell age.

Ella **tiene** veinte años.	*She's twenty years old.*
Él **tiene** hambre/sed/sueño/cansancio/ miedo/calor.	*He is hungry/thirsty/sleepy/ tired/ scared/hot.*

29.E Expressing change and state

Expresar cambio y estado

29.E.1 *To get / to be*: passive voice with *ser* and *estar* + *past participle*

a. The passive voice with **ser** is equivalent to the English passive voice with *to be* or *to get*. In this case, the verb expresses a change. The resulting state is described in Spanish with **estar** + *past participle*.

Passive voice with **ser**: 28.B
Verb phrases with the past participle: 26.E

Las cartas **son** escritas.	*The letters are/get written.*
Las cartas **están** escritas.	*The letters are written.*

b. Together with modal verbs, **ser** and **estar** are used as described in **a.**

Modal verb phrases with the infinitive: 26.B

Las cartas **deben / tienen que ser** escritas.	*The letters must be/get written.*
Las cartas **deben / tienen que estar** escritas.	*The letters must be written.*

29.E.2 *To be / to become* + infinitive: *es, fue, era*

While the *present* and the *imperfect* of **ser** are usually translated as *to be* because they describe states, the *preterite* can sometimes be translated as *to become* because it expresses change.

La situación **es** imposible de entender.	*The situation is impossible to understand.*
La situación **fue** imposible de entender.	*The situation became impossible to understand.*
La situación **era** imposible de entender.	*The situation was impossible to understand.*

29.E.3 *To become / to turn* with weather and time: Spanish equivalents

Changes in weather, time, days, and years that are expressed with *to become* or *to turn* in English can be expressed in Spanish in several ways.

Dio la una. / Dieron las tres.	*The clock struck one / three.*
Está amaneciendo. (Amaneció.)	*The sun is rising. (The sun rose.)*
Se hace (hizo) de día.	*It's becoming (It became) daylight.*
Se hace (hizo) de noche. /	*It is (was) getting dark. (It got dark.) /*
Anochece. (Anocheció.)	*The sun is setting. (The sun set.)*
Estamos a lunes. / Ya es lunes.	*It's Monday. / Now/Already it's Monday.*
Se está poniendo (volviendo) frío el tiempo.	*It is getting cold.*
Se puso (Se volvió) frío el tiempo.	*It got cold.*
Es verano (Estamos en verano) de nuevo.	*It's summer again. / We are in summer again.*

29.E.4 *To stay* with location: *quedarse*

To stay can be used in English with adverbs of place. In this case, the meaning is expressed in Spanish using **quedarse** (*to remain/stay*).

Hoy **estamos** en la escuela.	*Today, we're at school.*
Hoy **nos quedamos** en la escuela.	*Today, we're staying at school.*

29.E.5 *To become / to go* + adjective: *quedarse* and verbs that express change

a. Changes can also be conveyed with *to become/go* + *adjective* in English. In Spanish, **quedar(se)**, **ponerse**, and **volverse** can be used.

Verbs expressing change: 27.G

Ella **(se) quedó** ciega.	*She went (was) blind.*
Ella **se volvió** ciega.	*She became blind.*
Se puso loco.	*He went crazy.*
Me puse pálida.	*I became/went pale.*

Verbs expressing change: 27.G ▶

b. *To become/get + adjective* can be translated using many Spanish reflexive verbs.

alegrarse	*to become happy*	enojarse	*to get angry*
callarse	*to become quiet*	enriquecerse	*to become rich*
cansarse	*to get tired*	entristecerse	*to get sad*
curarse	*to get cured*	extinguirse	*to become extinct*
debilitarse	*to become weak*	irritarse	*to get annoyed*
emocionarse	*to get excited*	mejorarse	*to get better*
empobrecerse	*to become poor*	mojarse	*to get wet*
enfermarse	*to get sick*	perderse	*to get lost*

Me alegré mucho cuando recibí la noticia.   *I became very happy when I got the news.*
No **me canso** de mirar películas.   *I don't get tired of watching movies.*

c. The verb does not have to be reflexive (although it may also have a reflexive form).

enloquecer   *to go/become mad*
envejecer   *to get/become old*

Verbs expressing change: 27.G ▶

d. The verb **quedar(se)** can't be used with a *noun*. Other verbs, such as **convertirse** and **hacerse**, or verb phrases, such as **llegar a ser**, are used with a noun to express changes.

Los niños **se quedaron** callados.   *The children remained quiet.*
Ella **se convirtió** en una excelente abogada.   *She became an excellent lawyer.*
Él **llegó a ser** un médico famoso.   *Over time, he became a famous doctor.*
Ellos **se hicieron** políticos.   *They became politicians.*

Práctica

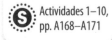
Actividades 1–10, pp. A168–A171

Use of *ser* and *estar*
Uso de ser *y* estar

30.A Overview

Aspectos generales

Both **ser** and **estar** mean *to be*, but they are used in different ways. In general, **ser** is used to describe the inherent and permanent nature and identity of something. **Estar** is used to describe the condition, state, or location of something.

| Marcos **es** un hombre. | *Marcos is a man.* |
| Juan **está** cansado. | *Juan is tired.* |

◀ **Ser** and **estar** are linking verbs: 17.B.1

30.B Use of *ser*

Usos de *ser*

30.B.1 Nouns with *ser*

Ser is used before nouns (with or without determiners), proper nouns, possessives, personal and indefinite pronouns, and professions. **Ser** identifies or defines the subject.

Soy **Raquel**. Soy **mujer**.	*I'm Raquel. I'm a woman.*
Soy **estudiante**.	*I'm a student.*
Raquel soy **yo**.	*I'm Raquel.*
Soy **una chica** joven.	*I'm a young girl.*
Julio es **mi primo**.	*Julio is my cousin.*
Esto es **algo** importante.	*This is something important.*

◀ *To be*: 29.A.1
Verb conjugation tables, B1–B20. See pattern 66.

◀ Determiners: Ch. 4
Indefinite pronouns: 7.D
Possessives: 9.C.2c, 9.D.3
Subject pronouns: 13.A
Ser with calendar and time: 29.C.2a

30.B.2 Adjectives with *ser*: **characteristics**

Ser describes permanent characteristics that define a person, thing, or idea in relation to others of the same kind. The characteristics are seen as belonging only to the subject. They constitute the subject's identity as an individual or as part of a group.

◀ Adjectives: Ch. 3

Identity: adjective with *ser*		
a.	**Appearance**	Soy alto. Mis ojos son negros.	*I'm tall. My eyes are black.*
b.	**Personality and other qualities**	Soy inteligente y trabajador.	*I'm intelligent and hard-working.*
c.	**Origin, nationality**	Soy español.	*I'm Spanish.*
d.	**Belief, ideology, religion**	Soy creyente. Soy católico.	*I'm a believer. I'm Catholic.*
e.	**Values relating to social norms or constructs**	Soy joven y no soy rico.	*I'm young and not rich.*

Some descriptive adjectives have different meanings when used with **ser** and **estar**: **aburrido/a** (*boring; bored*), **listo/a** (*smart; ready*), **malo/a** (*bad; sick*), **verde** (*green; not ripe*), **vivo/a** (*clever; alive*).

| Sofía, ¿**estás lista** para el examen? | *Sofía, are you ready for the test?* |
| Lo harás bien, ¡**eres** la más **lista** de la clase! | *You'll do great; you're the smartest in the class!* |

De: 12.B.4 ▶

30.B.3 Description: *ser + de*

Ser + de followed by nouns or pronouns describes characteristics of people and things: origin, ownership, what they are made of, etc.

Eva **es de** Almería.	*Eva is from Almería.*
Eva **es de** buen humor. (Tiene buen humor.)	*Eva is good-natured. (She has a good nature.)*
La casa **es de** Eva. Es su casa. La casa es suya.	*The house is Eva's. It's her house. The house is hers.*
La casa **es de** madera.	*The house is made of wood.*

30.B.4 Descriptions: *ser para*

Para: 12.B.6 ▶

Personal abilities and the purpose of things can be expressed using **ser** + *adjective* + **para** + *verb*. **Para** + *proper noun* or *pronoun* indicates the receiver.

Ricardo es **bueno para** hablar.	*Ricardo is good at talking.*
La copiadora es **para copiar**.	*The photocopier is for copying.*
La fiesta es **para disfrutarla**.	*The party is for having fun.*
El regalo es **para mí/Alejandra**.	*The present is for me/Alejandra.*

30.B.5 Appearance: *ser + con/a/sin*

The appearance of things is expressed using **ser** + **con/a/sin**.

Mi blusa es **con/sin botones**.	*My blouse has/doesn't have buttons.*
La falda es **a rayas**.	*The skirt is striped.*

30.B.6 Impersonal expressions with *ser*

Impersonal expressions: ▶
23.C.7–8

Spanish has many impersonal expressions with **ser** + *noun* or *adjective*.

¿**Es cierto** que hablas inglés?	*Is it true that you speak English?*
Fue difícil hacerlo.	*It was difficult to do.*
Es una lástima tener que irnos.	*It's a shame that we have to go.*

30.B.7 Personal impression: *ser* with indirect object pronouns

Indirect object pronouns: 13.F ▶

Ser can be used with indirect object pronouns and adjectives to express an opinion.

La situación **nos es indiferente**.	*The situation makes no difference to us.*
Ella **me es** muy **simpática**.	*She seems very nice to me.*
¿**Te fue difícil** llamarme?	*Was it difficult for you to call me?*
No les es fácil pagar de contado.	*It's not easy for them to pay cash.*

30.B.8 Other structures using *ser*

Passive voice with **ser**: 28.B ▶
Emphatic constructions: 15.B.8

Ser is also used in other structures such as the passive voice with **ser: El problema será resuelto**. (*The problem will be solved.*), and emphatic constructions such as **Fue ayer que ocurrió**. (*It was yesterday that it happened.*)

30.C Use of *estar*

Usos de *estar*

30.C.1 Adjectives and adverbs with *estar*: states

a. Adjectives that describe changeable physical or social states can be used with **estar**. The use of **estar** suggests that the state is temporary or is not a critical part of the subject's identity. Some adjectives about marital status can be used with **ser** or **estar** with the same meaning: **ser/estar casado, soltero, divorciado.**

Characteristics: *ser*	**States:** *estar*
El clima **es** inestable. *The weather is unstable.*	El clima **está** inestable. *The weather is (has become) unstable.*
El cielo **es** azul. *The sky is blue.*	El cielo **está** azul. *The sky is blue (today).*
Sandra **es** alegre. *Sandra is a happy person.*	Sandra **está** alegre. *Sandra is happy (at the moment).*
Ella **es** joven. *She is a young person.*	Ella **está** joven. *She is young (still).*
Ella **es** muy pobre. *She is very poor.*	Ella **está** muy pobre. *She is very poor (right now).*

b. Colors, sizes, and other physical characteristics can be described using **estar** when they change in relation to an objective or subjective standard.

Characteristics: *ser*	**States:** *estar*
La esmeralda **es** verde. *The emerald is green.*	Esta pintura **está** muy verde. *This paint is too green.*
El (árbol) bonsái **es** pequeño. *The bonsai (tree) is small.*	Los árboles **están** pequeños. *The trees are (still) small.*
El niño **es** grande y sano. *He is a big and healthy child.*	El niño **está** grande y sano. *The child looks big and healthy.*

c. Estar is used to describe people's health and well-being.

El niño **está** bien ahora. Antes **estaba** peor.   *The child is fine now. He was worse before.*

d. These expressions are used to express how clothes fit:
indirect object pronoun + **está(n)** + *adjective/adverb* (used in Spain) *indirect object pronoun* + **queda(n)** + *adjective/adverb* (used throughout the Spanish-speaking world, including Spain)

El sombrero **te está / te queda** grande.   *The hat is too big for you.*

e. The expression *indirect object pronoun* + **viene(n)** + *adverb* is used in a similar way.

El lunes **me viene** bien.   *Monday works for me.*

f. Both **ser** and **estar** can be used with the adverb **así**. The choice depends on whether it is an intrinsic characteristic or a temporary state.

Juan **es así**, siempre de mal humor.   *Juan is that way, always in a bad mood.*
Juan **está así** porque perdió su trabajo.   *Juan is that way because he lost his job.*

To be: 29.A.2
Verb conjugation tables, B1–B20. See pattern 33.

Adjectives with **ser**: 30.B.2
Gender and number of adjectives: 3.A
Estar in weather expressions: 29.C.1

Adjectives like **contento/a** and **enfermo/a** are used mostly with **estar** because they express conditions.

Remember to use **tener** to express age and some physical states: 29.D

Indirect object pronouns: 13.F

Adverbs of manner: 10.C.2

30.C.2 *Estar* **with a past participle**

The past participle in the passive voice with **ser**: 28.B

Reflexive verbs expressing change: 27.G

estar + *past participle*: 25.D.4c, 26.E, 28.C.3

Adjectives that convey the result of an action must be used with **estar**. The most common of such adjectives are the *past participle* forms used in the passive voice with **ser** or those derived from *reflexive verbs* of change (**sentarse, dormirse, despertarse, irritarse**).

Note that **estar** is used with **muerto/a** and **vivo/a**, since they are viewed as conditions.

Change	State: *estar*
Las casas **fueron construidas**. *The houses got built.*	Las casas **están construidas**. *The houses are built.*
El problema **ha sido resuelto**. *The problem has been solved.*	El problema **está resuelto**. *The problem is solved.*
Los niños **se duermen**. *The children are falling asleep.*	Los niños **están dormidos**. *The children are asleep.*
El vaso **se llena**. *The glass is being filled.*	El vaso **está lleno**. *The glass is full.*
Una persona **murió**. *A person died.*	Una persona **está muerta**. *A person is dead.*
El bebé **nació**. *The baby was born.*	El bebé **está vivo**. *The baby is alive.*
Me irrita el ruido. *The noise irritates me.*	**Estoy irritada** por el ruido. *I am irritated by the noise.*
Lisa **se enamoró**. *Lisa fell in love.*	Lisa **está enamorada**. *Lisa is in love.*

30.C.3 *Estar de* + **noun/adjective**

estar de: 12.B.4

With *nouns* or *adjectives* **estar de** denotes states, moods, jobs, or temporary work. **Andar** is an informal synonym in such sentences, while **encontrarse de** is more formal: **Andrea anda / se encuentra de viaje**. (*Andrea is on a trip*.)

Estoy **de viaje**.	*I'm on a trip.*
¿Estáis **de vacaciones**?	*Are you [pl.] on vacation?*
Estamos **de mal humor**.	*We're in a bad mood.*
¿Está usted **de profesor**?	*Are you working as a teacher?*

30.C.4 **Idiomatic expressions with** *estar*

Use of prepositions: 12.B

Estar is used in many idiomatic expressions.

estar con	No te preocupes, yo **estoy contigo**.	*Don't worry; I'm on your side.*
	En eso **estoy con** él. Creo que tiene razón.	*I agree with him on that. I think he's right.*
	Estoy con fiebre.	*I have a fever.*
estar en	**Estoy en** eso.	*I'm working on it.*
estar para	No **estoy para** bromas.	*I'm not in the mood for jokes.*
estar a punto de	**Estamos a punto de** irnos.	*We're about to leave.*
estar por	**Estoy por** salir.	*I'm about to head out.*
estar que + *verb*	La situación **está que** arde.	*The situation is very volatile.*
	Estoy que no puedo más.	*I'm exhausted. / I'm overwhelmed.*
estar visto	**Está visto** que de literatura no sabes nada.	*It's evident that you don't know anything about literature.*
estar por verse	Lo que va a suceder aún **está por verse**.	*It remains to be seen what will happen.*

30.C.5 **Impersonal expressions with** *estar*

Impersonal expressions with **estar** can be formed with *adverbs* and with *adjectives* derived from the *past participle*.

Impersonal expressions with **estar**: 23.C.8d

está permitido que	*it's allowed to*	**está mal** que	*it's bad that*
está bien que	*it's good that*	**está visto** que	*it's clear that*

30.C.6 *Estar* **+ present participle**

This structure refers to ongoing actions (the progressive tenses).

estar + present participle: 25.C.3
The present progressive: 17.F

Estamos escuchando música.   *We're listening to music.*

30.C.7 *Ser, estar,* **and** *haber*

a. Both **estar** and **haber** can express existence or presence. **Estar** is usually translated as *to be* and refers to the existence or presence of specific things or people. **Haber** is usually translated as *there is/are* and is used to express the existence of a thing or person, or the occurrence of an event.

Ser, estar, and haber: 29.A–29.C
Estar and haber with possessives: 9.D.6d

Hay dos personas esperando al abogado.	*There are two people waiting for the lawyer.*
Las dos personas de las que hablamos **están** en la sala de espera.	*The two people we talked about are in the waiting room.*

b. **Haber** is always used in the singular when it means *there is/are*.

Impersonal form of **haber**: 29.B.1
Impersonal constructions **había, hubo**: 18.E.12

Hubo tres accidentes el fin de semana.	*There were three accidents over the weekend.*
Había mucha nieve.	*There was a lot of snow.*
Dicen que **habrá** tormentas este fin de semana.	*They say there will be storms this weekend.*
Ha habido una pelea.	*There has been a fight.*

c. Both **ser** and **haber** can be used to talk about events. **Haber** points to an unspecified event. **Ser** is used to refer to specific events.

Hubo una fiesta.	*There was a party.*
La fiesta **fue** en un restaurante.	*The party was held at a restaurant.*

d. **Estar** and **haber** are usually interchangeable in relative clauses.

Relative clauses: 15.B

Vi los artículos nuevos que **había/estaban** en la tienda.	*I saw the new items that were in the store.*

30.D *Ser* **and** *estar* **with location**

Ser y estar con lugar

30.D.1 *Estar:* **physical location**

Estar implies a concrete physical location or place.

¿Dónde **estarán** mis llaves?	*Where are my keys?*
El auto **está** en el garaje.	*The car is in the garage.*

30.D.2 *Ser* **with location:** *is (located)*

In conversational Spanish, **ser** describes the location of addresses, buildings, cities, countries, and geographical places. A synonym in Spanish is the verb **quedar: ¿Dónde queda Mendoza?** (*Where is Mendoza [located]?*).

—¿Dónde queda tu casa?	*Where is your house?*
—**Es** en Connecticut.	*It's is in Connecticut.*

Ser is also used to indicate *when* an event takes place.

30.D.3 *Ser* **with location:** *to take place*

Where events and arrangements *take place* is implied with **ser**. In this case, it is not possible to use **estar**. Corresponding expressions are **tener lugar** (formal) and **celebrar**, which convey a celebration of something.

Quiero que la fiesta **sea** aquí.	*I want the party to be (held) here.*
El partido **será** en Monterrey.	*The game will be in Monterrey.*
¿Dónde **va a ser** tu boda?	*Where is your wedding going to be (held)?*
La celebración **fue** en el club.	*The celebration took place at the club.*
Las Fallas **son** en Valencia.	*The Fallas festival is in Valencia.*

30.E | Structures with *ser* and *estar*

Estructuras con *ser* y *estar*

		Ser	Estar
Nouns: Ch.2	Nouns	Él es **profesor**. *He is a teacher.*	Only with **estar de** + *profession*: Él **está de profesor**. *He is working as a teacher.*
Adjectives with **ser** and **estar**: 30.B.2, 30.C.1	Adjectives	La silla es **cómoda**. *The chair is comfortable.*	La silla está **cómoda**. *The chair feels comfortable.*
Passive voice with **ser**: 28.B Past participle: 19.A.1, 19.A.2, 25.D	Past participles	Las cuentas **fueron pagadas**. *The bills were paid.*	Las cuentas **están pagadas**. *The bills are paid.*
Prepositions: Ch.12	Prepositional phrases	Somos **de** Inglaterra. *We are from England.* Esto es **para** comer. *This is for eating.*	Estamos **en** la escuela. *We are in school.* Estamos **sin** dinero. *We are without money.*
Adverbs: Ch. 10	Adverbs	Él es **así**. *He is like that.* La fiesta es **aquí**. *The party is being held here.*	Está **así** porque su hermano está enfermo. *He is (being/feeling) like this because his brother is sick.* Estamos **aquí**. *We're here.*
Impersonal expressions with **ser**: 23.C.7, 23.C.8	Impersonal expressions	**Es importante que** entrenes. *It's important that you train.*	**Está bien que** entrenes. *It's good that you train.*
Emphatic constructions: 15.B.8	Emphatic constructions	**Es** hoy cuando viajo. *It is today that I travel.* **Fue** eso lo que dije. *That was what I said.*	*Not possible with* **estar**
estar + present participle: 25.C.3	Present participle (progressive tenses)	*Not possible with* **ser**	**Estamos** trabajando. *We're working.*

Práctica

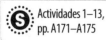 Actividades 1–13, pp. A171–A175

Indirect discourse
Discurso indirecto

Chapter 31

A. Overview
B. Indirect discourse: changes to verb tenses and mood

31.A Overview

Aspectos generales

The ability to relate what you have heard or what you know, think, or believe is important when communicating with other people. Direct and indirect discourse are the strategies used for this purpose.

31.A.1 Direct discourse

Also called *quoted speech*, direct discourse reproduces someone's exact words. In writing, quotation marks indicate that the words enclosed are being reproduced exactly. Dialogues use a dash for the same purpose. In speech (usually formal), a suitable introductory phrase and proper intonation announce the quotation.

◄ Use of quotation marks: 1.F.8
Use of the dash: 1.F.7

Direct discourse in writing	Direct discourse in speech
Carlos dijo: **"Esta fecha es muy importante para mí"**. *Carlos said: "This date is very important for me."*	Carlos dijo **lo siguiente**: **"Esta fecha es muy importante para mí"**. *Carlos said the following: "This date is very important for me."*

31.A.2 Indirect discourse

Also called *reported speech,* indirect discourse relates someone's statement without quoting his or her exact words. The same structure is used in writing and speech.

◄ **Decir** and other reporting verbs: 23.C.2

Indirect discourse	
Carlos dijo **que esa fecha era muy importante para él**.	*Carlos said (that) that date was very important for him.*

31.B Indirect discourse: changes to verb tenses and mood

Cambios en el tiempo o modo verbal

31.B.1 Overview

Several sentence components may have to change when reporting someone's words: subject pronouns, object and reflexive pronouns, possessives, demonstratives, adverbs of time and place, and *especially* the verb tense and/or mood. These changes are determined by the change of perspective needed when reproducing someone else's words in a different context. Usually if the reporting verb is in the present, the verb tenses stay the same.

Said on Monday	Iré al cine **mañana**.	*I'll go to the movies tomorrow.*
Reported on Monday	Dice que irá al cine **mañana**.	*He says he'll go to the movies tomorrow.*
Reported on Tuesday	Dijo / Ha dicho que iría al cine **hoy**.	*He (has) said he'd go to the movies today.*
Reported on Wednesday	Dijo que iría al cine **ayer**.	*He said he'd go to the movies yesterday.*
Reported on Sunday	Dijo que iría al cine **el martes**.	*He said he'd go to the movies on Tuesday.*

Decir and other reporting ▶ verbs: 23.C.2

31.B.2 Reporting information and commands

The most important thing to keep in mind when reporting your own or someone else's statements is whether the statement conveys *information* or a *command*. When information is reported, the mood of the verb does not change. When commands are reported, the imperative is replaced by the subjunctive.

	Direct discourse	Indirect discourse
Reporting information	La profesora dice: "Tú siempre **haces** los deberes". *The teacher says: "You always do your homework."*	La profesora dice que tú siempre **haces** los deberes. *The teacher says that you always do your homework.*
Reporting a command	La profesora dice: "**Haz** los deberes". *The teacher says: "Do your homework."*	La profesora dice que **hagas** los deberes. *The teacher says that you should do your homework.*

31.B.3 Changes in verb tenses

a. The following verb tenses change in indirect discourse when the reporting verb is used in the past.

Use of the imperfect: 18.E.10 ▶

Use of the past perfect: 19.E.3 ▶

Use of the conditional: 21.B.6 ▶

Regional variations in ▶ the use of the subjunctive in noun clauses: 23.Fa

	Type of change	Direct discourse	Indirect discourse
Indicative	Present → Imperfect	Ella **dijo**: "**Voy** de compras". *She said: "I am going shopping."*	Ella **dijo** que **iba** de compras. *She said that she was going shopping.*
	Preterite → Past perfect	Ella **dijo**: "**Fui** de compras". *She said: "I went shopping."*	Ella **dijo** que **había ido** de compras. *She said that she had gone shopping.*
	Present perfect → Past perfect	Ella **dijo**: "No **he comprado** nada". *She said: "I haven't bought anything."*	Ella **dijo** que no **había comprado** nada. *She said that she hadn't bought anything.*
	Future → Conditional	Ella **dijo**: "**Compraré** algo". *She said: "I will buy something."*	Ella **dijo** que **compraría** algo. *She said that she would buy something.*
	Future perfect → Conditional perfect	Ella **dijo**: "Esta tarde **habré terminado** mis compras". *She said: "I will have finished my shopping this afternoon."*	Ella **dijo** que esta tarde **habría terminado** sus compras. *She said that she would have finished her shopping this afternoon.*
Subjunctive	Present → Past	Ella **dijo**: "**Quiero** que me **acompañes**". *She said: "I want you to go with me."*	Ella **dijo** que **quería** que la **acompañara**. *She said that she wanted me to go with her.*
	Present perfect → Past perfect	Ella **dijo**: "No creo que me **hayan dado** un buen precio". *She said: "I don't believe they gave me a good price."*	Ella **dijo** que no creía que le **hubieran dado** un buen precio. *She said that she did not believe they had given her a good price.*
	Imperative → Past	Ella **dijo**: "¡**Espérame**!" *She said: "Wait for me!"*	Ella **dijo** que la **esperara**. *She said that I should wait for her.*

Ir a: 18.E.10c ▶

b. When a future statement is reported, it is also possible to use the *imperfect* of **ir a** + *infinitive*.

Iré la semana que viene. → Dijo que **iría** la semana siguiente. / Dijo que **iba a ir** la semana siguiente.

I will go next week. → *She said she would go next week. / She said she was going to go next week.*

31.B.4 Verb tenses that do not change

The following tenses do not change in indirect discourse. However, note that other changes to the sentence may be necessary, such as replacing subject, reflexive, and object pronouns.

		Direct discourse	Indirect discourse	
Indicative	Imperfect	Ella dijo: "**Me gustaban** mucho las tapas". *She said: "I used to like tapas a lot."*	Ella dijo que **le gustaban** mucho las tapas. *She said that she used to like tapas a lot.*	◀ Use of the imperfect: 18.E.10
	Past perfect	Ella dijo: "Nunca **me había divertido** tanto". *She said: "I'd never had so much fun."*	Ella dijo que nunca **se había divertido** tanto. *She said that she had never had so much fun.*	
	Conditional	Ella dijo: "**Tomaría** un crucero". *She said: "I would go on a cruise."*	Ella dijo que **tomaría** un crucero. *She said she would go on a cruise.*	◀ Use of the conditional: 21.B.6
	Conditional perfect	Ella dijo: "**Te habrías divertido** si hubieras venido a la fiesta". *She said: "You would have had fun if you had come to the party."*	Ella dijo que **me habría divertido** si hubiera ido a la fiesta. *She said I would have had fun if I had gone to the party.*	
Subjunctive	Past	Ella dijo: "**Me** gustaría que **tú me prepararas** un plato chileno". *She said: "I would like you to prepare a Chilean dish for me."*	Ella dijo que **le** gustaría que **yo le preparara** un plato chileno. *She said that she would like me to prepare a Chilean dish for her.*	
	Past perfect	Ella dijo: "**Te** habrías divertido si **hubieras venido** a la fiesta". *She said: "You would have had fun if you had come to the party."*	Ella dijo que **me** habría divertido si **hubiera ido** a la fiesta. *She said I would have had fun if I had gone to the party.*	

31.B.5 Other changes

a. Retelling and repeating imply a change of perspective and will necessarily require changes in other sentence elements such as object pronouns, reflexive pronouns, and possessives. Spanish and English share these perspectives and the same changes are required.

◀ Possessives: 9.B, 9.C
Pronouns after prepositions: 13.C
Direct object pronouns: 13.E.3
Indirect object pronouns: 13.F.2
Reflexive pronouns: 27.A

Direct discourse	Indirect discourse
Ella me dice: "**Te** voy a extrañar mucho". *She tells me: "I'm going to miss you a lot."*	Ella dijo que **me** iba a extrañar mucho. *She said she was going to miss me a lot.*
Ella dice: "No puedo poner**me** los zapatos". *She says: "I can't put on my shoes."*	Ella dijo que no podía poner**se** los zapatos. *She said she couldn't put on her shoes.*
Ella dice: "No encontré **mis** gafas en el estuche". *She says: "I didn't find my glasses in the case."*	Ella dijo que no había encontrado **sus** gafas en el estuche. *She said she hadn't found her glasses in the case.*

b. A change from direct discourse to indirect discourse may also imply a change in time perspective. In addition to changes in verb tenses, adverbs or time expressions may have to change, too.

◀ Adverbs of time: 10.B.2

Direct discourse	Indirect discourse
Fecha: 3 de enero Elena dice: "Publicaré las fotos **mañana**". *Elena says: "I will publish my photos tomorrow."*	Fecha: 15 de enero Elena dijo que publicaría las fotos **al día siguiente**. *Elena said that she would publish her photos the next day.*
Elena dice: "**Anoche** no pude dormir nada". *Elena says: "I couldn't sleep at all last night."*	Elena dijo que no había podido dormir nada **la noche anterior**. *Elena said that she hadn't been able to sleep at all the night before.*

In the shift to indirect discourse, **ahora** may become **entonces**, **ayer** may be changed to **el día anterior**, and **la semana pasada** may become **la semana anterior**.

Indirect questions:
14.B.1b, 14.B.9

31.B.6 Indirect questions

a. Questions can be reported indirectly or rephrased to make them more polite. Note that Spanish has the same word order in direct and indirect questions.

	Direct question	**Indirect or more polite question**
Present	—Señor, ¿**qué hora es**? *Sir, what time is it?*	—Señor, ¿podría decirme **qué hora es**? *Sir, could you tell me what time it is?*
Past	—¿Qué le **preguntaste** al señor? *What did you ask the man?*	—Le pregunté **qué hora era**. *I asked him what time it was.*

Que before indirect
questions: 16.C.1c

b. When yes/no questions are reported, **si** introduces the implied question. *If* or *whether* is used in the equivalent construction in English. In informal speech, **que** may be added to the indirect question.

—¿Qué le preguntaste al señor?   *What did you ask the man?*
—Le pregunté (que) **si** sabía la hora.   *I asked him if/whether he knew what time it was.*

c. Verbs referring to mental activity also form indirect questions with **si**.

Me pregunto **si** este producto es bueno.   *I wonder if/whether this product is good.*
No recuerdo **si** la cita es hoy.   *I don't recall if/whether the appointment is today.*

Question words: 1.E.7
Question formation: 14.A-14.B

d. Question words carry an accent in both direct and indirect questions.

—¿**Cuándo** llegará el avión?   *When will the plane arrive?*
—Nadie sabe **cuándo** llegará.   *No one knows when it will arrive.*

—¿**Cómo** se llamará esa chica?   *What is that girl's name?*
—No sé **cómo** se llama ella.   *I don't know what her name is.*

—¿**Dónde** podrán arreglarme el coche?   *Where can my car be fixed?*
—No sabemos **dónde** podrán arreglártelo.   *We don't know where it can be fixed.*

Práctica

 Actividades 1–10,
pp. A176–A179

Appendix

1. **Dividir** Lee la descripción de Anita y separa en sílabas la palabra subrayada en cada oración. **Atención: puede haber dos divisiones correctas para una palabra. Escríbelas.** `1.D`

   Modelo

   Es una pintora <u>extraña</u> y excepcional. _____*ex-tra-ña*_____

   1. Se trata de Anita, una artista <u>impresionante</u>. _____
   2. Algunos de sus cuadros reflejan personajes muy <u>simpáticos</u>. _____
   3. Uno de ellos es un mimo en una calle <u>europea</u>. _____
   4. Sus bocetos son tan precisos que no hace <u>correcciones</u> antes del óleo. _____
   5. Para <u>facilitar</u> su trabajo, ella prepara muchas paletas al tiempo. _____
   6. Compra sus pinceles por Internet y los recibe por correo <u>aéreo</u>. _____
   7. Mientas pinta, le encanta comer <u>cacahuates</u> o uvas pasas. _____
   8. Aunque vive en Ecuador, algunas de sus obras han cruzado el <u>Atlántico</u>. _____

2. **Partir** Separa en sílabas la última palabra de cada línea del siguiente aviso. `1.D`

   ¿Quieres ser mi compañera de viaje?

   Me llamo Daniel y soy un hombre
   de treinta y dos años de edad.
   Busco una mujer joven que quiera
   ir de vacaciones pronto a Europa
   y que le guste mucho ver ciudades
   nuevas y visitar muchos museos.
   Si te interesara, no dudes en llamarme.
   ¡Hasta pronto!

   _____*via-je*_____
   1. _____
   2. _____
   3. _____
   4. _____
   5. _____
   6. _____
   7. _____
   8. _____

3. **Sí o no** Indica con *Sí* o *No* si es posible separar en sílabas las vocales subrayadas. Si respondes *Sí*, muestra cómo lo harías. `1.D`

   Modelo

   t<u>ea</u>tro
   Sí, te-a-tro

   1. p<u>ia</u>no _____
   2. c<u>ua</u>dro _____
   3. f<u>eo</u> _____
   4. c<u>ao</u>s _____
   5. <u>ai</u>re _____
   6. r<u>ue</u>da _____
   7. mar<u>eo</u> _____
   8. barr<u>io</u> _____

4. Separar Separa en sílabas estas palabras. `1.D`

> **Modelo**
>
> callejón ____ca-lle-jón____

1. cepillo _____
2. excelente _____
3. pantalones _____
4. poeta _____
5. cielo _____

6. hacia _____
7. suave _____
8. aprender _____
9. empleado _____
10. oxígeno _____

11. empresa _____
12. Paraguay _____
13. anochecer _____
14. botellón _____
15. carruaje _____

5. Decidir Lee esta carta y decide si estas palabras llevan tilde o no. `1.E`

> Querida Juana:
>
> (1) ___Te___ (Te / Té) escribo desde Medellín. ¡Estamos tan cerca! No (2) _____ (se / sé) cuántos días me quedaré aquí, pero espero que puedas venir a visitarme. ¿Quieres que te (3) _____ (de / dé) mi número de teléfono? (4) _____ (Si / Sí) quieres, puedes llamarme por las tardes. (5) _____ (Tu / Tú) ya me has dado tu teléfono, ¿verdad? Hasta pronto.
>
> (6) _____ (Tu / Tú) amiga, Paula

6. Escoger Ordena las palabras en esta tabla según sean llanas, agudas o esdrújulas. `1.E`

> balón   ~~álbum~~   silla   ballets   lágrimas   césped   árbol
> palabra   razón   ídolos   cómprame   estoy   rápido   pasión

Llanas	Agudas	Esdrújulas
álbum		

7. Formar Forma una sola palabra con los dos elementos indicados. Recuerda poner o quitar la tilde si es necesario. `1.E`

> **Modelo**
>
> presenta + la = ___preséntala___

1. trae + los = _____
2. póster + es = _____
3. devuelve + los = _____
4. récord + s = _____

5. tomate + s = _____
6. inglés + es = _____
7. colección + es = _____
8. come + los = _____

8. **Corregir** En estas oraciones hay palabras que deben llevar tilde. ¡Corrígelas! **1.E**

   1. ¿Hoy es miercoles o jueves? _____

   2. Hace ocho dias que nadie me llama. ¡Me siento sola! _____

   3. Papa, regalanos camisetas de baloncesto para Navidad. ¡Por favor! _____

   4. ¿Quieres venir a tomar un te a casa? _____

   5. ¡Cuantos arboles hay en este bosque! _____

   6. La profesora me dijo que este calculo estaba mal. ¿Pero donde esta el error? _____

9. **Buscar** Lee la historia de Martín y subraya las palabras que tengan hiato. **1.E**

   > Hace poco estuve con Raúl, un gran amigo mío. Siempre lo veo los fines de semana, pero esta vez nos vimos aunque era lunes. Me contó que tuvo una pelea con su novia, María. Me dijo que le mandó a su casa un ramo de flores con un poema, pero sin ningún resultado. La realidad es que yo tampoco creo que haya una solución. Espero que ella lo llame y se reconcilien un día de estos.

10. **Hiato** En estas palabras, indica dónde está el hiato (si lo hay) y qué tipo de vocales lo forman: *fuertes* (F) y *débiles* (D). **1.E**

    Modelo

    toalla *(F, F)*

    1. oído _____   7. Mediterráneo _____
    2. maíz _____   8. reescribir _____
    3. aeroplano _____   9. Luis _____
    4. compañía _____   10. zanahoria _____
    5. cooperar _____   11. león _____
    6. repetía _____   12. tío _____

11. **¿Con tilde o sin ella?** Completa cada oración con la versión correcta de la palabra, con tilde o sin tilde. **1.E**

    Modelo

    _Tu_ (Tú/Tu) amigo Mark no habla francés.

    1. _____ (Él/El) hermano de Carla todavía no sabe escribir.

    2. ¡Cuántas veces te he dicho que no te tomes mi _____ (té/te)!

    3. _____ (Aún/Aun) si tuviera dinero, no compraría una casa en la playa.

    4. No debo engordar _____ (más/mas). De lo contrario, podría afectar mi salud.

    5. ¡Ya _____ (sé/se) cómo resolver este problema!

    6. _____ (Sí/Si) vamos a la playa, debemos llevar sombrero y protección solar.

    7. ¡Este libro es para _____ (mí/mi)!

    8. Él espera que su novia le _____ (dé/de) una nueva oportunidad.

    9. _____ (Éstas/Estas) sillas son muy económicas, ¡no pierda esta oportunidad!

    10. ¿_____ (Qué/Que) le diremos a tu padre?

12. Completar Incluye las palabras de la lista en este aviso publicitario. `1.E`

cómo   como   ~~Quién~~   quien   dónde   donde   que   qué

¿(1) ___Quién___ no soñó alguna vez con una luna de miel (2) _____ sea inolvidable? Podemos ayudarte a planear tu viaje tal (3) _____ lo desees, ¡con (4) _____ hayas elegido para pasar el resto de tu vida! ¿(5) _____ preferirías pasar tu luna de miel? ¿(6) _____ prefieres: playa, montañas o campo? Te damos consejos sobre los mejores lugares (7) _____ podrás disfrutar del romance. ¿(8) _____ puedes comunicarte con nosotros? Llámanos al 435 423 847 o visita nuestra página web (www.lunasllenasdemiel.com).

13. Reescribir Sin cambiar el sentido de la oración, usa los adjetivos de la lista para reescribir las palabras subrayadas con un adverbio que termine en -*mente*. `1.E`

~~ágil~~   atento   frecuente   público   rápido   sincero   teórico

Modelo

El corredor superaba los obstáculos con agilidad.   ___ágilmente___

1. Marta corrió <u>con rapidez</u> hasta la cocina. ¡Su comida se estaba quemando! _____
2. Lee cada frase <u>con atención</u> y encontrarás el error. _____
3. Debes cepillarte los dientes <u>con frecuencia</u> para no tener caries. _____
4. Dímelo <u>con sinceridad</u>, ¿te gusta mi nuevo corte de cabello? _____
5. <u>En teoría</u>, nada debería salir mal. Pero no siempre es así. _____
6. No me gusta que me llames "Juanita" <u>en público</u>, mamá. Dime "Juana", por favor. _____

14. Singular o plural Escribe el singular o el plural de estas palabras. `1.E`

1. ___margen___ → márgenes
2. aborigen → _____
3. _____ → condiciones
4. _____ → manteles
5. árbol → _____
6. _____ → intereses
7. _____ → meses
8. _____ → atunes

15. Seleccionar El señor González es un empresario con muchas actividades. Completa las oraciones con la mejor opción. `1.E`

1. 6:00 a. m. El señor González salió de su casa y su _____ lo llevó al gimnasio.
   a. chofer   b. chófer   c. Ambas opciones son posibles.
2. 7:30 a. m. Después de hacer ejercicio y jugar al _____, se dio una ducha y se dirigió a su trabajo.
   a. fútbol   b. futbol   c. Ambas opciones son posibles.
3. 10:30 a. m. González habló por teléfono con un empleado sobre un informe _____ de América Latina.
   a. economico-social   b. económico-social   c. Ambas opciones son posibles.
4. 1:30 p. m. González le escribe un correo electrónico a su secretaria. El asunto dice: "¿_____ EL INFORME?"
   a. DONDE ESTA   b. DÓNDE ESTÁ   c. DONDE ESTÁ
5. 6:00 p. m. González les comunica a sus empleados que les enviará el informe sobre la situación _____ de América Latina.
   a. político-económica   b. politico-economica   c. político-economica

16. Tildar Coloca la tilde donde haga falta. Como ayuda, las sílabas tónicas están subrayadas. `1.E`

> **Modelo**
>
> portatiles: portátiles

1. pa<u>is</u>	6. cora<u>zo</u>nes	11. ac<u>triz</u>	16. poe<u>si</u>a
2. <u>am</u>plio	7. <u>di</u>melo	12. holan<u>des</u>	17. <u>fi</u>sico-<u>qui</u>mico
3. gra<u>ma</u>tica	8. ac<u>tuar</u>	13. <u>de</u>biles	18. <u>can</u>talo
4. <u>ha</u>cia	9. <u>di</u>me	14. <u>cree</u>me	19. veinti<u>tres</u>
5. ra<u>zon</u>	10. <u>vi</u>	15. sutil<u>mente</u>	20. a<u>que</u>llo

17. Comas Escribe las comas donde sea necesario en el correo electrónico de Julia. `1.F`

> **Modelo**
>
> Hola, Guadalupe:

De:	julia@micorreo.com
Para:	guadalupe@micorreo.com
Asunto:	Bienvenida

¡Bienvenida a Córdoba amiga! ¡Qué bien que ya estés en la ciudad! No veo la hora de encontrarnos pero estoy un poco ocupada: por las mañanas voy a un curso de cocina. Estoy muy contenta con el curso. La profesora que es tan buena persona resultó ser mi vecina. ¿Puedes creerlo?

¿Te parece que mañana nos veamos? Podemos dar un paseo en barco ir a museos y caminar en el parque. Allá hace frío pero aquí calor. Para mí todo fue tan genial cuando llegué a esta ciudad. ¡Te encantará conocerla!

Un abrazo muy grande

Julia

18. Puntuar Escoge el signo de puntuación adecuado en cada parte e incorpóralo al relato de Lucía. `1.F`

Santiago de Chile____ (; / . / ,)
(1)
3 de febrero de 2015
Este es mi último día en Santiago y he visto todo lo que quería ver____ (: / , / ;) la Plaza de Armas,
(2)
el mercado central, el centro financiero y el teatro municipal. Para mí____ (; / , / :) lo más increíble
(3)
de esta ciudad es que tanta gente vive en ella. Santiago____ (; / , / :) que fue fundada en el siglo
(4)
XVI____ (; / , / :) ¡hoy tiene 6____ (; / , / :) 6 millones de habitantes!
(5)   (6)
Otra cosa que me encantó sobre esta ciudad fue la gente. ¡Conocí a personas tan amables! Por
ejemplo, a Juanita, la cocinera del hostal ____ (: / , / ;) a Pablo, el vendedor de periódicos____
(7)   (8)
(: / , / ;) y a Esther, la camarera de un bar.
Espero volver algún día... ¡y pronto!

19. Elegir Lee las oraciones y complétalas con los signos de puntuación de la lista. `1.F`

¡! ... () — —— « » : -

Modelo

__¡__No puede ser__!__ Dejé el celular en el taxi.

1. La asociación franco_____alemana de Lima hoy celebra su centenario.

2. Juan me miró a los ojos y me dijo_____"Quiero casarme contigo".

3. _____¡Hola, Carlos! Cuánto tiempo sin vernos.
   _____¡Hola, Manuela! Un gusto verte de nuevo.

4. Este año leí muchos poemas, pero el que más me gustó fue _____Al callarse_____, de Pablo Neruda.

5. Compramos muchísimas cosas para la fiesta: dulces, decoración, bebidas, comida_____

6. En Buenos Aires _____la capital de Argentina_____ hay cada vez más turistas.

20. Arreglar Corrige la puntuación en estas oraciones. `1.F`

Modelo

Como dice en *El Quijote*: —Confía en el tiempo, que suele dar dulces salidas a muchas amargas dificultades—.
Como dice en El Quijote: *"Confía en el tiempo, que suele dar dulces salidas a muchas amargas dificultades".*

1. Hoy hace tanto calor, ¡verdad!

2. El prefijo —**anti** significa "contrario".

3. Sara, Paula, Gastón, José, y Pedro fueron al cine el domingo.

4. El jefe de Silvina (que se llama Felipe (igual que el rey de España) no quiere que sus empleados lleguen ni un minuto tarde al trabajo.

5. Lee los capítulos 1.5 y resúmelos en una hoja.

6. Mi hermana que siempre está de mal humor hoy estaba sonriente.

7. —Vienes a la fiesta?
   —Sí si me invitas.

8. Hola. Roberto. Cómo estás?

21. Terminar Completa la historia de Ricardo con la opción correcta de cada caso. `1.G`

El (1) _____ (Lunes / lunes) pasado visité por primera vez el (2) _____ (Distrito Federal / distrito federal), la capital de México. Yo no lo sabía, pero es la octava ciudad más rica del mundo: ¡su PBI es de 315 000 millones de dólares! Los (3) _____ (Mexicanos / mexicanos) son muy simpáticos y serviciales. El señor (4) _____ (del Valle / Del Valle), el guía de nuestra excursión, no era de México, sino de (5) _____ (el Salvador / El Salvador). Creo que lo que más me interesó de esta excursión fue visitar la (6) _____ (Universidad nacional autónoma de México / Universidad Nacional Autónoma de México). Ojalá que pueda estudiar allí dentro de unos años.

22. Ortografía Completa las oraciones con la palabra adecuada. **Atención: usa con cuidado las mayúsculas y las minúsculas.** `1.G`

Modelo

En las vacaciones de _____*verano*_____ hace mucho calor; voy a la playa y tomo el sol.

1. El gentilicio de las personas que nacen en _____ es salvadoreño/a.

2. La _____ es el planeta que habitamos.

3. En el mes de _____ muchas personas celebran la Navidad.

4. El _____ es la estación más fría del año.

5. En español, el nombre del día _____ proviene del latín y significa "día de la luna".

23. ¿Mayúsculas? Reescribe las oraciones cambiando minúsculas a mayúsculas donde sea necesario. Sigue el modelo. `1.G`

Modelo

mi mamá nació en milán, pero no sabe hablar bien italiano.
Mi mamá nació en Milán, pero no sabe hablar bien italiano.

1. la gente fuera de españa no dice "euskadi", sino "país vasco".
   _____

2. en la sierra nevada de santa marta está el pico más alto de colombia.
   _____

3. arabia saudita limita con jordania y kuwait, entre otros países.
   _____

4. el río amazonas tiene un gran caudal.
   _____

5. una de las grandes capitales de la moda es parís.
   _____

6. la ciudad de río de janeiro es mi ciudad favorita.
   _____

24. Síntesis Emparejar Une los elementos de las dos columnas para formar oraciones sobre la acentuación, la puntuación y la ortografía. `1.D–1.G`

1. En una enumeración, antes de la **y**,
2. Las estaciones del año
3. Para expresar duda, inseguridad o temor,
4. Son ejemplos de palabras con acento diacrítico:
5. Los nombres propios
6. En algunos países, para expresar un decimal,
7. Son ejemplos de palabras con hiato:
8. Antes de las citas textuales
9. Son ejemplos de palabras con triptongo:

a. **maestro** y **coexistir**.
b. **aún** y **té**.
c. no se usa la coma.
d. se usa la coma.
e. se usan los puntos suspensivos.
f. se usan los dos puntos.
g. **Paraguay** y **Uruguay**.
h. se escriben en mayúscula inicial.
i. se escriben en minúscula.

25. Síntesis Finalizar Para cada afirmación encuentra la palabra que le corresponde y escríbela. `1.D–1.G`

agudas	ortográficas
diacrítico	puntuación
diptongo	~~sílabas~~
graves	tilde
hiatos	triptongo

1. Al final de una línea, si una palabra no cabe completa, puede dividirse por ellas. _____*sílabas*_____

2. Así se llaman dos vocales que suenan juntas y forman una sola sílaba. _____

3. También se llama de esta forma al acento gráfico que se marca en una sílaba. _____

4. La unión de tres vocales en una sílaba se denomina así. _____

5. **Andén, cantar, manatí, vendaval** son ejemplos de estas palabras. _____

6. El punto, la coma, el paréntesis, entre otros, son signos de este tipo. _____

7. Los contienen palabras como **baúl, país, río.** _____

8. **Bestia, golpe, mármol, póster** ejemplifican estas palabras. _____

9. Este tipo de normas indican que los nombres propios llevan mayúsculas iniciales y que en español los días de la semana se escriben con minúscula. _____

10. Así se llama el acento utilizado para diferenciar dos palabras que se deletrean de la misma forma. _____

 Practice more at **vhlcentral.com.**

Nouns
Chapter 2

1. Escoger Coloca estos sustantivos en la columna adecuada. `2.A`

~~fiscal~~	agente	representante	malabarista	ciclista	gerenta
~~profesora~~	~~portero~~	león	pájaro	poeta	yegua
artista	nuera	escritor	cirujana	actriz	toro

Masculino	Femenino	Masculino/Femenino
portero	profesora	fiscal

2. Cambiar Cambia el género de estos sustantivos. `2.A`

> **Modelo**
>
> la secretaria → _el secretario_

1. el accionista → _____
2. la madrina → _____
3. el periodista → _____
4. el cuñado → _____
5. el príncipe → _____
6. la yegua → _____

7. la doctora → _____
8. el cocodrilo macho → _____
9. la modelo → _____
10. el emperador → _____
11. el gallo → _____
12. la suegra → _____

3. Bogotá Lee esta descripción sobre la ciudad de Bogotá. Elige la opción correcta en cada oración. `2.A`

1. La ciudad de Bogotá es _____ capital de la República de Colombia.
   a. la   b. el
2. Está ubicada en _____ centro del país.
   a. la   b. el
3. Tiene _____ población de más de siete millones de habitantes.
   a. una   b. un
4. La ciudad ofrece _____ gran cantidad de museos, teatros y bibliotecas.
   a. una   b. un
5. _____ Bogotá es el río más extenso de los alrededores de la ciudad.
   a. La   b. El
6. _____ orquídea es la flor que se usa como símbolo de Bogotá.
   a. La   b. El
7. Los lugares turísticos más importantes son _____ jardín botánico, el observatorio nacional y el mirador de La Calera.
   a. la   b. el
8. _____ azul predomina en la bandera de esta ciudad.
   a. La   b. El

4. Elegir Localiza y subraya la palabra con distinto género de cada grupo. `2.A`

1. realidad   mal   poesía   foto
2. dolor   canal   verde   luz
3. canción   arroz   tema   cielo
4. heroína   problema   flor   libertad
5. inteligencia   gente   fantasma   mano
6. día   espíritu   color   sinceridad

7. tribu   confirmación   ayuda   mapa
8. amor   solicitud   viuda   cara
9. amanecer   poder   lunes   vejez
10. dilema   drama   idea   síntoma
11. rojo   abril   equis   planeta
12. tabú   rubí   clase   cine

5. Seleccionar Escoge la opción correcta para completar estas oraciones. `2.A`

1. _____ (La orden/El orden) vino directamente del jefe. Debemos obedecerle.
2. En la misa, _____ (la cura/el cura) rezó por la paz en el mundo.
3. Silvio, ¿puedes ayudarme? Se me cayó _____ (una pendiente/un pendiente) y se hace tarde para ir a la fiesta.
4. El libro fue publicado por _____ (la editorial/el editorial) municipal hace dos años.
5. Sin dudas, _____ (la rosa/el rosa) es mi color favorito para los vestidos de mis muñecas.
6. Me golpeé y ahora me duelen mucho _____ (la frente/el frente) y los ojos.

6. Completar Completa la composición con el artículo correcto en cada caso (*la* para femenino, *el* para masculino). `2.A`

> Tema: (1) __*El*__ barrio donde vivo
>
> Mi barrio es muy pequeño. Todo (2) _____ vecindario se conoce. Por (3) _____ tarde, todos los niños jugamos en (4) _____ calle. (5) _____ verdad es que todo es muy tranquilo. Solo debemos tener cuidado con (6) _____ tranvía y los coches.
>
> Tenemos muchos lugares para divertirnos. Por ejemplo, (7) _____ cine. Durante (8) _____ fin de semana, en (9) _____ programa hay películas infantiles. Si no hay una película interesante, vemos (10) _____ televisión o escuchamos (11) _____ radio. Pero (12) _____ parque es mi lugar favorito.
>
> En nuestra cuadra, viven muchas familias de distintos países. (13) _____ mitad de ellas viene de Latinoamérica. Lo cierto es que es muy divertido, porque todos somos diferentes, pero (14) _____ comunicación es muy buena siempre.

7. El plural Escribe el plural de estas palabras. `2.B`

> **Modelo**
>
> reloj *relojes*

1. vela _____
2. perro _____
3. canción _____
4. paquete _____
5. emoción _____
6. coche _____
7. papá _____
8. tren _____

9. pez _____
10. mujer _____
11. día _____
12. país _____
13. policía _____
14. champú _____
15. viernes _____

8. Encontrar Utiliza las palabras de la lista para completar las oraciones. Atención: ¡debes usarlas en plural! `2.B`

> ratón   pared   ~~señor~~   club   corazón   voz   paz   bus

1. __*Señores*__, pueden pasar al salón. La directora los espera.
2. ¡Cuántas historias de _____ rotos!
3. Hay _____ que nos llevan a Buenos Aires por un precio muy económico.
4. Hagamos las _____. No quiero más discusiones.
5. Los _____ de fútbol importantes tienen estadios gigantes.
6. Escucho _____ de niños gritando ¡y no puedo dormir!
7. Ten cuidado. Por la noche, siempre hay _____ en la cocina.
8. Quiero pintar las _____ de color rojo. ¿Qué te parece?

9. Precisar Roberto se equivocó en su informe. Completa los ajustes que le sugiere Natalia. `2.B`

> **Modelo**
>
> Cambia "La prueba demuestra…" por "Las _____ *pruebas* _____ demuestran…".

1. Cambia "el análisis técnico…" por: "los _____ técnicos …".
2. Cambia "La tesis descrita…" por "Las _____ descritas…".
3. Cambia "La tabla registra el espécimen…" por "La tabla registra los _____…".
4. Cambia "El uso de monitor digital…" por "El uso de _____ digitales…".
5. Cambia "el menú del informe..." por "los _____ de los informes...".
6. Cambia "El virus perdió…" por "Los _____ perdieron".

10. Regular o irregular Marca los plurales en cada frase e indica si son *regulares* (R) o *irregulares* (I). `2.B`

> **Modelo**
>
> Las crisis afectaron a los agricultores. *crisis (I), agricultores (R)*

1. Los miércoles jugamos a las cartas. _____
2. Mi tía compra los mejores tés en la tienda de la esquina. _____
3. En el tribunal, los jueces trabajan por la tarde. _____
4. ¡Quiero comprarme esos pantalones! _____
5. Los paréntesis amplían la información de la oración principal. _____
6. El profesor corrige las tesis de sus alumnos. _____
7. Me encantan los popurrís. _____
8. Con la computadora, puedes contar los caracteres de un texto fácilmente. _____

11. Indicar Escribe si estos sustantivos existen en plural y singular, o solamente en plural. `2.B`

> **Modelos**
>
> tesis *plural y singular*
> enseres *solo plural*

1. oasis _____
2. nupcias _____
3. gafas _____
4. prismáticos _____
5. víveres _____
6. tabúes _____
7. análisis _____
8. imágenes _____
9. jueves _____
10. tijeras _____
11. vacaciones _____
12. afueras _____

12. Plurales irregulares Identifica y escribe los 12 sustantivos de este texto que forman plurales irregulares. Recuerda que algunos tienen la misma forma en plural y en singular, otros solo poseen forma plural y otros presentan cambios en los acentos cuando pasan a plural. `2.B`

> **Nuevas pistas en caso de joven desaparecido**
>
> Después de la investigación en una mansión de las afueras de la ciudad y en sus alrededores, los investigadores formularon una nueva <u>hipótesis</u> sobre la desaparición del joven. El análisis indica que la casa estaba vacía, pero hallaron enseres tirados, unos prismáticos junto a una ventana, víveres regados en la cocina, unas tijeras y unas gafas con huellas digitales claras. En la basura encontraron varios recibos de un gimnasio que indican que el joven tenía un alto régimen de ejercicio: todos los días, de lunes a viernes. Al parecer, quienes vivían con él dejaron pistas suficientes para vincularlos a la investigación.

_____ *hipótesis* _____   _____   _____

_____   _____   _____

_____   _____   _____

_____   _____   _____

13. Relato Completa el relato de Cecilia con las opciones correctas. `2.C`

<u>Mi primer viaje en avión</u>

El viernes pasado fue la primera vez que viajé en avión. Pero fue un viaje (1) _____ (cortito / cortote), porque duró solo media hora. No puedo mentirles, siempre les tuve algo de (2) _____ (miedito / miedazo) a los aviones.

El avión era enorme. Tenía unas (3) _____ (alitas / alotas) y dos (4) _____ (turbinitas / turbinotas). Pero, por dentro, todo era distinto. En cada fila, había muchos (5) _____ (asientotes / asientitos) donde mi papá casi no podía sentarse y (6) _____ (ventanitas / ventanotas) que no me dejaban ver nada. ¡Parecía un (7) _____ (juguetito / juguetote)!

Cuando despegó, mi mamá me tomó la (8) _____ (manita / manota) y me dijo que me quedara (9) _____ (tranquilita / tranquilota). Mi hermano Daniel, que tiene solo tres años, se comportaba como un verdadero chico (10) _____ (grandote / grandecito). ¡Hasta quería ir a la cabina del piloto! Por suerte, el vuelo estuvo muy bien. Incluso pudimos ver unos (11) _____ (dibujotes / dibujitos) animados en una (12) _____ (pantallita / pantallota) que estaba enfrente de cada asiento. ¡No veo la hora de volver a volar!

14. Correo electrónico Gabriela, celosa por su hermana recién nacida, escribe un mensaje a Estela. Complétalo. `2.C`

Hola, Estela:

¿Cómo estás? Te escribo porque tengo un (1) _____ (problemón / problemita) y estoy un poco triste. Hace un mes que nació mi (2) _____ (hermanucha / hermanita), Sandra, y, al parecer, ya no le importo a nadie. Es verdad que Sandra nació un poco (3) _____ (debilita / debilota). Ahora está más (4) _____ (fuertucha / fuertecita), pero sigue siendo el centro de atención. Debe ser porque tiene unos (5) _____ (ojitos / ojazos) azules. ¡Son los ojos más grandes que he visto! También sus pequeñas (6) _____ (manitas / manotas) son tan dulces. Quiero que (7) _____ (mamaza / mamita) me preste atención de nuevo. ¿Qué puedo hacer? ¡Gracias por tu (8) _____ (ayudita / ayudota)!

Gabriela

15. Síntesis Decidir Decide si estas afirmaciones son ciertas o falsas. Si son falsas, corrígelas. `2.A–2.D`

> **Modelo**
>
> **Afueras** es el plural del sustantivo **afuera**. *Falso. Afuera no es un sustantivo. Afueras sí, pero solo se usa en plural.*

Cierto Falso

☐ ☐ 1. Es correcto decir **la serpiente hembra**. _____

☐ ☐ 2. Son despectivos **casucha**, **peliculón** y **flacucho**. _____

☐ ☐ 3. **Yerno** es el femenino de **nuera**. _____

☐ ☐ 4. En algunos países hispanohablantes, **azúcar** es masculino; en otros, es femenino.

☐ ☐ 5. Los diminutivos de **pescado**, **carro** y **pie** son **pescadito**, **carrito** y **piecito**.

☐ ☐ 6. **Enseres** solamente puede usarse en plural. _____

☐ ☐ 7. Es incorrecto usar **parienta** como femenino de **pariente**. _____

☐ ☐ 8. El aumentativo **-ito** indica afecto cuando uno se dirige a personas queridas.

☐ ☐ 9. El aumentativo de **nariz** es **narizota**. _____

☐ ☐ 10. **Perrazo** es un aumentativo. _____

16. Síntesis Identificar Elige la palabra que no pertenece al grupo. ¡Presta atención al género y al número! `2.A–2.D`

1. solterón   cincuentón   cuarentón   camión
2. viernes   veces   lunes   análisis
3. princesa   suegra   papá   emperatriz
4. almirante   representante   mariscal   abogado
5. programa   dilema   problema   arena
6. enero   jueves   rojo   flor
7. cita   playita   manchita   pastillita
8. dosis   tesis   crisis   bis
9. baldes   padres   cabezones   asistentes
10. clima   panorama   pasaje   madre

17. Síntesis Transformar **Convierte la palabra subrayada en cada línea según se indica.** `2.A–2.D`

1. vaca en sustantivo masculino plural: _____ *toros* _____
2. paciente en sustantivo femenino plural: _____
3. cara en sustantivo aumentativo singular: _____
4. asistente en sustantivo femenino singular: _____
5. dama en sustantivo masculino plural: _____
6. caballos en sustantivo femenino singular: _____
7. manteles en sustantivo despectivo singular: _____
8. papá en sustantivo femenino plural: _____
9. rubíes en sustantivo singular: _____
10. salón en sustantivo plural: _____
11. regímenes en sustantivo singular: _____
12. carácter en sustantivo plural: _____
13. jueza en sustantivo masculino plural: _____
14. profesional en sustantivo masculino plural: _____
15. canapé en sustantivo diminutivo plural: _____
16. tribu en sustantivo plural _____
17. reyes en sustantivo femenino plural: _____
18. ingeniero en sustantivo femenino plural: _____

18. Síntesis Profesiones **Escribe sobre cinco profesiones que te gustan o que admiras y explica por qué. Utiliza plurales en las oraciones.** `2.A–2.D`

> **Modelo**
>
> Admiro mucho a los médicos, porque curan a las personas y se ponen al servicio de los demás.

_____
_____
_____
_____
_____
_____
_____
_____
_____
_____
_____
_____
_____
_____
_____
_____

Practice more at **vhlcentral.com.**

1. Femenino Escribe en femenino la parte que aparece subrayada en cada oración. **3.A**

> **Modelo**
>
> Los jóvenes corteses pudieron entrar.
> _Las jóvenes corteses_

1. El electricista profesional trabajó el fin de semana. _____
2. El niño danzarín salta y salta sin parar. _____
3. El doctor alemán ahora vive en París. _____
4. Un ejecutivo importante renunció a su cargo. _____
5. He perdido mi gato negrote, mi juguete favorito. _____
6. El empleado gentil atiende a los clientes con una sonrisa. _____
7. El niño feliz jugaba en las hamacas del parque. _____
8. El fanático acosador no dejaba tranquila a la cantante. _____

2. Reescribir Reescribe los sustantivos y adjetivos según las pistas. **3.A**

> **Modelo**
>
> vendedor israelí → (femenino, plural)
> _vendedoras israelíes_

1. sabor agradable → (plural) _____
2. perro pequeñín → (femenino) _____
3. profesor conservador → (femenino) _____
4. niño albanés → (femenino) _____
5. político burgués → (femenino, plural) _____
6. salón posterior → (plural) _____
7. rostro paliducho → (plural) _____
8. joven bribón → (femenino) _____
9. plato tentador → (plural) _____
10. coche veloz → (plural) _____
11. publicación periódica → (plural) _____
12. aborigen guaraní → (plural) _____
13. herramienta útil → (plural) _____
14. actor inglés → (femenino) _____
15. hermano mayor → (femenino, plural) _____
16. café francés → (plural) _____

3. **Conversación** Completa la conversación con los adjetivos en el género y número adecuados. `3.B`

JULIETA ¿Tienes una idea (1) _____*clara*_____ (claro) de qué vestirás para la graduación?

MARTINA Sí, tengo una falda y unos zapatos (2) _____ (rojo) que me gustaría combinar con una blusa y una cartera (3) _____ (anaranjado).

JULIETA ¿No te parece que con algo (4) _____ (blanco) quedaría mejor? ¿O unos (5) _____ (bonito) zapatos y falda de color amarillo?

MARTINA No sé, siempre me gustan las vestimentas (6) _____ (colorido).

JULIETA Mira, yo podría prestarte un vestido con flores (7) _____ (amarillo) claro y tirantes (8) _____ (rojo).

MARTINA ¡Perfecto! Y podría entonces usar mis zapatos y cartera (9) _____ (verde).

JULIETA ¿Puedo verlos?

MARTINA Sí, aquí están. Y, ¿cómo luzco?

JULIETA ¡Como un (10) _____ (impactante) arco iris!

4. **Poema** Francisco escribió un poema para Andrea. Complétalo con los adjetivos indicados y asegúrate de que el género y el número sean los adecuados. `3.B`

Tienes unos (1) _____*hermosos*_____ (hermoso) y (2) _____ (grande) ojos,

y una mirada y sonrisa (3) _____ (bondadoso).

Unas cejas y cabellos (4) _____ (pelirrojo)...

Y una voz tan (5) _____ (fabuloso).

Y yo, un ser (6) _____ (afortunado), como pocos,

miro esas pupilas y pestañas (7) _____ (esplendoroso),

y, con mi corazón (8) _____ (jubiloso)

deseo que un buen día seas mi esposa.

5. **Escribir** En cada oración decide si el adjetivo entre paréntesis debe ir antes o después del sustantivo. `3.C`

> **Modelo**
>
> El _*fantástico*_ Chaplin _____
> hacía reír a grandes y chicos. (fantástico)

1. Todos dicen que es lindo, pero, para mí, es un _____ perro _____. (feíto)

2. Compré un _____ libro _____ en una feria de artículos usados. (agotado)

3. La _____ revista _____ *Saludables siempre* se publica cada dos meses. (médica)

4. La _____ película _____ del famoso director no tuvo el éxito esperado. (última)

5. Disculpe, señora, ya no tenemos más ese juguete. Se vendió como _____ pan _____. (caliente)

6. La _____ organización _____ lucha por los derechos de los trabajadores. (sindical)

7. La _____ situación _____ de ese país empeora día a día. (social)

8. Juana es una _____ amiga _____. Siempre me ayuda cuando lo necesito. (buena)

9. ¡Acabo de ganarme la lotería! Soy un _____ hombre _____. (rico)

10. El _____ soldado _____ sacó la mejor puntuación. (alto)

6. Adjetivos Escribe el adjetivo en la posición apropiada, ya sea antes o después del sustantivo. `3.C`

> **Modelo**
> _____ Editor _____: (estimado)
> *Estimado* Editor _____:

En la provincia oriental de Recodo, conseguir un (1) _____ trabajo _____ (digno) es duro. La (2) _____ oficina _____ (laboral) no ofrece una (3) _____ atención _____ (amable). Lo que es peor, los (4) _____ empleados _____ (maleducados) se ríen de la gente en su (5) _____ cara _____ (propia). La (6) _____ realidad _____ (cruda) es que no hay puestos de trabajo disponibles. Sin embargo, todos están en (7) _____ derecho _____ (pleno) de ser tratados cordialmente. Le pido que comunique esta situación a las (8) _____ autoridades _____ (nacionales)

Saludos,

Olivia P.

7. Ordenar Modifica el orden de los elementos para armar una oración que tenga sentido. `3.C`

1. En realidad, | concurso | tienen posibilidades | ambos | de ganar | participantes | famoso | el
   En realidad, ... _____

2. Pedí | pañuelo | un | expresamente | azul | que me enviaran
   Pedí... _____

3. muchas | romance | que buscan | personas | un | Hay | veraniego
   Hay... _____

4. nocturna | activa | deportistas | tienen | una | vida | Pocos
   Pocos... _____

5. mediterránea | calor | en esta | Hace | playa | mucho
   Hace... _____

6. principal | edificio | en la | El | concurrida | calle Posadas | se encuentra
   El... _____

8. Completar Completa las oraciones con el adjetivo y el sustantivo en el orden correcto. Cada palabra puede usarse una sola vez. `3.C`

menor	buen	ciertas	alta	noticias	lenguas	tensión	gusto
gran	malas	~~único~~	santo	padre	~~hijo~~	amigo	hermana

1. Todos mis amigos tienen hermanos, en cambio yo soy _____*hijo*_____ _____*único*_____.
2. ¡Qué bien decorada que está la casa! Ella tiene _____ _____.
3. ¡Cuidado con esos cables! ¡Son de _____ _____!
4. A menudo al Papa se lo denomina _____ _____.
5. Hablen bien o mal, no hago caso a lo que dicen las _____ _____.
6. Un amigo que está a tu lado en momentos difíciles es un _____ _____.
7. En este cajón, mi linda _____ _____ guarda sus juguetes.
8. Pienso que lo que dijeron en televisión no son _____ _____.

9. Resumen Lee el resumen de un capítulo de la novela *Caballero a caballo* y complétalo. Asegúrate de que el género y el número de los adjetivos sean los adecuados. **3.D**

En el (1) _____ (primero) capítulo de esta (2) _____ (grande) novela, conocemos al (3) _____ (bueno) caballero José de Salamanca, quien emprende un largo viaje en busca de su futura esposa. En la (4) _____ (tercero) jornada, se encuentra con la imagen de (5) _____ (Santo) Diego, quien le aconseja que no siga con su búsqueda, porque podría ser peligroso para su corazón. José de Salamanca no hace caso al supuesto (6) _____ (malo) augurio y sigue adelante. En la (7) _____ (cuarto) jornada de su travesía, recibe una (8) _____ (malo) noticia. Sus (9) _____ (grande) esperanzas se destrozan cuando se entera de que su princesa ya es la esposa del conde de Aranjuez.

10. Elegir Escoge la opción correcta para completar cada oración. **3.E**

1. Juan es _____ de los tres hermanos.
   a. el mayor   b. la menor   c. mayor
2. Carlos es _____ en matemáticas que Marta.
   a. más bueno   b. mejor   c. mayor
3. El libro es _____ de lo que pensaba.
   a. más bueno   b. mejor   c. menor
4. El accidente fue _____ de lo que imaginábamos.
   a. más malo   b. peor   c. el peor
5. Mi hermana es _____ que mi hermano. Ella nunca miente y siempre me ayuda.
   a. mejor   b. la más buena   c. más buena

11. Superlativos ¡Qué exagerada es Eloísa! Completa las oraciones con el superlativo usando el sufijo -*ísimo/a*. **3.E**

Modelo

Mi primer novio era romántico, en cambio mi novio actual es *romantiquísimo*.

1. Paula dice que su perro es muy flaco, pero el mío es _____.
2. Concepción me contó que su gato es muy tonto, pero el mío es _____.
3. Catalina siempre se queja de que su mochila es muy pesada, pero la mía es _____.
4. Mi hermana Sara dice que ella es muy ordenada, pero yo soy _____.
5. Clara cree que su profesora es muy simpática, pero la mía es _____.
6. A Joan la película le pareció muy triste, pero a mí me pareció _____.
7. Eva dice que tiene muchos amigos, pero yo tengo _____.
8. Mi mamá dice que soy muy exagerada, ¡pero yo digo que soy _____!
9. El café de hoy está algo amargo, pero el de anteayer estaba _____.
10. El servicio de buses no es nada veloz, en cambio el del metro es _____.
11. Mi gato en las mañanas casi no come y por la noche come muy poco. En general come _____.
12. El examen de portugués estuvo horrible, pero el de japonés sí estuvo _____.

12. Discusión Dos hermanas discuten sobre sus habitaciones. Completa el diálogo usando comparativos y superlativos. `3.E`

> **Modelo**
>
> **CONSTANZA** El baño de mi cuarto es _el más amplio_ (+ / amplio) de toda la casa.

MARIEL Pero mi ventana es (1) _____ (+ / grande) que la tuya.

CONSTANZA Te equivocas; mi ventana es (2) _____ (+ / grande) de la casa.

MARIEL Mi habitación es (3) _____ (+ / luminosa) que la tuya.

CONSTANZA ¡De ninguna manera! La mía es (4) _____ (+ / luminosa) del primer piso.

MARIEL Y mi cama es (5) _____ (+ / buena) que la tuya.

CONSTANZA ¿En qué mundo vives? Mi cama (6) _____ (+ / buena) de todas.

MARIEL Pero, ¿has visto qué tranquila es mi habitación? Es (7) _____ (– / ruidosa) que la tuya.

CONSTANZA Imposible. La mía es (8) _____ (– / ruidosa) de la casa.

MARIEL Claro, tú crees que siempre tienes la razón, porque eres la hermana (9) _____ (+ / vieja).

CONSTANZA ¿Ves? Me dices eso porque te aprovechas de ser (10) _____ (+ / joven) de la familia.

MARIEL Uy, ¡qué aburrida eres, Constanza!

CONSTANZA No, ¡tú eres (11) _____ (+ / aburrida) del mundo!

13. Síntesis Reunir Empareja un ejemplo con una sola afirmación, sin repetir tus respuestas. `3.A–3.E`

a. un problema técnico	g. el niño debilucho
b. una gran mujer	h. una forma mejor
c. las niñas y mujeres contentas	i. un hombre narigón
d. la primera vez	j. el caso más importante
e. el defensor ecologista	k. las casas y jardines caros
f. el pobre hombre	l. un diario político-económico

____ 1. Algunos adjetivos no varían con el género.

____ 2. Algunos adjetivos se apocopan (abrevian) cuando van delante de un sustantivo singular.

____ 3. Algunos adjetivos no se apocopan (abrevian) cuando van delante de un sustantivo femenino.

____ 4. Algunos adjetivos cambian de significado según estén delante o detrás de un sustantivo.

____ 5. Algunos adjetivos solo tienen una posición posible.

____ 6. Algunos adjetivos tienen comparativos irregulares.

____ 7. La mayoría de los adjetivos tienen superlativos regulares.

____ 8. Cuando hay varios sustantivos de distinto género antes de un adjetivo, este último toma la forma masculina en plural.

____ 9. Cuando hay varios sustantivos de igual género, el adjetivo toma el mismo género en plural.

____ 10. Algunos sustantivos forman adjetivos al agregar un sufijo aumentativo.

____ 11. Los adjetivos con sufijos expresivos se colocan después del sustantivo.

____ 12. Adjetivo compuesto que modifica un sustantivo y solo tiene una posición posible.

14. Síntesis Seleccionar Elige la opción que complete la afirmación. `3.A–3.E`

1. Una palabra que termina en **-és** y que no cambia de forma en femenino es _____.
   a. finlandés
   b. cortés

2. Otras formas de decir los adjetivos de color _____ son **anaranjado/a(s)** y **rosado/a(s)**.
   a. naranja y rosa
   b. lila y café

3. Los adjetivos que terminan en **í, -ú, -z, -l, -r, -s** no cambian de _____.
   a. número
   b. género

4. En español un adjetivo se puede escribir _____ un sustantivo para enfatizar o intensificar.
   a. antes de
   b. después de

5. Cuando varios adjetivos que describen un sustantivo son de diferente género o son masculinos, entonces los plurales toman la forma _____.
   a. femenina
   b. masculina

6. Algunos determinantes, como **ambo/a(s), mucho/a(s), otro/a(s)**, van _____ sustantivo.
   a. antes del
   b. después del

7. Para formar comparativos se agregan las palabras _____ antes del adjetivo.
   a. **más** o **menos**
   b. **súper** e **híper**

8. Algunos adjetivos comparativos como **mejor** o **exterior** no cambian en el _____.
   a. número
   b. género

9. En **sustancias placebo** o **públicos objetivo**, los segundos sustantivos que modifican los primeros funcionan como adjetivos y no varían en _____ ni en número.
   a. género
   b. extensión

10. Adjetivos como **bueno** y **primero** pierden _____ antes de un sustantivo masculino singular.
    a. la última consonante
    b. la última vocal

11. Adjetivos como **bueno/a(s), malo/a(s), joven/jóvenes** y **viejo/a(s)** tienen comparativos y superlativos tanto regulares como _____.
    a. irregulares
    b. positivos

12. Los adjetivos que terminan en **-e** o **-ista** no cambian de _____.
    a. número
    b. género

13. Es común usar adjetivos de colores a partir de nombres de _____.
    a. plantas o minerales
    b. animales o cosas

14. Terminaciones como **-ísimo/a** o **-bilísimo/a** indican que los adjetivos son _____ absolutos.
    a. superlativos
    b. comparativos

15. Síntesis Comparar Describe a cinco de tus amigos teniendo presente agregar por lo menos una oración con aumentativo o diminutivo, una con una comparación y una con un superlativo absoluto. `3.A–3.E`

> **Modelo**
>
> Paola es inteligentísima...

_____

_____

_____

_____

_____

_____

Practice more at **vhlcentral.com**.

1. **Los determinantes** Lee este artículo de un periódico escolar. Marca los determinantes que aparecen en él, menos los que se usan como pronombres. `4.A–4.B`

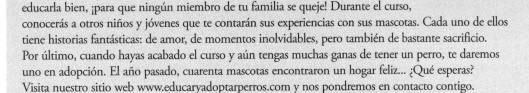

Amo educado, perro educado

¿Te gustan las mascotas? ¿Siempre quisiste tener una, pero tu mamá piensa que es demasiado trabajo? ¡Te tenemos una solución!

Somos un equipo de veterinarios que trabaja en un albergue con muchos perros abandonados. Algunos perros son cachorros, pero otros son más grandecitos. Estos animalitos buscan amor: ¡sabemos que tú puedes dárselo!

Sabemos que cuidar de un perro no es fácil y muchas madres no quieren encargarse de él. Por eso, te ofrecemos un curso introductorio al cuidado de animales: aprenderás cómo satisfacer todas las necesidades de tu mascota y cómo educarla bien, ¡para que ningún miembro de tu familia se queje! Durante el curso, conocerás a otros niños y jóvenes que te contarán sus experiencias con sus mascotas. Cada uno de ellos tiene historias fantásticas: de amor, de momentos inolvidables, pero también de bastante sacrificio.

Por último, cuando hayas acabado el curso y aún tengas muchas ganas de tener un perro, te daremos uno en adopción. El año pasado, cuarenta mascotas encontraron un hogar feliz... ¿Qué esperas? Visita nuestro sitio web www.educaryadoptarperros.com y nos pondremos en contacto contigo.

2. **Decidir** Para cada ejemplo, decide si la palabra subrayada funciona como *determinante, pronombre* o *adverbio*. `4.A–4.B`

Ejemplo	Determinante	Pronombre	Adverbio
1. Las grandes capitales tienen <u>muchos</u> problemas de contaminación.			
2. Comí <u>demasiado</u> esta noche. Mañana debería comer cosas más livianas.			
3. <u>Esta</u> es la última vez que limpio la cocina después de que tú cocinas.			
4. Ya tienes <u>bastantes</u> discusiones con tu jefe... ¡haz las paces de una vez!			
5. ¡Escuchen <u>todos</u>!, cuando esta casa sea mía, ¡haré fiestas todas las noches!			
6. ¡<u>Alguien</u> me quiere! Tengo una llamada perdida en mi teléfono celular.			
7. ¿Siempre de compras? Tienes que ahorrar. ¡No compres <u>más</u>!			
8. Con <u>tanto</u> humo de cigarrillo, no puedo respirar bien.			
9. Algunos compañeros son amables; <u>otros</u>, no.			
10. ¡<u>Esta</u> oportunidad de hacerme famoso es única!			
11. ¿Conoces el trabalenguas "<u>tres</u> tristes tigres"?			
12. "<u>Menos</u> televisión y más estudio", me dijo la maestra.			
13. <u>Aquella</u> es mi novia. ¿Acaso no es hermosa?			
14. No hables <u>tanto</u>: ¡estamos en la biblioteca!			
15. <u>Pocas</u> veces me duermo después de las doce de la noche.			
16. ¡Qué hermosa noche! ¡<u>Tantas</u> estrellas!			

3. Síntesis Escoger Elige la opción correcta para completar cada oración. `4.A–4.B`

1. En periódicos, revistas y publicidad, cuando el _____ de una oración es un sustantivo plural, puede omitirse el determinante.
   a. predicado   b. sujeto   c. pronombre   d. complemento indirecto

2. Hay cuatro grupos de determinantes: artículos, cuantificadores, _____ y posesivos.
   a. verbos   b. preposiciones   c. sustantivos   d. demostrativos

3. Los pronombres indefinidos **algo**, _____, **nada** y **nadie** nunca funcionan como determinantes.
   a. todo   b. cada   c. alguien   d. demás

4. Cuando los determinantes se encuentran solos, sin un sustantivo, funcionan como _____.
   a. verbos   b. pronombres   c. adjetivos   d. preposiciones

5. Los pronombres negativos indefinidos y los determinantes negativos requieren doble _____ si van después de un verbo.
   a. preposición   b. sustantivos   c. complemento   d. negación

6. Entre todos los determinantes, solamente _____ se pone antes de un artículo definido.
   a. este/a   b. otro/a(s)   c. todo/a(s)   d. varios/as

7. **Mucho** nunca puede ponerse antes de adjetivos o adverbios. En esos casos se pone _____.
   a. tanto/a(s)   b. muy   c. poco/a(s)   d. todo/a(s)

8. Dos o tres determinantes pueden usarse juntos, pero cuando se unen tres, el tercero casi siempre es un _____.
   a. número   b. adverbio   c. pronombre   d. sustantivo

: Practice more at **vhlcentral.com.**

Articles   Chapter 5

1. Seleccionar Elige el artículo apropiado, ya sea definido o indefinido, para cada uno de los sustantivos o adjetivos. `5.A`

Modelo

(la, las) _las_ españolas

1. (el, los) _____ teléfonos
2. (la, las) _____ gente
3. (una, unas) _____ cometas
4. (el, los) _____ orden
5. (lo, los) _____ bueno

6. (un, unos) _____ amigos
7. (la, las) _____ leona
8. (una, unas) _____ intelectuales
9. (un, unos) _____ canales
10. (el, la) _____ hacha

2. Elegir Elige la opción correcta en esta conversación. `5.B`

PABLO ¿Qué podríamos regalarles a tus padres para su aniversario de casados?

MARÍA No sé, no tengo (1) _____ (la/una/otra) idea clara.

PABLO Quizás podríamos comprarles (2) _____ (una/unos/otro) juego de platos; los que les regalamos hace (3) _____ (un/otro/unos) años se rompieron durante la mudanza. ¿Te acuerdas?

MARÍA Sí, es verdad. Pero, ¿cuánto dinero tenemos?

PABLO Creo que (4) _____ (un/otros/unos) ciento cincuenta dólares.

MARÍA Bien, el juego de platos me parece (5) _____ (un/otra/una) buena idea.

3. Carta Escribe en los espacios de esta carta el artículo correspondiente. Si no es necesario, escribe X. `5.B–5.C`

Estimado (1) __X__ doctor Pérez:

Quiero hacerle (2) _____ consulta. Estoy de vacaciones con mi hijo Joaquín en (3) _____ Salvador desde hace (4) _____ días. Desde ayer, al niño le duele (5) _____ cabeza y tiene fiebre. ¿Puede ser por (6) _____ vacuna que le dio antes del viaje? ¿O tal vez por (7) _____ calurosa que es esta ciudad?

Ayer fuimos a (8) _____ hospital en San Salvador y (9) _____ médico me dijo que no es nada grave. Pero yo quería preguntarle a usted, porque es su pediatra. No hay consejos como (10) _____ suyos.

Muchas gracias por su ayuda,

Paula Sánchez

4. Completar Completa la conversación con el artículo definido adecuado. `5.C`

Modelo

¿Tienes que ir a __la__ escuela el fin de semana?

1. ¡Cuántas veces te dije que no uses mi ropa. ¡Usa _____ tuya!
2. Hoy a _____ cuatro de la tarde podríamos ir al cine, ¿no?
3. En _____ Estados Unidos, la gente no duerme la siesta; pero en _____ Salvador, sí.
4. Me encantan las manzanas, sobre todo _____ verdes.
5. Mis vecinos, _____ Rodríguez, van de vacaciones todos los años a México.
6. Dile a _____ señora Pérez que no podremos ir a la cena _____ jueves.

5. Síntesis Unir Escribe en el espacio de la descripción, la letra del ejemplo correspondiente de la derecha. `5.A–5.C`

Descripción	Ejemplo
_____ 1. artículo en singular de una palabra que comienza por **a-** acentuada	a. En la tienda hay muchos modelos de televisores. Me voy a comprar uno rojo.
_____ 2. oración con una contracción de un artículo	b. Uno tiene pocas chances de ganar la lotería.
_____ 3. artículo indefinido utilizado como sujeto	c. Un hacha se entregará a cada leñador.
_____ 4. reemplazo de un posesivo antes de un sustantivo cuando la posesión es obvia	d. ¿Me prestas unos pesos para pagar el taxi?
_____ 5. determinantes que aparecen junto con artículos	e. ¡Acuérdate del mensaje!
_____ 6. artículo usado con un adjetivo en una oración en que se reconoce un sustantivo a partir del contexto	f. ¡Pedí un platillo! Ni te lo imaginas.
_____ 7. omisión del artículo definido en referencias de tiempo	g. El águila reposa en su nido.
_____ 8. artículo en singular antes de sustantivo que comienza por **ha-** acentuada	h. Nunca te rasques los ojos. Puedes lastimarte.
_____ 9. uso de un artículo indefinido para expresar un número aproximado	i. Ayer fue martes, ¿cierto?
_____ 10. uso enfático de artículos en exclamaciones	j. Todos los días cerramos todas las ventanas antes de salir.

6. Síntesis Anuncio Completa el anuncio con las palabras de la lista. `5.A–5.C`

del   el   la   las   los   otra   un   ~~un~~

Nuevo club escolar de artes marciales

Somos (1) _un_ grupo de alumnos (2) _____ noveno año de la escuela Campos Verdes y queremos organizar un club de aficionados a (3) _____ artes marciales.

¿Practicas taekwondo, karate o alguna (4) _____ arte marcial? ¿Quizás (5) _____ arte marcial que no conocemos?

Estamos en (6) _____ gimnasio de (7) _____ escuela todos (8) _____ jueves por la tarde. ¡Ven, que queremos conocerte!

7. Síntesis Clases Describe las clases que tengas en la semana: menciona cuál es el nombre de los profesores, de dónde provienen, etc. Utiliza artículos definidos e indefinidos. `5.A–5.C`

Modelo

Los miércoles tengo las clases de biología, matemáticas y español. La profesora de español es Catalina Mendoza, una argentina muy exigente…

_____
_____
_____
_____
_____
_____
_____
_____
_____
_____

Practice more at **vhlcentral.com.**

Quantifiers: Numbers   Chapter 6

1. Números Escribe estos números en letras. `6.A–6.B`

Modelo

19 674 _diecinueve mil seiscientos setenta y cuatro_

1. 28 _____
2. 132 _____
3. 1200 _____
4. 19 _____
5. 44 _____

6. 102 _____
7. 333 _____
8. 1 000 000 _____
9. 1981 _____
10. 57 _____

2. Reescribir Reescribe las oraciones usando números. `6.A–6.B`

> **Modelo**
> El monte Everest mide ocho mil ochocientos cincuenta metros de altura.
> *El monte Everest mide 8850 metros de altura.*

1. Camila nació el tres de agosto de mil novecientos ochenta y tres.

   _____

2. Tardaron ciento tres años en construir este castillo.

   _____

3. Para el lunes próximo, tengo que leer doscientas veintiuna páginas.

   _____

4. El empresario tiene un millón cuatrocientos mil dólares.

   _____

5. Necesitamos vender veintinueve mil unidades este mes.

   _____

6. El gobierno dio un subsidio de quinientos ocho dólares a cada vecino por la inundación.

   _____

7. Debo devolverte setecientos noventa y un pesos antes del treinta de enero.

   _____

8. Debido a la tormenta, se cayeron mil treinta y tres árboles.

   _____

3. Numerales colectivos Reescribe las oraciones usando las expresiones numéricas colectivas de la lista. `6.C`

| centenar | decena | docena | ~~millar~~ | sesentena | setentena | treintena | veintena |

> **Modelo**
> ¡Hay más de <u>mil</u> lugares que quiero visitar!
> *¡Hay más de un millar de lugares que quiero visitar!*

1. Hoy la tienda vendió <u>veinte</u> pares de zapatos en una tarde.

   _____

2. En México, hay más de <u>treinta</u> periódicos distintos.

   _____

3. Cuando ahorre más dinero, me compraré <u>cien</u> lápices de colores.

   _____

4. Si compro <u>diez</u> camisetas, cada una cuesta $8,59.

   _____

5. Sí, me llevaré <u>doce</u> rosas.

   _____

6. Asistieron al congreso <u>sesenta</u> especialistas.

   _____

4. En el mercado Completa la conversación entre Cintia y su madre con las palabras de la lista. `6.C`

> con (3)   más   es igual a   un (2)   por ciento   y

CINTIA ¿Cuánto costó toda la compra?

MADRE En total, costó diez dólares (1) _____*con*_____ cincuenta y cinco centavos.

CINTIA Ah, pensé que era más dinero. ¿Estás segura?

MADRE Sí, las verduras costaron ocho dólares; y la carne, cuatro (2) _____ cincuenta (3) _____ cinco centavos.

CINTIA Pero... ocho (4) _____ cuatro (5) _____ cincuenta y cinco... (6) _____ doce (7) _____ cincuenta y cinco.

MADRE ¡Qué brillante es mi hija! Me olvidé del descuento que hizo el verdulero.

CINTIA ¿Quizás (8) _____ veinticinco (9) _____ de descuento?

MADRE Increíble. ¡Ojalá tuviera (10) _____ diez por ciento de tu inteligencia!

5. Oraciones Forma oraciones con elementos de las tres columnas. `6.D`

1. No puede ser: es la	centenario	hombre que se casó en la familia.
2. No sé qué regalarles a mis padres para su	quinta	vez que lavo los platos.
3. Daniel fue el	milenaria	pieza se encuentra en el Museo Nacional.
4. El 30 de mayo es el	primer	de la fundación de mi pueblo.
5. Luis	trigésimo	era llamado "El Rey Sol".
6. En la actualidad, la	catorce	aniversario de casados.

_____

_____

_____

_____

_____

_____

6. Elegir Elige la opción correcta para completar las oraciones. `6.D`

1. El _____ (milenario/millonario) Juan Rodríguez pasa sus vacaciones en Mallorca.

2. La _____ (tercera/tercer) oportunidad es la última.

3. El papa Juan Pablo _____ (dos/segundo) murió en 2005.

4. 1/100 es un _____ (centésimo/milésimo).

5. En su _____ (trigésimo/treintavo) aniversario, la empresa realizará una gran fiesta.

6. En total, corrí diez vueltas, pero en la _____ (quinta/quincuagésima), paré a descansar un rato.

7. Enrique _____ (ocho/octavo) pertenecía a la casa Tudor.

8. En el _____ (décimo primero/décimo primer) piso, vive mi abuela Carolina.

7. Fracciones Escribe las fracciones en las dos formas posibles. **6.E**

Modelo

1/3 *un tercio* *una tercera parte*

1. 1/2 _____ _____
2. 1/13 _____ _____
3. 1/4 _____ _____
4. 4/5 _____ _____
5. 1/8 _____ _____
6. 2/7 _____ _____

8. Receta Lee la receta y reemplaza las fracciones y múltiplos en negrita por palabras. **6.E**

Cocina rápida: Recetas "en (1) *una millonésima* (**1/1 000 000**) de segundo y el (2) *cuádruple* (**4 veces**) de económicas en comparación con las del supermercado"

Hoy: Galletitas navideñas

Mezcle (3) _____ (**1/3**) de taza de azúcar con 250 gramos de harina, es decir, (4) _____ (**1/4**) de kilo de harina. Derrita al fuego (5) _____ (**1/5**) de una barra de mantequilla y agréguela a la primera mezcla. Estire la masa sobre una superficie plana y amásela. Colóquela en la nevera durante (6) _____ (**3/4**) de hora. Retire la masa y córtela en ocho partes iguales. Tome cada (7) _____ (**1/8**) y estire con un rodillo de amasar. Decore cada porción al gusto y llévelos al horno durante (8) _____ (**1/2**) hora. Finalmente retire del horno y deje enfriar durante el (9) _____ (**2 veces**) del tiempo de horneado, o sea, una hora aproximadamente. Como resultado tendrá unas galletitas que crecen el (10) _____ (**3 veces**) de la altura de la masa. Acompañe con leche o con su bebida preferida.

9. ¿Qué hora es? Escribe la hora de tantas maneras como puedas. **6.F**

1. *Son las ocho y cuarto.*
   Son las ocho y quince.
   _____
   _____

4. _____
   _____
   _____
   _____

2. _____
   _____
   _____

5. _____
   _____
   _____

3. _____
   _____
   _____

6. _____
   _____
   _____

10. **Contestar** Hoy es lunes y Marcos mira el calendario de esta semana. Escribe respuestas completas de acuerdo con el calendario. Debes escribir todos los números en letras. **6.F–6.G**

Lunes 1/10	Martes 2/10	Miércoles 3/10	Jueves 4/10	Viernes 5/10
8:40 a. m. Escuela	8.40 a. m. Escuela	8:40 a. m. Escuela	8:40 a. m. Escuela	8:40 a. m. Escuela
4:30 p. m. Natación	6:15 p. m. Regalo para la abuela	11:30 a. m. Examen de español		7:30 p. m. Cumpleaños de la abuela
		2:30 p. m. Dentista		

Modelo

¿En qué fecha y a qué hora es el examen de español?
El examen de español es el tres de octubre a las once y media de la mañana.

1. ¿Qué fecha es hoy?

2. ¿Qué sucede el tres de octubre?

3. ¿Qué debe hacer Marcos todos los días?

4. ¿A qué hora debe comprar el regalo para la abuela?

5. ¿A qué hora va a la escuela?

6. ¿Qué debe hacer el miércoles a las dos y media de la tarde?

7. ¿En qué fecha y a qué hora es la fiesta de cumpleaños de la abuela?

8. ¿Qué debe hacer Marcos en la tarde del lunes?

_____

_____

_____

_____

_____

_____

_____

_____

11. **Quinceañera** Completa la historia de Martina con las palabras de la lista. **6.H**

tenga   cumple   quinceañera   setentón   sesentona
~~cumplí~~   ser   sexagenaria   veinteañera

Un año más

Ayer (1) _____*cumplí*_____ quince años. La semana que viene, como toda (2) _____, celebro mi cumpleaños con una gran fiesta. Invité a cincuenta personas, entre familiares y amigos. El mismo día de la fiesta, mi abuela (3) _____ sesenta años. En broma, le digo que es una (4) _____, pero ella me dice que es una (5) _____ en perfecto estado físico. Ella me contó que, cuando ella era una (6) _____, había muchos jóvenes que estaban enamorados de ella. Pero ahora, solo tiene un vecino (7) _____ que la invita todos los domingos a bailar tango. ¡Qué graciosa que es mi abuela! Espero ser igual de divertida cuando (8) _____ su edad.

12. El tiempo Lee el pronóstico del tiempo y escribe las preguntas para las respuestas dadas. `6.I`

Hoy	Mañana	Pasado mañana
Temperatura: 10 °C	Temperatura: −1 °C/4 °C	Temperatura: −3 °C/8 °C

> **Modelo**
>
> *¿Cuál será la diferencia entre las temperaturas mínima y máxima mañana?*
> Mañana la diferencia entre las temperaturas máxima y mínima será de 5 °C.

1. ¿_____?
   Hoy hace 10 °C.

2. ¿_____?
   Mañana será de −1 °C.

3. ¿_____?
   Mañana será de 4 °C.

4. ¿_____?
   Serán de −3 °C y 8 °C.

5. ¿_____?
   No, aquí medimos la temperatura en grados centígrados.

13. Síntesis Seleccionar Elige la palabra que no pertenece al grupo. `6.B–6.J`

1. decenas   docenas   décadas   veintenas

2. tercio   cuarto   quinto   media

3. trigésimo   sexagésimo   décimo   veintiséis

4. máxima   mínima   promedio   próxima

5. cumplir   tener   celebrar   ser

6. sesentón   octogenario   veinteañero   quinceañero

7. décadas   siglos   milenios   millones

8. y veinte   y quince   y medio   y treinta

14. Síntesis Elegir Elige la opción correcta en cada oración. `6.B–6.J`

1. En la _____ de Hierro, comenzaron a fabricarse armas y herramientas de hierro.
   a. Época   b. Edad

2. Una _____ de huevos son diez huevos.
   a. decena   b. docena

3. Había _____ de personas en el festival.
   a. trescientos   b. cientos

4. _____ una y cuarto, nos encontramos en la estación.
   a. A las   b. A la

5. Debes llegar a las dos _____ diez, porque a las dos en punto sale el tren.
   a. menos   b. y

6. En América Latina, se dice "_____ de enero".
   a. primero   b. uno

7. Hoy estamos a cero _____.
   a. grados   b. grado

8. Un plan quinquenal dura _____ años.
   a. cinco   b. quince

15. Síntesis Clasificar Clasifica las palabras de la lista en la categoría apropiada. `6.B–6.J`

billón	cuarentena	~~decena~~	doceava parte	millar	trescientos	un quinto
ciento uno	~~cinco octavos~~	décimo cuarto	mil uno	quinto	trigésimo	la mitad

Colectivos	Cardinales	Ordinales	Fraccionarios
decena			*cinco octavos*

16. Síntesis Definiciones Escribe la palabra que corresponde a cada definición. `6.B–6.J`

> **Modelo**
>
> que se refiere a trescientos años de existencia o fundación *tricentenario*

1. período de mil años _____

2. la mitad de algo _____

3. que ocupa el lugar número diez en una serie ordenada de elementos _____

4. persona entre veinte y veintinueve años _____

5. una parte de las trece iguales en que se divide un todo _____

6. llegar a tener la edad o un número entero de años o meses _____

7. que ocupa el lugar número cien en una serie ordenada de elementos _____

8. que ha cumplido ochenta años y aún no ha llegado a los noventa _____

17. Síntesis Llamada Convierte los números en negrita en letras o si se encuentran en letras, pásalos a expresiones en números. Ten presentes las indicaciones entre paréntesis. `6.A–6.J`

SOFÍA Aló, ¿es la línea de emergencias, (1) *novecientos once* (**911**)?

EMERGENCIAS Sí. Por favor, díganos en qué podemos ayudarle.

SOFÍA Estaba mirando por la ventana, cuando en (2) _____ (**1/1000, fracción**) de segundo, un autobús se chocó contra un árbol.

EMERGENCIAS ¿Cuál es su dirección?

SOFÍA Avenida (3) _____ (**ciento treinta y cuatro**), número (4) _____ (**trescientos cincuenta y seis**).

EMERGENCIAS ¿Ve usted personas lesionadas?

SOFÍA Sí. Varias personas salen del autobús adoloridas. Veo una (5) _____ (**12, numeral colectivo**) por fuera y alrededor de una (6) _____ (**20, numeral colectivo**) todavía adentro.

EMERGENCIAS ¿Los lesionados son niños o adultos?

SOFÍA Parece que todos son adultos, entre (7) _____ (**25**) y (8) _____ (**60**) años.

EMERGENCIAS ¿Aproximadamente a qué horas sucedió?

SOFÍA Más o menos, (9) _____ (**9:42**) de la mañana.

EMERGENCIAS Está bien. En (10) _____ (**5**) minutos los bomberos y varias ambulancias deben llegar al lugar.

18. Síntesis Vivo en... Investiga datos actuales de tu estado, provincia o territorio: población, área, temperaturas promedio, etc. Escribe en letras los números cardinales y ordinales según requieras. `6.A–6.J`

> **Modelo**
>
> Vivo en el estado de Texas. La población total era de veintiséis millones novecientos cincuenta y seis mil novecientos cincuenta y ocho en dos mil catorce...

_____
_____
_____
_____

Practice more at **vhlcentral.com**.

1. **Completar** Completa las oraciones con las palabras de la lista. Atención: puedes usar una palabra más de una vez y hay algunas palabras que sobran. `7.A–7.B`

> algún   algunos   ningunas
> ~~alguna~~   nada   ninguna
> alguno   ningún   ninguno

Modelo

> ¿*Alguna* vez vendrás a visitarme?

1. No tienes _____ posibilidad de ganar la lotería. ¡Mejor ponte a trabajar!
2. _____ de los hombres de esta oficina está casado. Todos son solteros.
3. ¿Conoces _____ lugar divertido para ir de vacaciones?
4. No tengo _____ gafas de ese color. Mañana me compraré unas.
5. ¿_____ de ustedes podrá ir a la feria medieval? ¡Los demás están ocupadísimos!
6. No hay _____ problema, podemos posponer la cita para la semana próxima.

2. **Preguntas** Escribe las preguntas a estas respuestas. Asegúrate de incluir cuantificadores indefinidos en ellas. `7.A– 7.B`

Modelo

> ¿*Hay algún inconveniente con las maletas, señor*?
> No, no hay ningún inconveniente con las maletas.

1. ¿_____?
   No, ninguna de mis amigas vive en Perú.
2. ¿_____?
   Sí, hay un parque de diversiones cerca.
3. ¿_____?
   No, ningún compañero reprobó el examen.
4. ¿_____?
   No, ninguno de nosotros se comerá esta comida.
5. ¿_____?
   Sí, me comeré algunas frutas antes de dormir.
6. ¿_____?
   Sí, encontraré alguna oficina abierta en este barrio.

3. Reordenar Reordena las oraciones de forma correcta. 7.A–7.B

> **Modelo**
>
> conmigo / amigo / para / la película / No encontré / ver / ningún
> *No encontré ningún amigo para ver la película conmigo.*

1. para mí / No habrá / alguno / regalo / en este cumpleaños

   _____

2. de los / en el sur de Brasil / algunos / campos / Iré a

   _____

3. No, / come / de ellos / carne / ninguno

   _____

4. chico / nos guste / hay / ningún / que / No

   _____

5. Veré / que viven / en Colombia / a / parientes / algunos

   _____

6. ¿? / mexicana / este año / maestra / alguna / Tendremos

   _____

7. vestidos / algunos / mejores / de los / Nos probamos

   _____

8. lleva / tantos / avión / Ningún / como / este / pasajeros

   _____

4. Transformar Modifica las oraciones según se indica entre paréntesis, incorporando cuantificadores indefinidos. 7.A–7.B

> **Modelo**
>
> No queda ninguna de las tareas por terminar. (plural, afirmativo, interrogativo)
> *¿Quedan algunas tareas por terminar?*

1. ¿Ves algún motivo para celebrar? (singular, negativo)

   _____

2. Se dañaron algunos de los cuadros durante la mudanza. (singular, negativo)

   _____

3. Ninguno de los bancos estará en servicio el fin de semana. (singular, interrogativo)

   _____

4. Camila no tiene ninguna otra casa donde vivir. (afirmativo, interrogativo)

   _____

5. ¿Hay algunas buenas noticias? (singular, negativo, enunciado)

   _____

6. ¿Sus hijos maltratan a los animales de alguna manera? (singular, negativo)

   _____

5. Indicar En la carta, indica cuáles son los cuantificadores indefinidos que solo tienen forma afirmativa. Escríbelos. `7.C`

> Querida Eva:
>
> ¡Te extraño cada día más! ¿Cuándo podremos vernos? Ya sé que tenemos muchas actividades, pero deberíamos encontrarnos cualquier día de estos.
>
> ¿Sería demasiado estrés que nos viéramos el miércoles? Los demás días de la semana trabajo hasta muy tarde. En todo caso, podríamos coordinar para hacer las compras juntas u otra cosa que quieras.
>
> Deberíamos vernos alguna vez antes de fin de año, ¿no?
>
> Espero una respuesta pronto,
> Francisca

_____

_____

_____

_____

_____

_____

_____

_____

6. Cuantificadores Para cada ejemplo, indica si el cuantificador debe concordar en género y/o número con el sustantivo. `7.C`

Ejemplo	Sí	No
1. Ante **alguna** duda, consulte con su médico de cabecera.		
2. **Cada** uno ordena su habitación.		
3. Tengo **muchísimo** sueño.		
4. Hay **varias** alumnas que son excelentes deportistas.		
5. Habrá **más** contaminación si no cuidamos el planeta.		
6. Compra **menos** dulces la próxima vez.		

7. Escoger Elige la opción correcta para completar estas oraciones. `7.C`

1. No te preocupes, me encargaré de todo _____ (lo/los) demás.

2. Yo quería ir de viaje de estudios al sur, pero _____ (lo/las) demás eligieron el viaje al norte.

3. Necesito mucho _____ (menos / menos de) tiempo, ¡seis días son más que suficientes!

4. Si hago un poco _____ (más / más de) esfuerzo, me aceptarán en la universidad que quiera.

5. Tengo que arreglar _____ (otros detalles más / otros más detalles) y podremos irnos.

6. ¿Te acuerdas de que _____ (el otro / de otro) día hablamos sobre este tema?

7. Trabajemos _____ (otras tres / tres otras) horas y vámonos al parque.

8. El café no está muy dulce: quiero _____ (otro poco / otro poco de) azúcar.

8. Elegir Para cada oración, elige la opción correcta. **7.C**

> **Modelo**
>
> Mi médico dijo que es saludable comer _____cada_____ (cada/durante) cuatro horas.

1. Carmen y Sandra van a escuelas diferentes, pero _____ (ambas / cada una) juegan en el mismo equipo de hockey.

2. Ya tengo _____ (bastantes/demás) problemas con aprender francés. ¡Aprender también chino sería demasiado!

3. _____ (Todos/Ambos) los estudiantes deben hacer la tarea para el lunes próximo.

4. _____ (Ambos / Los tres) perros deben ir a la veterinaria: Pipo y Colita, hoy; y Huesito, mañana.

5. Estudié _____ (cada una de / demás) las lecciones del libro, de la primera a la última.

6. _____ (Más semanas / Todas las semanas) tengo clases de música.

9. La ciudad Completa la conversación entre Julia y Joaquín con las palabras de la lista. Si no es necesario agregar una palabra, indícalo con una X. **7.C**

> cualquier   cualquiera de   un   una   unos

JULIA ¿Vivirías para siempre en nuestra ciudad?

JOAQUÍN Sí, me encanta. Además, no podría vivir en ninguno de los pueblos cercanos.

JULIA Mmm... no sé, nuestra ciudad no tiene (1) _____ playa. Tampoco tiene (2) _____ bosque.

JOAQUÍN Pienso que el clima es ideal aquí. Hace (3) _____ poco de calor en el verano, pero no demasiado.

JULIA Puede ser... De (4) _____ manera, debo quedarme hasta que termine la escuela.

JOAQUÍN Sí, y para eso faltan (5) _____ cuatro años.

JULIA Es verdad, pero podría ir pensando en mudarme a (6) _____ las ciudades que tienen universidades importantes.

JOAQUÍN No es (7) _____ mala idea. Además, ¡tiempo es lo que nos sobra!

10. Sí o no En estos ejemplos, identifica el cuantificador indefinido e indica si funciona como pronombre o no. **7.C**

> **Modelo**
>
> Levantaron sus copas y ambos brindaron.
> _ambos: es pronombre_

1. Quería comprar libros, pero ninguno me pareció interesante. _____

2. Busquemos unas películas buenas y mirémoslas. _____

3. No me decido todavía: cualquiera me viene bien. _____

4. Algunos amigos de Juan viven en México. _____

5. Comunícate con cualquier integrante de nuestro personal. _____

6. ¡Todo me sale mal! _____

7. Al final, me arrepentí de comprar la cámara. No es necesario tener una. _____

8. La vecina de la esquina es amable; las demás, no. _____

11. Insertar Reescribe las oraciones insertando el cuantificador en el lugar adecuado de la oración. **7.C**

> **Modelo**
>
> Con una excepción, todos los alumnos aprobaron el curso. (demás)
> *Con una excepción, todos los demás alumnos aprobaron el curso.*

1. En nuestra tienda, le ofrecemos recetas: desde platos elaborados hasta platos rápidos. (varias)
_____

2. Con dos kilos, me veré mejor. (menos)
_____

3. Cinco días y comienzan las vacaciones. (más)
_____

4. Tengo sueño: mejor hablemos mañana. (bastante)
_____

5. Un día llegarás a casa y estaré esperándote con una gran sorpresa. (cualquiera)
_____

6. Hay cosas que tenemos que hablar. Necesitamos más tiempo. (varias)
_____

12. Contestar Contesta las preguntas con respuestas completas usando la palabra o frase indicada. **7.C**

> **Modelo**
>
> ¿Dedicas la mayor parte de tu tiempo a hacer deporte?
> Sí, *todo el tiempo hago deporte.* (todo el)

1. ¿Compraste las cosas que aparecían en la lista? Sí, _____. (todas)
2. ¿Esos pueblos son iguales entre sí? No, _____. (cada)
3. ¿Has estudiado para el examen? Sí, _____. (todo)
4. ¿Eres un experto en motocicletas? Sí, _____. (todo un)
5. ¿Sabes todo sobre acuarios? Sí, _____. (todo lo)

13. ¿*Nada* o *nadie?* Completa las oraciones con *nada* o *nadie*. **7.D**

> **Modelo**
>
> Yo creo que *nadie* de tu familia me pedirá más favores.

1. La vendedora de la tienda no fue _____ amable al atenderme.
2. No quiero a _____ más que a ti.
3. No tengo fuerzas para _____. Es mejor que descanse más.
4. El pronóstico no es _____ bueno: el paciente deberá quedarse en el hospital un largo tiempo.
5. ¿Tienes más hambre? Yo no quiero _____ más.
6. ¿Adivina quién me invitó a su cumpleaños? ¡_____ menos que el embajador de México!

14. Reemplazar Reemplaza las palabras subrayadas por un pronombre indefinido. **7.D**

> **Modelo**
>
> ¡No existe ninguna cosa que pueda compararse con un viaje en familia! *nada*

1. ¿Hay alguna persona que hable alemán aquí? _____
2. Ninguna persona viene de Colombia. _____
3. Al momento de elegir una playa en toda Latinoamérica, una persona elegiría una de Brasil. _____
4. Ninguna persona puede ayudarme. _____
5. No viajes con ninguna cosa que sea de valor. _____
6. Hay una cosa que debes saber. _____

15. Convertir Convierte estas oraciones afirmativas en negativas. **7.D**

> **Modelo**
>
> Mis primos entienden algo de alemán.
> *Mis primos no entienden nada de alemán.*

1. ¿Hay alguien que sea español? _____
2. Yo tenía que decirte algo. _____
3. Escucho algo cuando hablo por teléfono. _____
4. Ana recomienda a alguien de su grupo para el trabajo. _____
5. Me cuenta mucho sobre su abuelo, Pedro. _____

16. Reescribir Reescribe este relato de forma impersonal usando el pronombre *uno* en lugar del pronombre *tú*. **7.D**

Posibles soluciones para el insomnio

Muchas personas sufren de insomnio ocasionalmente. ¿Pero qué puedes hacer cuando esto se convierte en un problema frecuente?

Puedes hacer ejercicio por la tarde, aunque no demasiado tarde. De lo contrario, al momento de dormir, tienes un ritmo demasiado acelerado y no puedes conciliar el sueño.

Otra opción es no tomar bebidas con mucha cafeína. Cuando tomas mucho café o bebidas energéticas, estás más alerta y no puedes dormirte con tanta facilidad.

Muchos médicos recomiendan que no tengas un televisor en la habitación. Es mejor que la habitación sea un lugar donde solamente duermas.

Y, por último, debes intentar tener horarios regulares, es decir, una rutina.

17. Anuncio Completa este anuncio con la forma correcta de *mismo* o *propio*. `7.E`

> ¡Baje de peso ya!
>
> ¿No se siente cómodo con su (1) __*propio*__ cuerpo? ¿Tiene unos kilitos de más que lo hacen sentirse inseguro? ¡Siéntase bien consigo (2) _____ en treinta días! Gracias al revolucionario tratamiento que ofrecemos, bajará sus kilos de más de forma fácil y saludable, a su (3) _____ ritmo.
>
> Nuestro método es totalmente distinto de los demás: sin pastillas, sin mentiras, sin recetas mágicas. Se trata de buscar en uno (4) _____ las fuerzas y ganas para darle un rumbo nuevo a su (5) _____ vida. Llame ahora (6) _____ y le regalaremos un video explicativo donde podrá ver testimonios de muchos de nuestros clientes satisfechos.

18. Contradecir Cada vez que Patricia dice algo, Diego la contradice. Escribe los comentarios de Diego usando la palabra indicada. `7.E`

Modelo

> **PATRICIA** Yo conozco a alguien que puede reparar tu auto clásico.
> **DIEGO** *Tú no conoces a nadie que pueda reparar mi auto clásico*. (nadie)

1. **PATRICIA** Tu mamá siempre habla mucho.
   DIEGO _____. (poco)

2. **PATRICIA** Es bastante seguro que yo gane una beca.
   DIEGO _____. (nada)

3. **PATRICIA** En el último año, la economía de nuestro país creció mucho menos, en comparación con años anteriores.
   DIEGO _____. (más)

4. **PATRICIA** Este resfriado no es nada grave.
   DIEGO _____. (bastante)

5. **PATRICIA** Hace mucho que dejaste de trabajar.
   DIEGO _____. (tanto)

19. Síntesis Unir Une los elementos de las dos columnas para formar oraciones. `7.B–7.E`

1. No tengo ningún _____	a. con mis problemas. ¡No puedo solucionar los tuyos!
2. Algún _____	b. lugares donde podríamos festejar tu cumpleaños.
3. No hay forma _____	c. momento de tranquilidad.
4. Creo que hay bastantes _____	d. lado de la calle antes de cruzar.
5. Ya tengo bastante _____	e. madre la que me contó la verdad.
6. Elige cualquiera de _____	f. día seré rico y dejaré de trabajar.
7. Me ha dicho que en todo _____	g. momento estará conmigo.
8. Debes mirar a cada _____	h. alguna de entrar sin saber el código secreto.
9. Fue mi propia _____	i. mucho esta tarde.
10. Creo que he aprendido _____	j. las blusas; todas son hermosas.

20. Síntesis Decidir Decide a qué ejemplo hace referencia cada explicación. `7.B–7.E`

_____ 1. No tienes ninguna mascota.

_____ 2. ¿Hay algún problema?

_____ 3. Me gusta todo en esta tienda.

_____ 4. Me quedan unos cinco mil dólares en la cuenta.

_____ 5. Ambas sillas pertenecen a Marta.

_____ 6. Cada calle tiene un nombre distinto.

_____ 7. Uno debe cuidar su salud siempre.

_____ 8. Carla y Javier recibieron sendos galardones.

a. Es un cuantificador que se usa siempre en plural y que puede reemplazarse por "los/las dos".

b. Es un cuantificador que se usa en lugar de "aproximadamente" antes de un número.

c. Es un determinante que significa "uno cada uno" y se usa en el lenguaje escrito.

d. Este cuantificador se abrevia antes de sustantivos masculinos en singular.

e. Es un cuantificador que no concuerda en género ni en número con el sustantivo y solo indica una parte de un todo.

f. Esta forma negativa requiere una doble negación cuando se encuentra después del verbo.

g. Se usa cuando el hablante necesita expresarse de una forma impersonal.

h. Es un cuantificador indefinido que, en este caso, se usa como pronombre.

21. Síntesis Un mundo propio Imagina un mundo en el que eres el gobernante. Inventa diez normas para regular la educación, la salud, la convivencia, etc., usando cuantificadores y pronombres indefinidos. `7.B–7.E`

Modelo

Todas las personas tendrán alimento suficiente...

_____
_____
_____
_____
_____
_____
_____
_____
_____
_____

Practice more at **vhlcentral.com.**

1. Completar Carlos está en la zapatería y quiere comprarse zapatos nuevos. Observa las imágenes y completa las oraciones de la vendedora con determinantes demostrativos. `8.A`

1. ___Esos___ zapatos son clásicos y elegantes, ¿le quedan cómodos?

2. Si quiere algo más moderno, tiene _____ zapatos marrones, con rayas marrón claro, que están en el exhibidor.

3. O, si busca algo más informal, puedo ofrecerle _____ zapatillas color beige, están a un precio muy razonable.

4. ¿O prefiere _____ zapatos negros que le ofrecí al principio?

5. Me gustan los zapatos clásicos, llevo _____.

2. Elegir Selecciona la opción correcta para completar el artículo periodístico. `8.A`

Accidente automovilístico

(1) ___Esta___ (Aquella/Esta) madrugada, alrededor de las 5:30 a. m., dos coches chocaron en la intersección de las calles Colina y San Petersburgo. Según testigos, el conductor del coche azul cruzó la avenida con el semáforo en rojo. Los registros policiales indican que (2) _____ (esto/esta) no es la primera vez que este conductor comete una infracción de (3) _____ (esto/este) tipo. (4) _____ (Este/Aquel) tampoco es el primer accidente en esta intersección.

En la escena del accidente, un vecino, Francisco Gómez, declaró: "(5) _____ (Ese/Esto) ya pasó varias veces antes. (6) _____ (Aquel/Aquello) semáforo no está bien sincronizado con (7) _____ (aquel/aquello)".

Las autoridades de seguridad vial están analizando (8) _____ (eso/este) y otros casos de accidentes por cruzar semáforos en rojo. Sin embargo, afirman que (9) _____ (estas/estos) son casos de negligencia, y no de problemas técnicos.

3. **Descripción** Martín está en la habitación que tenía cuando era niño. Completa la descripción con las palabras de la lista. **8.A**

| aquellos | esas | esos | ~~Esta~~ | aquel | eso | este | estas |

(1) _____*Esta*_____ era mi habitación. Todo (2) _____ espacio de aquí era únicamente para mí, ¿no es genial? (3) _____ repisas que ves aquí están repletas de mis cómics favoritos. En (4) _____ cajones que están detrás de las repisas están mis juguetes de cuando era niño. Y (5) _____ oso gigante que ves al fondo es el primer peluche que me regalaron. ¿Ves (6) _____ que se ve por la ventana? Es un edificio de oficinas bastante feo. Allí antes había una casa de madera. ¡Qué tiempos (7) _____! Nos pasábamos allí todo el verano. ¡(8) _____ eran aventuras de verdad!

4. **Síntesis Demostrativos** Completa las oraciones con demostrativos. **8.A–8.B**

> **Modelo**
> Todo *esto* lo gané trabajando…
> ¡trabajando muchísimo!

1. La niña _____ que está allí no deja de mirarme: ¿qué querrá de mí?
2. _____ tres piedras que tengo en la mano son muy valiosas.
3. ¿Ves _____ que se mueve en el fondo del jardín? ¡Es mi perro!
4. Recibí dos veces la misma factura. Mira aquí: _____ hoy; y aquella, la semana pasada.
5. ¿Cómo armo _____? No entiendo las instrucciones.
6. _____… no sé la respuesta… no hice la tarea.
7. ¡Ay! ¡Ojalá tuviera tu edad! En _____ tiempos, todo parecía posible.
8. _____ vez no me olvidaré de llevar mi pasaporte.

5. **Síntesis Mochilas cruzadas** Varios compañeros de escuela con mochilas parecidas las confunden por error. Completa la conversación con los demostrativos apropiados. **8.A–8.B**

ANITA ¿Sabes si alguien se llevó (1) _*aquella / esa*_ mochila que puse al lado de la papelera?

PABLITO No sé… (2) _____ que tengo aquí es la mía.

ANITA Revísala otra vez, por favor. Si (3) _____ que tienes allí contiene un libro de cuentos, es la mía.

PABLITO A ver… Mmmmm… (4) _____… Tienes razón, acá está el libro. Y además (5) _____ no son mis cuadernos.

ANITA Para confirmar, dime si en (6) _____ mochila encuentras unos marcadores en el bolsillo de adelante.

PABLITO Sí, pero (7) _____ se ven muy gastados, y de marca Trazos.

ANITA Esos son.

PABLITO Entonces, ¿tú tienes la mía? En (8) _____ yo llevaba un diccionario.

ANITA No, (9) _____ que tengo aquí contiene un cuaderno, un libro de dibujo y una bolsa con lápices de colores.

PABLITO ¡(10) _____ no puede ser! ¿Dónde estará entonces?

6. Síntesis Escribir Identifica seis personas u objetos en tu salón de clases, tres de ellos cerca de ti y los otros tres, lejos de ti. Escribe oraciones en que expliques a un compañero dónde se encuentran ubicados estas personas u objetos. 8.A–8.B

> **Modelo**
>
> *Esta es mi silla y aquella es la silla del profesor.*

_____

_____

_____

_____

_____

_____

Practice more at **vhlcentral.com.**

Possessives | Chapter 9

1. Identificar Escribe en el espacio de cada oración si se utilizó un determinante posesivo tónico o uno átono. 9.A

> **Modelo**
>
> Mi interés en el tema es personal. *átono*
> El computador tuyo es muy rápido. *tónico*

1. Ese es mi número de teléfono. _____

2. No entiendo la tarea nuestra. _____

3. Acá tengo tus gafas. _____

4. El problema es vuestro. _____

5. Hablar cinco lenguas es el sueño mío. _____

6. No me gustan los comentarios tuyos. _____

7. Nuestra actuación fue maravillosa. _____

8. Vuestro sentido del gusto es buenísimo. _____

2. Conversación Completa la conversación con los determinantes posesivos correspondientes. 9.B

MAMÁ ¿Has hecho (1) ___*tu*___ tarea?

ANDRÉS Por supuesto, mamá. (2) _____ maestro es muy estricto.

MAMÁ ¿Y has ordenado (3) _____ habitación? Mañana viene (4) _____ amigo... ¿cómo se llama?

ANDRÉS Julio. Sí, mamá, hasta guardé todos (5) _____ juegos en el armario.

MAMÁ Bien hecho. Pero, ¿qué hiciste con (6) _____ camiseta de fútbol? Mañana debes llevarla a la escuela.

ANDRÉS No te preocupes, mamita. (7) _____ entrenador tiene todas (8) _____ camisetas en (9) _____ casa.

MAMÁ Así me gusta. ¡Solamente deseo que (10) _____ vidas sean ordenadas!

ANDRÉS ¡Sí, mamá! Y ya lo sabes, ¡(11) _____ deseos son órdenes!

3. Oraciones Completa las oraciones con los determinantes posesivos correspondientes. `9.C`

> **Modelo**
>
> Supongo que los cursos _suyos_ (ustedes) fueron pagados a tiempo.

1. No encuentro varios cuadernos _____ (yo). ¿Sabes dónde pueden estar?

2. Ayer me llamó una compañera _____ (tú).

3. En el periódico, publicaron muchos artículos _____ (nosotros).

4. ¿Te gustan las obras de Junot Díaz? Compré unas novelas _____ (él) a un precio muy bueno.

5. ¿Qué haremos con todos estos juguetes _____ (tú) cuando crezcas? Podríamos donarlos.

6. ¡Cómo extraño usar esas zapatillas _____ (yo)! Eran hermosas, ¿te acuerdas?

7. Un profesor _____ (nosotros) nos recomendó esta universidad.

8. En la fiesta, conocí a un amigo _____ (ella).

9. Esas amigas _____ (vosotros) que vinieron de visita son muy simpáticas.

10. ¿Estos libros de contabilidad son _____ (ustedes)?

4. Opciones Elige los posesivos correctos para completar el relato. `9.B–9.C`

> Mis regalos de Navidad
>
> Finalmente llegó la Navidad. (1) __Mis__ (Tus/Mis) papás me dieron muchos regalos.
>
> Bueno, primero, (2) _____ (su/mi) hermano, Pablo, abrió su regalo: un espectacular rompecabezas. Siempre fue (3) _____ (su/mi) sueño tener uno, y se le hizo realidad. Después fue mi turno. A diferencia de Pablo, el único deseo (4) _____ (suyo/mío) era una sencilla muñeca Patsy, ya sabes, la que sale en la televisión. Vi cuatro cajas, que parecían todas cosas (5) _____ (tuyas/mías) porque tenían mi nombre en ellas. En la primera caja, había una muñeca Patsy. Y en las demás, todos (6) _____ (sus/vuestros) accesorios. ¡Sí, y todo era (7) _____ (mío/nuestro)!
>
> En fin, pasé todo (8) _____ (su/mi) fin de semana jugando con mi muñeca Patsy, ¡y con todos (9) _____ (sus/tus) vestidos y zapatos!

5. Posesivos Completa las oraciones con los posesivos de la lista. `9.B–9.C`

> suya   míos   ~~nuestra~~   vuestro   mi   tus   sus   nuestros   tuyos

> **Modelo**
>
> La idea _nuestra_ es llegar al aeropuerto antes de mediodía.

1. Carla, _____ padres llamaron preocupados. ¡Quieren saber dónde estás!

2. Unos vecinos _____ se quejaron porque mi perro ladra. ¡Qué intolerancia hay en mi barrio!

3. Mis padres son mayores que los _____.

4. _____ compañera de cuarto, Alicia, estudia toda la noche y no me deja dormir.

5. Estos son _____ derechos como estudiantes. ¡Solamente nosotros podemos defenderlos!

6. ¿Has visto lo linda que es Paula? ¡_____ ojos son impactantes!

7. Es claro que Flavia organizó la fiesta sorpresa. Todo esto es obra _____.

8. Esto es _____, ¿no? Recuerdo que lo habéis dejado en mi casa.

6. Clasificar Clasifica estos determinantes posesivos según puedan usarse antes del sustantivo, después del sustantivo o en ambos lugares. Marca una X en la casilla que corresponda. `9.B–9.C`

Determinante	Posesivo antes del sustantivo	Posesivo después del sustantivo	Posesivo antes o después del sustantivo
1. su			
2. míos			
3. vuestros			
4. suyos			
5. nuestra			
6. tus			
7. mis			
8. tuya			
9. vuestra			
10. nuestros			

7. Reformular Reescribe estas oraciones cambiando los posesivos según la persona indicada. `9.B–9.C`

> **Modelo**
>
> ¡Qué egoísta eres! Nunca piensas en el bienestar suyo. (nosotros)
> *¡Qué egoísta eres! Nunca piensas en el bienestar nuestro.*

1. Esa compañera tuya no deja de llamar a casa. (vosotros)

   _____

2. Varios profesores míos dieron clases en universidades extranjeras. (tú)

   _____

3. ¡Nuestras madres hablan tanto! Escucharlas es agotador. (ellos)

   _____

4. ¿Puedes comprar ropa en la tienda de tu barrio? (yo)

   _____

5. Tus zapatos están sucios. Es necesario lavarlos antes de guardarlos. (vosotros)

   _____

6. Llamar a sus perros Guardián y Sultán solo pudo ser idea suya. (tú)

   _____

8. Átonos y tónicos Convierte los posesivos átonos (van antes del sustantivo) de las oraciones a tónicos (van después del sustantivo) o viceversa. 9.B–9.C

> **Modelo**
>
> La cualidad tuya de ser puntual es muy valiosa. *Tu cualidad de ser puntual es muy valiosa.*
> Nuestra cocina fue remodelada hace poco. *La cocina nuestra fue remodelada hace poco.*

1. Tus ojos son del color del cielo.

   _____

2. Nuestro sistema solar ya tiene ocho planetas.

   _____

3. Las uñas suyas están débiles.

   _____

4. ¿El televisor tuyo recibe señal digital?

   _____

5. Mis gafas están en el escritorio.

   _____

6. ¡No sabía que tu apartamento quedaba tan cerca!

   _____

7. El aporte mío es importante en la discusión.

   _____

8. No creo que el gusto suyo sea malo.

   _____

9. Pusimos nuestras esperanzas en el equipo más joven.

   _____

10. Tu alegría es contagiosa.

    _____

9. Completar Completa la conversación entre Luciana y el médico con determinantes posesivos o artículos definidos. 9.D

LUCIANA Hola, doctor. Le cuento (1) _mi_ inquietud: me pica (2) _____ lunar (*mole*) que tengo aquí en (3) _____ brazo. Además, (4) _____ piel es muy blanca.

MÉDICO Bueno, Luciana, primero unas preguntitas. ¿En (5) _____ familia, hay casos de cáncer?

LUCIANA No, nadie ha tenido cáncer.

MÉDICO ¿Te duele (6) _____ lunar?

LUCIANA No, no me duele, pero a veces me pica (7) _____ piel de alrededor.

MÉDICO Mmm... Bueno, haremos un examen el lunes que viene.

LUCIANA Bien, déjeme ver (8) _____ agenda... Perfecto, pero, ¿qué puedo hacer para solucionar la picazón?

MÉDICO Es importante que no te rasques (9) _____ piel.

LUCIANA Sí...

MÉDICO Ponte protector solar en (10) _____ brazos antes de salir de (11) _____ casa.

LUCIANA ¿Solamente allí?

MÉDICO Bueno, lo ideal es que te pongas protector en todo (12) _____ cuerpo.

LUCIANA Perfecto, entonces me cuido (13) _____ lunar hasta la próxima visita.

MÉDICO Luciana, ¡eres (14) _____ mejor paciente!

10. Seleccionar Escoge una frase de la lista para completar cada una de las oraciones. `9.D`

> mi amiga   mi general   mi papá   auto nuestro   ~~tu palabra~~
> valijas nuestras   tus bufandas   botas tuyas   lo mío

Modelo

> Para nosotros, _tu palabra_ es garantía más que suficiente.

1. ¿Recuerdas ese _____ que se descomponía en los días más importantes?

2. Aquí hay unas _____ de color marrón. ¿Las quieres todavía?

3. Para mi cumpleaños, vinieron _____ y la tuya.

4. Estaré listo a las 0700 horas, _____, como buen sargento que soy.

5. Mi tía tiene 46 años, y luego sigue _____, que tiene 43.

6. Aquí están _____ favoritas. ¿Qué hago con ellas?

7. En la casa de Andrea tenemos varias _____ que debemos buscar.

8. Papá, _____ siempre ha sido y será el tenis.

11. Elegir Completa las oraciones con *propio, propia, propios* o *propias*. Decide si va antes o después del sustantivo. `9.D`

Modelo

> Sofía dejó a su novio como muestra de _____ amor _propio_.

1. Te lo digo por _____ experiencia _____: cuida tus pertenencias en el aeropuerto.

2. Carina vive en su _____ mundo _____ y nunca presta atención en clase.

3. No puede ser que no me creas: ¡lo he visto con mis _____ ojos _____!

4. Le recomiendo ese abrigo que está en la vidriera: es una _____ chaqueta _____ para el invierno.

5. Yo tengo mi _____ habitación _____. ¿Y tú? ¿Compartes tu habitación con tu hermana?

6. Ella trabaja por su _____ cuenta _____, pero antes era empleada de una tienda.

12. Reescribir Reescribe cada frase subrayada diciendo exactamente a quién pertenece cada cosa. `9.D`

Regalos para adolescentes
Sugerencia: *Sol y lluvia*

En este libro, encontramos los relatos de Amparo, una hermosa y simpática joven que vive en una pequeña ciudad en el sur de (1) su país natal, Chile. Pero, al cabo de los primeros capítulos, en (2) su diario, es claro que (3) su vida no es de color de rosa: Amparo se encuentra con muchos problemas sin solución.

El autor de *Sol y lluvia*, Facundo Quesada, presentó (4) su libro y dio una conferencia de prensa. En (5) palabras suyas: "Esta historia es ideal para lectores adolescentes, porque pueden identificarse con Amparo. Al leer (6) su diario, ellos se dan cuenta de que no son de otro planeta: que tanto en (7) su vida como en (8) las suyas hay alegrías y tristezas, pero todo tiene una solución". Por esta razón y muchas otras, les recomendamos este libro para (9) sus hijos de entre doce y dieciséis años.

1. _el país natal de Amparo/ella_   4. _____   7. _____

2. _____   5. _____   8. _____

3. _____   6. _____   9. _____

13. Síntesis Historia Completa la historia con la opción correcta. `9.A–9.E`

De alumno a alumno

¿No consigues (1) _____ (tus/los) libros que te han pedido? ¿No sabes cómo hacer (2) _____ (las tareas tuyas / tus tareas)? No te rompas más (3) _____ (la/tu) cabeza tratando de hacerlas por (4) _____ (propia cuenta / cuenta propia).

¡Ofrecemos (5) _____ (una solución propia / tu solución) para estudiantes de primer año!

Somos un grupo de estudiantes de quinto año a punto de graduarnos y queremos que todos (6) _____ (vuestros compañeros / nuestros compañeros) de escuela tengan el mismo éxito que hemos tenido nosotros. Bajo el lema (*motto*) "Lo (7) _____ (mío/tuyo) es (8) _____ (mío/tuyo)", donamos nuestros libros y apuntes, y ayudamos a quienes tengan dificultades en matemáticas, ciencias y literatura. Puedes encontrarnos en el aula 43.

14. Síntesis Emparejar Escribe en el espacio del enunciado la letra del ejemplo que le corresponde. `9.A–9.E`

Enunciado

_____ 1. posesivo después de un sustantivo usado para dirigirse a una persona

_____ 2. aparición de una combinación de posesivos

_____ 3. utilización de posesivos con demostrativos

_____ 4. artículos que se emplean en lugar de los posesivos

_____ 5. indicación de áreas de interés o de pertenencia en general

_____ 6. reemplazo de **nuestro/a(s)**, tanto en español escrito como hablado

_____ 7. oración con **ser** o **parecer** que enfatiza la pertenencia

_____ 8. oración con una palabra que indica características de algo o alguien si va junto con **de + sustantivo/pronombre**

_____ 9. posesivo que puede usarse solo cuando no se menciona el sustantivo

_____ 10. oración en que se usa el artículo en lugar del posesivo, cuando se menciona una reacción física

Ejemplo

a. Esa manía nuestra de pagar sin revisar bien el producto nos va a costar mucho.

b. Lo suyo era surfear al atardecer.

c. La culpa no fue mía.

d. La velocidad de punta es propia de los guepardos.

e. Por fortuna los familiares suyos y nuestros se llevan de maravilla.

f. Me pica la cabeza. Mejor cambiaré de champú.

g. La camisa y el reloj me tallan.

h. En la foto del anuario mis hijos aparecen a la izquierda, ¿dónde está la tuya?

i. Madre mía, ya pronto iré a visitarte.

j. El profesor de nosotros nos dijo que la tarea era en parejas.

15. Síntesis Comparar Piensa en un familiar, como tu papá, tu mamá, o en una persona cercana y compara cinco de sus características con las tuyas o las de tus hermanos. Utiliza tanto posesivos átonos (van antes del sustantivo) como tónicos (van después del sustantivo). `9.A–9.E`

> **Modelo**
>
> *Mi mamá tiene el cabello claro; el mío es oscuro...*

_____
_____
_____
_____
_____

Practice more at **vhlcentral.com**.

Adverbs — Chapter 10

1. Adverbios o adjetivos Lee este texto e indica si las palabras subrayadas se utilizan como adverbios o adjetivos. `10.A`

> **El tren en Internet**
>
> (1) ¡<u>Ya</u> puede comprar sus billetes de tren muy (2) <u>fácilmente</u>! Ingrese en nuestro sitio web. En el buscador de horarios, elija la hora y el día en el que <u>desea</u> viajar. (3) <u>Luego</u>, busque la tarifa que (4) <u>mejor</u> se adecue a su bolsillo. Cuando la encuentre, haga clic (5) <u>rápidamente</u> sobre la opción escogida. No tiene (6) <u>demasiado</u> tiempo: en cinco minutos deberá concretar su compra. (7) <u>Ahora</u> pague su billete. Le ofrecemos una (8) <u>amplia</u> variedad de medios de pago. No olvide ingresar una dirección de correo electrónico, a la que le enviaremos (9) <u>inmediatamente</u> el billete que deberá imprimir. Preséntese en la estación (10) <u>pocos</u> minutos antes de la salida del tren... ¡y (11) <u>listo</u>! Disfrute de tiempo libre para hacer lo que (12) <u>más</u> le guste.

1. _____*adverbio*_____   5. _____   9. _____
2. _____   6. _____   10. _____
3. _____   7. _____   11. _____
4. _____   8. _____   12. _____

2. Relato Completa el relato de María Luisa con la opción correcta. `10.B`

Todos los días tengo algo para hacer por las tardes, después de la escuela. Es decir, (1) _____ (casi siempre / casi nunca) tengo tiempo libre. (2) _____ (Nunca/Siempre) me encontrarás en casa por las tardes. Si quieres verme, tendrás que ir al club, porque estoy allí (3) _____ (frecuentemente / rara vez).

(4) _____ (A veces / Pocas veces) me gustaría quedarme en casa, pero sé que es importante entrenar y socializar... ¡y no hay nada mejor que el club para eso! Bueno, entonces si quieres que nos veamos, (5) _____ (siempre/nunca) me busques en casa... ¡ya sabes dónde estoy (6) _____ (con poca frecuencia / con mucha frecuencia)!

3. Adverbios de tiempo Completa las oraciones con los adverbios de tiempo de la lista. `10.B`

temprano	nunca	ya (2)
cuándo	antes	tarde
pasado mañana	cuando	después

Modelo

_____ _Ya_ _____ verás qué divertida es esta amiga mía.

1. Dime _____ estarás en tu casa y pasaré a visitarte.

2. _____ hace frío, uso bufanda y guantes muy abrigados.

3. Los truenos se escuchan _____ de ver los relámpagos.

4. Mis abuelos dicen que _____ la vida era más tranquila.

5. Mañana es miércoles y _____ es jueves.

6. ¡Te despiertas demasiado _____! ¡Hoy es domingo y son las 7 a. m.!

7. _____ o temprano verás que tengo razón.

8. _____ no tengo más dinero. ¡Tendré que pedirles un poco a mis padres!

9. _____ jamás adivinarías a quién encontré en la calle.

10. _____ sabes la respuesta... ¡para qué me preguntas!

4. Seleccionar Elige la opción correcta para cada oración. `10.C`

1. _____ (Cómo/Como) me dijiste, compré las flores más lindas para Susana.

2. Día tras día me siento _____ (mal/peor): este remedio no cura mi tos.

3. Bate los huevos de esta manera, _____ (cómo/como) te estoy mostrando.

4. Esta carne no está _____ (bien/mejor) cocinada. ¡Parece cruda!

5. La próxima vez elegiré _____ (mejor/así) el destino de mis vacaciones.

6. Tu amiga es _____ (mal/bien) simpática. Invítala a todas nuestras fiestas.

5. Conversación Completa la conversación con *bien, mejor, así, cómo* y *como*. `10.C`

REBECA ¡Qué (1) __*bien*__! Si te mudas cerca de casa, podremos vernos todas las tardes.

CAMILA Sí… Me encantaría que fuera (2) _____, pero no sé (3) _____ haré para encontrar un apartamento a buen precio y bien ubicado.

REBECA Es verdad, aquí la gente vive (4) _____; por las noches siempre hay movimiento y todos quieren vivir aquí.

CAMILA Quizás sería (5) _____ buscar un apartamento en otro barrio, (6) _____ dijo mi madre.

REBECA No te preocupes, ya encontraremos un apartamento (7) _____ bonito para ti.

CAMILA ¡(8) _____ me gusta! Con esta actitud tan positiva, ¡encontraremos uno genial!

6. Oraciones Completa las oraciones con las palabras de la lista. `10.D`

| muy | todo lo que | casi | demasiado | cuánto | bastante | cuanto | poco | ~~suficiente~~ |

Modelo

¡No me pases la pimienta! El plato ya trae _____*suficiente*_____.

1. Mi instructor de yoga entrena _____. Creo que eso no es saludable.

2. _____ rompo mi computadora por llevarla en una mochila inadecuada.

3. No sabes _____ extrañé a mi perro durante las vacaciones.

4. Tu jefa nueva es _____ simpática. Mucho mejor que la anterior, ¿no?

5. _____ más aprendo matemáticas, más mejoro en geometría.

6. Me resulta _____ difícil estudiar más de dos horas seguidas.

7. Te juro que hice _____ pude para comprarte un regalo de aniversario.

8. Me siento lleno. Creo que hoy voy a almorzar _____.

7. Contradecir Cecilia siempre contradice a su madre. Reescribe las oraciones usando el adverbio adecuado. `10.D`

Modelo

MADRE En el supermercado debemos comprar mucho.
CECILIA *En el supermercado debemos comprar poco.*

1. **MADRE** Tardaremos más que la semana pasada.

   CECILIA _____

2. **MADRE** Tardaremos bastante.

   CECILIA _____

3. **MADRE** ¡Tendremos que pagar tanto por un taxi!

   CECILIA _____

4. **MADRE** Será mejor comprar poco para todo el mes.

   CECILIA _____

5. **MADRE** Vamos a terminar demasiado cansadas.

   CECILIA _____

8. ¿*Aquí*, *allí* o *allá*? Completa el relato de Cintia con *aquí*, *allí* y *allá*. `10.E`

¡Cómo me gusta mi ciudad nueva! (1) _____*Aquí*_____ puedo hacer mucho más que en Lobres, mi pueblo anterior. Es verdad que Lobres era más tranquilo. (2) _____ no nos preocupábamos por cerrar con llave las puertas de los carros o cerrar las ventanas por la noche. (3) _____ es diferente: tenemos que tener más cuidado con nuestros bolsos en la calle y estar más atentos. Lo bueno de vivir (4) _____ es que todos los días hay actividades: ir al cine, a museos, ver espectáculos al aire libre, de todo... Y por suerte, siempre puedo volver a Lobres cuando quiero. Voy para (5) _____ cada quince días a ver a mis padres. (6) _____ comemos muy rico, dormimos la siesta y disfrutamos de la tranquilidad del pueblo.

9. Reunir Une las oraciones de las columnas para que tengan sentido. `10.E`

1. Verás que más _____   a. cerca de los carros; es peligroso.
2. No camines muy _____   b. lejos de lo que pensábamos.
3. No estamos nada _____   c. fuera del teatro.
4. El teatro estaba mucho más _____   d. lejos del museo de la ciudad. ¡Tenemos que ir!
5. No te quedes demasiado _____   e. atrás: ¡te perderé de vista!
6. Hay mucha gente esperando _____   f. adelante hay una tienda con un cartel anaranjado.

10. Elegir Elige la opción correcta para cada oración. `10.E`

1. ¡La camisa azul está _____ (delante/adelante) de tus ojos. ¿Cómo no la ves?
2. ¡Cuidado! Si das dos pasos hacia _____ (detrás/atrás), pisarás al gato.
3. Ven _____ (dentro/adentro). Hace mucho frío para estar allí.
4. _____ (Debajo/Abajo) de esa cama, encontrarás muchas cajas.
5. Mira hacia _____ (encima/arriba): el techo tiene mucha humedad.
6. _____ (Dentro/Adentro) de la tienda, la temperatura es óptima.

11. Preguntas Escribe las preguntas para estas respuestas. Debes usar *dónde* o *adónde*. `10.E`

> **Modelo**
>
> *¿Dónde naciste?*
> Yo nací en Guatemala.

1. _____
   Iremos al centro comercial para comprar regalos.
2. _____
   Nos encontraremos en el restaurante chino a las diez.
3. _____
   Juana podrá dormir en mi cuarto.
4. _____
   Por la mañana, viajaremos a Jaén.
5. _____
   El avión aterrizará en el aeropuerto internacional.
6. _____
   Iremos a comer a la casa de la abuela.
7. _____
   Voy al gimnasio para levantar pesas.
8. _____
   Alfonso está en la biblioteca.

12. Completar Completa las oraciones con adverbios negativos, afirmativos o de duda. `10.F`

| no | quizás | sí (2) | también | tampoco | ~~tal vez~~ |

> **Modelo**
>
> El mesero no me trajo la cuenta. _Tal vez_ no me escuchó bien.

1. Qué bien que vendrás al cine. Te gustan las palomitas de maíz, ¿_____?
2. _____, iremos a la fiesta esta noche.
3. _____ termine de leer el libro este fin de semana... pero no estoy segura.
4. ¡Somos de la misma ciudad! Yo _____ vivo en Nueva York.
5. _____, mi madre vendrá por la tarde. ¿Necesitas hablar únicamente con ella?
6. Camila _____ tendrá vacaciones. Nos quedaremos las dos en la oficina.

13. Posición Coloca los adverbios en el lugar adecuado. `10.G`

> **Modelo**
>
> Juan Diego _____ corrió _____ _rápido_ _____ para alcanzar el bus en la estación. (rápido)

1. Los obreros perezosos _____ están _____ cansados. (siempre)
2. La bailarina _____ se vistió _____ para la presentación. (elegantemente)
3. Todos los equipos _____ jugaron _____ durante el campeonato. (limpio)
4. La vendedora _____ miró _____ al cliente cuando iba a pagar con cheque. (raro)
5. El capitán odia repetir órdenes. Por eso siempre _____ habla _____. (claro)
6. El anfitrión _____ presentó _____ a los invitados. (cuidadosa y graciosamente)
7. La enfermera dijo: "_____ respire _____ antes de aplicarle la inyección". (hondo)
8. El papá _____ sujetó _____ la correa del perro. Por eso escapó. (débilmente)

14. Adverbios Reemplaza las palabras subrayadas con adverbios terminados en -*mente*. `10.G–10.H`

> **Modelo**
>
> Al final todo se resolvío. _Finalmente_

1. Me di cuenta de que estaba enamorada de él con locura. _____
2. De repente, todos se habían ido ¡y yo estaba sola! _____
3. Te lo digo con sinceridad: ese vestido no es bonito. _____
4. Podríamos comunicarnos por teléfono, ¿te parece mejor? _____
5. La exhibición salió de maravilla. Ojalá hubieras venido. _____
6. Creo con firmeza en los ideales de nuestro partido. _____
7. Hazlo con tranquilidad y sin apuro. _____
8. Debes tratar a todos con cortesía. _____
9. Ahora sí que lo veo con claridad. _____

15. Convertir Transforma los adjetivos o las locuciones adverbiales entre paréntesis en adverbios. Ten presentes los acentos, donde sean necesarios. `10.G–10.H`

> **Modelo**
>
> Mi tía decora ___*magníficamente*___ la casa antes de las fiestas navideñas. (de forma magnífica)

1. Susana es una gran líder. Ella participa _____ en la toma de decisiones. (activa)

2. Liliana trata tan _____ a los demás que a todos les cae bien. (amistoso)

3. Jorge intentó _____ clavar una puntilla con un alicate. (de forma inútil)

4. La mamá le hablaba a su pequeño hijo _____. (con frecuencia)

5. El estudiante se dedicó _____ a repasar cuando ya poco podía hacer. (tardío)

6. Este periódico se encuentra _____ en puestos de revista. (por lo común)

7. Marcos se sube tan _____ al árbol que parece un mono. (rápido)

8. Puedes resolver el problema por lógica. No necesitas calcularlo _____. (de forma matemática)

9. Siempre habló de su novio _____. (con cariño)

10. No hay mejor forma para resolver las diferencias que _____. (de forma pacífica)

16. Emparejar Une las locuciones adverbiales con su significado. `10.H`

_____ 1. a lo grande   a. finalmente

_____ 2. a menudo   b. con todo lujo

_____ 3. en buenas manos   c. a largo plazo

_____ 4. por fin   d. bueno...

_____ 5. en fin   e. casi

_____ 6. de primera mano   f. con frecuencia

_____ 7. por poco   g. por experiencia propia

_____ 8. a la larga   h. a cargo de alguien responsable

17. Reescribir Reescribe las oraciones usando el comparativo. `10.I`

> **Modelo**
>
> Al paciente le duele poco a la madrugada, pero le duele mucho por las tardes.
> Al paciente por las tardes... *le duele peor que a la madrugada*.

1. Por la tarde, yo trabajo bien. Por la noche, trabajo muy bien.
   Por la noche... _____

2. Claudia dormía mal. Claudia ahora duerme bien.
   Claudia ahora... _____

3. Este año peso poco. El año pasado pesaba mucho.
   Este año... _____

4. Andrés lee rápido. Juan lee muy rápido.
   Andrés... _____

5. En España, se vive bien. En Francia, se vive muy bien.
   En España... _____

6. Mi hermana estudia frecuentemente. Mi hermano estudia muy pocas veces.
   Mi hermana... _____

18. Exageraciones Completa las exageraciones de Simón usando el superlativo absoluto. `10.I`

> **Modelo**
>
> Vimos una película que nos impactó fuertemente.
> No, vimos una película que *nos impactó fuertísimamente*.

1. Este hombre conduce lento.
   No, este hombre _____.

2. Dormimos tranquilamente toda la noche.
   No, dormimos _____.

3. Ulises comió mucho en casa.
   No, Ulises _____.

4. Isabel respondió las preguntas inteligentemente.
   No, Isabel _____.

5. Como no sabía el camino, Paula llegó tarde.
   No, como _____.

6. Nuestros padres vinieron pronto cuando conocieron la noticia.
   No, nuestros padres _____.

19. Síntesis Clasificar Clasifica estos adverbios según su clase. Marca con una X en la casilla que les corresponda. `10.A–10.I`

Adverbios	Tiempo	Modo	Cantidad	Lugar
1. nunca				
2. bastante				
3. allí				
4. rápidamente				
5. cerca				
6. rara vez				
7. mañana				
8. mucho				
9. peor				
10. con frecuencia				
11. poco				
12. delante				
13. tranquilamente				
14. arriba				
15. así				
16. demasiado				

20. Síntesis Completar Completa las oraciones con las palabras de la lista. `10.A–10.I`

allá	jamás	cuándo	suficiente	como	~~ahora~~
muy	primero	tampoco	bien	dónde	

Modelo

Antes no sabía lo que quería, pero _____*ahora*_____ lo sé perfectamente.

1. No quieres ir al cine y _____ al teatro. ¿Qué quieres hacer entonces?
2. _____ haría una excursión por la montaña. Sabes que le tengo fobia a las arañas.
3. _____ cortas la cebolla y luego la fríes.
4. La peluquería está más _____.
5. Estudia _____ bien este tema: seguramente será importante para el examen.
6. He comprado un teléfono _____ pequeño.
7. Ya he comido _____, creo que no comeré postre.
8. ¿A _____ vamos esta noche?
9. Haré la comida _____ tú me digas.
10. La maestra nos dijo exactamente _____ entregar la tarea.

21. Síntesis Reunir Encuentra los ejemplos de las afirmaciones y escribe en el espacio en blanco la letra correspondiente. `10.A–10.J`

_____ 1. un adverbio de tiempo utilizado en una pregunta indirecta

_____ 2. adverbios usados de manera frecuente en Latinoamérica en forma diminutiva

_____ 3. un adverbio utilizado de manera comparativa

_____ 4. uso de una locución adverbial que se interpreta así: de forma excelente

_____ 5. un adverbio de modo antes de un adjetivo que funciona como un adverbio intensificador

_____ 6. adverbio de lugar que indica una ubicación indefinida

_____ 7. adverbio de cantidad que expresa exceso o exageración

_____ 8. combinación de adverbios de tiempo que crean una negación muy fuerte

_____ 9. adverbio de lugar que indica que algo se encuentra cerca de quien habla

_____ 10. adverbio de tiempo que indica la más alta frecuencia

a. La presentadora expuso el tema a las mil maravillas.

b. Nunca jamás volveré a pedirte un favor.

c. Hijo, no dejes tu ropa sucia por ahí.

d. Aquí se recicla el papel.

e. No sé cuándo volverá mi primo.

f. Javier se ejercita demasiado.

g. Siempre desayuno cereal con leche y frutas.

h. Necesito estar bien despierto antes de presentar el examen.

i. Señor, enseguidita le ayudo.

j. El policía reaccionó más instintiva que lógicamente en esa situación.

22. Síntesis Describir Describe los tres lugares que más frecuentas y dónde están ubicados. Utiliza adverbios de tiempo, de modo, de cantidad y de lugar. `10.A-10.J`

> **Modelo**
>
> *En mi universidad, voy diariamente a la cafetería…*

_____

_____

_____

_____

_____

_____

🅢 Practice more at **vhlcentral.com.**

Comparison 🎾 ⟋   Chapter 11

1. Escoger Completa las oraciones con las opciones de la lista. `11.B`

> de (2)   de lo que
> que (3)   de los que
>   de las que

1. Me gusta más _____ pensaba.

2. Tengo más trabajo _____ tú.

3. Asisto a más _____ seis clases en la universidad.

4. Hoy me siento peor _____ ayer.

5. Compré más libros _____ tenía pensado.

6. Fotografié más plazas _____ pensaba.

7. A veces duermo menos _____ lo necesario.

8. No juego más _____ fútbol.

2. Irregulares Identifica cuáles de estos adjetivos y adverbios tienen comparativos irregulares. Escribe las formas irregulares. `11.B`

> **Modelo**   **Modelo**
>
> guapo *regular*   joven *irregular: menor*

1. malo _____   5. sucio _____   9. alto _____

2. rápido _____   6. oscuro _____   10. ordenado _____

3. poco _____   7. llano _____   11. blando _____

4. viejo (edad) _____   8. mucho _____   12. bueno _____

3. Completar Completa las oraciones usando el comparativo. `11.B`

El autobús es rápido.
El tren es muy rápido.
El tren _____*es más rápido que el autobús*_____ .

1. En Buenos Aires, hace calor.
En Lima, hace mucho calor.
En Lima, _____ .

2. La maestra de biología es joven.
La maestra de matemáticas es muy joven.
La maestra de matemáticas _____ .

3. Juana es buena en voleibol.
Carina es muy buena en voleibol.
Carina _____ .

4. Por la mañana llovió poco.
Por la tarde llovió mucho.
Por la mañana _____ .

5. *Ted* es mala.
Ted 2 es muy mala.
Ted 2 _____ .

4. Comparar Haz comparaciones entre Martín y Susana. Sigue el modelo. `11.B`

> **Modelo**
>
> Martín comió poco.   *Martín comió menos que Susana.*
> Susana comió mucho.   *Susana comió más que Martín.*

1. Martín corre 15 minutos por día.
Susana corre 30 minutos por día.
_____
_____

2. Martín tiene dos perros.
Susana tiene un perro.
_____
_____

3. Martín duerme 8 horas.
Susana duerme 9 horas.
_____
_____

4. Martín habla poco español.
Susana habla mucho español.
_____
_____

5. Martín hizo dos tortas.
Susana hizo una torta.
_____
_____

6. Martín es alto.
Susana es baja.
_____
_____

5. Reescribir Reescribe las oraciones usando las expresiones indicadas. `11.B`

> **Modelo**
>
> Mis horarios actuales son distintos a los que tenía antes. (diferentes)
> *Mis horarios actuales son diferentes de/a los que tenía antes.*

1. En agosto, tengo aproximadamente dos semanas de vacaciones. (más de)
_____

2. Durante el verano, voy más seguido al parque. (bastante)
_____

3. Vivimos en un barrio céntrico. (relativamente)
_____

4. Cuando estoy a dieta, bebo solamente agua mineral. (más que)
_____

5. Dormí la siesta y ahora tengo poco sueño. (menos)
_____

6. Mis manos son más delicadas que tus manos. (tuyas)
_____

6. Relato Completa el relato de Cecilia utilizando las opciones de la lista. 11.C

> tal como
> tan (3)
> misma
> igual
> tanto
> como
> mismo
> ~~tantas~~

¡Qué día!

Otra vez comenzaron las clases. Debo ir todos los días de 9 de la mañana a 12 del día y luego de 3 a 5 de la tarde ¡Cada año se consiguen (1) _____tantas_____ amistades como cuando sales de viaje!

Pero a veces me siento (2) _____ desorientado como cuando alguien comienza a trabajar en un lugar desconocido.

La maestra no es la (3) _____ que el año pasado. Ahora tenemos a la señorita Gómez, que es (4) _____ de aburrida que la señorita Albornoz, y nos hace trabajar (5) _____ como quiere. Y lo peor es que siempre nos manda hacer lo (6) _____ que hicimos el año pasado.

Solamente espero que este año no se me haga (7) _____ largo (8) _____ el año pasado. (9) _____ dijo mamá, no debería ser (10) _____ pesimista. Y tiene razón: mirándolo del lado positivo, ya falta un día menos para que terminen las clases.

7. Oraciones Forma oraciones lógicas combinando elementos de las tres columnas. 11.C

1. La historia no fue tal	tanto	como sea posible estas vacaciones.
2. Tamara tiene	tantos	de alta que yo.
3. Debo leer	igual	me la contaste. Fue más trágica.
4. Conduce exactamente a la	como	rápido como puedas, antes de que se enfríe.
5. Estela es	misma	mala suerte.
6. No entiendo cómo pude tener	tanta	velocidad que indica el cartel.
7. Come tu tarta	tan	libros que no ha leído aún.

_____
_____
_____
_____
_____
_____
_____

8. Contradecir Isabel contradice a su hermana Eugenia. Completa la conversación con expresiones que indiquen igualdad o desigualdad. `11.B–11.C`

EUGENIA ¿Qué te pareció la fiesta de ayer? Para mí, fue la mejor del año.

ISABEL De ninguna manera, (1) _____ *fue la peor del año* _____.

EUGENIA Pero había más invitados que en la fiesta de Juan. Eso no lo puedes negar...

ISABEL No, había (2) _____ que en esa fiesta.

EUGENIA Y la música era distinta todo el tiempo.

ISABEL No, era siempre (3) _____.

EUGENIA ¡Y bailamos muchísimo!

ISABEL No, ¡(4) _____!

EUGENIA Ay, Isabel, parece que no estuvimos en la misma fiesta. ¡Nunca me había divertido tanto!

ISABEL No, ¡nunca (5) _____!

EUGENIA ¿Y la comida? Yo comí muchísimo, ¿y tú?

ISABEL Yo comí (6) _____ y no bebí (7) _____ un vaso de agua.

EUGENIA ¡Qué increíble que seamos hermanas!

ISABEL ¡Sí! ¡Es increíble que seamos de la (8) _____ familia!

9. Comparaciones Cambia las comparaciones usando la palabra indicada. `11.B–11.C`

> **Modelo**
>
> Marta tiene una blusa tal como la de Ana María. (misma)
> *Marta y Ana María tienen la misma blusa.*

1. Catalina es más alta que su madre. (igual)

   _____

2. Tatiana tiene más vestidos que sus amigas. (tantos)

   _____

3. Mis notas son tan buenas como las tuyas. (mejores)

   _____

4. La primera parte de esta película es peor que la segunda. (tan)

   _____

5. Tú no comes más que yo. (tanto)

   _____

6. Mis calcetines son tal como los tuyos. (diferentes)

   _____

7. Daniel trabaja tanto como Pablo. (menos)

   _____

8. Mi camiseta es igual a la tuya. (distinta)

   _____

10. Anuncio Completa este anuncio publicitario con las palabras de la lista. `11.D`

verdaderamente	~~novedosísimo~~	lo más	lo mejor (2)	pequeñísimo
óptimo	ínfimo	practiquísimo	extraordinariamente	

Chaumanchas

En esta oportunidad, le ofrecemos *Chaumanchas*, el (1) _____novedosísimo_____ quitamanchas de bolsillo. Gracias a su envase (2) _____ pequeño, puede llevarlo con usted adonde vaya. Este quitamanchas es (3) _____ para madres de niños que se manchan todo el tiempo o para personas que viajan por negocios. *Chaumanchas* tiene una efectividad (4) _____ increíble: elimina manchas de aceite, grasa, tinta, ¡y muchísimas más!

¡Llame ya! ¡Le enviaremos este producto (5) _____ rápido posible! De esta manera, recibirá (6) _____ del mercado directamente en su hogar. Y (7) _____ de todo: con la compra de este (8) _____ producto, recibirá gratis un (9) _____ cepillo quitamanchas. *Chaumanchas*, el máximo poder quitamanchas en un (10) _____ envase.

11. Superlativo Reescribe las oraciones usando el superlativo. `11.D`

> **Modelo**
>
> Este auto es mejor que el resto de los autos. (todos)
> *Este auto es el mejor de todos.*

1. Los productos de nuestra compañía son mejores que los de la competencia. (mercado)

   _____

2. Sebastián es más alto que los compañeros de su clase. (clase)

   _____

3. Este sofá tiene una calidad peor que los demás sofás. (todos)

   _____

4. La música de esta radio es mejor que la de otras radios del país. (país)

   _____

5. Juanito es más pequeño que sus hermanos. (familia)

   _____

6. Mis ensaladas son más deliciosas que las demás. (concurso de cocina)

   _____

7. Mi padre es mayor que los demás padres. (todos)

   _____

12. Síntesis Seleccionar Completa las oraciones con la opción correcta. `11.B–11.D`

1. Caminar es _____ agotador que patinar.
   a. tan   b. más   c. tanto

2. Cómprate un colchón _____ que el que tienes y dormirás muy bien.
   a. más bueno   b. óptimo   c. mejor

3. Compré el mejor teléfono celular _____ tenían en la tienda.
   a. que   b. como   c. de

4. Tienes más _____ cien películas en tu tableta.
   a. que   b. como   c. de

5. Cristina es la empleada que _____ contacto tiene con los clientes.
   a. mejor   b. más   c. buenísimo

6. El fútbol es totalmente distinto _____ los demás deportes.
   a. como   b. a   c. que

7. Esta casa es _____ que las de los alrededores.
   a. mayor   b. más antigua c. menor

8. Aprender chino es más difícil _____ pensaba.
   a. de los que   b. de lo que   c. que

13. Síntesis Escribir Reescribe las oraciones a partir de las indicaciones dadas. `11.B–11.D`

> **Modelo**
>
> Las zapatillas de esta marca son buenas. + / el mercado
> *Las zapatillas de esta marca son las mejores del mercado.*

1. Roma es una ciudad romántica. – / Venecia
   _____

2. El carro azul es muy elegante. = / el carro rojo
   _____

3. Esta vendedora es realmente encantadora. + / el mundo
   _____

4. La tarea de hoy es fácil. – / la tarea de ayer
   _____

5. Este periódico es muy conocido. + / el país
   _____

6. Puedo comprar tantos zapatos como tú. – / tú
   _____

7. Tus tartas son las mejores que he probado. = / tartas de mi madre
   _____

8. La Plaza Mayor de Madrid es grandísima. + / España
   _____

14. Síntesis Películas Realiza cinco comparaciones de películas de distintos géneros utilizando comparativos. `11.B–11.D`

> **Modelo**
>
> *Las películas animadas son más cortas que las películas de terror...*

_____
_____
_____
_____
_____

Practice more at **vhlcentral.com.**

1. Artículo Completa el artículo con las preposiciones de la lista. `12.A`

de	durante	entre	hasta	sobre
desde	en	excepto	~~para~~	tras

Un lugar inolvidable

(1) _____*Para*_____ todos aquellos que desean pasar unas vacaciones de lujo, les recomendamos el hotel *Mar Azul*.

Este hotel se encuentra (2) _____ la costa del océano Atlántico y posee más de doscientas habitaciones. (3) _____ el siglo XX, allí se hospedaron innumerables famosos (4) _____ la farándula (*show business*) de América Latina; (5) _____ ellos, Luis Miguel y Santana.

(6) _____ 2004 (7) _____ 2006, el hotel permaneció cerrado al público por reformas. (8) _____ las remodelaciones, *Mar Azul* reabrió sus puertas, (9) _____ las zonas de sauna y masajes, que se abrieron (10) _____ 2007.

Desde entonces, el grandioso hotel alberga diariamente a más de 300 huéspedes.

2. Reformular Reescribe las oraciones usando las palabras de la lista. Haz los cambios necesarios. `12.A`

o	pro (2)	versus (2)	vía	y

Modelo

Los presidentes aprobaron planes en favor de la infancia.
Los países aprobaron planes en pro de la infancia.

1. Hoy en la televisión podremos ver el partido del Real Madrid contra el Barcelona.

   _____

2. Fui a París. Camino a París pasé por Londres.

   _____

3. Tobías trabaja para una organización que está a favor de los derechos de los animales.

   _____

4. Arriba de la nevera hay suciedad. Debajo de la nevera también hay suciedad.

   _____

5. Mira el gráfico del precio de alquiler frente al precio de compra.

   _____

6. ¿Nos encontramos enfrente del gimnasio? ¿Nos encontramos detrás del gimnasio?

   _____

3. Combinar Combina elementos de las tres columnas para formar oraciones lógicas. `12.A`

1. Yo no tengo nada en	sin	boleto.
2. Seamos sinceras,	entre	de su cama.
3. Mi casa está muy	contra	él y tú hay problemas.
4. Me encanta dormir la siesta	hacia	de tus amigos.
5. No puedes subir al autobús	bajo	el naranjo.
6. El papel de carta está	sobre	el escritorio.
7. Mi hermana cree que hay monstruos	debajo	el norte.
8. Las brújulas siempre apuntan	lejos	del parque de diversiones.

_____

_____

_____

_____

_____

_____

_____

_____

4. Carta Observa el mapa y completa la carta con las preposiciones de la lista. `12.A`

al lado de   cerca de   ~~de~~   delante de   en   hasta   lejos de   sobre

Querida Claudia:

¿Cómo estás? Te escribo para contarte sobre mi barrio nuevo... ¡que me encanta!

Vivo en una casa en la esquina (1) _____de_____ la calle Latina y la avenida América. (2) _____ mi casita, a la izquierda, está la escuela; y, a la derecha, la biblioteca. (3) _____ la avenida América, no muy (4) _____ mi casa, está el parque Robles. (5) _____ este parque, está el hospital. La semana pasada fuimos allí con mi mamá porque ella no se sentía muy bien. Mientras ella estaba con el médico, fui (6) _____ el kiosco, que queda justo (7) _____ diagonal al hospital, y me compré un refresco. Y, como estaba tan (8) _____ la heladería, me compré también un helado.

¿No te parece genial? ¡Es un barrio que lo tiene todo!

Espero que vengas a visitarme pronto.

Saludos,

Yolanda

	Iglesia	**A**		
		v		
	Hospital	**e**		
		n	Parque	
		i		
		d		
		a		
Calle Latina				
		A		
Escuela	Casa	**m**	Kiosco	Heladería
		é		
Biblioteca		**r**		
		i		
		c		
		a		

5. Reordenar Reordena las oraciones para que tengan sentido. `12.A`

> el reporte / todo / clima / el día / según / Lloverá / del
> *Lloverá todo el día según el reporte del clima.*

1. estoy / pro / de la / Yo / reforma constitucional / en

   _____

2. por / entre / gato / se perdió / El / las malezas

   _____

3. tu demora, / A / causa / el tren / de / perdimos

   _____

4. fue / a / Carola / una / por / barra de pan

   _____

5. Willy / Tengo / para / con / una obligación

   _____

6. y negra / es roja / fuera / por / dentro / La chaqueta / por

   _____

7. cuanto / En / a / deberás comprar / los zapatos, / unos nuevos

   _____

8. las entrevistas / Son / mejores / cara / cara / a

   _____

9. general, / las películas / lo / prefiero / de terror / Por

   _____

10. regreso / leche / Compraremos / de / al hostal

   _____

6. Terminar Completa estas oraciones con *a, con, de* y *en*. `12.B`

> ¿Me pasas, por favor, esa caja ___*de*___ cartón?

1. La pescadería está _____ dos cuadras de mi casa.
2. La cita es _____ las cuatro de la tarde.
3. Debes estar _____ silencio. La abuela duerme la siesta.
4. _____ gusto, te ayudo a poner la mesa.
5. Todas estas son carteras _____ Rocío.
6. Deja de hablar por teléfono _____ tu novio. ¡La factura será carísima!
7. Escríbele un mensaje de texto _____ Juan y dile que llegaremos tarde.
8. El maestro _____ español nos da muchísima tarea.
9. _____ agosto, iremos a las montañas.
10. _____ los nueve años, viajé por primera vez a Disney World.

7. Anuncio Completa este anuncio con *a, con* o *de*. Incluye el artículo o el pronombre personal si corresponde. `12.B`

Feria (1) ___*de*___ **las Naciones**: miles de culturas en un solo lugar
(2) _____ 20 (3) _____ 29 (4) _____ agosto, en el centro (5) _____ exposiciones
de la Ciudad de Buenos Aires, podrás visitar la Feria de las Naciones. Allí podrás comprar
productos (6) _____ todos los países (7) _____ mundo: salchichas (8) _____ Alemania,
perfumes (9) _____ Francia y mucho más. ¡Es como si estuvieras de viaje por todo el
mundo! Ven ¡y trae (10) _____ tus amigos!

8. ¿*Para* o *por*? Completa las oraciones con la preposición correcta. `12.B`

> **Modelo**
>
> El autobús que va ___*para*___ Quito sale a las ocho de la mañana.

1. No tengo tiempo _____ ir de compras contigo.
2. _____ las tardes, estudio muchísimo.
3. _____ el dolor de garganta, te recomiendo que tomes un té con miel.
4. _____ fin, estamos de vacaciones. Necesito descansar de la escuela.
5. Lucía trabaja _____ una compañía farmacéutica.
6. _____ mí, esa película fue la mejor del año.
7. ¿Viajas _____ placer?
8. La biblioteca es un lugar _____ leer, ¡silencio!

9. ¿Con *a* o sin ella? Decide si es necesario usar *a* en estas oraciones. Si no es necesario, escribe X. `12.B`

> **Modelo**
>
> ¡Préstale atención ___*a*___ tu hija! Quiere mostrarte lo que aprendió en la escuela.

1. Julia conoce _____ todos sus clientes.
2. ¿Por qué le trajiste flores _____ Paula si no es una ocasión especial?
3. Se buscan _____ profesores de física.
4. Tengo _____ demasiados compañeros de trabajo. No puedo invitarlos _____ todos.
5. Nos dijo el mecánico que debemos ponerle aceite _____ la motocicleta.
6. ¡Cuánto extraño _____ mi casa!
7. ¡Cómo me gustaría visitar _____ Ulises!
8. No encontramos _____ las maletas al bajar del avión.

10. Elegir Elige la opción correcta en cada oración. `12.B`

1. ¿_____ (Para/De) dónde vienes?

2. _____ (Desde/De) mañana, me despertaré temprano.

3. Recuerda pasar _____ (por/entre) la panadería antes de venir a casa.

4. Camina _____ (tras/hasta) la esquina. Cuando estés allí, dobla a la izquierda.

5. La tienda está abierta _____ (de/desde) 3 a 8.

6. ¿_____ (De/Para) dónde vamos esta noche?

7. _____ (Durante/En) tres días, llegarán mis padres.

8. La bicicleta está apoyada _____ (contra / encima de) la pared.

9. _____ (Salvo/Con) nuestra ayuda, usted podrá conseguir un puesto de trabajo.

10. _____ (Ante/Tras) una tormenta, siempre llega la calma.

11. Oraciones Completa las oraciones con la preposición correcta. `12.B`

> **Modelo**
>
> Solo hay una bella amistad *entre* tú y yo.

1. Llegamos a Boston _____ las ocho.

2. Vi _____ Juan en el parque.

3. Necesito una tabla _____ planchar nueva.

4. No llegué puntualmente _____ tu culpa.

5. Si no tienes el ensayo listo _____ el jueves, el profesor te quitará un punto.

6. Se movía _____ mucha lentitud.

7. Parece que este carro estuviera hecho _____ plástico.

8. La Casa Rosada se encuentra _____ la ciudad de Buenos Aires.

12. Preposiciones Vuelve a leer las oraciones de la *actividad 11*. Identifica la preposición a la que se refiere cada explicación. `12.B`

> **Modelo**
>
> Se usan otros dos pronombres en lugar de **mí** y **ti** después de esta preposición o de **según**, **excepto** y **salvo**. *entre*

1. Se usa para referirse a una causa o justificación. _____

2. Se usa para referirse a una fecha límite. _____

3. Se usa antes de un verbo para expresar propósito. _____

4. Se usa con sustantivos en locuciones adverbiales de modo. _____

5. Se usa con objetos directos cuando refieren a personas. _____

6. La preposición especifica dónde se encuentra una persona o cosa. _____

7. Se usa para referirse al material con el que están fabricados los objetos. _____

8. Se usa para referirse a una hora determinada. _____

13. Reescribir Reescribe estas oraciones usando la preposición entre paréntesis. `12.B`

> **Modelo**
>
> Debido a este aumento de salario, podré ahorrar un poco más de dinero. (con)
> *Con este aumento de salario, podré ahorrar un poco más de dinero.*

1. Karina cortó el papel usando unas tijeras. (con)

   _____

2. Isabela es española. (de)

   _____

3. Tengo mal humor. (de)

   _____

4. Llegó una carta destinada a ti. (para)

   _____

5. La señora que tiene cabello rubio se quedó dormida. (de)

   _____

6. Perdimos el barco a causa de la marea. (por)

   _____

14. Síntesis Seleccionar Elige la preposición correcta para completar estas oraciones. `12.A–12.C`

1. _____ tu ayuda, no podremos salvar el planeta.
   a. Con   b. Sin   c. En

2. _____ La Habana, verás qué amable que es la gente.
   a. De   b. En   c. Hasta

3. Hay un teléfono _____ la oficina de la directora.
   a. de   b. en   c. entre

4. _____ el año pasado, vivimos en este edificio.
   a. Desde   b. De   c. Entre

5. ¿Cuál es la diferencia _____ **casar** y **cazar**?
   a. en   b. de   c. entre

6. _____ la lluvia, tuvimos que quedarnos en casa.
   a. De   b. Sin   c. Por

7. _____ Guadalajara, hay 1000 kilómetros.
   a. Hasta   b. Entre   c. De

8. Todos, _____ María, quieren comer pastel.
   a. durante   b. excepto   c. sin

15. Síntesis Completar Completa las oraciones con las palabras de la lista. Escribe X si no se necesita preposición. `12.A–12.C`

~~ante~~	de	desde	en	entre	hasta	para	por	sin

> **Modelo**
>
> La policía prometió llevar a los culpables _____*ante*_____ la justicia.

1. _____ el momento, no hay pruebas de que los extraterrestres existan.

2. _____ dudas, aprobaremos este examen.

3. _____ la farmacia y la carnicería está la verdulería.

4. ¿Llegó un correo electrónico _____ mí?

5. _____ muchos motivos, no quiero ir de vacaciones con ella.

6. La boda se celebró _____ la iglesia de San Pablo.

7. ¿Se puede vivir _____ la caridad?

8. ¿Conoces _____ la casa de Juan?

16. Síntesis Simples o compuestas Completa las oraciones con preposiciones simples o compuestas. `12.A–12.C`

> **Modelo**
>
> Mi primo adora los animales y es miembro de una asociación ___*en contra del*___ maltrato animal.

1. _____ regreso a casa, me topé con una manifestación.

2. Los presidentes se reunieron con miras _____ resolver la situación.

3. Aunque este es un país rico, hay mucha gente que vive _____ la pobreza.

4. No sé qué le pasa. Está _____ muy mal humor.

5. Las discrepancias se resuelven _____ el diálogo.

6. Deja la correspondencia _____ la mesa, junto al teléfono.

17. Síntesis Asociar Relaciona los ejemplos con las explicaciones. `12.A–12.C`

____ 1. Se refiere a la ubicación de algo o alguien.

____ 2. Se refiere al destinatario de algo.

____ 3. Se usa para expresar un propósito con verbos de acción.

____ 4. Se usa para mostrar que alguien hace algo en tu lugar.

____ 5. Se usa con verbos de movimiento y sustantivos en España.

____ 6. En España, se usa la preposición **en** para esta misma frase.

____ 7. Se usa para expresar posesión.

____ 8. Se usa con el verbo **estar** para describir estado o situación.

____ 9. Se usa con el verbo **estar** para expresar un trabajo temporal.

____ 10. Se usa antes de un verbo en infinitivo para indicar el propósito o uso de algo.

a. Aprendo español **para** hablar bien con mis parientes de México.

b. **En** Barcelona, encontrarás gente de todo el mundo.

c. Mis amigos están **de** visita hasta el primero de octubre.

d. Hay un mensaje **para** ti. Léelo.

e. ¿Podrías buscar a Juanito **por** mí?

f. Florencia está **de** camarera en el bar de la esquina.

g. ¿La policía viene **a por** mí? ¡Yo no hice nada!

h. Necesito una mesa **de** planchar.

i. No me interesan las vidas **de** los famosos.

j. Entré **a** la casa y se cortó la luz.

18. Síntesis Llenar Completa los espacios en blanco con la preposición (simple o compuesta) adecuada. Como pista, tienes la primera letra de cada una. `12.A–12.C`

1. H_____ la playa hay dos kilómetros.

2. S_____ mi madre, "al que madruga, Dios lo ayuda".

3. C_____ tu casa vive la profesora de matemáticas.

4. J_____ mis amigos, organizaré una gran fiesta de cumpleaños.

5. H_____ fines del siglo veinte se inventó el Bluetooth.

6. E_____ marzo y junio aquí es otoño.

7. T_____ esa expresión dura se esconde una persona muy amable.

8. E_____ Juan, todos tienen menos de dieciocho años.

9. E_____ esa época, todos trabajábamos en la misma empresa.

10. C_____ ese vestido llamarás la atención de todos los invitados.

19. Síntesis Escribir Imagina que eres un guía escolar y que ayudas a los nuevos estudiantes a llegar a sus salones. Escribe varias indicaciones utilizando como mínimo diez preposiciones. `12.A–12.C`

> **Modelo**
>
> *¿El laboratorio? Camina por la derecha, hacia el salón de material audiovisual, hasta la cancha. Está justo al frente.*

_____

_____

_____

_____

_____

_____

_____

_____

_____

_____

_____

Practice more at **vhlcentral.com**.

Personal pronouns   Chapter 13

1. Reemplazar Reemplaza el texto subrayado con el pronombre adecuado. `13.A–13.B`

> **Modelo**
>
> Camila y yo jugamos a las cartas toda la tarde. _Nosotros/as_

1. ¿Sofía viene a la fiesta de fin de año? _____
2. Sandra y Facundo están durmiendo. _____
3. La abuela vendrá de visita el fin de semana. _____
4. Mi padre y yo somos arquitectos. _____
5. Romina y Laura son estudiantes de quinto año. _____
6. Mi hermana, mi padre y yo iremos de vacaciones a las montañas. _____

2. Pronombres Completa las oraciones. `13.A–13.B`

> **Modelo**
>
> La palabra _lo_ puede reemplazar una oración completa o una idea.

1. En muchas regiones de Latinoamérica se usa de manera informal el pronombre _____ en lugar de **tú**.
2. _____ y _____ son las abreviaturas de **usted** y **ustedes**.
3. El pronombre plural *you* en inglés tiene dos equivalentes en español: **ustedes** y _____.
4. La palabra _____ no tiene plural y se usa en español como sinónimo de **eso**.
5. En Latinoamérica, el pronombre plural _____ se utiliza tanto de manera formal como informal.

3. Decidir ¿Formal o informal? Decide quién dice cada oración. `13.A–13.B`

_____ 1. Le prometo que, de ahora en adelante, llegaré temprano todos los días.

_____ 2. ¿Podría decirme dónde está la juguetería, por favor?

_____ 3. No me molestes más, ¿acaso no ves que estoy estudiando?

_____ 4. Vosotros debéis respetar las reglas.

_____ 5. Ustedes prometieron organizar competencias deportivas para nosotros.

_____ 6. ¿Quieres darme tu teléfono celular?

a. un empleado a su jefe

b. un niño a su hermano

c. una niña a un anciano

d. un director de escuela a los alumnos

e. una amiga a otra

f. un alumno a las autoridades escolares

4. Oraciones Completa cada oración con la forma adecuada del pronombre después de la preposición. Sigue el modelo. `13.C`

Modelo

El fotógrafo se reprochaba a _sí_ (él) mismo por no empacar el trípode.

1. Lee este mensaje en privado. Es solo para _____ (tú).

2. Hoy discutimos con los vecinos. ¡Qué raro!, entre _____ (nosotros) nunca ha habido problemas.

3. Los turistas se llevaron con_____ (ellos) todos los recuerdos que compraron.

4. ¡Paren el autobús! No se vayan sin _____ (yo).

5. ¡Qué bueno que la policía estuvo con_____ (tú) durante la emergencia!

6. El gerente despidió a tres buenos compañeros. Muchos lloramos por _____ (ellos).

7. La profesora se enojó con_____ (yo) porque no traje la tarea.

8. Todos fuimos egoístas excepto _____ (tú), Mariana.

5. Completar Completa las oraciones con las palabras de la lista. `13.A–13.C`

vosotros	mí
yo	ti
él	conmigo
tú	consigo

Modelo

¿Vas _tú_ o voy yo al supermercado?

1. Para _____, este programa de televisión es muy malo. Pero es solo mi opinión, obviamente.

2. Carlos no está contento _____ mismo.

3. Entre Gabriela y _____ hay muchos conflictos. Debemos hablar sobre eso.

4. Según _____, todos deberíamos trabajar de lunes a lunes.

5. Rita es colombiana y _____ eres venezolano, ¿no?

6. _____ sabéis que es importante mantener la imagen de la empresa.

7. Tengo un regalo hermoso para _____. Te encantará.

8. _____ vivirás despreocupada. Verás que soy una persona muy tranquila.

6. Reescribir Reescribe las oraciones reemplazando el objeto directo por el pronombre correspondiente. **13.E**

> **Modelo**
>
> Ana María tenía el cabello desarreglado.
> *Ana María lo tenía desarreglado.*

1. Roberto compró naranjas en el mercado central. _____

2. Llamamos al abuelo porque lo extrañábamos. _____

3. Julia estudió muy bien la lección de gramática. _____

4. Finalmente la policía atrapó al ladrón. _____

5. Gonzalo buscó sus zapatillas debajo de la mesa. _____

6. Los funcionarios se toman un café a las dos de la tarde. _____

7. Constanza y Sofía quieren mucho a sus madres. _____

8. Traje los libros de la biblioteca. _____

7. Contestar Contesta las preguntas sobre los preparativos para una fiesta. Usa pronombres de objeto directo en tus respuestas. **13.E**

> **Modelo**
>
> ¿Quién compra los globos? (Enrique)
> *Enrique los compra.*

1. ¿Quién limpia la sala? (Isabel y Manuel) _____

2. ¿Quién trae las bebidas? (Ricardo) _____

3. ¿Quién hace el pastel? (Claudia) _____

4. ¿Quién prepara la paella? (Andrea) _____

5. ¿Quién compra el helado? (Victoria) _____

6. ¿Quién sirve los entremeses? (Sandra y Antonio) _____

8. Escribir Usa los fragmentos para escribir oraciones, reemplazando el objeto indirecto por el pronombre correspondiente. **13.F**

> **Modelo**
>
> la niña / echó / maíz / a las palomas en el parque
> *La niña les echó maíz en el parque.*

1. Julia / dio / una bufanda / a su hermana _____

2. dijiste / mentiras / a tus compañeros de clase _____

3. ellos / contaron historias de terror / a nuestros hermanos _____

4. el camarero / recomendó / una paella / a los turistas _____

5. tu madre / mostró / al cliente / la habitación _____

6. hoy leerás / a tu hermanito / un cuento de hadas _____

7. pedí / dinero / a mis padres _____

8. los músicos / ofrecieron / un gran espectáculo / al público _____

9. **Marcar** **Lee el relato de Josefina. Primero, marca todos los pronombres de objeto indirecto. Luego subraya el sujeto de las oraciones marcadas.** `13.F`

Soy una persona un poco complicada. No me gusta salir de casa. Me molesta mucho el ruido de los carros y motocicletas. Por eso, prefiero estar en casa.

Me gusta leer novelas: sobre todo, me interesan las novelas románticas. Además, me encanta ver comedias en la televisión. Ojalá algún día encuentre a mi pareja ideal. Un hombre a quien le guste mirar televisión conmigo, le interesen las noticias de la actualidad y le encante cocinar. ¿Os parecen demasiado grandes mis expectativas?

10. **Reescribir** **Reescribe las oraciones según el modelo.** `13.G`

> **Modelo**
>
> | Te voy a enseñar inglés. | Ella piensa prestarnos el dinero que necesitamos. |
> |---|---|
> | *Voy a enseñarte inglés.* | *Ella nos piensa prestar el dinero que necesitamos.* |

1. ¿Nos estás preparando la merienda?

   _____

2. Yo podría ayudarte con tus tareas.

   _____

3. Lucía me va a acompañar hasta la esquina.

   _____

4. El público está alentándolos.

   _____

5. La directora les va a enviar una carta de recomendación.

   _____

6. Estamos dándoles excelentes ideas para hacer un negocio.

   _____

11. **Contestar** **Lucas te hace muchas preguntas. Contéstalas usando el pronombre adecuado.** `13.G`

> **Modelo**
>
> **LUCAS** Primero que todo, ¿pediste el pastel desde ayer?
> **TÚ** *Sí, lo pedí desde ayer.*

1. **LUCAS** Falta poco para la fiesta. ¿Has comprado toda la decoración?

   TÚ Sí, _____.

2. **LUCAS** ¿Sería bueno decorar las ventanas?

   TÚ Sí, _____.

3. **LUCAS** ¿Has mandado las invitaciones?

   TÚ Sí, _____.

4. **LUCAS** ¿Has llamado a los invitados para confirmar su presencia?

   TÚ No, aún _____.

5. **LUCAS** ¿Me darás pronto la lista de invitados?

   TÚ Sí, _____.

6. **LUCAS** ¿Necesitas mi ayuda?

   TÚ ¡Gracias! Pero no _____.

12. Reemplazar Reescribe las oraciones reemplazando los complementos de objeto directo e indirecto por pronombres de objeto directo e indirecto. Ten presente la posición de los pronombres en cada oración. Sigue el modelo. **13.G**

> **Modelo**
>
> David está escribiendo una carta a sus padres.
> *David se la está escribiendo./David está escribiéndosela.*

1. Los organizadores prepararon una cena de bienvenida para nosotros. _____

2. A veces es difícil decir la verdad a los padres. _____

3. Enrique está pagando la renta a todos en la familia. _____

4. Mi hija compró la cobija al vendedor callejero sin mi permiso. _____

5. La alcaldía va a donar tabletas a los niños de escuelas públicas. _____

6. Es apropiado cambiar los televisores defectuosos a los clientes. _____

7. ¡No revises el celular a tu hijo tantas veces! _____

8. El entrenador logró conseguir uniformes para los jugadores del equipo. _____

9. Anita, ¿no has enseñado la canción a tu tía? _____

10. El médico dijo que ya podía suspender la medicina al paciente. _____

13. Completar Completa los comentarios que escribe Matías junto a cada quehacer usando pronombres para los objetos directos e indirectos. **13.G**

○	HACER TAREA ✓ *Ya la hice.* ✖ *No la he hecho.*
	LLAMAR TÍA ✓ (1)
	ARREGLAR COMPUTADORA ✖ (2)
	LLEVAR PAQUETE JUANA ✖ (3)
	BUSCAR PERRO ✓ (4)
	DAR COMIDA PERRO ✖ (5)
	DEVOLVER SILLA VECINO ✓ (6)

14. Unir Une los ejemplos con las explicaciones. **13.H**

___ 1. Se repite el objeto para enfatizar su identidad.

___ 2. Se debe repetir el objeto cuando los nombres propios están antepuestos al verbo.

___ 3. Se repite el objeto cuando hace referencia a cosas.

___ 4. Se repite el objeto cuando se hace referencia a conceptos abstractos.

___ 5. Se repite el objeto con **todo/a(s)**.

a. Los conocemos a todos.

b. Tienen que comprarle más memoria a mi computadora.

c. A Marta la vemos todos los jueves.

d. Esto jamás podremos recordarlo.

e. A mí no me mientas, ¿verdad?

15. Síntesis Emparejar Escoge la opción correcta para completar las oraciones. `13.A–13.H`

1. En la oración **Hace un ruido extraño**, algunos posibles pronombres sujeto son ____.

2. Si un objeto directo es una persona, antes se agrega ____.

3. Los pronombres sujeto **yo** y **tú** cambian a ____ después de casi todas las preposiciones.

4. Un ____ contesta las preguntas ¿a quién? o ¿para quién? se realiza la acción de la oración.

5. El ____ son dos formas de tratamiento informales en español.

6. Usar **le/les** en casos de pronombres masculinos de objeto directo en algunas zonas de América Latina y en España se denomina ____.

a. la preposición **a**

b. objeto indirecto

c. leísmo

d. él, ella, ello, eso

e. tuteo y voseo

f. mí, ti

16. Síntesis Escoger Selecciona los pronombres adecuados. `13.A–13.H`

1. Traje muchas flores para _____.
   te   tú   ti

2. El banco _____ entregó el préstamo ayer.
   mí   yo   me

3. ¿Me llevas a pasear _____, por favor?
   conmigo   contigo   consigo

4. _____ ya habéis confirmado la cantidad.
   Vosotros   Vos   Ustedes

5. A nadie _____ interesa jugar a las cartas.
   lo   la   le

6. A _____ me quieres, ¿no?
   mí   yo   me

7. A Daniela _____ conozco desde la universidad.
   le   ella   la

8. _____ lo di a ellas.
   Les   Se   Le

9. ¿_____ molestan mis ronquidos?
   Te   Ti   Tú

10. _____ daré una gran sorpresa a ustedes.
    Los   Les   Las

17. Síntesis Completar Completa la carta de Santiago con las palabras de la lista. `13.A–13.H`

nos   les   os (2)   me (2)   le   ti   vos

Queridos Juan y Alfredo:

Os escribo porque mis tíos (1) __*me*__ dieron una idea perfecta para mi negocio: ¡un servicio de piscinas móviles! Ya sé que probablemente no (2) _____ parecerá algo viable, pero si tan solo leyerais el plan de negocios que ellos escribieron... ¡es fantástico!

La idea (3) _____ vino a la mente un día de verano, de muchísimo calor. Mi tía (4) _____ dijo a mi tío:

—¿A (5) _____ te gustaría tener una piscina en casa?

Y, mi tío, que es argentino, le contestó con su tono característico:

—A mí (6) _____ parece que a (7) _____ el calor te hace mal... ¿no ves que no tenemos espacio?

Desde ese momento, no dejaron de pensar en tener una piscina, hasta que un día ambos se miraron entre sí, y se dijeron:

—¿Y si (8) _____ trajeran una piscina a nuestra casa?

Bueno, el plan de negocios es muy largo, pero si queréis, (9) _____ lo mando por correo postal.

¿(10) _____ enviaríais vuestras direcciones?

Saludos y hasta pronto,

Santiago

18. Síntesis Componer Escribe un párrafo sobre un regalo que hayas recibido y que te haya encantado, e indica quién te lo dio. Utiliza pronombres personales. `13.A–13.H`

> **Modelo**
>
> *Mi mejor amiga me dio una bufanda para mi cumpleaños en junio...*

_____

_____

_____

_____

_____

_____

_____

_____

_____

_____

_____

Practice more at **vhlcentral.com**.

Questions and question words ✎   Chapter 14

1. Reordenar Reordena las oraciones. Usa las mayúsculas como ayuda. `14.A`

> **Modelo**
>
> ? / por las mañanas / ¿ / Lees / el periódico
> *¿Lees el periódico por las mañanas?*

1. a comer, / ¿ / no es así / viene / ? / Úrsula

_____

2. hizo / frío, / verdad / Ayer /¿ / ?

_____

3. ¿ / Karina / Duerme / todavía / ?

_____

4. ¿ / toman / ? / Ustedes / el avión / de las 12, / no

_____

5. Tiene / las notas / el profesor / del examen / ¿ / ?

_____

6. Sabe / que / Florencia / la llamé / ¿ / ?

_____

2. Escribir Escribe dos tipos de preguntas posibles para estas respuestas, como en el modelo. `14.A`

> **Modelo**
>
> *¿Corrió Juana la maratón?*
> *Juana corrió la maratón, ¿no es cierto?*
> Sí, Juana corrió la maratón.

1. _____

   _____

   No, mi hermana no tiene quince años.

2. _____

   _____

   Sí, hoy debo ir a la escuela.

3. _____

   _____

   No, ellos no harán las compras hoy.

4. _____

   _____

   Sí, la primavera en Chile comienza el 21 de septiembre.

5. _____

   _____

   No, el edificio no fue construido en 1980.

6. _____

   _____

   No, no quiero pastel.

3. Elegir En cada pregunta, elige la opción correcta. `14.B`

1. ¿_____ (Quién/Cuál/Quiénes) fue el libertador de Venezuela?
   Simón Bolívar.

2. ¿_____ (Quién/Cuál/Quiénes) es tu fecha de nacimiento?
   El 30 de octubre de 1992.

3. ¿_____ (Qué/Cuál/Quiénes) fueron a tu cumpleaños?
   Mi tía Estela, mis padres y casi todos mis amigos.

4. ¿_____ (Quién/Cuál/Quiénes) era Dolores del Río?
   Era una actriz mexicana.

5. ¿_____ (Quién/Cuál/Qué) estás viendo en la tele?
   Una película de terror.

6. ¿_____ (Quién/Cuál/Quiénes) viven en esta casa?
   Solamente Víctor y su perro.

7. ¿_____ (Quién/Cuál/Qué) llamó por teléfono?
   Tu jefe.

8. ¿_____ (Quién/Cuál/Cuáles) es tu apellido?
   Fernández.

4. La entrevista Sabrina está en una entrevista de trabajo. Completa las preguntas del entrevistador con *qué, cuál* o *cuáles*. `14.B`

ENTREVISTADOR Buenos días, ¿(1) _____*cuál*_____ es su nombre?

SABRINA Me llamo Sabrina Pérez Garrido.

ENTREVISTADOR ¿(2) _____ son sus aptitudes para este trabajo?

SABRINA Bueno... soy estudiante de administración, hablo español e inglés, y tengo un buen dominio de la informática.

ENTREVISTADOR Bien, ¿(3) _____ piensa sobre esta compañía?

SABRINA Pienso que es una compañía de gran nivel, con una buena política de recursos humanos y una gran reputación a nivel mundial.

ENTREVISTADOR ¿(4) _____ son sus pasatiempos?

SABRINA Me gusta leer, hacer deportes y tomar fotografías.

ENTREVISTADOR ¿(5) _____ tipo de trabajo espera hacer para nosotros?

SABRINA Me gustaría ser asistente de gerencia.

ENTREVISTADOR Bien, ¿(6) _____ son sus expectativas salariales?

SABRINA No sé exactamente... escucho ofertas.

ENTREVISTADOR ¿(7) _____ es su número de teléfono?

SABRINA 309-987-0008.

ENTREVISTADOR Por último, ¿(8) _____ experiencia tiene en administración?

SABRINA Fui asistente de gerencia en una empresa de importaciones por dos años.

ENTREVISTADOR La llamaremos en cuanto tengamos novedades.

5. Completar Completa las preguntas con el pronombre interrogativo adecuado: *cuán, cuánto/a* o *cuántos/as*. `14.B`

> **Modelo**
>
> *¿Cuántas* mesas construyes por día?

1. ¿_____ kilos de tomates quiere, señora?
2. ¿_____ días de vacaciones tenemos?
3. ¿_____ costó la compra en el supermercado?
4. ¿_____ agua has bebido hoy?
5. ¿_____ empleadas tiene la compañía?
6. ¿_____ lejos está la próxima gasolinera?
7. ¿_____ trabajaste la semana pasada?
8. ¿_____ eficaz es este medicamento?

6. El mercado Completa esta conversación con las palabras de la lista. `14.B`

cuánto	cuántos	cuáles
qué	cómo (2)	cuán

VENDEDOR Buenos días. ¿(1) _____*Cómo*_____ está usted?

CLIENTE Muy bien, gracias, ¿y usted?

VENDEDOR Bien, gracias. ¿(2) _____ le puedo ofrecer?

CLIENTE Bueno, quisiera tomates. ¿(3) _____ me recomienda?

VENDEDOR Mire, hoy trajeron unos que están a buen precio. ¿(4) _____ kilos quiere?

CLIENTE ¿(5) _____ son de grandes?

VENDEDOR Son para ensalada, de tamaño medio.

CLIENTE Bien, entonces un kilo, por favor.

VENDEDOR Aquí tiene.

CLIENTE ¿(6) _____ le debo?

VENDEDOR Tres con cincuenta.

CLIENTE Aquí tiene. ¡Hasta luego!

7. Reescribir Reescribe estas preguntas usando *cómo*. `14.B`

> **Modelo**
> ¿Qué tal te gusta el café?
> *¿Cómo te gusta el café?*

1. ¿Cuán difícil es el problema?
   _____

2. ¿Cuán grande es la habitación?
   _____

3. ¿Qué altura tiene tu padre?
   _____

4. ¿Qué tal te sientes esta tarde?
   _____

5. ¿Qué te parece nuestro apartamento nuevo?
   _____

6. ¿Qué tan efectivo es este medicamento?
   _____

7. ¿Cuál es la importancia de la reunión?
   _____

8. ¿Cuán caros son estos videojuegos?
   _____

8. Preguntas indirectas Escribe las preguntas indirectas para estas preguntas directas. `14.B`

> **Modelo**
>
> ¿Qué programas de la televisión te aburren?
> Quisiera saber *qué programas de la televisión te aburren.*

1. ¿Quién es tu cantante favorito?
   Quiero saber _____.

2. ¿Cuántos años tiene Joaquín?
   Dime _____.

3. ¿Cuánto dinero hay en la cuenta?
   Dile a Carlos _____.

4. ¿Cómo se llama la persona que me espera?
   Recuerda decirme _____.

5. ¿Cuánto tiempo horneas la torta?
   Por favor, dime _____.

6. ¿Cuál es tu número de teléfono?
   Quisiera saber _____.

7. ¿Qué te gustaría beber en la cena?
   Quiero saber _____.

8. ¿Cómo manejas a diario el estrés?
   Cuéntame _____.

9. Preguntas Une los elementos de las tres columnas para formar preguntas. `14.B`

1. ¿Qué	preguntas	haces deporte?
2. ¿De qué	años	hicieron los periodistas?
3. ¿Con qué	altura	debes renovar tu licencia de conducir?
4. ¿Cada cuántos	hablan	es tu camiseta?
5. ¿A qué	frecuencia	de rápido?
6. ¿Cómo	talla	con tanto entusiasmo?
7. ¿De quién	nadas	sobre el nivel del mar está la ciudad de Quito?
8. ¿Cuántas	distancia	hay entre tu casa y la mía?

_____
_____
_____
_____
_____
_____
_____
_____
_____

10. Decidir Decide cuál de los dos palabras entre paréntesis es la adecuada para completar la oración. `14.B`

1. Explícame _____ (cómo/como) ir hasta el centro de la ciudad.

2. ¿_____ (Qué/Que) tal si tomamos un café en este bar?

3. No sé _____ (cuánto/cuanto) pueda cargar ese camión.

4. ¿De _____ (qué/que) forma se dice **alacena** en inglés?

5. ¿_____ (Cuántas/Cuantas) personas van al cine los fines de semana?

6. ¿_____ (Qué/Que) tan grande es la cocina?

7. Dime el _____ (porqué/porque) de tu visita.

8. Todavía no entendemos _____ (cómo/como) se dañaron todas las computadoras al tiempo.

11. Escoger Elige la opción correcta para cada oración. `14.B`

1. ¿_____ (A qué / Cuánta / Cuál) distancia está el hospital?

2. Realmente no sé _____ (porqué / cuándo / por qué) no me despertaste esta mañana.

3. ¿_____ (Cuál / Qué tal / Cómo) tus cosas? Hace tanto que no nos vemos.

4. ¿_____ (Hasta dónde / Dónde / Hasta cuándo) vas? Quizás puedo llevarte en el carro.

5. ¿_____ (Cómo/Cuán/Cuánto) son de caras esas bicicletas? Me gustaría comprar una nueva.

6. ¿_____ (Cuáles/Qué/Cuál) son tus zapatos, los verdes o los negros?

7. Desconozco totalmente el _____ (cuándo/cómo/porqué) del funcionamiento de las redes inalámbricas. Es una tecnología que no logro comprender.

12. Oraciones Reescribe las oraciones usando la palabra indicada. `14.B`

Modelo

Cuéntame en qué sitio trabaja tu mamá. (dónde)
Cuéntame dónde trabaja tu mamá.

1. Ismael quiere saber la razón de su despido. (porqué)

   _____

2. Dime el lugar en que viste tu teléfono por última vez. (dónde)

   _____

3. ¿A qué hora vendrás a buscarme? (cuándo)

   _____

4. ¿De qué manera puedo contactar contigo? (cómo)

   _____

5. ¿Por qué razón no viniste a mi fiesta de cumpleaños? (por qué)

   _____

6. ¿Cómo está la comida que preparé? (qué tal)

   _____

13. Exclamaciones Ricardo está asombrado con todo lo que ve. Completa las exclamaciones de Ricardo. `14.C`

Modelo

Ricardo piensa: Los parques de esta ciudad son grandes:
Ricardo dice: *¡Qué grandes son los parques de esta ciudad!*

1. Ricardo piensa: Hay tantas flores en este parque.
   Ricardo dice: _____

2. Ricardo piensa: Este barrio es muy elegante.
   Ricardo dice: _____

3. Ricardo piensa: Los restaurantes son tan caros.
   Ricardo dice: _____

4. Ricardo piensa: Las calles son tan limpias.
   Ricardo dice: _____

5. Ricardo piensa: Me gustaría vivir en esta ciudad.
   Ricardo dice: _____

14. Unir Une los elementos de las dos columnas para formar oraciones. `14.D`

1. ¿Qué tanta _____   a. tenemos que esperar para que deje de llover?

2. ¡Qué tanto _____   b. cosas sabes!

3. ¡Qué tantos _____   c. animales hay en este zoológico!

4. ¿Qué tanto _____   d. bueno es ese restaurante?

5. ¿Qué tan _____   e. hablas! No te callas un segundo.

6. ¡Qué tantas _____   f. gente hay en el concierto?

15. Síntesis La cantante Cristina es una famosa cantante. Completa la entrevista que le hicieron con las palabras de la lista. `14.A–14.D`

| cuál | ~~cuándo~~ | cuántos | cómo | no es cierto | qué (2) | qué tal |

CONDUCTOR Ante todo, Cristina, muchas gracias por darnos esta entrevista. ¿(1) _Cuándo_ fue tu última entrevista televisiva?

CRISTINA La última fue en agosto de este año. Estuve de gira y casi no he tenido tiempo para entrevistas.

CONDUCTOR ¿(2) _____ tu gira? ¿Estás contenta?

CRISTINA La verdad es que fue muy intensa. Muchísimos conciertos, muchas ciudades.

CONDUCTOR ¿(3) _____ fue la reacción del público ante este nuevo espectáculo que presentaste?

CRISTINA Mi público es muy efusivo: cantan, aplauden, bailan. Evidentemente les gustó, pero eso es lo que uno siempre espera, ¿(4) _____?

CONDUCTOR Sí, pero sabemos también que tuviste una asistencia increíble en tus conciertos. ¿(5) _____ espectadores te acompañaron?

CRISTINA No sabría decirte... ¡Pero no te imaginas con (6) _____ rapidez se agotaron las entradas!

CONDUCTOR ¡(7) _____ me alegro por ti!

CRISTINA Gracias. Ahora estoy preparando mi nuevo disco.

CONDUCTOR ¿(8) _____ tanto tendremos que esperar para escucharlo?

CRISTINA En dos meses saldrá a la venta. Espero que les guste.

CONDUCTOR Muchas gracias, Cristina. Esperamos verte pronto en el escenario.

16. Síntesis Reunir Une los ejemplos con las explicaciones. `14.A–14.D`

_____ 1. Es una afirmación seguida de una pregunta.

_____ 2. Es una pregunta para dar a elegir a alguien entre alternativas concretas.

_____ 3. Es una pregunta cuyo interrogativo concuerda en género y número con el sustantivo que modifica.

_____ 4. Es una abreviación de **cuánto** y se usa antes de adjetivos.

_____ 5. Es una pregunta indirecta.

_____ 6. Es un interrogativo que no varía en género ni en número cuando está seguido por verbos.

_____ 7. Es una expresión que se usa en Latinoamérica para decir **cuántos**.

_____ 8. Es una afirmación que contiene varios interrogativos usados como sustantivos.

a. ¿Cuánto costó la computadora?

b. ¿Cuántos kilos de patatas has comprado?

c. Explícame por qué no llegaste a tiempo.

d. ¡Qué tantos primos tienes!

e. ¿Qué prefieres beber, agua o jugo?

f. En este caso, es mejor conocer el cómo que el porqué.

g. ¿Cuán pesado es tu equipaje?

h. Aquí hace demasiado calor, ¿no?

17. Síntesis Personaje Si tuvieras la oportunidad de formular cinco preguntas a uno de los personajes que más admiras, ¿cuáles serían esas preguntas? Escribe cada una con un interrogativo diferente. `14.A–14.D`

> **Modelo**
>
> *(Alfonso Cuarón)*
> *Aparte de los Óscar, ¿cuál es el reconocimiento en el cine que le parece más valioso?*

_____

_____

_____

_____

_____

_____

_____

_____

_____

_____

:Ò: Practice more at **vhlcentral.com.**

Relative pronouns 🐾   Chapter 15

1. Antecedentes Marca los antecedentes de los pronombres relativos. En el caso de *cuyo/a*, subraya también la frase con la que concuerda. `15.A`

Busco relación estable

Me llamo Olivia y tengo 44 años. Busco a un hombre que tenga entre 45 y 55 años y que esté dispuesto a formar una pareja estable.

Me gustaría tener una pareja que no tenga hijos, preferentemente. Me gustan los hombres altos, elegantes y formales.

Soy activa y llevo una vida que podría definir como tranquila. Trabajo durante la semana y los fines de semana hago actividades al aire libre. El estilo de vida que llevo es un poco costoso, por lo tanto, preferiría un hombre cuyo salario sea superior o igual al mío.

Si eres un hombre que tiene estas cualidades, no dudes en llamar al teléfono que aparece abajo.

2. Oraciones Completa cada oración seleccionando el relativo adecuado. `15.A`

> **Modelo**
>
> Me siento preparado, *lo cual* (cuyo/lo cual/que) es bueno porque tengo un examen el viernes.

1. Le presento al empleado _____ (cuyo/la que/que) fue contratado la semana pasada.

2. Beberé _____ (cuyo/lo que/lo cual) tú bebas.

3. La escuela _____ (cuya/que/quien) está en la esquina es muy buena.

4. Los alumnos _____ (cuyos/los que/que) tengan buenas calificaciones podrán recibir becas.

5. Daniela, _____ (a quien/con la que/en la que) conocí en la escuela, ahora trabaja conmigo.

6. Elige la bufanda _____ (cuya/que/quien) más te guste.

3. Reordenar Reordena los elementos para formar oraciones lógicas. `15.A`

> **Modelo**
>
> Ruiz / que / carros / Los / son / hermanos / lavan / los
> _Los hermanos Ruiz son los que lavan los carros._

1. que / es la mujer / Lucila / las flores / me dio

   _____

2. donde / un lugar / puedo comprar / Encontré / productos orgánicos

   _____

3. que / Te / una mujer / ha llamado / se llama Elisa

   _____

4. Os gustó / que / os di / ¿ / el regalo / ?

   _____

5. donde / El barrio / está / vivo / muy lejos del centro

   _____

6. que / en el bar / Nos encontramos / te indiqué

   _____

4. Unir Une los elementos de las tres columnas para formar oraciones. `15.A`

1. Las tareas	quienes	currículum sea mejor.
2. La tienda	que	puerta es azul es demasiado oscura.
3. Todas las estudiantes	cuyo	hablé me recomendaron el mismo libro.
4. La habitación	con las que	olvidé el paraguas está cerrada.
5. Contrataremos a la candidata	cuya	cenamos anoche nos han invitado a su casa.
6. Los amigos con	donde	te encargué deben estar terminadas antes del 20 de junio.

_____

_____

_____

_____

_____

_____

5. ¿Explicativas o especificativas? Decide si estas proposiciones relativas son explicativas (_non-defining_) (ND) o especificativas (_defining_) (D). `15.B`

____ 1. Gastón, quien nunca duerme la siesta, siempre se va a dormir a las 8 de la noche.

____ 2. Las noches que son despejadas son las más frías.

____ 3. Me encanta la playa a la que fuimos la semana pasada.

____ 4. Mi nueva bicicleta, la cual compré en el mercado de las pulgas, funciona de maravilla.

____ 5. Los libros que compré ayer son carísimos.

____ 6. La niña a la que saludé es nuestra vecina.

6. Completar Completa las oraciones con *que, el que* y *la que*. `15.B`

> **Modelo**
>
> Tienes muchas fotos, pero prefiero _____*la que*_____ muestra todo tu rostro.

1. La situación en _____ estoy no es muy agradable.
2. Los colores _____ más me gustan son el rojo y el azul.
3. El banco en _____ estoy sentado es incómodo.
4. Las mujeres _____ trabajan conmigo son súper amables.
5. La discoteca en _____ te conocí es la mejor del pueblo.
6. Te diré el motivo por _____ no vine.
7. No le cuentes a nadie la idea _____ te di.

7. Relativos Completa las oraciones con las palabras de la lista. `15.B`

> cualquiera   cuyo   ~~las que~~   lo que   que (2)   quien   quienes

> **Modelo**
>
> Me gustan las actividades al aire libre,
> sobre todo *las que* se realizan en el mar.

1. Las personas _____ número de documento termine en 8 deberán presentarse el día lunes.
2. _____ quiera comer rico y barato vendrá a nuestro restaurante.
3. El _____ conduzca sin prudencia recibirá una sanción.
4. _____ más me interesa es la historia.
5. Todos los países _____ forman la Unión Europea tienen proyectos en común.
6. Me agradan las personas con _____ puedo hablar sobre literatura.

8. Combinar Combina las dos oraciones de manera lógica usando el pronombre relativo. `15.B`

> **Modelo**
>
> Estoy acostumbrado a conducir camiones. Los camiones son difíciles de parquear. (los cuales)
> *Estoy acostumbrado a conducir camiones, los cuales son difíciles de parquear.*

1. París tiene muchos puentes. París es mi ciudad favorita. (que)
   _____

2. La profesora se llama Silvia. Conocí a esta profesora ayer. (quien)
   _____

3. Trabajé para una empresa durante 20 años. La empresa está ahora en quiebra. (cual)
   _____

4. La semana que viene viajaré a Europa. Europa es mi continente favorito. (cual)
   _____

5. Mañana jugaré al baloncesto. No he jugado jamás antes al baloncesto. (cual)
   _____

9. Reescribir Reescribe las oraciones. Como ayuda, tienes las primeras palabras. `15.B`

> **Modelo**
>
> Nuestra madre con mucha dedicación sacó adelante a la familia.
> Fue así *como ella sacó adelante a la familia.*

1. Yo lavaré los platos.
   Soy yo _____.

2. El jefe pagará la multa.
   Es el jefe _____.

3. Comimos una exquisita paella en Valencia.
   Fue en Valencia _____.

4. Cervantes escribió *Don Quijote de la Mancha*.
   Fue Cervantes _____.

5. Ganamos la competencia el fin de semana pasado.
   Fue el fin de semana pasado _____.

6. Los estudiantes tienen demasiados reclamos.
   Son los estudiantes _____.

10. Adverbios relativos Reescribe las oraciones usando adverbios relativos. `15.C`

> **Modelo**
>
> Juega con tus amigos en el momento en que la cancha esté libre.
> *Juega con tus amigos cuando la cancha esté libre.*

1. La ciudad en la que vivo tiene doscientos mil habitantes.
   _____

2. Lo haré del modo en que tú me has dicho.
   _____

3. En la época en que nací, mis padres vivían en el extranjero.
   _____

4. ¿Te parece más agradable el lugar en que yo hago deporte?
   _____

5. Me gusta la manera en que crecen esas flores.
   _____

11. Síntesis Elegir Elige la opción correcta para cada oración. `15.A–15.D`

1. No me gusta nada la manera _____
   me hablas.
   a. la que   b. en la que   c. que

2. Como dice el dicho: "A _____ madruga,
   Dios lo ayuda".
   a. los   b. que   c. quien

3. Cecilia _____ es una compañera de trabajo.
   a. , quien es amiga de María,
   b. quien es amiga de María
   c. cuyo cabello es rubio

4. Mañana no tengo que trabajar, _____
   me alegra muchísimo.
   a. el que   b. que   c. lo cual

5. El químico _____ se fabricó este material
   es tóxico.
   a. con quien   b. con el que   c. cuyo

6. Te invitaré _____ que vaya de vacaciones.
   a. donde   b. adondequiera   c. adonde

7. El hombre _____ hablabas es el jefe.
   a. con que   b. con quien   c. quien

12. Síntesis Pronombres y adverbios relativos Completa las oraciones con el pronombre relativo o el adverbio relativo correcto. `15.A–15.C`

> **Modelo**
>
> El gimnasio _____*donde*_____ hago deporte ya tiene una nueva sede.

1. Para la época _____ se fundó esta ciudad, la economía era básicamente ganadera.

2. Este periódico, _____ nombre es *La Tribuna*, es uno de los más importantes del país.

3. Ayer conocí a tu padre, de _____ me hablaste tanto.

4. El mismo día _____ choqué con el carro, tú perdiste tu vuelo a Colombia.

5. El doctor _____ me atendió la semana pasada hoy está de vacaciones.

6. La Navidad más divertida _____ pasé fue la de 1998.

7. Te presentaré a las personas con _____ trabajo.

8. La casa _____ vivo es de alquiler.

9. Hoy me levanté muy temprano, _____ es un gran esfuerzo para mí.

10. Mi mejor amiga, _____ es fotógrafa, trabaja mucho.

11. El modo _____ trabaja mi hermano es muy particular.

12. Vimos una casa _____ muros estaban cubiertos de hierba.

13. Síntesis Escribir Escribe un párrafo sobre tu lugar favorito. Utiliza por lo menos dos pronombres relativos y un adverbio relativo. `15.A–15.C`

> **Modelo**
>
> *El lugar donde prefiero estar es la piscina de la escuela.*
> *Allá aprendo de mis amigos, quienes son mejores nadadores que yo…*

_____

_____

_____

_____

_____

_____

_____

_____

_____

_____

_____

_____

_____

_____

Practice more at **vhlcentral.com**.

Chapter 16

1. Decidir   En cada oración, decide cuál es la conjunción coordinante adecuada (*y/o*).   `16.B`

> **Modelo**
>
> Los bomberos apagan incendios ___y___ hacen rescates.

1. Tenemos entre cuatro _____ cinco dólares; no sé exactamente cuántos.

2. O bien comes ya mismo _____ bien esperas hasta las cuatro de la tarde.

3. Mi computadora nueva tiene cámara web _____ pantalla de 17 pulgadas.

4. Por cinco dólares puedes comprar una hamburguesa con papas fritas, ya sea con un refresco _____ con un jugo, tú eliges.

5. Sara es la cantante; _____ tú, el guitarrista.

6. ¿Cuándo _____ dónde nos encontraremos con Raquel? Pásame la información por mensaje de texto, por favor.

7. Se lo dices tú _____ se lo digo yo.

2. Usos   Empareja las conjunciones con sus usos.   `16.B`

_____ 1. y   a. unir elementos negativos

_____ 2. o   b. empezar una explicación

_____ 3. ni   c. expresar una suma

_____ 4. es decir   d. presentar alternativas

_____ 5. pues   e. expresar una consecuencia

3. Carta   Completa la carta con la opción correcta.   `16.B`

> Querida Gabriela:
>
> No sabes cuánto te extraño. Hace apenas un mes que te fuiste a vivir al D.F., (1) _____ (pero/pues) me parece que fue hace un año. (2) _____ (Ni/Tanto) Guadalupe (3) _____ (ni/como) yo te echamos de menos (4) _____ (pues/y) nos gustaría que volvieras pronto; (5) _____ (sin embargo / sino) sabemos que México es tu país favorito (6) _____ (y/e) que eres feliz allí.
>
> Por aquí todo sigue igual: (7) _____ (no/ni) peor (8) _____ (no/ni) mejor. Tenemos siete (9) _____ (o/u) ocho compañeros de clase nuevos, muy simpáticos todos. Uno de ellos habla a la perfección (10) _____ (tan/tanto) inglés como francés (11) _____ (y/o) español, (12) _____ (pero/pues) su madre es francesa, su padre es mexicano y él nació en Estados Unidos.
>
> Recuerda que, si quieres hablar con nosotras, nos puedes contactar (13) _____ (bien/ni) por chat, (14) _____ (sino/bien) por Skype.
>
> ¡Un abrazo fuerte!
>
> Milena

4. Conjunciones coordinantes Completa las oraciones con las conjunciones coordinantes de la lista. `16.B`

ni... ni...   e   pues   sino   no... ni...   y   pero   o

Modelo

¿Quieres un gato _____*o*_____ un perro como mascota?

1. Cuando lleguemos a casa, comeremos frutas _____ chocolates.

2. Mis padres se ducharán _____ irán a hacer las compras.

3. Ese vestido _____ es amarillo _____ naranja: es rosado.

4. _____ crudo, _____ demasiado cocido; quiero que el pavo esté en el punto justo.

5. Llegamos a tiempo a la fiesta, _____ nos olvidamos del regalo para el cumpleañero.

6. No es tu padre _____ tú quien debe hacer la tarea.

7. Voy a ducharme, _____ he hecho deporte ¡y no quiero oler mal!

5. Conjunciones subordinantes En esta conversación indica las conjunciones subordinantes. `16.C`

PACIENTE Buenos días, doctor Pérez.

DOCTOR Buenos días. Dígame: ¿qué lo trae por aquí?

PACIENTE A ver... desde hace dos días, cuando me levanto, me duele mucho el estómago.

DOCTOR Me ha dicho que le duele el estómago. ¿Suele comer alimentos poco saludables?

PACIENTE No... pero, pensándolo mejor, aunque no coma nada me duele la barriga. Eso sí, bebo café, me encanta.

DOCTOR Entonces usted no come, pero toma café. ¿Cuántas tazas toma por día?

PACIENTE Tomo solamente dos o tres en cuanto llego al trabajo, dos más una vez que tengo un tiempito libre, y tres más por la tarde porque me da sueño trabajar tanto.

DOCTOR ¡Y después me pregunta que cuál es el motivo de su dolor de estómago!

PACIENTE Creo que tiene razón, doctor. Debería tomar el café con un chorrito de leche, ¿no?

DOCTOR Mire, como usted no mide cuánto café toma, se lo prohibiré totalmente. Siempre que sienta ganas de tomarse un cafecito, tómese un té o, mucho mejor, un vaso de agua, de manera que su estómago no siga empeorando.

PACIENTE Muchas gracias, doctor.

DOCTOR ¡Cuídese! Adiós.

6. Elegir En cada oración, elige la opción correcta. `16.C`

1. Compré muchas frutas y verduras, _____ (de manera que / dado que) tendremos la nevera llenísima.

2. Venderemos nuestro carro, _____ (de modo que / puesto que) casi no lo usamos.

3. Tengo muchísimo sueño, _____ (porque / así que) dormiré un rato, ¿sí?

4. Alejandra quiere ir a la playa, _____ (de modo que / porque) quiere disfrutar de este hermoso día.

5. El supermercado está cerrado, _____ (así que / puesto que) tendremos que comer en el restaurante.

6. Voy a lavar los platos de una vez, _____ (a causa de que / de modo que) puedas ordenar lo que falta.

7. Clasificar Indica si las conjunciones son coordinantes o subordinantes. `16.B–16.C`

		Coordinantes	Subordinantes
1.	porque		
2.	ni… ni		
3.	y		
4.	tan pronto como		
5.	o		
6.	pero		
7.	aun cuando		
8.	hasta que		
9.	de modo que		
10.	sino		

8. ¿Temporal o causal? Indica si estas oraciones contienen conjunciones subordinantes temporales o causales. `16.C`

> **Modelo**
>
> Una vez que cese de llover, daremos un paseo. *temporal*

1. Antes de que llegaras, estaba hablando por teléfono con Luis. _____

2. Llegué tarde al trabajo, ya que perdí el tren de las 8. _____

3. Como no me has llamado, te llamo yo a ti. _____

4. Tan pronto como empezó la tormenta, la gente se refugió en las tiendas. _____

5. Cada vez que voy a visitarte, me esperas con una comida riquísima. _____

6. Dado que no se han cumplido las reglas, todos tendrán sus respectivas sanciones. _____

7. Puesto que vuestros perros ladran día y noche, deberéis mudaros a otro lugar. _____

8. Mientras tú cocinas, yo lavo la ropa. _____

9. Reescribir Reescribe las oraciones para que contengan cláusulas sustantivas (*noun clauses*). `16.C`

> **Modelo**
>
> Tengo frío. (dice/Rosa)
> *Rosa dice que tiene frío.*

1. ¿Cuál es tu número de teléfono? (pregunta/Leonel)

   _____

2. ¿Tienes la dirección electrónica de Carla? (pregunta/José)

   _____

3. El lechero vendrá a las nueve. (creen/Juan y Marina)

   _____

4. ¿Has oído el timbre? (pregunta/Estela)

   _____

5. Me gustaría dormir la siesta. (dice/Mirta)

   _____

10. Unir Combina las oraciones usando las conjunciones dadas. **16.C**

> **Modelo**
>
> Mis amigos son muy graciosos. Sin embargo, yo nunca me divierto con ellos.
> (aunque) *Aunque mis amigos son muy graciosos, yo nunca me divierto con ellos.*

1. Estudio muchísimo la gramática española. Sin embargo, siempre cometo los mismos errores.
   (a pesar de que) _____

2. Trabajaré mucho hoy. Por lo tanto, mañana podré descansar.
   (de modo que) _____

3. Martín cocina. Parece un experto.
   (como si) _____

4. Julia trabaja mucho. Patricia trabaja las mismas horas que Julia.
   (tanto... como) _____

5. Iremos a pasear. Iremos al lugar que tú quieras.
   (donde) _____

6. Tú y tu novio salen esta noche. Antes debes hacer todas tus tareas.
   (para que) _____

7. Yo como una gran cantidad de verduras. Tú comes tantas verduras como yo.
   (igual... que) _____

8. Debes ahorrar. Solamente así podrás comprar tu propia casa.
   (a fin de que) _____

11. Seleccionar En cada oración, elige la opción correcta. **16.D**

1. _____ dejes de quejarte porque la casa está sucia, mañana limpiaré hasta el último rincón.
   a. A menos que   b. En caso de que   c. Con tal de que

2. _____ el precio de los productos orgánicos no suba, seguiré comprándolos.
   a. Si   b. A menos que   c. Siempre y cuando

3. Los trabajadores no volverán a sus puestos de trabajo _____ les paguen los salarios atrasados.
   a. a menos que   b. en caso de que   c. si

4. _____ tengo tiempo, hago deportes.
   a. Con tal de que   b. En caso de que   c. Siempre que

5. _____ haya un incendio, baje por las escaleras.
   a. En caso de que   b. Siempre y cuando   c. Si

6. _____ no me llamas por mi cumpleaños, me enojaré muchísimo.
   a. A menos que   b. Si   c. Siempre que

7. _____ yo pueda trabajar, no te faltará nada.
   a. A menos que   b. Mientras   c. Si

8. _____ no elijas algo muy costoso, te compraré un regalo.
   a. A menos que   b. Si   c. Siempre que

12. Indicar Indica si las condiciones son (a) reales/posibles, (b) imaginarias/hipotéticas o (c) imposibles/irrealizadas. `16.D`

_____ 1. Si me acompañaras a la fiesta, ganaríamos el premio a la pareja de la noche.

_____ 2. Te invitaremos a cenar solamente si nos prometes que serás puntual.

_____ 3. Si tuvieras una mascota, comprenderías la responsabilidad de tener un animal a tu cargo.

_____ 4. Los abuelos no te habrían regalado ese CD si hubieran sabido que ya lo tenías.

_____ 5. Si saliera el sol, iríamos a patinar al parque.

_____ 6. Si mis hijos tienen clases por la mañana, podré anotarme en el curso de cerámica.

_____ 7. Nunca se lo habría contado a Silvia si me hubieras dicho que era un secreto.

_____ 8. Si haces ejercicio, te mantienes en forma.

13. Síntesis Emparejar Une las frases para formar oraciones lógicas. `16.B-16.D`

1. Aunque odio los teléfonos móviles, _____   a. en mi trabajo me piden que tenga uno.

2. Siempre que hago una pausa, _____   b. de modo que mi jefe no pudo comunicarse conmigo.

3. Para que mi jefe no se enfade, _____   c. así que no tengo excusas para no estar en contacto con mi jefe.

4. Me quedé sin batería en el teléfono, _____   d. porque no sabía usar el teléfono.

5. Sin querer borré todos los contactos, _____   e. mi jefe me dio un papel con todos los teléfonos.

6. Como borré todos los contactos, _____   f. mi jefe me llama por teléfono.

7. Ahora sé cómo usar el teléfono, _____   g. debo devolver sus llamadas de inmediato.

14. Síntesis ¿Cuáles? Indica si estas oraciones se refieren a conjunciones coordinantes, subordinantes o condicionales. `16.B-16.D`

> **Modelo**
>
> Se usan para hacer suposiciones. _conjunciones condicionales_

1. La conjunción más común de este tipo es **que**. _____

2. Unen dos palabras, frases u oraciones similares. _____

3. **Pero** y **sino** son ejemplos de este tipo de conjunción. _____

4. Se usan al comienzo de una cláusula sustantiva o una cláusula adverbial. _____

5. La conjunción más importante de este tipo es **si**. _____

15. Síntesis Conjunciones Identifica el tipo de conjunción que posee cada oración. `16.B-16.D`

_____ 1. Pórtate bien para que no te castiguen.

_____ 2. La reunión se aplazó, así que pudo terminar el reporte a tiempo.

_____ 3. Ana piensa empezar a estudiar, ya que su padre le pagará sus estudios.

_____ 4. Cada vez que entra en una librería, compra un libro.

_____ 5. Se siente solo a pesar de que tiene muchos amigos.

_____ 6. Este teléfono es más costoso, pero tiene más tiempo de garantía.

a. conjunción causal

b. conjunción concesiva

c. conjunción consecutiva

d. conjunción coordinante

e. conjunción de finalidad

f. conjunción temporal

16. Síntesis Completar Completa las oraciones con las conjunciones de la lista. Hay dos conjunciones que no debes usar. `16.B–16.D`

al mismo tiempo que	cada vez que	ni	pero	que si	sino
antes de que	cuando	o	pues	si	~~tanto... como~~
así que (2)	en caso de que	para que	que	sin embargo	y

Modelo

_____*Tanto*_____ Melisa _____*como*_____ Romina y Mariela son maestras.

1. Mamá me aseguró _____ Papá Noel vendría si me portaba bien.

2. El señor González no es tu amigo, _____ tu profesor, _____ háblale con respeto.

3. El secretario no redactó la carta _____ organizó las reuniones, _____ lo despidieron.

4. _____ dieran las doce, Cenicienta debía volver a su casa.

5. _____ la fiesta sea un éxito, debemos hacer mucha publicidad.

6. _____ no puedas venir, por favor, avísanos con antelación.

7. _____ hace frío, me gusta quedarme en casa y ver películas.

8. _____ pones atención, verás que aprenderás más rápido.

9. _____ te vas de vacaciones, la oficina es un caos.

10. No sé si reír _____ llorar.

11. Mis padres no han llegado aún. _____, avisaron que vendrían temprano.

12. No puedo salir esta tarde, _____ debo trabajar.

13. Adriana lavó la ropa, limpió la casa _____ preparó la cena.

14. Tengo muchos días de vacaciones, _____ me tomaré solamente una semana.

17. Síntesis Fin de semana Escribe un párrafo sobre tus planes para el fin de semana. Utiliza cinco conjunciones diferentes. `16.B–16.D`

Modelo

Voy a llevar mi ropa a la lavandería el sábado, pues quiero tiempo libre el domingo para ir al cine con mis amigos…

_____
_____
_____
_____
_____
_____
_____
_____
_____
_____
_____
_____

Practice more at **vhlcentral.com.**

1. Clasificar Indica si los verbos en este texto son *copulativos* (*linking*), *transitivos* o *intransitivos*. Escríbelos en la columna correcta. `17.B`

El famoso actor Julio Suárez, quien **protagonizó** telenovelas como *Amar es vivir* y *Enamorados siempre*, **sufrió** ayer un accidente de tránsito cuando **conducía** por el centro de Bogotá. Aunque Suárez no **tuvo** lesiones graves, el acompañante del artista aún **está** en el Hospital Central.

El accidente **sucedió** a las 20 horas del lunes 3 de agosto, cuando otro conductor **hizo** un giro peligroso para **ingresar** a una gasolinera y **chocó** el vehículo del prestigioso actor.

Suárez **está** preocupado por la salud de su amigo, a quien **conoció** cuando **era** aún un actor desconocido. "Ojalá que los conductores **sean** más prudentes al **conducir**", exclamó el artista.

Copulativo	Transitivo	Intransitivo

2. Elegir En cada oración, elige la opción correcta. `17.B`

1. ¡Cuántas veces soñé _____ (por/con) una fiesta como esta!

2. Horacio siempre se interesó _____ (por/en) la arquitectura de la ciudad.

3. ¿Confirmaste que asistiremos _____ (a/en) la reunión escolar?

4. ¡Ojalá quisieras jugar _____ (con/a) las cartas conmigo!

5. Volveremos _____ (a/en) vernos la semana que viene.

6. Mis padres se han encontrado _____ (en/con) los tuyos en el supermercado.

7. ¿Habéis disfrutado _____ (de/con) la playa?

3. Seleccionar En cada oración, elige la opción correcta. `17.B`

1. Juliana _____ de las escaleras y tuvo que ir al hospital.
   a. cayó   b. se cayó

2. No _____ despertarte: ¡dormías tan plácidamente!
   a. me atreví   b. me atreví a

3. Ayer _____ demasiado tarde.
   a. despertamos   b. nos despertamos

4. Quiero que _____ a la abuela hasta que yo vuelva.
   a. cuides   b. te cuides

5. Por favor, ¡_____ esa barba! ¡No te queda bien!
   a. afeita   b. aféitate

6. Estaba preparando la comida y _____ el dedo con un cuchillo.
   a. corté   b. me corté

7. No _____ la ropa y ahora no tenemos ni un par de calcetines limpios.
   a. lavamos   b. nos lavamos

4. Reescribir Reescribe las oraciones usando el verbo indicado. `17.B`

> **Modelo**
>
> Para mí, es muy divertido ir de compras. (divertir)
> *Me divierte ir de compras.*

1. Los alumnos detestan hacer la tarea. (disgustar)

   _____

2. ¿No te sientes triste por la despedida de Flor? (entristecer)

   _____

3. Adoro ir a las montañas en invierno. (fascinar)

   _____

4. ¡Qué sorpresa tu visita! (sorprender)

   _____

5. Tengo miedo de los fantasmas. (asustar)

   _____

5. Modo Para cada concepto, indica si se suele usar el indicativo, el subjuntivo o el imperativo. `17.C`

> **Modelo**
>
> deseos *subjuntivo*

1. duda _____

2. hechos _____

3. suposiciones _____

4. preferencias _____

5. órdenes _____

6. emociones _____

7. incertidumbre _____

8. lo desconocido _____

6. Conjugar Conjuga estos verbos en presente de indicativo. `17.D`

> **Modelo**
>
> trabajar (usted) *trabaja*

1. completar (nosotros) _____

2. cumplir (vosotros) _____

3. beber (tú) _____

4. viajar (ellos) _____

5. insistir (ella) _____

6. leer (yo) _____

7. responder (él) _____

8. investigar (vos) _____

7. Completar Completa las oraciones usando los verbos de la lista conjugados en presente de indicativo. **17.D**

> cocer   conseguir   ejercer   exigir   ~~introducir~~   recoger   traducir

Modelo

¿ _Introduzco_ (yo) la moneda en esta ranura?

1. ¿Cuánto tiempo _____ (yo) esta pasta?
2. Te _____ que me ayudes a limpiar la casa.
3. _____ (yo) la profesión desde hace veinte años.
4. Yo _____ los juguetes y tú los guardas en el armario.
5. No _____ (yo) olvidarte: sueño contigo todas las noches.
6. ¿Cómo _____ (yo) esta palabra? No se me ocurre cómo hacerlo.

8. Oraciones Completa las oraciones con los verbos conjugados en presente de indicativo. **17.D**

Modelo

Tú _____ _quieres_ _____ (querer) esta almohada, así que voy a usar aquella.

1. Julio y Daniel _____ (adquirir) los boletos para el partido.
2. Mariana _____ (entender) muy bien los problemas de Fernanda.
3. Yo _____ (jugar) al tenis dos veces por semana.
4. Nosotros _____ (preferir) la calidad sobre la cantidad.
5. ¿Tú _____ (dormir) la siesta después del almuerzo?
6. Lucía y Rosa _____ (mentir) sobre la hora a la que llegaron.
7. Vosotros _____ (servir) la cena y yo lavo los platos.
8. Juan Manuel _____ (probar) el sabor de la salsa antes de echarla a las papas.

9. Reescribir Reescribe las oraciones usando el sujeto indicado. **17.D**

Modelo

Volvemos a las nueve y media de la noche. (ellos)
Vuelven a las nueve y media de la noche.

1. ¿Por qué incluyes a Juana en tu lista de invitados, pero no a mí? (vos)
   _____

2. ¿Continuáis con las clases de guitarra? (tú)
   _____

3. No confiamos en el criterio de Emiliano. (yo)
   _____

4. Siempre perdéis el hilo de la conversación. (ellos)
   _____

5. Nosotros te defendemos si pasa algo. (yo)
   _____

6. Te pedimos un gran favor. (yo)
   _____

10. Un estreno Completa el texto con los verbos conjugados en presente de indicativo. **17.D**

acostarse	comenzar	convertirse	deducir	perseguir	repetirse	soñar
afligir	~~contar~~	decidir	empezar	recordar	situarse	

El martes que viene se estrenará en todas las salas del país la película *La escuela*. Este drama
(1) _____*cuenta*_____ con la participación de estrellas, como el joven actor Tomás Rapal y la ya
consagrada Gabriela Perotti.

La historia (2) _____ en un pequeño pueblo y es protagonizada por un niño llamado Juan
que (3) _____ el año en una escuela nueva. Ese primer día de clases (4) _____
en una pesadilla, porque sus compañeros lo maltratan y lo (5) _____ por los pasillos de
la escuela.

Esa noche, cuando Juan (6) _____ en la cama, (7) _____ hacer todo lo posible
para que sus compañeros lo acepten. Sin embargo, al día siguiente, Juan nota que la situación
del día anterior (8) _____. Al final del día, Juan (9) _____ que no será fácil
enfrentarse a sus compañeros y que debe hacer algo para adaptarse a la nueva escuela.

Así (10) _____ esta magnífica historia: un niño que (11) _____ con ser
aceptado. Sin duda, esta situación nos (12) _____ nuestra niñez y los problemas que
(13) _____ a los más pequeños en esta difícil etapa de la vida. Una película totalmente
recomendable para ver en familia.

11. Calendario Completa las oraciones según lo que dice el calendario con los verbos conjugados en
presente de indicativo. **17.D**

○	**Lunes**
	9:30 poner a lavar ropa
	11:00 salir de paseo con la abuela
	15:00 traer al perro de la veterinaria
	17:00 hacer resumen de literatura
	20:00 componer canción para Paola
	22:00 proponer casamiento a Paola

Bueno, hoy es un día muy especial y complicado, pero
ya tengo todo organizado en mi mente. Si a las 9:30
(1) _____*pongo*_____ a lavar la ropa, a las 10:30 puedo colgarla,
justo cuando (2) _____ de paseo con la abuela.
Después de una larga caminata con ella, (3) _____
a casa al perro que está en la veterinaria. Duermo una breve
siesta y a las 17:00 (4) _____ el resumen de literatura.
Después, me baño y me visto bien elegante con mi ropa
recién lavada. A las 20:00, uso toda mi inspiración y le
(5) _____ una canción a Paola. Con esa canción, le
(6) _____ casamiento. ¡No hay forma de que diga que no!

12. Llenar Completa las oraciones con los verbos conjugados en presente de indicativo. **17.D**

Modelo

Yo no ___*intervengo*___ (intervenir) en las disputas de mis amigos.

1. Yo no te _____ (oír) bien si no hablas claro.

2. La escultura _____ (tener) más de trescientos años.

3. ¿Finalmente _____ (venir) tu familia a visitarte?

4. Tú siempre _____ (maldecir) cuando conduces. No debes hacerlo frente a los niños.

5. O te _____ (atener) a las reglas de la casa o te buscas otro lugar donde vivir.

6. Cuando _____ (decir, yo) algo, quiero que me escuches.

7. ¿Los bebés _____ (oír) también cuando están en el vientre de su mamá?

13. Escribir Escribe oraciones completas siguiendo el modelo. `17.D`

> **Modelo**
>
> yo – dar – flor / tú – dar – beso
> *Yo te doy una flor si tú me das un beso.*

1. yo – decir – la verdad / tú – decir – la verdad – también

_____

2. ellos – ver – el documental / yo – verlo – también

_____

3. yo – estar – de buen humor / vosotros – estar – de buen humor – también

_____

4. yo – ir – a la fiesta / tú – ir – también

_____

5. yo – traer – el pastel / vosotros – traer – un regalo

_____

14. Indicar Para cada oración, indica por qué se utiliza el presente de indicativo. `17.E`

Ejemplos	Acciones presentes	Costumbres	Hechos intemporales
1. Hoy hago ejercicios en el parque.			
2. La Luna es un satélite de la Tierra.			
3. Cuatro más ocho son doce.			
4. A las 7 abre la panadería.			
5. Por la noche, comemos en el salón.			
6. En Argentina, se habla español.			
7. Ahora mismo llamo a la tía.			

15. Escoger Para cada oración, indica por qué se utiliza el presente de indicativo. `17.E`

_____ 1. En 1816, se declara la independencia de Argentina.
   a. presente histórico   b. hechos intemporales

_____ 2. El domingo cocino un riquísimo pollo.
   a. presente para dar órdenes   b. presente para referirse al futuro

_____ 3. ¿Te doy dinero para el metro?
   a. presente para dar órdenes   b. presente de confirmación

_____ 4. Si duermo mal, estoy cansadísimo al día siguiente.
   a. cláusulas condicionales   b. hechos intemporales

_____ 5. ¡Ya mismo dejas lo que haces y vienes aquí!
   a. presente para dar órdenes   b. presente para referirse al futuro

_____ 6. ¿Tomamos un café?
   a. presente de confirmación   b. presente para referirse al futuro

16. Unir Une las frases para formar oraciones lógicas. `17.F`

1. Gonzalo trabaja en una fábrica _____
2. Los niños leen cuentos de terror _____
3. Ulises está trabajando _____
4. Estoy llegando a tu casa, _____
5. Los profesores están leyendo tu examen _____
6. Llego tarde, _____
7. Mis colegas están viajando a Europa _____
8. Te escribo por correo electrónico _____
9. Estoy trabajando en mi tesis _____

a. y no quiere que lo molesten ahora.
b. y siempre tienen miedo a la hora de dormir.
c. baja a abrirme la puerta.
d. y además estudia ingeniería.
e. no me esperes para comer.
f. y no pueden creer los errores ortográficos que tiene.
g. la semana que viene.
h. y espero terminarla pronto.
i. en este momento porque tienen que ir a una conferencia en Madrid.

17. Presente progresivo Escribe oraciones completas siguiendo el modelo. `17.F`

> **Modelo**
>
> Juan Carlos / escuchar / música
> *Juan Carlos está escuchando música.*

1. ellos / jugar / al baloncesto _____
2. nosotros / mirar / televisión _____
3. yo / servir / la cena _____
4. Elena / leer / una revista _____
5. ¿ / qué / hacer / tú / ? _____

18. Síntesis ¿Presente o presente progresivo? Completa las oraciones con el verbo conjugado en presente o presente progresivo. `17.A–17.F`

> **Modelo**
>
> Ellos _____*aprenden*_____ mucho en sus clases este semestre.

1. A Elena le _____ (encantar) las flores rojas.
2. Roberto _____ (casarse) con Susana en mayo.
3. _____ (llamar, yo) a la puerta, ¡pero no me abres! ¿Por qué?
4. Por el contexto, _____ (deducir, yo) que ese término está relacionado con la física.
5. Todavía _____ (elegir, yo) qué voy a comer. ¿Tú ya elegiste?
6. Tu recuerdo me _____ (perseguir) día y noche.
7. Mi esposa y yo _____ (construir) una casa en el bosque. En noviembre, estará terminada.
8. ¿Por qué no _____ (empezar, tú) a cocinar mientras yo limpio el comedor?
9. En este momento no _____ (poder, yo) atenderte.
10. Mi amiga _____ (llegar) de Australia la semana que viene.
11. No puede atender el teléfono porque en este instante _____ (dormir).
12. Si no _____ (descansar), te vas a enfermar.

19. Síntesis Verbos Conjuga estos verbos en presente y presente progresivo. Si no es posible conjugar el verbo en presente progresivo, coloca una X. `17.A–17.F`

Modelo

dar (yo) *doy estoy dando*

1. perder (ellos) _____ _____
2. atravesar (yo) _____ _____
3. querer (ellos) _____ _____
4. costar (él) _____ _____
5. poder (vos) _____ _____
6. promover (yo) _____ _____
7. confesar (nosotros) _____ _____
8. estar (vosotros) _____ _____
9. destruir (tú) _____ _____
10. oír (ella) _____ _____
11. deber (tú) _____ _____
12. salir (yo) _____ _____

20. Síntesis Hábitos Escribe un párrafo de por lo menos cinco oraciones en presente de indicativo en las que menciones actividades diarias. Incluye por lo menos dos verbos que posean cambios en la raíz y uno irregular. `17.A–17.F`

Modelo

Por las mañanas me despierto a las siete de la mañana…

_____
_____
_____
_____
_____
_____
_____
_____
_____
_____
_____
_____
_____
_____
_____
_____
_____

Practice more at **vhlcentral.com.**

1. Verbos Lee el texto e indica los verbos conjugados en pretérito perfecto simple. `18.B`

De:	francisco_gutierrez@universidad.edu
Para:	oficina_de_objetos_perdidos@universidad.edu
Asunto:	Libros perdidos

Me llamo Francisco y el día lunes 23 de agosto tuve una clase en el aula 213. Estuve allí desde las nueve hasta las doce. Cuando salí, olvidé un bolso con libros debajo de la silla. Son un libro de Matemáticas, otro de Física y uno de Química; los compré en la librería universitaria y escribí mi nombre en la primera hoja.

Si alguien los encontró, les pido que me escriban o me llamen al teléfono que aparece abajo.

¡Muchas gracias!
Teléfono: 932 80 394

2. Conjugar Conjuga estos verbos en pretérito perfecto simple. `18.B`

Modelo

huir (usted) _____ *huyó* _____

1. abrazar (yo) _____
2. andar (vosotros) _____
3. traer (tú) _____
4. oír (nosotras) _____
5. destruir (ustedes) _____

6. pagar (yo) _____
7. reír (usted) _____
8. venir (nosotras) _____
9. leer (ella) _____
10. practicar (yo) _____

3. Completar Completa las oraciones usando el pretérito perfecto simple. `18.B`

Modelo

Nosotros _____ *perdimos* _____ (perder) el avión anoche.

1. Ayer yo _____ (jugar) al fútbol durante tres horas.
2. Yo ya te _____ (explicar) tres veces el argumento de la película.
3. El lunes yo _____ (tocar) el timbre de tu casa, pero nadie _____ (contestar).
4. _____ (caerse) el aceite al piso. Ten cuidado.
5. Es increíble lo rápido que _____ (reconstruirse) la ciudad después de la inundación.
6. Carolina _____ (sentirse) mal todo el día y ahora está en el hospital.
7. ¿Quién _____ (poner) un calcetín en la nevera?
8. El chofer _____ (conducir) a una velocidad superior a la permitida.

4. Reescribir Reescribe las oraciones con el sujeto indicado. `18.B`

> **Modelo**
>
> Ayer fui a la estación de tren para comprar los boletos. (nosotros)
> *Fuimos a la estación de tren para comprar los boletos.*

1. Cristina averiguó el teléfono del chico que vio en el autobús. (yo)

_____

2. ¿Por qué llegaron tarde tus compañeros? (tú)

_____

3. ¿Oíste tú también un ruido fuerte? (él)

_____

4. Dormimos muy bien anoche. (ellos)

_____

5. Nunca supimos el motivo del incendio. (yo)

_____

6. Carla y Juan hicieron la comida. (ella)

_____

5. Cambiar Escribe estos verbos en pretérito imperfecto. `18.D`

> **Modelo**
>
> (ustedes) mienten _____ *mentían* _____

1. (yo) estuve _____
2. (yo) duermo _____
3. (tú) comiste _____
4. (nosotros) vivimos _____
5. (nosotros) somos _____

6. (nosotros) vemos _____
7. (vosotros) vais _____
8. (ellos) compraron _____
9. (nosotros) estamos _____
10. (yo) supe _____

6. Unir Decide si las explicaciones hacen referencia al pretérito perfecto simple (PPS) o al pretérito imperfecto (PI). Luego une las explicaciones con los ejemplos. `18.B–18.E`

Explicación	Ejemplo
1. Se usa para constatar datos históricos. _____	a. Ya iba a llamarte cuando sonó el timbre.
2. Se usa para expresar cómo solía ser una persona en el pasado. _____	b. El famoso pintor nació el 3 de mayo de 1599.
3. Se usa para expresar una acción en el pasado que no sucedió debido a una interrupción. _____	c. El autobús se descompuso en el medio de la ruta.
4. Se usa para enfatizar la simultaneidad de dos acciones en el pasado. _____	d. Mi novio siempre me regalaba flores cuando venía a visitarme.
5. Se usa para expresar cortesía. _____	e. Mi bisabuelo era amable, simpático y muy culto.
6. Se usa para indicar que algo sucedió en el pasado. _____	f. Quería pedirle un favor.
7. Se usa para enfatizar el fin de una acción y el comienzo de otra. _____	g. Llevaba cinco años sin ir al cine.
8. Se usa para expresar la duración de tiempo. _____	h. Ese día salí de casa a las 10, tomé el autobús a las 11 y llegué al trabajo a tiempo.

7. Elegir Elige la opción correcta. `18.B–18.E`

1. ¿Qué día _____ (visitabas/visitaste) el museo? Me pareció haberte visto.

2. Cuando _____ (cumplí/cumplía) ocho años, me regalaron mi primera bicicleta.

3. Cuando era estudiante, _____ (me desperté / me despertaba) temprano y _____ (desayuné/desayunaba) con mucha tranquilidad.

4. El día _____ (fue/estaba) soleado, pero de repente _____ (se nublaba / se nubló) y _____ (comenzaba/comenzó) a llover.

5. Juguemos a que _____ (teníamos/tuvimos) una gran mansión para nosotras y que _____ (fuimos/éramos) millonarias.

6. Cuando _____ (fui/iba) a salir de casa, _____ (me acordé / me acordaba) de que era el cumpleaños de mi madre.

7. Mi primera maestra _____ (se llamó / se llamaba) Claudia.

8. A las ocho de la mañana, _____ (hubo/había) sol, pero de todos modos _____ (decidí/decidía) no ir al parque.

9. _____ (Fui/Iba) camino a casa cuando _____ (me encontré / me encontraba) con Pedro.

8. Seleccionar Escoge la forma correcta de los verbos en la composición de Eduardo. `18.B–18.E`

Mi escuela nueva

El 7 de septiembre de 2010 (1) _____ (**iba/fui**) por primera vez a mi escuela nueva. Me (2) _____ (**impactaba/impactó**) la belleza del edificio: tenía tres pisos, dos jardines gigantes y una cancha de fútbol propia. Cuando (3) _____ (**entraba/entré**) en la clase, todos mis compañeros me saludaron con una sonrisa. La directora incluso me (4) _____ (**daba/dio**) un regalo de bienvenida. Cuando (5) _____ (**terminaba/terminó**) la clase, mis compañeros me (6) _____ (**invitaban/invitaron**) a tomar un helado. En mi escuela anterior, mis compañeros (7) _____ (**eran/fueron**) aburridos y antipáticos. ¡Qué suerte que (8) _____ (**decidía/decidí**) cambiarme de escuela! Estoy contentísimo.

9. ¿Pretérito perfecto simple o pretérito imperfecto? Decide qué tiempo verbal debes usar y completa las oraciones con los verbos de la lista. `18.B–18.E`

aliviar	decir	haber	ir (2)	sacar	ser
dar	doler	hacer	llegar	sentarse	

El martes pasado (1) ____*fui*____ al dentista porque me (2) _____ la muela. ¡(3) _____ tanto que no (4) _____ al dentista! Por suerte, no (5) _____ mucha gente en la sala de espera.

En cuanto (6) _____ en el sillón, el dentista me (7) _____ una inyección con anestesia que (8) _____ totalmente el dolor. Después, me (9) _____ que abriera bien grande la boca ¡y me (10) _____ la muela! ¡Todo (11) _____ tan rápido que no (12) _____ a tener miedo!

10. Discurso indirecto Completa las oraciones de Catalina, que está enojada con su mejor amigo. Haz todos los cambios necesarios. `18.E`

> Tomás dijo: "Quiero que vengas a visitarme".
> Catalina: Me dijiste que *querías que fuera a visitarte*, pero después no parecías tan contento de verme.

1. Tomás dijo: "Es muy importante ser puntual".
   Catalina: Me dijiste que _____ ,
   pero cuando llegué a tu casa, ¡no estabas!

2. Tomás dijo: "Tengo una sorpresa para ti".
   Catalina: Me dijiste que _____ ,
   pero todo era una mentira.

3. Tomás dijo: "Prefiero estar a solas contigo porque hace mucho que no nos vemos".
   Catalina: Me dijiste que _____ ,
   pero invitaste a tres amigos más.

4. Tomás dijo: "Espero ver todas las fotos de tus últimas vacaciones".
   Catalina: Me dijiste que _____ ,
   ¡pero te aburriste a la segunda foto!

5. Tomás dijo: "Hace tres meses que no paso tiempo con amigos".
   Catalina: Me dijiste que _____ ,
   ¡pero un amigo tuyo me dijo que diste una fiesta el sábado pasado!

6. Tomás dijo: "Eres mi mejor amiga".
   Catalina: Me dijiste que _____ ,
   ¡pero tus acciones dicen lo contrario!

11. Completar Completa las oraciones con el verbo conjugado en pretérito perfecto simple o pretérito imperfecto. `18.F`

> ¿Recuerdas cuántos años _____*teníamos*_____ (tener, nosotros) cuando nos mudamos a esta casa?

1. Finalmente, el caballo _____ (poder) adelantarse y ganó la carrera.

2. Nuestros vecinos no _____ (querer) hacer un fondo común para las reparaciones del edificio porque no tenían el dinero.

3. Ayer discutimos con Fernando, porque él _____ (querer) ir al cine y yo no.

4. Cuando conocí a Marta, en 2010, ella _____ (tener) un novio que se llamaba Omar.

5. ¿Recuerdas el club del barrio? Allí siempre se _____ (poder) jugar al baloncesto y al fútbol incluso sin ser socio.

6. Ayer _____ (saber, yo) que me contrataron para trabajar en la tienda de juguetes más grande del país; estoy muy contento.

7. Los señores Vega _____ (conocer) al nuevo profesor en la reunión.

8. Roberto no _____ (poder) trabajar ayer.

9. Esta mañana yo _____ (tener) una visita inesperada.

10. Nosotros no _____ (saber) dónde estabas.

11. Carmen _____ (conocer) Puerto Rico muy bien. Por eso la contrataron como guía.

12. Mis hermanos menores _____ (querer) esquiar, pero se cayeron muchas veces.

12. Síntesis El pasado Completa las oraciones con los verbos de la lista en el tiempo verbal indicado. `18.A–18.F`

Pretérito perfecto simple	Pretérito imperfecto
haber	ir
traducir	saber
oír	ser
pedir	haber
hacer	preparar

1. La directora nos _____ que nos comportáramos bien durante la ceremonia escolar.

2. Yo no _____ que tenías 18 años. ¡Pareces mayor!

3. ¿Quiénes _____ esta torta? ¡Está riquísima!

4. Graciela _____ al inglés este libro sobre historia suramericana.

5. Cuando yo _____ a llamarte, se cortó la luz.

6. La abuela siempre nos _____ el desayuno.

7. De pronto, _____ un ruido y salté de la cama.

8. Soñé que _____ una famosísima actriz.

9. En los años sesenta, _____ un gran movimiento de liberación femenina.

10. En esa época, _____ mucha gente que no sabía leer.

13. Síntesis Relato Completa el relato de Diego con el pretérito perfecto simple o el pretérito imperfecto. `18.A–18.F`

Pilar y yo (1) ____ *nos conocimos* ____ (conocerse) en el primer año de la escuela primaria cuando (2) _____ (tener) seis años y desde ese momento no nos separamos nunca.

Este año (3) _____ (decidir) festejar nuestros cumpleaños juntos. Pilar (4) _____ (enviar) todas las invitaciones y yo (5) _____ (comprar) las comida y las bebidas.

En el día de la fiesta el sol (6) _____ (brillar) y casi no (7) _____ (hacer) frío.

(8) _____ (Parecer) que todo iba a salir perfecto. Sin embargo, nadie (9) _____ (aparecer) a la hora esperada. Pilar y yo no (10) _____ (saber) por qué la gente no había venido.

De pronto, ambos (11) _____ (correr) a buscar las invitaciones. Cuando las (12) _____ (leer), ¡no (13) _____ (poder) creerlo! ¡La hora (14) _____ (ser) incorrecta!

Por suerte, dos horas después (15) _____ (comenzar) a llegar los invitados. La fiesta (16) _____ (estar) genial. (17) _____ (Hacer) mucho tiempo que nosotros no (18) _____ (divertirse) tanto en una fiesta de cumpleaños.

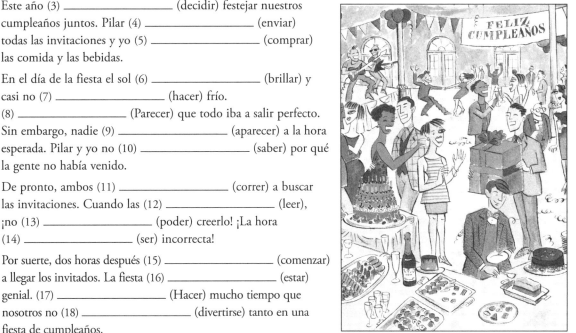

14. Síntesis Lo pasado es pasado Escribe un párrafo en el que menciones algo que te sucedió en el pasado. Describe la situación, en qué momento de tu vida pasó, cómo te sentiste, cómo era el lugar, etc. Utiliza el pretérito perfecto simple y el pretérito imperfecto. **18.A–18.F**

> **Modelo**
>
> *Cuando tenía 13 años, tuve una experiencia terrible. Era la hora del recreo en la escuela y mientras montaba en columpio, me pegaron un balonazo y me caí del columpio…*

_____

_____

_____

_____

_____

Practice more at **vhlcentral.com.**

The present perfect and the past perfect Chapter 19

1. Completar Completa las oraciones con los verbos conjugados en pretérito perfecto compuesto. **19.A**

> **Modelo**
>
> Nuestro jefe nos _____ *ha invitado* _____ (invitar) a una conferencia en Las Bahamas.

1. Nosotros _____ (estudiar) toda la tarde.

2. Todavía no _____ (terminar) mis tareas.

3. ¡Por fin los trabajadores _____ (recibir) un aumento de sueldo!

4. Vosotros ya _____ (esperar) demasiado.

5. Las autoridades _____ (actuar) de forma muy responsable.

6. Roberto no _____ (llegar) todavía.

2. Reordenar Reordena las oraciones y conjuga los verbos en pretérito perfecto compuesto. **19.A**

> **Modelo**
>
> ¡ / te / de mí / Tan pronto / olvidar / !
> *¡Tan pronto te has olvidado de mí!*

1. ¿ / comer (tú) / Alguna vez / paella / ?

_____

2. no / vender / Lucía / todavía / su bicicleta

_____

3. Este año / en / esta zona / transformarse / un centro financiero

_____

4. En mi vida / un carro / tener / rojo

_____

5. ¿ / cuál será / mostrar / te / tu oficina / Tus jefes / ?

_____

3. Indicar Indica qué verbos tienen participios regulares y cuáles tienen participios pasados irregulares o las dos opciones. Escribe los participios. `19.A`

comprar	concurrir	describir
estar	descubrir	aumentar
sonreír	ver	hacer
leer	freír	morir

Regulares	Irregulares
comprado	

4. Participios irregulares Completa las oraciones conjugando los verbos en pretérito perfecto compuesto. `19.A`

Modelo

Yo te _____ *he escrito* _____ (escribir) un mensaje de texto.

1. El músico aún no _____ (componer) la canción que le pidió el director de cine porque estaba muy enfermo.

2. ¿_____ (Leer, vosotros) bien qué dice ese cartel?

3. Veo que ya _____ (volver, tú).

4. ¿Quién _____ (abrir) la puerta?

5. Mi madre _____ (traer) unas flores hermosas.

6. ¿Dónde _____ (poner) Olivia el azúcar?

7. Hasta ahora, los estudiantes no _____ (resolver) el problema matemático; es muy difícil.

8. Nosotros _____ (decir) la verdad.

9. Yo _____ (imprimir) el documento para todos.

10. Gabriel _____ (romper) unos vasos. Debe tener más cuidado.

5. Decidir Decide por qué en estas oraciones se utiliza el pretérito perfecto compuesto. Indica *acción continua, acción incompleta* o *experiencia*, según el caso. `19.B`

Ejemplos	Explicación
1. ¿Has dormido alguna vez en una tienda de campaña?	
2. Hemos ido al centro comercial todos los días.	
3. Todavía no he conseguido hablar con mi abuela.	
4. ¡En mi vida he comido tanto como hoy!	
5. Juana está realmente bella hoy, ¿la has visto?	
6. Siempre he querido tener un pececito.	
7. Hasta hoy, no hemos tenido problema alguno.	
8. Muchas veces nos hemos ido a dormir sin comer.	
9. Lorena está haciendo dieta, pero aún no ha podido bajar de peso.	

6. Variaciones regionales Indica si el uso corresponde al español de Latinoamérica o al de España. `19.C`

Modelos

> Ya he visto el último episodio de la serie. _____*España*_____
> Ya vendieron todas las boletas para el concierto. ____*Latinoamérica*____

1. ¡Por fin te he encontrado en casa! _____

2. Hace un momento he visto a Sandra en el balcón. _____

3. Ya hemos viajado a Lima en avión. _____

4. Sí, ya almorcé. _____

5. ¿Por qué te has levantado tan temprano esta mañana? _____

6. Finalmente Luis Fernando terminó de comer. _____

7. ¿Ya te conté sobre la nueva profesora? _____

8. Hoy he hablado con los vecinos. _____

7. El pretérito pluscuamperfecto Completa las oraciones usando el pretérito pluscuamperfecto. `19.D`

Modelo

> Sofía me contó que ya _____*había oído*_____ (oír) las noticias.

1. Cuando llegué, todos los autobuses ya _____ (salir).

2. Yo nunca _____ (imaginar) que algo así podía sucederme.

3. Una semana antes, nosotros _____ (recibir) una carta de la tía, en la que decía que estaba muy bien de salud.

4. Mi hermanito no _____ (entender) la letra de la canción hasta que yo se la expliqué.

5. No pudimos viajar porque _____ (olvidar) el pasaporte en casa.

6. Roberto nos dijo que su perro _____ (comerse) su tarea de matemáticas.

7. Hasta ese momento, jamás _____ (probar, nosotros) el helado con sabor a café.

8. ¿Tú ya _____ (distribuir) los folletos cuando descubrieron el error?

8. **¿Por qué?** Indica por qué se utiliza el pretérito pluscuamperfecto en estas oraciones. Escribe el número de la oración en la columna correcta. `19.E`

Acción previa en el pasado	Discurso indirecto

1. El cliente llamó al camarero y le dijo que había visto una mosca en su sopa.
2. No, todavía no había recibido tu mensaje cuando me llamaste.
3. Nos preguntaron si habíamos notado algún cambio en la casa.
4. Llegaste justo cuando yo había salido de casa.
5. ¿Ya habías conocido a Francisco cuando te graduaste?
6. Invitamos a Eduardo a una fiesta, pero nos dijo que la noche anterior no había dormido mucho y estaba cansado.
7. ¿Vosotros os habíais mudado ya cuando vine a vivir a Chile?

9. **Modificar** Modifica las oraciones de manera lógica usando el pretérito pluscuamperfecto. `19.E`

Modelo

Me fui de casa y luego tú llegaste. (cuando)
Cuando llegaste a casa, yo ya me había ido.

1. Apagué mi teléfono celular y luego tú me llamaste. (cuando)
   _____
2. Nos levantamos de la cama y luego sonó el despertador. (cuando)
   _____
3. Laura estudió mucho y luego aprobó el examen. (porque)
   _____
4. Natalia dejó la dieta y luego subió de peso. (porque)
   _____
5. Terminamos de comer y luego llegó Raúl. (cuando)
   _____
6. Pablo se rompió la pierna esquiando y luego no pudo ir a la fiesta. (porque)
   _____

10. **Síntesis Unir** Une las frases para crear una narración lógica. `19.A–19.D`

1. Todavía no me _____
2. Sin duda, este último año _____
3. Al buscar mi bolso, me di cuenta de que _____
4. Le pregunté al camarero si _____
5. Me contestó que, cuando ocurrió el hecho, él todavía no _____
6. Hasta ahora, nadie _____
7. Jamás me _____

a. me lo habían robado.
b. había empezado su turno.
c. he sentido tan indefensa como hoy.
d. ha encontrado mi bolso ni al ladrón.
e. he tenido mucha mala suerte.
f. he recuperado de esta amarga situación por la que pasé.
g. había visto a alguien sospechoso.

11. **Síntesis ¿Cuál?** Completa las oraciones con pretérito perfecto compuesto o pluscuamperfecto. `19.A–19.D`

> **Modelo**
>
> ¿Tú _____*has comido*_____ (comer) pulpo alguna vez?

1. Todavía no _____ (encontrar) al amor de mi vida. ¿Lo encontraré algún día?

2. Siempre _____ (anhelar) tener un carro; pero, ahora que lo tengo, no lo uso.

3. El doctor me dijo que yo _____ (cometer) un error al no consultar antes por mi dolor de espalda.

4. ¿No _____ (terminar) tu tarea todavía? Ya llega el profesor.

5. Nosotros _____ (dormir) todos los días hasta las once de la mañana. Deberíamos despertarnos más temprano.

6. _____ (nevar) muchísimo y por eso no podíamos usar las bicicletas.

7. Ella solamente quería saber si tú _____ (limpiarse) los pies antes de entrar a la casa.

8. Hasta ahora, ya _____ (tomar, yo) cinco clases de salsa.

9. Julián no me _____ (devolver) el libro de matemáticas. Lo llamaré para pedírselo.

10. Todos _____ (imprimir) sus ensayos, ¡pero yo no! Por suerte, corrí a casa y lo imprimí de inmediato.

12. **Síntesis Seleccionar** Escoge la opción que corresponda al tiempo verbal del fragmento subrayado en cada oración. `19.A–19.G`

1. Cuando se despertó, supo que <u>había dormido</u> más de la cuenta.
   - a. pretérito perfecto compuesto
   - b. pretérito pluscuamperfecto
   - c. pretérito anterior

2. El fotógrafo comenzó a tomar fotos cuando <u>hubo iniciado</u> el evento.
   - a. pretérito perfecto compuesto
   - b. pretérito pluscuamperfecto
   - c. pretérito anterior

3. El carpintero ya <u>había construido</u> dos mesas cuando lo supervisaron.
   - a. pretérito perfecto compuesto
   - b. pretérito pluscuamperfecto
   - c. pretérito anterior

4. Internet <u>ha resuelto</u> problemas de comunicación en comunidades alejadas.
   - a. pretérito perfecto compuesto
   - b. pretérito perfecto simple
   - c. pretérito pluscuamperfecto

5. Los niños <u>trajeron</u> alegría al hogar.
   - a. pretérito perfecto compuesto
   - b. pretérito perfecto simple
   - c. pretérito pluscuamperfecto

6. Nadie <u>ha dicho</u> al jefe que ya están funcionando las máquinas reparadas.
   - a. pretérito perfecto compuesto
   - b. pretérito perfecto simple
   - c. pretérito pluscuamperfecto

13. **Síntesis Escribir** Escribe un párrafo sobre tres cosas que has hecho desde el semestre pasado y dos cosas que habías hecho antes para mejorar las calificaciones. `19.A–19.G`

> **Modelo**
>
> *Para mejorar mi español, desde el semestre pasado he tomado varios cursos de conversación. Y en el semestre anterior a ese, me había inscrito en un club de repaso…*

_____

_____

_____

_____

Practice more at **vhlcentral.com.**

1. Completar   Completa las oraciones con el futuro simple. **20.B**

> **Modelo**
>
> El famoso artista _____*dará*_____ (dar) un gran concierto en México.

1. ¿La abuela _____ (cocinar) para nosotros el domingo?

2. ¿Tú me _____ (ayudar) con la mudanza?

3. Los periodistas dicen que nosotros _____ (elegir) al candidato conservador.

4. Si te comes toda la comida, yo te _____ (regalar) un riquísimo chocolate.

5. Las reuniones se _____ (cancelar) hasta nuevo aviso.

6. Según los expertos, los precios de los alimentos _____ (subir) un tres por ciento este año.

2. Verbos   Para cada verbo, indica cuál es la raíz usada para conjugarlo en futuro simple. **20.B**

> **Modelo**
>
> decir *dir-*

1. hacer _____
2. salir _____
3. valer _____
4. tener _____
5. venir _____
6. saber _____
7. caber _____
8. poner _____
9. haber _____
10. querer _____

3. En el futuro   Completa el texto con los verbos de la lista conjugados en futuro simple. **20.B**

> hacer   poder   querer   salir   ~~tener~~   valer   venir

Cuando sea grande, (1) _____*tendré*_____ muchísimo dinero y compraré una casa que (2) _____ millones de dólares. (3) _____ fiestas a las que (4) _____ muchísimas personas de todas partes del mundo. Seré tan famoso que (5) _____ en las portadas de todas las revistas y todos los medios (6) _____ hacerme entrevistas. Pero la gran pregunta es: ¿cómo (7) _____ ganar tanto dinero?

4. Transformar Convierte estas oraciones a futuro simple. `20.B`

> **Modelo**
>
> Mi papá contiene la respiración por más de un minuto bajo el agua.
> *Mi papá contendrá la respiración por más de un minuto bajo el agua.*

1. A veces la prensa te dice realidades a medias.

   _____

2. Los artistas componen nuevas canciones para el próximo álbum.

   _____

3. Tú sostienes a tu familia solo.

   _____

4. Los mensajes provienen de un remitente desconocido.

   _____

5. El niño de Jorge se duerme con una lámpara encendida.

   _____

5. Seleccionar En estas oraciones, indica por qué se emplea el futuro simple. `20.C`

1. Creo que mañana entregarán las notas del examen.
   a. suposición sobre el futuro   b. acción en el futuro

2. Las personas de este signo conocerán a mucha gente este año.
   a. predicción   b. consecuencia en el futuro

3. No robarás.
   a. acción en el futuro   b. leyes/reglas

4. No habrá trenes mañana debido a la huelga general.
   a. suposición sobre el presente   b. acción en el futuro

5. Este año iré de vacaciones al Caribe.
   a. acción en el futuro   b. suposición sobre el futuro

6. Alicia estará en la plaza. Ve y fíjate.
   a. suposición sobre el presente   b. suposición sobre el futuro

6. Indicar En cada oración, indica por qué se usa el futuro simple. `20.C`

> a. acciones futuras   d. suposiciones sobre el futuro
> b. suposiciones sobre el presente   e. pronósticos
> c. leyes/reglas   f. consecuencias en el futuro

1. ¿Quién será esa chica que nos está saludando? _____
2. Seguramente Estela será nuestra profesora de matemáticas este año. _____
3. Si trabajáis mucho, tendréis muy buenas notas. _____
4. Los trabajadores dispondrán de un día de vacaciones por cada veinte días trabajados. _____
5. Este fin de semana, lloverá en el norte del país. _____
6. Volverás a Chile algún día. _____

7. Unir Une los elementos de las dos columnas para formar oraciones lógicas. Usa cada respuesta solo una vez. **20.C**

1. Hoy yo _____   a. estaré invitado a la boda?
2. Por favor, tráigame _____   b. un hospital nuevo en 2025.
3. ¿Le compramos _____   c. un vaso de agua.
4. Seré _____   d. penas de hasta ocho años por ese delito.
5. Habrá _____   e. lavo los platos, ¿sí?
6. ¿Yo también _____   f. un regalo?
7. Me llevo _____   g. rico algún día, sin duda.
8. Se construirá _____   h. esa bufanda colorida.

8. Reordenar Ordena las palabras para crear oraciones. Conjuga los verbos en futuro simple. **20.C**

> **Modelo**
>
> hoy / Como / ser / todos estos días, / ser / un día lluvioso
> *Como todos estos días, hoy será un día lluvioso.*

1. tarde / esta / también / llegar / Nosotros / noche
   _____

2. al cine / Yo / del mes / ir / al final
   _____

3. imprudentes / sancionados / Ser / todos los conductores
   _____

4. en / de días / Tus heridas / sanar / un par
   _____

5. ? / valer / de cuero / Cuánto / ¿ / esa chaqueta
   _____

6. nevar / en las montañas / Mañana / mucho
   _____

7. el viernes / No / clase / haber
   _____

8. de la ciudad / Celebrarse / en julio / el bicentenario
   _____

9. Emparejar Une las oraciones con las explicaciones. **20.D**

_____ 1. ¿Vas a comerte toda la ensalada?

_____ 2. Casi no hay más helado. Si no te apuras, vas a quedarte sin nada.

_____ 3. Mañana a las doce viene la abuela.

_____ 4. Ya vendrá tu madre, no llores más.

_____ 5. Ya van a abrir los negocios.

a. Se describe una acción explicitándose mediante adverbios que tendrá lugar en el futuro.

b. Se expresa una predicción.

c. Se expresa una intención de algo que se hará inmediatamente.

d. Se describe un evento con gran probabilidad de suceder de inmediato.

e. Se describe una acción o un hecho inminente.

10. Futuro compuesto Completa las oraciones con los verbos conjugados en futuro compuesto. `20.E`

> **Modelo**
>
> En octubre, yo ya _____*me habré mudado*_____ (mudarse) a San Francisco.

1. El lunes a esta hora, _____ (terminar, nosotros) la mudanza.

2. ¿Dónde _____ (quedar) mi cepillo de dientes? No lo veo por ningún lado.

3. ¿_____ (Haber) disturbios después del partido de fútbol?

4. Si no asistes a las clases de francés, _____ (desperdiciar) el dinero que pagaste.

5. ¡Qué increíble! Dentro de un mes, _____ (graduarse, nosotros).

6. Mario _____ (cansarse) de esperar. Por eso, se fue sin nosotros.

7. Cuando me vieron con esa camiseta, _____ (pensar) que soy fanático de Boca Juniors.

8. Ana ya _____ (conseguir) entradas. Por eso no te llamó para comprar tu entrada extra.

9. Si trabajáis este verano, antes de graduaros ya _____ (obtener) experiencia laboral.

10. No sé exactamente cuántos kilos de carne compré, pero _____ (comprar) unos cinco o seis kilos.

11. Elegir En cada oración, elige la opción correcta. `20.F`

1. Ya _____ (comeremos / habremos comido) en cualquier momento.

2. ¿A Lucas le _____ (habrá gustado / gustará) realmente mi regalo? No parecía demasiado sorprendido al abrirlo.

3. Según las encuestas, el candidato liberal _____ (habrá obtenido / obtendrá) un cincuenta por ciento de los votos.

4. ¿Quién _____ (se encargará / se habrá encargado) de la decoración del salón? Es realmente una obra de arte.

5. Según el periódico, mañana _____ (lloverá / habrá llovido) por la tarde.

6. Si haces ejercicio, _____ (tendrás / habrás tenido) una vida más saludable.

7. Creo que _____ (habrá / habrá habido) muchísimo para ver en la exposición de mañana.

8. ¿Dónde _____ (irá / habrá ido) tu hermana? Hace un ratito estaba aquí.

12. ¿Futuro simple o compuesto? Completa las oraciones con el futuro simple o el futuro compuesto. `20.F`

> contar   ~~estar~~   jugar   subir   valer   venir

> **Modelo**
>
> Si nos acostamos temprano, mañana _____*estaremos*_____ más descansados.

1. ¿Te das cuenta de que dentro de una hora ya _____ más de cuatro horas seguidas? En lugar de eso, deberías estudiar más.

2. ¿Cuánto _____ esa hermosa blusa?

3. ¿_____ tu hermana a cenar? Ya lleva una hora de retraso.

4. ¿Piensas que los precios _____ en diciembre por la Navidad?

5. ¿Vanesa le _____ la verdad a su madre sobre sus malas calificaciones? Yo no lo creo, porque su madre dice a todos que su hija es la mejor alumna de la clase.

13. Síntesis Escoger Lee el texto y elige la forma verbal más apropiada. `20.B–20.F`

Planes para estas vacaciones

Si todo sale bien, dentro de quince días (1) _____ (estaré / habré estado) en
Río de Janeiro, disfrutando de la playa y de la compañía de mis amigos. Pero primero tengo que hacer
varias cosas.

Esta semana (2) _____ (tengo / habré tenido) una reunión con mi jefe para
pedirle que me aumente el sueldo y me dé algunos días más de vacaciones. Seguramente me
(3) _____ (habrá dicho / dirá) que no al principio; pero después de una hora,
(4) _____ (acepta / aceptará) mi pedido. Pensándolo bien, ahora mismo lo
(5) _____ (habré llamado / voy a llamar) para adelantar la reunión.

La semana que viene ya (6) _____ (habré recibido / recibiré) mi aumento de sueldo
y con ese dinero (7) _____ (podré / habré podido) comprar los pasajes de avión y
los regalos para mis amigos. A Juanita quiero comprarle un libro con fotos de San Francisco; y a Pablo,
una camiseta de béisbol. Estoy segura de que (8) _____ (quedarán / habrán quedado)
boquiabiertos con los regalos.

Por último, espero que el tiempo sea bueno. Según el pronóstico, (9) _____
(habrá llovido / lloverá) muy poco. Espero que así sea, porque de lo contrario (10) _____
(habré gastado / gastaré) muchísimo dinero para estar todo el día dentro del hotel.

---

14. Síntesis Planes Escribe un párrafo de por lo menos cinco oraciones sobre tus planes para el futuro: la
educación, el trabajo, el matrimonio, hijos, etc. Utiliza el futuro simple, el futuro compuesto y otras
formas de expresar el futuro en español. `20.A–20.F`

> **Modelo**
>
> *Iré a la escuela de posgrado para estudiar la literatura española…*

_____
_____
_____
_____
_____
_____
_____
_____
_____
_____
_____
_____
_____
_____
_____
_____

Practice more at **vhlcentral.com.**

1. Completar Completa las oraciones con los verbos conjugados en el condicional simple. **21.A**

Modelo

Ustedes _____*llegarían*_____ (llegar) más rápido en metro.

1. ¿_____ (Tener, tú) una manta de más? No encuentro la mía y tengo frío.

2. Si hiciéramos ejercicio, _____ (poder, nosotros) ir de excursión a las montañas.

3. ¿Te _____ (gustar) venir a cenar a mi casa?

4. Si me preguntaras a mí, no _____ (saber) qué decirte.

5. La mujer policía nos dijo que el tren _____ (pasar) a las 17 horas.

6. ¿Crees que _____ (valer) la pena comprar una bicicleta nueva?

7. _____ (Deber, tú) trabajar menos horas. Luces muy cansado.

8. _____ (Querer) vender mi carro. ¿Cuánto dinero me _____ (dar, usted) por él?

9. Si pudieras viajar a cualquier parte, ¿adónde _____ (ir)?

10. Me _____ (encantar) ir al concierto esta noche.

11. Ellos no vinieron a clase ayer. ¿Dónde _____ (estar)?

12. Supimos que _____ (haber) una reunión hoy.

2. Verbos Completa las oraciones con los verbos de la lista conjugados en el condicional simple. **21.A**

| caber | decir | poner | querer | saber | ser | valer | ~~vivir~~ |

Modelo

En tu lugar, yo _____*viviría*_____ en un apartamento del centro.

1. ¿Crees que este sofá _____ en mi habitación?

2. Si supieras la verdad, ¿me la _____?

3. Si tuviera más espacio en el comedor, _____ aquí una mesa para ocho personas.

4. _____ conveniente que no gastaras tanto dinero en tecnología.

5. Constanza _____ tener más tiempo libre para hacer deportes.

6. ¿Crees que tus padres _____ en un pueblo pequeño?

7. Me robaron el canasto de la bicicleta. ¿Quién _____ un canasto tan viejo y roto?

8. ¿_____ acompañarme a la fiesta el viernes? Puedo pasarte a buscar.

9. Si estuviéramos en tu situación, no _____ qué hacer.

10. ¿Crees que _____ la pena invertir en acciones de esa compañía?

11. ¿Qué le _____ a vuestro actor favorito?

12. Acabo de comprar este cuadro y no sé dónde se vería mejor. ¿Usted dónde lo _____?

3. **¿Por qué?** Decide por qué se usa el condicional simple en estas oraciones: consejo, suposición o deseo. `21.B`

   1. ¿Te gustaría que te regalara una planta para tu graduación?
      a. consejo   b. suposición   c. deseo

   2. ¿Cómo le iría a Tamara en su primer día de clases?
      a. consejo   b. suposición   c. deseo

   3. Preferiría quedarme en casa.
      a. consejo   b. suposición   c. deseo

   4. Deberíais ordenar vuestras habitaciones: vendrán los abuelos este fin de semana.
      a. consejo   b. suposición   c. deseo

   5. Sería mejor que llegaras temprano. Necesito ayuda en la cocina.
      a. consejo   b. suposición   c. deseo

   6. Se cree que los griegos tendrían un sistema de comunicación eficiente.
      a. consejo   b. suposición   c. deseo

   7. A nosotros nos gustaría pintar la cocina de color verde. ¿Qué te parece la idea?
      a. consejo   b. suposición   c. deseo

   8. En tu lugar, yo seguiría con las clases de pintura. ¡Eres un genio para las artes!
      a. consejo   b. suposición   c. deseo

4. **Emparejar** Une las explicaciones sobre el condicional simple con los ejemplos. `21.B`

   1. Se usa para expresar deseos. _____

   2. Se usa para dar consejos y sugerencias. _____

   3. Se usa para expresar cortesía. _____

   4. Se usa para expresar duda o probabilidad en el pasado. _____

   5. Se usa para expresar un futuro desde un punto de vista pasado. _____

   6. Se usa para hacer una invitación. _____

   a. No sé a qué hora nos acostamos anoche. Serían las dos de la mañana.

   b. Deberías hablar más español que inglés. Así aprenderás más rápido.

   c. Me gustaría viajar al Congo.

   d. Nos prometiste que nos llamarías al mediodía.

   e. ¿Querrías ir al cine conmigo?

   f. ¿Te importaría cerrar la ventana?

5. **Oraciones** Completa las oraciones de Lucas de forma lógica y conjuga el verbo entre paréntesis. `21.B`

   1. Si estudiara más español, _____

   2. Si tuviera más dinero, _____

   3. Si mis amigos fueran más deportistas, _____

   4. Si mi madre me diera más libertad, _____

   5. Si tuviera videojuegos nuevos, _____

   6. Si no tuviera que ir a la escuela tan temprano, _____

   7. Si me encontrara con mi banda de música favorita, _____

   a. _____ (armar) un equipo de fútbol.

   b. _____ (poder) viajar a México.

   c. _____ (comprar) más ropa.

   d. _____ (dormir) más horas.

   e. _____ (salir) hasta tarde con mis amigos.

   f. _____ (venir) más amigos a visitarme.

   g. les _____ (decir) que me encanta su música.

6. Consejos Escribe los consejos que le da Estela a su hermanita enferma con los verbos conjugados en el condicional simple. `21.B`

> **Modelo**
> (en tu lugar / ponerse una bufanda)
> *En tu lugar, yo me pondría una bufanda.*

1. (en tu lugar / tomar mucho té)

   _____

2. (en tu lugar / guardar cama)

   _____

3. (deber / dormir más por la noche)

   _____

4. (en tu lugar / ir al médico)

   _____

5. (en tu lugar / no tomar medicamentos)

   _____

6. (en tu lugar / estar contenta por no ir a la escuela)

   _____

7. Condicional compuesto Completa las oraciones con los verbos conjugados en condicional compuesto. `21.C`

> **Modelo**
> Me _____ *habría gustado* _____ (gustar) pasar más tiempo con vosotros, pero tuve que trabajar muchísimo.

1. Si yo hubiera tenido más tiempo, _____ (hacer) las compras.
2. Si nos hubiéramos conocido antes, quizás _____ (ser) marido y mujer.
3. Si Olivia no se hubiera mudado a otro barrio, _____ (compartir) muchas más tardes juntas.
4. Me _____ (ir) mejor en el examen si me hubiera preparado mejor.
5. En tu lugar, yo no _____ (comer) tanto. Ahora te duele la barriga.
6. Con tu ayuda, _____ (tardar, nosotros) mucho menos en hacer la mudanza. ¡Pero no nos ayudaste!

8. Decidir Decide si el condicional compuesto se usa para expresar (a) *una situación imaginaria que contrasta con el presente* o (b) *una circunstancia hipotética del pasado.* `21.D`

1. Sin el cinturón de seguridad, el accidente habría sido mucho más grave. _____
2. Te habría invitado a la fiesta si hubiera sabido que estabas en la ciudad. _____
3. Si hubiera estado en tu lugar, yo habría visitado más museos. _____
4. Me aseguraste que, para esta fecha, habrías terminado el trabajo. _____
5. Si Pamela hubiera llevado una vianda para el viaje, no habría tenido que pagar ocho dólares por un chocolate. _____
6. Si Pedro hubiera sabido que yo estaba enferma, me habría llamado. _____

9. Elegir Escoge la forma correcta del verbo en el aviso publicitario. `21.D`

¿Qué (1) _____ (pasaría / habría pasado) si usted hubiera sabido los números de la pasada lotería de Navidad? ¿Se imagina cómo habría sido su vida? Piense cuántas casas (2) _____ (compraría / habría comprado) con ese dinero. Pero, claro, usted jamás (3) _____ (ganaría / habría ganado) la lotería porque no tenía... ¡la fabulosa BOLA DE CRISTAL®! El revolucionario producto que adivina el futuro.

Usted que ahora está solo, si hubiera tenido la BOLA DE CRISTAL®, (4) _____ (sabría / habría sabido) dónde encontrar al amor de su vida. ¡Incluso (5) _____ (habría tenido / tendría) al alcance de su mano todas las técnicas para conquistarlo!

Por eso, no siga perdiendo el tiempo. Deje atrás su pasado lleno de tristezas ¡y compre ya la BOLA DE CRISTAL®! ¡Debería (6) _____ (haberlo hecho / hacerlo) hace tiempo!

Llame ya al teléfono que aparece en pantalla y termine con sus incertidumbres.

10. Síntesis Escoger En cada oración, elige la opción correcta. `21.A–21.D`

1. No te preocupes, de todas maneras, ellos no _____ nuestra propuesta. Tenían muchas otras mejores.
   a. habrían aceptado   b. aceptarían

2. ¿_____ volver a casa ahora o más tarde? Haremos lo que tú quieras.
   a. Habrías preferido   b. Preferirías

3. Si me hubieras avisado, _____ una comida vegetariana.
   a. habría cocinado   b. cocinaría

4. ¿_____ estudiar más tiempo español antes de ir a Guatemala? Yo creo que fue el momento ideal para ti.
   a. Habrías preferido   b. Preferirías

5. Si hubiera sabido que dormías, no _____ la puerta.
   a. habría tocado   b. tocaría

6. Otra vez llegamos tarde. _____ menos en metro.
   a. Tardaríamos   b. Habríamos tardado

7. Supe que _____ una exposición de tu pintor favorito y corrí a decírtelo.
   a. habría   b. habría habido

8. ¡_____ prestarte dinero si tanta falta te hacía!
   a. Podría   b. Habría podido

9. ¿Dónde _____ Natalia ayer por la tarde? No estaba en la oficina.
   a. estaría   b. habría estado

10. Tú _____ la verdad desde un principio. Las cosas serían más claras entre nosotros ahora.
    a. dirías   b. deberías haber dicho

11. Síntesis ¿Condicional simple o compuesto? **Completa las oraciones con los verbos conjugados en condicional simple o condicional compuesto, según corresponda.** `21.A–21.D`

> **Modelo**
>
> ¿Tú _____*votarías*_____ (votar) de nuevo por Justo Juárez si se presentara a elecciones?

1. Si hubieras llevado el teléfono celular, nosotros no _____ (tener) este desencuentro.
2. Si fuera de vacaciones a Chile, me _____ (gustar) conocer Valparaíso.
3. Yo te _____ (regalar) otro libro si hubiera sabido que este ya lo tenías.
4. Con un mayor control del tránsito, la gente _____ (conducir) a la velocidad permitida.
5. ¿_____ (Votar) por ese candidato si hubieras sabido que solamente decía mentiras?

12. Síntesis Completar **Completa las oraciones con los verbos conjugados en condicional simple o condicional compuesto.** `21.A–21.D`

> **Modelo**
>
> En tu lugar, yo no _____*habría escrito*_____ (escribir) en los bancos de la escuela. Ahora te castigarán por ello.

1. Si supieras el esfuerzo que me costó aprender español, ¡no _____ (decir) que hablo mal!
2. ¿Te _____ (gustar) casarte conmigo? ¡Te amo tanto!
3. Nuestras mascotas _____ (ser) más obedientes si les hubiéramos enseñado modales a tiempo.
4. ¿_____ (ser) posible reservar una habitación para dos personas?
5. Las autoridades confirmaron que _____ (solucionar) la crisis energética para comienzos de 2030.
6. ¿Cuánto crees que _____ (valer) el alquiler de un apartamento como este?
7. Con una buena política de salud, este invierno _____ (haber) menos enfermos de gripe. Pero como ves, no fue así.

13. Síntesis Explicar **Explica qué habrías hecho tú en estas situaciones. Usa las frases de la lista.** `21.A–21.D`

> echarle la culpa a otro camarero — ~~llamar al cerrajero~~
> pedir disculpas — decirle que la pintura era buena

1. *Yo habría llamado al cerrajero* .
   _____
2. _____
   _____
3. _____
   _____
4. _____
   _____

14. Síntesis Lotería Si mañana te ganaras la lotería, ¿qué harías? Escribe lo que harías, utilizando cinco verbos en condicional. `21.A–21.D`

> **Modelo**
>
> *Si me ganara la lotería, llevaría de viaje a mi familia por todo el mundo…*

_____

_____

_____

_____

_____

🪄 Practice more at **vhlcentral.com**.

The subjunctive 🎾 Chapter 22

1. ¿Indicativo o subjuntivo? Lee el texto e indica si los verbos subrayados están en modo indicativo (I) o subjuntivo (S). `22.A`

Querida Lucía:

Te escribo porque (1) _____ tengo un gran dilema. (2) _____ Me gustaría tener una mascota, ya sea un gato o un perro. Probablemente (3) _____ busque un gato, porque son más independientes y no (4) _____ necesitan tanto cuidado.

En todo caso, dudo que mis padres (5) _____ acepten mi propuesta. Por eso, (6) _____ voy a buscar la forma de convencerlos. ¿Se te (7) _____ ocurren buenos argumentos que (8) _____ puedan convencerlos?

También pensé en llegar un día a casa con un gato o perro sin hacer muchas preguntas antes. Pero no (9) _____ quiero que mi mamá (10) _____ se enoje y (11) _____ me grite durante todo un día.

¿Qué (12) _____ me recomiendas que (13) _____ haga? Quiero tener una mascota y sé que (14) _____ podré hacerme cargo de ella.

Hasta pronto,
Raúl

2. Completar Completa las oraciones con los verbos de la lista conjugados en presente de subjuntivo. `22.B`

| charlar | comprender | ~~correr~~ | escribir | ladrar | transmitir | vivir |

> **Modelo**
>
> ¿Conoces algún animal que _____*viva*_____ más de cien años?

1. El entrenador espera que los jugadores _____ las reglas del juego.

2. Por más que _____ (tú), no podrás alcanzar el autobús.

3. ¿Hay algún canal de televisión que _____ el partido en directo?

4. Me gustaría que _____ (nosotros) con más tranquilidad en la sala.

5. La dueña del apartamento no quiere un perro que _____ si está solo.

6. Mi hermana me pide siempre que le _____ un correo electrónico cada semana.

3. Explicar Silvina le explica a su amiga las actividades que deben hacer para la próxima clase. Completa las oraciones siguiendo el modelo. `22.B`

> **Modelo**
>
> **PROFESORA** Mañana deberán llegar temprano a clase.
> **SILVINA** La profesora quiere que *mañana lleguemos temprano a clase.*

1. **PROFESORA** Deberán aprender de memoria el himno nacional.
   SILVINA La profesora quiere que _____.
2. **PROFESORA** Cada uno pasará al frente y lo cantará.
   SILVINA Ella quiere que cada uno _____.
3. **PROFESORA** Si lo desean, pueden cantar el himno en parejas.
   SILVINA Nos ha permitido que _____.
4. **PROFESORA** No deberán cometer ni un solo error al cantar la letra.
   SILVINA Ella no admitirá que _____.
5. **PROFESORA** Posiblemente la directora los escuchará cantar.
   SILVINA Dijo que es posible que _____.
6. **PROFESORA** Si todo sale bien, los mejores cantantes formarán parte del coro.
   SILVINA Ella espera que _____.

4. Subjuntivo Completa las oraciones con los verbos que tengan cambios ortográficos en presente de subjuntivo. `22.B`

> **Modelo**
>
> Entiendo por qué te disgusta tanto que la salsa de tomate te _____*salpique*_____ (salpicar) toda la ropa.

1. Espero que tus primos _____ (averiguar) pronto cómo arreglar los frenos de la bicicleta.
2. Ya hay pocos tigres siberianos. Espero que no se _____ (extinguir) estas especies de felinos.
3. ¡Es increíble que Daniel _____ (roncar) tan fuerte y no se despierte!
4. Te quedarás sin dinero. No conviene que tú lo _____ (sacar) todo de la cuenta.
5. Me encanta que mis papás se _____ (abrazar). Se quieren mucho.

5. Llenar Completa las oraciones con los verbos que tengan cambios ortográficos en presente de subjuntivo. `22.B`

> **Modelo**
>
> Una posibilidad es que _____*te dediques*_____ (dedicarse) a dar clases de matemáticas. Así podrás ganar dinero extra.

1. Es mejor que tú _____ (escoger) el regalo que prefieras. No conozco realmente tus gustos.
2. Espero que el pueblo _____ (elegir) bien a su futuro presidente.
3. Tu padre y yo no queremos que tus amigos _____ (seguir) llamando a la hora de comer.
4. Los profesores nos recomiendan que _____ (buscar) la bibliografía en sitios de Internet confiables.
5. Los jueces no permiten que sus vidas privadas _____ (influir) en sus trabajos.

6. Nota Completa la nota que escribió Renata a su hermanita menor con los verbos conjugados en presente de subjuntivo. **22.B**

agregar   apagar   cargar   destruir   poder   ~~salir~~   seguir   tocar (2)

Querida hermanita:

Sé que ya sabes cómo cuidar a mi tortuga, pero quiero asegurarme de que todo (1) _____ *salga* _____ bien.

Ante todo, te ruego que no (2) _____ el plato de Manuelita con demasiada lechuga. Ella come muy poco. Otra cosa importante: te sugiero que (3) _____ agua fresca al bebedero todas las mañanas.

Recuerda que a ella no le gusta que la (4) _____ demasiado. No es muy cariñosa y además se asusta cuando viene alguien nuevo. Por la noche, es mejor que (5) _____ la luz, así ella duerme mejor.

Mantén las puertas cerradas para que ella no (6) _____ las plantas que me regaló la abuela. Sé que quizás exagero, pero no quiero que Manuelita (7) _____ esas plantas con flores tan lindas.

Ojalá que (8) _____ recordar todo lo que te expliqué y te agradezco muchísimo tu ayuda. Sé que es mucho pedir que (9) _____ mis instrucciones al pie de la letra, pero sabes que Manuelita es como mi hija y quiero que siempre esté bien.

¡Nos vemos el lunes!
Renata

7. Conjugar Conjuga estos verbos en presente de subjuntivo en la persona indicada. **22.B**

Modelo

salir – yo *salga*

1. traer – tú _____
2. insinuar – ustedes _____
3. enviar – ella _____
4. guiar – nosotras _____
5. conocer – yo _____
6. decir – él _____
7. valer – ellas _____
8. tener – vosotros _____
9. convencer – tú _____
10. hacer – usted _____
11. caer – yo _____
12. venir – nosotros _____

8. Oraciones Completa las oraciones con los verbos que sean irregulares o tengan cambios ortográficos en presente de subjuntivo. `22.B`

| ampliar | ~~conducir~~ | decir | evaluar | oír | poner | ver |

> **Modelo**
>
> Te prohíbo que _____*conduzcas*_____ a una velocidad mayor a la permitida.

1. Ojalá _____ (ellos) esta carretera. Es muy angosta y hay muchos accidentes de tránsito.

2. Es mejor que le _____ al pintor que vienes de parte mía. Así te hará un descuento.

3. Esperemos que el gobierno pronto _____ los daños producidos por la catástrofe y _____ en marcha un plan de recuperación de los bosques quemados.

4. No estoy seguro de que la abuela _____ bien la música. Quizás deberíamos subir el volumen.

5. El profesor quiere que los estudiantes _____ este documental sobre los efectos del cambio climático.

9. Verbos con cambio de raíz Completa las oraciones con el verbo conjugado en presente de subjuntivo. `22.B`

> **Modelo**
>
> Espero que tú _____*cierres*_____ (cerrar) bien la puerta del apartamento.

1. No conviene que Rafael _____ (mentir) sobre su experiencia.

2. Carlos está cansado de que _____ (perder) su equipo favorito.

3. El niño espera que las cometas _____ (volar) hasta las nubes.

4. Victoria desea que Marcos le _____ (pedir) matrimonio en un restaurante elegante.

5. Necesitamos que los técnicos _____ (resolver) el problema de la red.

10. Contradecir Juancito contradice siempre a su amiga, Teresa. Completa lo que dice, siguiendo el modelo. `22.B`

> **Modelo**
>
> **TERESA** Las clases comenzarán a las doce.
> **JUANCITO** No es verdad que *las clases comiencen a las doce.*

1. **TERESA** Empieza a estudiar veinte días antes del examen.
   JUANCITO No es necesario que _____.

2. **TERESA** Te contaré una historia increíble.
   JUANCITO No quiero que me _____.

3. **TERESA** Seguramente la comida costará unos veinte dólares.
   JUANCITO No creo que _____.

4. **TERESA** Llueve muchísimo.
   JUANCITO No puede ser que _____.

5. **TERESA** Te despertaré a las nueve con el desayuno.
   JUANCITO No quiero que me _____.

6. **TERESA** Probablemente te devolveré los libros a fin de mes.
   JUANCITO Es poco probable que me _____.

11. Reescribir Reescribe las oraciones usando la persona indicada entre paréntesis como sujeto de cada verbo subrayado. `22.B`

> **Modelo**
>
> <u>Haremos</u> todo lo que <u>podamos</u> para recaudar dinero para los pobres.
> (tú) *Harás todo lo que puedas para recaudar dinero para los pobres.*

1. Es mejor que no <u>pensemos</u> en cosas negativas.
   (yo) _____

2. Cuando <u>descendáis</u> las escaleras, <u>veréis</u> a la derecha una gran puerta.
   (tú) _____

3. Los profesores no pretenden que <u>entiendas</u> todo el texto.
   (nosotros) _____

4. La niña insiste en que sus padres le <u>cuenten</u> un cuento cada noche.
   (yo) _____

5. Quiero que <u>oláis</u> el nuevo perfume que me compré.
   (tú) _____

12. Verbos Completa las oraciones con los verbos de la lista conjugados en presente de subjuntivo. `22.B`

> divertirse   dormir   herir   morir   preferir

> **Modelo**
>
> Otra posibilidad es que _____*durmamos*_____ (nosotros) en una tienda de campaña.

1. Es posible que Lucas _____ volver a casa más temprano. Mejor dale las llaves a él.

2. Quiero que _____ tiempo suficiente, así podréis estar atentos en el seminario de mañana.

3. Vamos a ponerle un bozal al perro para que no _____ a los niños.

4. Ojalá que _____ (nosotros) en la fiesta de Guido.

5. El día que mi perro _____ será el día más triste de mi vida.

13. Tabla Completa la tabla con los verbos conjugados en presente de subjuntivo. `22.B`

Pronombre	adquirir	jugar
yo	(1)	juegue
tú, vos	(2)	(6)
usted, él, ella	(3)	(7)
nosotros/as	(4)	juguemos
vosotros/as	adquiráis	(8)
ustedes, ellos/as	(5)	(9)

14. Artículo Completa el artículo con los verbos conjugados en presente de subjuntivo. `22.B`

adquirir   costar   divertirse   dormir   enfriarse   guiar   organizar   ~~pensar~~   querer   volver

---

"Acampar es incómodo"

Aquí ofrecemos consejos sobre cómo acampar, justamente para quienes (1) _____*piensen*_____ que acampar es un sufrimiento.

- Es importante que realmente (2) _____ (ustedes) ir de campamento. Ir a regañadientes (*reluctantly*) o porque no tienen reserva de hotel es un mal comienzo.
- Si eligen un campamento libre, hablen con un guardaparques que los (3) _____ y siempre tengan a mano un mapa de la zona.
- Les recomendamos que (4) _____ (ustedes) un equipamiento adecuado para el clima del lugar al que vayan. Quizás el equipo (5) _____ más de lo que habían presupuestado, pero un equipamiento bueno es siempre una buena inversión.
- Es fundamental que (6) _____ (ustedes) el campamento: separar las áreas donde comerán, dormirán o descansarán.
- Cuando (7) _____ (ustedes), les recomendamos abrigarse bien la cabeza y los pies. No queremos que estas zonas (8) _____, porque luego es muy difícil recuperar el calor.

Esperamos que (9) _____ (ustedes) en su próximo campamento ¡y que (10) _____ (ustedes) a hacerlo una y otra vez!

---

15. Construir Construye oraciones negativas usando el presente de subjuntivo. `22.B`

> **Modelo**
>
> Creo que Juan tiene miedo a las arañas.
> No creo que Juan *tenga miedo a las arañas.*

1. Me parece que llueve.
   No me parece que _____.
2. La policía piensa que el asesino todavía está en los alrededores.
   La policía no piensa que _____.
3. Creo que Luis recuerda el día en que nos conocimos.
   No creo que Luis _____.
4. Estoy segura de que ellos prefieren ir de vacaciones a la playa.
   No estoy segura de que ellos _____.
5. Sandra se sabe de memoria toda la lección.
   No creo que Sandra _____.
6. Creo que hoy llego a tiempo para ver la telenovela.
   No creo que _____.
7. Me parece que Juan y Carlos van a venir a la fiesta.
   No creo que _____.
8. Estoy segura de que vosotros podéis participar en el evento.
   No creo que _____.

16. **Indicar** **Indica qué oraciones incluyen verbos conjugados en pretérito imperfecto de subjuntivo. Subráyalos.** `22.C`

1. Espero que la temperatura sea agradable este fin de semana. No quiero llevar mucho abrigo.

2. Me pareció raro que no te comieras toda tu comida.

3. Me gustaría que hablásemos a solas sobre este tema.

4. Si los trabajadores pidieran un aumento de sueldo, con gusto se lo daría.

5. Es mejor que no haya postre. Ya comimos demasiado.

6. ¡Ojalá pudiéramos ir de vacaciones a Cusco este verano!

7. No creo que sepas todas las respuestas. ¡Solamente el profesor las sabe!

8. Te pedí que te cambiases la camisa. ¡Esa está sucia!

17. **Formas** **El pretérito imperfecto de subjuntivo tiene dos formas. Escribe junto a cada verbo las dos formas correspondientes a la forma *yo*.** `22.C`

Modelo

venir _____*viniera*_____   _____*viniese*_____

1. subir	_____	_____	8. concluir	_____	_____
2. pedir	_____	_____	9. desear	_____	_____
3. caber	_____	_____	10. querer	_____	_____
4. ser	_____	_____	11. poseer	_____	_____
5. poner	_____	_____	12. decir	_____	_____
6. lastimar	_____	_____	13. estar	_____	_____
7. hacer	_____	_____	14. dormir	_____	_____

18. **Completar** **Completa las oraciones con los verbos conjugados en pretérito imperfecto de subjuntivo.** `22.C`

Modelo

Fue fundamental para el rescate que los bomberos _____*llegaran*_____ (llegar) de inmediato.

1. Si yo _____ (hablar) quechua, podría ser traductor en una comunidad indígena.

2. ¡Cómo me gustaría que _____ (viajar, nosotros) a la India!

3. Hasta ayer necesitaba un empleado que _____ (trabajar) por las tardes.

4. Habíamos preparado todo para que los agasajados _____ (sorprenderse) al entrar.

5. Compré comida para que _____ (cocinar, nosotros) juntos.

19. **Conjugar** **Conjuga estos verbos en pretérito imperfecto de subjuntivo.** `22.C`

Modelo

andar (usted) _____*anduviera*_____

1. divertir (yo) _____

2. saber (nosotros) _____

3. tener (ellos) _____

4. caer (vosotros) _____

5. leer (tú) _____

6. producir (ella) _____

7. ser (ustedes) _____

8. distribuir (ellos) _____

9. dar (yo) _____

10. morir (él) _____

20. Reescribir Reescribe las oraciones usando el pretérito imperfecto de subjuntivo. `22.C`

> **Modelo**
>
> Quiero que te sientas como en casa.
> Quería que _____*te sintieras como en casa*_____.

1. Te pido que me prestes atención.
   Te pedí que _____.

2. Podemos ir al cine si realmente quieres.
   Podríamos ir al cine si realmente _____.

3. Te llamo para que me incluyas en tu lista de invitados.
   Te llamé para que _____.

4. No quiero que destruyan ese edificio antiguo tan hermoso.
   No quería que _____.

5. Me alegra que puedas venir a nuestra fiesta.
   Me alegró que _____.

6. Julia nos recomienda que tengamos cuidado con nuestros bolsos.
   Julia nos recomendó que _____.

7. Le recomiendo que vaya a esa panadería y que pruebe las galletas.
   Le recomendé que _____.

21. Verbos Escribe los verbos en pretérito perfecto de subjuntivo. `22.D`

> **Modelo**
>
> atender (él) _____*haya atendido*_____

1. tardar (ellos) _____
2. ser (nosotros) _____
3. compartir (vosotros) _____
4. pedir (ustedes) _____
5. beber (yo) _____
6. escribir (tú) _____

7. probar (ella) _____
8. descubrir (nosotros) _____
9. traducir (ellos) _____
10. jugar (vos) _____
11. creer (usted) _____
12. escribir (vosotros) _____

22. Completar Completa las oraciones conjugando los verbos en el pretérito perfecto de subjuntivo. `22.D`

> **Modelo**
>
> Dudo que Julieta _____*haya preguntado*_____ (preguntar) por Martín.

1. No es verdad que _____ (querer) leer tu diario íntimo. Jamás lo haríamos.

2. Nos alegra tanto que _____ (venir, ustedes).

3. Esperamos que _____ (pasar, usted) un día estupendo en nuestro spa.

4. En mi familia no hay nadie que _____ (divorciarse).

5. Verás que la escuela te parecerá más fácil una vez que _____ (aprobar) los primeros exámenes.

23. Indicar Indica qué oraciones incluyen verbos conjugados en pretérito pluscuamperfecto de subjuntivo. Subráyalos. `22.E`

1. Si hubieras llegado temprano a casa, no te habrías perdido el exquisito postre que hizo Camila.

2. No sabía que hoy era tu cumpleaños.

3. Cuando hayan aprendido todas las palabras, les haré una pequeña prueba.

4. Entre mis amigos, no encontré a nadie que hubiera ido a Quito.

5. Me habría bastado con que me hubieras mandado un mensaje de texto. Estuve esperándote dos horas bajo la lluvia.

6. Si hubiésemos salido antes, no habríamos perdido el tren.

7. No pensé que hubieses disfrutado de la fiesta tanto como yo.

8. Nunca pensé que pudiese haber tanta gente allí.

9. Te habría invitado a la reunión si hubiera sabido que ya habías vuelto de tu viaje.

10. Es necesario que cenemos temprano esta noche.

11. Si hubierais ido al concierto anoche, habríais escuchado una música estupenda.

12. En tu lugar, yo no me casaría con él.

24. Oraciones Completa las oraciones con el verbo conjugado en el pretérito pluscuamperfecto de subjuntivo. `22.E`

> **Modelo**
>
> Si tan solo _____*hubiera sabido*_____ (saber) que querías ir a la playa, te habría invitado.

1. En toda la universidad no encontré a dos profesores que _____ (graduarse) después de 2005.

2. Si _____ (conocer) antes a tu hermana, la habría invitado a mi casamiento.

3. ¡Ojalá _____ (poder, nosotros) trabajar en esta escuela!

4. Si vosotros _____ (subir) a la torre, habríais visto toda la ciudad.

5. Si _____ (cerrar, tú) la puerta, el gato no se habría escapado.

25. Identificar Identifica el tiempo de subjuntivo de los verbos subrayados. `22.F–22.G`

1. Cualquiera que <u>fuere</u> la nacionalidad de los turistas, se deberán solicitar los pasaportes en todos los casos.
   a. futuro   b. futuro perfecto   c. pretérito imperfecto   d. pretérito pluscuamperfecto

2. Se tendrán en cuenta aquellos currículos que <u>se hubieren recibido</u> antes del 20 de agosto.
   a. futuro   b. futuro perfecto   c. pretérito imperfecto   d. pretérito pluscuamperfecto

3. Quien <u>tuviere</u> algo en contra de esta unión, deberá informarlo por escrito.
   a. futuro   b. futuro perfecto   c. pretérito imperfecto   d. pretérito pluscuamperfecto

4. A donde <u>fueres</u>, haz lo que vieres.
   a. futuro   b. futuro perfecto   c. pretérito imperfecto   d. pretérito pluscuamperfecto

5. Quien <u>hubiere sido</u> culpable de este delito, deberá pagar por ello.
   a. futuro   b. futuro perfecto   c. pretérito imperfecto   d. pretérito pluscuamperfecto

6. Me pareció tan extraño que Tamara no <u>fuera</u> a clase.
   a. futuro   b. futuro perfecto   c. pretérito imperfecto   d. pretérito pluscuamperfecto

26. Síntesis Tiempo Identifica el tiempo de subjuntivo de los verbos subrayados. `22.A–22.H`

1. Que te <u>haya invitado</u> a comer a casa no significa que no tengas que ayudarme a cocinar.
   a. pretérito perfecto   b. pretérito pluscuamperfecto   c. futuro perfecto

2. Vaya a donde <u>fuere</u>, el fantasma de mis pesadillas me persigue.
   a. presente   b. futuro   c. pretérito imperfecto

3. Hicimos comidas sin carne para que los vegetarianos <u>pudiesen</u> disfrutar del banquete.
   a. presente   b. futuro   c. pretérito imperfecto

4. Si tu hermana nos <u>pidiera</u> ayuda, seríamos los primeros en ayudarla.
   a. presente   b. futuro   c. pretérito imperfecto

5. Ojalá nos <u>divertamos</u> en la casa de Paula.
   a. presente   b. futuro   c. pretérito imperfecto

6. Quien <u>hubiere desobedecido</u> a las autoridades será castigado con diez años de prisión.
   a. pretérito perfecto   b. pretérito pluscuamperfecto   c. futuro perfecto

7. Hicimos muchísimo para que todo <u>saliera</u> tal como lo planeamos.
   a. presente   b. futuro   c. pretérito imperfecto

8. Habría sido mejor que Juan Gabriel <u>hubiera traído</u> ropa para cambiarse.
   a. pretérito perfecto   b. pretérito pluscuamperfecto   c. futuro perfecto

9. Mis padres quieren que yo <u>sea</u> responsable.
   a. presente   b. futuro   c. pretérito imperfecto

10. Te sentirás mejor cuando <u>hayas comido</u> algo.
    a. pretérito perfecto   b. pretérito pluscuamperfecto   c. futuro perfecto

27. Escribir Piensa en cinco noticias recientes que hayas escuchado y escribe cinco reacciones ante ellas utilizando expresiones como *es bueno/malo/terrible que* con el subjuntivo. `22.A–22.H`

Modelo
Es terrible que miles de personas hayan muerto al intentar emigrar a Europa…

_____

_____

_____

_____

_____

_____

_____

_____

_____

_____

_____

_____

_____

_____

Practice more at **vhlcentral.com.**

1. Completar   Completa las oraciones con los verbos de la lista conjugados en subjuntivo. Usa cada verbo solo una vez. `23.B`

avisar	~~llegar~~
cambiar	reconciliarse
cumplir	regalar
divertir	venir

Modelo

Tal vez (nosotros) ____*lleguemos*____ tarde mañana a causa del tráfico.

1. ¡Que te _____ muchísimo en la fiesta!

2. ¡Ojalá me _____ la muñeca que tanto quiero! Creo que ellos ya saben qué quiero.

3. ¡Ojalá nos _____ antes sobre el retraso del tren! Habríamos aprovechado para ver más la ciudad.

4. ¡Que _____ muchísimos años más, hermanita!

5. Posiblemente _____ de visita la tía Carolina. Ábrele la puerta, ¿sí?

6. Quizás el gobierno _____ su política económica en los próximos años.

7. Ojalá que _____. Hacen muy buena pareja.

2. Unir   Une las frases para formar oraciones lógicas. `23.B`

1. Ojalá Roberto no traiga postre de chocolate; ____

2. Ojalá Roberto no hubiera traído una tarta de limón: ____

3. Probablemente Roberto compre algo de postre, ____

4. Quizás fuera Roberto ____

5. Ojalá Roberto haya disfrutado ____

6. Ojalá Roberto disfrute ____

a. así que yo no compraré nada.

b. de la cena que hice.

c. el que trajo la torta de naranja.

d. siempre estar conmigo.

e. yo ya compré uno.

f. me la comí toda y ahora me duele la barriga.

3. Consejos   Escribe oraciones siguiendo el modelo. `23.C`

Modelo

Estudia después de cada clase. (exigirte)
Te exijo que estudies después de cada clase.

1. Sé puntual. (sugerirte)

_____

2. Ayuda a tus compañeros. (aconsejarte)

_____

3. Siempre haz los ejercicios de matemáticas. (recomendarte)

_____

4. Llámame por la tarde si tienes preguntas. (pedirte)

_____

5. Presta atención a mis consejos. (rogarte)

_____

6. Recuerda todo lo que te digo. (necesitar)

_____

4. Completar Completa las oraciones con un elemento de cada lista. `23.C`

que	~~aburrirse~~
el que	elegir
es que	retrasarse
hace que	tener
el hecho de que	aprobar
~~lo que pasa~~	bajar

Modelo

_____Lo que pasa_____ no es que _____me aburra_____, es que tengo que irme.

1. La huelga del transporte _____ todos los vuelos _____.
2. _____ no _____ el examen no es excusa para bajar los brazos. ¡Te queda medio año por delante!
3. _____ te _____ "mejor compañero" habla muy bien de ti.
4. _____ _____ los precios no es algo muy frecuente en este país.
5. No _____ yo _____ poco dinero, es que todo aquí es muy caro.

5. Decidir Lee estas oraciones y decide si en cada caso se expresa deseo o se brinda información. `23.C`

Modelo

Mamá dice que te acuestes ahora mismo. _____deseo_____

1. Agustina insistió en que le trajeran un café. _____
2. Manuela le gritó a su hermana que se quedara tranquila. _____
3. Mi novia insiste en que soy el chico más lindo del mundo. _____
4. El policía me indicó que estacionara. _____
5. Las autoridades afirmaron que los pasajeros están a salvo. _____
6. Insisto en que me dejen hablar con un abogado. _____
7. Te advierto que no me hagas enojar. _____
8. Mi padre dice que él tiene la razón. _____

6. Reescribir Reescribe las oraciones siguiendo el modelo. `23.C`

Modelo

¿Te visitan tus padres? ¡Cuánto me alegra!
Me alegra que te visiten tus padres.

1. ¿Te robaron la maleta? ¡Qué indignante! _____
2. ¿Estás fumando? ¡Cómo me molesta! _____
3. ¿Los vecinos están haciendo una fiesta? ¡Cómo me enfada eso! _____
   _____
4. ¿Has perdido el tren? ¡Qué frustrante! _____
5. ¿Has ganado la lotería? ¡Qué sorpresa! _____

7. Elegir En cada oración, elige la opción correcta. `23.C`

1. Temo que la inyección me _____. ¡Mira lo grande que es la aguja!
   a. duele   b. dolerá

2. Esperaba con ansias a que me _____ sobre la beca.
   a. contestan   b. contestaran

3. Creo que la camarera _____ muy amable.
   a. es   b. sea

4. No pienso que la profesora nos _____ buenas notas.
   a. da   b. dé

5. Parece como si _____ ocho grados bajo cero.
   a. hace   b. hiciera

6. ¿Piensas que _____ mejor esperar a que bajen los precios?
   a. es   b. sea

7. Siento que esto _____ en un gran problema pronto.
   a. se convierta   b. se convertirá

8. ¿Indicativo o subjuntivo? Completa las oraciones con los verbos conjugados en indicativo o subjuntivo según corresponda. `23.C`

1. Desconfío de que me _____ (has contado / hayas contado) la verdad sobre tus calificaciones.

2. Pero no dudo en absoluto que _____ (seas/eres) una buena persona.

3. Aunque no niego que _____ (haya pensado / he pensado) lo contrario.

4. Es cierto también que esto ya _____ (ha sucedido / haya sucedido) antes.

5. No hay certeza alguna de que _____ (vayas/vas) a cambiar de actitud.

6. Pero, al fin y al cabo, estoy convencido de que nuestra amistad _____ (sobreviva/sobrevivirá) a este conflicto.

7. Te aconsejo que _____ (dejas/dejes) de fumar.

8. Admito que no _____ (haya leído / he leído) ese libro.

9. Fue muy importante que nos _____ (dijeras/dijiste) la verdad.

10. Estoy muy acostumbrado a que los vecinos _____ (hagan/hacen) mucho ruido.

9. Mensaje electrónico Completa el mensaje electrónico de Tomás con los verbos conjugados en subjuntivo. `23.C`

De:	tomasito@email.com
Para:	leandroj@email.com, vanesam@email.com
Asunto:	El trabajo en grupo

Fue increíble que se (1) _____ (comportar) de esa manera la clase pasada. No es justo que yo siempre (2) _____ (tener) que hacer las tareas por ustedes. ¡Es terrible que (3) _____ (pensar) de esa manera!

Leandro, fue un error que no (4) _____ (venir) a la reunión del sábado pasado. No era el trato que solo un miembro del grupo (5) _____ (trabajar) por todos. Está bien que ahora (6) _____ (querer) compensar tu error, pero ya es demasiado tarde.

Y tú, Vanesa, ¿acaso estás acostumbrada a que la gente te (7) _____ (esperar)? Estoy harto de que (8) _____ (llegar) tarde a todas las reuniones.

A los dos, les repito lo que ya les dije la semana pasada: más vale que (9) _____ (cambiar) de actitud. Me da igual que la profesora los (10) _____ (desaprobar): si esto no cambia, le contaré todo.

10. Unir Une las frases para formar oraciones lógicas. Usa cada opción solo una vez. `23.C`

1. Queríamos _____
2. Te aconsejamos _____
3. A tus padres les ha molestado _____
4. A los empleados les molesta _____
5. Es la tercera vez que les pido _____
6. Ayer Julio nos pidió dos veces _____
7. La lluvia les impidió _____

a. que no hayamos limpiado la casa después de la reunión.
b. que no descuides tu bolso.
c. que limpien la sala después de usarla.
d. ir de excursión a la montaña.
e. ver la película de vampiros.
f. que los clientes no saluden al entrar.
g. que no habláramos muy alto.

11. Oraciones Reescribe las oraciones usando *lo + adjetivo/adverbio* y *lo que*. `23.C`

> **Modelo**
>
> El sistema de transporte funciona muy mal. Eso es lo que veo.
> *Lo que veo es que el sistema de transporte funciona muy mal.*

1. Pasa a buscarme tú. Eso es lo lógico.

   _____

2. Eres realmente hermosa. Eso es lo cierto.

   _____

3. La gente es simpática. Eso es lo más común.

   _____

4. El tren llegó a tiempo. Eso fue lo más normal.

   _____

5. Por suerte, no nos robaron. Eso habría sido lo peor.

   _____

6. Mi familia iba a la playa en verano. Eso era lo más corriente.

   _____

12. Escoger Para cada oración, elige la opción correcta. `23.D`

1. La junta directiva elegirá a un delegado que es muy responsable.
   a. La junta también tomará en cuenta la experiencia de los candidatos en esa área.
   b. Se llama Juan Carlos Gómez y tiene experiencia en esa área.

2. Buscamos un sillón que tenga dos metros de largo.
   a. En el comedor, no nos entraría uno más grande.
   b. Lo vimos la semana pasada en un catálogo.

3. Los niños quieren un muñeco que dice frases en español.
   a. Se llama "Sr. Caballín", pero no lo encuentro en ninguna juguetería.
   b. Les compraré el primero que vea.

4. Te llevaré a un museo donde haya una exposición de arte.
   a. He estado allí antes y he visto exposiciones súper interesantes.
   b. Seguramente encontraremos uno por aquí cerca.

5. Necesito un diccionario que tenga imágenes.
   a. Lo vi en Internet y ahora no recuerdo el nombre.
   b. Creo que me ayudaría a memorizar las palabras más rápido.

13. Seleccionar **En cada oración, elige la opción correcta.** `23.D`

1. _____ (Jamás/Siempre) he sido una alumna que tiene buenas notas.

2. _____ (En ninguna parte / En muchas partes) del mundo hay aeropuertos donde se pueda fumar.

3. En tu casa _____ (no había / había) un par de cuadros que me encantaban.

4. _____ (No existe nadie / Existe alguien) que pueda resolver este acertijo.

5. Contrata a cualquiera que _____ (pueda trabajar / puede trabajar) los fines de semana.

6. Busco a la persona que _____ (quiera/quiere) alquilar mi habitación. Su nombre es Manuel, pero no recuerdo su apellido.

14. Completar **Completa las oraciones con los verbos conjugados en indicativo o subjuntivo.** `23.C–23.D`

> **Modelo**
>
> En Argentina, no había comida que me ___*encantara*___ (encantar) más que el asado.

1. Lo que _____ (decidir) Marta será respetado por todos.

2. Lo que no me conviene es que _____ (subir) la tasa de interés.

3. Quienes te _____ (acabar) de saludar son los vecinos del primer piso.

4. Me gustaría tener una casa que _____ (tener) una piscina climatizada en la sala, pero no creo que exista.

5. Nunca he conocido a nadie que le _____ (gustar) comer comida picante en el desayuno.

15. Reescribir **Reescribe las oraciones con las palabras dadas.** `23.D`

> **Modelo**
>
> Necesito un par de tijeras que corten bien.
> Jamás he tenido *un par de tijeras que hayan cortado bien.*

1. Busco un hombre que sea cariñoso.
   Buscaba _____.

2. Quiero estudiar una profesión que me haga feliz.
   Habría querido _____.

3. Necesito un par de lentes que cuesten menos de 90 dólares.
   Necesitaba _____.

4. Quiero tener amigos que sean sociables.
   Habría querido _____.

5. Busco un libro que sea en inglés.
   Buscaba _____.

6. Deseo ver una película que no se trate de superhéroes.
   Deseaba _____.

7. Necesito una mascota que me obedezca.
   Nunca he tenido _____.

16. Oraciones Reescribe las oraciones usando la conjunción o adverbio relativo indicado. `23.E`

>
> Ellos comen todo lo que quieren. (cuanto)
> *Ellos comen cuanto quieren.*

1. Juan Manuel habla castellano como un español. (como si)

   _____

2. Hice la tarea y nadie me ayudó. (sin que)

   _____

3. Si no llegas puntualmente, me habré ido. (como)

   _____

4. Dado que no tienes dinero, te prestaré un poco. (como)

   _____

5. ¡Ni loca te presto dinero! (ni que)

   _____

17. Carta Lee la carta de Joaquín y elige la opción correcta. `23.E`

> Querida Alicia:
> ¿Cómo estás? Luego de (1) _____ (que reciba/recibir) tu mensaje de texto, me
> quedé un poco preocupado. Imagínate que, tan pronto como lo (2) _____ (leyera/
> leí), corrí hasta este cibercafé para comunicarme contigo.
> ¿Estás más tranquila? ¡Qué mala suerte con estos ladrones! Pero cuántas veces te dije que,
> cada vez que (3) _____ (camines/caminas) por el centro, lleves tu bolso delante
> de ti. Estas son las cosas que pasan cuando (4) _____ (descuidas/descuides) tus
> pertenencias. Te recomiendo que vayas a la comisaría ya mismo. Después de que
> (5) _____ (hagas/haces) la denuncia, la policía comenzará a buscar tus
> documentos. Hasta que (6) _____ (recuperes/recuperas) tu pasaporte, usa tu
> documento de identidad mexicano. Por favor, apenas (7) _____ (lees/leas) mi
> mensaje, llámame por teléfono.
>
> Un abrazo,
> Joaquín

18. Conjunciones Completa las oraciones con las palabras de la lista. `23.E`

> tanto que   ~~a causa de que~~   para   tan ... que   porque (2)   a fin de que

>
> _A causa de que_ perdimos el autobús, ahora tenemos que esperar dos horas.

1. Ando en bicicleta no _____ me guste, sino _____ no perjudica el medio ambiente.
2. _____ no haya desempleo, el gobierno puso en marcha un plan de generación de puestos de trabajo.
3. Llovía _____ no pudimos ir al concierto.
4. La probabilidad de ganar el concurso no es _____ baja _____ debamos desanimarnos.
5. Tengo que pedir un crédito _____ comprar la casa.

19. **Reescribir** Reescribe las oraciones usando la conjunción indicada. **23.E**

> **Modelo**
>
> No me invitaron a la fiesta. De todas maneras, no habría ido a esa fiesta. (aunque)
> *Aunque me hubieran invitado a la fiesta, no habría ido.*

1. No tengo hambre, pero comeré una porción de pizza. (si bien)

   _____

2. Podría venir mucha gente a la fiesta. Sin embargo, habrá lugar para todos. (por + *sustantivo* + que)

   _____

3. Hacía mucho calor. Sin embargo, los niños jugaron en el parque. (pese a que)

   _____

4. No compraría esa casa aun teniendo el dinero. (aunque)

   _____

5. Ni siquiera viviendo en Barcelona me sería fácil aprender catalán. (aun cuando)

   _____

20. **Subordinadas condicionales** Conjuga adecuadamente los verbos indicados para completar las oraciones. **23.E**

> **Modelo**
>
> No hay de qué preocuparse en el centro de la ciudad, siempre que _____ *esté* _____ (estar) atento.

1. Les dejo este folleto en caso de que ustedes _____ (querer) comprar nuestros productos.
2. Yo te ayudo con la tarea, a no ser que tu hermano _____ (preferir) intentarlo primero.
3. Si Juan David _____ (haber) entrenado más, habría llegado de primero.
4. Tendrás acceso a Internet, siempre y cuando tú _____ (recargar) tu plan telefónico.
5. Haremos el asado sin problemas a menos que _____ (llover) esta noche.
6. Mi mamá disfrutará mucho el viaje con tal de que no _____ (marearse) en el crucero.
7. Si se dañaran las líneas telefónicas, de todas formas nosotros _____ (poder) hablarte vía Internet.
8. Llevaré un libro por si acaso _____ (aburrirse).

21. **Escribir** Escribe oraciones a partir de las frases dadas. **23.E**

> **Modelo**
>
> Si me dijeras que ganaste la lotería, (yo / no / creerte)
> *Si me dijeras que ganaste la lotería, yo no te creería.*

1. Podrías venir a cenar a casa _____.
   (a no ser que / ya / tener / planes)

2. Lleva el paraguas _____.
   (por si acaso / llover)

3. Compraré bebida de más _____.
   (en caso de que / esta noche / venir / más invitados)

4. Solo serás exitoso _____.
   (si / esforzarte)

5. Habrías llegado a tiempo _____.
   (si / el metro / funcionar / bien)

22. Síntesis Sueños Completa el texto con la opción correcta. `23.A–23.E`

¿Que cuáles (1) _____ (son/sean) mis sueños? ¡Qué pregunta! Bueno, esperaba que me (2) _____ (hagas/hicieras) una pregunta más concreta.

A ver... No es que (3) _____ (haya/hay) algo con lo que sueñe en realidad. Me gusta vivir el momento y disfrutar del día a día. Pero, para ser sincera, a veces sueño con encontrar un hombre que me (4) _____ (quiere/quiera) y que me (5) _____ (apoye/apoya). Sería tan romántico estar en pareja ¡y para toda la vida! Quizás yo (6) _____ (sea/fuera) un poco desconfiada, pero para establecer una relación duradera, a menos que la otra persona me (7) _____ (demuestra/demuestre) con sinceridad sus sentimientos, yo no doy señales de los míos.

Y hablando de sueños o ambiciones... si yo (8) _____ (tengo/tuviera) un mejor trabajo, aportaría suficiente dinero en caso de que mi pareja (9) _____ (exige/exigiera) compartir por igual las necesidades del hogar. Además, deseo estar en una empresa donde me (10) _____ (paguen/pagaran) más y (11) _____ (tenga/tuviera) que trabajar menos. ¡Eso sí que no creo que se (12) _____ (haga/hace) realidad! Pero soñar no cuesta nada.

23. Síntesis Completar Completa las oraciones con las palabras o frases de la lista. `23.A–23.E`

No pienso	Siento
Es sorprendente	Comprendo
Que	Parece como si
El que	Estoy convencido
Es aconsejable	

Modelo

_____Es sorprendente_____ que una actriz tan mala recibiera un Oscar.

1. ¡_____ duerman bien!
2. _____ que no gasten dinero en hoteles caros.
3. _____ hayas sido amable conmigo hoy no me dice nada.
4. _____ que hoy será un gran día.
5. _____ que nos espere un futuro brillante.
6. _____ la gente no tuviera ganas de trabajar.
7. _____ que no hayas llegado a tiempo. El tránsito en esta ciudad es un caos.
8. _____ de que seremos los vencedores.

24. Síntesis Clasificar Agrupa las palabras y frases de la lista, según puedan utilizarse solo en indicativo, solo en subjuntivo o en ambos casos. `23.A–23.E`

~~aunque~~	es obvio	ojalá	siempre que
como	~~esperar a que~~	para que	sin que
de tal modo que	hacer que	puesto que	tal vez
~~es claro~~	hay certeza de	si	vale la pena que

Solo en indicativo	Solo en subjuntivo	En ambos casos
es claro	esperar a que	aunque

25. Síntesis Emparejar Une los ejemplos con las explicaciones. `23.A–23.E`

_____ 1. Dormiré en una cama que sea cómoda.

_____ 2. Lo lógico es que durmamos en una tienda de campaña.

_____ 3. No había una sola persona que hablara español.

_____ 4. Cuando estudies más, tendrás buenas notas.

_____ 5. Los precios son tan altos que no podemos comprar ni un café.

_____ 6. Por si acaso no me despierto, llámame por teléfono por la mañana.

_____ 7. Si tocas el fuego, te quemarás.

_____ 8. El pueblo desconfía de que el gobernador sea honesto.

a. Usamos el subjuntivo con expresiones que hacen referencia a normas, reglas o preferencias consideradas las mejores, las peores, etc.

b. Usamos el subjuntivo en subordinadas temporales cuando la oración hace referencia a una acción futura.

c. Usamos el subjuntivo en subordinadas relativas cuando nos referimos a algo cuyas características imaginamos o deseamos.

d. Usamos el indicativo para expresar una condición cuando la relación condición-resultado es segura.

e. Usamos el indicativo con esta expresión.

f. Usamos el subjuntivo cuando afirmamos que el antecedente de la cláusula relativa no existe.

g. Usamos el indicativo en comparaciones implícitas.

h. Usamos el subjuntivo con verbos que expresan duda.

26. Síntesis Composición Describe a tu compañero/a ideal, tanto física como intelectualmente. Incluye cinco usos diferentes del subjuntivo. `23.A–23.E`

Modelo

No es necesario que mi compañero ideal sea un deportista profesional, pero sí insisto en que se mantenga en forma...

_____

_____

_____

_____

_____

Practice more at **vhlcentral.com.**

1. Completar Completa las oraciones con el verbo conjugado en imperativo afirmativo de *tú*. `24.B`

Modelo

_____*Repite*_____ (repetir) las instrucciones.

1. _____ (descansar) unas horas y te paso a buscar a las 8.
2. _____ (limpiar) tus gafas. ¡Están muy sucias!
3. _____ (comer) toda tu comida si quieres el postre.
4. _____ (esperar) hasta que venga la abuela.
5. _____ (leer) en voz alta las primeras frases del libro.
6. _____ (ordenar) la habitación: ¡es un desastre!
7. _____ (ir) a visitar a tus abuelos.
8. _____ (poner) las bolsas sobre la mesa.
9. _____ (tener) bien a mano el pasaporte.
10. _____ (comprar) este libro. Te lo recomiendo.

2. Reescribir Reescribe las oraciones con el verbo conjugado en imperativo afirmativo de *tú*. `24.B`

Modelo

Tienes que salir ahora. ¡_____*Sal ahora*_____!

1. Tienes que venir a casa a buscar el DVD. ¡_____!
2. Tienes que ser amable con nosotros. ¡_____!
3. Tienes que poner cada libro en su lugar. ¡_____!
4. Tienes que hacer todo lo que yo te digo. ¡_____!
5. Tienes que ir a la farmacia ya mismo. ¡_____!
6. Tienes que decir "permiso" antes de entrar. ¡_____!

3. Mandatos Una amiga argentina te da consejos para cuando llegues a Buenos Aires. Escribe sus mandatos usando el imperativo afirmativo de *vos*. `24.C`

Modelo

(salir del aeropuerto)
Salí del aeropuerto.

1. (tener cuidado con tus maletas) _____
2. (pedir un mapa en la estación) _____
3. (preguntar dónde tomar el autobús 152) _____
4. (ser simpática con el chofer del autobús) _____
5. (buscar la calle Juramento) _____
6. (tocar el timbre del apartamento 1B) _____

4. Contestar Eres jefe de redacción del periódico escolar. Contesta las preguntas de tus compañeros. **24.C**

> **Modelo**
>
> **COMPAÑEROS** ¿Debemos escribir artículos?
> (No, corregir | artículos | redactados)
> **TÚ** *No, corregid los artículos redactados.*

1. **COMPAÑEROS** ¿Debemos entrevistar al director?
   (No, entrevistar | profesor de música)
   TÚ _____

2. **COMPAÑEROS** ¿Llamamos por teléfono al profesor de música?
   (No, enviar | mensaje electrónico)
   TÚ _____

3. **COMPAÑEROS** ¿Debemos pensar en preguntas sobre música contemporánea?
   (No, hacer | preguntas | música clásica)
   TÚ _____

4. **COMPAÑEROS** ¿Debemos escribir el artículo para el lunes?
   (No, escribir | artículo | miércoles)
   TÚ _____

5. **COMPAÑEROS** ¿Podemos hacer un descanso ahora?
   (Sí, descansar | una hora)
   TÚ _____

5. Reescribir Reescribe las oraciones en imperativo negativo. **24.D**

> **Modelo**
>
> Ten prisa.
> *No tengas prisa.*

1. Haz ejercicio cuatro veces por semana.
   _____

2. Leed todos los libros de la biblioteca.
   _____

3. Tirad los periódicos viejos a la basura.
   _____

4. Sé cordial con los turistas.
   _____

5. Aparca tu carro enfrente de mi casa.
   _____

6. Venid a cenar a casa.
   _____

7. Sal de ahí.
   _____

8. Ayudad a vuestros amigos.
   _____

6. Completar Completa las oraciones con los verbos de la lista conjugados en imperativo de *usted,* *ustedes* o *nosotros.* `24.E`

| decir | hacer | jugar | pedir | respetar | subir | tomar |

Modelo

No _____*digamos*_____ que somos estudiantes. Es mejor que crean que somos profesionales.

1. Hoy no _____ a la pelota. Ayer practicamos demasiadas horas.

2. _____ el tren de las 8:50, profesor. Lo esperaré en la estación.

3. Alumnos, _____ las normas de la escuela; de lo contrario, habrá sanciones para todos.

4. _____ lo que quiera, señor Juárez. La empresa pagará la cuenta del restaurante.

5. _____ hasta el quinto piso. Allí los estará esperando la coordinadora.

6. Jamás _____ trampa en la competencia deportiva. El entrenador se enojaría muchísimo con nosotros.

7. Órdenes Utiliza las palabras para crear órdenes afirmativas y negativas con las formas *usted, ustedes* y *nosotros/as.* `24.E`

Modelo

ustedes: pintar las paredes / no ensuciar el piso
Pinten las paredes. No ensucien el piso.

1. nosotros: ir al cine / no sentarse a ver televisión
_____

2. ustedes: averiguar los hechos / no insinuar las causas
_____

3. nosotras: dormir lo suficiente / no quedarse despiertas hasta tarde
_____

4. usted: tener confianza / no pensar en perder
_____

5. nosotros: elegir según nuestros gustos / no ir a dejarse convencer por los vendedores
_____

6. ustedes: venir elegantes / no traer sandalias
_____

7. usted: decir la verdad / no mentir más
_____

8. ustedes: apagar las luces / no desperdiciar energía
_____

9. nosotros: trabajar duro / no ser perezosos
_____

10. usted: dar un paseo / no jugar videojuegos
_____

8. Oraciones Escribe las oraciones siguiendo el modelo. **24.F**

> **Modelo**
>
> ¿Me traes una bebida?
> *Tráeme una bebida.*
> *Tráemela.*

1. ¿Nos das un abrazo?
   _____
   _____

2. ¿Os quitáis el abrigo?
   _____
   _____

3. ¿Me cortas el cabello?
   _____
   _____

4. ¿Nos regalas unas rosas?
   _____
   _____

5. ¿Me manda una postal, señorita Álvarez?
   _____
   _____

6. ¿Nos comemos la torta?
   _____
   _____

9. Consejos Completa los consejos de salud que da el Doctor Salvador a sus televidentes. **24.B–24.F**

Buenos días, damas y caballeros. Hoy hablaremos sobre cómo llevar una vida saludable.

Si quieren vivir durante mucho tiempo y gozar de buena salud, sigan mis consejos. Primero, no (1) _____*fumen*_____ (fumar) más. El cigarrillo causa cáncer de pulmón a ustedes y a quienes los rodean. ¡(2) _____ (Decidirse) de una vez y (3) _____ (terminar) con ese vicio! Segundo, (4) _____ (olvidarse) de las comidas con gran contenido graso y, además, ¡(5) _____ (hacer) deporte! (6) _____ (Caminar), (7) _____ (correr), lo que ustedes quieran... ¡y no (8) _____ (mirar) tanta televisión! Por último, (9) _____ (dormir), como mínimo, ocho horas diarias.

¡(10) _____ (Ser) inteligentes y (11) _____ (cuidarse)! ¡Hasta la próxima!

10. Mandatos Completa los mandatos del cocinero español a sus empleados. **24.B–24.F**

Julia y Lucía, (1) _____*cortad*_____ (cortar) la zanahoria en tiritas muy finas. Tú, Marcelo, (2) _____ (tener) más cuidado cuando lavas las patatas: tienen tierra todavía. Y tú, Ester, (3) _____ (ir) al depósito y (4) _____ (traer) dos kilos de cebollas. (5) _____ (Prestar, vosotros) atención a lo que os digo. ¡No (6) _____ (distraerse, vosotros)!

¡(7) _____ (Hacer, nosotros) de este restaurante el mejor de toda España! Y ahora, (8) _____ (poner, nosotros) manos a la obra.

11. Reescribir Reescribe las oraciones usando la estructura indicada. `24.G`

1. ¡Venid a casa ya mismo!
   (infinitivo) _____

2. Lea el folleto del medicamento.
   (imperativo impersonal) _____

3. ¡Trabajen duro!
   (**A** + infinitivo) _____

4. ¡Tomad un plato cada uno!
   (infinitivo) _____

5. Prohibido adelantarse.
   (imperativo negativo de **usted**) _____

6. ¡Poner más empeño!
   (imperativo afirmativo de **usted**) _____

12. La cortesía Reescribe las oraciones usando los comienzos indicados. `24.G`

1. ¡Hagan silencio!
   ¿Podrían _____?

2. ¡A trabajar, todos!
   ¡Pongámonos _____!

3. ¡Dame el teléfono de este cliente!
   ¿Me _____?

4. ¡Cállate la boca!
   ¡A ver _____!

5. ¡Ayúdame con los paquetes!
   ¿Por qué _____?

6. ¡Paga el café que te traje!
   Que _____.

7. ¡Habla más despacio!
   ¿Puedes _____?

8. ¡Lleven las bolsas a la cocina!
   ¿Querrían _____?

9. ¡Lea las instrucciones!
   ¿Por qué _____?

10. ¡Dígame la verdad!
    Que _____.

13. Síntesis La reunión La directora, Tomás y sus padres tienen una reunión. Completa los mandatos informales (dirigidos a Tomás) y formales (dirigidos a sus padres). `24.B–24.G`

> ayudarlo con las tareas para el hogar
> enseñarle buenos modales
> ~~llegar puntualmente~~
> molestar a tus compañeros
> prestar atención a la clase
> recompensarlo con dinero

Tomás, (1) _____*llega puntualmente*_____ o te quedarás fuera de la escuela. Y a ustedes, les pido por favor, (2) _____ a Tomás. Le contesta mal a todos los profesores y eso es inadmisible. Otra cosa, Tomás, (3) _____. La profesora Menéndez se queja de que no sabes ni siquiera en qué asignatura estás.

Y, usted, señor Pérez, no (4) _____. Es evidente que Tomás no es el autor de frases como "La situación político-financiera de Azerbaiyán es inverosímil".

Ah, me olvidaba: ¡no (5) _____ cuando aprueba un examen, señores padres! Él tiene el deber de estudiar... ¡sin recibir nada a cambio!

Por último, Tomás, ¡no (6) _____! Te quedarás sin amigos en poco tiempo.

14. Síntesis Emparejar Une el ejemplo de la izquierda con el tipo de imperativo al que corresponde de la derecha. `24.B–24.G`

1. No prestes atención a lo que dicen.
2. ¡A bailar toda la noche!
3. ¿Podría usted cuidar mi puesto en la fila?
4. ¡Bebe mucha agua antes, durante y después de hacer deporte!
5. Prohibido nadar.
6. Opiná sobre esta bebida sabor a tamarindo.
7. ¡No nos subamos a ese taxi!
8. Traducid las obras completas al español.
9. Andá a la tienda por un jabón.
10. Haz el bien sin mirar a quién.

a. imperativo negativo de **nosotros**
b. imperativo regular afirmativo para **tú**
c. imperativo afirmativo de **vosotros**
d. imperativo afirmativo para la forma **vos**
e. imperativo irregular para **tú**
f. imperativo afirmativo del verbo **ir** para la forma **vos**
g. mandato en infinitivo
h. imperativo de cortesía, introducido por un verbo en condicional
i. imperativo negativo de **tú**
j. imperativo impersonal

15. Síntesis Redactar Escribe cinco consejos para algunos de tus amigos o miembros de tu familia. Utiliza mandatos afirmativos y negativos para *tú, ustedes* y *nosotros*. `24.B–24.G`

> **Modelo**
> *Compartamos todo el tiempo posible con la familia...*

_____
_____
_____
_____
_____

Practice more at **vhlcentral.com.**

1. Tabla   **Completa la tabla clasificando las formas no personales de los verbos que aparecen en el texto.**   `25.A`

> Querida Natalia:
>
> Desde hace dos años, mi familia viene festejando Halloween, también llamada "Noche de Brujas". Nos encanta disfrazarnos de personajes que dan miedo. Claro, tener el mejor disfraz no es fácil. El año pasado estuve diseñando mi traje durante una semana. Pero al probármelo, me quedaba demasiado ajustado, por lo que terminé comprando un disfraz ya confeccionado en una tienda.
>
> Este año tengo mucho por hacer. ¿Quieres ayudarme? Por lo visto, deberé tener más cuidado cuando haga mi disfraz. Si estás decidida a ayudarme, todas las sugerencias serán bien recibidas.
>
> Avísame qué te parece lo que te he propuesto.
>
> ¡Hasta pronto!
>
> Leandro

Infinitivo	Gerundio	Participio
		llamada

2. Elegir   **En cada oración, elige la mejor opción.**   `25.B`

1. Me gustaría _____ alegre.
      a. estar   b. que yo esté   c. Ambas opciones son posibles.

2. No permitiremos _____ sin entrada.
      a. que ingresen   b. ingresar   c. Ambas opciones son posibles.

3. Lucía está cansada y quiere _____ la siesta.
      a. dormir   b. que ella duerma   c. Ambas opciones son posibles.

4. El delincuente se declaró inocente. El testigo asegura _____.
      a. mentir   b. que miente   c. Ambas opciones son posibles.

5. No se te permitirá _____ con tanto equipaje.
      a. que viajes   b. viajar   c. Ambas opciones son posibles.

6. Tenemos muchos asuntos _____.
      a. por discutir   b. que debemos discutir   c. Ambas opciones son posibles.

3. Unir Une las frases para formar oraciones lógicas. Usa cada opción solo una vez. `25.B`

1. Te dije que salieras _____   a. de correr.

2. Eran las seis cuando vine _____   b. gritar y vinimos corriendo.

3. Te oímos _____   c. caminando de la mano.

4. Por favor, no _____   d. a cerrar el negocio.

5. Nos vieron _____   e. molestar.

6. Vamos _____   f. a abrirme la puerta cuando llegara.

4. Reemplazar Reemplaza el texto subrayado por una frase con infinitivo. `25.B`

> **Modelo**
> Es útil que estudie español.
> *Es útil estudiar español.*

1. El sonido de las campanas no me dejó dormir.
   _____

2. La caminata es una buena forma de ejercicio.
   _____

3. La compra de la casa nos llenó de deudas.
   _____

4. No es bueno que beba refrescos.
   _____

5. El baile me divierte.
   _____

6. Te recomiendo que comas frutas y verduras.
   _____

5. Reescribir Reescribe las oraciones usando el infinitivo. `25.B`

> **Modelo**
> Si hubiéramos seguido caminando, habríamos llegado al muelle.
> *De haber seguido caminando, habríamos llegado al muelle.*

1. Me alegré tanto cuando te vi.
   Al _____.

2. Si hubieras estudiado más, hoy tendrías mejores calificaciones.
   De _____.

3. Cuando amaneció, la playa estaba desierta.
   Al _____.

4. Si es tan complicado el viaje, mejor nos quedamos aquí.
   De _____.

5. Cuando llegue Juan, llámame por teléfono.
   Al _____.

6. Gerundio Convierte los infinitivos en gerundios. `25.C`

> **Modelo**
>
> decir _____diciendo_____

1. oler _____
2. ampliar _____
3. caer _____
4. conducir _____
5. entender _____
6. destruir _____
7. hacer _____

8. dormir _____
9. leer _____
10. pedir _____
11. oír _____
12. tocar _____
13. sentir _____
14. venir _____

7. Completar Completa las oraciones con el gerundio de los verbos de la lista. `25.C`

> bajar ~~necesitar~~
> comer pensar
> viajar trabajar

> **Modelo**
>
> Mi hermana anda _____necesitando_____ una bicicleta nueva. Le regalaré una para su cumpleaños.

1. Por más que me digas que es malo para la salud, yo sigo _____ carne.
2. Ayer me quedé _____ en lo que me dijiste. ¿De veras te quieres mudar?
3. Mi padre lleva treinta años _____ en la misma compañía. ¡Es increíble!
4. Emilio viene _____ de peso desde el verano pasado. ¡Parece que va a desaparecer!
5. Al final, los estudiantes terminaron _____ a Cancún.

8. Escoger En cada oración, elige la opción correcta. `25.C`

1. En la tienda, había dos cajas _____ (conteniendo/que contenían) rompecabezas de mil piezas.
2. ¿No me ves? ¡Estoy _____ (parando/parado) frente a ti!
3. El autobús chocó contra un árbol _____ (resultando heridos los pasajeros/habiendo esquivado una vaca).
4. Cocina la pasta en agua _____ (que hierve/hirviendo) durante cinco minutos.
5. No me puedo imaginar a mi abuelo _____ (cantando/cantar) en una banda de rock.
6. Me encanta la foto de tu madre _____ (abrazando/que abraza) a tu padre.
7. La policía salió en busca del delincuente _____ (capturándolo/y lo capturó) unos minutos después.

9. Clasificar Clasifica los ejemplos de gerundio según los usos mencionados en la lista. `25.C`

> a. causa   b. concesión   c. condición   d. método   e. modo   f. propósito   g. simultaneidad

1. Siendo tan jóvenes, parecen muy responsables. ___
2. Lloviendo mañana, iremos al cine en vez de al parque. ___
3. Los alumnos salieron corriendo de la escuela. ___
4. Nos llamaron diciendo que había huelga. ___

5. Me dormí pensando en el problema. ___
6. No queriendo ver a Juan, me fui de la fiesta. ___
7. Pablo se hizo famoso cantando boleros. ___

10. Reescribir   Reescribe las oraciones usando el gerundio. `25.C`

> **Modelo**
>
> Si presionas el botón de ese modo, lo romperás.
> *Presionando el botón de ese modo, lo romperás.*

1. El jefe nos llamó para decirnos que estábamos despedidos.
   _____

2. Como no te encontré, me fui a casa.
   _____

3. Mientras caminábamos, cantábamos.
   _____

4. Como vi que no había comida, decidí irme al mercado.
   _____

5. Me quebré la pierna mientras practicaba esquí.
   _____

6. Si leo el libro, aprenderé mucho sobre la historia de Chile.
   _____

7. Le escribí a mi hermana para explicarle por qué yo no podía ir.
   _____

8. Mi tío diseñó videojuegos y se hizo rico.
   _____

11. Participio   Utiliza los verbos indicados para crear participios pasados que permitan completar cada oración. `25.D`

> **Modelo**
>
> La calle está totalmente _____*cubierta*_____ (cubrir) por nieve.

1. El pájaro ha _____ (beber) agua fresca de la fuente.

2. Después del fin de semana, María Teresa se siente _____ (descansar).

3. Mis papás han _____ (creer) siempre en mí.

4. La autora ha _____ (escribir) una antología de cuentos.

5. Las autoridades han _____ (decir) que tenemos que evacuar.

6. Por favor, cambia las flores del jarrón. Están casi _____ (morir).

7. El obrero ha _____ (trabajar) de sol a sol.

8. Los revisores han _____ (incluir) sus comentarios en el informe.

9. Al abrir la caja, vi dos platos que están _____ (romper).

10. Los jugadores han _____ (poner) todo su empeño.

11. Las nuevas computadoras portátiles han _____ (satisfacer) nuestras necesidades.

12. Aún no se han _____ (ver) los resultados de la campaña.

12. Seleccionar En cada oración, elige la opción correcta. `25.D`

1. Los comentarios _____ realizados por usuarios anónimos.
   a. son   b. están

2. El enigma _____ resuelto por el famoso científico Juan Carlos Luz.
   a. será   b. estará

3. La tienda _____ cerrada a las ocho.
   a. estuvo   b. fue

4. La paciente _____ atendida por la doctora Pérez.
   a. ha sido   b. ha estado

5. La ciudad _____ conquistada por los indígenas en 1450.
   a. estuvo   b. fue

6. El templo _____ construido de piedras y lodo.
   a. está   b. es

7. Las clases _____ suspendidas hasta nuevo aviso.
   a. han estado   b. han sido

13. Relato Completa el relato de Cristina con el participio adecuado del verbo indicado. `25.D`

Hoy me he (1) _____*despertado*_____ (despertar) muy (2) _____ (confundir). Soñé que era (3) _____ (elegir) presidenta del país. Sí, como has (4) _____ (oír). Lo más (5) _____ (confundir) de todo era que yo nunca me había (6) _____ (presentar) a elecciones. Después de haber (7) _____ (asumir) el cargo, me acusaban de ser una gobernante corrupta, que había (8) _____ (robar) millones de dólares al pueblo. Después de un juicio de cinco minutos y sin prueba alguna, estaba (9) _____ (prender) de por vida. Por suerte, en cuanto estuve lo suficientemente (10) _____ (despertar), me di cuenta de que estaba sana y salva.

14. Oraciones Escribe oraciones siguiendo el modelo. `25.D`

Modelo

Se ha cocinado un pollo.
El pollo está cocinado.

1. Se ha redactado la renuncia.
   _____

2. Se ha divorciado Julia.
   _____

3. Se han casado Juan y Paula.
   _____

4. Se ha soltado al perro.
   _____

5. Se ha corregido el ensayo.
   _____

6. Se ha resuelto el problema.
   _____

15. Síntesis Unir Une las frases para formar oraciones lógicas. Usa cada opción solo una vez. `25.A–25.D`

1. No soy capaz _____   a. acordándome de cuánto te gustan.
2. Compré fresas _____   b. comiendo palomitas de maíz.
3. Vimos una película _____   c. de dormir en una tienda de campaña.
4. A la tienda, entró una mujer alterada _____   d. al sentarme en el sofá.
5. Cómo me gusta _____   e. el cantar de los pájaros.
6. Me quedé dormida _____   f. atenta a las palabras de su amiga.
7. Luciana estaba _____   g. dando gritos y saltando.

16. Síntesis Completar Completa las oraciones con la forma no personal del verbo indicado. `25.A–25.D`

> **Modelo**
>
> Juan camina _____*moviendo*_____ (mover) los brazos de un lado al otro.

1. Nadie se hace rico _____ (vender) artesanías.
2. De _____ (continuar) la huelga, no podremos viajar a Alicante.
3. Segundo, _____ (desconectar) el suministro eléctrico.
4. Quiero comprar el cuadro que se llama "Mujer _____ (tejer)".
5. Me encanta el refrán que dice "A lo _____ (hacer), pecho".
6. _____ (pagar) con la tarjeta de crédito, te endeudarás sin saberlo.
7. Al _____ (oír) la puerta, el gato se escondió debajo del sofá.

17. Síntesis Artículo Completa el artículo con la forma no personal adecuada de los verbos de la lista. `25.A–25.D`

> decidir   golpear   liberar   ~~presumir~~   quedarse   recibir   ser

> Carlos Castaño, el (1) _____*presunto*_____ asesino de la cantante
> Úrsula Gómez, ha sido (2) _____ en el día de ayer.
> (3) _____ declarado inocente por el jurado, Castaño ahora
> ha (4) _____ demandar al Estado. Dos días antes, el jurado
> había (5) _____ una carta de una vecina de Gómez. En ella,
> la vecina describe que vio a una mujer (6) _____ a Gómez la
> noche del 8 de diciembre. Al (7) _____ sin sospechosos, la
> policía ha reanudado la búsqueda.

18. Síntesis Emparejar Une los ejemplos con las explicaciones. `25.A–25.D`

____ 1. Para expresar propósito, el gerundio puede usarse con verbos de comunicación.

____ 2. Los verbos de movimiento como este llevan la preposición **a** o **de**.

____ 3. Por lo general, se usa el infinitivo junto a verbos de deseo para indicar que el sujeto de la acción deseada es quien expresa el deseo.

____ 4. Hay algunos verbos en español que permiten formar tiempos compuestos con el participio regular o el irregular. Solo la forma irregular se usa como adjetivo.

____ 5. Se puede usar el gerundio para referirse al objeto de los verbos que expresan una representación, ya sea mental o física.

____ 6. Esta estructura funciona como un adverbio para indicar que la acción está ocurriendo paralelamente a otra.

____ 7. Los sustantivos y adjetivos pueden ser modificados por una preposición más infinitivo.

____ 8. Hay verbos que al parecer tienen dos formas de participio pasado, pero se emplea el participio regular para formar tiempos compuestos con **haber**.

a. Baja a recibir el pedido del supermercado, por favor.

b. He impreso el pasaje del tren en la casa de Irma.

c. Al salir, cerré la puerta.

d. Nuestra prima nos escribió contándonos que se casaba.

e. Quiero ganar la lotería.

f. ¡Tenemos tantas cosas por hacer!

g. Me imagino a Marina patinando sobre hielo ¡y me da risa!

h. Nunca he sido tan bien atendido en un restaurante.

19. **Síntesis Escribir** Escribe cinco oraciones en las que menciones lo que hiciste ayer, lo que estás haciendo ahora mismo y lo que vas a hacer mañana. Usa verbos en infinitivo, gerundios y participios. `25.A–25.D`

> **Modelo**
>
> *Mañana debo terminar la lectura de la nueva novela que compré…*

_____

_____

_____

_____

_____

Practice more at **vhlcentral.com**.

Verb phrases and modal verbs | Chapter 26

1. **Elegir** En cada oración, elige la opción correcta. `26.B`

1. No _____ (deberías/debes de) salir tan desabrigada si tienes tos.

2. ¿Finalmente _____ (pudiste/podías) hablar con María? Yo la llamé varias veces y me atendió el contestador.

3. ¿_____ (Debes/Sabes) hablar alemán? Hay una clienta que necesita ayuda ¡y no habla ni un poquito de español!

4. Cuando encienda la lavadora, _____ (debería titilar/titilará) una luz verde.

5. No _____ (debías/debiste) haberle puesto tanta sal a la ensalada. ¡Es imposible comerla!

6. En las montañas, _____ (parece/puede) haber mucha nieve. Es un día perfecto para esquiar.

7. Por supuesto que sé montar en bicicleta, pero hoy no _____ (puedo/debo de) hacerlo. ¡Me duele la rodilla!

2. **Completar** Completa las oraciones conjugando los verbos modales de la lista. `26.B`

> deber   haber   poder   tener   venir

> **Modelo**
>
> ___Deben___ de ser tres o cuatro los que aún no han pagado la cuota del club. No estoy segura.

1. Esta mesa no _____ a costar más de 300 dólares, ¿la compramos?

2. ¿_____ probar la ensalada? Se ve tan rica y tengo tanta hambre.

3. No tenemos otra opción: _____ de sacar esa muela, aunque no quieras.

4. Lucía _____ de haberse quedado dormida. Son las 10 y todavía no ha llegado al trabajo.

5. Los alumnos _____ de asistir, como mínimo, a un 75% de las clases.

6. Como las habitaciones de todos los hoteles estaban reservadas, mis padres _____ que dormir en el auto.

7. Elisa y tú _____ hacer la presentación para el miércoles próximo.

8. Al final, los arreglos de la casa _____ a costarnos más de dos mil pesos.

9. Me quedé en casa porque _____ que estudiar para el examen.

10. ¿Sabías que las bolsas de plástico _____ causar la muerte de muchas mascotas que se meten en ellas y se asfixian?

3. **Decidir** Decide si estos ejemplos de perífrasis verbales expresan *tiempo*, una *fase* u *orden*. `26.C`

   1. Juana se puso a llorar en cuanto vio a su hija en el traje de novia. _____

   2. Empezaremos por meter toda la ropa en cajas. Luego, las rotularemos. _____

   3. No acostumbramos beber café por las mañanas. _____

   4. ¡Deja de llamarme por teléfono! _____

   5. Volveremos a vernos pronto, ¿no? _____

   6. Todo nuestro trabajo vino a resultar en vano. ¡Todo por no leer bien las instrucciones! _____

   7. Cuando llegaste, estaba por escribirte un mensaje de texto. _____

   8. ¡Justo vengo a olvidarme el trabajo en casa! _____

4. **Carta** Completa la carta con las perífrasis verbales de la lista. `26.C`

volveré a	fui a	para de	puso a	acababa de	~~empiezo por~~	suelo	terminaré por

   Querida hermana:

   ¿Cómo estás? (1) ____Empiezo por____ decirte que te extraño muchísimo. Bien sabes que yo no
   (2) _____ quejarme, pero estos primeros días aquí en Chile no han sido fáciles.

   No te imaginas qué frío que es el clima aquí. ¡No (3) _____ llover! Ayer (4) _____
   salir de casa, muy bien vestida para ir a una entrevista y, de pronto, se (5) _____ llover a
   cántaros. Por supuesto, no (6) _____ salir sin paraguas.

   Otra cosa, mi compañera de cuarto es muy maleducada. Nunca limpia, tampoco cocina y me trata mal.
   ¡Qué mala suerte que tengo! ¿Cómo (7) _____ parar a esta habitación?

   Bueno, veré qué hago en las próximas semanas. Seguramente (8) _____ mudarme
   a otra habitación.

   Tu hermana menor

5. **Unir** Une los elementos de las tres columnas para formar oraciones lógicas. `26.C`

1. Después de probar con el canto,	volvería a	estudiar pintura.
2. En esas dos horas, el profesor no	dejó de	robar en la tienda.
3. Me juró que no	iría a	comer dulces, ¡pero este bombón es tentador!
4. Un rato después de salir el sol,	suelo	hablar ni un segundo.
5. Es verdad que no	pasé a	hacer las compras por iniciativa propia.
6. Natalia nunca	entró a	nublarse y a la media hora llovía sin parar.

   _____
   _____
   _____
   _____
   _____
   _____

6. Escoger En cada oración, elige la opción correcta. `26.D`

1. La falta de agua potable _____ (anda/continúa) siendo el problema más grave de las zonas más pobres del país.

2. Tomás _____ (sigue/lleva) buscando trabajo unos cuatro meses.

3. La paciente _____ (va/está) recuperándose de la operación. Por favor, déjenla dormir.

4. _____ (Sigo/Llevo) esperando el llamado de Pablo.

5. El niñito ese _____ (está/vive) molestando en clase. Hablaré con sus padres.

7. Gerundio Usa los verbos de la lista para formar perífrasis verbales de gerundio de los verbos indicados. Usa cada verbo solo una vez. `26.D`

~~andar~~	pasarse
estar	seguir
ir	venir
llevar	vivir

Modelo

Mi padre _____*anda necesitando*_____ (necesitar) una corbata nueva. Se la regalaré para su cumpleaños.

1. ¿Te das cuenta de que _____ (hablar) por teléfono desde que llegué?

2. Mi madre _____ (criticar) a todas sus vecinas. ¡Es insoportable!

3. El perro _____ toda la tarde _____ (ladrar) y los vecinos se quejaron.

4. Los impuestos _____ (aumentar) hasta que fue casi imposible pagarlos.

5. ¡Hace cuánto que te _____ (pedir) que arregles el grifo de la cocina!

6. Juana _____ (vivir) dos años en Ecuador.

7. Yo _____ (trabajar) hasta las 8 de la noche. ¿Tú qué quieres hacer?

8. Emparejar Une las explicaciones con los ejemplos. `26.D`

1. _____ Expresa un proceso en aumento que tiene un límite o resultado.

2. _____ Expresa una acción constante, habitual o que se repite.

3. _____ Expresa una acción referida a un período de tiempo.

4. _____ Expresa un proceso en curso que se da intermitentemente.

5. _____ Expresa un proceso que comenzó en el pasado y continúa hasta ahora.

6. _____ Expresa un proceso en curso (con una expresión de tiempo), pero es más enfático que **estar** + **gerundio**.

a. Llevo tres horas esperándote en la esquina. ¿Dónde te metiste?

b. La humedad de esa pared fue creciendo hasta que finalmente el dueño decidió repararla.

c. Mi primita se pasó toda la tarde llorando por su mamá.

d. Ya nos venía pareciendo que faltaba dinero de la caja y ahora descubrimos que el vendedor nos robaba.

e. Juan y su novia viven peleándose por cualquier cosa.

f. Lucas anda preguntando por ti. ¿Por qué no lo llamas?

9. Reescribir Reescribe las oraciones usando perífrasis de participio. `26.E`

> **Modelo**
>
> Ya escribí veinte capítulos del libro. (llevar)
> *Llevo escritos veinte capítulos del libro.*

1. Mamá le prohibió a Luisito que use vasos de vidrio. (tener)
   _____
2. Gonzalo ha ganado tres carreras. (llevar)
   _____
3. Mis amigos no han comprado las entradas para mañana. (tener)
   _____
4. Este director ha dirigido más de veinte películas. (llevar)
   _____
5. La carta se escribió con tinta roja. (estar)
   _____

10. Completar Completa las oraciones conjugando los verbos de la lista. `26.E`

> ~~estar~~   quedar (2)   seguir   venir   ver

> **Modelo**
>
> Ya _____*está*_____ preparado todo para el concierto de esta noche.

1. La profesora _____ encantada con tu trabajo final. Seguramente te pondrá una buena nota.
2. El nombre de la empresa _____ impreso en los sobres. No hace falta escribir nada.
3. _____ decidido que se cerrará el restaurante hasta el verano próximo.
4. Federica _____ preocupada por la salud de su perrito. Hace una semana que está enfermo.
5. Al final, nos _____ obligados a tomar una decisión drástica.

11. Síntesis Indicar Indica si cada enunciado se refiere a un *infinitivo*, un *gerundio*, un *participio* o *los tres*. `26.A–26.E`

> **Modelo**
>
> Puede expresar una necesidad. *infinitivo*

1. Expresa una acción en curso. _____
2. Se usa con **deber** y **poder**. _____
3. Puede expresar una posibilidad. _____
4. Se usa con **resultar** y **verse**. _____
5. Puede expresar una obligación. _____
6. Concuerda en género y número con un sujeto u objeto. _____
7. Se usa con **andar** y **continuar**. _____
8. Expresa el resultado de una acción o proceso. _____
9. Puede expresar el comienzo de una acción. _____
10. Se usa con verbos auxiliares. _____

12. Síntesis Verbos Completa las perífrasis con el infinitivo, participio o gerundio de los verbos de la lista. `26.B–26.E`

| despertarte | dormir (2) | gastar | perjudicar | tener | ~~ver~~ |

> **Modelo**
>
> Acabo de _____ver_____ a la chica más linda del mundo.

1. Perdona, no quería _____. ¡Te llamaré más tarde!
2. Marta está _____ desde las 2 de la tarde.
3. Todos resultamos _____ por la crisis económica.
4. No suelo _____ la siesta, ¡pero hoy estaba tan cansada!
5. Sigo _____ pesadillas con fantasmas. ¡Todo por ver esa película!
6. Llevamos _____ demasiado dinero en este negocio.

13. Síntesis Emparejar Une las explicaciones con los ejemplos. `26.B–26.E`

___ 1. Indica una acción que está a punto de empezar.

___ 2. Indica una acción que se está desarrollando.

___ 3. Indica una acción acabada.

___ 4. Indica una destreza.

___ 5. Indica una acción que se repite varias veces.

___ 6. Indica una obligación.

___ 7. Indica una posibilidad.

___ 8. Indica un deseo.

a. Carla sabe esquiar muy bien.

b. Estaba por cocinar algo cuando apareciste con una pizza.

c. Suelo comer un yogur como cena.

d. Puedo comerme tres platos de sopa cuando tengo hambre.

e. Hemos de vender más de veinte productos por día.

f. Me estoy rompiendo la cabeza con este crucigrama.

g. Queremos ir a la playa.

h. Tengo estudiada toda la lección uno.

14. Síntesis Escribir ¿Qué obligaciones, necesidades, costumbres o posibilidades tienes en casa o en tu escuela? Redacta cinco de estas, utilizando verbos modales con infinitivos o perífrasis verbales con gerundios y participios. `26.B–26.E`

> **Modelo**
>
> En mi escuela, siempre tengo que llevar bien puesto mi uniforme...

_____

_____

_____

_____

_____

_____

_____

_____

Practice more at **vhlcentral.com**.

1. Indicar Indica los pronombres y verbos reflexivos. `27.A`

> Juan:
>
> Hoy me desperté a las siete de la mañana. Apenas escuché el despertador, me senté en la cama y te llamé por teléfono para despertarte. El teléfono sonó, sonó y sonó, pero no atendiste.
>
> Como todavía era temprano, no me preocupé y decidí darme un baño largo. Después, me cepillé los dientes y me peiné.
>
> Dos minutos después de salir de la ducha, me di cuenta de mi error: ¡me había equivocado de número de teléfono! Ahora me siento tan mal por esta situación. Llegaste tarde al trabajo, tu jefe se enojó contigo y casi pierdes tu trabajo.
>
> ¡Espero que sepas disculparme!
>
> Lucas

2. Pronombres Coloca las preposiciones y los pronombres en el orden adecuado y realiza los cambios necesarios en el caso de la preposición *con*. `27.A`

> **Modelo**
>
> La actriz se evalúa _____*a sí misma*_____ para mejorar su actuación. (misma, sí, a)

1. Los filósofos reflexionan _____ con frecuencia. (sí, sobre, mismos)

2. Me sorprendí _____ por la reacción airada. (con, mismo, mí)

3. Javier se ríe _____ sin problema. (de, mismo, sí)

4. ¡Tu hijito se entretiene tanto _____! (sí, con, mismo)

5. Camila se felicitó _____ después de la gran presentación. (sí, a, misma)

6. ¿Te enfureciste _____ por no aprobar el examen? (mismo, ti, con)

3. Escribir Escribe las oraciones usando pronombres y verbos reflexivos. Sigue el modelo. `27.A`

> **Modelo**
>
> dormirse / yo / las once
> *Me duermo a las once.*
> *Me voy a dormir a las once.* OR *Voy a dormirme a las once.*

1. afeitarse / Oscar / las siete
   _____
   _____

2. reunirse / ellos / miércoles
   _____
   _____

3. reírse / vosotros / mucho
   _____
   _____

4. pelearse / nosotros / nunca
   _____
   _____

5. ponerse / Gabriela / tacones
   _____
   _____

6. dormirse / tú / siempre
   _____
   _____

4. Reescribir Reescribe las oraciones usando *el uno al otro, los unos a los otros*, etc. `27.B`

> **Modelo**
>
> Los novios, Camila y Marcos, se besan mutuamente.
> *Los novios, Camila y Marcos, se besan el uno al otro.*

1. Juan e Isabel se apoyan mutuamente.

   _____

2. Los alumnos y los profesores siempre se critican mutuamente.

   _____

3. Federica y su amiga se respetan mutuamente.

   _____

4. Los trabajadores se ayudan mutuamente.

   _____

5. Mi madre y mi hermana se miraron entre sí con tristeza.

   _____

5. ¿Sí o no? Indica si estos ejemplos contienen verbos reflexivos. Escribe *sí* o *no*. `27.C–27.D`

> **Modelo**
>
> Mi hermano no sabe defenderse. *sí*

1. Me he maquillado demasiado, ¿no? _____
2. Juan durmió al niño y comenzó a estudiar. _____
3. ¿Te manchaste la camisa otra vez? _____
4. Despiértenme a las nueve. _____
5. Quita tus cosas de mi armario. _____
6. Los invitados deberán vestirse de etiqueta. _____

6. Elegir En cada oración, elige la opción correcta. `27.C–27.D`

1. Florencia se bañó _____ rápidamente y salió al cine.
   a. a sí misma   b. X

2. El pobre perrito ya no puede levantarse _____.
   a. por sí mismo   b. X

3. Me acosté _____ muy temprano.
   a. a mí mismo   b. X

4. ¿El niño ya es capaz de ducharse _____?
   a. por sí mismo   b. X

5. ¿A qué hora te despiertas _____ para ir a trabajar?
   a. X   b. a ti misma

6. Una vez que crezca, la niña podrá vestirse _____.
   a. X   b. por sí sola

7. Clasificar Clasifica los verbos según sean únicamente reflexivos o no. `27.C–27.D`

arrepentirse   cansarse   atreverse
jactarse   ~~lavarse~~   quemarse
abstenerse   conocerse   levantarse
odiarse   quejarse   despedirse

Únicamente reflexivos	Reflexivos/No reflexivos
	lavarse

8. Oraciones Completa las oraciones usando los verbos de la lista para expresar una acción "completa". `27.C–27.D`

andar   comer   conocer   creer   saber   ~~ver~~

Modelo

Nosotros _____*nos vemos*_____ todas las películas de Alfonso Cuarón.

1. Yo _____ todos los restaurantes vegetarianos de la ciudad.

2. ¿De veras _____ lo que dice mi hermanita? ¡No seas tonta!

3. Cuando tienen hambre, esos niños _____ tres platos de sopa cada uno.

4. Andrea _____ de memoria los nombres de todas las actrices de la telenovela.

5. ¿_____ toda Barcelona? Supongo que estás cansada.

9. Emparejar Une los ejemplos con las explicaciones. `27.C–27.D`

_____ 1. Es un verbo que implica reciprocidad.

_____ 2. Es un verbo que solamente puede ser reflexivo.

_____ 3. Es un verbo que expresa una acción "completa".

_____ 4. Es un verbo que implica que uno mismo no realizó la acción.

_____ 5. Es un verbo cuyo sujeto es afectado indirectamente por la acción.

a. ¡De qué color más raro te teñiste el cabello!

b. Me aprendí todo el vocabulario para el examen.

c. Las mujeres no nos llevamos bien entre nosotras.

d. ¡Te quejas y te quejas todo el día!

e. ¡Qué lindo vestido que me mandé a hacer!

10. **Completar** Completa las oraciones conjugando los verbos de la lista. Agrega el pronombre adecuado a cada verbo. `27.C–27.D`

abrazar	aprender	casar	confesar	duchar	mirar	pelear
apoyar	arrepentir	comprometer	conocer	escribir	~~odiar~~	reunir

Modelo

Es algo muy raro, pero mi perro y mi gato no _____*se odian*_____.

1. Los enamorados _____ a los ojos y _____ su amor.

2. Estamos tan contentos. _____ el 20 de octubre y _____ el 1.° de diciembre.

3. Los hermanos siempre _____ mutuamente.

4. María y Julia _____ todo el día y sin ningún motivo.

5. Las amigas _____ cuando se reencontraron después de tantos años.

6. Aníbal _____ con agua fría porque se había acabado el agua caliente.

7. Es verdad que Ana _____ todos los nombres la primera vez que los oyó.

8. Los directivos _____ la semana próxima para analizar las nuevas propuestas.

9. Ellos _____ cuando eran niños y _____ cartas desde entonces.

10. No _____ de haberle dicho la verdad, aunque no le haya gustado oírla.

11. **Escoger** En cada oración, elige la opción correcta. `27.E`

1. _____ (Anima/Anímate) a tu amiga a que venga a la fiesta.

2. _____ (Me decidí/Decidí) no comprar una casa en las montañas.

3. Josefina _____ (se saltó/saltó) el almuerzo: piensa que así podrá adelgazar más rápido.

4. _____ (Jugamos/Nos jugamos) el pellejo en este partido. ¡Debemos ganarlo sí o sí!

5. No _____ (te deshagas/deshagas) el trabajo que con tanto esfuerzo logramos hacer.

6. ¡_____ (Cómanse/Coman) todo el chocolate! A mí no me gusta.

12. **Contestar** Escribe las respuestas usando reflexivos que expresan acciones involuntarias. Sigue el modelo. `27.F`

Modelo

¿Qué le pasó a la botella? (romper)
Se rompió.

1. ¿Qué le pasó a tu motocicleta? (descomponer)

_____

2. ¿Qué le pasó a la batería de tu teléfono? (descargar)

_____

3. ¿Qué les pasó a los adornos que te regalé? (caer)

_____

4. ¿Qué le pasó al ovillo de lana? (enredar)

_____

5. ¿Qué les pasó a los edificios? (derrumbar)

_____

13. Escribir Escribe oraciones siguiendo el modelo. **27.F**

> **Modelo**
> Se descompuso la radio. (yo)
> *Se me descompuso la radio.*

1. Se quebró la madera. (tú)
_____

2. Se cerró la puerta. (él)
_____

3. Se rompió la tetera. (yo)
_____

4. Se derramó la leche. (nosotros)
_____

5. Se agotó la batería. (mi auto)
_____

6. Se olvidaron los nombres. (ellos)
_____

14. Completar Completa las oraciones con verbos que expresen cambio. Como pista, tienes los adjetivos que corresponden a dichos verbos. **27.G**

> ~~alegre~~   emocionado/a   enamorado/a   muerto/a   rico/a   rojo/a   separado/a

> **Modelo**
> Ignacio _____*se alegró*_____ al oír las buenas noticias anoche.

1. Cuando se dio cuenta de que todos lo miraban, Juan _____.
2. Mi madre _____ tanto cuando nos graduamos.
3. Mi gato _____ en 2010.
4. Los empresarios _____ a raíz del aumento de los bienes inmuebles.
5. Las adolescentes pronto _____ de la estrella de la música pop.
6. La diputada _____ de su marido y ahora se ve más feliz.

15. Reescribir Reescribe las oraciones usando el verbo indicado. **27.G**

> **Modelo**
> La mala noticia me preocupa todavía. (quedarse)
> *Me quedé preocupado con la mala noticia.*

1. La oficina es un caos cuando tú no estás. (convertirse)
_____

2. Tu perrito se entristece apenas sales de la sala. (ponerse)
_____

3. Mi prima se enriqueció con su tienda de perfumes. (hacerse)
_____

4. Ahora Madrid es una ciudad muy cara. (volverse)
_____

5. Algún día, seré muy rico. (llegar a ser)
_____

16. Síntesis Seleccionar En cada oración, elige la opción correcta. `27.A–27.G`

1. El ladrón _____ de los objetos robados.
   a. se deshizo   b. deshizo

2. El cabello _____ cada día más.
   a. se cae   b. se me cae

3. ¡Qué tonta soy! _____ los libros en casa.
   a. Se me olvidaron   b. Se olvidaron

4. Juan es tan ingenuo. _____ todo lo que le dicen.
   a. Cree   b. Se cree

5. _____ que vendrías más temprano.
   a. Se me ocurrió   b. Me ocurrió

6. Isabela _____ al bebé y se puso a leer.
   a. se acostó   b. acostó

17. Síntesis Emparejar Empareja los pistas con los verbos adecuados. `27.A–27.G`

_____ 1. cambio emocional	a. tutearse
_____ 2. reciprocidad	b. arrodillarse
_____ 3. acción "completa"	c. graduarse
_____ 4. cambio significativo	d. entristecerse
_____ 5. rutina diaria	e. saberse
_____ 6. cambio físico	f. olvidarse
_____ 7. acción involuntaria	g. vestirse
_____ 8. cambio social	h. convertirse

18. Síntesis Decidir Decide qué oración es la intrusa. `27.A–27.G`

1. a. Me leí el libro en una tarde.
   b. Me caí de las escaleras.
   c. Me conozco Venezuela de cabo a rabo.

2. a. No te atreviste a llamarme.
   b. El jefe se quejó mucho ayer.
   c. La empresa se declaró en quiebra.

3. a. Luisa se operó el lunes.
   b. La ventana se abrió.
   c. El vidrio se rompió.

4. a. Has avergonzado a tu hermana.
   b. El delincuente escapó de la guardia policial.
   c. ¿Te has burlado de mí?

5. a. Nos casamos en junio.
   b. Te irritaste un poco, ¿no?
   c. Se me olvidó traer dinero.

6. a. ¡Se hizo demasiado tarde!
   b. Se volvió para decirme algo.
   c. El barrio se ha vuelto un lugar concurrido.

19. Síntesis Redactar Escribe sobre tu rutina diaria utilizando por lo menos cinco verbos reflexivos. `27.A–27.G`

> **Modelo**
>
> *Todos los días me despierto a las seis de la mañana…*

_____

_____

_____

_____

_____

_____

_____

_____

_____

Practice more at **vhlcentral.com.**

Passive and impersonal constructions ◗ | Chapter 28

1. Elegir En cada oración, elige la opción correcta. `28.B–28.C`

1. La prensa de los Estados Unidos _____ muy _____ por no ser imparcial.
   a. fueron; criticados   b. fue; criticada

2. Las cartas que escribió la niña _____ hace dos semanas.
   a. fue enviada   b. fueron enviadas

3. La habitación ya _____ por el señor vestido de azul.
   a. ha sido pagada   b. ha sido pagado

4. El contrato de trabajo y el acuerdo de confidencialidad _____ por todas las partes interesadas.
   a. será firmado   b. serán firmados

5. La fila de prioridad de embarque _____ por todos los pasajeros.
   a. deberá ser respetada   b. deberá ser respetado

2. Reordenar Reordena los elementos para formar oraciones completas. `28.B–28.C`

> **Modelo**
>
> fue / El conserje / despertado / los visitantes / por / .
> *El conserje fue despertado por los visitantes.*

1. cruelmente / por / fueron / Los animalitos / tratados / el cazador / .

_____

2. información / serán / Quienes den / recompensados / .

_____

3. los lectores / fueron / enviados / Los periódicos / a / esta tarde / .

_____

4. El problema / el jefe del departamento / había sido / por / resuelto / .

_____

5. por / confeccionado / El vestido de novia / fue / el afamado diseñador / .

_____

3. Convertir Convierte las oraciones en oraciones pasivas con *ser*. `28.B–28.C`

> **Modelo**
>
> Ambos países firmaron un acuerdo de cooperación.
> *Un acuerdo de cooperación fue firmado por ambos países.*

1. El Senado aprobó hoy la ley de alimentos orgánicos.
   _____

2. Miles de fanáticos vieron el partido.
   _____

3. La crítica elogió el documental.
   _____

4. Los arqueólogos chilenos descubrieron tres tumbas egipcias.
   _____

5. La policía controló la identidad de los pasajeros.
   _____

4. Reescribir Reescribe las oraciones en voz pasiva siguiendo el modelo. `28.B–28.C`

> **Modelo**
>
> Juan cambiará una lámpara de la cocina.
> *Una lámpara de la cocina será cambiada por Juan.*
> *La lámpara ya está cambiada.*

1. La policía prenderá al delincuente.
   _____
   _____

2. Mi madre hará el pastel para mi cumpleaños.
   _____
   _____

3. Ulises redactará una carta de queja.
   _____
   _____

4. Todos los trabajadores pagarán los aportes de la jubilación.
   _____
   _____

5. El directorio de la compañía publicará una revista.
   _____
   _____

6. Un arquitecto diseñará el monumento.
   _____
   _____

5. Oraciones   Escribe las oraciones siguiendo el modelo. **28.D**

> **Modelo**
>
> café: hacer
> *Primero, se hace el café.*

1. papas: pelar

_____

2. tarta: hornear

_____

3. casa: construir

_____

4. bombilla de luz: apagar

_____

5. cabello: lavar

_____

6. galletas: decorar

_____

7. mesa: poner

_____

8. muebles: sacudir

_____

9. libro: abrir

_____

10. zanahorias: cortar

_____

6. Tareas   Crea las oraciones sobre las tareas pendientes de cada día. Utiliza construcciones pasivas con los verbos modales. **28.D**

> **Modelo**
>
> lunes / deber / limpiar el pasillo
> *El lunes se debe limpiar el pasillo.*

1. martes / tener que / pintar la puerta

_____

2. miércoles / haber de / lavar la ropa

_____

3. jueves / ir a / sacar la basura

_____

4. viernes / deber / planchar la ropa

_____

5. sábado / poder / hacer fiesta

_____

7. Seleccionar **Elige la mejor opción.** `28.B–28.D`

1. Ayer vi que, en el restaurante de la esquina, _____ camareros. ¿Te interesa?
   a. se buscan   b. se busca   c. Ambas opciones son posibles.

2. _____ que al final del cuento el príncipe siempre conquista el corazón de la mujer de sus sueños.
   a. Se supone   b. Se suponen   c. Ambas opciones son posibles.

3. Esta enfermedad ya _____ por los expertos de nuestro país.
   a. ha sido estudiada   b. se ha estudiado   c. Ambas opciones son posibles.

4. Los detalles de la reunión _____ durante esta semana.
   a. se prepararán   b. serán preparados   c. Ambas opciones son posibles.

5. La naranja es la fruta que más _____ en España.
   a. se exporta   b. se exportan   c. Ambas opciones son posibles.

6. Las instrucciones _____ con antelación.
   a. deberían comunicarse   b. se deberían comunicar   c. Ambas opciones son posibles.

7. Las cuentas del hogar _____ por correo electrónico a la brevedad.
   a. se envía   b. se envían   c. Ambas opciones son posibles.

8. Completar **Completa las oraciones con los verbos de la lista. Deberás elegir entre oraciones pasivas con _ser_ y oraciones pasivas reflejas.** `28.B–28.D`

> aceptar   agregar   detener   firmar   mojar   reparar   ~~saber~~

Modelo

> No _____ _se sabe_ _____ aún dónde está el dinero robado.

1. La antena de mi casa está rota y _____ por un profesional la semana que viene.

2. _____ todas las solicitudes que cumplan con los requisitos.

3. La lavadora no funciona sin detergente. Antes de encenderla, _____ la pastilla en este recipiente.

4. Ayer dejé abierta la ventana de la habitación y _____ todos mis apuntes con la lluvia.

5. Las prescripciones de medicamentos siempre _____ por los médicos.

9. Escribir **Escribe oraciones siguiendo el modelo.** `28.E`

Modelo

> pincel - pintar. _Con el pincel, se pinta._
> oficina - trabajar. _En la oficina, se trabaja._

1. cuchillo - cortar
   _____

2. pimienta - condimentar
   _____

3. cuchara - probar
   _____

4. tenedor - comer
   _____

5. lápiz - escribir
   _____

6. ayuntamiento - debatir
   _____

7. escuela - aprender
   _____

8. comedor - comer
   _____

10. Oraciones   Escribe oraciones siguiendo el modelo. **28.E**

> **Modelo**
>
> Los pasajeros serán controlados al subir al autobús.
> *Se controlará a los pasajeros al subir al autobús.*
> *Se los controlará al subir al autobús.*

1. Los estudiantes fueron clasificados por especialización.

_____

_____

2. Los peatones deben ser respetados.

_____

_____

3. Las enfermeras son contratadas por un año.

_____

_____

4. Todo el pueblo es encuestado cada diez años.

_____

_____

5. Los trabajadores son evaluados cada trimestre.

_____

_____

11. Indicar   En el siguiente texto, indica dónde está expresado el objeto indirecto. **28.F**

Primero, se redactaron las normas de seguridad. Una vez redactadas, la gerencia se las enseñó a los miembros del departamento de documentación. Cuando estaban listas, se las enviaron a todos los trabajadores de la planta.

Hubo diversas reacciones de parte de los trabajadores. Se le informó a la gerencia que muchas de las normas eran obsoletas y se le advirtió que debían hacerse modificaciones con urgencia.

Ahora se han reformado las normas. Mañana por la tarde se las presentará al gerente general. Esta vez seguramente se las aprobará sin objeciones.

12. ¿Pasiva o impersonal?   Decide si estas oraciones son construcciones pasivas con *se* o impersonales con *se*. **28.G**

> **Modelo**
>
> Nunca se supo el porqué de su decisión. _____*pasiva*_____

1. En el instituto que está cerca de casa se enseñan más de veinte idiomas. _____

2. Se contratan camareros con experiencia. _____

3. Cuando se estudia, se aprueba sin problemas. _____

4. Se dicen muchas mentiras en la prensa amarilla. _____

5. Se elogió a nuestra directora en el discurso de inauguración. _____

6. Se vendieron más de cuarenta videojuegos en un día. _____

7. Se cree cada vez menos en los gobernantes. _____

8. Aquí se trabaja muchísimo. _____

13. Completar Completa las oraciones con las palabras de la lista. 28.H

| habían | es | había | han | hay | ~~hubo~~ | era |

Modelo

¿ _____Hubo_____ problemas entre Martín y tú? Veo que ya no se hablan.

1. _____ demasiada nieve y no podemos salir de casa.

2. Este mes, se _____ vendido más de mil ejemplares de la novela.

3. Mis artículos _____ sido publicados en la revista *Lugares* ¡y yo no me había enterado!

4. _____ tanto sol que tuve que ponerme a la sombra.

5. _____ invierno, pero parece primavera.

6. ¡Ya _____ hora de que me llamaras!

14. Reescribir Reescribe las oraciones usando las pistas. 28.H

Modelo

Te recomiendo que estudies mucho para el examen. (importar)
Importa estudiar mucho para el examen.

1. Nunca se sabe cómo estará el tiempo al día siguiente. (uno)

_____

2. Se hace lo que se puede. (gente)

_____

3. Es conveniente tener un botiquín de primeros auxilios. (convenir)

_____

4. No se puede respirar en esta habitación llena de humo. (una)

_____

5. Se puede reconocer fácilmente un disco compacto falso. (tú)

_____

6. Ha caído muchísima lluvia en la última semana. (llover)

_____

7. Abundan los libros sobre historia medieval en esta biblioteca. (haber)

_____

8. El clima está frío en esa época del año. (hacer)

_____

15. Síntesis Indicar Indica si cada enunciado se refiere a construcciones pasivas con *ser, se* (P) o construcciones impersonales con *se* (I). 28.B–28.H

1. Hay una **a** personal. _____

2. Solo se puede formar con verbos transitivos. _____

3. El verbo siempre es singular. _____

4. El objeto directo de la oración activa es el sujeto. _____

5. El verbo puede ser singular o plural. _____

6. No hay sujeto gramatical. _____

16. Síntesis Escoger Escoge el tipo de oración pasiva o impersonal según corresponda, ya sea pasiva con *ser*, pasiva con *se* o impersonal con *se*. `28.B–28.H`

1. La alarma fue desactivada por accidente.
   a. pasiva con **ser**   b. pasiva con **se**   c. impersonal con **se**

2. Se galardonó la película con ocho estatuillas.
   a. pasiva con **ser**   b. pasiva con **se**   c. impersonal con **se**

3. Se recomiendan materiales cien por ciento reutilizables.
   a. pasiva con **ser**   b. pasiva con **se**   c. impersonal con **se**

4. El asesino fue perseguido día y noche por los investigadores.
   a. pasiva con **ser**   b. pasiva con **se**   c. impersonal con **se**

5. Se premiará por su desempeño a los mejores deportistas.
   a. pasiva con **ser**   b. pasiva con **se**   c. impersonal con **se**

6. Los cheques serán firmados en el dorso por el cliente.
   a. pasiva con **ser**   b. pasiva con **se**   c. impersonal con **se**

7. Se permite el ingreso de mascotas.
   a. pasiva con **ser**   b. pasiva con **se**   c. impersonal con **se**

8. Los conductores fueron multados por exceso de velocidad.
   a. pasiva con **ser**   b. pasiva con **se**   c. impersonal con **se**

9. Se sostiene a la familia con el sudor de la frente.
   a. pasiva con **ser**   b. pasiva con **se**   c. impersonal con **se**

10. Se consideran soluciones pacíficas para el conflicto.
    a. pasiva con **ser**   b. pasiva con **se**   c. impersonal con **se**

11. Los trabajadores han sido contratados por sus méritos.
    a. pasiva con **ser**   b. pasiva con **se**   c. impersonal con **se**

12. Se cambian libros usados.
    a. pasiva con **ser**   b. pasiva con **se**   c. impersonal con **se**

17. Síntesis Titulares Imagina que eres el/la redactor(a) de un diario escolar. Escribe cinco sucesos que hayan pasado en tu lugar de estudio como si fueran titulares para el periódico. Utiliza formas pasivas con *ser* o *se* e impersonales con *se*. `28.B–28.H`

> **Modelo**
> *Ayer fueron abiertas las inscripciones para el club escolar de música.*

_____

_____

_____

_____

_____

_____

_____

_____

Practice more at **vhlcentral.com.**

1. Seleccionar Elige lo que expresan *ser* o *estar* en cada oración, ya sea cualidad esencial, condición o ubicación. `29.A`

1. Mi tía está enferma.
   a. cualidad esencial   b. condición   c. ubicación

2. Los delfines son muy inteligentes.
   a. cualidad esencial   b. condición   c. ubicación

3. Las llaves estaban dentro del carro.
   a. cualidad esencial   b. condición   c. ubicación

4. La lavadora está dañada.
   a. cualidad esencial   b. condición   c. ubicación

5. El postre está sobre la mesa.
   a. cualidad esencial   b. condición   c. ubicación

6. Esos cuchillos son de acero inoxidable.
   a. cualidad esencial   b. condición   c. ubicación

2. Conversación Completa la conversación con los verbos *haber* o *estar*. `29.B`

LUCIANO Hola, soy Luciano, ¿(1) ____*está*____ Paula?

JOSEFINA Aquí no (2) _____ ninguna Paula, debes haberte equivocado de número de teléfono.

LUCIANO Seguramente (3) _____ un malentendido.

JOSEFINA Mira, yo vivo aquí y puedo asegurarte que no (4) _____ nadie en esta casa que se llame así.

LUCIANO ¿(5) _____ alguna posibilidad de que estés confundida?

JOSEFINA ¡No (6) _____ posibilidad alguna! Vivo con mi compañera de piso ¡y no se llama Paula!

LUCIANO ¿Y (7) _____ tu compañera contigo ahora?

JOSEFINA No, ahora (8) _____ en la universidad.

LUCIANO Bueno, dile que llamó Luciano y que se (9) _____ olvidado unos libros con su nombre en el aula.

JOSEFINA ¿Paula? ¿No será Laura?

LUCIANO "Laura", "Paula", ¡qué más da! ¡(10) _____ una letra de diferencia!

3. Elegir En cada oración, elige la opción correcta. `29.C`

1. _____ (Está/Es) oscuro y _____ (es/son) las cuatro de la tarde. ¡Qué feo es el invierno!

2. ¿_____ (Será/Estará) nevando en la montaña ahora?

3. _____ (Es/Estamos) a martes y Juan todavía no ha pagado el alquiler.

4. ¡Esas camisas ya no se usan! _____ (Estamos/Es) en 2015, ¡no en 1980!

5. Ayer _____ (estuvo/fue) nublado y las fotos salieron muy oscuras.

6. _____ (Es/Son) la una: ¿dónde está Carlos?

7. ¿Hoy _____ (estamos/es) lunes o martes?

8. _____ (Es/Está) otoño, pero todavía hace calor.

9. _____ (Estaba/Era) lloviendo cuando salimos del cine.

10. Mi abuela piensa que _____ (está/es) 2000.

4. Diario Completa el diario de Julián con las palabras de la lista. `29.C`

está	hizo	estuvo	estamos	son
es	hace	hubo (2)	hará	~~es~~

Hoy (1) _____es_____ 8 de julio y (2) _____ las tres de la tarde. A pesar de que (3) _____ verano, (4) _____ mucho frío afuera y (5) _____ lloviendo a cántaros.

Ayer también (6) _____ mal tiempo. (7) _____ nublado y (8) _____ mucho viento.

¡Qué mal! Hoy (9) _____ a viernes y en toda la semana no (10) _____ ni un solo día lindo. ¿(11) _____ menos frío mañana? Me fijaré ya mismo en el pronóstico.

5. Completar Completa las oraciones con la forma apropiada de *ser, estar* o *tener*. `29.D`

> **Modelo**
>
> ¿ _Tenéis_ calor? Si os parece, bajaré la calefacción un poco.

1. Ayer no dormí bien y ahora _____ muchísimo sueño.
2. Ema _____ menor que Graciela.
3. El perro seguramente _____ hambriento. Dale un poco de comida.
4. ¿Los niños les _____ miedo todavía a los payasos?
5. Este edificio _____ más de doscientos años, ¿puedes creerlo?
6. ¡Qué cansada que _____! Mejor me quedaré en casa.

6. Traducir Traduce las siguientes oraciones usando las palabras indicadas. `29.E`

> **Modelo**
>
> The sun is rising.
> _Está amaneciendo_. (amanecer)

1. It's becoming night.
   _____ (hacer)

2. It turned cold.
   _____ (ponerse)

3. The clock struck five.
   _____ (dar)

4. It's winter again.
   _____ (de nuevo)

5. Now it's Friday.
   _____ (ya)

6. It became day.
   _____ (hacer)

7. Cambios Traduce las siguientes oraciones siguiendo el modelo. `29.E`

> **Modelo**
> He got sick.
> *Se enfermó.*
> *Se puso enfermo.*

1. She got tired.

_____

_____

2. She became happy.

_____

_____

3. My grandfather became weak.

_____

_____

4. I got better.

_____

_____

5. They became sad.

_____

_____

6. We became quiet.

_____

_____

7. He went crazy.

_____

_____

8. The dog got wet.

_____

_____

9. My friends and I got angry.

_____

_____

10. The children got excited.

_____

_____

8. Síntesis Emparejar Une el verbo con el uso que le corresponde. `29.A–29.E`

1. ___ junto con un sustantivo, expresar un cambio   a. ser
2. ___ decir la edad   b. ponerse
3. ___ junto con un pronombre indefinido, indicar la presencia   c. haber
4. ___ decir la hora   d. convertirse
5. ___ junto con un adjetivo, indicar un cambio   e. estar
6. ___ junto con un pronombre sujeto, indicar la presencia   f. tener

9. Síntesis Escoger En cada oración, elige la opción correcta. `29.B–29.E`

1. ¿_____ (Está/Hay) alguien que se llame Ángela en tu clase?
2. José ya _____ (tiene/es) veinticuatro años.
3. Mi hermanito _____ (es/está) cansado.
4. Las lámparas _____ (están/fueron) destruidas por vándalos.
5. En verano, _____ (se hace/anochece) de noche muy tarde.
6. _____ (Estamos/Es) en abril y todavía los árboles no tienen hojas.
7. Hoy _____ (fui/me quedé) en casa porque me dolía la barriga.
8. Sara se _____ (convirtió/puso) tan triste cuando vio que te habías ido.
9. Antonio _____ se (quedó/hizo) escritor.
10. ¿_____ (Están/Hay) Silvia y Susana en la escuela?

10. Síntesis Redactar Escribe por lo menos cinco oraciones sobre cambios de tus compañeros de clase o de personas conocidas. `29.A–29.E`

> **Modelo**
>
> *Jorge Luis se puso furioso cuando supo las notas finales…*

_____
_____
_____
_____
_____
_____
_____
_____
_____
_____
_____
_____
_____
_____
_____
_____
_____
_____
_____
_____
_____

Practice more at **vhlcentral.com.**

Use of *ser* and *estar*   Chapter 30

1. Preposiciones Completa las oraciones con las preposiciones de la lista. `30.B`

> a   con   de   para   sin

> **Modelo**
>
> El mantel que me regalaron es ___*a/de*___ cuadros.

1. Me llamo Juliana y soy _____ Medellín, Colombia.
2. Esta casa es ideal _____ hacer una fiesta, ¿no te parece?
3. La chaqueta es _____ Diego.
4. ¡Todos esos regalos son _____ ti!
5. ¿Has visto un pañuelo azul? Es _____ lunares blancos.
6. No me gustan los bolsos que son _____ cremallera (*zipper*). ¡Son un imán para los ladrones!

2. Reescribir Reescribe estas oraciones usando *ser* y las palabras indicadas. `30.B`

> **Modelo**
>
> Para mí, no es fácil dormir con la luz del día. (me)
> *No me es fácil dormir con la luz del día.*

1. La hermana de Juan me parece muy amable. (me)

   _____

2. ¿De veras sabes andar a caballo? (cierto)

   _____

3. ¡Siento tanto que no nos hayamos visto! (lástima)

   _____

4. Profesora, nos pareció muy difícil hacer la tarea. (nos)

   _____

5. Nací en Bogotá y viví ahí hasta los quince años. (de)

   _____

6. Marcos habla muy bien inglés. (bueno)

   _____

7. Construyeron la casa con madera. (de)

   _____

3. Unir Une las frases para formar oraciones lógicas. Usa cada opción solo una vez. `30.C`

1. Luis está _____
2. En este restaurante, no está _____
3. En Alemania, está _____
4. La directora está _____
5. Guillermo, estoy _____
6. En la oficina, la cosa está _____
7. Solo por dos meses, Romina está _____

a. que arde... mejor hablaré con mi jefe mañana.

b. por llegar a tu casa. ¿Bajas a abrirme la puerta?

c. permitido fumar, ¿no ves el cartel?

d. de camarera en el bar de la esquina.

e. con mucha tos. Le llevaré un té.

f. mal visto saludar con un beso a alguien que acabas de conocer.

g. de vacaciones durante todo enero. Llámala por teléfono si es algo urgente.

4. Oraciones Reescribe las oraciones usando *estar* y la preposición indicada. `30.C`

> **Modelo**
>
> Justo iba a comprarte una camisa del mismo color. (por)
> *Estaba por comprarte una camisa del mismo color.*

1. Nos acompaña nuestro queridísimo Presidente. (con)

   _____

2. Tengo dolor de garganta desde hace una semana. (con)

   _____

3. Casi salgo de casa sin las llaves. (a punto de)

   _____

4. Pronto comenzarán las obras del metro nuevo. (por)

   _____

5. Mi padre siempre fue partidario de los liberales. (con)

   _____

5. ¿*Ser* o *estar*? En cada oración, elige la opción correcta. `30.B–30.C`

1. Mira, los dedos de mis manos _____ azules por el frío.
   a. son   b. están

2. Ese pantalón te _____ muy grande. ¿No ves que se te cae cuando caminas?
   a. es   b. está

3. Las cosas en esta casa _____ así. Si no te gusta, puedes irte a otro lado.
   a. son   b. están

4. Natalia _____ de muy mal humor ahora. Mejor habla con ella mañana.
   a. está   b. es

5. ¡_____ cansado de ser el único que limpia en esta casa!
   a. Soy   b. Estoy

6. ¡Qué grande que _____ tu hija! ¡Cuánto ha crecido en el último verano!
   a. es   b. está

7. Te conviene comprar una cama que _____ de madera aunque cueste más que las de metal.
   a. sea   b. esté

8. Por lo general, la clase de física _____ muy aburrida.
   a. es   b. está

6. Escoger Completa el texto con *ser* o *estar* según corresponda. `30.B–30.C`

> ¡Qué linda que (1) _____ (es/está) Barcelona! Sin duda, en este momento (2) _____ (está/es) entre mis ciudades favoritas para vivir.
>
> El clima (3) _____ (está/es) caluroso en verano, pero no muy frío en invierno. Además, (4) _____ (es/está) la playa ahí nomás. ¿Qué más se puede pedir?
>
> También me encanta la gente, que (5) _____ (está/es) de buen humor para atendernos. (6) _____ (Es/Está) como estar en casa. ¡(7) _____ (Estoy/Soy) muerta de ganas de mudarme a esta ciudad!

7. Elegir En cada oración, elige entre *ser* o *estar*, según corresponda. `30.B–30.C`

1. Hace un rato que no escucho las voces de Juanito y Pedrito. Ya _____ (serán/estarán) dormidos.

2. ¿Sabes de quién _____ (está/es) enamorada Isabel?

3. La decisión _____ (fue/estuvo) aceptada por toda la empresa.

4. ¿Creías que _____ (era/estaba) satisfecha con mis notas? ¡De ninguna manera!

5. ¡Qué triste que _____ (es/está) el perrito! ¿Le pasa algo?

6. ¡Hoy sí que _____ (estás/eres) trabajadora, Paula! No paras ni un minuto.

7. ¿_____ (Es/Está) verdad que lanzarás un disco nuevo el año que viene?

8. Mis hijos _____ (están/son) muy listos: saben hablar latín.

8. ¿*Haber* o *estar*? Completa la conversación con la opción correcta. `30.C`

SABRINA Sabes que en la esquina (1) _____ (está/hay) un parque gigante, ¿no?

TERESA ¿Estás segura? ¿En qué esquina (2) _____ (está/hay)?

SABRINA En la esquina de la avenida Naciones Unidas y Terrazas.

TERESA Ah, sí, ¿a qué venía eso?

SABRINA Allí (3) _____ (hay/está) un concierto esta tarde.

TERESA Genial. ¿(4) _____ (Habrá/Habrán) bandas conocidas?

SABRINA No lo sé, pero el año pasado (5) _____ (hubo/estuvo) muy bien.

TERESA ¿Y sabes si (6) _____ (estará/habrá) lluvia?

SABRINA Mmm... dicen que (7) _____ (habrá/estará) nuboso, pero no muy frío.

TERESA Perfecto. ¿Y tienes entradas? (8) _____ (Hay/Están) dos compañeras de la uni que vendrán a casa a comer y me gustaría ir con ellas.

SABRINA ¡Por supuesto! La entrada es libre y (9) _____ (está/hay) abierto a todo el público.

9. Unir Une las frases para formar oraciones lógicas. `30.D`

1. Mi casa está _____   a. la fiesta de aniversario de los abuelos.

2. Dime dónde será _____   b. en Pamplona, en julio. ¿Quieres que vayamos?

3. Lucía, estoy _____   c. muy lejos de la tuya.

4. Los sanfermines son _____   d. aquí en la esquina, ¿no me ves?

5. Las flores están _____   e. en el auto. Tráelas, por favor.

10. Síntesis Seleccionar En cada oración, elige la opción correcta. `30.B–30.E`

1. La cama _____ (está/es) muy cara ahora. La semana pasada el precio era menor.

2. _____ (Es/Está) importante que vengas a la reunión del jueves.

3. ¿_____ (Estabas/Eras) durmiendo? ¡Discúlpame!

4. _____ (Fue/Estuvo) Francisco quien te llamó ayer, no Federico.

5. Por suerte, la comida ya _____ (está/es) hecha. En un minuto podremos comer.

6. Quiero que _____ (seamos/estemos) felices para toda la vida.

7. _____ (Es/Está) bien que estudies mucho, pero también tienes que descansar un poco.

8. Los mangos _____ (son/están) verdes: no los comas.

11. Síntesis Completar Completa el texto de Rodrigo con los verbos adecuados. `30.B–30.E`

Mi equipo de fútbol favorito

(1) _____ (Está/Es) sabido que en España hay dos equipos de fútbol muy importantes: el Real Madrid y el FC Barcelona. El problema (2) _____ (es/está) que yo (3) _____ (soy/estoy) del Real Madrid, a pesar de (4) _____ (estar/ser) de la ciudad de Barcelona. Me (5) _____ (es/está) tan difícil vivir en Barcelona ¡y ver cómo las banderas del Barcelona (6) _____ (son/están) hasta en la sopa! Por eso, (7) _____ (soy/estoy) a punto de lanzar una campaña para reclutar más fanáticos del Real en Barcelona. Si (8) _____ (eres/estás) conmigo, envíame un mensaje electrónico a mejormadrid@barcelona.es

12. Síntesis Verbos Completa las oraciones con los verbos de la lista. `30.B–30.E`

estábamos	están	fue	son (2)	estuvo
ha	está (2)	será	hubo	~~es~~

1. Marina ___*es*___ abogada, pero ahora _____ de profesora de historia en una escuela.
2. _____ evidente que _____ problemas de organización en el desfile del mes pasado. Este mes será diferente.
3. ¿El perro _____ en mi habitación? Las paredes _____ llenas de barro.
4. Aunque los novios _____ de Buenos Aires, la boda _____ en Córdoba.
5. _____ en el cine cuando nos llamaste. _____ prohibido usar el teléfono celular allí.
6. _____ habido muchas peleas entre ellos, pero _____ muy amigos.

13. Síntesis Escribir Redacta un párrafo de por lo menos cinco oraciones sobre ti mismo/a. Puedes decir de dónde eres, cómo es tu apariencia, cómo te sientes, dónde te encuentras, etc., usando los verbos *ser* y *estar*. `30.B–30.E`

Modelo

Estoy en casa es este momento. Soy un joven responsable y activo…

_____
_____
_____
_____
_____
_____
_____
_____
_____
_____

Practice more at **vhlcentral.com.**

1. Indicar Indica si cada frase se refiere al discurso directo (D) o al discurso indirecto (I). `31.A`

1. discurso citado _____

2. discurso reportado _____

3. entre comillas _____

4. no es una cita exacta _____

5. las palabras exactas de alguien _____

2. Elegir En cada oración, elige la forma apropiada del verbo. `31.B`

1. Andrés dijo: "Quiero que me ayudes con la tarea".
Andrés dijo que quería que lo _____ (ayudar/ayudara) con la tarea.

2. Los niños dijeron: "Iremos al parque por la tarde".
Los niños dijeron que _____ (irían/iríamos) al parque por la tarde.

3. José y Roberto me dijeron: "Haz la presentación por nosotros".
José y Roberto me dijeron que _____ (hiciste/hiciera) la presentación por ellos.

4. Sandra nos dijo: "He olvidado las llaves dentro de mi casa".
Sandra nos dijo que se _____ (hubiera olvidado/había olvidado) las llaves dentro de su casa.

5. La directora dijo: "No me parece que ustedes se hayan comportado bien".
La directora dijo que no le parecía que ustedes se _____ (habían/hubieran) comportado bien".

6. Mi madre dijo: "Voy a la peluquería y vuelvo en una hora".
Mi madre dijo que _____ (iría/iba) a la peluquería y que _____ (volvería/volvía) en una hora.

7. Mi hermano me dijo: "Son las seis. Te llamo en una hora".
Mi hermano me dijo que _____ (serían/eran) las seis y que me _____ (llamaría/llamaba) en una hora.

8. El doctor me dijo: "Toma el jarabe".
El doctor me dijo que _____ (tomara/hubiese tomado) el jarabe.

3. Emparejar Une las oraciones en discurso directo con las oraciones en discurso indirecto. Hay tres oraciones en discurso indirecto que no debes usar. `31.B`

_____ 1. Él dijo: "Me duelen los pies".

_____ 2. Ella dijo: "Quisiera una sopa".

_____ 3. Él dijo: "Mañana nos despertaremos temprano".

_____ 4. Ella dijo: "Anoche escuché ruidos raros".

_____ 5. Él dijo: "Aún no se ha secado mi ropa".

_____ 6. Ella dijo: "Ahora quiero una sopa".

a. Él dijo que había escuchado ruidos raros la noche anterior.

b. Él dijo que le dolían los pies.

c. Él dijo que aún no se había secado su ropa.

d. Ella dijo que había escuchado ruidos raros la noche anterior.

e. Él dijo que mañana se despertarían temprano.

f. Ella dijo que quería una sopa.

g. Ella dijo que en ese momento quería una sopa.

h. Él dijo que al día siguiente se despertarían temprano.

i. Él dijo que aún no se había secado mi ropa.

4. Completar   Escribe la forma correcta del verbo en discurso indirecto. **31.B**

> **Modelo**
>
> Nosotros dijimos: "Nos encantará cenar con ustedes".
> Nosotros dijimos que nos _____ *encantaría* _____ cenar con ustedes.

1. Él dijo: "Nunca he reprobado un examen".
   Él dijo que nunca _____ un examen.

2. Tú me dijiste: "Me encantaría que me fueras a buscar al aeropuerto".
   Tú me dijiste que te _____ que te fuera a buscar al aeropuerto.

3. El vecino nos dijo: "No hagan más ruido: no puedo dormir".
   El vecino nos dijo que no _____ más ruido porque no
   _____ dormir.

4. Laura nos dijo: "Me caí de la bicicleta".
   Laura nos dijo que _____ de la bicicleta.

5. Los clientes de la mesa dos dijeron: "Nos gustaban más los platos del cocinero anterior".
   Los clientes de la mesa dos dijeron que les _____ más los platos
   que hacía el cocinero anterior.

6. Él dijo: "En una hora habré terminado de trabajar y estaré de vacaciones".
   Él dijo que en una hora _____ de trabajar y
   _____ de vacaciones.

7. Juan me explicó: "No te puedo contar la verdad porque me voy a meter en problemas".
   Juan me explicó que no me _____ contar la verdad porque
   se _____ a meter en problemas.

5. Nota   Lee el mensaje electrónico que escribió Daniela y completa la nota de Emilio a Juan reescribiendo las oraciones en discurso indirecto. **31.B**

> ¡Hola!
> ¡Estoy tan feliz porque nos vemos mañana! Llegaré a las nueve y media a la Estación del Sur.
> Te esperaré en las escaleras del edificio principal. ¡No te olvides de pasar a buscarme!
> No he tenido vacaciones con amigos desde 2012. Quiero que disfrutemos lo máximo posible.
> Llama a Juan y avísale sobre mi llegada.
> Daniela

> Juan:
> Hoy recibí un *correo electrónico* de Daniela.
>
> 1. Dijo que _____ *estaba muy feliz porque nos veríamos al día siguiente* _____.
>
> 2. Me confirmó que _____
>
> 3. Dijo que _____ y que _____
>   _____.
>
> 4. Luego explicó que _____ y que _____
>   lo máximo posible.
>
> 5. Por último, me pidió que _____ y que _____
>   _____.
>
> Saludos,
> Emilio

6. Escribir Escribe las oraciones en discurso indirecto. `31.B`

> **Modelo**
>
> (viernes) Mi mejor amiga dijo: "No iré a la fiesta de mañana".
> (Hoy es sábado.) *Mi mejor amiga dijo que no iría a la fiesta de hoy.*

1. (martes) Tu hermana dijo: "Anoche dormí doce horas".
   (Hoy es viernes.) _____

2. (viernes) La profesora nos dijo: "Estudien para el examen de la semana que viene".
   (Hoy es sábado.) _____

3. (lunes) El presidente dijo: "Me entrevistaré con el presidente ecuatoriano pasado mañana".
   (Hoy es miércoles.) _____

4. (domingo) Juana me dijo: "Nos veremos el martes por la noche".
   (Hoy es lunes.) _____

5. (viernes) Mi tutor me dijo: "Mañana no tendremos clases".
   (Hoy es domingo.) _____

7. Oraciones Decide si en estas oraciones se da información (I) o una orden (O). Luego, escribe las oraciones en discurso indirecto. Sigue el modelo. `31.B`

> **Modelo**
>
> "Le agradezco su visita". _I_   *Me dijo que me agradecía mi visita.*

1. "Pase y mire sin compromiso". _____ _____

2. "Por favor, no se siente allí". _____ _____

3. "Los pantalones están en oferta". _____ _____

4. "Llévese dos pantalones por 20 dólares". _____ _____

5. "La tienda cierra a las nueve". _____ _____

6. "Apúrese a comprar". _____ _____

8. Reordenar Reordena los elementos para formular preguntas indirectas. `31.B`

> **Modelo**
>
> si / Me pregunto / es / esta película / divertida / .
> *Me pregunto si esta película es divertida.*

1. ¿ / está / podría / dónde / el correo más cercano / decirme / Señora, / ?
   _____

2. mi papá / me pasa a buscar / si / a las cinco / No recuerdo / o / a las seis / .
   _____

3. ¿ / cumple /cuándo / años / Sabes / Cristina / ?
   _____

4. si / no / tenía calor / Le / con esa chaqueta / pregunté / .
   _____

5. era / el nombre / supe / cuál / Nunca / de esa chica tan bonita / .
   _____

6. ¿ / hora / decirme / a qué / Puedes / comeremos / ?
   _____

9. Síntesis Transformar Completa las oraciones para transformar el discurso directo en indirecto. `31.A–31.B`

> **Modelo**
>
> Esta noche habré lavado la ropa.
> Manuel dijo *que esta noche habría lavado la ropa.*

1. ¿Cuánto tiempo se tarda para llegar en tren a Barcelona?
   Me gustaría saber _____.

2. ¡He perdido mi cartera!
   Marina me dijo _____.

3. ¡No me molestes más!
   Cecilia me pidió _____.

4. Señor, ¿cómo será el tiempo mañana?
   Le pregunté al señor _____.

5. Señora, ¿tiene cambio de veinte dólares?
   Señora, quisiera saber _____.

6. Ayer trabajé hasta las diez de la noche.
   Mi hermana me contó _____.

7. Nunca había tenido un accidente de tránsito.
   Mi tío me dijo _____.

8. Nos gustaría que nos mostraras las fotos de tu viaje.
   Mis padres me pidieron _____.

9. Si hubiéramos tenido tiempo, te habríamos visitado.
   Mis primos me dijeron _____.

10. Compraría una computadora nueva si tuviera dinero ahorrado.
    Le expliqué a mi jefe _____.

10. Síntesis Escribir Escribe por lo menos cinco comentarios u órdenes de personas con quienes compartiste tiempo ayer, utilizando el discurso indirecto. `31.A–31.B`

> **Modelo**
>
> *Ayer mi mamá me dijo que no olvidara empacar todos los libros…*

_____
_____
_____
_____
_____
_____
_____
_____
_____

Practice more at **vhlcentral.com.**

Verb conjugation tables

Pages **B5–B20** contain verb conjugation patterns. Patterns 1–3 include the simple tenses of three model **-ar**, **-er**, and **-ir** regular verbs. Patterns 4 to 80 include spell-changing, stem-changing, and irregular verbs. Charts are also provided for the formation of compound tenses (**p. B5**) and progressive tenses (**p. B6**). For the formation of reflexive verbs, see **27.A.** To see a list of irregular participles, see **19.A.2** and **25.D.2.**

Spell-changing, stem-changing, and irregular verbs

In patterns 4 to 80, the superscript numbers in parentheses identify the type of irregularity:

[1]Stem-changing verbs (**pensar** → **pienso**)

[2]Verbs with spelling changes (**recoger** → **recojo**)

[3]Verbs with accent changes or verbs that require replacing **u** with **ü** (**reunir** → **reúno**; **averiguar** → **averigüe**)

[4]Verbs with unique irregularities (sometimes in addition to stem or spelling changes) (**poner** → **puse**)

Note: Any form that deviates from the regular verb patterns is indicated in **bold** font.

Voseo

Vos conjugations are included in the present indicative and in the imperative. These are the **vos** forms included in the verb charts in the RAE's *Nueva gramática*. For more information about the **voseo**, see **13.B.2, 22.B.b, 24.C,** and **24.D.**

tú/vos   hablas/hablás   habla/hablá

Terminology

The Spanish names of the verb tenses used in this handbook correspond to the names used in the *Nueva gramática* published by the **Real Academia Española**.

English terminology used in this handbook	Spanish terminology used in this handbook	Traditional Spanish terminology	Terminology used by Andrés Bello
Simple present	Presente	Presente	Presente
Imperfect	Pretérito imperfecto	Pretérito imperfecto	Copretérito
Preterite	Pretérito perfecto simple	Pretérito indefinido	Pretérito
Present perfect	Pretérito perfecto compuesto	Pretérito perfecto	Antepresente
Past perfect	Pretérito pluscuamperfecto	Pretérito pluscuamperfecto	Antecopretérito
Simple future	Futuro (simple)	Futuro (simple)	Futuro
Future perfect	Futuro compuesto	Futuro compuesto/perfecto	Antefuturo
Conditional	Condicional (simple)	Condicional simple/presente Potencial simple	Pospretérito
Conditional perfect	Condicional compuesto	Condicional compuesto/perfecto Potencial compuesto/perfecto	Antepospretérito

Tenses not included in the charts

The following tenses are rarely used in contemporary Spanish. They have been excluded from the verb tables in this handbook.

Pretérito anterior (indicativo): See **19.F.**	Cuando **hubo terminado** la fiesta, fuimos a casa.
Futuro simple (subjuntivo): See **22.F.**	Adonde **fueres**, haz lo que vieres.
Futuro compuesto (subjuntivo): See **22.G.**	"Será proclamado Alcalde el concejal que **hubiere obtenido** más votos..."

Negative imperative

The verb forms for the negative imperative are not included in the verb charts. They are the same as the forms of the present subjunctive.

Verb chapters

The following chapters cover verb tense formation and usage.

Indicative			Subjunctive		
	Present	Chapter 17		All tenses – Formation	Chapter 22
	Preterite and Imperfect	Chapter 18			
	Present perfect and Past perfect	Chapter 19		All tenses – Usage	Chapter 23
	Future and Future perfect	Chapter 20			
	Conditional and Conditional perfect	Chapter 21		**Imperative**	Chapter 24

Verbs with stem changes, verbs with spelling changes, and irregular verbs

The list below includes common verbs with stem changes, verbs with spelling changes, and irregular verbs, as well as the verbs used as models/patterns in the charts on **pp. B5–B20**. The number in brackets indicates where in the verb tables you can find the conjugated form of the model verb.

abastecer (*conocer* [15])
aborrecer (*conocer* [15])
abstenerse (*tener* [69])
abstraer (*traer* [73])
acaecer (*conocer* [15])
acentuar (*graduar* [37])
acoger (*proteger* [54])
acontecer (*conocer* [15])
acordar (*contar* [16])
acostar (*contar* [16])
acrecentar (*pensar* [49])
actuar (*graduar* [37])
adherir (*sentir* [65])
adolecer (*conocer* [15])
adormecer (*conocer* [15])
adquirir [4]
aducir (*conducir* [14])
advertir (*sentir* [65])
afligir (*exigir* [35])
agradecer (*conocer* [15])
ahumar (*rehusar* [57])
airar (*aislar* [5])
aislar [5]
alentar (*pensar* [49])
almorzar [6]
amanecer (*conocer* [15])
amoblar (*contar* [16])
amortiguar (*averiguar* [10])
ampliar (*enviar* [29])
andar [7]
anegar (*negar* [45])
anochecer (*conocer* [15])
apaciguar (*averiguar* [10])

aparecer (*conocer* [15])
apetecer (*conocer* [15])
apretar (*pensar* [49])
aprobar (*contar* [16])
arrepentirse (*sentir* [65])
ascender (*entender* [28])
asentar (*pensar* [49])
asentir (*sentir* [65])
asir [8]
atañer (*tañer* [68])
atardecer (*conocer* [15])
atender (*entender* [28])
atenerse (*tener* [69])
atestiguar (*averiguar* [10])
atraer (*traer* [73])
atravesar (*pensar* [49])
atribuir (*destruir* [23])
aunar (*rehusar* [57])
avergonzar [9]
averiguar [10]
balbucir (*lucir* [43])
bendecir [11]
buscar (*tocar* [71])
caber [12]
caer [13]
calentar (*pensar* [49])
cegar (*negar* [45])
ceñir (*teñir* [70])
cerrar (*pensar* [49])
cimentar (*pensar* [49])
cocer (*torcer* [72])
coercer (*vencer* [75])
coger (*proteger* [54])

cohibir (*prohibir* [53])
colgar (*rogar* [61])
comenzar (*empezar* [27])
comer [2]
compadecer (*conocer* [15])
comparecer (*conocer* [15])
competir (*pedir* [48])
componer (*poner* [51])
comprobar (*contar* [16])
concebir (*pedir* [48])
concernir (*discernir* [24])
concluir (*destruir* [23])
concordar (*contar* [16])
conducir [14]
confesar (*pensar* [49])
confiar (*enviar* [29])
conmover (*mover* [44])
conocer [15]
conseguir (*seguir* [64])
consentir (*sentir* [65])
consolar (*contar* [16])
constituir (*destruir* [23])
construir (*destruir* [23])
contar [16]
contener (*tener* [69])
continuar (*graduar* [37])
contradecir (*predecir* [52])
contraer (*traer* [73])
contrariar (*enviar* [29])
convalecer (*conocer* [15])
convencer (*vencer* [75])
converger (*proteger* [54])
convertir (*sentir* [65])

corregir (*elegir* [26])
corroer (*roer* [60])
costar (*contar* [16])
creer [17]
criar (*enviar* [29])
cruzar [18]
dar [19]
decaer (*caer* [13])
decir [20]
deducir (*conducir* [14])
defender (*entender* [28])
degollar [21]
delinquir [22]
demoler (*mover* [44])
demostrar (*contar* [16])
denegar (*negar* [45])
derretir (*pedir* [48])
desafiar (*enviar* [29])
desaguar (*averiguar* [10])
desalentar (*pensar* [49])
desandar (*andar* [7])
desaparecer (*conocer* [15])
desasir (*asir* [8])
descafeinar (*aislar* [5])
descolgar (*rogar* [61])
desconsolar (*contar* [16])
desdecir (*predecir* [52])
desentenderse (*entender* [28])
desfallecer (*conocer* [15])
desfavorecer (*conocer* [15])
deshacer (*hacer* [39])
deslucir (*lucir* [43])
desmerecer (*conocer* [15])
desoír (*oír* [46])
despedir (*pedir* [48])
despertar (*pensar* [49])
desplegar (*negar* [45])
desteñir (*teñir* [70])
destruir [23]
desvestir (*pedir* [48])
detener (*tener* [69])
diferir (*sentir* [65])
digerir (*sentir* [65])
diluir (*destruir* [23])
dirigir (*exigir* [35])
discernir [24]
disentir (*sentir* [65])
disminuir (*destruir* [23])
distender (*entender* [28])
distinguir (*extinguir* [36])
distraer (*traer* [73])
distribuir (*destruir* [23])
divertir (*sentir* [65])
doler (*mover* [44])
dormir [25]
efectuar (*graduar* [37])

ejercer (*vencer* [75])
elegir [26]
embellecer (*conocer* [15])
embestir (*pedir* [48])
emerger (*proteger* [54])
empalidecer (*conocer* [15])
emparentar (*pensar* [49])
empequeñecer (*conocer* [15])
empezar [27]
empobrecer (*conocer* [15])
encarecer (*conocer* [15])
enceguecer (*conocer* [15])
encender (*entender* [28])
encerrar (*pensar* [49])
encontrar (*contar* [16])
endurecer (*conocer* [15])
enfriar (*enviar* [29])
enfurecer (*conocer* [15])
engullir (*zambullir* [80])
enloquecer (*conocer* [15])
enmendar (*pensar* [49])
enmudecer (*conocer* [15])
enriquecer (*conocer* [15])
ensordecer (*conocer* [15])
entender [28]
enterrar (*pensar* [49])
entorpecer (*conocer* [15])
entrelucir (*lucir* [43])
entreoír (*oír* [46])
entretener (*tener* [69])
entristecer (*conocer* [15])
envejecer (*conocer* [15])
enviar [29]
equivaler (*valer* [74])
erguir [30]
errar [31]
escarmentar (*pensar* [49])
escoger (*proteger* [54])
esforzar (*almorzar* [6])
esparcir [32]
espiar (*enviar* [29])
establecer (*conocer* [15])
estar [33]
estremecer (*conocer* [15])
estreñir (*teñir* [70])
europeizar [34]
evaluar (*graduar* [37])
exceptuar (*graduar* [37])
excluir (*destruir* [23])
exigir [35]
expedir (*pedir* [48])
extender (*entender* [28])
extinguir [36]
extraer (*traer* [73])
fallecer (*conocer* [15])
favorecer (*conocer* [15])

fingir (*exigir* [35])
florecer (*conocer* [15])
fluir (*destruir* [23])
fortalecer (*conocer* [15])
forzar (*almorzar* [6])
fotografiar (*enviar* [29])
fraguar (*averiguar* [10])
fregar (*negar* [45])
freír (*reír* [58])
gobernar (*pensar* [49])
graduar [37]
gruñir (*zambullir* [80])
guiar (*enviar* [29])
haber [38]
habituar (*graduar* [37])
hablar [1]
hacer [39]
helar (*pensar* [49])
hendir (*discernir* [24])
herir (*sentir* [65])
herrar (*pensar* [49])
hervir (*sentir* [65])
homogeneizar (*europeizar* [34])
huir (*destruir* [23])
humedecer (*conocer* [15])
impedir (*pedir* [48])
incluir (*destruir* [23])
inducir (*conducir* [14])
infligir (*exigir* [35])
influir (*destruir* [23])
ingerir (*sentir* [65])
inquirir (*adquirir* [4])
insinuar (*graduar* [37])
instituir (*destruir* [23])
instruir (*destruir* [23])
interferir (*sentir* [65])
introducir (*conducir* [14])
invernar (*pensar* [49])
invertir (*sentir* [65])
investir (*pedir* [48])
ir [40]
judaizar (*europeizar* [34])
jugar [41]
leer (*creer* [17])
liar (*enviar* [29])
llegar [42]
llover (*mover* [44])
lucir [43]
malcriar (*enviar* [29])
maldecir (*bendecir* [11])
malentender (*entender* [28])
malherir (*sentir* [65])
maltraer (*traer* [73])
manifestar (*pensar* [49])
mantener (*tener* [69])
maullar (*rehusar* [57])

mecer (*vencer* [75])
medir (*pedir* [48])
mentir (*sentir* [65])
merecer (*conocer* [15])
merendar (*pensar* [49])
moler (*mover* [44])
morder (*mover* [44])
morir (p.p. muerto) (*dormir* [25])
mostrar (*contar* [16])
mover [44]
mugir (*exigir* [35])
mullir (*zambullir* [80])
nacer (*conocer* [15])
negar [45]
nevar (*pensar* [49])
obedecer (*conocer* [15])
obstruir (*destruir* [23])
obtener (*tener* [69])
ofrecer (*conocer* [15])
oír [46]
oler [47]
oscurecer (*conocer* [15])
padecer (*conocer* [15])
palidecer (*conocer* [15])
parecer (*conocer* [15])
pedir [48]
pensar [49]
perder (*entender* [28])
permanecer (*conocer* [15])
perpetuar (*graduar* [37])
perseguir (*seguir* [64])
plegar (*negar* [45])
poblar (*contar* [16])
poder [50]
poner [51]
poseer (*creer* [17])
predecir [52]
preferir (*sentir* [65])
presentir (*sentir* [65])
prevaler (*valer* [74])
prevenir (*venir* [76])
probar (*contar* [16])
producir (*conducir* [14])
prohibir [53]
promover (*mover* [44])
proponer (*poner* [51])
proseguir (*seguir* [64])
proteger [54]
proveer (*creer* [17])
pudrir/podrir [55]
quebrar (*pensar* [49])
querer [56]
recaer (*caer* [13])
recoger (*proteger* [54])
recomendar (*pensar* [49])
recomenzar (*empezar* [27])

reconducir (*conducir* [14])
reconocer (*conocer* [15])
recordar (*contar* [16])
recostar (*contar* [16])
reducir (*conducir* [14])
reforzar (*almorzar* [6])
refregar (*negar* [45])
regir (*elegir* [26])
rehusar [57]
reír [58]
releer (*creer* [17])
relucir (*lucir* [43])
remendar (*pensar* [49])
remover (*mover* [44])
rendir (*pedir* [48])
renegar (*negar* [45])
reñir (*teñir* [70])
renovar (*contar* [16])
repetir (*pedir* [48])
replegar (*negar* [45])
reproducir (*conducir* [14])
requerir (*sentir* [65])
resarcir (*esparcir* [32])
resolver (p.p. resuelto) (*mover* [44])
restringir (*exigir* [35])
resurgir (*exigir* [35])
retorcer (*torcer* [72])
retrotraer (*traer* [73])
reunir [59]
reventar (*pensar* [49])
revertir (*sentir* [65])
revolcar (*volcar* [78])
robustecer (*conocer* [15])
rociar (*enviar* [29])
rodar (*contar* [16])
roer [60]
rogar [61]
saber [62]
sacar (*tocar* [71])
salir [63]
salpimentar (*pensar* [49])
satisfacer (*hacer* [39])
seducir (*conducir* [14])
seguir [64]
sembrar (*pensar* [49])
sentar (*pensar* [49])
sentir [65]
ser [66]
servir (*pedir* [48])
situar (*graduar* [37])
sobrecoger (*proteger* [54])
sobresalir (*salir* [63])
sobreseer (*creer* [17])
sofreír (*reír* [58])
soler [67]
soltar (*contar* [16])

sonar (*contar* [16])
sonreír (*reír* [58])
soñar (*contar* [16])
sosegar (*negar* [45])
sostener (*tener* [69])
subyacer (*yacer* [79])
sugerir (*sentir* [65])
sumergir (*exigir* [35])
suponer (*poner* [51])
surgir (*exigir* [35])
sustituir (*destruir* [23])
sustraer (*traer* [73])
tañer [68]
tatuar (*graduar* [37])
temblar (*pensar* [49])
tener [69]
tentar (*pensar* [49])
teñir [70]
tocar [71]
torcer [72]
tostar (*contar* [16])
traducir (*conducir* [14])
traer [73]
transferir (*sentir* [65])
trascender (*entender* [28])
traslucirse (*lucir* [43])
trastocar (*volcar* [78])
trocar (*volcar* [78])
tropezar (*empezar* [27])
uncir (*esparcir* [32])
urgir (*exigir* [35])
valer [74]
valuar (*graduar* [37])
variar (*enviar* [29])
vencer [75]
venir [76]
ver [77]
verter (*entender* [28])
vestir (*pedir* [48])
vivir [3]
volar (*contar* [16])
volcar [78]
volver (p.p. vuelto) (*mover* [44])
yacer [79]
zambullir [80]
zurcir (*esparcir* [32])

Verb conjugation tables

Regular verbs: simple tenses

Infinitivo / Gerundio / Participio	Pronombres personales	INDICATIVO					SUBJUNTIVO		IMPERATIVO
		Presente	Pretérito imperfecto	Pretérito perfecto simple	Futuro simple	Condicional simple	Presente	Pretérito imperfecto	
1 hablar	yo	hablo	hablaba	hablé	hablaré	hablaría	hable	hablara o hablase	
hablando	tú/vos	hablas/hablás	hablabas	hablaste	hablarás	hablarías	hables	hablaras o hablases	habla/hablá
hablado	Ud., él, ella	habla	hablaba	habló	hablará	hablaría	hable	hablara o hablase	hable
	nosotros/as	hablamos	hablábamos	hablamos	hablaremos	hablaríamos	hablemos	habláramos o hablásemos	hablemos
	vosotros/as	habláis	hablabais	hablasteis	hablaréis	hablaríais	habléis	hablarais o hablaseis	hablad
	Uds., ellos/as	hablan	hablaban	hablaron	hablarán	hablarían	hablen	hablaran o hablasen	hablen
2 comer	yo	como	comía	comí	comeré	comería	coma	comiera o comiese	
comiendo	tú/vos	comes/comés	comías	comiste	comerás	comerías	comas	comieras o comieses	come/comé
comido	Ud., él, ella	come	comía	comió	comerá	comería	coma	comiera o comiese	coma
	nosotros/as	comemos	comíamos	comimos	comeremos	comeríamos	comamos	comiéramos o comiésemos	comamos
	vosotros/as	coméis	comíais	comisteis	comeréis	comeríais	comáis	comierais o comieseis	comed
	Uds., ellos/as	comen	comían	comieron	comerán	comerían	coman	comieran o comiesen	coman
3 vivir	yo	vivo	vivía	viví	viviré	viviría	viva	viviera o viviese	
viviendo	tú/vos	vives/vivís	vivías	viviste	vivirás	vivirías	vivas	vivieras o vivieses	vive/viví
vivido	Ud., él, ella	vive	vivía	vivió	vivirá	viviría	viva	viviera o viviese	viva
	nosotros/as	vivimos	vivíamos	vivimos	viviremos	viviríamos	vivamos	viviéramos o viviésemos	vivamos
	vosotros/as	vivís	vivíais	vivisteis	viviréis	viviríais	viváis	vivierais o vivieseis	vivid
	Uds., ellos/as	viven	vivían	vivieron	vivirán	vivirían	vivan	vivieran o viviesen	vivan

Compound tenses

INDICATIVO								SUBJUNTIVO			
Pretérito perfecto compuesto		Pretérito pluscuamperfecto		Futuro compuesto		Condicional compuesto		Pretérito perfecto compuesto		Pretérito pluscuamperfecto	
he	hablado	había	hablado	habré	hablado	habría	hablado	haya	hablado	hubiera o hubiese	hablado
has	comido	habías	comido	habrás	comido	habrías	comido	hayas	comido	hubieras o hubieses	comido
ha	vivido	había	vivido	habrá	vivido	habría	vivido	haya	vivido	hubiera o hubiese	vivido
hemos		habíamos		habremos		habríamos		hayamos		hubiéramos o hubiésemos	
habéis		habíais		habréis		habríais		hayáis		hubierais o hubieseis	
han		habían		habrán		habrían		hayan		hubieran o hubiesen	

Progressive tenses

INDICATIVO

Presente		Pretérito imperfecto		Pretérito perfecto simple		Futuro simple		Condicional simple	
estoy		estaba		estuve		estaré		estaría	
estás		estabas		estuviste		estarás		estarías	
está	hablando	estaba	hablando	estuvo	hablando	estará	hablando	estaría	hablando
estamos	comiendo	estábamos	comiendo	estuvimos	comiendo	estaremos	comiendo	estaríamos	comiendo
estáis	viviendo	estabais	viviendo	estuvisteis	viviendo	estaréis	viviendo	estaríais	viviendo
están		estaban		estuvieron		estarán		estarían	

SUBJUNTIVO

Pretérito perfecto		Pretérito imperfecto	
esté		estuviera o estuviese	
estés		estuvieras o estuvieses	
esté	hablando	estuviera o estuviese	hablando
estemos	comiendo	estuviéramos o estuviésemos	comiendo
estéis	viviendo	estuvierais o estuvieseis	viviendo
estén		estuvieran o estuviesen	

Note: Perfect progressive tenses are formed using a conjugated form of **haber** + **estado** + *gerundio*, as in **he estado comiendo, hubiera estado corriendo**, etc.

Verbs with stem changes, verbs with spelling changes, and irregular verbs

Infinitivo	Pronombres personales	INDICATIVO					SUBJUNTIVO		IMPERATIVO
Gerundio Participio		Presente	Pretérito imperfecto	Pretérito perfecto simple	Futuro simple	Condicional simple	Presente	Pretérito imperfecto	
4 **adquirir** [1] (i:ie)	yo	**adquiero**	adquiría	adquirí	adquiriré	adquiriría	**adquiera**	adquiriera o adquiriese	
	tú/vos	**adquieres/** adquirís	adquirías	adquiriste	adquirirás	adquirirías	**adquieras**	adquirieras o adquirieses	**adquiere/** adquirí
adquiriendo	Ud., él, ella	**adquiere**	adquiría	adquirió	adquirirá	adquiriría	**adquiera**	adquiriera o adquiriese	**adquiera**
adquirido	nosotros/as	adquirimos	adquiríamos	adquirimos	adquiriremos	adquiriríamos	adquiramos	adquiriéramos o adquiriésemos	adquiramos
	vosotros/as	adquirís	adquiríais	adquiristeis	adquiriréis	adquiriríais	adquiráis	adquirierais o adquirieseis	adquirid
	Uds., ellos/as	**adquieren**	adquirían	adquirieron	adquirirán	adquirirían	**adquieran**	adquirieran o adquiriesen	**adquieran**

Infinitivo / Gerundio / Participio	Pronombres personales	INDICATIVO Presente	Pretérito imperfecto	Pretérito perfecto simple	Futuro simple	Condicional simple	SUBJUNTIVO Presente	Pretérito imperfecto	IMPERATIVO
5 aislar [(3)] (i:í)	yo	**aíslo**	aislaba	aislé	aislaré	aislaría	**aísle**	aislara o aislase	
aislando	tú/vos	**aíslas/aislás**	aislabas	aislaste	aislarás	aislarías	**aísles**	aislaras o aislases	**aísla/aislá**
aislado	Ud., él, ella	**aísla**	aislaba	aisló	aislará	aislaría	**aísle**	aislara o aislase	**aísle**
	nosotros/as	aislamos	aislábamos	aislamos	aislaremos	aislaríamos	aislemos	aisláramos o aislásemos	aislemos
	vosotros/as	aisláis	aislabais	aislasteis	aislaréis	aislaríais	aisléis	aislarais o aislaseis	aislad
	Uds., ellos/as	**aíslan**	aislaban	aislaron	aislarán	aislarían	**aíslen**	aislaran o aislasen	**aíslen**
6 almorzar [(1, 2)] (o:ue) (z:c)	yo	**almuerzo**	almorzaba	**almorcé**	almorzaré	almorzaría	**almuerce**	almorzara o almorzase	
	tú/vos	**almuerzas/almorzás**	almorzabas	almorzaste	almorzarás	almorzarías	**almuerces**	almorzaras o almorzases	**almuerza/almorzá**
almorzando	Ud., él, ella	**almuerza**	almorzaba	almorzó	almorzará	almorzaría	**almuerce**	almorzara o almorzase	**almuerce**
almorzado	nosotros/as	almorzamos	almorzábamos	almorzamos	almorzaremos	almorzaríamos	**almorcemos**	almorzáramos o almorzásemos	**almorcemos**
	vosotros/as	almorzáis	almorzabais	almorzasteis	almorzaréis	almorzaríais	**almorcéis**	almorzarais o almorzaseis	almorzad
	Uds., ellos/as	**almuerzan**	almorzaban	almorzaron	almorzarán	almorzarían	**almuercen**	almorzaran o almorzasen	**almuercen**
7 andar [(4)]	yo	ando	andaba	**anduve**	andaré	andaría	ande	**anduviera o anduviese**	
	tú/vos	andas/andás	andabas	**anduviste**	andarás	andarías	andes	**anduvieras o anduvieses**	anda/andá
andando	Ud., él, ella	anda	andaba	**anduvo**	andará	andaría	ande	**anduviera o anduviese**	ande
andado	nosotros/as	andamos	andábamos	**anduvimos**	andaremos	andaríamos	andemos	**anduviéramos o anduviésemos**	andemos
	vosotros/as	andáis	andabais	**anduvisteis**	andaréis	andaríais	andéis	**anduvierais o anduvieseis**	andad
	Uds., ellos/as	andan	andaban	**anduvieron**	andarán	andarían	anden	**anduvieran o anduviesen**	anden
8 asir [(4)]	yo	**asgo**	asía	así	asiré	asiría	**asga**	asiera o asiese	
	tú/vos	ases/asís	asías	asiste	asirás	asirías	**asgas**	asieras o asieses	ase/así
asiendo	Ud., él, ella	ase	asía	asió	asirá	asiría	**asga**	asiera o asiese	**asga**
asido	nosotros/as	asimos	asíamos	asimos	asiremos	asiríamos	**asgamos**	asiéramos o asiésemos	**asgamos**
	vosotros/as	asís	asíais	asisteis	asiréis	asiríais	**asgáis**	asierais o asieseis	asid
	Uds., ellos/as	asen	asían	asieron	asirán	asirían	**asgan**	asieran o asiesen	**asgan**
9 avergonzar [(1,2)] (o:üe) (z:c)	yo	**avergüenzo**	avergonzaba	**avergoncé**	avergonzaré	avergonzaría	**avergüence**	avergonzara o avergonzase	
	tú/vos	**avergüenzas/avergonzás**	avergonzabas	avergonzaste	avergonzarás	avergonzarías	**avergüences**	avergonzaras o avergonzases	**avergüenza/avergonzá**
avergonzando	Ud., él, ella	**avergüenza**	avergonzaba	avergonzó	avergonzará	avergonzaría	**avergüence**	avergonzara o avergonzase	**avergüence**
avergonzado	nosotros/as	avergonzamos	avergonzábamos	avergonzamos	avergonzaremos	avergonzaríamos	**avergoncemos**	avergonzáramos o avergonzásemos	**avergoncemos**
	vosotros/as	avergonzáis	avergonzabais	avergonzasteis	avergonzaréis	avergonzaríais	**avergoncéis**	avergonzarais o avergonzaseis	avergonzad
	Uds., ellos/as	**avergüenzan**	avergonzaban	avergonzaron	avergonzarán	avergonzarían	**avergüencen**	avergonzaran o avergonzasen	**avergüencen**

Verb conjugation tables

Infinitivo / Gerundio / Participio	Pronombres personales	INDICATIVO					SUBJUNTIVO		IMPERATIVO
		Presente	Pretérito imperfecto	Pretérito perfecto simple	Futuro simple	Condicional simple	Presente	Pretérito imperfecto	
10 averiguar (3) (u:ü) averiguando averiguado	yo	averiguo	averiguaba	**averigüé**	averiguaré	averiguaría	**averigüe**	averiguara o averiguase	
	tú/vos	averiguas/averiguás	averiguabas	averiguaste	averiguarás	averiguarías	**averigües**	averiguaras o averiguases	averigua/averiguá
	Ud., él, ella	averigua	averiguaba	averiguó	averiguará	averiguaría	**averigüe**	averiguara o averiguase	**averigüe**
	nosotros/as	averiguamos	averiguábamos	averiguamos	averiguaremos	averiguaríamos	**averigüemos**	averiguáramos o averiguásemos	**averigüemos**
	vosotros/as	averiguáis	averiguabais	averiguasteis	averiguaréis	averiguaríais	**averigüéis**	averiguarais o averiguaseis	averiguad
	Uds., ellos/as	averiguan	averiguaban	averiguaron	averiguarán	averiguarían	**averigüen**	averiguaran o averiguasen	**averigüen**
11 bendecir (4) **bendiciendo** bendecido o **bendito**	yo	**bendigo**	bendecía	**bendije**	bendeciré	bendeciría	**bendiga**	**bendijera** o **bendijese**	
	tú/vos	**bendices**/bendecís	bendecías	**bendijiste**	bendecirás	bendecirías	**bendigas**	**bendijeras** o **bendijeses**	**bendice**/bendecí
	Ud., él, ella	**bendice**	bendecía	**bendijo**	bendecirá	bendeciría	**bendiga**	**bendijera** o **bendijese**	**bendiga**
	nosotros/as	bendecimos	bendecíamos	**bendijimos**	bendeciremos	bendeciríamos	**bendigamos**	**bendijéramos** o **bendijésemos**	**bendigamos**
	vosotros/as	bendecís	bendecíais	**bendijisteis**	bendeciréis	bendeciríais	**bendigáis**	**bendijerais** o **bendijeseis**	bendecid
	Uds., ellos/as	**bendicen**	bendecían	**bendijeron**	bendecirán	bendecirían	**bendigan**	**bendijeran** o **bendijesen**	**bendigan**
12 caber (4) cabiendo cabido	yo	**quepo**	cabía	**cupe**	**cabré**	**cabría**	**quepa**	cupiera o cupiese	
	tú/vos	cabes/cabés	cabías	cupiste	**cabrás**	**cabrías**	**quepas**	cupieras o cupieses	cabe/cabé
	Ud., él, ella	cabe	cabía	cupo	**cabrá**	**cabría**	**quepa**	cupiera o cupiese	**quepa**
	nosotros/as	cabemos	cabíamos	**cupimos**	**cabremos**	**cabríamos**	**quepamos**	cupiéramos o cupiésemos	**quepamos**
	vosotros/as	cabéis	cabíais	cupisteis	**cabréis**	**cabríais**	**quepáis**	cupierais o cupieseis	cabed
	Uds., ellos/as	caben	cabían	cupieron	**cabrán**	**cabrían**	**quepan**	cupieran o cupiesen	**quepan**
13 caer (4) (y) cayendo caído	yo	**caigo**	caía	caí	caeré	caería	**caiga**	**cayera** o **cayese**	
	tú/vos	caes/caés	caías	**caíste**	caerás	caerías	**caigas**	**cayeras** o **cayeses**	cae/caé
	Ud., él, ella	cae	caía	**cayó**	caerá	caería	**caiga**	**cayera** o **cayese**	**caiga**
	nosotros/as	caemos	caíamos	**caímos**	caeremos	caeríamos	**caigamos**	**cayéramos** o **cayésemos**	**caigamos**
	vosotros/as	caéis	caíais	**caísteis**	caeréis	caeríais	**caigáis**	**cayerais** o **cayeseis**	caed
	Uds., ellos/as	caen	caían	**cayeron**	caerán	caerían	**caigan**	**cayeran** o **cayesen**	**caigan**
14 conducir (2) (c:zc) conduciendo conducido	yo	**conduzco**	conducía	**conduje**	conduciré	conduciría	**conduzca**	**condujera** o **condujese**	
	tú/vos	**conduces**/conducís	conducías	**condujiste**	conducirás	conducirías	**conduzcas**	**condujeras** o **condujeses**	conduce/conducí
	Ud., él, ella	conduce	conducía	**condujo**	conducirá	conduciría	**conduzca**	**condujera** o **condujese**	**conduzca**
	nosotros/as	conducimos	conducíamos	**condujimos**	conduciremos	conduciríamos	**conduzcamos**	**condujéramos** o **condujésemos**	**conduzcamos**
	vosotros/as	conducís	conducíais	**condujisteis**	conduciréis	conduciríais	**conduzcáis**	**condujerais** o **condujeseis**	conducid
	Uds., ellos/as	conducen	conducían	**condujeron**	conducirán	conducirían	**conduzcan**	**condujeran** o **condujesen**	**conduzcan**

Verb conjugation tables

Infinitivo / Gerundio / Participio	Pronombres personales	INDICATIVO					SUBJUNTIVO		IMPERATIVO
		Presente	Pretérito imperfecto	Pretérito perfecto simple	Futuro simple	Condicional simple	Presente	Pretérito imperfecto	
15 conocer (2) (c:zc) / conociendo / conocido	yo	**conozco**	conocía	conocí	conoceré	conocería	**conozca**	conociera o conociese	
	tú/vos	conoces/conocés	conocías	conociste	conocerás	conocerías	**conozcas**	conocieras o conocieses	conoce/conocé
	Ud., él, ella	conoce	conocía	conoció	conocerá	conocería	**conozca**	conociera o conociese	**conozca**
	nosotros/as	conocemos	conocíamos	conocimos	conoceremos	conoceríamos	**conozcamos**	conociéramos o conociésemos	**conozcamos**
	vosotros/as	conocéis	conocíais	conocisteis	conoceréis	conoceríais	**conozcáis**	conocierais o conocieseis	conoced
	Uds., ellos/as	conocen	conocían	conocieron	conocerán	conocerían	**conozcan**	conocieran o conociesen	**conozcan**
16 contar (1) (o:ue) / contando / contado	yo	**cuento**	contaba	conté	contaré	contaría	**cuente**	contara o contase	
	tú/vos	**cuentas**/contás	contabas	contaste	contarás	contarías	**cuentes**	contaras o contases	**cuenta**/contá
	Ud., él, ella	**cuenta**	contaba	contó	contará	contaría	**cuente**	contara o contase	**cuente**
	nosotros/as	contamos	contábamos	contamos	contaremos	contaríamos	contemos	contáramos o contásemos	contemos
	vosotros/as	contáis	contabais	contasteis	contaréis	contaríais	contéis	contarais o contaseis	contad
	Uds., ellos/as	**cuentan**	contaban	contaron	contarán	contarían	**cuenten**	contaran o contasen	**cuenten**
17 creer (2, 3) (y) / creyendo / creído	yo	creo	creía	creí	creeré	creería	crea	**creyera** o **creyese**	
	tú/vos	crees/creés	creías	**creíste**	creerás	creerías	creas	**creyeras** o **creyeses**	cree/creé
	Ud., él, ella	cree	creía	**creyó**	creerá	creería	crea	**creyera** o **creyese**	crea
	nosotros/as	creemos	creíamos	**creímos**	creeremos	creeríamos	creamos	**creyéramos** o **creyésemos**	creamos
	vosotros/as	creéis	creíais	**creísteis**	creeréis	creeríais	creáis	**creyerais** o **creyeseis**	creed
	Uds., ellos/as	creen	creían	**creyeron**	creerán	creerían	crean	**creyeran** o **creyesen**	crean
18 cruzar (2) (z:c) / cruzando / cruzado	yo	cruzo	cruzaba	**crucé**	cruzaré	cruzaría	**cruce**	cruzara o cruzase	
	tú/vos	cruzas/cruzás	cruzabas	cruzaste	cruzarás	cruzarías	**cruces**	cruzaras o cruzases	cruza/cruzá
	Ud., él, ella	cruza	cruzaba	cruzó	cruzará	cruzaría	**cruce**	cruzara o cruzase	**cruce**
	nosotros/as	cruzamos	cruzábamos	cruzamos	cruzaremos	cruzaríamos	**crucemos**	cruzáramos o cruzásemos	**crucemos**
	vosotros/as	cruzáis	cruzabais	cruzasteis	cruzaréis	cruzaríais	**crucéis**	cruzarais o cruzaseis	cruzad
	Uds., ellos/as	cruzan	cruzaban	cruzaron	cruzarán	cruzarían	**crucen**	cruzaran o cruzasen	**crucen**
19 dar (4) / dando / dado	yo	**doy**	daba	**di**	daré	daría	**dé**	diera o diese	
	tú/vos	das	dabas	**diste**	darás	darías	des	dieras o dieses	da
	Ud., él, ella	da	daba	**dio**	dará	daría	**dé**	diera o diese	**dé**
	nosotros/as	damos	dábamos	**dimos**	daremos	daríamos	demos	diéramos o diésemos	demos
	vosotros/as	**dais**	dabais	**disteis**	daréis	daríais	**deis**	dierais o dieseis	dad
	Uds., ellos/as	dan	daban	**dieron**	darán	darían	den	dieran o diesen	den
20 decir (1, 4) (e:i) / diciendo / dicho	yo	**digo**	decía	**dije**	**diré**	**diría**	**diga**	dijera o dijese	
	tú/vos	**dices**/decís	decías	**dijiste**	**dirás**	**dirías**	**digas**	dijeras o dijeses	**di**/decí
	Ud., él, ella	**dice**	decía	**dijo**	**dirá**	**diría**	**diga**	dijera o dijese	**diga**
	nosotros/as	decimos	decíamos	**dijimos**	**diremos**	**diríamos**	**digamos**	dijéramos o dijésemos	**digamos**
	vosotros/as	decís	decíais	**dijisteis**	**diréis**	**diríais**	**digáis**	dijerais o dijeseis	decid
	Uds., ellos/as	**dicen**	decían	**dijeron**	**dirán**	**dirían**	**digan**	dijeran o dijesen	**digan**

Verb conjugation tables

Infinitivo / Gerundio / Participio	Pronombres personales	INDICATIVO					SUBJUNTIVO		IMPERATIVO
		Presente	Pretérito imperfecto	Pretérito perfecto simple	Futuro simple	Condicional simple	Presente	Pretérito imperfecto	
21 degollar (1, 3) (go:güe) degollando degollado	yo	**degüello**	degollaba	degollé	degollaré	degollaría	**degüelle**	degollara o degollase	
	tú/vos	**degüellas**/degollás	degollabas	degollaste	degollarás	degollarías	**degüelles**	degollaras o degollases	**degüella**/degollá
	Ud., él, ella	**degüella**	degollaba	degolló	degollará	degollaría	**degüelle**	degollara o degollase	**degüelle**
	nosotros/as	degollamos	degollábamos	degollamos	degollaremos	degollaríamos	degollemos	degolláramos o degollásemos	degollemos
	vosotros/as	degolláis	degollabais	degollasteis	degollaréis	degollaríais	degolléis	degollarais o degollaseis	degollad
	Uds., ellos/as	**degüellan**	degollaban	degollaron	degollarán	degollarían	**degüellen**	degollaran o degollasen	**degüellen**
22 delinquir (2) (qu:c) delinquiendo delinquido	yo	**delinco**	delinquía	delinquí	delinquiré	delinquiría	**delinca**	delinquiera o delinquiese	
	tú/vos	**delinques**/delinquís	delinquías	delinquiste	delinquirás	delinquirías	**delincas**	delinquieras o delinquieses	delinque/delinquí
	Ud., él, ella	delinque	delinquía	delinquió	delinquirá	delinquiría	**delinca**	delinquiera o delinquiese	**delinca**
	nosotros/as	delinquimos	delinquíamos	delinquimos	delinquiremos	delinquiríamos	**delincamos**	delinquiéramos o delinquiésemos	**delincamos**
	vosotros/as	delinquís	delinquíais	delinquisteis	delinquiréis	delinquiríais	**delincáis**	delinquierais o delinquieseis	delinquid
	Uds., ellos/as	delinquen	delinquían	delinquieron	delinquirán	delinquirían	**delincan**	delinquieran o delinquiesen	**delincan**
23 destruir (2) (y) destruyendo destruido	yo	**destruyo**	destruía	destruí	destruiré	destruiría	**destruya**	**destruyera** o **destruyese**	
	tú/vos	**destruyes**/destruís	destruías	destruiste	destruirás	destruirías	**destruyas**	**destruyeras** o **destruyeses**	**destruye**/destruí
	Ud., él, ella	**destruye**	destruía	**destruyó**	destruirá	destruiría	**destruya**	**destruyera** o **destruyese**	**destruya**
	nosotros/as	destruimos	destruíamos	destruimos	destruiremos	destruiríamos	**destruyamos**	**destruyéramos** o **destruyésemos**	**destruyamos**
	vosotros/as	destruís	destruíais	destruisteis	destruiréis	destruiríais	**destruyáis**	**destruyerais** o **destruyeseis**	destruid
	Uds., ellos/as	**destruyen**	destruían	**destruyeron**	destruirán	destruirían	**destruyan**	**destruyeran** o **destruyesen**	**destruyan**
24 discernir (1) (e:ie) discerniendo discernido	yo	**discierno**	discernía	discerní	discerniré	discerniría	**discierna**	discerniera o discerniese	
	tú/vos	**disciernes**/discernís	discernías	discerniste	discernirás	discernirías	**disciernas**	discernieras o discernieses	discierne/discerní
	Ud., él, ella	**discierne**	discernía	discernió	discernirá	discerniría	**discierna**	discerniera o discerniese	**discierna**
	nosotros/as	discernimos	discerníamos	discernimos	discerniremos	discerniríamos	discernamos	discerniéramos o discerniésemos	discernamos
	vosotros/as	discernís	discerníais	discernisteis	discerniréis	discerniríais	discernáis	discernierais o discernieseis	discernid
	Uds., ellos/as	**disciernen**	discernían	discernieron	discernirán	discernirían	**disciernan**	discernieran o discerniesen	**disciernan**
25 dormir (1) (o:ue) durmiendo dormido	yo	**duermo**	dormía	dormí	dormiré	dormiría	**duerma**	**durmiera** o **durmiese**	
	tú/vos	**duermes**/dormís	dormías	dormiste	dormirás	dormirías	**duermas**	**durmieras** o **durmieses**	**duerme**/dormí
	Ud., él, ella	**duerme**	dormía	**durmió**	dormirá	dormiría	**duerma**	**durmiera** o **durmiese**	**duerma**
	nosotros/as	dormimos	dormíamos	dormimos	dormiremos	dormiríamos	**durmamos**	**durmiéramos** o **durmiésemos**	**durmamos**
	vosotros/as	dormís	dormíais	dormisteis	dormiréis	dormiríais	**durmáis**	**durmierais** o **durmieseis**	dormid
	Uds., ellos/as	**duermen**	dormían	**durmieron**	dormirán	dormirían	**duerman**	**durmieran** o **durmiesen**	**duerman**

Infinitivo / Gerundio / Participio	Pronombres personales	INDICATIVO Presente	Pretérito imperfecto	Pretérito perfecto simple	Futuro simple	Condicional simple	SUBJUNTIVO Presente	Pretérito imperfecto	IMPERATIVO
26 elegir (1, 2) (e:i) (g:j)	yo	elijo	elegía	elegí	elegiré	elegiría	elija	eligiera o eligiese	
	tú/vos	eliges/elegís	elegías	elegiste	elegirás	elegirías	elijas	eligieras o eligieses	elige/elegí
	Ud., él, ella	elige	elegía	eligió	elegirá	elegiría	elija	eligiera o eligiese	elija
eligiendo	nosotros/as	elegimos	elegíamos	elegimos	elegiremos	elegiríamos	elijamos	eligiéramos o eligiésemos	elijamos
elegido o **electo**	vosotros/as	elegís	elegíais	elegisteis	elegiréis	elegiríais	elijáis	eligierais o eligieseis	elegid
	Uds., ellos/as	eligen	elegían	eligieron	elegirán	elegirían	elijan	eligieran o eligiesen	elijan
27 empezar (1, 2) (e:ie) (z:c)	yo	empiezo	empezaba	empecé	empezaré	empezaría	empiece	empezara o empezase	
	tú/vos	empiezas/empezás	empezabas	empezaste	empezarás	empezarías	empieces	empezaras o empezases	empieza/empezá
empezando	Ud., él, ella	empieza	empezaba	empezó	empezará	empezaría	empiece	empezara o empezase	empiece
empezado	nosotros/as	empezamos	empezábamos	empezamos	empezaremos	empezaríamos	empecemos	empezáramos o empezásemos	empecemos
	vosotros/as	empezáis	empezabais	empezasteis	empezaréis	empezaríais	empecéis	empezarais o empezaseis	empezad
	Uds., ellos/as	empiezan	empezaban	empezaron	empezarán	empezarían	empiecen	empezaran o empezasen	empiecen
28 entender (1) (e:ie)	yo	entiendo	entendía	entendí	entenderé	entendería	entienda	entendiera o entendiese	
	tú/vos	entiendes/entendés	entendías	entendiste	entenderás	entenderías	entiendas	entendieras o entendieses	entiende/entendé
entendiendo	Ud., él, ella	entiende	entendía	entendió	entenderá	entendería	entienda	entendiera o entendiese	entienda
entendido	nosotros/as	entendemos	entendíamos	entendimos	entenderemos	entenderíamos	entendamos	entendiéramos o entendiésemos	entendamos
	vosotros/as	entendéis	entendíais	entendisteis	entenderéis	entenderíais	entendáis	entendierais o entendieseis	entended
	Uds., ellos/as	entienden	entendían	entendieron	entenderán	entenderían	entiendan	entendieran o entendiesen	entiendan
29 enviar (3) (i:í)	yo	envío	enviaba	envié	enviaré	enviaría	envíe	enviara o enviase	
	tú/vos	envías/enviás	enviabas	enviaste	enviarás	enviarías	envíes	enviaras o enviases	envía/enviá
	Ud., él, ella	envía	enviaba	envió	enviará	enviaría	envíe	enviara o enviase	envíe
enviando	nosotros/as	enviamos	enviábamos	enviamos	enviaremos	enviaríamos	enviemos	enviáramos o enviásemos	enviemos
enviado	vosotros/as	enviáis	enviabais	enviasteis	enviaréis	enviaríais	enviéis	enviarais o enviaseis	enviad
	Uds., ellos/as	envían	enviaban	enviaron	enviarán	enviarían	envíen	enviaran o enviasen	envíen
30 erguir (4)	yo	irgo o yergo	erguía	erguí	erguiré	erguiría	irga o yerga	irguiera o irguiese	
	tú/vos	irgues o yergues/erguís	erguías	erguiste	erguirás	erguirías	irgas o yergas	irguieras o irguieses	irgue o yergue/erguí
irguiendo	Ud., él, ella	irgue o yergue	erguía	irguió	erguirá	erguiría	irga o yerga	irguiera o irguiese	irga o yerga
erguido	nosotros/as	erguimos	erguíamos	erguimos	erguiremos	erguiríamos	irgamos o yergamos	irguiéramos o irguiésemos	irgamos o yergamos
	vosotros/as	erguís	erguíais	erguisteis	erguiréis	erguiríais	irgáis o yergáis	irguierais o irguieseis	erguid
	Uds., ellos/as	irguen o yerguen	erguían	irguieron	erguirán	erguirían	irgan o yergan	irguieran o irguiesen	irgan o yergan

Infinitivo / Gerundio Participio	Pronombres personales	INDICATIVO					SUBJUNTIVO		IMPERATIVO
		Presente	Pretérito imperfecto	Pretérito perfecto simple	Futuro simple	Condicional simple	Presente	Pretérito imperfecto	
31 errar (4) (y) errando errado	yo	**yerro** o erro	erraba	erré	erraré	erraría	**yerre** o erre	errara o errase	
	tú/vos	**yerras** o erras/errás	errabas	erraste	errarás	errarías	**yerres** o erres	erraras o errases	**yerra** o erra/errá
	Ud., él, ella	**yerra** o erra	erraba	erró	errará	erraría	**yerre** o erre	errara o errase	**yerre** o erre
	nosotros/as	erramos	errábamos	erramos	erraremos	erraríamos	erremos	erráramos o errásemos	erremos
	vosotros/as	erráis	errabais	errasteis	erraréis	erraríais	erréis	errarais o erraseis	errad
	Uds., ellos/as	**yerran** o erran	erraban	erraron	errarán	errarían	**yerren** o erren	erraran o errasen	**yerren** o erren
32 esparcir (2) (c:z) esparciendo esparcido	yo	**esparzo**	esparcía	esparcí	esparciré	esparciría	**esparza**	esparciera o esparciese	
	tú/vos	esparces/esparcís	esparcías	esparciste	esparcirás	esparcirías	**esparzas**	esparcieras o esparcieses	esparce/esparcí
	Ud., él, ella	esparce	esparcía	esparció	esparcirá	esparciría	**esparza**	esparciera o esparciese	**esparza**
	nosotros/as	esparcimos	esparcíamos	esparcimos	esparciremos	esparciríamos	**esparzamos**	esparciéramos o esparciésemos	**esparzamos**
	vosotros/as	esparcís	esparcíais	esparcisteis	esparciréis	esparciríais	**esparzáis**	esparcierais o esparcieseis	esparcid
	Uds., ellos/as	esparcen	esparcían	esparcieron	esparcirán	esparcirían	**esparzan**	esparcieran o esparciesen	**esparzan**
33 estar (4) estando estado	yo	**estoy**	estaba	**estuve**	estaré	estaría	**esté**	**estuviera** o **estuviese**	
	tú/vos	**estás**	estabas	**estuviste**	estarás	estarías	**estés**	**estuvieras** o **estuvieses**	**está**
	Ud., él, ella	**está**	estaba	**estuvo**	estará	estaría	**esté**	**estuviera** o **estuviese**	**esté**
	nosotros/as	estamos	estábamos	**estuvimos**	estaremos	estaríamos	estemos	**estuviéramos** o **estuviésemos**	estemos
	vosotros/as	estáis	estabais	**estuvisteis**	estaréis	estaríais	estéis	**estuvierais** o **estuvieseis**	estad
	Uds., ellos/as	**están**	estaban	**estuvieron**	estarán	estarían	**estén**	**estuvieran** o **estuviesen**	**estén**
34 europeizar (2, 3) (z:c) (i:í) europeizando europeizado	yo	**europeizo**	europeizaba	**europeicé**	europeizaré	europeizaría	**europeice**	europeizara o europeizase	
	tú/vos	**europeizas**/europeizás	europeizabas	europeizaste	europeizarás	europeizarías	**europeices**	europeizaras o europeizases	**europeiza**/europeizá
	Ud., él, ella	**europeiza**	europeizaba	europeizó	europeizará	europeizaría	**europeice**	europeizara o europeizase	**europeice**
	nosotros/as	europeizamos	europeizábamos	europeizamos	europeizaremos	europeizaríamos	**europeicemos**	europeizáramos o europeizásemos	**europeicemos**
	vosotros/as	europeizáis	europeizabais	europeizasteis	europeizaréis	europeizaríais	**europeicéis**	europeizarais o europeizaseis	europeizad
	Uds., ellos/as	**europeizan**	europeizaban	europeizaron	europeizarán	europeizarían	**europeicen**	europeizaran o europeizasen	**europeicen**
35 exigir (2) (g:j) exigiendo exigido	yo	**exijo**	exigía	exigí	exigiré	exigiría	**exija**	exigiera o exigiese	
	tú/vos	exiges/exigís	exigías	exigiste	exigirás	exigirías	**exijas**	exigieras o exigieses	exige/exigí
	Ud., él, ella	exige	exigía	exigió	exigirá	exigiría	**exija**	exigiera o exigiese	**exija**
	nosotros/as	exigimos	exigíamos	exigimos	exigiremos	exigiríamos	**exijamos**	exigiéramos o exigiésemos	**exijamos**
	vosotros/as	exigís	exigíais	exigisteis	exigiréis	exigiríais	**exijáis**	exigierais o exigieseis	exigid
	Uds., ellos/as	exigen	exigían	exigieron	exigirán	exigirían	**exijan**	exigieran o exigiesen	**exijan**
36 extinguir (2) (gu:g) extinguiendo extinguido	yo	**extingo**	extinguía	extinguí	extinguiré	extinguiría	**extinga**	extinguiera o extinguiese	
	tú/vos	extingues/extinguís	extinguías	extinguiste	extinguirás	extinguirías	**extingas**	extinguieras o extinguieses	extingue/extinguí
	Ud., él, ella	extingue	extinguía	extinguió	extinguirá	extinguiría	**extinga**	extinguiera o extinguiese	**extinga**
	nosotros/as	extinguimos	extinguíamos	extinguimos	extinguiremos	extinguiríamos	**extingamos**	extinguiéramos o extinguiésemos	**extingamos**
	vosotros/as	extinguís	extinguíais	extinguisteis	extinguiréis	extinguiríais	**extingáis**	extinguierais o extinguieseis	extinguid
	Uds., ellos/as	extinguen	extinguían	extinguieron	extinguirán	extinguirían	**extingan**	extinguieran o extinguiesen	**extingan**

Infinitivo Gerundio Participio	Pronombres personales	INDICATIVO Presente	Pretérito imperfecto	Pretérito perfecto simple	Futuro simple	Condicional simple	SUBJUNTIVO Presente	Pretérito imperfecto	IMPERATIVO
37 graduar [3] (u:ú) graduando graduado	yo	**graduo**	graduaba	gradué	graduaré	graduaría	**gradúe**	graduara o graduase	
	tú/vos	**graduas**/graduás	graduabas	graduaste	graduarás	graduarías	**gradúes**	graduaras o graduases	**gradúa**/graduá
	Ud., él, ella	**gradua**	graduaba	graduó	graduará	graduaría	**gradúe**	graduara o graduase	**gradúe**
	nosotros/as	graduamos	graduábamos	graduamos	graduaremos	graduaríamos	graduemos	graduáramos o graduásemos	graduemos
	vosotros/as	graduáis	graduabais	graduasteis	graduaréis	graduaríais	graduéis	graduarais o graduaseis	graduad
	Uds., ellos/as	**graduan**	graduaban	graduaron	graduarán	graduarían	**gradúen**	graduaran o graduasen	**gradúen**
38 haber [4] habiendo habido	yo	**he**	había	**hube**	**habré**	**habría**	**haya**	**hubiera** o **hubiese**	
	tú/vos	**has**	habías	**hubiste**	**habrás**	**habrías**	**hayas**	**hubieras** o **hubieses**	
	Ud., él, ella	**ha**	había	**hubo**	**habrá**	**habría**	**haya**	**hubiera** o **hubiese**	
	nosotros/as	**hemos**	habíamos	**hubimos**	**habremos**	**habríamos**	**hayamos**	**hubiéramos** o **hubiésemos**	
	vosotros/as	habéis	habíais	**hubisteis**	**habréis**	**habríais**	**hayáis**	**hubierais** o **hubieseis**	
	Uds., ellos/as	**han**	habían	**hubieron**	**habrán**	**habrían**	**hayan**	**hubieran** o **hubiesen**	
39 hacer [4] haciendo hecho	yo	**hago**	hacía	**hice**	**haré**	**haría**	**haga**	**hiciera** o **hiciese**	
	tú/vos	haces/hacés	hacías	**hiciste**	**harás**	**harías**	**hagas**	**hicieras** o **hicieses**	**haz**/hacé
	Ud., él, ella	hace	hacía	**hizo**	**hará**	**haría**	**haga**	**hiciera** o **hiciese**	**haga**
	nosotros/as	hacemos	hacíamos	**hicimos**	**haremos**	**haríamos**	**hagamos**	**hiciéramos** o **hiciésemos**	**hagamos**
	vosotros/as	hacéis	hacíais	**hicisteis**	**haréis**	**haríais**	**hagáis**	**hicierais** o **hicieseis**	haced
	Uds., ellos/as	hacen	hacían	**hicieron**	**harán**	**harían**	**hagan**	**hicieran** o **hiciesen**	**hagan**
40 ir [4] yendo ido	yo	**voy**	**iba**	**fui**	iré	iría	**vaya**	**fuera** o **fuese**	
	tú/vos	**vas**	**ibas**	**fuiste**	irás	irías	**vayas**	**fueras** o **fueses**	**ve**/**andá**
	Ud., él, ella	**va**	**iba**	**fue**	irá	iría	**vaya**	**fuera** o **fuese**	**vaya**
	nosotros/as	**vamos**	**íbamos**	**fuimos**	iremos	iríamos	**vayamos**	**fuéramos** o **fuésemos**	**vamos**
	vosotros/as	**vais**	**ibais**	**fuisteis**	iréis	iríais	**vayáis**	**fuerais** o **fueseis**	**id**
	Uds., ellos/as	**van**	**iban**	**fueron**	irán	irían	**vayan**	**fueran** o **fuesen**	**vayan**
41 jugar [1,2] (u:ue) (g:gu) jugando jugado	yo	**juego**	jugaba	**jugué**	jugaré	jugaría	**juegue**	jugara o jugase	
	tú/vos	**juegas**/jugás	jugabas	jugaste	jugarás	jugarías	**juegues**	jugaras o jugases	**juega**/jugá
	Ud., él, ella	**juega**	jugaba	jugó	jugará	jugaría	**juegue**	jugara o jugase	**juegue**
	nosotros/as	jugamos	jugábamos	jugamos	jugaremos	jugaríamos	**juguemos**	jugáramos o jugásemos	**juguemos**
	vosotros/as	jugáis	jugabais	jugasteis	jugaréis	jugaríais	**juguéis**	jugarais o jugaseis	jugad
	Uds., ellos/as	**juegan**	jugaban	jugaron	jugarán	jugarían	**jueguen**	jugaran o jugasen	**jueguen**
42 llegar [2] (g:gu) llegando llegado	yo	llego	llegaba	**llegué**	llegaré	llegaría	**llegue**	llegara o llegase	
	tú/vos	llegas/llegás	llegabas	llegaste	llegarás	llegarías	**llegues**	llegaras o llegases	llega/llegá
	Ud., él, ella	llega	llegaba	llegó	llegará	llegaría	**llegue**	llegara o llegase	**llegue**
	nosotros/as	llegamos	llegábamos	llegamos	llegaremos	llegaríamos	**lleguemos**	llegáramos o llegásemos	**lleguemos**
	vosotros/as	llegáis	llegabais	llegasteis	llegaréis	llegaríais	**lleguéis**	llegarais o llegaseis	llegad
	Uds., ellos/as	llegan	llegaban	llegaron	llegarán	llegarían	**lleguen**	llegaran o llegasen	**lleguen**

Infinitivo / Gerundio / Participio	Pronombres personales	INDICATIVO Presente	Pretérito imperfecto	Pretérito perfecto simple	Futuro simple	Condicional simple	SUBJUNTIVO Presente	Pretérito imperfecto	IMPERATIVO
43 lucir [2] (c:zc) luciendo lucido	yo	**luzco**	lucía	lucí	luciré	luciría	**luzca**	luciera o luciese	
	tú/vos	**luces/lucís**	lucías	luciste	lucirás	lucirías	**luzcas**	lucieras o lucieses	luce/lucí
	Ud., él, ella	luce	lucía	lució	lucirá	luciría	**luzca**	luciera o luciese	**luzca**
	nosotros/as	lucimos	lucíamos	lucimos	luciremos	luciríamos	**luzcamos**	luciéramos o luciésemos	**luzcamos**
	vosotros/as	lucís	lucíais	lucisteis	luciréis	luciríais	**luzcáis**	lucierais o lucieseis	lucid
	Uds., ellos/as	lucen	lucían	lucieron	lucirán	lucirían	**luzcan**	lucieran o luciesen	**luzcan**
44 mover [1] (o:ue) moviendo movido	yo	**muevo**	movía	moví	moveré	movería	**mueva**	moviera o moviese	
	tú/vos	**mueves/movés**	movías	moviste	moverás	moverías	**muevas**	movieras o movieses	**mueve/mové**
	Ud., él, ella	**mueve**	movía	movió	moverá	movería	**mueva**	moviera o moviese	**mueva**
	nosotros/as	movemos	movíamos	movimos	moveremos	moveríamos	movamos	moviéramos o moviésemos	movamos
	vosotros/as	movéis	movíais	movisteis	moveréis	moveríais	mováis	movierais o movieseis	moved
	Uds., ellos/as	**mueven**	movían	movieron	moverán	moverían	**muevan**	movieran o moviesen	**muevan**
45 negar [1, 2] (e:ie) (g:gu) negando negado	yo	**niego**	negaba	**negué**	negaré	negaría	**niegue**	negara o negase	
	tú/vos	**niegas/negás**	negabas	negaste	negarás	negarías	**niegues**	negaras o negases	**niega/negá**
	Ud., él, ella	**niega**	negaba	negó	negará	negaría	**niegue**	negara o negase	**niegue**
	nosotros/as	negamos	negábamos	negamos	negaremos	negaríamos	**neguemos**	negáramos o negásemos	**neguemos**
	vosotros/as	negáis	negabais	negasteis	negaréis	negaríais	**neguéis**	negarais o negaseis	negad
	Uds., ellos/as	**niegan**	negaban	negaron	negarán	negarían	**nieguen**	negaran o negasen	**nieguen**
46 oír [3,4] (y) oyendo oído	yo	**oigo**	oía	oí	oiré	oiría	**oiga**	**oyera u oyese**	
	tú/vos	**oyes/oís**	oías	**oíste**	oirás	oirías	**oigas**	**oyeras u oyeses**	**oye/oí**
	Ud., él, ella	**oye**	oía	**oyó**	oirá	oiría	**oiga**	**oyera u oyese**	**oiga**
	nosotros/as	**oímos**	oíamos	**oímos**	oiremos	oiríamos	**oigamos**	**oyéramos u oyésemos**	**oigamos**
	vosotros/as	oís	oíais	**oísteis**	oiréis	oiríais	oigáis	**oyerais u oyeseis**	oíd
	Uds., ellos/as	**oyen**	oían	**oyeron**	oirán	oirían	**oigan**	**oyeran u oyesen**	**oigan**
47 oler [1] (o:hue) oliendo olido	yo	**huelo**	olía	olí	oleré	olería	**huela**	oliera u oliese	
	tú/vos	**hueles/olés**	olías	oliste	olerás	olerías	**huelas**	olieras u olieses	**huele/olé**
	Ud., él, ella	**huele**	olía	olió	olerá	olería	**huela**	oliera u oliese	**huela**
	nosotros/as	olemos	olíamos	olimos	oleremos	oleríamos	olamos	oliéramos u oliésemos	olamos
	vosotros/as	oléis	olíais	olisteis	oleréis	oleríais	oláis	olierais u olieseis	oled
	Uds., ellos/as	**huelen**	olían	olieron	olerán	olerían	**huelan**	olieran u oliesen	**huelan**
48 pedir [1] (e:i) pidiendo pedido	yo	**pido**	pedía	pedí	pediré	pediría	**pida**	**pidiera o pidiese**	
	tú/vos	**pides/pedís**	pedías	pediste	pedirás	pedirías	**pidas**	**pidieras o pidieses**	**pide/pedí**
	Ud., él, ella	**pide**	pedía	**pidió**	pedirá	pediría	**pida**	**pidiera o pidiese**	**pida**
	nosotros/as	pedimos	pedíamos	pedimos	pediremos	pediríamos	**pidamos**	**pidiéramos o pidiésemos**	**pidamos**
	vosotros/as	pedís	pedíais	pedisteis	pediréis	pediríais	**pidáis**	**pidierais o pidieseis**	pedid
	Uds., ellos/as	**piden**	pedían	**pidieron**	pedirán	pedirían	**pidan**	**pidieran o pidiesen**	**pidan**

Infinitivo / Gerundio Participio	Pronombres personales	INDICATIVO Presente	Pretérito imperfecto	Pretérito perfecto simple	Futuro simple	Condicional simple	SUBJUNTIVO Presente	Pretérito imperfecto	IMPERATIVO
49 pensar [(1)] (e:ie) pensando pensado	yo	**pienso**	pensaba	pensé	pensaré	pensaría	**piense**	pensara o pensase	
	tú/vos	**piensas/pensás**	pensabas	pensaste	pensarás	pensarías	**pienses**	pensaras o pensases	**piensa/pensá**
	Ud., él, ella	**piensa**	pensaba	pensó	pensará	pensaría	**piense**	pensara o pensase	**piense**
	nosotros/as	pensamos	pensábamos	pensamos	pensaremos	pensaríamos	pensemos	pensáramos o pensásemos	pensemos
	vosotros/as	pensáis	pensabais	pensasteis	pensaréis	pensaríais	penséis	pensarais o pensaseis	pensad
	Uds., ellos/as	**piensan**	pensaban	pensaron	pensarán	pensarían	**piensen**	pensaran o pensasen	**piensen**
50 poder [(1,4)] (o:ue) pudiendo podido	yo	**puedo**	podía	**pude**	**podré**	**podría**	**pueda**	**pudiera** o **pudiese**	
	tú/vos	**puedes/podés**	podías	**pudiste**	**podrás**	**podrías**	**puedas**	**pudieras** o **pudieses**	**puede/podé**
	Ud., él, ella	**puede**	podía	**pudo**	**podrá**	**podría**	**pueda**	**pudiera** o **pudiese**	**pueda**
	nosotros/as	podemos	podíamos	**pudimos**	**podremos**	**podríamos**	podamos	**pudiéramos** o **pudiésemos**	podamos
	vosotros/as	podéis	podíais	**pudisteis**	**podréis**	**podríais**	podáis	**pudierais** o **pudieseis**	poded
	Uds., ellos/as	**pueden**	podían	**pudieron**	**podrán**	**podrían**	**puedan**	**pudieran** o **pudiesen**	**puedan**
51 poner [(4)] poniendo puesto	yo	**pongo**	ponía	**puse**	**pondré**	**pondría**	**ponga**	**pusiera** o **pusiese**	
	tú/vos	pones/ponés	ponías	**pusiste**	**pondrás**	**pondrías**	**pongas**	**pusieras** o **pusieses**	**pon/poné**
	Ud., él, ella	pone	ponía	**puso**	**pondrá**	**pondría**	**ponga**	**pusiera** o **pusiese**	**ponga**
	nosotros/as	ponemos	poníamos	**pusimos**	**pondremos**	**pondríamos**	**pongamos**	**pusiéramos** o **pusiésemos**	**pongamos**
	vosotros/as	ponéis	poníais	**pusisteis**	**pondréis**	**pondríais**	**pongáis**	**pusierais** o **pusieseis**	poned
	Uds., ellos/as	ponen	ponían	**pusieron**	**pondrán**	**pondrían**	**pongan**	**pusieran** o **pusiesen**	**pongan**
52 predecir [(1,4)] (e:i) prediciendo predicho	yo	**predigo**	predecía	**predije**	**prediciré** o **prediré**	prediciría o **prediría**	**prediga**	**predijera** o **predijese**	
	tú/vos	**predices/predecís**	predecías	**predijiste**	**predecirás** o **predirás**	predecirías o **predirías**	**predigas**	**predijeras** o **predijeses**	**predice/predecí**
	Ud., él, ella	**predice**	predecía	**predijo**	**predecirá** o **predirá**	prediciría o **prediría**	**prediga**	**predijera** o **predijese**	**prediga**
	nosotros/as	predecimos	predecíamos	**predijimos**	**prediciremos** o **prediremos**	prediciríamos o **prediríamos**	**predigamos**	**predijéramos** o **predijésemos**	**predigamos**
	vosotros/as	predecís	predecíais	**predijisteis**	**predeciréis** o **prediréis**	predeciríais o **prediríais**	**predigáis**	**predijerais** o **predijeseis**	predecid
	Uds., ellos/as	**predicen**	predecían	**predijeron**	**predecirán** o **predirán**	predecirían o **predirían**	**predigan**	**predijeran** o **predijesen**	**predigan**
53 prohibir [(3)] (i:í) prohibiendo prohibido	yo	**prohíbo**	prohibía	prohibí	prohibiré	prohibiría	**prohíba**	prohibiera o prohibiese	
	tú/vos	**prohíbes/prohibís**	prohibías	prohibiste	prohibirás	prohibirías	**prohíbas**	prohibieras o prohibieses	**prohíbe/prohibís**
	Ud., él, ella	**prohíbe**	prohibía	prohibió	prohibirá	prohibiría	**prohíba**	prohibiera o prohibiese	**prohíba**
	nosotros/as	prohibimos	prohibíamos	prohibimos	prohibiremos	prohibiríamos	prohibamos	prohibiéramos o prohibiésemos	prohibamos
	vosotros/as	prohibís	prohibíais	prohibisteis	prohibiréis	prohibiríais	prohibáis	prohibierais o prohibieseis	prohibid
	Uds., ellos/as	**prohíben**	prohibían	prohibieron	prohibirán	prohibirían	**prohíban**	prohibieran o prohibiesen	**prohíban**

Infinitivo / Gerundio Participio	Pronombres personales	INDICATIVO					SUBJUNTIVO		IMPERATIVO
		Presente	Pretérito imperfecto	Pretérito perfecto simple	Futuro simple	Condicional simple	Presente	Pretérito imperfecto	
54 proteger (2) (g:j) protegiendo protegido	yo	**protejo**	protegía	protegí	protegeré	protegería	**proteja**	protegiera o protegiese	
	tú/vos	proteges/protegés	protegías	protegiste	protegerás	protegerías	**protejas**	protegieras o protegieses	protege/protegé
	Ud., él, ella	protege	protegía	protegió	protegerá	protegería	**proteja**	protegiera o protegiese	**proteja**
	nosotros/as	protegemos	protegíamos	protegimos	protegeremos	protegeríamos	**protejamos**	protegiéramos o protegiésemos	**protejamos**
	vosotros/as	protegéis	protegíais	protegisteis	protegeréis	protegeríais	**protejáis**	protegierais o protegieseis	proteged
	Uds., ellos/as	protegen	protegían	protegieron	protegerán	protegerían	**protejan**	protegieran o protegiesen	**protejan**
55 pudrir/podrir (4) pudriendo podrido	yo	pudro	pudría o podría	pudrí o podrí	pudriré o podriré	pudriría o podriría	pudra	pudriera o pudriese	
	tú/vos	pudres/pudrís	pudrías o podrías	pudriste o podriste	pudrirás o podrirás	pudrirías o podrirías	pudras	pudrieras o pudrieses	pudre/pudrí o podrí
	Ud., él, ella	pudre	pudría o podría	pudrió o podrió	pudrirá o podrirá	pudriría o podriría	pudra	pudriera o pudriese	pudra
	nosotros/as	pudrimos o podrimos	pudríamos o podríamos	pudrimos o podrimos	pudriremos o podriremos	pudriríamos o podriríamos	pudramos	pudriéramos o pudriésemos	pudramos
	vosotros/as	pudrís o podrís	pudríais o podríais	pudristeis o podristeis	pudriréis o podriréis	pudriríais o podriríais	pudráis	pudrierais o pudrieseis	pudrid o podrid
	Uds., ellos/as	pudren	pudrían o podrían	pudrieron o podrieron	pudrirán o podrirán	pudrirían o podrirían	pudran	pudrieran o pudriesen	pudran
56 querer (1,4) (e:ie) queriendo querido	yo	**quiero**	quería	quise	querré	querría	**quiera**	quisiera o quisiese	
	tú/vos	**quieres/querés**	querías	quisiste	querrás	querrías	**quieras**	quisieras o quisieses	**quiere**/queré
	Ud., él, ella	**quiere**	quería	quiso	querrá	querría	**quiera**	quisiera o quisiese	**quiera**
	nosotros/as	queremos	queríamos	**quisimos**	**querremos**	**querríamos**	queramos	**quisiéramos o quisiésemos**	queramos
	vosotros/as	queréis	queríais	**quisisteis**	**querréis**	**querríais**	queráis	**quisierais o quisieseis**	quered
	Uds., ellos/as	**quieren**	querían	**quisieron**	**querrán**	**querrían**	**quieran**	**quisieran o quisiesen**	**quieran**
57 rehusar (3) (u:ú) rehusando rehusado	yo	**rehúso**	rehusaba	rehusé	rehusaré	rehusaría	**rehúse**	rehusara o rehusase	
	tú/vos	**rehúsas/rehusás**	rehusabas	rehusaste	rehusarás	rehusarías	**rehúses**	rehusaras o rehusases	**rehúsa**/rehusá
	Ud., él, ella	**rehúsa**	rehusaba	rehusó	rehusará	rehusaría	**rehúse**	rehusara o rehusase	**rehúse**
	nosotros/as	rehusamos	rehusábamos	rehusamos	rehusaremos	rehusaríamos	rehusemos	rehusáramos o rehusásemos	rehusemos
	vosotros/as	rehusáis	rehusabais	rehusasteis	rehusaréis	rehusaríais	rehuséis	rehusarais o rehusaseis	rehusad
	Uds., ellos/as	**rehúsan**	rehusaban	rehusaron	rehusarán	rehusarían	**rehúsen**	rehusaran o rehusasen	**rehúsen**
58 reír (1) (e:i) riendo reído	yo	**río**	reía	reí	reiré	reiría	**ría**	riera o riese	
	tú/vos	**ríes/reís**	reías	**reíste**	reirás	reirías	**rías**	**rieras o rieses**	**ríe**/reí
	Ud., él, ella	**ríe**	reía	**rio**	reirá	reiría	**ría**	**riera o riese**	**ría**
	nosotros/as	**reímos**	reíamos	**reímos**	reiremos	reiríamos	**riamos**	**riéramos o riésemos**	**riamos**
	vosotros/as	reís	reíais	**reísteis**	reiréis	reiríais	**riáis**	**rierais o rieseis**	**reíd**
	Uds., ellos/as	**ríen**	reían	**rieron**	reirán	reirían	**rían**	**rieran o riesen**	**rían**

Infinitivo / Gerundio / Participio	Pronombres personales	INDICATIVO Presente	Pretérito imperfecto	Pretérito perfecto simple	Futuro simple	Condicional simple	SUBJUNTIVO Presente	Pretérito imperfecto	IMPERATIVO
59 reunir [(3)] (u:ú) reuniendo reunido	yo	**reúno**	reunía	reuní	reuniré	reuniría	**reúna**	reuniera o reuniese	
	tú/vos	**reúnes**/reunís	reunías	reuniste	reunirás	reunirías	**reúnas**	reunieras o reunieses	**reúne**/reuní
	Ud., él, ella	**reúne**	reunía	reunió	reunirá	reuniría	**reúna**	reuniera o reuniese	**reúna**
	nosotros/as	reunimos	reuníamos	reunimos	reuniremos	reuniríamos	reunamos	reuniéramos o reuniésemos	reunamos
	vosotros/as	reunís	reuníais	reunisteis	reuniréis	reuniríais	reunáis	reunierais o reunieseis	reunid
	Uds., ellos/as	**reúnen**	reunían	reunieron	reunirán	reunirían	**reúnan**	reunieran o reuniesen	**reúnan**
60 roer [(3, 4)] (y) **royendo roído**	yo	roo o **roigo** o **royo**	roía	roí	roeré	roería	roa o **roiga** o **roya**	**royera** o **royese**	
	tú/vos	roes/roés	roías	**roíste**	roerás	roerías	roas o **roigas** o **royas**	**royeras** o **royeses**	roe/roé
	Ud., él, ella	roe	roía	**royó**	roerá	roería	roa o **roiga** o **roya**	**royera** o **royese**	roa o **roiga** o **roya**
	nosotros/as	roemos	roíamos	**roímos**	roeremos	roeríamos	roamos o **roigamos** o **royamos**	**royéramos** o **royésemos**	roamos o **roigamos** o **royamos**
	vosotros/as	roéis	roíais	**roísteis**	roeréis	roeríais	roáis o **roigáis** o **royáis**	**royerais** o **royeseis**	roed
	Uds., ellos/as	roen	roían	**royeron**	roerán	roerían	roan o **roigan** o **royan**	**royeran** o **royesen**	roan o **roigan** o **royan**
61 rogar [(1, 2)] (o:ue) (g:gu) rogando rogado	yo	**ruego**	rogaba	**rogué**	rogaré	rogaría	**ruegue**	rogara o rogase	
	tú/vos	**ruegas**/rogás	rogabas	rogaste	rogarás	rogarías	**ruegues**	rogaras o rogases	**ruega**/rogá
	Ud., él, ella	**ruega**	rogaba	rogó	rogará	rogaría	**ruegue**	rogara o rogase	**ruegue**
	nosotros/as	rogamos	rogábamos	rogamos	rogaremos	rogaríamos	**roguemos**	rogáramos o rogásemos	**roguemos**
	vosotros/as	rogáis	rogabais	rogasteis	rogaréis	rogaríais	**roguéis**	rogarais o rogaseis	rogad
	Uds., ellos/as	**ruegan**	rogaban	rogaron	rogarán	rogarían	**rueguen**	rogaran o rogasen	**rueguen**
62 saber [(4)] sabiendo sabido	yo	**sé**	sabía	**supe**	**sabré**	**sabría**	**sepa**	**supiera** o **supiese**	
	tú/vos	sabes/sabés	sabías	**supiste**	**sabrás**	**sabrías**	**sepas**	**supieras** o **supieses**	sabe/sabé
	Ud., él, ella	sabe	sabía	**supo**	**sabrá**	**sabría**	**sepa**	**supiera** o **supiese**	**sepa**
	nosotros/as	sabemos	sabíamos	**supimos**	**sabremos**	**sabríamos**	**sepamos**	**supiéramos** o **supiésemos**	**sepamos**
	vosotros/as	sabéis	sabíais	**supisteis**	**sabréis**	**sabríais**	**sepáis**	**supierais** o **supieseis**	sabed
	Uds., ellos/as	saben	sabían	**supieron**	**sabrán**	**sabrían**	**sepan**	**supieran** o **supiesen**	**sepan**
63 salir [(4)] saliendo salido	yo	**salgo**	salía	salí	**saldré**	**saldría**	**salga**	saliera o saliese	
	tú/vos	sales/salís	salías	saliste	**saldrás**	**saldrías**	**salgas**	salieras o salieses	**sal**/salí
	Ud., él, ella	sale	salía	salió	**saldrá**	**saldría**	**salga**	saliera o saliese	**salga**
	nosotros/as	salimos	salíamos	salimos	**saldremos**	**saldríamos**	**salgamos**	saliéramos o saliésemos	**salgamos**
	vosotros/as	salís	salíais	salisteis	**saldréis**	**saldríais**	**salgáis**	salierais o salieseis	salid
	Uds., ellos/as	salen	salían	salieron	**saldrán**	**saldrían**	**salgan**	salieran o saliesen	**salgan**

Infinitivo / Gerundio / Participio	Pronombres personales	INDICATIVO					SUBJUNTIVO		IMPERATIVO
		Presente	Pretérito imperfecto	Pretérito perfecto simple	Futuro simple	Condicional simple	Presente	Pretérito imperfecto	
64 seguir [(1,2)] (e:i) (gu:g) **siguiendo** seguido	yo	**sigo**	seguía	seguí	seguiré	seguiría	**siga**	**siguiera** *o* **siguiese**	
	tú/vos	**sigues/seguís**	seguías	seguiste	seguirás	seguirías	**sigas**	**siguieras** *o* **siguieses**	**sigue/seguí**
	Ud., él, ella	**sigue**	seguía	**siguió**	seguirá	seguiría	**siga**	**siguiera** *o* **siguiese**	**siga**
	nosotros/as	seguimos	seguíamos	seguimos	seguiremos	seguiríamos	**sigamos**	**siguiéramos** *o* **siguiésemos**	**sigamos**
	vosotros/as	seguís	seguíais	seguisteis	seguiréis	seguiríais	**sigáis**	**siguierais** *o* **siguieseis**	seguid
	Uds., ellos/as	**siguen**	seguían	**siguieron**	seguirán	seguirían	**sigan**	**siguieran** *o* **siguiesen**	**sigan**
65 sentir [(1)] (e:ie) **sintiendo** sentido	yo	**siento**	sentía	sentí	sentiré	sentiría	**sienta**	**sintiera** *o* **sintiese**	
	tú/vos	**sientes/sentís**	sentías	sentiste	sentirás	sentirías	**sientas**	**sintieras** *o* **sintieses**	**siente/sentí**
	Ud., él, ella	**siente**	sentía	**sintió**	sentirá	sentiría	**sienta**	**sintiera** *o* **sintiese**	**sienta**
	nosotros/as	sentimos	sentíamos	sentimos	sentiremos	sentiríamos	**sintamos**	**sintiéramos** *o* **sintiésemos**	**sintamos**
	vosotros/as	sentís	sentíais	sentisteis	sentiréis	sentiríais	**sintáis**	**sintierais** *o* **sintieseis**	sentid
	Uds., ellos/as	**sienten**	sentían	**sintieron**	sentirán	sentirían	**sientan**	**sintieran** *o* **sintiesen**	**sientan**
66 ser [(4)] siendo sido	yo	**soy**	**era**	**fui**	seré	sería	**sea**	**fuera** *o* **fuese**	
	tú/vos	**eres/sos**	**eras**	**fuiste**	serás	serías	**seas**	**fueras** *o* **fueses**	**sé**
	Ud., él, ella	**es**	**era**	**fue**	será	sería	**sea**	**fuera** *o* **fuese**	**sea**
	nosotros/as	**somos**	**éramos**	**fuimos**	seremos	seríamos	**seamos**	**fuéramos** *o* **fuésemos**	**seamos**
	vosotros/as	**sois**	**erais**	**fuisteis**	seréis	seríais	**seáis**	**fuerais** *o* **fueseis**	sed
	Uds., ellos/as	**son**	**eran**	**fueron**	serán	serían	**sean**	**fueran** *o* **fuesen**	**sean**
67 soler [(1)] (o:ue) soliendo solido	yo	**suelo**	solía	*soler is a defective verb (it does not exist in certain tenses)			**suela**		
	tú/vos	**sueles/solés**	solías				**suelas**		
	Ud., él, ella	**suele**	solía				**suela**		
	nosotros/as	solemos	solíamos				solamos		
	vosotros/as	soléis	solíais				soláis		
	Uds., ellos/as	**suelen**	solían				**suelan**		
68 tañer [(4)] **tañendo** tañido	yo	taño	tañía	tañí	tañeré	tañería	taña	**tañera** *o* **tañese**	
	tú/vos	tañes/tañés	tañías	tañiste	tañerás	tañerías	tañas	**tañeras** *o* **tañeses**	tañe/tañé
	Ud., él, ella	tañe	tañía	**tañó**	tañerá	tañería	taña	**tañera** *o* **tañese**	taña
	nosotros/as	tañemos	tañíamos	tañimos	tañeremos	tañeríamos	tañamos	**tañéramos** *o* **tañésemos**	tañamos
	vosotros/as	tañéis	tañíais	tañisteis	tañeréis	tañeríais	tañáis	**tañerais** *o* **tañeseis**	tañed
	Uds., ellos/as	tañen	tañían	**tañeron**	tañerán	tañerían	tañan	**tañeran** *o* **tañesen**	tañan
69 tener [(1,4)] (e:ie) teniendo tenido	yo	**tengo**	tenía	**tuve**	**tendré**	**tendría**	**tenga**	**tuviera** *o* **tuviese**	
	tú/vos	**tienes/tenés**	tenías	**tuviste**	**tendrás**	**tendrías**	**tengas**	**tuvieras** *o* **tuvieses**	**ten/tené**
	Ud., él, ella	**tiene**	tenía	**tuvo**	**tendrá**	**tendría**	**tenga**	**tuviera** *o* **tuviese**	**tenga**
	nosotros/as	tenemos	teníamos	**tuvimos**	**tendremos**	**tendríamos**	**tengamos**	**tuviéramos** *o* **tuviésemos**	**tengamos**
	vosotros/as	tenéis	teníais	**tuvisteis**	**tendréis**	**tendríais**	**tengáis**	**tuvierais** *o* **tuvieseis**	tened
	Uds., ellos/as	**tienen**	tenían	**tuvieron**	**tendrán**	**tendrían**	**tengan**	**tuvieran** *o* **tuviesen**	**tengan**

Verb conjugation tables

Infinitivo Gerundio Participio	Pronombres personales	INDICATIVO Presente	Pretérito imperfecto	Pretérito perfecto simple	Futuro simple	Condicional simple	SUBJUNTIVO Presente	Pretérito imperfecto	IMPERATIVO
70 **teñir** [1, 4] (e:i) **tiñendo** teñido	yo	**tiño**	teñía	teñí	teñiré	teñiría	**tiña**	**tiñera** o **tiñese**	
	tú/vos	**tiñes**/teñís	teñías	teñiste	teñirás	teñirías	**tiñas**	**tiñeras** o **tiñeses**	**tiñe**/teñí
	Ud., él, ella	**tiñe**	teñía	**tiñó**	teñirá	teñiría	**tiña**	**tiñera** o **tiñese**	**tiña**
	nosotros/as	teñimos	teñíamos	teñimos	teñiremos	teñiríamos	**tiñamos**	**tiñéramos** o **tiñésemos**	**tiñamos**
	vosotros/as	teñís	teñíais	teñisteis	teñiréis	teñiríais	**tiñáis**	**tiñerais** o **tiñeseis**	teñid
	Uds., ellos/as	**tiñen**	teñían	**tiñeron**	teñirán	teñirían	**tiñan**	**tiñeran** o **tiñesen**	**tiñan**
71 **tocar** [2] (c:qu) tocando tocado	yo	toco	tocaba	**toqué**	tocaré	tocaría	**toque**	tocara o tocase	
	tú/vos	tocas/tocás	tocabas	tocaste	tocarás	tocarías	**toques**	tocaras o tocases	toca/tocá
	Ud., él, ella	toca	tocaba	tocó	tocará	tocaría	**toque**	tocara o tocase	**toque**
	nosotros/as	tocamos	tocábamos	tocamos	tocaremos	tocaríamos	**toquemos**	tocáramos o tocásemos	**toquemos**
	vosotros/as	tocáis	tocabais	tocasteis	tocaréis	tocaríais	**toquéis**	tocarais o tocaseis	tocad
	Uds., ellos/as	tocan	tocaban	tocaron	tocarán	tocarían	**toquen**	tocaran o tocasen	**toquen**
72 **torcer** [1, 2] (o:ue) (c:z) torciendo torcido, **tuerto**	yo	**tuerzo**	torcía	torcí	torceré	torcería	**tuerza**	torciera o torciese	
	tú/vos	**tuerces**/torcés	torcías	torciste	torcerás	torcerías	**tuerzas**	torcieras o torcieses	**tuerce**/torcé
	Ud., él, ella	**tuerce**	torcía	torció	torcerá	torcería	**tuerza**	torciera o torciese	**tuerza**
	nosotros/as	torcemos	torcíamos	torcimos	torceremos	torceríamos	**torzamos**	torciéramos o torciésemos	**torzamos**
	vosotros/as	torcéis	torcíais	torcisteis	torceréis	torceríais	**torzáis**	torcierais o torcieseis	torced
	Uds., ellos/as	**tuercen**	torcían	torcieron	torcerán	torcerían	**tuerzan**	torcieran o torciesen	**tuerzan**
73 **traer** [4] **trayendo** traído	yo	**traigo**	traía	**traje**	traeré	traería	**traiga**	**trajera** o **trajese**	
	tú/vos	traes/traés	traías	**trajiste**	traerás	traerías	**traigas**	**trajeras** o **trajeses**	trae/traé
	Ud., él, ella	trae	traía	**trajo**	traerá	traería	**traiga**	**trajera** o **trajese**	**traiga**
	nosotros/as	traemos	traíamos	**trajimos**	traeremos	traeríamos	**traigamos**	**trajéramos** o **trajésemos**	**traigamos**
	vosotros/as	traéis	traíais	**trajisteis**	traeréis	traeríais	**traigáis**	**trajerais** o **trajeseis**	traed
	Uds., ellos/as	traen	traían	**trajeron**	traerán	traerían	**traigan**	**trajeran** o **trajesen**	**traigan**
74 **valer** [4] valiendo valido	yo	**valgo**	valía	valí	**valdré**	**valdría**	**valga**	valiera o valiese	
	tú/vos	vales/valés	valías	valiste	**valdrás**	**valdrías**	**valgas**	valieras o valieses	vale/valga
	Ud., él, ella	vale	valía	valió	**valdrá**	**valdría**	**valga**	valiera o valiese	**valga**
	nosotros/as	valemos	valíamos	valimos	**valdremos**	**valdríamos**	**valgamos**	valiéramos o valiésemos	**valgamos**
	vosotros/as	valéis	valíais	valisteis	**valdréis**	**valdríais**	**valgáis**	valierais o valieseis	valed
	Uds., ellos/as	valen	valían	valieron	**valdrán**	**valdrían**	**valgan**	valieran o valiesen	**valgan**
75 **vencer** [2] (c:z) venciendo vencido	yo	**venzo**	vencía	vencí	venceré	vencería	**venza**	venciera o venciese	
	tú/vos	vences/vencés	vencías	venciste	vencerás	vencerías	**venzas**	vencieras o vencieses	vence/vencé
	Ud., él, ella	vence	vencía	venció	vencerá	vencería	**venza**	venciera o venciese	**venza**
	nosotros/as	vencemos	vencíamos	vencimos	venceremos	venceríamos	**venzamos**	venciéramos o venciésemos	**venzamos**
	vosotros/as	vencéis	vencíais	vencisteis	venceréis	venceríais	**venzáis**	vencierais o vencieseis	venced
	Uds., ellos/as	vencen	vencían	vencieron	vencerán	vencerían	**venzan**	vencieran o venciesen	**venzan**

Verb conjugation tables

Infinitivo / Gerundio / Participio	Pronombres personales	INDICATIVO					SUBJUNTIVO		IMPERATIVO
		Presente	Pretérito imperfecto	Pretérito perfecto simple	Futuro simple	Condicional simple	Presente	Pretérito imperfecto	
76 venir (1,4) (e:ie) **viniendo** venido	yo	**vengo**	venía	**vine**	**vendré**	**vendría**	**venga**	**viniera** o **viniese**	
	tú/vos	**vienes/venís**	venías	**viniste**	**vendrás**	**vendrías**	**vengas**	**vinieras** o **vinieses**	**ven/vení**
	Ud., él, ella	**viene**	venía	**vino**	**vendrá**	**vendría**	**venga**	**viniera** o **viniese**	**venga**
	nosotros/as	venimos	veníamos	**vinimos**	**vendremos**	**vendríamos**	**vengamos**	**viniéramos** o **viniésemos**	**vengamos**
	vosotros/as	venís	veníais	**vinisteis**	**vendréis**	**vendríais**	**vengáis**	**vinierais** o **vinieseis**	venid
	Uds., ellos/as	**vienen**	venían	**vinieron**	**vendrán**	**vendrían**	**vengan**	**vinieran** o **viniesen**	**vengan**
77 ver (4) viendo **visto**	yo	**veo**	**veía**	**vi**	veré	vería	**vea**	viera o viese	
	tú/vos	ves	**veías**	viste	verás	verías	**veas**	vieras o vieses	ve
	Ud., él, ella	ve	**veía**	**vio**	verá	vería	**vea**	viera o viese	**vea**
	nosotros/as	vemos	**veíamos**	vimos	veremos	veríamos	**veamos**	viéramos o viésemos	**veamos**
	vosotros/as	veis	**veíais**	visteis	veréis	veríais	**veáis**	vierais o vieseis	ved
	Uds., ellos/as	ven	**veían**	vieron	verán	verían	**vean**	vieran o viesen	**vean**
78 volcar (1,2) (o:ue) (c:qu) volcando volcado	yo	**vuelco**	volcaba	**volqué**	volcaré	volcaría	**vuelque**	volcara o volcase	
	tú/vos	**vuelcas/volcás**	volcabas	volcaste	volcarás	volcarías	**vuelques**	volcaras o volcases	**vuelca/volcá**
	Ud., él, ella	**vuelca**	volcaba	volcó	volcará	volcaría	**vuelque**	volcara o volcase	**vuelque**
	nosotros/as	volcamos	volcábamos	volcamos	volcaremos	volcaríamos	**volquemos**	volcáramos o volcásemos	**volquemos**
	vosotros/as	volcáis	volcabais	volcasteis	volcaréis	volcaríais	**volquéis**	volcarais o volcaseis	volcad
	Uds., ellos/as	**vuelcan**	volcaban	volcaron	volcarán	volcarían	**vuelquen**	volcaran o volcasen	**vuelquen**
79 yacer (4) yaciendo yacido	yo	**yazco** o **yazgo** o **yago**	yacía	yací	yaceré	yacería	**yazca** o **yazga** o **yaga**	yaciera o yaciese	
	tú/vos	yaces/yacés	yacías	yaciste	yacerás	yacerías	**yazcas** o **yazgas** o **yagas**	yacieras o yacieses	**yace** o **yaz/yacé**
	Ud., él, ella	yace	yacía	yació	yacerá	yacería	**yazca** o **yazga** o **yaga**	yaciera o yaciese	**yazca** o **yazga** o **yaga**
	nosotros/as	yacemos	yacíamos	yacimos	yaceremos	yaceríamos	**yazcamos** o **yazgamos** o **yagamos**	yaciéramos o yaciésemos	**yazcamos** o **yazgamos** o **yagamos**
	vosotros/as	yacéis	yacíais	yacisteis	yaceréis	yaceríais	**yazcáis** o **yazgáis** o **yagáis**	yacierais o yacieseis	yaced
	Uds., ellos/as	yacen	yacían	yacieron	yacerán	yacerían	**yazcan** o **yazgan** o **yagan**	yacieran o yaciesen	**yazcan** o **yazgan** o **yagan**
80 zambullir (4) **zambullendo** zambullido	yo	zambullo	zambullía	zambullí	zambulliré	zambulliría	zambulla	**zambullera** o **zambullese**	
	tú/vos	zambulles/zambullís	zambullías	zambulliste	zambullirás	zambullirías	zambullas	**zambulleras** o **zambulleses**	zambulle/zambullí
	Ud., él, ella	zambulle	zambullía	**zambulló**	zambullirá	zambulliría	zambulla	**zambullera** o **zambullese**	zambulla
	nosotros/as	zambullimos	zambullíamos	zambullimos	zambulliremos	zambulliríamos	zambullamos	**zambulléramos** o **zambullésemos**	zambullamos
	vosotros/as	zambullís	zambullíais	zambullisteis	zambulliréis	zambulliríais	zambulláis	**zambullerais** o **zambulleseis**	zambullid
	Uds., ellos/as	zambullen	zambullían	**zambulleron**	zambullirán	zambullirían	zambullan	**zambulleran** o **zambullesen**	zambullan

El voseo en América Latina

México

Cuba

Honduras

Guatemala

Nicaragua

El Salvador

Costa Rica

Panamá

Venezuela

Colombia

Ecuador

Perú

Bolivia

Paraguay

Chile

Argentina

Uruguay

N
W — E
S

SCALE

0   500   1000 Miles

0   500   1000 Kilometers

Quesada Pacheco, Miguel Ángel (2002):
"El Español de América". San José, Costa Rica,
Editorial Tecnológica de Costa Rica, p.106.

Glosario combinatorio

In English, you can see somebody *in the flesh*, while in Spanish, you can see someone **en carne y hueso** (lit. *in flesh and bone*). In English, you are *fed up **with** something or someone* and in Spanish, you can be **harto *de* algo o alguien**. This glossary provides a sample of word combinations like these, which will help expand your vocabulary by giving a glimpse of the common, established word combinations that native speakers use. It will also help you with your grammar by showing that certain verbs take different prepositions from the ones used in English, or that no preposition is needed at all.

These types of word combinations are commonly called *collocations*. Not all word combinations are considered collocations. Many are free combinations with countless options. For example, the phrase **un hermano joven** is a free combination. The adjective, **joven**, can be used together with countless nouns (**un niño joven, una muchacha joven, un profesor joven, una estudiante joven,** etc.). **Un hermano gemelo**, on the other hand, is a collocation. The use of the adjective **gemelo** is restricted to a limited number of nouns.

Lexical collocations usually involve nouns, adjectives, adverbs, and verbs. *Grammatical* collocations usually involve a main word and a preposition or a dependent clause.

Compare these other examples. You can look up these collocations in the glossary!

Free combinations	Collocations
caer en un pozo, caerse en la calle	caer en la cuenta
surtir gasolina, surtir un medicamento	surtir efecto
va al cine, va a la escuela	va de veras

Compare these Spanish and English collocations:

Spanish collocations	English collocations
fuego lento	*low heat*
trabajar **en** algo	*to work **on** something*
hacer la vista gorda	*to turn a blind eye*

How to find collocations in this glossary

Follow these simple rules:

• If there is a noun, look under the noun.

• If there are two nouns, look under the first.

• If there is no noun, look under the adjective.

• If there is no adjective, look under the verb.

In addition, common expressions that are introduced by prepositions are also cross-listed under the preposition.

Abbreviations

adj.	adjective	*f.*	feminine noun	*p.p.*	past participle
adv.	adverb	*fam.*	familiar	*prep.*	preposition
algn	alguien	*form.*	formal	*pron.*	pronoun
Am. L.	Latin America	*m.*	masculine noun	sb	somebody
Arg.	Argentina	*Méx.*	Mexico	sth	something
Esp.	Spain	*pl.*	plural	*v.*	verb

a *prep.* to, at

a altas horas de la madrugada/noche in the wee/small hours of the morning/night

a base de with/of; on the basis of (Esto está hecho a base de verduras.)

a bordo de onboard

a caballo on horseback

a cada rato every so often/often

a cámara lenta in slow motion

a cambio de algo in return for sth

a cargo de, al cargo de in charge of

a causa de because of

a ciegas blindly

a ciencia cierta for sure

a como dé lugar, ~ como diera lugar however possible

a costa de at the expense of (No veo la gracia de reírse a costa de los demás.)

a cucharadas by the spoonful

a cuenta on account

a dieta on a diet

a escondidas secretly, behind sb's back

a eso de around (a certain time)

a este fin, ~ tal fin with this aim

a falta de lacking/for lack of

a fin de with the purpose of

a fin de cuentas, al final de cuentas, al fin y al cabo after all

a fondo in depth

a fuego lento on/at/over low heat

a fuerza de by virtue of/because of

a futuro in the future (Deberíamos evaluar los proyectos a futuro.)

a gusto at ease/at home/comfortable (No me siento a gusto aquí.)

a gusto del consumidor *fam.* however you like

a la carrera, ~ las carreras in a hurry

a la derecha (de) to/on the right (Gira a la derecha. Da un paso a la derecha, por favor.)

a la fuerza by force

a la hora de when it is time to (A la hora de escribir, prefiero hacerlo en un lugar tranquilo.)

a la izquierda (de) to/on the left (Si miran a la izquierda, verán uno de los mayores atractivos de la ciudad. María está a la izquierda de Juana.)

a la larga in the long run (Estoy segura de que Pedro, a la larga, comprenderá que es por su bien.)

a la manera de algn sb's way (Hagámoslo a mi manera.)

a la primera de cambio at the first opportunity

a la sombra de in the shadow of

a la vez at the same time

a la vista in sight, on view

a las mil maravillas wonderfully (¡Todo salió a las mil maravillas!)

a lo grande luxuriously, in style (Festejaremos tu cumpleaños a lo grande.)

a lo largo de throughout

a lo loco in a crazy way (Está gastando el dinero a lo loco.)

a lo mejor probably, likely

a los efectos de algo in order to do sth

a manera de algo by way of / as (Traje este dibujo a manera de ejemplo.)

a mano by hand

a (la) mano close at hand (¿Tienes tu planilla a (la) mano?)

a más tardar at the very latest

a mediados de in mid-/by mid- (Voy a retirar las cosas que faltan a mediados del mes que viene.)

a medias halfway/half

a medida que as/when/only (Resolveremos los problemas a medida que vayan surgiendo.)

a menos que unless

a menudo often

a modo de by way of, as (Usó su cuaderno a modo de pantalla.)

a no ser que if not

a nombre de algn addressed to sb

a oscuras in the dark

a partir de from, starting from

a pesar de in spite of

a pie on foot

a poco de algo shortly after sth

a por *Esp.* to go and get (Iré a por ti en dos horas.)

a primera hora, ~ última hora first thing/ at the last moment

a principios de at the beginning of (Supongo que nos mudaremos a principios de año.)

a propósito on purpose, by the way (¡Lo hiciste a propósito! Ayer me encontré con Mario; a propósito, me preguntó cuánto vale tu coche.)

a prueba de impervious to sth, resistant (¿Tu reloj es a prueba de agua?)

a raíz de as a result of

a rayas striped

a razón de at a rate of

a regañadientes reluctantly

a renglón seguido immediately afterward (Las instrucciones se detallan a renglón seguido.)

a sabiendas knowingly

a salvo safe (Mi familia está a salvo, gracias a Dios.)

a simple vista to the naked eye

a solas alone (No me gusta quedarme a solas con ella.)

a su regreso on one's return

a su vez in turn

a tiempo on time

a todo volumen very loud, at full volume

a tontas y a locas without thinking

a través de through

a trueque de in exchange for

a veces sometimes (A veces me olvido de hacer las compras.)

a ver all right, now, so; let's see (A ver, ¿qué está pasando acá? Llamémoslo a ver qué nos dice.)

a vista de pájaro bird's-eye view

al aire libre outdoors

al descubierto exposed

al día up-to-date

al día siguiente, al otro día on the next day

al efecto, a tal efecto, ~ este efecto for a particular purpose

al fin at last

al final at/in the end (Al final, ¿qué vas a hacer en las vacaciones?)

al igual que just as

al lado de beside, next to

al menos at least

al mismo tiempo que at the same time as

al pie de la letra literally, exactly (Siguieron nuestras instrucciones al pie de la letra.)

al pie de la montaña, ~ los pies de la montaña at the foot of the mountain

al principio at first

al (poco) rato shortly after

al través diagonally

abastecer *v.* to supply

abastecer a algn de algo, ~ a algn con algo to supply sb with sth

abogar *v.* to defend, to fight for

abogar por algn/algo, ~ en favor de algn/ algo to defend sb, to fight for sth (El defensor abogó a favor de los inmigrantes. Toda su vida abogó por los derechos de los trabajadores.)

abstenerse *v.* to abstain

abstenerse de algo to refrain/abstain from sth

abuelo/a *m./f.* grandfather/grandmother

abuelo/a materno/a, ~ paterno/a maternal/paternal grandfather/mother

abundar *v.* to abound

abundar de algo, ~ en algo to abound in

aburrirse *v.* to be bored

aburrirse con algo/algn, ~ de algo/algn, ~ por algo to be bored with sb/sth, to get tired of sb/sth

abusar *v.* **1** to impose, to take advantage, to abuse

abusar de algo to impose on sb (Silvia abusó de mi amabilidad.)

abusar de algn to abuse sb

2 to make excessive use

abusar de algo to make excessive use of sth (No debes abusar del alcohol.)

abuso *m.* abuse, breach

abuso de autoridad, ~ de confianza abuse of authority, breach of trust

acabar *v.* to finish, to end

acabar con algo, ~ de hacer algo to finish sth off, to have just done sth (Acaba con eso de una vez. Acabo de despertarme.)

acabar por algo to end up doing sth (Este niño acabará por volverme loca.)

nunca acabar never-ending (Esto es un asunto de nunca acabar.)

acceder *v.* **1** to gain access, to access

acceder a algo to gain access to sth; to access sth (He podido acceder a los datos.)

2 to obtain

acceder a un cargo/trabajo to obtain/get a position/job

3 to agree

acceder a algo to agree to sth (Lucas accedió a los deseos de Sara.)

acción *f.* action

acción de armas, ~ de guerra military action

acción de gracias thanksgiving

buena/mala acción good/bad deed

novela/película de acción action novel/movie

pasar a la acción, entrar en ~ to go into action

poner algo en acción to put/turn sth into action

aceptar *v.* to accept

aceptar algo, ~ a algn (como algo) to accept sth/sb (Susana aceptó la oferta. ¿Acepta a Sandro como su legítimo esposo?)

acercarse *v.* to approach

acercarse a algo/algn to approach sth/sb

acercarse algo to come closer (Se acercan las fiestas.)

aconsejar *v.* to advise

aconsejar (algo) a algn to advise/give advice to sb

acordar *v.* **1** to agree

acordar algo con algn to agree to sth with sb

2 to award

acordar algo a algn *Am. L.* to award sth to sb (El premio le fue acordado por unanimidad.)

acordarse *v.* to remember

acordarse de algo/algn to remember sth/sb

acostumbrado/a *adj.* **1** used to

estar acostumbrado/a a algo to be used to sth

2 trained

estar bien/mal acostumbrado/a to be well/badly trained (Lo que pasa es que nos tienen mal acostumbrados.)

acostumbrar *v.* **1** to get used (to)

acostumbrar a algn a algo to get sb used to sth

2 to be accustomed

acostumbrar algo, ~ a algo to be accustomed to/in the habit of doing sth

acostumbrarse *v.* to get used (to)

acostumbrarse a algo/algn to get used to sth/sb

acudir *v.* **1** to attend

acudir a algo to attend sth (Debo acudir a la cita.)

2 to come

acudir en ayuda de algn to come to sb's aid/to help sb (Nadie acudió en su ayuda.)

3 to resort to

acudir a algo/algn to resort to sth/sb (No es necesario acudir a la violencia. Tuvo que acudir a su hermano mayor.)

acuerdo *m.* **1** agreement

estar de acuerdo con algo/algn to agree with sth/sb

estar de acuerdo en algo to agree on sth

hacer algo de común acuerdo to do sth by mutual agreement

llegar a un acuerdo, alcanzar un ~, ponerse de ~ to reach an agreement

2 accordance

de acuerdo con according to, complying with (Procederemos de acuerdo con lo hablado.)

acusar *v.* **1** to blame, to charge

acusar a algn de algo to blame/charge sb for sth

2 to show signs of (Su mirada acusaba cansancio.)

3 to acknowledge

acusar recibo de algo to acknowledge receipt of sth

acuse *m.* acknowledgement

acuse de recibo acknowledgement of receipt (¿Me traes el acuse de recibo firmado, por favor?)

adaptarse *v.* to adapt

adaptarse a algo to adapt to sth

adelantado/a *adj.* advanced

por adelantado in advance

adelante *adv.* forward

más adelante farther

además *adv.* besides

además de apart from (Además de feo, es maleducado. Además de ser sabroso, es muy saludable.)

administración *f.* administration; management

administración de negocios, ~ de empresas business administration

administración pública civil/public service

admirar *v.* to admire

admirar algo, ~ a algn to admire sth/sb

admirarse *v.* to be amazed

admirarse de algo to be amazed at sth

adolecer *v.* to suffer from

adolecer de algo to suffer from sth

advertir *v.* to warn

advertir a algn de algo, ~ a algn que to warn sb of sth, to warn sb that (¿Has advertido a Juan de los riesgos? Te advierto que es muy peligroso.)

aficionado/a *m./f.* fan

ser aficionado a algo to be a fan of sth

agarrarse *v.* **1** to hold on

agarrarse a algo, ~ de algo to hold on to sth

2 to have a fight

agarrarse con algn to have a fight with sb

agencia *f.* agency

agencia de colocaciones employment agency

agencia de contactos dating agency

agencia de prensa/noticias news/press agency

agencia de publicidad advertising agency

agencia de viajes travel agency

agencia inmobiliaria real estate agency

agradar *v.* to appeal

agradarle algo/algn a algn to be to sb's liking (Me agrada tu actitud. Me agrada la nueva maestra.)

agradecer *v.* to be grateful, to thank

agradecerle algo a algn, agradecer a algn por algo to thank sb for sth (Te agradezco el regalo. Le agradezco por haberme ayudado.)

agua *f.* water

agua bendita holy water

agua corriente running water

agua de lluvia rainwater

agua de mar seawater

agua dulce fresh water

agua mineral (con/sin gas) mineral water (carbonated/still)

agua oxigenada peroxide

agua potable drinking water

agua salada salt water

aguas servidas/residuales sewage

como agua para chocolate *Méx.* furious

estar con el agua al cuello to be up to one's neck in problems

estar más claro que el agua to be crystal clear

ahora *adv.* now

por ahora for the time being

aire *m.* air

aire acondicionado air conditioning (Las habitaciones del hotel tienen aire acondicionado.)

al aire libre outdoors

en el aire on air

salir al aire to go out on the air (Nuestro programa sale al aire martes y jueves a las 6 de la tarde.)

alcance *m.* range

de corto/largo alcance short/long-range

alcanzar *v.* **1** to reach

alcanzar algo, ~ a algn to reach sth, to catch up with sb

2 to pass

alcanzar algo a algn to pass sth to sb

3 to manage to

alcanzar a hacer algo to manage to do sth (No alcancé a terminar el trabajo.)

alegrar *v.* to bring happiness

alegrar a algn to make sb happy

alegrarse *v.* to be glad, to be happy

alegrarse de algo, ~ por algo/algn to be glad about sth, to be happy for sb

alejarse *v.* to move away

alejarse de algo/algn to move away from sth/sb

alimentar *v.* to feed

alimentar a algo/algn to feed sth/sb

alimentar algo to fuel sth (Sus comentarios alimentaron el clima de violencia.)

alimentarse *v.* to live, to run

alimentarse con algo, ~ de algo to live/run on sth

allí *adv.* there

de allí en adelante from then on

alma *f.* soul

alegrarse en el alma to be overjoyed

alma de la fiesta life/soul of the party

alma gemela soul mate

como (un) alma en pena like a lost soul

con toda el alma with all one's heart

del alma darling/dearest/best (Es mi amigo del alma.)

llegarle a algn al alma to be deeply touched by sth (Las palabras del sacerdote me llegaron al alma.)

sentir algo en el alma to be terribly sorry about sth (Siento en el alma haber sacado ese tema.)

alrededor *adv.* around

alrededor de around

altura *f.* height

estar a la altura de las circunstancias to rise to the occasion

quedar a la altura de algo/algn to be equal to sth/sb

amanecer *v.* to dawn; to wake up/begin at dawn/to start the day (¿A qué hora amanece? ¿Amaneciste bien? Hoy amaneció lloviendo.)

amanecer *m.* dawn, daybreak

amenazar *v.* to threaten

amenazar (a algn) con algo to threaten (sb) with sth

amigo/a *m./f.* friend

amigo/a íntimo/a intimate friend

mejor amigo/a best friend

(no) ser amigo/a de algo to (not) be fond of sth (No soy muy amigo de las fiestas.)

amo/a *m./f.* master/mistress

ama de casa homemaker

ama de llaves housekeeper

animarse *v.* to feel like

animarse a hacer algo to feel like doing sth, to dare (to) do sth

aniversario *m.* anniversary

aniversario de boda, ~ de bodas wedding anniversary

ansioso/a *adj.* eager

estar ansioso/a de algo, estar ~ por algo to be anxious/eager to do sth (Estoy ansioso de verlos. Está muy ansiosa por los exámenes.)

anteojos *m.* glasses

anteojos bifocales bifocals

anteojos de sol, ~ oscuros sunglasses

antes *adv.* before

antes de before (Antes de ir a la escuela se detuvo en la plaza.)

antes de Jesucristo, ~ de Cristo BC

antes (de) que before (Llámalo antes de que sea tarde. Lo haré antes que me olvide.)

antes que nada, ~ de nada first of all

antojarse *v.* to feel like

antojársele algo a algn to feel like/crave sth

apartarse *v.* to separate

apartarse de algo/algn to separate from sth/sb

apasionarse *v.* to have a passion for

apasionarse con algo, ~ por algo/algn to have a passion for sth/sb (Mi hijo está apasionado con su nueva guitarra. Marcos está apasionado por esa mujer.)

apetecer *v.* to feel like

apetecerle algo a algn *Esp.* to feel like (Me apetece un paseo.)

apiadarse *v.* to take pity

apiadarse de algo/algn to take pity on sth/sb

apoderarse *v.* to seize

apoderarse de algo/algn to seize sth/sb (El ejército se apoderó del edificio. El miedo se apoderó de todos nosotros.)

apoyar *v.* **1** to rest

apoyar algo en un lugar to rest sth somewhere

2 to support

apoyar a algn (en algo) to support sb (in sth)

apoyar algo to support sth (El presidente apoyó nuestra causa inmediatamente.)

apoyarse *v.* to lean, to base

apoyarse en algo, ~ contra algo to lean on sth (Ellos se apoyan mucho en su familia. Se apoyó contra la pared porque estaba mareado.)

aprender *v.* to learn

  aprender a hacer algo to learn to do sth (Debes aprender a escuchar a los demás.)

apresurarse *v.* to hurry

  apresurarse a hacer algo to hurry to do sth (Se apresuraron a dejar todo como estaba.)

  apresurarse en algo to hurry to do sth (Me parece que se apresuró en su respuesta.)

apropiarse *v.* to appropriate

  apropiarse de algo to appropriate sth

aprovechar *v.* to make the best of

aprovecharse *v.* to take advantage

  aprovecharse de algo/algn to take advantage of sth/sb

apuro *m.* rush (¿Por qué tanto apuro para terminar el examen?)

  poner en un apuro to put in a predicament/tight spot (Su comentario me puso en un apuro.)

  tener apuro to be in a hurry; to be urgent (Tengo mucho apuro./El proyecto tiene apuro.)

aquí *adv.* here

  por aquí around here

arrepentirse *v.* to regret

  arrepentirse de algo to regret sth

arriba *adv.* up

  de arriba abajo up and down, from top to bottom

  para arriba y para abajo back and forth

arriesgarse *v.* to risk

  arriesgarse a algo to risk sth/to take a risk

ascender *v.* to rise

  ascender a algo/algn to promote, to be promoted (El coronel ascendió a general rápidamente. Parece que van a ascender a Pérez.)

  ascender a un lugar to rise to/reach a place or position

asegurarse *v.* to assure, secure

  asegurarse de algo to assure oneself of sth

asistir *v.* **1** to attend, to witness

  asistir a algo to attend sth, to witness sth (Asistió a la clase. Asistimos a la coronación del rey.)

  2 to assist

  asistir a algn to assist sb (Asistió al médico durante la operación.)

asombrarse *v.* to be amazed

asombrarse ante algo, ~ con algo, ~ de algo, ~ por algo to be amazed at sth

aspirar *v.* to hope, to seek

  aspirar a algo to hope to become sth (Sandra aspira a convertirse en una cantante famosa.)

  aspirar a la mano de algn to seek sb's hand in marriage

asustado/a *adj.* afraid

  estar asustado/a de to be afraid of

asustar *v.* to frighten

  asustar a algn (con algo) to frighten sb (with sth)

asustarse *v.* to get frightened

  asustarse ante algo, ~ con algo, ~ de algo, ~ por algo to get frightened about sth

atención *f.* attention

  llamar la atención to attract/call attention to

  llamarle a algn la atención sobre algo to draw sb's attention to sth

  prestar atención a algo/algn to pay attention to sth/sb

atender *v.* to pay attention

  atender a algo/algn to pay attention to/ to attend to sth/sb (Debes atender a tus hijos. No atiende a sus deberes.)

atreverse *v.* to dare

  atreverse a algo, ~ con algo to dare to do sth

  atreverse con algn to dare or take on sb

auge *m.* peak

  en auge flourishing

aumento *m.* increase

  aumento de algo increase in sth (Estoy preocupada por su aumento de peso. La policía tomará medidas por el aumento de la violencia en los estadios de fútbol.)

  pedir un aumento, solicitar un ~ to ask for a pay raise

  sufrir un aumento, experimentar un ~ to experience an increase in sth (Los servicios de luz y de gas sufrirán fuertes aumentos. El precio del petróleo experimentó un aumento por tercera semana consecutiva.)

auxilio *m.* help; aid (in an emergency)

  acudir en auxilio de algn to go to sb's aid

  pedir auxilio to ask for help

prestar auxilio to help

primeros auxilios first aid

avance *m.* advance; news summary

avance científico, ~ de la ciencia scientific breakthrough

avance informativo news summary

ave *f.* bird

ave de mal agüero bird of ill omen

ave de paso rolling stone

ave de rapiña bird of prey

aventurarse *v.* to venture

aventurarse a algo, ~ en algo to venture to do sth

aventurarse por un lugar to venture somewhere

avergonzarse *v.* to be ashamed

avergonzarse de algo/algn, ~ por algo/algn to be ashamed of sth/sb

avisar *v.* to inform

avisar a algn de algo to let sb know about sth

ayudar *v.* to help

ayudar (a algn) a algo, ~ con algo, ~ en algo to help (sb) with sth

B

bajar *v.* to go down

bajar a hacer algo to come down to do sth (¿Cuándo bajará a saludarnos?)

bajar algo de algo, ~ a algn de algo to get sb/sth down from sth (Baja la muñeca de la repisa, por favor. ¿Bajarías al niño del caballo?)

bajar de algo to get off sth (Los pasajeros ya están bajando del avión.)

banda *f.* strip

banda de sonido, ~ sonora soundtrack

banda magnética magnetic strip

basarse *v.* to base

basarse en algo to be based in/on sth

base *f.* base

a base de with/of; on the basis of (Esto está hecho a base de verduras.)

con base en based on

bastar *v.* to be enough

bastar algo (para), ~ con algo (para), ~ a algn algo to be enough (for) (Basta que yo diga algo para que mis hijos hagan

lo contrario. Basta con marcar 911 para obtener ayuda. A mí me basta con tu palabra.)

bastar y sobrar to be more than enough (Con eso basta y sobra.)

batalla *f.* battle

batalla campal pitched battle

dar batalla to cause a lot of problems/grief (Los problemas de salud le han dado mucha batalla.)

de batalla everyday (Son mis zapatos de batalla.)

beca *f.* grant, scholarship

beca de estudios study grant

beca de investigación research grant

boda *f.* wedding, a special anniversary

bodas de oro golden (wedding) anniversary; golden jubilee

bodas de plata silver (wedding) anniversary; silver jubilee

bolsa *f.* **1** bag

bolsa de agua caliente hot-water bottle

bolsa de (la) basura garbage bag

bolsa de compras, ~ de la compra shopping bag

bolsa de dormir sleeping bag

bolsa de hielo ice pack

2 stock market

bolsa de cereales grain exchange

bolsa de comercio commodities exchange

bolsa de valores stock exchange

bordo *m.*

a bordo de onboard

bote *m.* boat

bote a remos, ~ de remos rowboat

bote inflable inflatable dinghy/raft

bote salvavidas lifeboat

brecha *f.* breach, opening

abrir brecha to break through

brecha generacional generation gap

estar en la brecha to be in the thick of things

seguir en la brecha to stand one's ground

brindar *v.* **1** to toast

brindar (con algo) por algo/algn, ~ a la salud de algn to toast sb/sth

2 to give, to provide

brindar algo a algn to provide sb with sth
(Le brindaremos toda la información
que necesite.)

broma *f.* joke

celebrar una broma to laugh at a joke

de broma, en ~ as a joke (No le creas,
lo dijo en broma. ¿Te asustaste?
¡Era de broma!)

**fuera de broma, fuera de bromas, bromas
aparte** all joking apart/aside

**hacerle una broma a algn, gastarle una ~
a algn** to play a joke on sb

ni en broma no way

no estar para bromas to not be in the
mood for jokes

bromear *v.* to joke

bromear (con algn) sobre algo to joke
about sth (with sb)

bueno/a *adj.* good

por las buenas o por las malas one way or
the other

burlar *v.* to evade

burlar (a) algo/algn to evade, to get
around, to slip past (El delincuente burló
la vigilancia y huyó. Marcia burló a su
jefe con engaños.)

burlarse *v.* to make fun of

burlarse de algo/algn to make fun
of sth/sb

C

caballo *m.* horse

a caballo on horseback

caballo de carrera, ~ de carreras racehorse

caballo de fuerza horsepower

caber *v.* to fit

caber en algo, ~ por un lugar to fit
somewhere, to fit through sth

no caber en uno/a mismo/a to be
beside oneself

cabo *m.* end

atar los cabos sueltos to tie up the
loose ends

dejar cabos sueltos to leave loose ends

llevar algo a cabo to carry sth out

caer *v.* **1** to fall

caer de bruces to fall on one's face

2 to stoop

caer bajo to stoop low

3 to show up

caer de improviso to show up without
warning

4 caer bien/mal, ~ en gracia to be liked/
disliked, to be fond of

cajero/a *m./f.* cashier

cajero automático, ~ permanente ATM

calidad *f.* quality

calidad de vida standard of living

cámara *f.* camera

cámara de cine movie camera

cámara de video video camera

cámara digital digital camera

cámara fotográfica camera

en cámara lenta, a ~ lenta in slow motion

cambiar *v.* to change

cambiar algo a algo, ~ algo en algo to
change sth into sth (Necesito cambiar
estos dólares a pesos. ¿Me puede cambiar
estos bolívares en pesos?)

cambiar algo por algo to change sth
for sth

cambiar de algo to change sth
(¡Cámbiate de ropa!)

cambiarle algo a algo to change sth in sth
(El relojero le cambió la pila a mi reloj.)

cambiarle algo a algn to exchange
sth with sb

cambio *m.* **1** change

a la primera de cambio at the first
opportunity

cambio de aires, ~ de ambiente change
of scenery

2 exchange

a cambio de algo in return for sth

en cambio on the other hand
(El vestido azul es feo; el rojo, en
cambio, es hermoso.)

en cambio de instead of

camino *m.* way; road

**abrir el camino, allanar el ~, preparar
el ~** to pave the way

camino vecinal minor/country road

**estar camino a algo, estar ~ de algo, estar
en el ~ a algo** on the way to (Me crucé
con él camino al dentista. La vi camino
del club. Esa tienda queda en el camino a
la escuela.)

estar en camino to be on one's way (Ya deben estar en camino, no los llames por teléfono.)

por el camino on the way (Vamos, te lo diré por el camino.)

candelero *m.* candlestick

estar en el candelero to be in the limelight

cansado/a *adj.* tired

estar cansado/a de algo to be tired of sth

cansarse *v.* to get tired

cansarse con algo, ~ de algo/algn to get tired of sth/sb (Mi madre se cansa con la rutina. ¿No te cansas de repetir siempre lo mismo?)

capaz *adj.* capable

ser capaz de algo to be capable of sth

cara *f.* face

cara a cara face to face

echar en cara algo a algn to reproach sb for sth (No me eches en cara lo que has hecho por mí.)

carecer *v.* to lack

carecer de algo to lack sth

cargar *v.* **1** to load

cargar a algn de algo to burden sb with sth

cargar algo con algo to load sth with sth

cargar algo en algo to load sth into/onto sth

2 to carry

cargar con algo to carry sth

3 to charge

cargar contra algn to charge against sb

cargo *m.* **1** charge

a cargo de, al ~ de in charge of

hacerse cargo de algo/algn to take charge of sth, to take care of sb

2 position, job

cargo público public office

desempeñar un cargo to hold a position

carne *f.* **1** flesh

carne de cañón cannon fodder

de carne y hueso quite human

en carne propia by personal experience

en carne y hueso in the flesh

2 meat

carne de res beef/red meat

echar toda la carne al asador, poner

toda la ~ al asador to put all one's eggs in one basket

carrera **1** race

a la carrera, a las carreras in a hurry

carrera armamentista, ~ armamentística, ~ de armamentos arms race

carrera contra reloj race against time

2 university course of study

seguir una carrera, hacer una ~ to study for a degree

3 career

hacer carrera to carve out/make a career

casarse *v.* to marry; to get married

casarse con algn to marry sb

casarse en primeras/segundas nupcias to marry/remarry

casarse por poder to get married by proxy

caso *m.* **1** case

caso fortuito misadventure

en caso contrario otherwise

en caso de que in case of

en cualquier caso, en todo ~ in any case

no hay/hubo caso there is/was no way

no tiene caso to be pointless

ser un caso perdido to be a hopeless case

2 attention

hacer caso a algn to pay attention to sb

hacer caso de algo to take notice of sth

hacer caso omiso de algo to ignore (Hizo caso omiso de todas las advertencias de su familia.)

casualidad *f.* chance

de casualidad, por ~ by accident

causa *f.* cause

a causa de, por ~ de because of

causa perdida lost cause

ceder *v.* **1** to hand over

ceder algo a algn to hand sth over to sb

2 to give up

ceder en algo to give sth up

3 to give in

ceder a algo, ~ ante algo/algn to give in to sth/sb

celebrar *v.* to celebrate

celebrar algo, ~ por algo to celebrate sth

ceniza *f.* ash

reducir algo a cenizas to reduce sth to ashes

centro *m.* center

  centro comercial shopping mall

  centro de gravedad center of gravity

  centro de mesa centerpiece

  ser el centro de las miradas to have all eyes on sb

ceñirse *v.* to stick to

  ceñirse a algo to stick to sth (Deberías ceñirte al reglamento.)

cerca *adv.* close

  cerca de near, close to

cerciorarse *v.* to make certain

  cerciorarse de algo to make certain of sth

cerco *m.* siege

  cerco policial police cordon

  levantar el cerco, alzar el ~ to raise the siege

  poner cerco a algo to lay siege to sth

cesar *v.* to cease

  cesar de hacer algo to cease doing sth (No cesa de insultarnos.)

  sin cesar nonstop (Se trabajó sin cesar en el rescate de los mineros.)

charlar *v.* to chat

  charlar (con algn) de algo, ~ (con algn) sobre algo to chat about sth (with sb)

cheque *m.* check

  cheque de viaje, ~ de viajero traveler's check

  cheque en blanco blank check

  cheque sin fondos, ~ sobregirado overdrawn check

chocar(se) *v.* to collide

  chocarse con algo/algn, ~ contra algo/algn to collide/crash against sth/sb

ciencia *f.* science

  a ciencia cierta for sure

  ciencias ocultas occultism

  de ciencia ficción science fiction

  no tiene ninguna ciencia there is nothing difficult about it

cinturón *m.*

  cinturón de seguridad seat belt, safety belt

cita *f.* date, appointment

  cita a ciegas blind date

  concertar una cita to arrange an appointment

  darse cita to arrange to meet (Se dieron cita en la puerta de la iglesia.)

  pedir cita to make an appointment

  tener una cita con algn to have an appointment/date with sb

citarse *v.* to make an appointment

  citarse con algn to make an appointment with sb

coincidir *v.* to agree

  coincidir con algn en algo to agree with sb on sth

comentar *v.* to discuss

  comentar algo con algn to discuss sth with sb

comenzar *v.* to begin

  comenzar a hacer algo to begin to do sth (¿Cuándo comenzarás a trabajar?)

  comenzar por algo to begin by sth (Puedes comenzar por pedirme disculpas.)

compadecerse *v.* to take pity on

  compadecerse con algn, ~ de algn to take pity on sb

comparar *v.* to compare

  comparar algo con algo, ~ algo/algn a algo/algn, ~ a algn con algn to compare sth/sb with sth/sb else (Estuve comparando tu camiseta con la mía y la tuya es más grande. Si comparas un triángulo a un cuadrado, te darás cuenta. ¡Deja de compararme con mi hermano!)

compararse *v.* to compare oneself

  compararse con algn to compare oneself to sb

compensar *v.* to compensate

  compensar (a algn) con algo to compensate (sb) by doing sth (¿Me compensarás con un rico pastel?)

  compensar (a algn) por algo to compensate (sb) for sth (Decidimos compensarlo por su buen desempeño en el trabajo.)

competir *v.* **1** to compete

  competir con algn por algo, ~ contra algn por algo to compete with/against sb for sth **2** to rival

  competir en algo to compete in sth (Los dos artefactos compiten en calidad y precio.)

complacer *v.* to please

  complacer a algn con algo, ~ a algn en algo to please sb with sth

complacerse *v.* to take pleasure in

complacerse con algo, ~ de algo, ~ en algo to take pleasure in sth (Nos complace con su visita, Su Señoría. Mi hermana se complace en ayudar a los demás.)

completo/a *adj.* complete

por completo completely

componerse *v.* to be made up

componerse de algo to be made up of sth

comprar *v.* to buy

comprar algo a algn to buy sth from/for sb

comprometerse *v.* 1 to commit

comprometerse a algo, ~ en algo to commit to do sth

2 to get engaged

comprometerse con algn to get engaged to sb

comunicar *v.* 1 to inform, to communicate

comunicar algo a algn to communicate sth to sb

2 comunicar algo con algo to connect sth with sth (Este corredor comunica las habitaciones con la sala.)

comunicarse *v.* to communicate

comunicarse (con algn) mediante algo, ~ (con algn) por algo to communicate (with sb) through sth (Ellos se comunican mediante gestos. Trataré de comunicarme por señas.)

con *prep.* with

con base en based on

con buen pie, ~ el pie derecho off to a good start (Creo que no comenzaron con buen pie. Nuestra relación comenzó con el pie derecho.)

con dureza harshly

con el fin de with the purpose of

con erguida frente, ~ la frente bien alta, ~ la frente en alto, ~ la frente levantada with one's head held high

con este fin with this aim

con frecuencia frequently, often (¿Vienes a este bar con frecuencia?)

con la guardia baja with one's guard down

con las propias manos with one's own hands

con mal pie, ~ el pie izquierdo badly

con miras a with the purpose of

con motivo de due to, because of

con permiso with your permission/excuse me

con respecto a regarding

con tal (de) que provided that, as long as

con toda el alma with all one's heart

con toda seriedad seriously

con todas las de la ley rightly (No puedes quejarte, ella te ha ganado con todas las de la ley.)

concentrarse *v.* to concentrate

concentrarse en algo to concentrate on sth

condenar *v.* to condemn

condenar a algn a algo to condemn sb to sth (Su mal carácter lo condenó a la soledad.)

condenar a algn por algo to condemn sb for sth (Lo condenaron por robo.)

confiar *v.* 1 to entrust

confiar algo a algn to entrust sb with sth (Le confío la seguridad de mis hijos.)

2 to trust

confiar en algo/algn to trust sth/sb

3 to confide

confiar algo a algn to confide sth to sb (Me confió sus más oscuras intenciones.)

conflicto *m.* conflict

conflicto armado/bélico armed conflict

conflicto de ideas clash of ideas

conflicto de intereses conflict of interests

conflicto laboral labor dispute

conflicto limítrofe border dispute

conformarse *v.* to be happy

conformarse con poco to be happy with very little

confundir *v.* to mix up

confundir algo con algo, ~ a algn con algn to mix sth/sb up with sth/sb else

confundirse *v.* to mistake

confundirse con algo/algn to mistake sth/sb for sth/sb else

confundirse de algo to get sth wrong (Susana se confundió de coche.)

confundirse en algo to make a mistake in sth

conocer *v.* to know

conocer a algn to know sb

conocer de algo to know about sth

consentir *v.* to agree

consentir algo (a algn) to allow (sb) to do sth (Les consienten todo a sus nietos.)

consentir en algo to agree to sth (El ministro consintió en apoyar al candidato.)

consiguiente *adj.* consequent

por consiguiente therefore

consistir *v.* **1** consist

consistir en algo to consist of sth (La prueba consiste en una serie de actividades prácticas.)

2 to consist of/lie in

consistir en algo to consist of sth (¿En qué consiste la gracia?)

constar *v.* **1** to be stated (La edad no consta en el documento.)

constarle a algn algo to be sure that (Me consta que la carta fue enviada.)

hacer constar/que conste to state (Hagamos constar que pagamos la multa.)

que conste for the record, to set the record straight (Que conste que yo nunca le mentí./Jamás le mentí, que conste.)

2 to consist of

constar de algo to consist of sth (El libro consta de una serie de capítulos.)

consultar *v.* to consult

consultar algo a algn, ~ algo con algn, ~ a algn sobre algo to consult about sth with sb

contar 1 to tell

contar algo a algn to tell sth to sb

2 to count

contar con algo/algn to count on sth/sb

contentarse *v.* to be pleased

contentarse con poco to be pleased with very little

contento/a *adj.* happy

estar contento/a con algo, estar ~ de algo, estar ~ por algo to be happy with/ about sth (Estamos contentos con los resultados. ¿Estás contenta de haber ido? Están contentos por la visita del gobernador.)

contestar *v.* to answer, to reply

contestar (a) algo, ~ algo a algn to answer sth to sb

contra *prep.* against

contra reembolso cash on delivery

contrario/a *adj.* opposite

de lo contrario if not/otherwise/on the contrary (Termina tu comida; de lo contrario, te quedarás sin postre.)

contribuir *v.* to contribute

contribuir a algo to contribute to sth (Yo contribuí al progreso de la empresa.)

contribuir con algo to contribute sth (Los vecinos contribuyeron con alimentos y ropa.)

control *m.* control

a control remoto, por ~ remoto by remote control (Funciona a control remoto. Eso se maneja por control remoto.)

control antidoping drug test

control de armas gun control

control de calidad quality control

convalecer *v.* to convalesce

convalecer de algo to convalesce from sth

convencer *v.* to persuade

convencer a algn de algo to persuade sb of sth

convencerse *v.* to believe, to accept

convencerse de algo to accept sth (Debes convencerte de que eso terminó.)

convenir *v.* **1** to agree on

a convenir negotiable (La remuneración es a convenir.)

convenir con algn en algo, ~ con algo to agree on sth with sb (Debo convenir con mi exmarido en los horarios de visita. Convenimos con el dictamen de la auditoría.)

2 to be advisable

convenir a uno algo to be good for sb (Me conviene esperar unos días.)

conversar *v.* to talk

conversar (con algn) de algo, ~ (con algn) sobre algo to talk about sth with sb

convertirse *v.* **1** to turn into

convertirse en algo/algn to turn into sth/ sb (Se convirtió en una persona despreciable.)

2 to convert

convertirse a algo to convert to sth (Se convirtió al cristianismo.)

convocar *v.* to call, to summon

  convocar a algn a algo, ~ a algn para algo to summon sb to sth

coro *m.* chorus

  hacerle coro a algn to back sb up

corredor(a) *m./f.* **1** runner

  corredor(a) de coches/automóviles race car driver

  corredor(a) de fondo long-distance runner

  corredor(a) de vallas hurdler

  2 agent

  corredor(a) de bolsa stockbroker

  corredor(a) de seguros insurance broker

cosa *f.* thing

  cualquier cosa anything

  no ser cosa de broma, no ser ~ de risa to not be a joke

  no ser cosa fácil to not be easy (Convencerlo no va a ser cosa fácil.)

  poca cosa hardly anything

costa *f.* coast, coastline

  a costa de at the expense of (No veo la gracia de reírse a costa de los demás.)

  costas expenses (Después del juicio, tuvo que pagar las costas judiciales.)

costar *v.* to cost

  costarle a uno algo to lose/to cost one/sb sth (Una pequeña distracción le costó el empleo.)

coste *m.* cost *Esp.*

costo *m.* cost *Am. L.*

costumbre *f.* habit

  como de costumbre, para no perder la ~ as always/usual (Olvidaste tu tarea, para no perder la costumbre. Llegó tarde, como de costumbre.)

  de costumbre usual (Nos vemos en el lugar de costumbre.)

  tener la costumbre de algo, tener algo por ~ to be in the habit of sth

crédito *m.* credit; loan

  a crédito on credit

  dar crédito a algn/algo to believe (No les dio crédito a mis palabras.)

creer *v.* to believe

  creer en algn/algo to believe in sb/sth

creerse *v.* to trust

  creerse de algn *Méx.* to trust sb

crisis *f.* crisis

  crisis cardíaca heart failure, cardiac arrest

  crisis de identidad identity crisis

  crisis de los cuarenta midlife crisis

  crisis energética energy crisis

  crisis nerviosa nervous breakdown

cuando *adv.* when

  cada cuando, de ~ en ~ from time to time

  cuando más, ~ mucho at the most

  cuando menos at the least

  cuando quiera whenever (Cuando quiera que llegue el momento.)

cuanto *adv.* as much as

  cuanto antes as soon as possible

  cuanto más let alone (Es un momento difícil para todos, cuanto más para su esposa.)

  en cuanto as soon (as) (Iré en cuanto pueda.)

  en cuanto a regarding (En cuanto a la inflación, estamos tomando todas las medidas necesarias.)

  por cuanto insofar as

cubierto/a *adj.* covered

  estar cubierto/a de algo, estar ~ por algo to be covered with sth

cucharada *f.* spoonful

  a cucharadas by the spoonful

cuenta *f.* **1** calculation

  a fin de cuentas, al fin de ~ after all

  hacer cuentas, sacar ~ to do calculations

  2 count

  caer en la cuenta de algo, darse ~ de algo to realize sth

  llevar la cuenta to keep count

  más de la cuenta too much (He comido más de la cuenta.)

  3 account

  a cuenta on account

  abrir/cerrar una cuenta to open/close an account

  cuenta a plazo fijo time deposit/fixed-term account

  cuenta corriente (de cheques) checking account

  cuenta de ahorros savings account

  4 consideration

  darse cuenta de algo to realize sth

tener algo en cuenta, tomar algo en ~ to take sth into account

cuidar *v.* to look after

cuidar algo, ~ a algn, ~ de algo/algn to look after sth/sb

cuidarse *v.* **1** to take care

cuidarse de algo/algn to take care of sth/sb

2 to avoid

cuidarse de algo to avoid doing sth (Cuídate de lo que dices por ahí.)

culpa *f.* fault

echarle la culpa de algo a algn to blame sb for sth

tener la culpa de algo to be sb's fault

culpar *v.* to blame

culpar a algn de algo, ~ a algn por algo to blame sb for sth

culto *m.* worship

rendir culto a algo/algn to worship sth/sb

cumplir *v.* to carry out, fulfill, keep

cumplir con algo/algn to keep (Yo siempre cumplo con mi palabra.)

D

dar *v.* **1** to find

dar con algo/algn to find sth/sb (No logro dar con él.)

2 to give

dar algo a algn to give sth to sb

dar de comer a algn to feed sb

3 to hit

dar algo contra algo to hit sth against sth

4 to face

dar a (algo) to face (sth) (Mi ventana da al jardín.)

de *prep.* of, from

de a each (Nos tocan de a cinco galletas cada una.)

de a ratos, ~ rato en rato from time to time

de acuerdo con according to (Procederemos de acuerdo con lo hablado.)

de allí en adelante from then on

de broma as a joke (¿Te asustaste? ¡Era de broma!)

de buen/mal modo, ~ buenos/malos modos in a good/bad way

de buena ley genuine (Es oro de buena ley.)

de buena/mala gana willingly/unwillingly

de buena/mala manera in a good/bad way

de carne y hueso quite human

de casualidad by accident

de ciencia ficción science fiction

de corto/largo alcance short-/long-range

de costumbre usual

de cualquier forma, ~ una u otra forma, ~ todas formas, ~ cualquier manera, ~ todas maneras, ~ cualquier modo, ~ todos modos anyway, in any case

de cuando en cuando from time to time

de derecha right-wing (Jamás votaré a un partido de derecha.)

de enfrente across the street

de entre semana working day (No puedo salir contigo de entre semana, tengo mucho trabajo.)

de esa manera in that way

de frente face-to-face

de golpe, ~ golpe y porrazo suddenly

de gusto for the fun of it

de izquierda left-wing (Sectores de izquierda se opusieron a la medida.)

de la derecha on the right (Me gusta el coche de la derecha.)

de la izquierda on the left (Busca en el cajón de la izquierda.)

de la mano hand in hand

de lo contrario if not/on the contrary/ otherwise (Termina tu comida; de lo contrario, te quedarás sin postre.)

de lujo luxury (Iván y Paola se alojarán en un hotel de lujo durante su luna de miel.)

de mala muerte lousy (No vayas a ese restaurante, es de mala muerte.)

de manera que so (that) (¿De manera que la decisión ya está tomada?)

de modo que in such a way that

de nada you're welcome

de ningún modo no way

de ninguna manera certainly not

de nuevo again

de pie standing (Ponte de pie cuando entre la maestra.)

de plano outright (Se negó de plano a participar en el negocio.)

de primera mano firsthand

de pronto suddenly

de propina for a tip (¿Cuánto has dejado de propina?)

de regreso a back at (¿Cuándo estarás de regreso a la oficina?)

de repente suddenly

de rodillas down on one's knees

de tal modo que, ~ modo que in such a way that (Estudió mucho, de tal modo que aprobó el examen. Ya es tarde, de modo que me voy a casa.)

de través *Méx.* diagonally

de un día para el otro overnight

de un golpe all at once

de una vez (por todas) once and for all

de veras really

de vez en cuando once in a while

de vista by sight (A su hermana la conocemos solo de vista.)

del alma darling/dearest/best (Es mi amigo del alma.)

del mismo modo, de igual modo in the same way

debajo *adv.* under

por debajo de under

debatir *v.* to discuss

debatir (con algn) sobre algo to discuss sth (with sb)

deber *v.* to owe

deber algo a algn to owe sth to sb

decidido/a *adj.* determined

estar decidido a algo to be determined to do sth

decidir *v.* to decide

decidir sobre algo to make a decision about sth

decidirse *v.* to decide, to make up one's mind

decidirse a hacer algo to decide to do sth

decidirse por algo to decide on sth

dedicar *v.* to devote, to dedicate

dedicar algo a algn to devote sth to sb (Debes dedicarle más tiempo a tu familia.)

dedicarse *v.* to devote oneself

dedicarse a algo to devote oneself to sth

defender *v.* to defend

defender algo, ~ a algn to defend sth/sb

defenderse *v.* to defend oneself

defenderse de algo/algn to defend oneself against sth/sb

degenerar *v.* to degenerate

degenerar en algo to degenerate/lead into sth

dejar *v.* **1** to stop

dejar de hacer algo to stop doing sth
2 to leave

dejar a algn to leave sb

dejar algo mucho que desear to leave much to be desired
3 to let, to allow

dejar a algn hacer algo to let sb do sth
4 to fail

dejar de hacer algo to give up/stop doing sth/to fail to do sth (No dejes de llamarme cuando llegues.)

delante *adv.* ahead

por delante ahead (Aún nos queda mucho por delante.)

por delante de in front of, opposite (Ayer pasé por delante de tu casa.)

deliberar *v.* to deliberate

deliberar sobre algo to deliberate on sth

delito *m.* crime

cometer un delito, incurrir en un ~ to commit a crime

demandar *v.* **1** to require (Esta tarea demanda mucha concentración.)
2 to sue

demandar por daños y perjuicios to sue for damages

demás *pron.* the rest

estar por demás hacer algo there is no point in doing sth

lo demás, los/las ~ the rest

por demás extremely (Te comportas de una manera por demás grosera.)

por lo demás apart from that

y demás and the like (Se aceptan perros, gatos y demás.)

demora *f.* delay

sin demora without delay

dentro *adv.* inside

por dentro de in, inside of

depender *v.* **1** to depend

depender de algo/algn to depend on sth/sb

2 to report

depender de algn to report to sb

derecha *f.* right

a la derecha (de) to/on the right (of) (Gira a la derecha. Da un paso a la derecha, por favor.)

de derecha right-wing (Jamás votaré a un partido de derecha.)

de la derecha on the right (Me gusta el coche de la derecha.)

descansar *v.* **1** to take a break

descansar de algo/algn to take a break from sth/sb (Necesitaba descansar de los niños por un día.)

2 to rest upon

descansar en algo, ~ sobre algo to rest upon sth (Su pierna descansaba sobre unas almohadas.)

desconfiar *v.* to mistrust

desconfiar de algo/algn to mistrust sth/sb

descubierto/a *adj.* uncovered

al descubierto exposed (Sus numerosas estafas quedaron al descubierto.)

desde *prep.* since

desde el principio, ~ un principio from the beginning

desear *v.* to wish

desear algo (a algn) to wish sb sth

desembocar *v.* to culminate

desembocar en algo to culminate in sth

deseoso/a *adj.* anxious/eager

estar deseoso/a de to be anxious/eager about

desgracia *f.* misfortune

por desgracia unfortunately

deshacerse *v.* to get rid

deshacerse de algo/algn to get rid of sth/sb

desistir *v.* to give up

desistir de algo, ~ en algo to give up sth (Desistió de vender su casa. Nunca desistió en su empeño por ser el mejor de la clase.)

despedir *v.* **1** to see off

despedir a algn to see sb off

2 to fire

despedir a algn to fire sb

despedirse *v.* to say goodbye

despedirse de algo/algn to say goodbye to sth/sb

desposeer *v.* to strip

desposeer a algn de algo to strip sb of sth

desprenderse 1 to let go

desprenderse de algo/algn to let go of sth/sb (Deberías desprenderte de los objetos que ya no usas.)

2 to emerge

desprenderse de algo to emerge from sth (Los datos se desprenden de una serie de encuestas.)

después *adv.* later

después de Jesucristo, ~ de Cristo AD

después de todo after all

después (de) que after, as soon as (Después de que hablé contigo, encendí el televisor.)

destinar *v.* to allocate

destinar algo a algo, ~ algo para algo to set sth aside for sth

detalle *m.* **1** detail

al detalle retail (Esa tienda vende al detalle.)

con todo detalle in great detail

dar detalles to go into details

entrar en detalles to go into details

2 little gift; nice gesture (Estuvo en París y me trajo un detallecito.)

¡Qué detalle! How thoughtful!

tener un detalle con algn to do sth nice for sb (¿Puedes creer que después de que lo ayudé tanto no tuvo ningún detalle conmigo?)

detenerse *v.* **1** to stop

detenerse a hacer algo to stop to do sth

2 to dwell

detenerse en algo to dwell on sth (Concéntrate en lo importante, no te detengas en detalles.)

detrás *adv.* behind

(por) detrás de behind, in the back of

devolver *v.* to return

devolver algo a algn to return sth to sb

día *m.* day

al día up-to-date

al día siguiente, al otro ~ the next day

de un día para otro overnight

día de por medio *Am. L.* every other day

día festivo public holiday

día hábil, ~ laborable working day

día tras día day after day

hoy en día nowadays

diente *m.* tooth

armado hasta los dientes armed to the teeth

diente de ajo garlic clove

diente de leche baby tooth

salirle los dientes a algn to be teething (¡Ya le está saliendo el primer dientito!)

dieta *f.* diet

dieta habitual staple diet

estar/ponerse a dieta to be/go on a diet

diferir *v.* **1** to differ

diferir de algo to differ from sth (Su nuevo trabajo difiere de los anteriores.)

2 to disagree

diferir de algn, ~ entre sí to disagree with sb

difícil *adj.* difficult

ser algn difícil to be difficult (Es una persona muy difícil.)

ser difícil de hacer to be difficult to do (Es una asignatura muy difícil de estudiar.)

Dios *m.* God

Dios mediante God willing

Dios mío/santo for Heaven's sake

por Dios for Heaven's sake

si Dios quiere God willing

dirigir *v.* to address

dirigir algo a algn to address sth to sb

dirigirse *v.* **1** to head for

dirigirse a un lugar to head for a place

2 to address

dirigirse a algn to address sb

discrepar *v.* to disagree

discrepar (con algn) en algo, ~ (con algn) sobre algo to disagree (with sb) on sth

disculparse *v.* to apologize

disculparse (ante/con algn) de algo, ~ (ante/con algn) por algo to apologize (to sb) for sth

discutir *v.* to argue

discutir con algn por algo, ~ con algn sobre algo to argue with sb about sth

discutirle algo a algn to argue sth with sb

disfrutar *v.* to enjoy

disfrutar de algo to enjoy sth

disgustado/a *adj.* annoyed

estar disgustado/a con algn, estar ~ por algo to be annoyed with sb/sth

disgustar *v.* to dislike

disgustarle algo/algn (a algn) to dislike sth/sb

disgustarse *v.* to get upset

disgustarse con algo, ~ por algo to get upset because of sth

disponer *v.* to possess

disponer de algo/algn to have sth/sb at one's disposal

disponerse *v.* to prepare

disponerse a hacer algo, ~ para hacer algo to prepare to do sth

dispuesto/a *adj.* willing

estar dispuesto/a a to be willing to

distanciarse *v.* to distance

distanciarse de algo/algn to distance oneself from sth/sb

distinguir *v.* **1** to differentiate

distinguir algo de algo to tell sth from sth else

2 to honor

distinguir a algn con algo to honor sb with sth

distinguirse *v.* to stand out

distinguirse en algo to stand out in sth

distinguirse por algo to stand out for sth

disuadir *v.* to dissuade

disuadir a algn con algo to dissuade sb with sth

disuadir a algn de algo to dissuade sb from sth

divorciarse *v.* to get divorced

divorciarse de algn to get divorced from sb

doler *v.* to hurt

dolerle a uno/a algo to have a pain somewhere (Me duele la cabeza.)

dominio *f.* **1** mastery

ser de dominio público to be public knowledge

tener dominio de uno/a mismo/a to have self-control

tener el dominio de algo to have command of sth

2 field

entrar en el dominio de algo to be in the
field of sth (Eso entra en el dominio de
la Economía.)

duda *f.* doubt

  sin duda without (a) doubt

dudar *v.* 1 to doubt

  dudar de algo/algn to doubt sth/sb

  2 to hesitate

  dudar en hacer algo to hesitate in
doing sth (No dudes en llamarme si
necesitas algo.)

dureza *f.* harshness

  con dureza harshly

E

echar *v.* 1 to dismiss/fire

  echar a algn to dismiss/fire sb

  2 to start

  echar a andar algo to start sth

  3 to miss

  **echar de menos algo, ~ de menos a
algn** to miss sth/sb

echarse *v.* to start

  echarse a hacer algo to start to do sth
(Los niños se echaron a llorar.)

edad *f.* age

  desde temprana edad from an early age

  edad adulta, mayoría de ~ adulthood

  edad escolar school age

  sacarse la edad, quitarse la ~ to take years
off one's age

  ser de edad to be elderly

  ser de edad madura, ser de mediana ~ to
be middle-aged

efectivo *m.* cash

  en efectivo (in) cash

efecto *m.* 1 effect

  efecto invernadero greenhouse effect

  efecto retroactivo backdated

  efecto secundario side effect

  efectos especiales/sonoros
special/sound effects

  en efecto in fact

  estar bajo los efectos de algo to be under
the influence of sth

  hacer efecto, tener ~ to take effect
(Esos medicamentos ya no me hacen
efecto. La nueva ley tendrá efecto a
partir del año próximo.)

surtir efecto to have an effect

  2 purpose

  a los efectos de algo in order to do sth

  al efecto, a tal ~, a este ~ for a
particular purpose

ejemplo *m.* example

  por ejemplo for example

embargo *m.* seizure/embargo

  sin embargo however

empeñarse *v.* to strive, to insist

  empeñarse en hacer algo to strive to
do sth, to insist on doing sth (Debes
empeñarte en lograr tus objetivos. Mi
padre se empeñó en que fuera a visitarlo.)

empezar *v.* to begin

  empezar a to begin to

  empezar por, ~ con to begin with

en *prep.* in, inside, on

  en algún momento at some
point, sometime

  en alguna parte somewhere

  en auge flourishing

  en broma as a joke (No le creas, lo
dijo en broma.)

  en buenas manos in good hands (Me
marcho, pero los dejo en buenas manos.)

  en cámara lenta in slow motion

  en cambio however

  en carne propia by personal experience

  en carne y hueso in the flesh

  en caso contrario otherwise

  en caso de que in case of

  en cierto modo in a way

  en contra (de) against (No tengo nada en
contra de tus compañeros de trabajo. Te
recomiendo no ponerte en su contra.)

  en cualquier caso, ~ todo caso in any case

  en cuanto as soon (as)

  en cuanto a regarding

  en cuanto a algo/algn as regards sth/
sb (En cuanto a la inflación, estamos
tomando todas las medidas necesarias.)

  en efectivo (in) cash

  en el aire on air

  en el futuro, ~ lo futuro in the future
(En el futuro, envía los trabajos por
correo electrónico. En lo futuro, sé más
organizado con los archivos.)

en especie, ~ especies in kind

en fin finally, well then (En fin, creo que eso es todo.)

en frente de in front of

en la margen derecha/izquierda on the right/left bank (En la margen izquierda del río hay más árboles que en la margen derecha.)

en lontananza *form.* in the distance

en (propia) mano hand delivery

en nombre de algo/algn in the name of sth/sb

en pie up (awake), on one's feet, standing, valid (Estuve en pie todo el día. Lo único que quedó en pie fue la antigua capilla. ¿Sabes si la oferta sigue en pie?)

en pie de guerra ready for war

en (un) principio in the beginning

en pro o en contra (de), ~ pro y ~ contra for or against (Hay muchas opiniones en pro y en contra de nuestra propuesta.)

en punto o'clock/on the dot

en razón de because of (No debes discriminar en razón de la edad o la raza de las personas.)

en resumen all in all/in summary

en seguida right away

en suma in short

en torno a about (El argumento de la película gira en torno a las relaciones amorosas.)

en vez de, ~ lugar de, ~ cambio de instead of

en virtud de in virtue of

en vista de que in view of the fact that

enamorado/a *adj.* in love

estar enamorado/a de algn to be in love with sb

enamorarse *v.* to fall in love

enamorarse de algo/algn to fall in love with sth/sb

encantado/a *adj.* glad/enchanted

estar encantado de to be glad about/ pleased with

encantar *v.* to love, to really like; to enchant/put a spell on

encantarle a algn algo to love sth (Me encantan tus zapatos.)

encargar *v.* to ask

encargar algo a algn to ask sb to do sth (Me encargó una botella de vino. Le encargamos a José que cuidara de nuestras plantas.)

encargarse *v.* to take care

encargarse de algo to take care of sth

encariñarse *v.* to get attached

encariñarse con algo/algn to get attached to sth/sb

encima *adv.* on top

encima de on top of, on

por encima de over

encomendar *v.* to entrust

encomendar algo a algn to entrust sth to sb (Le encomendaron el sector administrativo.)

encontrar *v.* to find

encontrar algo, ~ a algn to find sth/sb

encontrarse *v.* to meet

encontrarse con algn to meet sb

enemigo/a *adj.* enemy

ser enemigo/a de algo to be against sth (Soy enemigo de la violencia.)

enemistado/a *adj.* estranged

estar enemistado/a con algn to be estranged from sb

energía *f.* energy, power

energía atómica atomic power

energía eólica wind energy

energía hidráulica water power

energía nuclear nuclear energy

energía renovable renewable energy

energía solar solar energy

enfadarse *v.* to get angry

enfadarse con algn por algo to get angry at sb for sth

enfermar *v.* **1** to make ill

enfermar de algo *Esp.* to get sick

2 to drive mad *Am. L.* (¡Me enferma esa actitud!)

enfermarse *v.* to get sick

enfermarse de algo *Am. L.* to get sick

enfrentar *v.* to confront

enfrentar a algn con algn to bring sb face-to-face with sb

enfrentar algo, ~ a algn to face sth/sb

enfrentarse *v.* to confront

enfrentarse a algo to face sth

enfrentarse a algn, ~ con algn to confront sb

enfrente *adv.* **1** opposite
de enfrente across the street
enfrente de in front of, opposite
2 in front
enfrente de algo in front of sth

enojar *v.* to anger
enojar a algn algo to make sb angry

enojarse *v.* to get angry
enojarse con algn por algo to get angry at sb for sth

enorgullecerse *v.* to be proud
enorgullecerse de algo/algn, ~ por algo to be proud of sth/sb

enseguida *adv.* immediately
(Te llamaré enseguida.)

enseñar *v.* **1** to teach
enseñar algo a algn to teach sth to sb
2 to show
enseñar algo a algn to show sth to sb

entender *v.* to understand
entender algo, ~ a algn to understand sth/sb
entender de algo to know all about sth
entenderle algo a algn to understand sth sb does (Discúlpame, pero no te entiendo la letra.)

entenderse *v.* **1** to communicate
entenderse con algn to communicate with sb (Se entiende con su primo por señas.)
2 to get along
entenderse con algn to get along with sb (¡Qué suerte que los chicos se entienden!)
3 to deal
entenderse con algn to deal with sb (Es mejor entenderse con el encargado.)

enterarse *v.* to hear, to find out
enterarse de algo to find out about sth

entero/a *adj.* whole
por entero completely

entrar *v.* **1** to go into
entrar a algo *Am. L.* to go into a place (Nunca he entrado a ese cine.)
entrar en algo to go into sth (Entremos en ese banco. No quiere entrar en razón.)
2 to enter
entrar en algo to enter sth (Entramos en una nueva etapa.)

3 to start
entrar a hacer algo to start to do sth (¿A qué hora entras a trabajar?)
entrar como algo to start as sth (Quieren que entre a la editorial como traductora.)

entre *prep.* between
entre horas between meals (No comas golosinas entre horas.)

entregarse *v.* **1** to devote oneself
entregarse a algo/algn to devote oneself to sth/sb
2 to give
entregarse a algo/algn to give oneself over to sth/sb

entristecerse *v.* to grow sad
entristecerse por algo, ~ con algo, ~ a causa de algo to grow sad because of sth

entrometerse *v.* to meddle
entrometerse en algo to meddle in sth

entusiasmarse *v.* to get excited
entusiasmarse por algo, ~ con algo/algn to get excited about sth/sb

enviar *v.* to send
enviar a algn por algo/algn to send sb out for sth/sb
enviar algo a algn to send sth to sb

envidiar *v.* to envy
envidiar algo a algn to envy sb because of sth

equivocarse *v.* to be wrong, to make a mistake
equivocarse en algo, ~ con algo/algn to be wrong/to make a mistake about sth/sb

escalera *f.* ladder, staircase
escalera caracol, ~ de caracol, ~ espiral spiral staircase
escalera de emergencia fire escape
escalera de mano ladder
escalera mecánica escalator

escandalizarse *v.* to be shocked
escandalizarse por algo to be shocked about sth

esconderse *v.* to hide
esconderse de algo/algn to hide from sth/sb

escondido/a *adj.* hidden
a escondidas secretly, behind sb's back

escribir *v.* to write

escribir a máquina to type

escribir algo a algn to write sth to sb

escribir sobre algo to write about sth

escribirse *v.* to write

escribirse con algn to write to each other

escuchar *v.* to hear

escuchar algo de algn, ~ algo sobre algn to hear sth about sb

esforzarse *v.* to strive

esforzarse en algo, ~ por algo to strive to do sth

eso *pron.* that

a eso de around (Llegué a eso de las ocho.)

por eso that's why

especializarse *v.* to major, to specialize

especializarse en algo to major/specialize in sth

especie *f.* 1 kind

en especie, en especies in kind

ser una especie de algo to be a sort of

2 species

especie en peligro (de extinción) endangered species

especie humana human race

especie protegida protected species

especular *v.* to speculate

especular sobre algo to speculate about sth

esperar *v.* 1 to wait

esperar algo, ~ a algn to wait for sth/sb

2 to hope (Espero que no llueva.)

estación *f.* station

estación de autobuses, ~ de ómnibus bus station

estación de bomberos fire station

estación de policía police station

estación de tren, ~ de trenes train station

estación del metro, ~ del subterráneo subway station

estafar *v.* to defraud/con/rip off

estafar (algo) a algn to defraud sb (out of sth)

estrella *f.* star

estrella de cine movie star

estrella de mar starfish

estrella en ascenso rising star

estrella fugaz shooting star

tener buena/mala estrella to be (born) lucky/unlucky

ver (las) estrellas to see stars

estudiar *v.* to study

estudiar algo to study sth

estudiar para algo to study for sth

evitar *v.* to avoid

evitar algo, ~ a algn to avoid sth/sb

exaltarse *v.* to get worked up

exaltarse por algo to get worked up about sth

exhortar *v.* to urge

exhortar a algn a hacer algo to urge sb to do sth (Los exhortó a continuar con su tarea.)

exigir *v.* to demand

exigir algo a algn to demand sth from sb

exponer *v.* 1 to expose

exponer algo a algo, ~ a algn a algo to expose sth/sb to sth (Es una tela muy delicada, no debes exponerla al sol.)

2 to explain, to describe

exponer algo a algn to explain sth to sb (Marcelo le expuso el problema claramente.)

exponerse *v.* to expose oneself

exponerse a algo to expose oneself to sth (No sé por qué te expones a esos peligros.)

extrañar *v.* to miss

extrañar algo, ~ a algn to miss sth/sb

extrañarse *v.* to be surprised

extrañarse de algo to be surprised at sth

F

fácil *adj.* easy

ser fácil de hacer to be easy to do (Es muy fácil de convencer.)

falta *f.* 1 lack

a falta de lacking/for lack of

echar algo en falta to be lacking (Aquí lo que se echa en falta es interés por el trabajo.)

falta de algo lack of sth

falta de educación bad manners

falta de pago nonpayment

2 fail

sin falta without fail

3 mistake

falta de ortografía spelling mistake

faltar *v.* to be missing

faltarle algo a algn, ~ algn a algn to be in
want of sth/sb (A ese muchacho le falta un
objetivo en la vida. Le falta un amigo que lo
aconseje.)

familia *f.* family

de buena familia from a good family

familia de acogida foster family

familia numerosa large family

familia política in-laws

sentirse como en familia to feel at home

tener familia to have children (Mi prima
tuvo familia la semana pasada.)

venirle/ser de familia to run in the family

familiarizarse *v.* to become familiar

familiarizarse con algo to become familiar
with sth

fascinar *v.* to fascinate

fascinar a algn to fascinate sb (Me fascinan
los cuentos de terror.)

felicitar *v.* to congratulate

felicitar a algn por algo to congratulate sb
on sth

fiarse *v.* to trust

fiarse de algo/algn to trust sth/sb

fijarse *v.* to notice

fijarse en algo/algn to notice sth/sb

fin *m.* 1 end

al fin, por ~ at last

al fin y al cabo after all

el fin del mundo the end of the world

en fin finally, well then

fin de semana weekend

poner fin a algo to put an end to sth

por fin finally

2 purpose

a este fin, a tal ~, con este ~ with this aim

con el fin de, a ~ de with the purpose of

el fin de algo the purpose of sth

**sin fines de lucro, sin fines
lucrativos** not-for-profit

un fin en sí mismo an end in itself

final *m.* end

al final at/in the end

fondo *m.* depth

a fondo in depth

forma *f.* 1 shape

en plena forma in top form

estar en forma, mantenerse en ~
to be/keep fit

tomar forma to take shape

2 way

**de cualquier forma, de una ~ o de otra,
de todas formas** anyway, in any case

forma de pago method of payment

forma de ser the way sb is

fortuna *f.* fortune

amasar una fortuna, hacer una ~ to make
a fortune

por fortuna fortunately

probar fortuna to try one's luck

frecuencia *f.* frequency

con frecuencia frequently, often (¿Vienes a
este bar con frecuencia?)

frente *f.* 1 forehead

**con erguida frente, con la ~ bien alta,
con la ~ en alto, con la ~ levantada** with
one's head held high

de frente, frente a ~ face-to-face

2 *m.* front

el frente de algo the front of sth

estar al frente de algo to be in charge
of sth

hacer frente a algo/algn to face up to
sth/sb

hacer un frente común to form a
united front

3 *adv.* opposite

frente a in front of, opposite

fuego *m.* fire

a fuego lento on/at/over low heat

**abrir fuego contra algo/algn, abrir ~
sobre algo/algn** to open fire on sth/sb

estar entre dos fuegos to be between a rock
and a hard place

fuego a discreción fire at will

fuegos artificiales, ~ de artificio fireworks

jugar con fuego to play with fire

prender fuego a algo, pegar ~ a algo to
set sth on fire

sofocar el fuego to put out the fire

fuera *adv.* outside

fuera de out/outside of

por fuera de out/outside of

fuerza *f.* strength, force

a fuerza de by (dint of)

a la fuerza by force

fuerza bruta brute force

fuerza de gravedad force of gravity

fuerza de trabajo workforce

fuerza de voluntad willpower

fuerza pública, fuerzas del orden, fuerzas de orden público police

por fuerza necessarily

por fuerza mayor, por causas de ~ mayor force majeure

fundarse *v.* to base

fundarse en algo to be based on sth (¿En qué se fundan tus sospechas?)

futuro *m.* future

con/sin futuro sth/sb with good/no prospects (Es una profesión sin futuro. Ese es un muchacho con futuro.)

en el futuro, en lo ~, a ~ in the future (En el futuro, envía los trabajos por correo electrónico. En lo futuro, sé más organizado con los archivos. Deberíamos evaluar los proyectos a futuro.)

futuro cercano, ~ próximo near future

no tener ningún futuro to have no future (Con esta crisis, nuestra empresa no tiene ningún futuro.)

G

gana *f.* desire

de buena/mala gana willingly/unwillingly

tener ganas de hacer algo, sentir ~ de hacer algo to feel like doing sth

ganar *v.* to win, to beat

ganar a algn en algo to beat sb in sth (No quiero jugar contigo, siempre me ganas en todo.)

ganar a algn para algo to win sb over to sth (Su intención es ganar al directorio para nuestro proyecto.)

general *adj.* general

por lo general in general

genio *m.* **1** temper

tener buen/mal genio, estar de buen/mal ~ to be even-/bad-tempered

2 genius

ser un genio con algo, ser un genio de algo to be a genius at/very talented in sth (María es un genio con la pelota. Juan es un genio de las letras.)

gestión *f.* **1** process; procedure (Estoy haciendo las gestiones para abrir una tienda de ropa.)

2 management

gestión de proyectos project management

3 (*pl.*) negotiations

golpe *m.* **1** knock, blow

de golpe, de ~ y porrazo suddenly

de un golpe all at once

2 punch, hit

golpe bajo hit below the belt

golpe de efecto dramatic effect

golpe de estado coup d'état

golpe de fortuna, ~ de suerte stroke of luck

gozar *v.* to enjoy

gozar de algo to enjoy sth (Mi abuela goza de buena salud, gracias a Dios.)

gracia *f.* grace

no verle la gracia a algo to not find sth funny (No le veo la gracia a sus chistes.)

grande *adj.* big, large

a lo grande luxuriously, in style (Festejaremos tu cumpleaños a lo grande.)

guardia *f.* guard

bajar la guardia to lower one's guard

con la guardia baja with one's guard down

estar de guardia to be on duty/on call

guardia de seguridad security guard

guardia municipal, ~ urbana police/municipal guard

guiarse *v.* to follow

guiarse por algo to follow sth (Nos guiamos por un antiguo mapa.)

gustar *v.* to like

gustar de algo, ~ a uno algo/algn to like sb/sth

gusto *m.* **1** taste

a gusto del consumidor *fam.* however you like

hacer algo a gusto, hacer algo al ~ to do sth as you please

tener buen/mal gusto to have good/bad taste

tener gusto a algo to taste of sth

2 pleasure

a gusto at ease (No me siento
a gusto aquí.)

con mucho gusto with pleasure

**darle el gusto a algn, hacerle el ~ a
algn** to indulge sb

de gusto, por ~ for the fun of it

mucho gusto, tanto ~ nice to meet you

tener el gusto de algo to be pleased
to do sth

**tomarle el gusto a algo, agarrarle el ~ a
algo** to get to like sth

H

habituarse *v.* to get used to
habituarse a algo to get used to sth

hablar *v.* to talk
hablar a algn to talk to sb
**hablar acerca de algo/algn, ~ de algo/
algn, ~ sobre algo/algn** to talk about
sth/sb
hablar de más to talk too much
ni hablar no way (¿Lo harías? ¡Ni hablar!)

hacer *v.* to do
hacer algo por algn to do sth for sb

hacerse *v.* to become
hacerse de algo/algn to become of sb/sth
(¿Qué se hizo del coche que tenías? No
sé qué se hizo de Juan, hace años que no
lo veo.)

harto/a *adj.* fed up
estar harto/a de to be fed up with

hasta *prep.* until
hasta ahora, ~ la fecha, ~ el momento so far
hasta entonces until then
hasta que until (Hasta que llegue a casa,
no estaré tranquilo.)
hasta tanto until such time as
no... hasta not until

hermano/a *m./f.* brother/sister
**hermano/a gemelo/a, hermano/a
mellizo/a** twin brother/sister
hermano/a mayor/menor older/younger
brother/sister
medio/a hermano/a half brother/sister

hijo/a *m./f.* son/daughter
**como cualquier hijo de vecino, como
todo ~ de vecino** like everybody else
hijo/a adoptivo/a adopted son/daughter

hijo/a ilegítimo/a illegitimate
son/daughter
hijo/a único/a only child

hincapié *m.* emphasis
hacer hincapié en algo to emphasize sth

hora *f.* hour; time
a altas horas de la madrugada/noche in
the wee/small hours of the morning/night
a la hora de when it is time to
(A la hora de escribir, prefiero hacerlo en
un lugar tranquilo.)
a primera hora, a última ~ first thing, at
the last moment
dar la hora, decir la ~ to tell the time
entre horas between meals (No
comas golosinas entre horas.)
ser hora de to be time to
ya ser hora de to be about time (Ya era
hora de que volvieras.)

horario *m.* schedule
horario de trabajo work schedule

horno *m.* oven
horno de microondas microwave oven

huelga *f.* strike
declararse en huelga to go on strike
estar de huelga, estar en ~ to be on strike
huelga de brazos caídos sit-down strike
huelga de hambre hunger strike

huir *v.* to run away, to flee
huir de algo/algn to run away from sth/sb
huirle a algn to avoid sb

I

idea *f.* idea
hacerse a la idea de algo to come to terms
with sth

idéntico/a *adj.* identical
ser idéntico/a a algn to be identical to sb

igual *adj.* equal
al igual que just as
da igual que it doesn't matter
igual a algo/algn, ~ que algo/algn the
same as sth/sb (Mi brazalete es igual al
tuyo. Es igual que su madre.)
igual de algo the same as (Está igual de
alta que la última vez que la vi.)
**ser igual algo que algo, dar ~ algo que
algo** (two or more things) to be equal/
the same

ilusionado/a *adj.* hopeful

    estar ilusionado/a con to be hopeful for

ilusionarse *v.* to be excited

    ilusionarse con algo/algn to be excited about sth/sb

impedir *v.* to prevent

    impedir a algn hacer algo to prevent sb from doing sth

importar *v.* to care

    importarle algo a algn to care about sth

impuesto *m.* tax

    evasión de impuestos tax evasion

    impuesto a/sobre la renta income tax

    impuesto al valor agregado/añadido, ~ sobre el valor agregado/añadido value-added tax

    impuesto directo/indirecto direct/indirect tax

    libre de impuestos tax-free

imputar *v.* to attribute/charge/hold responsible

    imputarle algo a algn to attribute sth to sb

indemnizar *v.* to compensate

    indemnizar a algn con algo to give sth to sb in compensation

    indemnizar a algn por algo to compensate sb for sth

indignar *v.* to outrage

    indignar algo a algn to be outraged by sth (Esa decisión ha indignado a todos los vecinos.)

indignarse *v.* to be outraged, to become indignant

    indignarse con algn por algo to get angry at sb for sth

inducir *v.* to lead

    inducir a algn a algo to lead sb to do sth (Las declaraciones del político pueden inducir a la gente a la venganza.)

inferir *v.* to infer

    inferir algo de algo to infer sth from sth (Eso es lo que se infiere de las pruebas.)

influir *v.* to influence

    influir en algo/algn, ~ a algn en algo to influence sth/sb

informar *v.* to inform

    informar a algn de algo, ~ a algn sobre algo to inform sb of sth

informarse *v.* to inquire

    informarse de algo, ~ sobre algo to inquire about sth

ingresar *v.* to join, to enter

    ingresar en algo, ~ a algo to join sth

inmiscuirse *v.* to interfere, to meddle

    inmiscuirse en algo to interfere in sth

inscribirse *v.* to register

    inscribirse dentro de algo to register within sth (Esta medida se inscribe dentro de nuestra política de inmigración.)

    inscribirse en algo to enroll in/sign up for sth

insistir *v.* to insist

    insistir en algo, ~ sobre algo to insist on sth

inspirarse *v.* to be inspired

    inspirarse en algo to be inspired by sth

instar *v.* to urge

    instar a algn a algo to urge sb to do sth

interés *m.* interest

    de interés + [*adj.*], of + [*adj.*] + interest (Es un programa de interés humano/político.)

    despertar (el) interés to arouse interest (El experimento despertó mucho interés.)

    poner interés en algo to take interest in sth

    por el interés de algn for sb's own interest (Lo hizo por su propio interés.)

    tener interés en algo to be interested in sth

interesar *v.* to concern, to interest

    interesar a algn en algo to interest sb in sth (Logré interesarlo en nuestra idea.)

    interesar algo/algn a algn to be interested in sth/sb (A mí no me interesa lo que piensan los demás. A Juan no le interesan los chismes.)

interesarse *v.* to take interest

    interesarse en algo/algn, ~ por algo/algn to take interest in sth/sb

invitar *v.* to invite

    invitar a algn a algo to invite sb to sth

ir *v.* to go

ir a hacer algo to go to do sth

ir (a) por algo/algn to go to get sth/sb

irritar *v.* to annoy

irritar a algn algo to annoy sb (Me irrita su personalidad.)

irritar a algn con algo to annoy sb with sth (Marcela irritó a su hermana con sus insultos.)

irritarse *v.* to get annoyed

irritarse con algo, ~ por algo to get annoyed at sth (Se irritó por lo que dije. Siempre se irrita con las críticas de sus colegas.)

irse *v.* to leave

irse de un lugar to leave a place

izquierda *f.* left

a la izquierda (de) to/on the left (of) (Si miran a la izquierda, verán uno de los mayores atractivos de la ciudad. María está a la izquierda de Juana.)

de izquierda left-wing (Sectores de izquierda se opusieron a la medida.)

de la izquierda on the left (Busca en el cajón de la izquierda.)

J

jactarse *v.* to brag

jactarse de algo to brag about sth

juego *m.* **1** game

estar algo en juego to be at stake (No puedo hacer eso, mi carrera está en juego.)

juego de azar game of chance

juego de ingenio guessing game

juego de mesa, ~ de tablero, ~ de salón board game

juego de palabras pun

poner algo en juego to put at stake (No voy a poner en juego nuestro futuro.)

2 play

juego limpio/sucio fair/foul play

seguirle el juego a algn to play along with sb

ser un juego de niños to be child's play

3 set

hacer juego con algo to match sth

juego de llaves set of keys

juego de té/café tea/coffee set

jugar *v.* to play

jugar a algo to play sth (¿Quieres jugar al avioncito?)

jugar con algo/algn to play with sth/sb (Estás jugando con tu futuro. ¡Estoy harta de que juegues conmigo!)

jugar contra algo/algn to play against sth/sb (Mañana jugaremos contra un equipo muy bueno.)

jugarse *v.* to risk

jugarse algo to put sth at risk (¿No ves que me estoy jugando el puesto con esto?)

juicio *m.* **1** judgement; sense

estar en su sano juicio to be in one's right mind

juicio de valor value judgement

perder el juicio to go out of one's mind, to go crazy

tener poco juicio to not be very sensible

2 opinion

a juicio de algn in sb's opinion (A mi juicio, lo que hizo está mal.)

dejar algo al juicio de algn to leave sth up to sb (Dejo la decisión a tu juicio.)

3 trial

ir a juicio to go to court

juicio político political trial

llevar a juicio to take to court

junto *adv.* close

junto a close to, next to

jurar *v.* to swear (Juro que soy inocente.)

jurar por algo/algn to swear to sth/sb (Lo juró por sus hijos. Le juró por Dios que era cierto.)

justificar *v.* to justify, to excuse

justificar a algn to make excuses for sb (No intentes justificarlo, es un irresponsable.)

justificar algo to justify sth (Debes justificar todas tus ausencias.)

juzgar *v.* to judge

a juzgar por algo judging by

juzgar algo, ~ a algn por algo to judge sth/sb for sth

juzgar por uno mismo to judge for oneself

lado *m.* side

al lado de beside, next to

por otro lado on the other hand

lamentar *v.* to regret (Lamento lo sucedido.)

lamentarse *v.* to deplore; to complain

lamentarse de algo/algn to deplore sth/sb, to complain about sth/sb (Me lamento de la falta de interés de los jóvenes por la lectura.)

largo/a *adj.* long

a la larga in the long run (Estoy segura de que Pedro, a la larga, comprenderá que es por su bien.)

a lo largo de throughout

lástima *f.* 1 shame, pity

darle lástima a algn to be a shame (Me da lástima dejar esta casa.)

¡Qué lástima! What a pity!

2 sympathy

sentir lástima por algn to feel sorry for sb (Siento lástima por esa pobre madre.)

lejos *adv.* far

lejos de far from

lente *m./f.* lens

lentes de contacto (duro/a(s), blando/a(s)) (hard/soft) contact lenses

ley *f.* law

con todas las de la ley rightly (No puedes quejarte, ella te ha ganado con todas las de la ley.)

conforme la ley, según dispone la ~ in accordance with the law

de buena ley genuine (Es oro de buena ley.)

la ley de la selva, la ~ de la jungla the law of the jungle

ley de la oferta y la demanda law of supply and demand

ley de ventaja advantage

ley seca Prohibition

promulgar/dictar una ley to promulgate/enact a law

violar la ley to break the law

libertad *f.* freedom, liberty

dejar a algn en libertad to free/release sb

libertad bajo fianza, ~ bajo palabra, ~ provisional bail

libertad condicional parole

libertad de cátedra academic freedom

libertad de conciencia freedom of conscience

libertad de cultos, ~ de culto freedom of worship

libertad de expresión, ~ de palabra freedom of expression/speech

libertad de prensa freedom of the press

libre *adj.* free

libre de hacer algo free to do sth (Eres libre de decir lo que quieras.)

limitarse *v.* to limit oneself

limitarse a algo to limit oneself to do sth (Por favor, limítese a responder la pregunta.)

limosna *f.* alms

dar limosna to give money (to beggars)

pedir limosna to beg

vivir de limosnas to live off begging

limpio/a *adj.* clean

limpio/a de algo purified of, unblemished by (Es un producto limpio de impurezas.)

pasar algo en limpio, pasar algo a ~ to make a clean copy of sth

sacar algo en limpio to get sth clear

listo/a *adj.* ready

estar listo para algo to be ready to do sth

llanto *m.* crying

romper en llanto to burst into tears

llave *f.* 1 key

bajo siete llaves hidden away

la llave de oro, las llaves de la ciudad the keys to the city

llave de contacto, ~ de encendido ignition key

llave en mano for immediate occupancy (Nos especializamos en construir casas llave en mano.)

llave inglesa monkey wrench

llave maestra master key

2 valve

llave de paso stopcock, main valve

llave del gas gas jet

llegar *v.* 1 to arrive

llegar a un lugar to arrive somewhere

2 to become

llegar a ser algo to become sth/sb (Si sigue así, Agustín llegará a ser un gran escritor.)

llenar *v.* to fill

llenar a algn de algo to fill sb with sth
(El embarazo los llenó de alegría.)

llenar algo de algo, ~ algo con algo to
fill sth with sth

llenarse *v.* to fill

llenarse de algo, ~ algo de algo to fill with
sth (La maceta se llenó de insectos. Los
ojos se le llenaron de lágrimas.)

llevar *v.* to take

llevar algo a algn to take sth to sb

llevarle... años a algn to be... years older
than sb

llevarse *v.* **1** to take away

llevarse algo, ~ a algn to take sth/sb away

2 to get along

llevarse bien/mal con algn to get along/
to not get along with sb

loco/a *adj.* **1** crazy

a lo loco in a crazy way (Está gastando el
dinero a lo loco.)

**estar loco/a con algo, estar ~ de algo,
estar ~ por algo/algn** to be crazy with/
from sth/for sth/sb (Está loco con sus
novelas. Está loca de alegría. Está loco por
su novia.)

loco/a de atar, ~ de remate stark
raving mad

2 anxious

estar loco/a por algo to be most anxious
to do sth (Estamos locos por comenzar
a entrenar.)

lograr *v.* to succeed, to achieve sth (Creo
que lo lograrás.)

lontananza *f.* distance

en lontananza in the distance

lotería *f.* lottery

ganarse la lotería, sacarse la ~ to win
the lottery

sacarse la lotería con algn to strike it
lucky with sb

ser una lotería to be a lottery (Comprar un
apartamento en ese barrio es una lotería.)

tocarle la lotería a algn to win the lottery

luchar *v.* to fight

luchar contra algo to fight against sth
(Está luchando contra una enfermedad
muy grave.)

luchar por algo/algn to fight for sth/sb
(Luchamos por los derechos de
los ciudadanos.)

luego *adv.* after

luego de after

lugar *m.* place

a como dé lugar, a como diera ~ *Am. L.*
however possible

dar lugar a algo to provoke sth (Eso dará
lugar a disputas.)

dejar a algn en mal lugar to put sb in an
awkward position

en lugar de instead of

lugar común cliché (Este discurso está
lleno de prejuicios y lugares comunes.)

sin lugar a dudas without a doubt

tener lugar to take place

lujo *m.* luxury

con lujo de detalles with a wealth of detail

darse el lujo de, permitirse el ~ de to have
the satisfaction of

de lujo luxury (Iván y Paola se alojarán en
un hotel de lujo durante su luna de miel.)

luna *f.* moon

estar con luna, estar de ~ to be in a foul/
bad mood

**estar en la luna (de Valencia), vivir en la
~ (de Valencia)** to have one's head in
the clouds

luna creciente waxing moon

luna de miel honeymoon

luna llena full moon

luna menguante waning moon

luna nueva new moon

luto *m.* mourning

estar de luto por algn to be in mourning
for sb

guardar luto a algn to be mourning for sb

ir de luto, llevar ~ to wear mourning
clothes

luto riguroso deep mourning

ponerse de luto to go into mourning

quitarse el luto to come out of mourning

M

madrugada *f.* early morning

de madrugada early in the morning
(Llegamos de madrugada.)

madrugar *v.* to get/wake up very early

mal *m.* **1** evil

mal menor lesser of two evils

2 illness

echarle el mal de ojo a algn, darle el ～ de ojo a algn to give sb the evil eye

mal de altura, mal de las alturas altitude sickness

mal de Alzheimer/de Chagas/de Parkinson/de San Vito Alzheimer's/ Chagas'/Parkinson's/Huntington's disease

mal de amores lovesickness

mal *adj./adv.* bad

estar mal de algo to be short of sth (Desde que Juan se quedó sin trabajo, la familia ha estado muy mal de dinero.)

nada mal not bad at all

malo/a *adj.* bad

mandar *v.* **1** to send

mandar a algn to send sb

mandar algo a algn to send sth to sb

2 to order

mandar a algn a hacer algo to order sb to do sth (¡No me mandes a callar!)

manera *f.* way

a la manera de algn sb's way (Hagámoslo a mi manera.)

a manera de algo by way of (Traje este dibujo a manera de ejemplo.)

de buena/mala manera in a good/bad way

de cualquier manera, de todas maneras anyway, in any case

de esa manera in that way

de manera que so (¿De manera que la decisión ya está tomada?)

de ninguna manera certainly not

manga *f.* sleeve

sacar algo de la manga off the top of one's head

mano *f.* hand

a (la) mano close at hand (¿Tienes tu planilla a (la) mano?)

a mano by hand

con las propias manos with sb's own hands

de la mano hand in hand

de primera mano firsthand

dejar algo en las manos de algn to leave sth in the hands of sb

en buenas manos in good hands (Me marcho, pero los dejo en buenas manos.)

en (propia) mano hand delivery

ir de mano en ～, pasar de ～ en ～ to pass around

irse algo de las manos to get out of hand

levantar la mano to put one's hand up

manos en alto, arriba las manos, manos arriba hands up

tender una mano, ofrecer una ～, dar una ～, echar una ～ to lend a hand

tomarle la mano a algo, agarrarle la ～ a algo to get the hang of sth

maravilla *f.* wonder

a las mil maravillas wonderfully (¡Todo salió a las mil maravillas!)

maravillarse *v.* to be amazed/astonished

maravillarse de algo/algn, ～ con algo/ algn, ～ ante algo to be amazed at sth/sb

margen *f.* bank, side *m.* margin

estar al margen de la sociedad/ley to be on the fringes of society/the law

ganar por un amplio/estrecho margen to win by a comfortable/narrow margin

mantenerse al margen de algo to keep out of sth

margen de beneficio, ～ comercial, ～ de ganancias profit margin

margen de error margin of error

margen de tolerancia range of tolerance

nota al margen margin note

mayor *adj.* greater, older

por mayor wholesale

mediados *m.* middle

a mediados de in the middle of (Voy a retirar las cosas que faltan a mediados del mes que viene.)

medida *f.* measure

a medida que as (Resolveremos los problemas a medida que vayan surgiendo.)

medio/a *adj.* half

a medias halfway

meditar *v.* to meditate

meditar sobre algo to meditate on sth

mejor *adj.* better

a lo mejor maybe

menor *adj.* lesser

por menor retail

menos *adj.* less

a menos que unless

al menos at least

por lo menos at least

menudo/a *adj.* small, slight (Es un hombre muy menudo.)

   a menudo often

   menudo... *Esp.* what a…, such a… (¡Menudo lío! ¡Caí en menuda trampa!)

mercado *m.* market

   mercado al aire libre open-air market

   mercado cambiario, ~ de divisas foreign exchange market

   mercado de abastos, ~ de abasto market

   mercado de las pulgas, ~ de pulgas flea market

   mercado negro black market

   mercado persa bazaar

mesa *f.* table

   bendecir la mesa to say grace

   levantar la mesa, quitar la ~, recoger la ~ to clear the table

   mesa auxiliar side table

   mesa de centro, ~ ratona coffee table

   mesa de comedor/cocina dining room/ kitchen table

   mesa de dibujo drawing board

   mesa de negociaciones, ~ negociadora negotiating table

   mesa de noche, ~ de luz bedside table

   mesa plegable folding table

   poner la mesa to set the table

   sentarse a la mesa to sit at the table

meta *f.* **1** finish line

   llegar a la meta to reach the finish line

   2 goal

   alcanzar una meta to reach a goal

   ponerse algo por meta to set oneself a goal

   tener una meta, trazarse una ~ to set a goal for oneself

meterse *v.* **1** to get involved

   meterse en algo to get involved in sth

   2 to pick on

   meterse con algn to pick on sb

   3 to become

   meterse a algo to become sth (Juan se metió a periodista, pero no sabe escribir bien.)

miedo *m.* fear

   tener miedo a algo/algn to be afraid of sb/sth

   tener miedo de algo to be afraid of sth

mira *f.* view

   con miras a with the purpose of

mismo/a *adj.* same

   dar lo mismo que to make no difference

misterio *m.* mystery

   dejarse de misterio to stop being mysterious (¡Dejaos ya de tanto misterio y contadnos cuándo os vais a casar!)

   novela de misterio mystery novel

moda *f.* fashion

   estar a la moda, estar de ~, ponerse de ~ to be in fashion

   estar de última moda to be very fashionable

   estar pasado de moda to be out of fashion

   ir a la moda to be trendy

modo *m.* way, manner

   a modo de as, by way of (Usó su cuaderno a modo de pantalla.)

   de buen/mal modo, de buenos/malos modos in a good/bad way

   de cualquier modo, de todos modos anyway, in any case

   de modo que in such a way that

   de ningún modo no way

   de tal modo que, de ~ que so (that) (Estudió mucho, de tal modo que aprobó el examen. Ya es tarde, de modo que me voy a casa.)

   del mismo modo, de igual ~ in the same way

   en cierto modo in a way

   modo de empleo instructions for use

   ni modo not a chance

   no es modo de hacer las cosas no way of going about things

molestar *v.* to bother

   molestar a algn to bother sb

molestarse *v.* **1** to get upset

   molestarse con algn por algo to get upset with sb about sth

   2 to take the trouble

   molestarse en hacer algo to take the trouble to do sth

momento *m.* moment

   en algún momento at some point, sometime

morirse *v.* to die

   morirse de algo to die of sth, to be really hungry, thirsty... (Se murió de pulmonía. ¡Me muero de hambre!)

morirse por algo to die for sth (¡Me muero por conocerlo personalmente!)

motivo *m.* reason
  con motivo de because of, in order to
  por motivos de fuerza mayor force majeure
  por ningún motivo under no circumstances

mozo/a *m./f.* 1 young man/woman
  buen mozo, buena moza good-looking boy/girl
  2 waiter/waitress *Arg.*

muela *f.* molar; back tooth
  muela de juicio wisdom tooth

muerte *f.* death
  amenaza de muerte death threat
  de mala muerte lousy (No vayas a ese restaurante, es de mala muerte.)
  estar condenado a muerte to be sentenced to death
  hacer algo a muerte to do sth to death
  herido de muerte fatally wounded

muerto/a *adj.* dead
  muerto/a de cansancio, ~ de sueño dead-tired
  muerto/a de frío freezing
  muerto/a de hambre starving
  muerto/a de miedo frightened to death
  muerto/a de risa dying of laughter

N

nada *pron.* nothing
  como si nada as if it were nothing
  de nada, por ~ you're welcome
  nada de algo not to need any of sth (No necesitamos nada de combustible.)
  nada de nada not a thing

necesidad *f.* need
  por necesidad out of necessity

negar *v.* to deny
  negar algo a algn to deny sth to sb

negarse *v.* to refuse, to deny
  negarse a hacer algo to refuse to do sth
  negarse algo to deny oneself sth (Se niega todo para que su hija pueda estudiar.)

negociar *v.* to negotiate
  negociar algo con algn to negotiate sth with sb

nombre *m.* name
  a nombre de algn addressed to sb
  en nombre de algo/algn in the name of sth/sb
  no tener nombre to be beyond belief (Lo que has hecho no tiene nombre.)
  nombre artístico stage name
  nombre completo full name
  nombre de guerra, ~ de batalla alias, pseudonym
  nombre de mujer/varón girl's/boy's name
  nombre de pila first name

notar *v.* to notice
  hacerse notar to draw attention to oneself
  notar algo to notice sth

nube *f.* cloud
  por las nubes sky-high (Los precios están por las nubes.)

nuevo/a *adj.* new
  de nuevo again

O

obligar *v.* to force
  obligar a algn a hacer algo to force sb to do sth

obra *f.* work
  obra benéfica, ~ de beneficencia, ~ de caridad act of charity
  obra de arte work of art
  obra de consulta reference book
  obra de teatro theater play
  obra maestra masterpiece

obstinarse *v.* to refuse to give way
  obstinarse en algo to persist in sth (Se obstina en dificultar las cosas.)

ocuparse *v.* to be in charge
  ocuparse de algo/algn to be in charge of sth/sb

ofender *v.* to offend
  ofender a algn to offend sb

ofenderse *v.* to be offended
  ofenderse con algn por algo to be offended by sb because of sth

ojo *m.* eye
  a los ojos de la sociedad in the eyes of society
  guiñar el ojo to wink
  ¡Ojo! Be careful!, Watch out!

tener (buen) ojo to be sharp (Mi hermano tiene muy buen ojo para estas cosas.)

oler *v.* to smell

oler a algo to smell like sth (La habitación olía a jazmines.)

oler algo to smell sth (Huele este perfume, es francés.)

olvidarse *v.* to forget

olvidarse de algo/algn to forget about sth/sb

olvidársele algo a algn to forget about sth

opinar *v.* to have an opinion

opinar (algo) de algo/algn, ~ sobre algo/algn to have an opinion about sth/sb (¿Qué opinas de la reforma económica? El ministro opinó sobre las nuevas medidas. Pablo opina que su nuevo jefe es un tirano.)

opinión *f.* opinion

cambiar de opinión to change one's mind (Mi hermano cambió de opinión sobre las vacaciones.)

oponerse *v.* to oppose

oponerse a algo/algn to oppose sth/sb

optar *v.* to choose

optar por algo to choose sth

ordenar *v.* to order

ordenar algo a algn to order sb to do sth

orgulloso/a *adj.* proud

estar orgulloso/a de to be proud of

oscuro/a *adj.* dark

a oscuras in the dark

P

padecer *v.* to suffer

padecer de algo to suffer from sth

pagar *v.* to pay

pagar al contado, ~ en efectivo to pay in cash

pagar algo a algn to pay sth to sb

pagar algo con algo to pay for sth with sth

pagar (algo) por algo to pay (sth) for sth

para *prep.* for, to

no ser para tanto to not exaggerate/to not be so bad (No te quejes por eso, que no es para tanto.)

para con with (Son muy buenos para con los niños.)

para siempre forever

parada *f.* stop

parada de autobús, ~ de ómnibus bus stop

parada de metro subway stop

parada de taxi taxi stand

parecer *v.* **1** to seem

al parecer, ~ que apparently, evidently, it would seem/appear

2 to have an opinion

a mi parecer in my opinion

parecer mentira to seem impossible

parecerse *v.* to be like

no parecerse en nada a algo/algn not to be/look alike at all

parecerse a algo/algn to be/look like sth/sb

parecido/a *adj.* **1** similar

ser parecido/a a algo/algn to be similar to sth/sb

2 good-looking

ser bien/mal parecido/a to be good-/bad-looking

pareja *f.* **1** couple; pair

formar parejas to get into pairs

vivir en pareja to live together

2 partner

la pareja the other one (No encuentro la pareja de este calcetín.)

tener pareja to have a partner (Después de tanto tiempo de soltería, finalmente tengo pareja.)

parte *f.* part

en alguna parte somewhere

por otra parte besides (La película es interesante y, por otra parte, no tengo nada que hacer.)

participar *v.* to take part

participar en algo to take part in sth

partido *m.* game, match

sacar partido de algo to take advantage of sth

tomar partido to take sides

partir *v.* to leave

a partir de starting

pasaje *m.* ticket

pasaje de ida one-way ticket

pasaje de ida y vuelta round-trip ticket

sacar un pasaje to buy a ticket

paseo *m.* walk

estar de paseo to be visiting

mandar a algn a paseo to tell sb
to get lost

paseo marítimo esplanade

paso *m.* **1** passage, passing; path

dicho sea de paso by the way (Dicho sea
de paso, te queda muy bien ese color.)

el paso del tiempo the passage of time

2 way

abrir paso to make way

abrirse paso to make one's way

ceder el paso to yield

cerrar el paso to block the way

3 pass

paso fronterizo border crossing

4 step

a pasos agigantados by leaps and bounds

con paso firme firmly, purposefully

dar un paso en falso to stumble; to make
a false move

paso a paso step by step

5 rate, speed

a este paso at this rate

a paso de hormiga/tortuga at a
snail's pace

pata *f.* leg

estirar la pata *fam.* to kick the bucket

meter la pata *fam.* to put one's foot in
one's mouth

pata delantera/trasera front/hind leg

patas para arriba *fam.* upside down

saltar en una pata to jump for joy

paz *f.* peace

**dejar en paz algo, dejar en ~ a algn, dejar
a algn vivir en ~** to let sth/sb alone

descansar en paz rest in peace

estar en paz, quedar en ~ *fam.* to be
at peace

firmar la paz to sign a peace agreement

hacer las paces to make up

pedir *v.* to ask for; to request

pedir algo a algn to ask sb (for) sth
(Pidió un adelanto a su jefe. Pidió a su
secretaria que escribiera una carta.)

pedir algo por algo to ask sth for sth
(¿Cuánto pide por la bicicleta?)

pedir prestado to borrow

pelearse *v.* to quarrel

pelearse con algn por algo to quarrel with
sb over sth

pelo *m.* hair

**andar con los pelos de punta, estar con
los ~ de punta** to be in a real state

caérsele el pelo a algn to lose one's hair

cortarle el pelo a algn to cut sb's hair

cortarse el pelo to have one's hair cut

no tener ni un pelo de tonto to not be a fool

no tener pelos en la lengua to not mince
one's words

pelo lacio, ~ liso straight hair

pelo rizado curly hair

ponerle a algn los pelos de punta to make
sb's hair stand on end

por un pelo just barely (¡Nos salvamos por
un pelo!)

traído por los pelos, traído de los ~
far-fetched

pena *f.* sorrow

vale la pena que it's worth it that/to (Vale
la pena que te esfuerces, tendrás una
buena recompensa.)

pensar *v.* to think

pensar algo de algn to think sth of sb
(Pienso que Susana es muy cruel.)

pensar en algo/algn to think about sth/sb

percatarse *v.* to notice

percatarse de algo to notice sth

permiso *m.* permission

dar permiso, pedir ~ to give/ask for
permission

(con) permiso excuse me

permitir *v.* to allow

permitir algo a algn to allow sb to do sth

persistir *v.* to persist

persistir en algo to persist in sth

pertenecer *v.* to belong

pertenecer a algn to belong to sb (Este
reloj le pertenecía a mi bisabuelo.)

pesar *m.* regret, sorrow

a pesar de, pese a in spite of

mal que le pese a algn whether sb likes
it or not

pie *m.* foot

a pie on foot

al pie de la letra literally, exactly (Siguieron
nuestras instrucciones al pie de la letra.)

al pie de la montaña, a los pies de la montaña at the foot of the mountain

con buen pie, con el ~ derecho off to a good start (Creo que no comenzaron con buen pie. Nuestra relación comenzó con el pie derecho.)

con mal pie, con el ~ izquierdo badly

dar pie a algo to give rise to sth

dar pie con bola *fam.* to get sth right (Últimamente todo me sale mal, no doy pie con bola.)

de pie standing (Ponte de pie cuando entre la maestra.)

en pie up (awake), on one's feet, standing (Estuve en pie todo el día. Lo único que quedó en pie fue la antigua capilla. ¿Sabes si la oferta sigue en pie?)

en pie de guerra ready for war

hacer pie to be able to touch the bottom (No puedo hacer pie en esa piscina.)

nacer de pie to be born lucky

nota a pie de página, nota al ~ de página footnote

perder pie, no hacer ~ to get out of one's depth (Si pierdes pie, llámame enseguida.)

pie de fotografía caption

pie de imprenta imprint

pie equino clubfoot

pie plano flat foot

pila *f.* **1** battery

funcionar a pila(s), funcionar con pila(s) to run on batteries

2 pile, loads

pila de algo, pilas de algo mountains of sth

plano *m.* level

de plano outright (Se negó de plano a participar en el negocio.)

plantado/a *adj.* planted

dejar plantado/a a algn to stand sb up (¡No puedo creer que te dejara plantado!)

plantado de algo planted with sth (El campo está plantado de trigo.)

plazo *m.* **1** period

corto plazo short-term

dar un plazo to give a deadline (Nos dieron un plazo de 30 días para comenzar a pagar.)

largo plazo long-term

medio plazo, mediano ~ middle-term

2 installment

pagar a plazos to pay in installments

poco *pron.* little

a poco de algo shortly after sth

dentro de poco soon

poco antes de algo shortly before sth

poco y nada very little, to hardly do sth (Hicieron poco y nada por sus compañeros.)

por poco almost (¡Por poco le creo sus mentiras!)

poder *v.* to be possible

puede (ser) que it might/could be (Puede ser que salgamos campeones este año, estamos jugando bien. Puede que mañana llegue tarde a casa, tengo una reunión con mi jefa.)

poner *v.* **1** to put

poner algo en marcha to start sth

poner algo / a algn en un lugar to put sth somewhere, to put sb in his/her place

2 to make (something change)

poner a algn de una manera to make sb feel some way (Ese poema me pone triste.)

ponerse *v.* to begin

ponerse a hacer algo to begin to (Ponte a hacer la tarea ahora mismo.)

por *prep.* by, for, in

por adelantado in advance

por ahora for the time being

por aquí around here

por casualidad by accident

por causa de because of

por completo, ~ entero completely

por consiguiente, ~ lo tanto therefore

por cuanto insofar as

por delante ahead (Aún nos queda mucho por delante.)

por delante de in front of, opposite (Ayer pasé por delante de tu casa.)

por demás extremely (Te comportas de una manera por demás grosera.)

por dentro de in, inside of

por desgracia unfortunately

por detrás de behind, in the back of

por Dios for heaven's sake

por ejemplo for example

por el camino on the way (Vamos, te lo cuento por el camino.)

por el principio at the beginning

por encima de over

por entre in between (Los niños se metieron por entre los invitados y los perdimos de vista.)

por escrito in writing

por eso that's why

por fin finally

por fortuna fortunately

por fuera de out, outside of

por fuerza necessarily

por fuerza mayor, ~ causas de fuerza mayor, ~ motivos de fuerza mayor force majeure

por gusto for the fun of it

por las buenas o por las malas one way or the other

por las nubes sky-high

por lo demás apart from that

por lo general, ~ regla general in general

por lo menos at least

por lo pronto, ~ de pronto, ~ el pronto for a start

por lo tanto therefore

por lo visto apparently

por mayor wholesale

por menor retail

por nada you're welcome

por necesidad out of necessity

por ningún motivo under no circumstances

por otra parte, ~ otro lado besides (La película es interesante y, por otra parte, no tengo nada que hacer.)

por poco almost (¡Por poco le creo sus mentiras!)

por principio on principle

por siempre jamás forever and ever

por suerte luckily

por supuesto of course

por un pelo just barely (¡Nos salvamos por un pelo!)

por... vez for the... time

preferir *v.* to prefer

preferir algo a algo to prefer sth to sth

preguntar *v.* to ask

preguntar algo a algn to ask sb sth

preguntar (a algn) por algo/algn to ask (sb) about sth/sb

preocupado/a *adj.* worried

estar preocupado/a por to be worried about

preocupar *v.* to worry

preocupar a algn to worry about sth

preocuparse *v.* to be worried

preocuparse de algo to take interest in sth (No se preocupó más del tema.)

preocuparse por algo/algn to be worried about sth/sb (Estoy preocupada por la educación de mis hijos.)

prescindir *v.* **1** to do without

prescindir de algo/algn to do without sth/sb

prescindir de los servicios de algn to dispense with sb's services

2 to disregard

prescindir de algo to disregard sth

3 to dispense

prescindir de algo to dispense with sth (Decidió prescindir de los detalles.)

presenciar *v.* to witness

presenciar algo to witness sth

prestar *v.* to lend

prestar algo a algn to lend sth to sb

primero/a *adj.* first

ser el/la primero/a en hacer algo to be the first one to do sth (Eres el primero en ocuparse de los niños.)

principio *m.* **1** beginning

a principios de at the beginning of (Supongo que nos mudaremos a principios de año.)

al principio at first

desde el principio, desde un ~ from the beginning

en (un) principio in the beginning

por el principio at the beginning

2 principle

cuestión de principios question of principles

por principio on principle

ser algn de principios to be someone with principles

prisa *f.* haste

  correr prisa to be in a rush

  darse prisa to hurry

privar *v.* to deprive

  privar a algn de algo to deprive sb of sth

privarse *v.* to deprive oneself

  privarse de algo to deprive oneself of sth

procurar *v.* **1** to try, to aim to/at

  procurar hacer algo to try to do sth
    (Procura terminar el proyecto esta semana.)

  2 to obtain

  procurar algo para algn to obtain sth for
    sb (Procuraremos alimentos
    para los refugiados.)

prohibir *v.* to ban/forbid

  prohibirle a algn algo to forbid sb
    to do sth

  prohibirle algo a algn to ban sb from
    doing sth

pronto *adv.* soon

  de pronto suddenly

  ¡hasta pronto! see you soon!

  lo más pronto posible as soon as possible

  por lo pronto, por de ~, por el ~ for
    a start

  tan pronto como as soon as, once

propina *f.* tip

  dar propina to tip

  de propina for a tip (¿Cuánto has dejado
    de propina?)

  dejar una propina to leave a tip

proponer *v.* to propose, suggest

  **proponer a algn para algo, ~ a algn como
  algo** to propose sb as sth

  proponer algo a algn to propose sth to sb

proporcionar *v.* to provide

  proporcionar algo a algn to provide sb
    with sth (Me proporcionó todos los
    materiales necesarios.)

propósito *m.* intention, purpose

  a propósito on purpose, by the way
    (¡Lo hiciste a propósito! Ayer me encontré
    con Mario; a propósito, me preguntó
    cuánto vale tu coche.)

  propósito de enmienda promise to
    mend one's ways

  sin propósito aimlessly

  tener buenos propósitos to have
    good intentions

proteger *v.* to protect

  **proteger algo de algo/algn, ~ a algn de
  algo/algn, ~ algo contra algo** to protect
  sth/sb from/against sth/sb

protegerse *v.* to protect oneself

  **protegerse de algo/algn, ~ contra
  algo/algn** to protect oneself from/against
  sth/sb

protestar *v.* to protest

  protestar contra algo/algn to protest
    against sth (Los manifestantes protestan
    contra el gobierno.)

  protestar por algo to complain about sth
    (Protestan por la falta de trabajo.)

provecho *m.* benefit

  sacar provecho de algo to benefit from sth

prueba *f.* proof

  a prueba de impervious to, resistant (¿Tu
    reloj es a prueba de agua?)

punto *m.* point

  **anotarse un punto con algo, marcarse un
  ~ con algo** to get ten out of ten on sth

  en punto o'clock/on the dot

  estar a punto de hacer algo to be about to
    do sth

  poner punto final a algo to end

  punto álgido culminating point, climax
    (La crisis económica alcanzó su
    punto álgido.)

  punto de apoyo fulcrum

  punto decimal decimal point

  punto final period

  punto y aparte period, new paragraph

  punto y coma semicolon

  punto y seguido period

  puntos suspensivos ellipsis

Q

quedar *v.* **1** to fit

  quedarle algo bien/mal a algn to fit well/
    badly (¿Me queda mal el vestido?)

  2 to cause an impression

  quedar bien/mal con algn to make a
    good/bad impression on sb (No quiero
    quedar mal con mis suegros.)

  3 to agree

  quedar en algo con algn to agree to do sth
    with sb (Quedamos en no volver a hablar
    del tema.)

quedarse *v.* to stay

quedarse con algo to keep sth

quedarse dormido to oversleep

quejarse *v.* to complain

quejarse de algo/algn to complain about sb/sth (¿De qué te quejas? No deja de quejarse de sus vecinos.)

quejarse por algo, ~ de algo to complain of sth (Marta se queja por el costo de vida. Tu hijo se queja de un fuerte dolor de muelas.)

quiebra *f.* bankruptcy

declararse en quiebra, irse a la ~ to go bankrupt

quitar *v.* to take away

quitar algo a algn to take sth away from sb

R

rabo *m.* tail

con el rabo entre las piernas, con el ~ entre las patas with one's tail between one's legs

raíz *f.* root

a raíz de as a result of

echar raíces to take roots

raíz cuadrada/cúbica square/cube root

rato *m.* while

a cada rato the whole time

al (poco) rato shortly thereafter

de a rato, de a ratos, de ~ en ~ from time to time

hace rato for some time

pasar el rato to spend time/hang out

ratos libres, ~ de ocio spare time

tener para rato to be a while

raya *f.* **1** line

a rayas striped

pasarse de la raya to overstep the mark, to go too far, to push one's luck

tener a algn a raya, mantener a algn a ~ to keep sb under control

2 part

llevar raya al medio/al costado to part one's hair in the middle/to one side

razón *f.* **1** reason

atender razones, atenerse a ~, avenirse a ~ to listen to reason

darle la razón a algn to admit sb is right

en razón de because of (No debes discriminar en razón de la edad o la raza de las personas.)

entrar en razón to see reason

perder la razón to lose one's mind

razón de ser raison d'être/reason for being (¡Esta masacre no tiene razón de ser!)

razón social registered name

tener (la) razón, llevar la ~ to be right

2 rate

a razón de at a rate of

3 information

dar razón de algo/algn to give information about sth/sb

rechazar *v.* to reject

rechazar a algn por algo to reject sb for sth

rechazar algo a algn to reject sth from sb

reclamar *v.* to claim, to demand

reclamar algo de algn to demand sth from sb

recomendar *v.* to recommend

recomendar algo a algn to recommend sth to sb

recompensar *v.* to reward

recompensar a algn por algo to reward sb for sth (Deberías recompensar a tus alumnos por su esfuerzo.)

reconciliarse *v.* to reconcile

reconciliarse con algo to become reconciled to sth (Se reconcilió con su idea de la familia.)

reconciliarse con algn to make up with sb (Marcia se reconcilió con su marido.)

recordar *v.* to remind

recordar algo a algn to remind sb of sth

recuperarse *v.* to recover

recuperarse de algo to recover from sth

recurso *m.* **1** resource

agotar todos los recursos to exhaust all the options

como último recurso as a last resort

recurso natural, recursos naturales natural resource(s)

recursos económicos economic/financial resources

recursos energéticos energy resources

recursos humanos human resources

sin recursos without means/without resources

2 appeal

interponer/presentar un recurso to file an appeal

red *f.* net

caer en las redes de algn to fall into sb's trap

reembolso *m.* refund

contra reembolso cash on delivery

referir *v.* **1** to tell

referir algo a algn to tell sth to sb (Nos refirió sus experiencias como maestro rural.)

2 to refer

referir a algn a algo to refer sb to sth (Nos refirió al segundo párrafo de la nota.)

referirse *v.* to refer

referirse a algo/algn to refer to sth/sb (No entiendo a qué te refieres. No me estaba refiriendo a ti.)

reflexionar *v.* to reflect

reflexionar sobre algo/algn to think about sth/sb

refugiado/a *m./f.* refugee

refugiado/a político/a political refugee

refugiado/a de guerra war refugee

regalar *v.* to give as a gift

regalar algo a algn to give sth to sb as a gift

regañadientes *adv.* reluctantly

a regañadientes reluctantly

regla *f.* rule

por regla general in general

regreso *m.* return

a su regreso on one's return

de regreso a back at/to (¿Cuándo estarás de regreso a la oficina?)

emprender el regreso to set off on the return trip

reírse *v.* to laugh

reírse de algo/algn to laugh at sth/sb

reírse por algo to laugh because of sth

remedio *m.* **1** remedy

santo remedio to do the trick (¿Tienes tos? Prepara un vaso de leche tibia con miel y santo remedio.)

2 solution

no tener remedio to be hopeless/to

have no solution (Olvídalo, nuestro matrimonio no tiene remedio.)

3 option

no tener más remedio que, no quedar más ~ que, no haber más ~ que, no haber otro ~ que to have no option but to

renglón *m.* line

a renglón seguido immediately afterward (Las instrucciones se detallan a renglón seguido.)

renunciar *v.* **1** to resign

renunciar a algo to resign from sth (Renunció a su trabajo y salió a recorrer el mundo.)

2 to renounce

renunciar a algo to renounce sth (Decidimos renunciar a la lucha armada.)

reñir *v.* to quarrel

reñir con algn to quarrel with sb

reojo *m.* the corner of the eye

mirar de reojo a algn to look at sb out of the corner of one's eye

repente *m.* sudden movement

de repente suddenly

repercutir *v.* **1** to impact

repercutir en algo/algn to have an impact on sth/sb

2 to pass on

repercutir algo en algn, ~ sobre algn to pass sth on to sb

reponerse *v.* to recover

reponerse de algo to recover from sth

reprochar *v.* to reproach

reprochar algo a algn to reproach sb for sth

reputación *f.* reputation

tener reputación de to have a reputation as (Tiene reputación de buen cocinero.)

resentirse *v.* to get upset

resentirse con algn por algo to get upset with sb because of sth

resignarse *v.* to resign oneself

resignarse a algo to resign oneself to sth

resistirse *v.* to be reluctant, to resist

resistirse a algo to resist sth

respecto *m.* matter, regard

con respecto a regarding

respetar *v.* to respect

respetar a algn por algo to respect sb
for sth

responder *v.* to answer

**responder algo a algn, responder a
algo** to answer sb about sth

responder por algo/algn to be held
responsible

responsabilizar *v.* to blame

responsabilizar a algn de algo to blame
sb for sth (La víctima responsabilizó a la
policía del fracaso de la operación.)

responsable *adj.* responsible

ser responsable de algo to be responsible
for sth

resumen *m.* summary

en resumen all in all

hacer un resumen to summarize

reunirse *v.* to meet

reunirse con algn to meet with sb

revista *f.* **1** magazine

revista de chistes comic book

revista de modas fashion magazine

revista del corazón *Esp.* gossip magazine

2 revue

teatro de revista vaudeville-style comedy

3 review

pasar revista a algo to review sth

rivalizar *v.* to compete

rivalizar con algn por algo to compete
with sb for sth

rodilla *f.* knee

de rodillas down on one's knees

hincar la rodilla to go down on
one's knee

pedir algo de rodillas to beg on
one's knees

rogar *v.* to beg

rogar algo a algn to beg sb for sth

romper *v.* to break

romper algo to break sth

romper con algn to break up with sb

S

saber *v.* **1** to know

(de) haberlo sabido had sb known

**saber algo de algo/algn, ~ algo sobre
algo/algn** to know sth about sth/sb
(Mi padre sabe algo de física. ¿Sabes algo

de Mariano? ¿Alguien sabe algo
sobre la fiesta?)

2 to taste

saber a algo to taste like sth (Esto sabe
a nueces.)

sabiendas *adv.* knowingly

a sabiendas knowingly

salida *f.* exit; way out

no verle salida a algo not to see a way
out of sth (No le veo la salida a
este problema.)

salir *v.* **1** to leave

salir de algo to leave from sth

salir para algo to leave for sth (Salgo para
Colombia esta misma noche.)

salir por algo to leave via sth (¡No querrás
que salga por la chimenea!)

2 to go

salir a algo to go out onto/into/for (Salieron
al balcón. ¿Salimos a comer?)

salir con algn to go out with sb

3 to take after

salir a algn to take after sb (El bebé salió a
su padre.)

saludar *v.* to greet

saludar a algn to greet sb

salvo/a *adj.* safe

a salvo safe (Mi familia está a salvo, gracias
a Dios.)

ponerse a salvo to reach safety

satisfecho/a *adj.* satisfied

estar satisfecho/a de to be satisfied
by/with

seguir *v.* to follow

seguir algo, ~ a algn to follow sth/sb

seguro/a *adj.* **1** safe

hacer algo sobre seguro to play safe
with sth

2 sure

estar seguro/a de algo to be sure about sth

sentado/a *adj.* seated

esperar sentado/a to not hold one's breath

sentido *m.* **1** sense

sentido común common sense

sentido de algo sense of sth (Su sentido
del deber es admirable.)

sentido de (la) orientación sense of
direction

tener sentido to make sense
2 consciousness
perder el sentido to lose consciousness
recobrar el sentido to regain consciousness
sentir *v.* 1 to feel
sentir algo hacia algn, ~ algo por algo/ algn to feel sth for sth/sb
2 to regret
sentir algo to regret sth (Siento mucho haberte dicho eso.)
sentirse 1 to feel
sentirse bien/mal to feel well/ill
2 to be offended
sentirse con algn *Méx.* to be offended by sb (Está sentida con su hermana porque le mintió.)
ser *v.* to be
a no ser que if not, unless
ser de algo/algn to become (¿Qué fue del aumento que te iban a dar? ¿Qué será de nuestros amigos?)
ser *m.* being
el ser y la nada being and nothingness
ser humano human being
ser sobrenatural supernatural being
ser vivo, ~ viviente living being
serie *f.* series
coches/motores de serie production cars/ engines
fuera de serie out of this world
producción en serie, fabricación en ~ mass production
serie numérica numerical sequence
seriedad *f.* seriousness
con toda seriedad seriously
falta de seriedad irresponsibility, lack of seriousness
servir *v.* to serve
servir a algo/algn to serve sth/sb
siempre *adv.* always
casi siempre almost always
como siempre as usual
¡hasta siempre! farewell!
para siempre forever
por siempre jamás forever and ever
siempre que whenever, provided that (Me viene a visitar siempre que puede. Te ayudaré, siempre que prometas contarme toda la verdad.)

siempre y cuando if (Iré siempre y cuando me acompañes.)
silencio *m.* silence
guardar silencio to keep silent
sin *prep.* without
sin cesar nonstop
sin demora without delay
sin embargo however
sin falta without fail
sin fines de lucro, ~ fines lucrativos not-for-profit
sin lugar a dudas, ~ duda without a doubt
sin propósito aimlessly
sobrar *v.* to have in excess
sobrar algo a algn to have sth in excess (Les sobraba el dinero.)
solidarizarse *v.* to support
solidarizarse con algo/algn to support sth/ sb (Nos solidarizamos con su reclamo. La presidenta se solidarizó con los trabajadores despedidos.)
solo/a *adj.* alone
a solas alone (No me gusta quedarme a solas con ella.)
sombra *f.* shadow
a la sombra de in the shadow of
soñar to dream
soñar con algo/algn to dream about sth/sb
sorprender *v.* to surprise
sorprender a algn con algo to surprise sb with sth
sorprenderse *v.* to be surprised
sorprenderse de algo, ~ por algo to be surprised by sth
sospechar *v.* to suspect
sospechar algo, ~ de algn to suspect sth/sb
subasta *f.* auction
sacar algo a subasta to put sth up for auction
subir *v.* to get on
subir a algo to get on/onto sth
suceder *v.* to happen
suceder algo a algn for sth to happen to sb
suerte *f.* 1 chance
caer en suerte, tocar en ~ to fall to one's lot

echar algo a la suerte, echar algo a suertes to toss a coin for sth
la suerte está echada the die is cast
2 luck
buena/mala suerte good/bad luck
desear buena suerte a algn to wish luck to sb
estar de suerte to be in luck
por suerte luckily
probar suerte to try one's luck
traer buena/mala suerte, dar buena/mala ~ to bring good/bad luck
sufrir to suffer
sufrir de algo to suffer from sth
sufrir por algo/algn to suffer because of sth/sb
sugerir *v.* to suggest
sugerir algo a algn to suggest sth to sb
suma *f.* sum
en suma in short
suplicar *v.* to beg, to implore
suplicar a algn por algo/algn to beg sb to do sth
supuesto/a *adj.* so-called
por supuesto of course
sustituir *v.* to replace
sustituir a algn to replace sb
sustituir algo con algo, ~ algo por algo to replace sth with sth

T

tablón *m.* board
tablón de anuncios bulletin board
taller *m.* workshop, garage
taller mecánico, ~ de reparación garage
tanto *pron.* so, so much
otro tanto the same
por (lo) tanto therefore
tanto... como... both... and...
tardar *v.* to take (time)
a más tardar at the very latest
tardar en algo to take a long time to
tarde *adv.* late
hacerse tarde to be getting late
más vale tarde que nunca better late than never
ser tarde para algo to be too late for sth
tarde o temprano sooner or later

tarjeta *f.* card
tarjeta de crédito credit card
tarjeta de débito debit card
tarjeta postal postcard
tasa *f.* **1** tax; fee (Debo pagar las tasas.)
2 rate
tasa de desempleo unemployment rate
tasa de interés interest rate
tasa de mortalidad/natalidad mortality rate/birthrate
telón *m.* curtain
telón de fondo background
temer *v.* to fear
temer a algo/algn to be afraid of sth/sb
temer por algo/algn to fear for sth/sb
tender *v.* to tend
tender a algo to tend to sth (Siempre tiendo a preocuparme por todo.)
tener *v.* to have
tener que ver to pertain/have sth to do (No tiene nada que ver con este asunto.)
terminar *v.* to finish
terminar con algo/algn to finish with sth/sb
terminar de hacer algo to finish sth
tiempo *m.* time
a tiempo on time
al mismo tiempo que at the same time as
tiempo libre free time
tirar *v.* **1** to throw
tirar algo a algn to throw sth to sb, to throw sth at sb
2 to pull
tirar de algo to pull sth
3 to shoot
tirar a dar to shoot to wound
tirar a matar to shoot to kill
tirar a traición to shoot in the back
tomar *v.* to take
tomar a algn por algo to take sb for sth (A nadie le gusta que lo tomen por tonto.)
tono *m.* pitch, tone
estar a tono con to keep up with, to be in tune with
fuera de tono inappropriate, out of place
no venir a tono to be out of place
subido de tono risqué

tonto/a *adj.* silly

  a tontas y a locas without thinking

toparse *v.* to encounter

  toparse con algo/algn to run into sth/sb

torno *m.* lathe

  en torno a around (El argumento de la película gira en torno a las relaciones amorosas.)

trabajar *v.* to work

  trabajar en algo, ~ con algo to work on/in/with sth

  trabajar para algn to work for sb

  trabajar por algo to work for sth

traducir *v.* to translate

  traducir algo a algo to translate sth into sth

transformarse *v.* to become

  transformarse en algo/algn to become sth/sb

transporte *m.* transportation

  transporte aéreo air freight

  transporte marítimo shipping

  transporte público public transportation

tratar *v.* **1** to try

  tratar de hacer algo to try to do sth

  2 to treat

  tratar bien/mal a algn to treat sb well/badly

  3 to deal

  tratar con algn to deal with sb

  4 to call

  tratar a algn de algo to call sb sth (¡Me trató de mentiroso!)

tratarse *v.* **1** to socialize

  tratarse con algn to socialize with sb

  2 to address

  tratarse con respeto to show respect for each other, to treat (each) other with respect

  tratarse de usted/tú to address each other as "usted"/"tú"

  3 to be about

  tratarse de to be about (¿De qué se trata la novela?)

través *m.* crossbeam

  a través de through

  al través diagonally

  de través *Méx.* diagonally

trepar *v.* to climb

  trepar a algo, ~ por algo to climb up sth

treparse *v.* to climb

  treparse a algo to climb sth

tropezar *v.* **1** to stumble

  tropezar con algo to stumble over sth (Se tropezó con la silla.)

  2 to run into

  tropezar con algo/algn to run into sth/sb (¿A que no sabes con quién me tropecé hoy?)

trueque *m.* barter

  a trueque de in exchange for

U

último/a *adj.* last

  ser el/la último/a en hacer algo to be the last one to do sth (Fue el último en dejar el barco.)

V

vacilar *v.* to hesitate

  vacilar en algo to hesitate to do sth (No vaciló en la respuesta.)

  vacilar entre algo y algo to hesitate over sth (Estoy vacilando entre seguir con este empleo y buscar uno nuevo.)

valer *v.* **1** to be worth

  más vale que it's better that (Más vale que traigas lo que te pedí la semana pasada.)

  valer más/menos to be more/less valuable

  2 to be useful

  valer de algo a algn to be useful (Mis protestas no valieron de nada.)

  valer para algo to be good at sth

valerse *v.* **1** to use

  valerse de algo/algn to make use of sth/sb

  2 to manage

  valerse por uno/a mismo/a to manage on one's own (No puede valerse por sí misma.)

vanguardia *f.* vanguard; avant-garde

  estar/ir a la vanguardia (de algo) to be at the forefront (of sth)

vengar *v.* to avenge

  vengar algo to avenge sth

vengarse *v.* to take revenge

  vengarse de algo, ~ de algn por algo to take revenge (on sb) for sth

ver *v.* to see

  a ver all right, now, so; let's see (A ver, ¿qué está pasando acá? Llamémoslo a ver qué nos dice.)

veras *f. pl.* truth (Lo dijo entre veras y bromas.)

  de veras really (Te lo digo de veras.)

vestirse *v.* to get dressed; to dress up

  vestirse de algo to dress up as sth

vez *f.* time

  a la vez at the same time

  a su vez in turn

  a veces sometimes (A veces me olvido de hacer las compras.)

  alguna vez sometime (Deberíamos invitarlos a cenar alguna vez.)

  cada vez que each/every time (that)

  de una vez (por todas) once and for all

  de vez en cuando once in a while

  en vez de instead of

  por... vez for the... time

  una vez que once (Una vez que termines la tarea, podrás jugar con la computadora.)

  una y otra vez time after time

vilo *m.*

  estar en vilo, seguir en ~ to be in the air

  levantar a algn en vilo to lift sb up off the ground

  mantenerse en vilo to be in suspense

virtud *f.* virtue

  en virtud de by virtue of

  virtudes curativas healing powers

vista *f.* sight

  a la vista in sight

  a primera vista at first sight

  a simple vista to the naked eye

  a vista de pájaro bird's-eye view

  de vista by sight (A su hermana la conocemos solo de vista.)

  en vista de que in view of

  estar con la vista puesta en algo/algn, tener la ~ puesta en algo/algn to have one's eye on sth/sb

  hacer la vista gorda to turn a blind eye

  perder algo de vista, perder a algn de ~ to lose sight of sth/sb

  perderse de vista to disappear from view

  saltar a la vista to be blindingly obvious

  tener algo en vista, tener a algn en ~ to have sth/sb in view/mind

vistazo *m.* look

  dar/echar un vistazo a algo to have a quick look at sth (Échale un vistazo al modelo y dime qué te parece.)

visto *p.p.* seen

  por lo visto apparently

volumen *m.* volume

  a todo volumen at full volume

  subir/bajar el volumen to turn the volume up/down

  volumen de ventas volume of sales

volver *v.* to return

  volver a hacer algo to do sth again

votar *v.* to vote

  votar a algn, ~ por algn to vote for sb

  votar a favor de algo, ~ en contra de algo to vote for/against sth

voz *f.* voice

  cambiar de voz, mudar de ~ to change one's voice

  correr la voz to spread the word

  dar la voz de alarma to raise the alarm

Index

condicional compuesto
see conditional perfect
condicional simple
see conditional
conditional **21**
  in impersonal constructions **21.B.8**
  in indirect discourse **21.B.6**
  in polite requests **21.B.4**
  irregular verbs **21.A.2**
  regular verbs **21.A.1,** Verb conjugation
    tables **p. B5**
  to express assumptions about
    the past **21.B.2**
  to express imagined possibility or
    characteristic **21.B.1**
  to express wishes **21.B.3**
  to give advice **21.B.5**
  Verb conjugation tables **pp. B1-B20**
  with **si** clauses **16.D.2, 21.B.7, 23.E.8b**
conditional clauses **16.D**
  conjunctions **16.D.1**
  donde, como, mientras 16.D.2c
  indicative mood **16.D.2, 17.E.9, 20.C.4,**
    20.F.4, 21.B.7, 21.D.2, 23.E.8
  punctuation **1.F.2d, 16.D.2b**
  si clauses **16.D.2**
  subjunctive mood **16.D.2, 21.B.7, 21.D.2,**
    23.E.7, 23.E.8
conditional perfect **21.C**
  English *should have* **21.D.3**
  in impersonal constructions **21.D.4**
  to express imagined possibility or
    characteristic **21.D.1**
  with **si** clauses **21.D.2, 23.E.8c**
conjunctions 16
  see coordinating conjunctions;
    subordinating conjunctions
conmigo, contigo, consigo 12.B.3,
  13.C.1, 13.C.2, 27.A.2
consequence
  coordinating conjunctions **16.B.6**
  subordinating conjunctions **16.C.5**
consonants and digraphs **1.B, 1.C.5, 1.C.6,**
  1.D.1, 1.D.4, 1.D.5
coordinating conjunctions **16.B**
  ni 16.B.4
  o 16.B.3
  pero 16.B.5

pues 16.B.6
sin embargo 16.B.5
sino 11.B.1l, 16.B.5
structure **16.B.1**
to express consequence or introduce
  explanations **16.B.6**
y 16.B.2
corchetes
  see punctuation, brackets
cuál(es), cual(es)
  interrogatives **14.B.3, 14.Da**
  relative clauses **15.A.2, 15.B.4**
cualquier, cualquiera, cualesquiera
  see indefinite pronouns; indefinite
    quantifiers; relative clauses
cuán 10.D.1, 14.B.5d
cuándo, cuando
  adverb of time **10.B.1**
  as a noun **14.B.10**
  interrogatives **14.B.1, 14.B.8**
  relative adverbs **15.C.1, 23.D**
cuandoquiera 15.D.1a
cuánto, cuanto
  adverbs of quantity **10.D.1**
  as a noun **14.B.10**
  interrogatives **14.B.1, 14.B.5**
  relative adverbs **23.D**
cuyo/a 15.A.2, 15.B.6

D

dates **5.C.2, 6.G**
days **1.G.1, 2.A.3b, 5.C.2**
definite article
  country names **5.C.6**
  days and dates **5.C.2**
  direct address and titles **5.C.4**
  el with prepositions **a** or **de 5.A.4**
  family names **5.C.11**
  forms **5.A.1**
  in exclamations **5.C.10**
  instead of possessives **5.C.7, 9.D.4**
  names of languages **5.C.5**
  placement **5.C.8**
  time **5.C.3**
  use **5.C.1**
  with proper names **5.D**
  without nouns **5.C.9**

lo 5.A.2
in abstract noun phrases with superlative
meaning **11.D.3**
in impersonal expressions **23.C.10**
lo más/menos + *adjective/adverb* + **que**
11.D.4c
lo más/menos + *adverb* + *adjective* or *clause*
10.I.2e, 11.D.2d
lo + *possessives* **9.D.5**
lo que 11.D.4b, 15.B.7b, 23.C.10
location
adverbial clauses of place **16.C.10, 23.E.1**
adverbs of place and direction **10.E.2**
adverbs of place and prepositions **10.E.4**
estar with location **30.D.1**
prepositions to express **12.B.7**
ser with location **30.D.2, 30.D.3**

M

manner
adverbial clauses **16.C.9, 23.E.1**
adverbs **10.C**
maps
Equatorial Guinea **p. xxi**
Mexico, Central America, and Caribbean
p. xxiii
South America **p. xxii**
Spain **p. xxi**
Spanish speakers in the U.S. **p. xxiv**
spread of **vos p. B21**
más
idiomatic expressions with **más 7.F.1**
lo más/menos + *adverb* + *adjective* or *clause*
10.I.2e, 11.D.2d
nadie más 7.D.4
see also comparison; indefinite quantifiers
menos
lo más/menos + *adverb* + *adjective* or *clause*
10.I.2e, 11.D.2d
see also comparison; indefinite quantifiers
mismo/a, mismos/as 7.E.5, 11.C.5,
27.A.2, 27.D.1
months **1.G.1, 2.A.3b**
mucho/a(s)
see indefinite pronouns; indefinite
quantifiers

N

nada
see indefinite pronouns
nadie más
see indefinite pronouns
ni
see coordinating conjunctions
ningún, ninguno/a
see indefinite pronouns; indefinite
quantifiers
noun clauses
el hecho de que 23.C.1c
es que 23.C.1d
hacer que + *subjunctive* **23.C.1b**
in impersonal expressions with **que**
23.C.7, 23.C.8
indirect questions with **si 16.C.1c**
subordinating conjunctions **16.C.1**
to give personal opinions and thoughts
23.C.5
vs. infinitive **23.C.9, 25.B.5**
with sense verbs **23.C.4**
with verbs of denial or doubt **23.C.6**
with verbs of emotion **23.C.3**
with verbs of will, influence, or
necessity **23.C.1**
nouns 2
agreement with adjectives **3.B**
agreement with articles **5.A.1, 5.A.3**
comparison **11.B.1, 11.C.2, 11.C.4**
expressive suffixes **2.C**
gender **2.A**
in prepositional phrases **12.A.2c**
infinitives as **2.A.3e, 25.B.1**
interrogatives as **14.B.10**
noun phrases with neuter article **lo**
5.A.2, 11.D.3
number **2.B**
with **ser 30.B.1**
see also noun clauses
number
adjectives **3.A.1–3.A.3**
articles **5.A.1, 5.A.3**
demonstratives **8.A.1, 8.A.2**
determiners **4.B.4**
expressive suffixes **2.C.4**
indefinite quantifiers **7.C.1**

after nouns, use **9.C.2–9.D, 11.B.1f**
agreement **9.A, 9.B, 9.C**
articles instead **9.D.4, 27.D.1c**
as pronouns **9.C.2b–9.C.2d**
before nouns **9.B**
definite and indefinite meaning of **9.D.6**
in direct address **9.D.8**
lo + *possessives* **9.D.5**
short forms vs. long forms **9.A**
using before and after nouns **9.D.7**
with adverbs of place **9.E**
prepositions **12**
 a 12.B.2
 compound **12.A.2**
 con 12.B.3, 13.C.1, 13.C.2
 de 12.B.4
 en 12.B.5
 idiomatic expressions with **estar 30.C.4**
 para 12.B.6
 por 12.B.6
 prepositional phrases **12.A.2c**
 pronouns after **12.B.1, 12.B.3, 13.C**
 simple **12.A.1**
 to express direction **12.B.7**
 to express location **12.B.7**
 to express time **12.B.7**
 use **12.B**
 verb phrases with the infinitive **26.C**
 with adverbs of place **10.E.3, 10.E.4**
 with relative pronouns **15.A.3b**
 with verbs **17.B.2, 17.B.3d**
present indicative **17**
 in conditional clauses **17.E.9, 23.E.8a**
 irregular verbs **17.D.5**
 regular verbs **17.D.1,** Verb conjugation tables **p. B5**
 to express confirmation of wishes or requests **17.E.7**
 to express continuity of past actions **17.E.8, 18.E.11**
 to express future meaning **17.E.4, 17.F.4a, 20.A, 20.D.2**
 to express habits **17.E.2, 28.B.2**
 to express imperative meaning **17.E.6**
 to express involvement in past actions **17.E.5**
 to express present actions **17.E.1**

to express timeless facts **17.E.3**
 Verb conjugation tables **pp. B1-B20**
 verbs with spelling changes **17.D.2, 17.D.3**
 verbs with stem changes **17.D.4**
 vs. present progressive **17.F.2, 17.F.4**
present participle
 in progressive tenses **17.F.1, 25.C.3**
 placement of object pronouns **13.G.2, 13.G.5**
present perfect (indicative) **19**
 auxiliary verb **haber 19.A**
 past participles, irregular **19.A.2**
 past participles, regular **19.A.1**
 regional variations **19.C**
 to refer to continuous actions **19.B.3**
 to refer to incomplete actions **19.B.2**
 to refer to life experiences **19.B.1**
 vs. preterite **19.C.1, 19.C.3**
 with **si** clauses **23.E.8a**
present progressive **17.F**
presente
 see present indicative
preterite (indicative) **18**
 impersonal constructions **18.E.12**
 irregular verbs **18.B.5**
 regular verbs **18.B.1,** Verb conjugation tables **p. B5**
 stem-changing verbs **18.B.3**
 to refer to a sequence of events **18.C.3**
 to refer to an action in the past **18.C.2, 19.C**
 to refer to the beginning and end of an action **18.C.1**
 use **18.C**
 Verb conjugation tables **pp. B1-B20**
 verbs that change meaning **18.F**
 verbs with irregular stems **18.B.4**
 verbs with spelling changes **18.B.2**
 vs. present perfect **19.C.1, 19.C.3**
 vs. **pretérito anterior 19.Gb**
 with **si** clauses **23.E.8a**
pretérito anterior (indicative) **19.F, 19.G**
 auxiliary verb **haber 19.F**
 past participles, irregular **19.A.2**
 past participles, regular **19.A.1**
 use **19.G**

About the author

Ana Beatriz Chiquito is a Professor of Spanish at the University of Bergen, Norway, and for nearly twenty years has been affiliated with the Center for Educational Computing Initiatives at MIT as a Visiting Research Engineer. Professor Chiquito holds degrees in Linguistics, Social Sciences, and Teacher Education, and has been a Visiting Professor at the University of Massachusetts, Boston; the Universidad Católica de Quito; the Universidad de Costa Rica; the Norwegian School of Economics and Business Administration; and at the UNDP Program in Public Administration in Ecuador. Professor Chiquito has extensive international experience designing and developing e-learning applications for language education at all levels and for over thirty years has led research projects in Spanish linguistics, sociolinguistics, and e-learning in Latin America, Spain, Norway, and the United States. She has also co-authored several textbooks and e-learning applications for Spanish as a foreign language for the U.S. and European markets. A native of Colombia, she now divides her time between the Boston area and Norway.

Credits

Photography Credits

All images © Vista Higher Learning unless otherwise noted.

Cover: *Nomade* (2010), Jaume Plensa. Acero inoxidable pintado, 800 x 550 x 530 cm. Port Vauban, Musée Picasso, Antibes, France/Cahir Davitt/John Warburton Lee/SuperStock/© 2015 Artists Rights Society (ARS), New York/VEGAP, Madrid.

Actividades: A21: Martín Bernetti; **A39:** (all) Paula Díez.

Index: D16: Turi Aksdal.